THE ARCHEOLOGY OF THE NEW TESTAMENT
The Life of Jesus and the Beginning
of the Early Church

THE
ARCHEOLOGY
OF THE NEW TESTAMENT

The Life of Jesus and the Beginning
of the Early Church

BY JACK FINEGAN

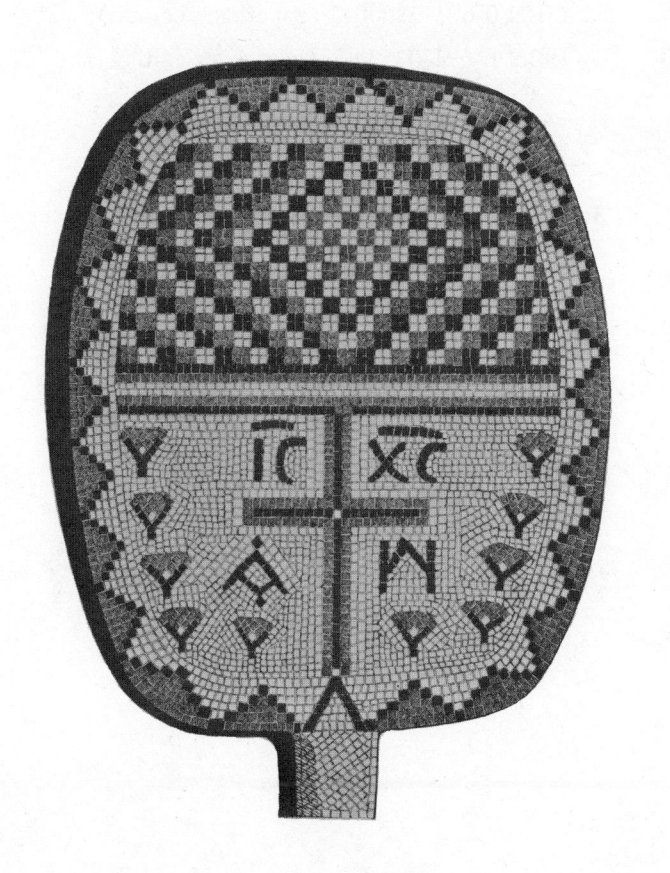

PRINCETON, NEW JERSEY · PRINCETON UNIVERSITY PRESS

Preface

This book might properly be dedicated to the remembrance of Melito of Sardis, the first pilgrim to Palestine of whom we are informed. A Christian leader in Asia Minor, in 160 he "went to the East and came to the place (τόπος) where these things were preached and done." Others, unknown to us, may have preceded him in such pilgrimage, certainly many others followed. In 212 Alexander of Cappadocia, earlier a student in the great Christian university in Alexandria, went to Jerusalem "for the purpose of prayer and investigation of the places." The "places" (τόποι), as in the case of Melito, were the sites of sacred history, and the "investigation" was ἱστορία, which means learning by inquiry and is the root of the English word "history." A few years later Origen, who had been a fellow student with Alexander in Alexandria, later head of the Alexandrian school, and after that resident in Palestine, tells how he too "visited the places to learn by inquiry of the footsteps of Jesus and of his disciples." Information he obtained in this way was used by Origen in his scholarly works of exegesis and apology. In this connection he remarks upon occasion that in a given place something "is pointed out" (δείκνυται). Eusebius also uses this word repeatedly in connection with the geographical and historical information which he brings together in his famous *Onomasticon*, and the use of the identical phrase suggests that in many cases his information comes from far back in the times when the same things were pointed out to many of his predecessors in these investigations.

To these men, therefore, and to many others also identified in our "Chronological List of Ancient Sources," it was important to learn by investigation, in the very places where it had transpired, as much as possible about the history of Jesus and his early followers. In contrast with the widely spread modern opinion that historical inquiry is irrelevant to faith, such investigation was obviously deemed significant by these men with respect to the witness which they bore—some to the point of martyrdom—to the facts of the Christian faith.

In modern times New Testament archeology has also been concerned to conduct investigations in "the place where these things were preached and done." In the *Biblical Researches* based upon his travels in Palestine in 1838 and 1852, Edward Robinson discussed many New Testament sites as well as Old Testament ones. Likewise the work of the Palestine Exploration Fund and the British School of Archaeology in Jerusalem, of the American School of Oriental Research in Jeru-

salem, of the Dominican *École Biblique et Archéologique Française* and of the *Studium Biblicum Franciscanum*, both in Jerusalem, of the Department of Antiquities of Jordan, of the Department of Antiquities and Museums in Israel, of the Department of Archaeology of the Hebrew University, of the Israel Exploration Society, and of other institutions and individuals, has at least in part had to do with sites and objects related to the New Testament and early Palestinian Christianity and to the environment thereof.

In its procedure archeology must be as rigorously scientific as possible. What can be found and dealt with are therefore tangible things, inscriptions, objects, tombs, architectural remains, and the like. These are proper subjects of investigation in their own right. Archeology may be concerned with them simply because they exist, or with respect to their bearing on the history of culture, the history of art, etc. In themselves they are obviously not of the substance of the Biblical faith, whether of the Old Testament or of the New Testament. But insofar as the Biblical faith both of the Old Testament and of the New Testament has to do with events which happened at particular times and places, the investigation of any and all materials which cast light upon those times and places is of importance and relevance.

The present book has to do, then, with any things which can be found, chiefly in Palestine, which are connected with or cast light upon the life of Jesus and the existence of the early Christian church. The archeological sites and objects are presented in photographs, with some related drawings, maps, and plans, and the ancient sources, such as those mentioned above, are utilized along with the New Testament to help in identifying and interpreting these objects and sites. Since the purpose is the same as that expressed by Origen, namely, "to learn by inquiry of the footsteps of Jesus and of his disciples," the order of presentation is in general the same as that of the records in the New Testament, chiefly in the Gospels, concerning the life of Jesus and of his earliest followers.

Specifically this means that we first investigate sites connected with John the Baptist, then go on to Bethlehem and Nazareth, Samaria and Galilee, Jerash as an example of the Decapolis cities, Caesarea as the Roman capital, Jericho, the Mount of Olives, Jerusalem, and Emmaus. In Jerusalem the climactic sacred site is reached at the Church of the Holy Sepulcher, earlier known as the Anastasis, the Church of the Resurrection. Here the rock of Calvary and the traditional tomb have been so cut away and built upon that it is difficult to see how they may have looked prior to these enterprises, but we try to envision the earlier situation and give a hypothetical reconstruction of the tomb. Then we go on to assemble some additional information on ancient Jewish burial places. This gives perspective with regard to the tomb reconstruction just mentioned, and it also prepares for the last part of our undertaking, namely, to ask if the earliest followers of Jesus have left any tangible signs referring to him. Here we are involved with the history of the cross mark, and the earliest examples of this mark—where the question must at least be raised of possible connection with the Christian faith —are on burial monuments.

Since the pictures are arranged in a sequence along the lines just indicated, the discussion which accompanies and elucidates them is also intended to be connected and consecutive, and not just the isolated notes of a catalogue. At the same time, the division of the text into numbered sections agreeing with the numbers of the illustrations makes it possible to consult directly and immediately any particular picture or group of pictures, and subject or group of subjects. It also facilitates cross-reference: for example, as early as No. 2, the reader is referred to No. 207, and also back to No. 1.

The sites and objects have almost all been seen and studied personally by the author. Many of the photographs he has made himself, others are gathered from the sources to which acknowledgment is made in the notes at the end of the sections. Acknowledgment is also made to Professor Jerry Vardaman of The Southern Baptist Theological Seminary, Louisville, Kentucky, for a number of photographs and a number of suggestions which have been incorporated into the text and the bibliographies, usually with his name attached. For the cartography of maps and plans Nos. 7, 19, 33, 41, 52, 76, 107, 135, and 143 acknowledgment is made to Evelyn Bingham.

With this book in hand one may go, it is hoped, either in actuality or in imagination and study, "to the East . . . to the place where these things were preached and done."

J.F.

Contents

〰〰

THE LIFE OF JOHN THE BAPTIST

THE LIFE OF JESUS

BETHLEHEM

NAZARETH

SAMARIA

CONTENTS

CONTENTS

CONTENTS

X

CONTENTS

CATACOMBS

BETH SHE'ARIM

ROME

SARCOPHAGI

OSSUARIES

THE CROSS

HISTORY OF THE CROSS MARK

CONTENTS

Chronological List of Ancient Sources

With respect to the identification of Gospel sites the following are the most important ancient sources, with approximate dates in parenthesis.

Josephus (90). The Jewish historian was born in 37/38 in Jerusalem, participated in the Jewish War and, after the fall of Jerusalem, settled in Rome. He wrote a long account of *The Jewish War* which probably appeared c. 75, and in the thirteenth year of Domitian (93/94), when he himself was fifty-six years of age, completed his *Jewish Antiquities* (*Ant.* xx 12, 1 §267). His work, *Against Apion*, replied to criticisms on the *Antiquities*, and the *Life* of Josephus responded to another history of the Jewish War by Justus of Tiberias in which Josephus was criticized for his part in the war. In Josephus' *Life* (65 §§359-360), he speaks of Herod Agrippa II as no longer alive, hence must have written this work after the decease of that king. The exact date of Agrippa's death is unknown. He struck no coins later than 95; no inscription of his (over twenty are known) dates later than 93. He must, however, have lost much, if not all, of his territory before the last year of the emperor Domitian (96), since an inscription from Ahire, under his control formerly, refers to the sixteenth year of Domitian. The date of the death of Josephus himself is also unknown. All references are to Josephus' works, ed. H. St. J. Thackeray, Ralph Marcus, Allen Wikgren, and Louis H. Feldman, 9 vols. LCL; for the date of the death of Agrippa II see an unpublished paper by Jerry Vardaman.

The Protevangelium of James (150). A legendary account of Mary, daughter of Joachim and Anne, child wife of the widowed Joseph, and mother of Jesus. The oldest manuscript is Papyrus Bodmer v, probably of the third century, ed. M. Testuz. O. Cullmann, HSNTA pp. 370-388.

Justin Martyr (150). Born soon after 100 of a pagan Greek family at Flavia Neapolis (modern Nablus, cf. No. 44) in Palestine, Justin became a Christian at Ephesus, founded a school at Rome, and was beheaded under the prefect of Rome, Junius Rusticus, in 165. Eusebius, *Church History* IV, 1ff., mentions eight treatises by Justin. Three are extant in a poor manuscript of 1364, namely, two *Apologies Against the Gentiles*, and a *Dialogue with the Jew Trypho*. The *First Apology* was written c. 150-155; the *Second Apology* was a sort of postscript, and the *Dialogue* was written after the *First Apology*. ANF I.

Melito of Sardis (160). Bishop of Sardis, he wrote a number of works the titles of which are given by Eusebius (*Ch. Hist.* IV 26). The last which Eusebius mentions, and therefore possibly but not certainly the last which Melito wrote, was an *Apology* addressed to the Emperor Marcus Aurelius (161-180). From the quotations given by Eusebius it appears that this was written after the death of the emperor's brother, Lucius Verus, i.e., after the year 169. The work by Melito, which is of particular interest in the present connection, was a treatise in six books named *Extracts*, as both Eusebius (*Ch. Hist.* IV 26, 12 ἐν δὲ ταῖς γραφείσαις αὐτῷ Ἐκλογαῖς) and Jerome (*Lives of Illustrious Men* 24) call it, and addressed to an otherwise unknown Onesimus. It contained a list of the accepted books of the OT canon, and consisted chiefly of quotations from these Scriptures, no doubt quotations believed to have to do with Christ. As he tells of this work Eusebius (*Ch. Hist.* IV 26, 13) quotes from its Preface. In the Preface Melito gives an account of the cause and circumstances of the writing. Onesimus had expressed a wish to have extracts made from the Law and the Prophets concerning the Savior and the Christian faith, and along therewith desired to know accurately the number and order of the ancient books. Melito continues: "Accordingly when I went to the East and came to the place where these things were preached and done (ἀνελθὼν οὖν εἰς τὴν ἀνατολὴν καὶ ἕως τοῦ τόπου γενόμενος ἔνθα ἐκηρύχθη καὶ ἐπράχθη), I learned accurately the books of the Old Testament, and send them to you. . . . From these I have also made the extracts. . . ."

Here then was the first pilgrim journey to the East of which we are informed. This bishop in Asia Minor desired to obtain dependable information, particularly concerning the OT canon, in the homeland of the Christian faith. At the same time he desired to see with his own eyes the very place (τόπος) where these things were preached and done, i.e., the actual scene of Gospel history. From this statement we can conclude that the important places in Gospel history were actually being shown to visitors at that time, in the middle of the second century. So the authenticity of the faith was confirmed to Melito and others like him, and they were able to bear witness to it. For the significance of Melito in this respect, see Hans Windisch, "Die ältesten christlichen Palästinapilger," in ZDPV 48 (1925), pp. 145-147.

Alexander of Cappadocia (212). Alexander was a friend of Origen and together with him a student under Pantaenus and Clement in Alexandria (Eusebius, *Ch. Hist.* VI 14, 8-9). Later he was bishop in some city in Cappadocia (*Ch. Hist.* VI 11). In the first year of Caracalla (211) Asclepiades was made bishop of Antioch (Eusebius, *Chronicle,* ed. Helm, 2d ed. 1956, p. 213) and Alexander wrote a letter of congratulation (*Ch. Hist.* VI 11) in which he described himself as a prisoner. The next year he went to Jerusalem, where he was made bishop along with the then aged Narcissus (*Chronicle,* p. 213). In Jerusalem he established a library from which Eusebius, a century later, gathered materials (*Ch. Hist.* VI 20). Alexander died a martyr under Decius (250) (Jerome, *Lives of Illustrious Men* 62). When he tells about Alexander's trip to Jerusalem Eusebius (*Ch. Hist.* VI 11, 2) says that he went "for the purpose of prayer and investigation of the places" (εὐχῆς καὶ τῶν τόπων ἱστορίας ἕνεκεν). By the "places" (τόποι) must almost certainly be meant the places that were of special significance in the Christian faith, i.e., the sacred places of Gospel events. Even as the Ethiopian once came to Jerusalem to worship (Ac 8:27), and Paul hastened to be there, if possible, on the day of Pentecost (Ac 20:16), so the bishop desired to pray in Jerusalem and presumably at the sacred places in the city. Furthermore he was concerned with ἱστορία, i.e., investigation in the sense of learning by inquiry, with respect to "the places." Herodotus (II 99) links the same word with seeing and judging when he says that what he writes about Egypt is the outcome "of my own sight and judgment and inquiry" (ὄψις τε ἐμὴ καὶ γνώμη καὶ ἱστορίη). So Alexander desires to conduct "investigation of the places," in order that he may bear witness, as he finally did even unto martyrdom. While neither Melito of Sardis nor Alexander of Cappadocia have left us writings in which are actual descriptions of specific places in the Holy Land, it is evident that both of them undertook to visit the sacred places to confirm the authenticity of the sacred history, and that they might be able to bear witness thereto. Nor were they the only such travelers who had this objective as early as their times, i.e., in the second and third centuries. What is told by other writers who traveled to the Holy Land later in the third and following centuries was presumably the same sort of information already provided by local traditions in Palestine to Melito and Alexander and their contemporaries. For the significance of Alexander in this respect, see Windisch in ZDPV 48 (1925), pp. 150-151.

Origen (230). Born c. 185, probably at Alexandria, Origen was appointed head of the catechetical school in that city in 202/203. About 212 he traveled to Rome. About 215 he visited Palestine and lectured in Caesarea (Eusebius, *Ch. Hist.* VI 19, 16). In 230 he visited Palestine again and a year later settled permanently in Caesarea where he founded a school. In 218-222 he lectured in Antioch, and in 244 visited Arabia. In the persecution by Decius (250) he was imprisoned and tortured, probably at Caesarea, and died at the age of about seventy, probably in 253/254, at Tyre. During his residence in Palestine, and in connection with his exegetical and text-critical study of the Bible, Origen visited various places of sacred history. This is evident from a statement in his *Commentary on John* (VI 24 GCS Origines IV, p. 149 ANF IX, p. 370) where he gives "Bethabara" as the reading to be preferred in Jn 1:28. Having declared his conviction that we should read not "Bethany" but "Bethabara" in this passage (cf. below No. 9), he adds: "We have visited the places to learn by inquiry of the footsteps of Jesus and of his disciples and of the prophets (γενόμενοι ἐν τοῖς τόποις ἐπὶ ἱστορίαν τῶν ἰχνῶν Ἰησοῦ καὶ τῶν μαθητῶν αὐτοῦ καὶ τῶν προφητῶν)." Here again, as in the case of Melito (above), there is interest in the *topos* or "place" where the things of Christian history were preached and done and, as in the case of Alexander (above), in the *historia* or investigation of these places. In another case Origen appeals to the apologetic significance of an attested site of a Gospel event. Writing *Against Celsus* (I 51 GCS Origenes I, p. 102 ANF IV, p. 418 cf. below No. 20) he says that if any one wishes to have additional evidence with respect to the birth of Jesus in Bethlehem, let him know that in accordance with the history in the Gospel concerning his birth, the cave in Bethlehem is pointed out where he was born and the manger in the cave where he was wrapped in swaddling clothes (ὅτι ἀκολούθως τῇ ἐν τῷ εὐαγγελίῳ περὶ τῆς γενέσεως αὐτοῦ ἱστορίᾳ δείκνυται τὸ ἐν Βηθλεὲμ σπήλαιον, ἔνθα ἐγεννήθη, καὶ ἡ ἐν τῷ σπηλαίῳ φάτνη, ἔνθα ἐσπαργανώθη). The word δείκνυται, "is pointed out," is very important. It means, almost certainly that in his investigation of the footsteps of Jesus, Origen went himself to Bethlehem and was personally shown, no doubt by the Christians of the place, the evidential cave. To him this was a witness to the truth of the Gospel history. Although Origen is the first Christian to leave explicit eyewitness testimony of this sort to places of the Gospel history, there is little doubt that such places were also "shown" to his predecessors such as Alexander and Melito. After him, Eusebius also uses the same formula, "is pointed out," at a number of points in the *Onomasticon* (see below), namely, with respect to Akeldama (p. 38), Ainon (p. 40), Bethania, Bethabara, Bezatha (p. 58), and Sychar (p. 164). Since the notations of Eusebius are in much the same style as that of Origen about Bethlehem and employ the characteristic δείκνυται, it is quite possible that Eusebius derived materials for the *Onomasticon* from these earlier researches of Origen. For Origen's numerous writings see GCS and ANF. For his significance among the early visitors to the places of Gospel history, see Windisch in ZDPV 48 (1925), pp. 152-154. As Windisch remarks (*ibid.*, p. 155), the journeys in Palestine of Melito, Alexander, Origen, and other early visitors to places which were shown as places of Gospel history are a testimony to the relatively early date of the traditions attaching to these places. While the genuineness of the sites is not proved by this alone, it is at any rate clear that Melito and the others would not have made their journeys if they had not believed that the places they wished to see were still identifiable and accessible.

Eusebius (325). He was born in Palestine, probably at Caesarea, in 263. At the school which Origen had founded here, the presbyter Pamphilus developed a great library and was the teacher and friend of Eusebius, who called himself Eusebius Pamphili, i.e., the spiritual son of Pamphilus. Eusebius was elected bishop of Caesarea in 313, the same year in which the edict of Constantine brought peace to the church. He was active in the Council of Nicaea (325), took part in the dedication of the Church of the Holy Sepulcher in Jerusalem (335), lectured in Constantinople in the same year, and died in 339 or 340. The *Chronicle* of Eusebius was published c. 303 and is extant in late Armenian manuscripts (ed. Karst, GCS), and a Latin version was made by Jerome probably in 381 and is preserved in manuscripts as early as the fifth century (ed. Helm, GCS). The *Church History* records events down to the victory of Constantine over Licinius (324). The *Life of Constantine* was written after the death of the emperor (337), whom Eusebius so greatly admired, and tells of church buildings which Constantine erected (LPPTS I). The *Onomasticon* (περὶ τῶν τοπικῶν ὀνομάτων τῶν ἐν τῇ θείᾳ γραφῇ) was the fourth part of a work on biblical geography, the writing of which was suggested by Bishop Paulinus of Tyre. Since the latter died in 331, this work was probably composed before that date, say, therefore, about 330. The first three parts of the work, which are not extant, were an Interpretation of the Ethnological Terms of the Hebrew Scriptures in Greek, a Topography of Ancient Judea, and a Plan of Jerusalem and the Temple. The fourth part, which is extant and is commonly called the *Onomasticon*, is an alphabetical list of place names in the Bible, with notes on the situation and history of these localities. While the work is alphabetically arranged in that it goes through the letters of the alphabet from Alpha to Omega, under each letter it takes up biblical books in order and then in each book takes up place names generally in the order of their occurrence. Under the letter Alpha and in the book of Genesis, for example, we find Ararat (᾿Αραράτ) (Gen 8:4), Accad (᾿Αχάδ) (Gen 10:10), Ai (᾿Αγγαί) (Gen 12:8), and so on, in that order. That the work may rest, at least in part, upon material gathered by Origen, has been pointed out just above. In addition to the Greek text of the *Onomasticon* as written by Eusebius, we also have a Latin translation of the work which was made by Jerome in 390, in which are not a few corrections and additions representing additional information which Jerome is able to supply. Greek and Latin texts ed. Klostermann, GCS.

Helena (325). This lady was the mother of Constantine. She died c. 327 at the age of eighty, having made a pilgrimage to the Holy Land shortly before her death. Eusebius tells of her journey in *The Life of Constantine* III 41-47. This imperial example, and the increased freedom for such travel under the Christian emperors, must have contributed considerably to the henceforth greatly augmented interest in pilgrimages to Palestine.

The Bordeaux Pilgrim (333). This anonymous pilgrim made a journey from Bordeaux to Jerusalem and back by way of Rome to Milan. His is the oldest pilgrim account, and is called *Itinerarium a Burdigala Hierusalem usque.* ed. Geyer pp. 1-33; LPPTS I; CCSL CLXXV, pp. 1-26.

Cyril of Jerusalem (348). Probably born in Jerusalem c. 315, he became bishop of Jerusalem in 347/348 and, in the Easter season of that year, gave a series of twenty-four catechetical lectures in the Church of the Holy Sepulcher, lectures which were afterward published from the shorthand notes of a member of the congregation. NPNFSS VII; LPPTS XI.

Epiphanius (367). Born c. 315 in the vicinity of Eleutheropolis near Gaza in Palestine, c. 335 he visited the monks of Egypt, then founded a monastery at Eleutheropolis and headed it for thirty years. In 367 he became bishop of Salamis on the island of Cyprus, but continued in close touch with Palestine personally and through correspondence. He wrote *Ancoratus,* "The Firmly-Anchored Man," in 374; *Panarion,* "Medicine Chest," also cited as *Haereses,* in 374-377; Greek text ed. K. Holl, GCS 25, 31, 37; and *De mensuris et ponderibus,* "On Weights and Measures," in 392, a Bible dictionary dealing with canon and versions of the OT, measures and weights in the Bible, and the geography of Palestine, Eng. tr. of the complete Syriac version, ed. James E. Dean, SAOC 11, 1935.

Aetheria (385). A nun, probably from the north of Spain or the south of France, who made a pilgrimage to the holy places (385-388). She left a plain record, only a part of which was found in 1884. It goes also under the name of Sylvia, and is called *Peregrinatio ad loca sancta.* ed. Geyer pp. 35-101; LPPTS I; Hélène Pétré, *Éthérie, Journal de voyage.* Sources Chretiennes, 21. Paris: Les Éditions du Cerf, 1957; CCSL CLXXV, pp. 37-90.

Jerome (385). Born in Dalmatia c. 347, Jerome was educated in Rome and baptized there, afterward lived in Aquileia, and undertook a pilgrimage to the Near East. He was a friend and secretary of Pope Damasus and, during his sojourn in Rome in 382-385, he undertook the revision of the Latin Bible. He became the center of an ascetical circle in which several ladies of the Roman aristocracy were associated, including the widows Marcella and Paula and the latter's daughter, Eustochium. In 385 Jerome went to Palestine and lived in a cave at the Church of the Nativity in Bethlehem until his death in 420. Paula and Eustochium followed Jerome to Palestine. Paula built three convents for women which she headed, and one monastery for men with Jerome as the head. In addition to his translation and revision of the *Onomasticon* of Eusebius, made in 390, as mentioned above, Jerome's own writings were numerous. CCSL, NPNFSS.

In his *Letter* 46 (NPNFSS VI, p. 65) which he wrote from Bethlehem in 386 in the name of Paula and Eustochium to invite their friend Marcella to visit the Holy Land, Jerome expressed his deep feelings concerning the experiences one would have at the sacred sites. He wrote in part:

Will the time never come when a breathless messenger shall bring the news that our dear Marcella has reached the shores of Palestine, and when every band of monks and every troop of virgins shall unite in a song of welcome? In our excitement we are already hurrying to meet you; without waiting for a vehicle, we hasten off at once on foot. We shall clasp you by the hand, we shall look upon your face; and when, after long waiting, we at last embrace you, we shall find it hard to tear ourselves away. Will the day never come when we shall together enter the Savior's cave, and together weep in the sepulcher of the Lord with his sister and with his mother? Then shall we touch with our lips the wood of the cross, and rise in prayer and resolve upon the Mount of Olives with the ascending Lord. We shall see Lazarus come forth bound with grave clothes, we shall look upon the waters of Jordan purified for the washing of the Lord. Thence we shall pass to the folds of the shepherds, we shall pray together in the mausoleum of David. We shall see the prophet, Amos, upon his crag blowing his shepherd's horn. We shall hasten, if not to the tents, to the monuments of Abraham, Isaac and Jacob, and of their three illustrious wives. We shall see the fountain in which the eunuch was immersed by Philip. We shall make a pilgrimage to Samaria, and side by side venerate the ashes of John the Baptist, of Elisha, and of Obadiah. We shall enter the very caves where in the time of persecution and famine the companies of the prophets were fed. If only you will come, we shall go to see Nazareth, as its name denotes, the flower of Galilee. Not far off Cana will be visible where the water was turned into wine. We shall make our way to Tabor, and see the tabernacles

there which the Saviour shares, not, as Peter once wished, with Moses and Elijah, but with the Father and with the Holy Spirit. Thence we shall come to the Sea of Gennesaret, and when there we shall see the spots where the five thousand were filled with five loaves and the four thousand with seven. The town of Nain will meet our eyes, at the gate of which the widow's son was raised to life. Hermon too will be visible, and the torrent of Endor, at which Sisera was vanquished. Our eyes will look also on Capernaum, the scene of so many of our Lord's signs—yes, and on all Galilee besides. And when accompanied by Christ, we shall have made our way back to our cave through Shiloh and Bethel, and those other places where churches are set up like standards to commemorate the Lord's victories, then we shall sing heartily, we shall weep copiously, we shall pray unceasingly. Wounded with the Saviour's shaft, we shall say one to another: "I have found him whom my soul loveth; I will hold him and will not let him go."

Although Jerome expressed such feelings as these about the visitation of the holy places, and chose himself to reside at Bethlehem, he also spoke elsewhere about how little the places themselves could mean apart from faith. In his *Letter* 58 (NPNFSS VI, pp. 119-120) written c. 395 to his friend Paulinus of Nola, he declared that access to the courts of heaven was as easy from Britain as from Jerusalem, and assured Paulinus that nothing was lacking to his faith although he had not seen Jerusalem, and that he, Jerome, was none the better for living where he did. The Palestinian hermit Hilarion (died 371, Jerome wrote his life in 390, NPNFSS VI, pp. 303-315) provided a good example, Jerome told Paulinus, because although he was a native of and dweller in Palestine he only allowed himself to visit Jerusalem for a single day, "not wishing on the one hand when he was so near to neglect the holy places, nor yet on the other to appear to confine God within local limits." Indeed, said Jerome, "the spots which witnessed the crucifixion and the resurrection profit those only who bear their several crosses, who day by day rise again with Christ, and who thus show themselves worthy of an abode so holy."

Paula (386). The husband of this distinguished and wealthy Roman woman died in 380, and she became a pupil and companion of Jerome. She settled at Bethlehem, and studied Hebrew, Greek, and Latin. Her daughter, Eustochium, was with her at Bethlehem, while other children were in the West. In his *Letter* 108 Jerome wrote in 404 to Eustochium to console the daughter upon the death of the mother, and described Paula's journey to the East including Egypt and the Holy Land. NPNFSS VI, pp. 195-212; LPPTS I.

xvi

Paulinus of Nola (403). Born at Bordeaux in 353, Paulinus was a pupil and friend of the Roman rhetorician, Ausonius. He adopted the monastic life, and lived in Nola in Italy from 394 onward, where he died as bishop in 431. He wrote poems, and letters to Augustine, Sulpicius Severus, and others. MPL 61, CSEL XXIX-XXX.

Sozomen (425). Born at Bethelia near Gaza in Palestine, Sozomen became a civil servant at Constantinople. His *Church History* was intended as a continuation of the work of Eusebius, and covered the period from 324 to 425. NPNFSS II.

Socrates (439). Also a civil servant in Constantinople, in which city he was born c. 380, Socrates wrote a *Church History* in seven books, intended to be a continuation of that of Eusebius, covering the period from the abdication of Diocletian in 305 down to 439. NPNFSS II.

Peter the Iberian (451). The son of a prince in Georgia, he came to Jerusalem in 451 where he was consecrated as a priest. He became bishop of Majuma near Gaza and died there in 485. R. Raabe, *Petrus der Iberer*, 1895 (cited as Raabe, as quoted in Kopp; cf. M.-J. Lagrange in RB 5 [1896], pp. 457-460).

The Jerusalem Breviary (sixth century). A brief enumeration of the sanctuaries in Jerusalem, probably written in the early sixth century. *Breviarius de Hierosolyma,* ed. Geyer pp. 151-155; LPPTS II; CCSL CLXXV, pp. 109-112.

Theodosius (530). This author is known only from the pilgrim itinerary which he has left, but it is of value for its concise notations on the holy places as they were known in the early sixth century. *Theodosius de situ terrae sanctae,* ed. Geyer pp. 135-150; LPPTS II; CCSL CLXXV, pp. 115-125.

The Madaba Mosaic Map (560). The ancient Moabite town of Medeba (Num 21:30; Jos 13:9, 16) is today the village of Madaba in Transjordan, sixteen miles east and south of where the Jordan flows into the Dead Sea. The place was occupied by Christians from Kerak around 1880, and in 1884 the existence of the mosaic was first reported to the Greek Orthodox Patriarch of Jerusalem, whose librarian visited the site in 1896. The mosaic was the floor of an ancient church, and at the time a new Greek Orthodox church was being built over the old one and the mosaic was already much damaged. The librarian published the first drawings of the map in 1897, and Palmer and Guthe made the first copy in color in 1902. The principal preserved fragment of the map is 10.50 meters long by 5 meters wide. The geographical area represented extends from Aenon (near Scythopolis) in the north to the Canopic branch of the Nile in the south, and from the Mediterranean Sea in the west to Charachmoba (Kerak) on

the east. The map is oriented in the literal sense of the word, i.e., the viewer is looking eastward. The inscriptions, which are in Greek, are written so as to be read by one looking in this direction. If a river runs from east to west the letters of its name are written in a vertical line. Buildings normally show the western façade. The intention of the map was obviously to depict the Bible lands and, in its original form, the map must have covered biblical Palestine and parts of adjacent lands connected with the Bible. The principal source was undoubtedly the *Onomasticon* of Eusebius, with which it corresponds in many points. Some other sources must have been used too and one of these may have been an early road map. The center of the map is the city of Jerusalem, shown in a large oval, and most precisely the center is the base of the column shown inside the northern gate of the city, the column no doubt being the point from which road distances from Jerusalem were measured. On the map the sea is deep green, the plains light brown, the mountains dark brown. In the cities, specially in Jerusalem, the normal representation is to use red roofs for churches or monasteries, and yellow or gray roofs for palaces or public buildings. Brown areas appear to be squares. The doors of the principal basilicas are yellow cubes, which may represent either polished brass or lights shining from inside. The inscriptions are usually in black, but in the mountains where the background is dark they are lettered in white, and in occasional instances a specially important place is indicated in red letters. The neuter article τό is used to signify a sacred place, often one marked by a church. The script of the inscriptions employs an oval alphabet such as is also found, for example, in numerous sixth century inscriptions in the churches at Gerasa (C. B. Welles in Kraeling, *Gerasa,* p. 367). As may also be seen in some of those inscriptions, Omicron and Upsilon are often written in a ligature. Some abbreviations and punctuation marks are employed, and consonantal Iota is marked with two dots. The date of the map is probably between 560 and 565. Except for the *Tabula Peutingeriana,* a Roman road map of the third century copied in a manuscript of the thirteenth century, the Madaba mosaic map is the only extant ancient cartographical representation of Palestine. P. Palmer and H. Guthe, *Die Mosaikkarte von Madeba,* I, Pls. Leipzig, 1906; R. T. O'Callaghan, "Madaba (Carte de)," in DB Supplément 5 (1957), cols. 627-704; Michael Avi-Yonah, *The Madaba Mosaic Map with Introduction and Commentary.* Jerusalem: The Israel Exploration Society, 1954; Victor Gold, "The Mosaic Map of Madeba," in BA 21 (1958), pp. 50-71; Herbert Donner and Heinz Cüppers, "Die Restauration und Konservierung der Mosaikkarte von Madeba," in ZDPV 83 (1967), pp. 1-33.

The Anonymous of Piacenza (570). The title of this work is *Antonini Placentini Itinerarium*, but it has been shown (Grisar in ZKT 1902, pp. 760-770 and 1903, pp. 776-780) that it describes a pilgrimage not by, but rather under the protection of, Antoninus Martyr, the latter being the patron saint of Placentia, i.e., Piacenza, in Italy, hence the work is now cited as the Anonymous of Piacenza. It describes the sanctuaries, and the legends attaching to them, at the height of the Byzantine period, ed. Geyer pp. 157-218; LPPTS II; CCSL CLXXV, pp. 129-174.

Sophronius (634). A native of Damascus, Sophronius became a monk at Jerusalem, and also visited Egypt, Rome, and Constantinople. He was made patriarch of Jerusalem in 634. In his time the Persians, i.e., the Neo-Persians or Sasanians, invaded Palestine (614), and he died in the year (638) that Jerusalem was captured by the Muslims under the Caliph 'Umar. The poems (*Anacreontica*) of Sophronius describe the holy places in Jerusalem and Bethlehem. MPG 87, 3 cols. 3147-4014; LPPTS XI.

The Jerusalem Calendar (before 638). The *Kalendarium Hierosolymitanum*, also known as the Georgian Festival Calendar, is preserved in various manuscripts and lists the stations at which the Georgian Church in Jerusalem celebrated the festivals of the church year prior to the Muslim invasion in 638. H. Goussen, *Über georgische Drucke und Handschriften* in *Liturgie und Kunst*, M.-Gladbach, 1923 (cited as Goussen, as quoted in Kopp).

Arculf (670). A Frankish bishop and pilgrim, he visited the Near East and stayed nine months in Jerusalem, being the first Christian traveler there of importance after the rise of Islam. On the return journey Arculf's ship was driven by contrary winds to Britain and he came to Iona. There he related his experiences to Adamnan, Abbot of Iona (679-704), and the latter wrote down the narrative of the journey including ground plans of churches copied from Arculf's wax tablets. The work was in three books, the first concerning Jerusalem, the second about other sites in the Holy Land, and the third about Constantinople. *Adamnai de locis sanctis libri tres*, ed. Geyer pp. 219-297; LPPTS III; CCSL CLXXV, pp. 183-234.

Bede (720). Bede or Baeda, commonly called "the Venerable," lived about 672-735 and spent almost his entire life in the monastery at Wearmouth and Jarrow in Northumbria. About 701 the narrative by Adamnan of the journey of Arculf was presented to the Northumbrian king, Aldfrith the Wise, at York, and became known to Bede. He included some extracts from it in his *Ecclesiastical History of the English Nation* (731), and founded upon it his own treatise, *De locis sanctis*, which became the standard guidebook to the holy places for the pilgrims of the Middle Ages. *Baedae liber de locis sanctis*, ed. Geyer pp. 299-324; LPPTS III; CCSL CLXXV, pp. 251-280.

Epiphanius, or Epiphanius Hagiopolita (750-800). In the title of his "narration" (Διήγησις Ἐπιφανίου Μοναχοῦ τοῦ Ἁγιοπολίτου . . .) he calls himself a monk and a resident of the holy city, i.e., of Jerusalem. His work is an itinerary, written in Greek, and based in part upon an earlier travel account, the latter probably of about the time of Arculf (670). MPG CXX; for other editions and for the date and sources see A. M. Schneider, "Das Itinerarium des Epiphanius Hagiopolita," in ZDPV 63 (1940), pp. 143-154.

Bernard (870). A Frankish monk, he was the last pilgrim from the West to write an account of the holy places before the time of the Crusaders. T. Tobler and A. Molinier, *Itinera Hierosolymitana* I 2 (Geneva 1880).

Eutychius (940). Sa'id ibn al-Bitriq, known as Eutychius or Eutychius of Alexandria, was born in Fustat (Cairo) in 877 and was the Melchite patriarch of Alexandria 933-940. He wrote in Arabic a theological and historical work entitled *The Book of the Demonstration*, in which paragraphs 310ff., probably based upon an earlier source, describe the Christian sanctuaries in Palestine. Pierre Cachia and W. Montgomery Watt, *Eutychius of Alexandria, The Book of the Demonstration (Kitāb al-Burhān)*. CSCO 192, 193, 209, 210. Louvain: Secrétariat du Corpus SCO, 1960-61; also *Annales*, MPG 111; LPPTS XI, pp. 35-70.

Muqaddasi (985). Shams ad Din Abu Abdallah Muhammad ibn Ahmad, known as al-Muqaddasi, "the Jerusalemite," was an Arabian traveler and author. Born at Jerusalem in A.H. 336 = A.D. 946, he made his first pilgrimage at the age of twenty in A.H. 356 = A.D. 967, and completed his *Description of the Lands of Islam* nearly twenty years later in A.H. 375 = A.D. 985. From this work the Description of the Province of Syria, including Palestine, is translated from the Arabic by Guy Le Strange in LPPTS III.

Saewulf (1102). Scandinavian pilgrim and later monk in England, his description of Jerusalem and the holy land is the first we have to cover the period immediately after the conquest of Jerusalem by the Crusaders on July 15, 1099. LPPTS IV.

Daniel (1106). Daniel was a Russian abbot and made a journey in the Holy Land in 1106/1107. His record reflects the traditions preserved by the Greek Orthodox church from before the Crusades. LPPTS IV.

Peter the Deacon (1137). *Petrus Diaconus* was librarian in Monte Cassino, Italy. In 1137 he compiled a *Book concerning the Holy Places*, utilizing earlier pilgrim writings including the narrative of Aetheria, from which he probably preserves materials otherwise missing. *Petri diaconi liber de locis sanctis*, ed. Geyer pp. 103-121.

Phocas (1185). Joannes Phocas was a Greek monk from Crete who described in some detail his travels from Antioch on the Orontes to Jerusalem and elsewhere in the Holy Land. MPG 133; LPPTS V.

Anonymous I (1098), II (1170), III, IV, V, VI, VII (1145), VIII (1185). These are short descriptions of the holy places by unknown authors of the eleventh and twelfth centuries (with more precise dates given when known), i.e., from the time of the Crusades (Jerusalem was taken by the Crusaders in 1099 and by Saladin in 1187). LPPTS VI.

Ernoul (1231). His reports also are from the time of the Crusades, but are preserved only fragmentarily. H. Michelant and G. Raynaud, *Itinéraires à Jérusalem* (Geneva 1882).

Burchard of Mount Sion (1283). He was a German Dominican and presumably received his appellation because of extended residence in Jerusalem. His book, entitled "A Description of the Holy Land," is considered the best of its kind from the time of the Crusades. LPPTS XII.

Quaresmius (1626). Franciscus Quaresmius was born at Lodi in Lombardy in 1583 and died at Milan in 1650. He held high offices in the Franciscan order and in 1616 went to Jerusalem in the position of Guardian. Between 1616 and 1626 he wrote a comprehensive history of the Holy Land and of the custody of the holy places, known as *Elucidatio terrae sanctae*. F. Quaresmius, *Historica, theologica et moralis terrae sanctae elucidatio*, ed. Cypriano da Treviso. Venice, 2 vols. 1880-81.

REFERENCES

William Smith and Henry Wace, *A Dictionary of Christian Biography.* Boston: Little, Brown and Company, 4 vols. 1877-87 (cited as SWDCB); Johannes Quasten, *Patrology.* Westminster, Maryland: The Newman Press, 3 vols. 1950-60; Clemens Kopp, *Die heiligen Stätten der Evangelien.* Regensburg: Friedrich Pustet, 1959 (cited as Kopp), pp. 480-486; Berthold Altaner, *Patrology.* New York: Herder and Herder, 1960.

TABLE OF ARCHEOLOGICAL PERIODS
IN PALESTINE

Neolithic	before 4500 B.C.
Chalcolithic	4500-3200 B.C.
Early Bronze	3200-2100 B.C.
Middle Bronze	2100-1500 B.C.
Late Bronze	1500-1200 B.C.
Iron I	1200-900 B.C.
Iron II	900-539 B.C.
Persian (Iron III)	539-332 B.C.
Hellenistic	332-63 B.C.
Roman	63 B.C.-A.D. 323
Byzantine	A.D. 323-638
Arabic	A.D. 638-1517
Turkish	A.D. 1517-1918

A NOTE ON MEASURES OF LENGTH AND STATEMENTS OF DIRECTION

In the ancient sources such as have just been listed there are various references to distances and directions. The most important measures of length are:

Hebrew

Cubit. The English word is derived from Greek κύβιτον and Latin *cubitum* which mean "elbow," hence is a measure approximately equal to the distance from the elbow to the finger tips. The usual Hebrew word is אמה which means "forearm" and "cubit," and this is usually rendered in the LXX by the Greek word πῆχυς which has the same two meanings. Dt 3:11 mentions the "cubit of a man" which RSV renders as the "common cubit." As the etymology of "cubit" suggests, the length of this ordinary cubit was presumably the average length of the forearm, say about 17.5 inches or in round numbers 18 inches, i.e., one and one-half English feet. Ezk 40:5 refers to a cubit which was a cubit and a handbreadth in length. RSV calls this a "long cubit." If the additional handbreadth be taken as nearly three inches additional this would make a long cubit of about 20.4 inches. The Siloam Tunnel (No. 139) is 1,749 feet long by Vincent's measurement, and the Hebrew inscription found in it says that it was 1,200 cubits in length. This gives a cubit 17.49 inches in length. Other evidence makes it probable that this same value of very close to seventeen and one-half inches is that of Josephus and of *Middoth* as they give measurements of the Jerusalem temple. R. B. Y. Scott in BA 22 (1959), pp. 22ff.; O. R. Sellers in IDB IV, pp. 837f.; R. Pearce S. Hubbard in PEQ 1966, p. 131.

Greek

Foot, πούς, Attic 295.7 millimeters, Olympic 320.5 mm., as compared with English 304.8 mm., say approximately one English foot.

Stadion or Stade, στάδιον, 600 feet, no matter what the length of the foot, Attic stadion 607 English feet, Olympic stadion (as measured from the race course at Olympia) 630.8 English feet, say approximately 600 English feet.

Roman

Foot, *pes*, 296 mm., say approximately one English foot.

Pace or Step (probably actually a double pace), *passus*, 5 *pedes*, say approximately 5 English feet.

Stadium, *stadium*, 125 *passus*, 625 *pedes*, say approximately 600 English feet.

Mile, *mille passus*, a thousand paces, indicated by a *miliarium* or milestone, also called a *lapis* or (mile)-stone (in Greek *mille* is used as a loan word in the form μίλιον, and a milestone is called a σημεῖον, literally a mark or sign), 5,000 Roman feet, 8 *stadia,* approximately 4,854 English feet, 2 Roman miles = approximately 1 4/5 English miles, 5 Roman miles = approximately 4 1/2 English miles.

English and Metric Equivalents

12 inches = 1 foot
5,280 feet = 1 mile
1 millimeter = 0.039 inches
1 centimeter = 0.39 inches
1 meter = 39.37 inches
1 kilometer = 0.62 miles

Examples of the use of some of the foregoing measures: Josephus says that the façade of the Temple edifice was of equal height and breadth, each dimension being a hundred cubits (ἀνὰ πήχεις ἑκατόν), i.e., about 150 feet (*War* v 5, 4 §207); Origen states that Bethany was fifteen stadia from Jerusalem (ἀπέχει τῶν Ἱεροσολύμων σταδίους δέκα πέντε), i.e., about 1 7/10 miles from the city (*Commentary on John* VI 24 GCS Origenes IV p. 149); Eusebius and Jerome locate Bethany at the second mile from Aelia (ἐν δευτέρῳ Αἰλίας σημείῳ; *in secundo ab Aelia miliario*), i.e., about 1 4/5 miles from Jerusalem (*Onomasticon*, pp. 58-59), and place Bethennim (the Ain of Jos 15:32) two miles from a certain terebinth tree (ἀπὸ β′ σημείων τῆς τερεβίνθου; *in secundo lapide a terebintho*) (*Onomasticon*, pp. 24-25); and the Bordeaux Pilgrim states that the spring of the prophet Elisha is 1,500 paces from the city of Jericho (*a ciuitate passos mille quingentos*), i.e., slightly less than a mile and one-half (Geyer p. 24; CCSL CLXXV, p. 18).

As for directions it is often customary, as in the *Onomasticon*, to distinguish only the four cardinal directions, and "to the east" (πρὸς ἀνατολάς or πρὸς ἡλίου ἀνατολάς; *ad orientalem plagam*), for example, can mean east or anywhere in the eastern quarter such as northeast (*Onomasticon*, p. 20 Line 16, p. 64 Line 25).

With the above tabulation of measures readily available references are often allowed to stand in our text to cubits, stadia, etc., without giving conversion into English units. Also it is the case that some archeological reports use centimeters and meters while others employ inches, feet, and yards, and it has been deemed simpler and more accurate to reproduce the reported figures in whatever system is employed rather than to convert all into a single system, and again it is assumed that this will cause no difficulty.

LIST OF ABBREVIATIONS

AAA
Acta apostolorum apocrypha. ed. C. Tischendorf, 1851. Vol. 1 ed. R. A. Lipsius 1891; vols. 2, 1 and 2 ed. M. Bonnet 1898 and 1903; 3 vols. reprinted 1959.

AASOR
The Annual of the American School of Oriental Research in Jerusalem.

Abel, *Géographie*
F.-M. Abel, *Géographie de la Palestine.* Vol. ɪ, 1933, Vol. ɪɪ, 1938. Paris: J. Gabalda et Cie.

AJA
American Journal of Archaeology.

ANEP
James B. Pritchard, *The Ancient Near East in Pictures Relating to the Old Testament.* Princeton: Princeton University Press, 1954.

ANET
James B. Pritchard, ed., *Ancient Near Eastern Texts Relating to the Old Testament.* Princeton: Princeton University Press, 2d ed. 1955.

ANF
Alexander Roberts and James Donaldson, eds., rev. by A. Cleveland Coxe, *The Ante-Nicene Fathers, Translations of the Writings of the Fathers down to A.D. 325.* 10 vols. 1885-87.

ARAB
Daniel D. Luckenbill, *Ancient Records of Assyria and Babylonia.* Chicago: University of Chicago Press, 2 vols. 1926-27.

ASR
Anatolian Studies presented to Sir William Mitchell Ramsay, edited by W. H. Buckler and W. M. Calder. Manchester: University Press, 1923.

Assemani
Joseph Assemani, *Ephraem Syri Opera omnia quae exstant Graece, Syriace, Latine.* Rome: Typographia Pontificia Vaticana, 6 vols. 1732-46.

ASV
American Standard Version.

Avi-Yonah, *Abbreviations*
M. Avi-Yonah, *Abbreviations in Greek Inscriptions (The Near East, 200 B.C.-A.D. 1100).* ǫᴅᴀᴘ 9 (1940) Supplement.

Avi-Yonah, *Madaba Mosaic*
Michael Avi-Yonah, *The Madaba Mosaic Map, with Introduction and Commentary.* Jerusalem: The Israel Exploration Society, 1954; with this cf. the same author's *Map of Roman Palestine.* London: Oxford University Press, 2d ed. 1940.

BAC
Bullettino di archeologia cristiana.

Badè, *Tombs*
William F. Badè, *Some Tombs of Tell en-Nasbeh discovered in 1929.* Berkeley: Palestine Institute Publication No. 2, 1931.

Bagatti
P. B. Bagatti and J. T. Milik, *Gli scavi del "Dominus flevit" (Monte Oliveto-Gerusalemme).* Part ɪ, *La necropoli del periodo romano.* Pubblicazioni dello Studium Biblicum Franciscanum No. 13. Jerusalem: Tipografia dei PP. Francescani, 1958.

Barrois
A.-G. Barrois, *Manuel d'archéologie biblique*, Paris: A. et J. Picard et Cie. Vol. ɪ, 1939; Vol. ɪɪ, 1953.

BASOR
Bulletin of the American Schools of Oriental Research.

BCH
Bulletin de correspondance hellénique.

BJRL
Bulletin of the John Rylands Library.

Cagnat
René Cagnat, *Cours d'épigraphie latine.* Paris: Fontemoing, 4th edition. 1914.

CAP
R. H. Charles, ed., *The Apocrypha and Pseudepigrapha of the Old Testament in English with Introductions and Critical and Explanatory Notes to the Several Books.* Oxford: Clarendon Press, 2 vols. 1913.

Casey
The Excerpta ex Theodoto of Clement of Alexandria edited with Translation, Introduction, and Notes, by Robert P. Casey. Studies and Documents, ɪ. London: Christophers, 1934.

CCSL
Corpus Christianorum Series Latina.

CEMA
K. A. C. Creswell, *Early Muslim Architecture.* Oxford: Clarendon Press, Vol. ɪ, 1932; Vol. ɪɪ, 1940.

CIG
Corpus inscriptionum graecarum. Berlin: G. Reimer, 1828-97.

CIL
Corpus inscriptionum latinarum. Berlin: G. Reimer, 1893-1943.

Clermont-Ganneau
Charles Clermont-Ganneau, *Archaeological Researches in Palestine during the Years 1873-1874.* London: Palestine Exploration Fund, Vol. ɪ, 1899; Vol. ɪɪ, 1896.

CRAI
Comptes rendus des séances de l'Académie des Inscriptions et Belles-Lettres.

Cramer
Maria Cramer, *Das altägyptische Lebenszeichen im christlichen (koptischen) Ägypten, Eine kultur- und religionsgeschichtliche Studie auf archäologischer Grundlage.* Wiesbaden: Otto Harrassowitz, 3d ed., 1955.

Crowfoot, *Early Churches*
J. W. Crowfoot, *Early Churches in Palestine.* The Schweich Lectures of the British Academy, 1937. London: The British Academy, 1941.

CSCO
Corpus Scriptorum Christianorum Orientalium.

CSEL
Corpus scriptorum ecclesiasticorum latinorum.

DACL
Dictionnaire d'archéologie chrétienne et de liturgie. 1924ff.

Dalman, *Jerusalem*
Gustaf Dalman, *Jerusalem und sein Gelände*. Gütersloh: C. Bertelsmann, 1930.

Dalman, *Sacred Sites*
Gustaf Dalman, *Sacred Sites and Ways, Studies in the Topography of the Gospels*. tr. Paul P. Levertoff. New York: The Macmillan Company, 1935.

DB
Dictionnaire de la Bible.

Dean
Epiphanius' Treatise on Weights and Measures, The Syriac Version, ed. by James E. Dean. SAOC 11. Chicago: The University of Chicago Press, 1935.

De Rossi
G. B. de Rossi, *La Roma sotterranea cristiana*. 1864-77.

Diehl
E. Diehl, ed., *Inscriptiones latinae christianae veteres*. 3 vols. Berlin: Weidmann, 1961.

DJD
Discoveries in the Judaean Desert.

Dölger
Dölger, ΙΧΘΥC. Münster in Westf.: Aschendorf. Vol. I, Das Fisch-Symbol in frühchristlicher Zeit, 2d ed. 1928; Vol. IV, Die Fisch-Denkmäler in der frühchristlichen Plastik, Malerei und Kleinkunst, Tafeln, 1927.

DM
The Mishnah translated from the Hebrew with Introduction and Brief Explanatory Notes, by Herbert Danby. London: Humphrey Milford, Oxford University Press, 1933, rev. ed. 1964.

EB
Encyclopaedia Biblica, ed. by T. K. Cheyne and J. Sutherland Black. New York: The Macmillan Company, 4 vols. 1899-1903.

Eusebius, *Onomasticon*
ed. Erich Klostermann, GCS Eusebius 3:1.

FAWR
Jack Finegan, *The Archeology of World Religions, The Background of Primitivism, Zoroastrianism, Hinduism, Jainism, Buddhism, Confucianism, Taoism, Shinto, Islam, and Sikhism*. Princeton: Princeton University Press, 1952. Princeton Paperback edition in three volumes, 1965.

FHBC
Jack Finegan, *Handbook of Biblical Chronology, Principles of Time Reckoning in the Ancient World and Problems of Chronology in the Bible*. Princeton: Princeton University Press, 1964.

FHRJ
Jack Finegan, *Hidden Records of the Life of Jesus*. Philadelphia: United Church Press, 1969.

FLAP
Jack Finegan, *Light from the Ancient Past, The Archeological Background of Judaism and Christianity*. Princeton: Princeton University Press, 2d. ed. 1959.

Frey
Jean-Baptiste Frey, *Corpus Inscriptionum Iudaicarum, Recueil des inscriptions juives qui vont du IIIᵉ siècle avant Jésus-Christ au VIIᵉ siècle de notre ère*. Città del Vaticano: Pontificio Istituto di Archeologia Cristiana. Vol. I, Europe, 1936; Vol. II, Asie-Afrique, 1952.

Galling, "Nekropole"
K. Galling, "Die Nekropole von Jerusalem," in PJ 32 (1936), pp. 73-101.

Galling, *Reallexikon*
Kurt Galling, *Biblisches Reallexikon* (Handbuch zum Alten Testament, ed. Otto Eissfeldt, 1). Tübingen: J. C. B. Mohr (Paul Siebeck), 1937.

GBT
Lazarus Goldschmidt, *Der babylonische Talmud*. Leipzig: Otto Harrassowitz, 9 vols. 1899-1935.

GCS
Die griechischen christlichen Schriftsteller der ersten drei Jahrhunderte, herausgegeben von der Kirchenväter-Commission der königl. preussischen Akademie der Wissenschaften.

Geffcken
Joh. Geffcken, ed., *Die Oracula Sibyllina*. Leipzig: J. C. Hinrichs, 1902.

Geyer
P. Geyer, *Itinera Hierosolymitana saeculi* IIII-VIII. CSEL 39. Vindobonae: F. Tempsky; Lipsiae: G. Freytag, 1898.

Goodenough
Erwin R. Goodenough, *Jewish Symbols in the Greco-Roman Period*. New York: Pantheon Books, Inc., Bollingen Series XXXVII, 1953ff.

Harris and Mingana
Rendel Harris and Alphonse Mingana, *The Odes and Psalms of Solomon*. Manchester: University Press, Vol. I, 1916; Vol. II, 1920.

HERE
James Hastings, ed., *Encyclopaedia of Religion and Ethics*, 12 vols. 1910-22.

HSNTA
Edgar Hennecke, *New Testament Apocrypha*, ed. Wilhelm Schneemelcher, tr. R. McL. Wilson, Vol. I, *Gospels and Related Writings*, 1963; Vol. II, *Writings Relating to the Apostles; Apocalypses and Related Subjects*, 1965. Philadelphia: The Westminster Press.

HTR
The Harvard Theological Review.

HUCA
Hebrew Union College Annual.

IDB
The Interpreter's Dictionary of the Bible. 4 vols. New York and Nashville: Abingdon Press, 1962.

IEJ
Israel Exploration Journal.

JAC
Jahrbuch für Antike und Christentum.

JAOS
Journal of the American Oriental Society.

JBL
Journal of Biblical Literature.

JE
The Jewish Encyclopedia, ed. Isidore Singer. 12 vols. New York and London: Funk & Wagnalls Company, 1901-05.

JEA
The Journal of Egyptian Archaeology.

JJS
The Journal of Jewish Studies.

JPOS
The Journal of the Palestine Oriental Society.

JQR
The Jewish Quarterly Review.

JRS
The Journal of Roman Studies.

JSS
Journal of Semitic Studies.

Kenyon, Jerusalem
Kathleen M. Kenyon, *Jerusalem, Excavating 3000 Years of History.* London: Thames and Hudson, 1967.

Klijn
A. F. J. Klijn, *The Acts of Thomas.* Supplements to Novum Testamentum, v. Leiden: E. J. Brill, 1962.

KLT
Kleine Texte für theologische und philologische Vorlesungen und Übungen, ed. Hans Lietzmann.

Kopp
Clemens Kopp, *Die heiligen Stätten der Evangelien.* Regensburg: Friedrich Pustet, 1959. References are to the German edition. The condensed English edition is: *The Holy Places of the Gospels.* New York: Herder and Herder, 1963.

Kraeling, Bible Atlas
Emil G. Kraeling, *Rand McNally Bible Atlas.* Chicago: Rand McNally & Company, 1956.

Kraeling, Gerasa
Gerasa, City of the Decapolis, ed. Carl H. Kraeling. New Haven: American Schools of Oriental Research, 1938.

LA
Studii Biblici Franciscani Liber Annus.

Lagrange
M.-J. Lagrange, *L'Évangile de Jésus-Christ.* Études bibliques. Paris: J. Gabalda et Cie., new ed., 1954.

LCL
The Loeb Classical Library.

Lefebvre
Gustave Lefebvre, *Recueil des inscriptions grecques-chretiennes d'Egypte.* Cairo: Imprimerie de l'Institut Français d'Archéologie Orientale, 1907.

LPPTS
The Library of the Palestine Pilgrims' Text Society.

LXX
The Septuagint. Henry Barclay Swete, ed., *The Old Testament in Greek according to the Septuagint.* I, 4th ed. 1909; II, 3d ed. 1907; III, 3d ed. 1905. Alfred Rahlfs, ed., *Septuaginta, id est Vetus Testamentum Graece iuxta LXX interpretes.* 2 vols. 1935. *Septuaginta, Vetus Testamentum Graecum auctoritate Societatis Litterarum Gottingensis editum.* 1931ff.

MPG
Jacques Paul Migne, *Patrologiae cursus completus. Series graeca.*

Müller-Bees
Die Inschriften der jüdischen Katakombe am Monteverde zu Rom entdeckt und erklärt von D. Dr. Nikolaus Müller, nach des Verfassers Tode vervollständigt und herausgegeben von Dr. Nikos A. Bees. Schriften herausgegeben von der Gesellschaft zur Förderung der Wissenschaft des Judentums. Leipzig: Otto Harrassowitz, 1919. Cf. Harry J. Leon in *AJA* 31 (1927), pp. 392-394.

NBAC
Nuovo bullettino di archeologia cristiana.

Nötscher
Friedrich Nötscher, *Biblische Altertumskunde* (Die Heilige Schrift des Alten Testaments.) Bonn: Peter Hanstein, 1940.

NPNF
Philip Schaff, ed., *A Select Library of the Nicene and Post-Nicene Fathers,* First Series. 14 vols. 1886-89.

NPNFSS
Philip Schaff and Henry Wace, eds., *A Select Library of Nicene and Post-Nicene Fathers of the Christian Church,* Second Series. 14 vols. 1890-1900.

NT
New Testament.

NTAM
New Testament Archaeology Monographs, ed. Jerry Vardaman. Louisville, Ky.: Southern Baptist Theological Seminary.

NTS
New Testament Studies.

O'Callaghan
R. T. O'Callaghan, "Madaba (Carte de)," in DB Supplément 5 (1957), cols. 627-704.

Oesterley
W. O. E. Oesterley, *II Esdras (The Ezra Apocalypse).* London: Methuen & Co. Ltd., 1933.

OIP
Oriental Institute Publications, The University of Chicago.

OP
The Oxyrhynchus Papyri, ed. Bernard P. Grenfell and Arthur S. Hunt, *et al.* London: Egypt Exploration Fund, 1898ff.

OT
Old Testament.

Pack
Roger A. Pack, ed., Artemidorus, *Onirocriticon.* Leipzig: B. G. Teubner, 1963.

Parrot, Golgotha
André Parrot, *Golgotha and the Church of the Holy Sepulchre.* Studies in Biblical Archaeology No. 6. New York: Philosophical Library, 1957.

Pearlman and Yannai
Moshe Pearlman and Yaacov Yannai, *Historical Sites in Israel.* Tel Aviv–Jerusalem: Massadah–P.E.C. Press Ltd., 2d ed. 1965.

PEFQS
Palestine Exploration Fund Quarterly Statement.

PJ
Palästinajahrbuch des Deutschen evangelischen Instituts für Altertumswissenschaft des Heiligen Landes zu Jerusalem.

Preisigke, Namenbuch
Friedrich Preisigke, *Namenbuch, enthaltend alle griechischen, lateinischen, ägyptischen, hebräischen, arabischen und sonstigen semitischen und nichtsemitischen Menschennamen, soweit sie in griechischen Urkunden (Papyri, Ostraka, Inschriften, Mumienschildern usw.) Ägyptens sich vorfinden.* Heidelberg: 1922.

PSBF
Pubblicazioni dello Studium Biblicum Franciscanum; Publications of the Studium Biblicum Franciscanum.

PWRE
Pauly-Wissowa, *Real-Encyclopädie der classischen Altertumswissenschaft.*

QDAP
The Quarterly of the Department of Antiquities in Palestine.

Rabin
Chaim Rabin, *The Zadokite Documents.* Oxford: Clarendon Press, 2d ed. 1958.

RAC
Rivista di Archeologia Cristiana.

Ramsay, *Phrygia*
W. M. Ramsay, *The Cities and Bishoprics of Phrygia.* Oxford: Clarendon Press, Vol. I, 1895; Vol. I, Part II (cited as II), 1897.

RAO
C. Clermont-Ganneau, *Recueil d'archéologie orientale.* Paris: Ernest Leroux, 1888-1924.

RB
Revue Biblique.

REJ
Revue des Études Juives.

RFAC
Reallexikon für Antike und Christentum, ed. Theodor Klauser. Stuttgart: Hiersemann Verlag, 1950ff.

RSV
Revised Standard Version.
SAOC
Studies in Ancient Oriental Civilization.

SBT
I. Epstein, ed., *The Babylonian Talmud.* London: The Soncino Press, 1935ff.

Schwartz
Eduard Schwartz, *Eusebius Werke, Die Kirchengeschichte.* GCS IX 1-3. Leipzig: J. C. Hinrichs, 3 vols. 1903-09.

SHJP
Emil Schürer, *A History of the Jewish People in the Time of Jesus Christ.* New York: Charles Scribner's Sons, 5 vols. 1896. Revisions of the German edition 1901-09, and photographic reprint by George Olms Verlagsbuchhandlung, Hildesheim, 1964. New revised edition, ed. Matthew Black and Geza Vermes, to be published by T. and T. Clark, Edinburgh.

Simons, *Jerusalem*
J. Simons, *Jerusalem in the Old Testament, Researches and Theories.* Leiden: E. J. Brill, 1952.

Smith, *Geography*
George Adam Smith, *The Historical Geography of the Holy Land.* London: Hodder and Stoughton, 25th ed. 1931. Reprint in Fontana Library, London, Collins, 1966.

Smith, *Jerusalem*
George Adam Smith, Jerusalem, *The Topography, Economics and History from the Earliest Times to A.D. 70.* New York: A. C. Armstrong and Son, 2 vols. 1908.

SMR
H. Freedman and Maurice Simon, eds. *Midrash Rabbah.* London: Soncino Press, 1939ff.

Styger
Paul Styger, *Die römischen Katakomben.* Berlin: Verlag für Kunstwissenschaft, 1933.

SWDCB
William Smith and Henry Wace, *A Dictionary of Christian Biography.* Boston: Little, Brown and Company, 4 vols. 1877-87.

Tell en-Nasbeh
Tell en-Nasbeh Excavated under the Direction of the Late William Frederic Badè, by Chester C. McCown *et al.* Berkeley and New Haven: The Palestine Institute of Pacific School of Religion and The American Schools of Oriental Research, 2 vols., 1947.

Testa
P. E. Testa, *Il simbolismo dei giudeo-cristiani.* PSBF No. 14. Jerusalem: Tipografia dei PP. Francescani, 1962.

Vincent, *Jérusalem*
L.-Hugues Vincent and M.-A. Steve, *Jérusalem de l'Ancien Testament, recherches d'archéologie et d'histoire.* Paris: Librairie Lecoffre, J. Gabalda et Cie, Éditeurs, 3 parts, 1954-56.

Vincent, *Jérusalem nouvelle*
Jérusalem recherches de topographie, d'archéologie et d'histoire. Vol. II, *Jérusalem nouvelle* by Hugues Vincent and F.-M. Abel, 4 Fascicules and Volume of Plates. Paris: Librairie Lecoffre, J. Gabalda, Éditeur. 1914-26.

VT
Vetus Testamentum.

Watzinger
Carl Watzinger, *Denkmäler Palästinas, Eine Einführung in die Archäologie des Heiligen Landes.* Vol. I, *Von den Anfängen bis zum Ende der israelitischen Königszeit*, 1933. Vol. II, *Von der Herrschaft der Assyrer bis zur arabischen Eroberung*, 1935. Leipzig: J. C. Hinrichs.

Wilpert, "La croce"
G. Wilpert, "La croce sui monumenti delle catacombe," in NBAC 8 (1902), pp. 5-14.

YCS
Yale Classical Studies.

ZÄS
Zeitschrift für ägyptische Sprache und Alterthumskunde.

ZAW
Zeitschrift für die alttestamentliche Wissenschaft.

ZDPV
Zeitschrift des Deutschen Palästina-Vereins.

ZHT
Zeitschrift für die historische Theologie.

ZKT
Zeitschrift für katholische Theologie.

ZNW
Zeitschrift für die neutestamentliche Wissenschaft.

ZTK
Zeitschrift für Theologie und Kirche.

The Life of Jesus and the Beginning
of the Early Church

The Life of John the Baptist

1. A View of Ain Karim and the Church of St. John the Baptist

The forerunner of Jesus was known as John the Baptist and was the son of a priest Zechariah and his wife Elizabeth. When Mary visited the home of Zechariah and Elizabeth she went "into the hill country, to a city of Judah" (Lk 1:39); and when John was born and named the events were the subject of conversation "through all the hill country of Judea" (Lk 1:65). The word here rendered "hill country" is ὀρεινή. In the *Natural History* (V 15), which was completed in A.D. 77, Pliny uses the same word in Latin as the name of the district in which, he says, Jerusalem was formerly (*Orinen, in qua fuere Hierosolyma*). Certainly the name was appropriate to the mountainous region in which Jerusalem was located. Therefore the home of Zechariah and Elizabeth, which was the birthplace of John, was somewhere in the hilly area around Jerusalem. About A.D. 150 *The Protevangelium of James* (22:3) represents Elizabeth as fleeing to save John when Herod slaughtered the children, and as going up into the hill country where a mountain was rent asunder and received her. Legendary as this is, the reference is at any rate also to the hill country. Theodosius (530) (Geyer p. 140; LPPTS II, p. 10; CCSL CLXXV, p. 117) states that it was a distance of five miles from Jerusalem to the place where Elizabeth, the mother of John the Baptist, lived. This agrees with the distance (7.50 kilometers) from Jerusalem westward to the village of Ain Karim ("Spring of the Vineyard"). This village is mentioned by name in the Jerusalem Calendar (before 638) when it gives this as the place of a festival, celebrated on the 28th of August, in memory of Elizabeth: "In the village of Enquarim, in the church of the just Elizabeth, her memory" (Goussen p. 30). Eutychius of Alexandria (940) writes: "The church of Bayt Zakariya in the district of Aelia bears witness to the visit of Mary to her kinswoman Elizabeth" (CSCO 193, p. 135). When Jerusalem was rebuilt by Hadrian (135) it was called Aelia Capitolina, so the church just referred to "in the district of Aelia" was in the vicinity of Jerusalem and probably at Ain Karim. Whether the church of Elizabeth mentioned in the Jerusalem Calendar and the church of Zechariah spoken of by Eutychius were two different churches or were one and the same is not fully clear, but the latter will appear more probable in the light of what follows from Daniel. Daniel (1106) describes two separate churches which were evidently at Ain Karim. Proceeding from the monastery of the Holy Cross west of Jerusalem it was, he says (LPPTS IV, pp. 51ff.), four versts (the Russian verst equals 3,500 feet or about two-thirds of an English mile) to the house of Zacharias, the house where the holy Virgin came to greet Elizabeth. "A church now occupies this place," he writes; "on entering it there is, to the left, beneath the low altar, a small cavern, in which John the Forerunner was born." Half a verst from there, Daniel continues, is the mountain which gave asylum to Elizabeth and her son when the soldiers of Herod

were pursuing them, and this place is also marked with a small church. The church described by Daniel at the site of the house of Zacharias is presumably the same as the church of Zakariya mentioned by Eutychius; it may well be also the same as the church of Elizabeth listed in the Jerusalem Calendar since it marks the place, according to Daniel, where Mary visited Elizabeth. The second church, where the rock received Elizabeth and John, was obviously related to the narrative in *The Protevangelium of James* rather than to the account in the canonical Gospels.

The spring which provides water for the village of Ain Karim must have encouraged settlement in this region from an early time, and pottery from the Middle Bronze Age has been found at or near Ain Karim (G. Ernest Wright in BASOR 71 [Oct. 1938], pp. 28f.). The town may be the same as the Karem (Καρέμ) listed in Jos 15:59 LXX among the cities of the tribe of Judah.

The photograph shows the village as it lies in the hill country, with the Church of St. John the Baptist near the center of the picture. The church has been in the hands of the Franciscans since 1674. In 1941-1942 they conducted excavations in the area immediately west of the church and the adjoining monastery. In the area were uncovered several rock-cut chambers and graves as well as wine presses with mosaic floors and small chapels with mosaic pavements. The southern rock-cut chamber contained pottery of a type which has been found elsewhere around Jerusalem in association with coins of the Herodian dynasty and belongs therefore to the period from about the first century B.C. up to A.D. 70. This chamber must have existed, then, in about the first century B.C., and it is evidence for a community here at the very time of Zechariah, Elizabeth, and John. The other finds show a continuity of the community not only during Roman but also Byzantine and early Arab times. As for St. John's church itself, the present structure may be mainly from the eleventh century (Abel, *Géographie* II, pp. 295f.) but lower portions of the walls probably still remain from the Byzantine period. At the front end of the left aisle is a grotto which must correspond with the small cavern mentioned by Daniel.

Sylvester J. Saller, *Discoveries at St. John's, 'Ein Karim, 1941-1942.* PSBF 3. Jerusalem: Franciscan Press, 1946. Photograph: courtesy École Biblique et Archéologique Française.

2. The Church of the Visitation at Ain Karim

The other ancient church at Ain Karim is known as the Sanctuary of the Visitation. It is located across the village to the southwest from St. John's. In the vicinity are two rock-cut chambers with ledges around the walls, tombs therefore of a type known in Palestine from the end of the Late Bronze Age and in use even in the Roman period (see No. 207). In 1938 the Franciscans conducted excavations in the ancient ruins at the Visitation Church. The early sanctuary was built against a rocky declivity, and both Byzantine and medieval walls were found. In the crypt a recess contains an oval gray rock, 91 x 104 x 70 centimeters in size, with a natural depression in the center. It is venerated as the *pietra del nascondimento*, the "stone in which John was concealed," in obvious dependence on *The Protevangelium of James* (cf. above No. 1).

QDAP 8 (1939), pp. 170-172; Bellarmino Bagatti, *Il santuario della Visitazione ad 'Ain Karim (Montana Judaeae), esplorazione archeologica e ripristino.* PSBF 5. Jerusalem: Franciscan Press, 1948. Photograph: courtesy École Biblique et Archéologique Française.

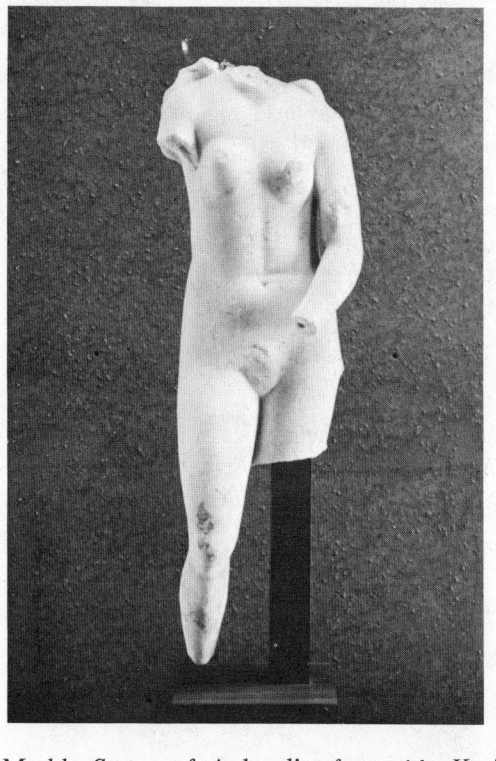

3. Marble Statue of Aphrodite from Ain Karim

In the excavations at Ain Karim this marble statue of Aphrodite or Venus was found in two broken pieces. As joined together again the total height of the figure is 72 centimeters. The statue appears to be a copy of a work of Praxiteles (340 B.C.) and, with its strong and vigorous lines, is thought to belong to the first century of the Christian era. According to Herodotus (I 105) the goddess Aphrodite was worshiped in a temple in Ascalon as early as in the time of Psammetichus (Psamtik I, 663-610 B.C.) of Egypt. According to Jerome (*Letter 58 to Paulinus*, 3) there was from the time of Hadrian to the reign of Constantine—a period of about 180 years—on the rock at Jerusalem, where the cross had

stood, a marble statue of Venus which was an object of worship. This was done away with when the Church of the Holy Sepulcher was built and dedicated in 335 (Eusebius, *Life of Constantine* III 26). The statue here shown, made of marble as was the one Jerome describes at Calvary, presumably stood at Ain Karim during the Roman period too, and was also overthrown in the Byzantine period, perhaps somewhat later than the one in Jerusalem.

While the evidence noted thus far seems to point to Ain Karim, there were other traditions. Among the Christian sanctuaries of the Arab period (seventh-tenth centuries) there were two churches of St. John the Baptist at Jerusalem, one on the summit of the Mount of the Olives, the other at the foot of the Mount. Concerning the latter a Slavonic text (*Archives de l'Orient Latin*, II, p. 392; J. T. Milik in RB 67 [1960], p. 562 cf. p. 357) earlier than Daniel (1106) says that the place at the foot of the Mount was that of the house of Zechariah where John was born and from which Elizabeth went into the mountains with her child.

Saller, *Discoveries at St. John's, 'Ein Karim*, pp. 108-115, 190 n. 1, Pl. 30, 1 a-c. Photograph: courtesy Palestine Archaeological Museum.

4. A View of the Wilderness of Judea

Although John was born in a city in the "hill country" of Judah (No. 1), it is stated of him in Lk 1:80 that he was in the wilderness or, literally, in the deserts ($\dot{\epsilon}\nu$ $\tau\alpha\hat{\imath}\varsigma$ $\dot{\epsilon}\rho\dot{\eta}\mu o\iota\varsigma$) till the day of his manifestation to Israel, i.e., until the day of his public appearance. Like the Hebrew מדבר, which it generally translates in the LXX, the Greek $\ddot{\epsilon}\rho\eta\mu o\varsigma$ is the desolate, empty, lonely land. It may be stony or sandy, or it may be a grassland. It may be the haunt of nomads. But it is not cultivated, and

it is not permanently settled.

Since the birthplace of John was in the land of Judea, the wilderness in which he spent his youth was presumably the wilderness of Judea. The latter is definable from biblical references. Num 21:20 states that Mount Pisgah looks down upon Jeshimon. The latter name means desolated or deserted, and probably describes the barren terraces of marl on either side of the Jordan above the Dead Sea, and the steep hills behind Jericho and on the west side of the Dead Sea. Jos 15:61-62 lists six "cities" which were in the wilderness of Judah. Among them are the following, whose probable locations are in the area just described and whose names are obviously characteristic for desert sites: Beth-arabah, "House of the Arabah (i.e., the 'arid region' containing the Jordan and Dead Sea and extending to the Gulf of Aqabah)," probably to be identified with Ain Gharba, southeast of Jericho; 'Ir-hammelah, "City of Salt," probably the later Qumran; and En-gedi, "Spring of the Kid," still today a hot spring called Ain Jidi on the west shore of the Dead Sea twenty miles south of Qumran. In all, the area of this wilderness (see map, No. 7) is some thirty-five miles from north to south and fifteen miles from east to west.

This view in the wilderness of Judea is taken from the road between Jerusalem and Jericho. In the distance an ancient trail runs across the hills.

Smith, *Geography*, pp. 312-316. Photograph: JF.

5. Khirbet Qumran

Since Zechariah and Elizabeth were already of advanced age at the birth of John, it may be supposed that the child was left without father and mother at a relatively early time. How this child could live "in the wilderness" (Lk 1:80) is difficult to understand, unless there were those there who could receive him and help him. Josephus says of the Essenes who disdained marriage that "they adopt other men's children while yet pliable and docile, and regard them as their kin and mould them in accordance with their own principles" (*War* II, viii, 2 §120). It is at least possible, therefore, that John could have been taken in as a child by such a group. This possibility encounters real problems, of course, since an antipathy existed between the Essenes and the regular temple priests (Vardaman). Zechariah, John the Baptist's father, was of the priestly family of Abijah (Lk 1:5), one of the regular line of priestly courses or families.

Pliny locates the Essenes "on the west side of the Dead Sea, but out of range of the noxious exhalations of the coast" (*Natural History* V xv 73), and the well-known ruins at Qumran are probably to be recognized as this very Essene center. The photograph looks across the ruins from the southeast toward the steep cliffs in the background, in which the first of the famous Dead Sea Scrolls were found. From here it is only a few miles around the curving northwestern shore of the Dead Sea to the Jordan River, and that is where John made his public appearance. A prior association with nearby Qumran is therefore at least hypothetically possible.

William H. Brownlee in *Interpretation* 9 (1955), p. 73. Photograph: JF.

6. Column VIII of the Manual of Discipline

In their center above the Dead Sea the Qumran community was located on the edge of the wilderness of Judea, the limestone hills of which fall off precipitously to the marl terrace on which their buildings were constructed (No. 5). In Israelite experience and thought the wilderness was of great importance. It was a place of political refuge and a base for revolutionary action. When Saul pursued David, David took refuge in the wilderness of En-gedi (I Sam 24:1). When Antiochus Epiphanes persecuted the Jews, "Many who were seeking righteousness and justice went down to the wilderness to dwell there, they, their sons, their wives, and their cattle, because evils pressed heavily upon them" (I Macc 2:29), and there in the wilderness, when they were hunted out by the enemy and refused to defend themselves on the sabbath, they died. Judas Maccabeus kept himself and his companions alive in the wilderness (II Macc 5:27). An Egyptian led four thousand *sicarii* into the wilderness (Ac 21:38).

The wilderness was also unforgettably associated with the thought of the exodus. The first exodus, from Egypt, was across the wilderness of Sinai. The second exodus, from Babylon, was across the wilderness between Babylonia and Palestine and, in connection with it, Isaiah (40:3) heard a voice crying:

In the wilderness prepare the way of the Lord,
 make straight in the desert a highway for our God.

This passage in Isaiah was of decisive importance in the thought of the Qumran community. A manuscript found in Cave 1 at Qumran refers in its opening line to the "order" (*serek*) of the community, hence is designated as 1QS and commonly known as the Manual of Discipline. Column VIII of this manuscript is shown in the photograph (No. 6). In the middle of the column the text states that, according to these rules, the men of the community will separate themselves from the midst of perverse men to go to the wilderness to prepare the way, i.e., to do what the Scripture instructs when it says,

In the wilderness prepare the way of . . . .
 make straight in the desert a highway for our God.

This is an exact quotation of Is 40:3 except that, as may be seen in Line 14 of Column VIII, four dots stand in the place of the four letter name of the Lord (YHWH), which was too holy to write or pronounce. Then it is further explained that this reference really means to study the Law which God commanded through Moses, so as to do, as occasion arises, according to all that was revealed in it and according to what the prophets also revealed through God's Holy Spirit. It was, therefore,

with deliberate intent that the Qumran community established itself in the wilderness, there to study and do the Law, and thus to prepare the way of the Lord. The purpose was, as it were, to make a third exodus and a third conquest of the promised land, a conquest which would be both "concurrent with, and instrumental in, the ushering in of the Kingdom of God" (Williams). Significantly enough, the same crucial passage in Isaiah is cited in all four Gospels (Mt 3:3; Mk 1:3; Lk 3:4; Jn 1:23) to describe the work of John the Baptist as he made his public appearance and, according to Jn 1:23, he himself cited the passage with respect to his own work. The relationship of John in his public work with Qumran was, therefore, not only one of geographical nearness but also of similarity of thought form. Yet the work to which John addressed himself was not that deemed most important at Qumran, namely, the study of the Law, but rather something that was distinctively different, namely, the preaching of a baptism of repentance.

Millar Burrows, *The Dead Sea Scrolls of St. Mark's Monastery*, Vol. II, Fascicle 2, *Plates and Transcription of the Manual of Discipline*. New Haven: The American Schools of Oriental Research, 1951; William H. Brownlee, *The Dead Sea Manual of Discipline, Translation and Notes*. BASOR Supplementary Studies Nos. 10-12, pp. 32-33; Theodor H. Gaster, *The Dead Sea Scriptures in English Translation*. Garden City, New York: Doubleday & Company, Inc., 1956, p. 56; George H. Williams, *Wilderness and Paradise in Christian Thought*. New York: Harper & Brothers, 1962, p. 19. Photograph: Burrows, *op.cit.*, Pl. VIII, courtesy American Schools of Oriental Research.

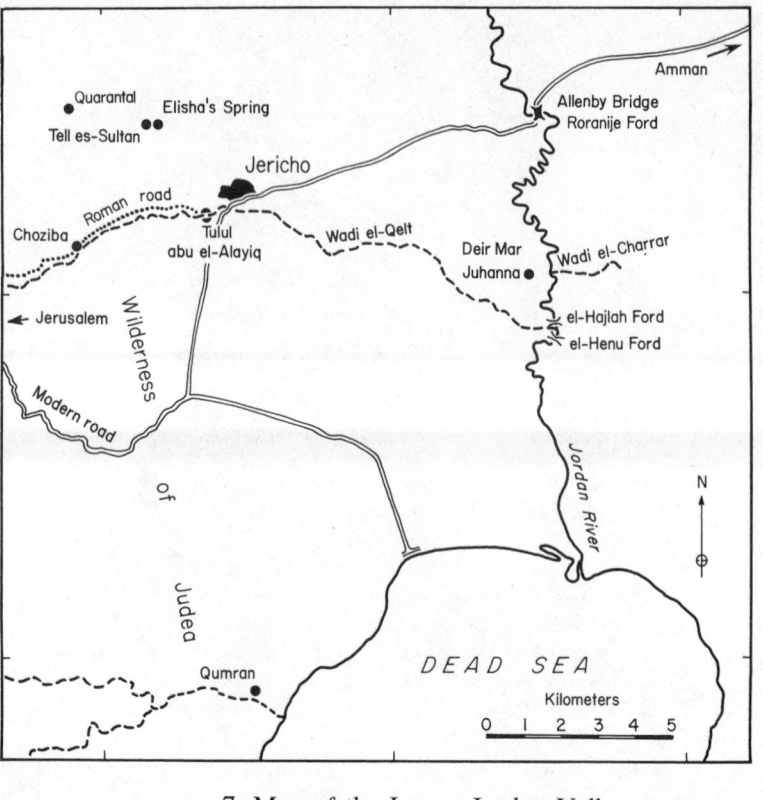

7. Map of the Lower Jordan Valley

When John the Baptist came on the scene of his public work he was found in "the region about the Jordan" (Lk 3:3) and was baptizing people in the Jordan (Mt. 3:6; Mk 1:5). The sketch map shows sites on the Lower Jordan and in the adjacent valley as far westward as Jericho.

Map: JF, cf. Kopp, p. 141.

8. The Jordan River near the Monastery of St. John

When John chose to baptize in the Jordan river it was presumably first of all because this stream provided adequate water for the ceremony of immersion ($\beta\alpha\pi\tau\iota\zeta\omega$ Mt 3:6, etc., in LXX for טבל IV K 5:14, "to dip"). It is also true that a connection was recognized between John and Elijah (Mk 1:2 cites Mal 4:5; see also Mt 11:14; 17:12; Mk 9:13), and John clothed himself in the same garb as Elijah (Mt 3:4; Mk 1:6; cf. II K 1:8). At the close of his life (II K 2) Elijah was at Jericho and Gilgal and then went across the Jordan, therefore it could be that John's choice of a Jordan locale in which to work was related to his enactment of the role of Elijah. Since all the people, as it seemed, of Jerusalem and Judea went out to John (Mt 3:5; Mk 1:5), it is probable that his place of preaching and baptizing was at a point on the river to which a main road or roads came down. As may be seen on the preceding Map of the Lower Jordan Valley (No. 7), the main road east from Jericho to Amman crosses the river today by a bridge at what used to be the Roranije ford. This point is five miles on the road from Jericho and about nine miles on the river upstream from where the Jordan enters the Dead Sea. Below the Roranije ford there were three other ancient crossings. The next was about four and one-half miles downstream where the Deir Mar Juhanna or Monastery of St. John stands on a low hill seven hundred yards west of the river and, on the other side, the Wadi el-Charrar comes in from the east. The photograph shows the river in this area. Another mile below was the el-Hajlah ford, near where the Wadi el-Qelt comes in from the west. Half again as far southward was the el-Henu crossing. The circumstances of John's work noted above make it probable that his activity was somewhere in this general area.

Photograph: JF.

9. Baptism in the Jordan near the Monastery of St. John

In Jn 1:28 (cf. Jn 10:40) there is reference to a specific point for John's work when it is stated that he was baptizing "in Bethany beyond the Jordan." In the NT the well-known Bethany is the village on the slope of the Mount of Olives near Jerusalem, and this Bethany beyond the Jordan is not mentioned except in the Fourth Gospel. While in Jn 1:28 the best and earliest manuscripts read Bethany (Βηθανία), there is also a variant reading of Bethabara (Βηθαβαρά). The latter reading is now preserved only in some relatively late manuscripts (Π = 041 ninth century, Ψ = 044 eighth-ninth centuries, Sinaitic and Curetonian Syriac, etc.), but Origen was acquainted with it and was convinced that it was correct. Bethany, he explains in his *Commentary on John* (VI 24 GCS Origenes IV, p. 149; ANF IX, p. 370), was the town of Lazarus, Martha, and Mary, only fifteen stadia (less than two miles) from Jerusalem, but the river Jordan is about 180 stadia (over twenty miles) distant and there is no place named Bethany in its neighborhood. "They say," however, Origen declares, "that Bethabara is pointed out on the banks of the Jordan, and that John is said to have baptized there." His further contribution to the subject is the suggestion that in etymology Bethany means "House of obedience," and Bethabara "House of preparation," the latter obviously being the more appropriate to the work of the one who prepared the way before the face of the Christ. Eusebius also, in the *Onomasticon* (p. 58), lists Bethany as the village of Lazarus at the Mount of Olives, and gives Bethabara (Βηθααβαρά) as the place where John baptized and where even until now, as he says,

many of the brethren aspire to receive the washing. Yet one other textual variant appears in Jn 1:28 in the hand of the second corrector of Codex Sinaiticus and the margin of the Harklean Syriac, namely, Betharaba (Βηθαραβά). This can be explained as a simple error for Bethabara or as an equation of the place with the Betharabah listed in Jos 15:6 which was probably located southeast of Jericho (cf. above No. 4).

In the itinerary of the Bordeaux Pilgrim (333), after a description of the Dead Sea, it is said (Geyer p. 24; LPPTS I, p. 26; CCSL CLXXV, p. 19): "From there to the Jordan, where the Lord was baptized by John, is five miles. Here there is a place by the river, a little hill on the far bank, where Elijah was caught up into heaven." The distance of five Roman miles, or about four and one-half English miles, upstream from the Dead Sea would have brought the pilgrim to about the point of the Monastery of St. John. The little hill on the east side would be the Jebel Mar Elyas or Mount of St. Elijah, which is less than a mile and one-half up the Wadi el-Charrar. Jewish tradition must have pointed to this as the place where Elijah was taken up. According to II K 2:4, 6, 8-11, the place of that event was indeed east of the Jordan across from Jericho. By the hill are abundant springs and the waters here might well have been used for baptizing when the Jordan was in flood.

Theodosius (530) (Geyer pp. 145-146; LPPTS II, pp. 14-15; CCSL CLXXV, pp. 121-122) also says that it was five (Roman) miles from the Dead Sea to the place where the Lord was baptized, and declares that the place was marked by a marble column with an iron cross. He also says that there was a Church of St. John the Baptist

9

here, but does not make it plain whether the church was on the west bank or the east. It could have been where the Monastery of St. John is now. As to the place where the Lord was baptized, however, he says explicitly that it was on the east side (*trans Iordanem*) and he mentions there a little mountain where Elijah was taken up, obviously identical with the hill mentioned by the Bordeaux Pilgrim.

The Anonymous of Piacenza (570) mentions (Geyer p. 165; LPPTS II, pp. 8-9; CCSL CLXXV, p. 134) the same hill and the spring, two Roman miles (slightly less than one and one-half English miles) from the Jordan, where John used to baptize. The valley itself is where Elijah was found when the raven brought him bread and meat. Wadi el-Charrar was, accordingly, identified with "the

brook Cherith that is east of the Jordan" (1 K 17:5) and, with this identification, it appears more clearly than ever that John chose to do his work in surroundings associated with Elijah. The place where Jesus himself was baptized (Geyer pp. 166-168; LPPTS II, pp. 10-12; CCSL CLXXV, pp. 135-136), however, was at the Jordan. At the place a wooden cross stood in the water and above the Jordan, not far from the river, was the Monastery of St. John. At Epiphany, says the Anonymous, many people come here to the river to be baptized. The photograph pictures the preparation for the conduct of baptism by the Greek Orthodox Church at this traditional place on the Jordan River near the Monastery of St. John.

Photograph: JF.

10. The Region of Jericho on the Madaba Mosaic Map
North is at *left* on Madaba mosaic

The area which has just been under discussion is depicted in detail on the Madaba Mosaic Map. We will now show this area in photographs of three slightly overlapping sections (Nos. 10-12). The first photograph reproduces the area around Jericho. Extending up a little above the middle of the picture are the dark mountains of the wilderness of Judea. Beyond is the lighter plain of the Jordan and in the extreme upper right-hand corner the curve of the shore of the Dead Sea. On the edge of the plain and near the mountains are, from left to right:

Archelais (Αρχελαις) (Josephus, *Ant.* XVII 13, 1 §340; XVIII 2, 2 §31); the place of Saint Elisha (Τὸ τοῦ ἁγίου Ἐλισαιου), undoubtedly the spring cleansed by Elisha (II K 2:19-22) and visited by the Bordeaux Pilgrim (Geyer p. 24; LPPTS I, p. 25; CCSL CLXXV, p. 18) at 1,500 paces from Jericho, shown here with a sanctuary from under the southern tower of which a stream flows toward the city; and Jericho (·Ι· εριχω). Farther out in the plain are Galgala, the place which is also called the Twelve Stones (Γαλγαλα τὸ καὶ Δωδεκαλιθον), marking the site of Jos 4:20, located by Eusebius (*Onomasticon* pp. 64-67) two miles from Jericho in an eastward direction (πρὸς ἡλίου ἀνατολάς Jos 4:19 LXX), and shown here with a wall in which are embedded twelve white stones; and the Threshing Floor of Atad which is now Bethagla ("Αλων 'Ατὰθ ἡ νῦν Βηθαγλά), the site of Gen 50:10-11, located by Eusebius (*Onomasticon* p. 8) three miles from Jericho and two miles from the Jordan, i.e., on the west side as shown here. The fact that the passage in Genesis puts the place "beyond the Jordan" can be explained by supposing that the statement is phrased from the point of view of Joseph's party as they came up from Egypt. On the other hand the site may have been originally in Transjordan and transferred to the west side for the convenience of visiting pilgrims. It is not, however, mentioned in any of the ancient pilgrim itineraries. From Archelais to Bethagla many palm trees are shown and they are particularly numerous around Jericho. Both Josephus (*Ant.* XVIII 2, 2 §31) and Pliny (*Nat. Hist.* XIII 9, 44) mention the date palms at Archelais, and Josephus (*Ant.* XVII 13, 1 §340) tells of a whole plain planted with palm trees at Jericho.

Photograph: courtesy Victor R. Gold.

11. The Lower Jordan on the Madaba Mosaic Map
North is at *left* on Madaba mosaic.

This photograph overlaps the east edge of the preceding section and repeats in whole or in part the legends for Galgala and Bethagla (see No. 10). Looking beyond these legends we see the Jordan River flowing down through the plain and into the Dead Sea. In the river are several fish and the one farthest downstream is turning back, evidently in distaste, from the salt water of the Dead Sea in which are no living creatures. Upstream there is a construction which reaches across the river, with a boat beneath it. This is perhaps a ferry guided by a rope across the river. On the west bank at this point is a tower built upon an arch and approached by a ladder. Eusebius (*Onomasticon*, p. 154) mentions a certain Magdalsenna (Μαγδαλσεννά) which marked the border of Judea and was eight miles north of Jericho; since Magdal can be Hebrew "tower" (מגדל) and the location is approximately correct, this tower may mark that site. On either side of the river crossing is a large desert shrub, perhaps a thorn bush, and these mark the plains of Jericho on this side of the river and the plains of Moab in Transjordan. In Transjordan a lion, the representation of which is badly damaged, is chasing a gazelle. Also partly damaged are two unidentified villages with many date palms.

Coming to the banks of the river and the names associated with the work of John the Baptist, we have on the west side the name Bethabara and, under it, a legend in red letters (partly obscured by the leg of the photographer's tripod) identifying the place of St. John (and) of the baptism (Βεθαβαρὰ τὸ τοῦ ἁγίου Ἰωάννου τοῦ βαπτίσματος), and a church building. In Jn 1:28 Bethany (or Bethabara) is located beyond the Jordan and both the Bordeaux Pilgrim and Theodosius (cf. above No. 9) mention the place of the baptism of Jesus in some connection with the hill from which Elijah was caught up, which was on the east side of the river. If John was working thus on the east side of the river and if Jesus was baptized in the river itself (Mk 1:9), the actual place would presumably have been near the east bank. The transfer of Bethabara and of the traditional place of the baptism to the west bank, as shown here in the Madaba Mosaic, would make the spot more convenient for pilgrims to visit, and this may account for the change.

On the map we see on the east side of the river at about the place we would have expected to find Bethabara and the hill of Elijah, a site with an inscription reading, Aenon, there now Sapsaphas (Αἰνὼν ἔνθα νῦν ὁ Σαπσαφάς). Since the map shows the Aenon identified as near Salim (Jn 3:23) farther up the river (cf. No. 12) this is not that Aenon, at least in the opinion of the map maker, although his use of the name here may mean that one tradition did localize the other Aenon at this place. Since the name Aenon is doubtless derived from the Hebrew word for "springs" (עינים), it could refer here to the springs by the hill from which Elijah was supposed to have been taken up, springs which could have been used for baptism by John as well as

the Jordan itself, and which are probably to be identified with the spring where John was said to baptize, two miles from the Jordan, as mentioned by the Anonymous of Piacenza (Geyer p. 199: LPPTS II, p. 9; CCSL CLXXV, p. 134; and cf. above No. 9). Sapsaphas may mean "willow" (Avi-Yonah in IDB I, p. 52). A Sapsas is mentioned by John Moschus (MPG 87, col. 2851), who also says that the patriarch Elias of Jerusalem (494-518) built a church and monastery there. No buildings are shown at this site on the Madaba Map, but there is an object on the right side which may be a tree, and a representation on the left side which could stand for a cave. Around 840 Epiphanius Monachus (MPG 120, col. 272) mentions a cave of the forerunner about a mile beyond the Jordan (πέραν τοῦ Ἰορδάνου ὡς ἀπὸ μιλίου ἑνός ἐστι τὸ σπήλαιον τοῦ προδρόμου), which may be what is meant here.

F.-M. Abel in RB 41 (1932), pp. 248-252 and Pl. V facing p. 240; Sylvester J. Saller and Bellarmino Bagatti, *The Town of Nebo (Khirbet el-Mekhayyat), with a Brief Survey of Other Ancient Christian Monuments in Transjordan.* PSBF 7. Jerusalem: Franciscan Press, 1949, p. 226 No. 59 and Pl. 54 No. 1; Wolfgang Wiefel, "Bethabara jenseits des Jordan (Joh. 1, 28)," in ZDPV 83 (1967), pp. 72-81. Photograph: courtesy Victor R. Gold.

12. Upper Portion of the Jordan on the
Madaba Mosaic Map

North is at *left* on Madaba mosaic.

This is the uppermost part of the river which is preserved in the fragmentary mosaic map at Madaba. As

also in the lower course of the river (see No. 11), there is a boat in the stream and a construction across the river, probably a ferry. Below this, a tributary river, evidently the Jabbok (Wadi Zerqa), comes in from the far side and creates a disturbance in the Jordan. On the west bank at this point is a village labeled Κορεους, Coreus. This is doubtless the Coreae (Κορέαι) which Josephus (*War* I 6, 5 §134; IV 8, 1 §449; *Ant.* XIV 3, 4 §49; 5, 2 §83) mentions as below Scythopolis and on the border of Judea, a point through which Pompey marched in 63 B.C. and Vespasian in A.D. 68. It is identified with Tell el-Mazar at the lower end of Wadi Far 'ah (BASOR 62 [Apr. 1936], p. 14). Upstream on the west side opposite the ferry is a place labeled Αἰνὼν ἡ ἐγγὺς τοῦ Σαλήμ, clearly intended to be the Aenon near Salim (Αἰνὼν ἐγγὺς τοῦ Σαλίμ) of Jn 3:23. The location is in agreement with Eusebius (*Onomasticon* p. 40) who places the Aenon of Jn 3:23 at eight miles south of Scythopolis, and also with a description given by Aetheria (Geyer pp. 56-58; LPPTS I, pp. 30-32; CCSL CLXXV, pp. 54-56). The latter came down into the Jordan valley to a village called Sedima which, she was given to understand, had been the Salem of King Melchizedek. Two hundred paces from there she was shown a garden called The Garden of St. John. Here was a spring which flowed into a pool and in this, she says, it appeared that John had baptized. On the Madaba Map the pool may be represented by the row of bluish-greenish cubes above the name Aenon. In the area indicated, some twelve kilometers south of Tell el-Husn (ancient Beth-shean and Scythopolis), there is in fact a region of abundant springs (Ain ed-Deir and others) (RB 22 [1913], pp. 222-223). The marches of Pompey and Vespasian down the Jordan valley and through this region, referred to above, show that this was on a main route of travel. If John the Baptist worked here as well as at the lower fords of the Jordan (cf. above No. 8), he was in both cases in regions where large numbers of people would go by.

Photograph: courtesy Victor R. Gold.

13. Baptismal Pool and Apse in the Byzantine Church in the Desert of St. John near Hebron

While the area dealt with in the preceding sections (Nos. 4-12) appears best to correspond with the indications in the Gospels as to where the work of John the Baptist was centered, there are also other but later traditions. In the pilgrim record known as Anonymous II (1170) there is mention of returning from Hebron toward Jerusalem and of passing the Church of St. John the Baptist, where he preached baptism and repentance and where there was an unfailing spring of water in the midst of the desert (LPPTS VI, p. 11). The combination of church and desert and spring in the vicinity of Hebron corresponds with a valley five miles west of that city, in which are a spring still called Ain el-Ma'-mudiyyeh, "spring of baptism," and the ruins of a small Byzantine church. The church was probably built in

the time of Justinian (527-565). As shown in the photograph, there is in the apse a circular baptistery over four feet deep, with four marble steps leading down into it. A conduit opens in the wall at one side which conducts water to the baptistery from the spring. Another location for the "desert of John," for which the attestation is even later, is about a mile and one-half west of Ain Karim at Ain el-Khabis, the "Spring of the Hermit." It is mentioned first by Ulrich Brunner, who made a trip from Würzburg to Jerusalem in 1470 (ZDPV 29 [1906], p. 43). At the place there are now a church and monastery built by the Franciscans.

"Le désert de Saint Jean près d'Hébron," in RB 53 (1946), I, "La tradition," by Clemens Kopp, pp. 547-558; II, "Les monuments," by A.-M. Steve, pp. 559-575; "Die Jerusalemfahrt des Kanonikus Ulrich Brunner vom Haugstift in Würzburg (1470)," ed. Reinhold Röhricht, in ZDPV 29 (1906), pp. 1-50. Photograph: RB 53 (1946), Pl. IX, courtesy École Biblique et Archéologique Française.

14. Machaerus

The death of John the Baptist is related in Mt 14:3-12 and Mk 6:17-29. The king who ordered John beheaded was Herod Antipas, tetrarch of Galilee and Perea from 4 B.C. to A.D. 39. At his birthday banquet, it is stated in Mk 6:21, there were present "the leading men of Galilee." This could suggest that the banquet was held in the city of Tiberias, which Herod Antipas built as his capital on the Sea of Galilee (Josephus, *Ant.* XVIII 2, 3 §36). Josephus (*Ant.* XVIII 5, 2 §119), however, states that John was brought in chains to Machaerus and there put to death. The site of Machaerus, shown in this photograph, is some fifteen miles southeast of the mouth of the Jordan, in the wild and desolate hills that overlook the Dead Sea from the east. The fortress on this site was built originally by Alexander Jannaeus (103-76 B.C.), destroyed by Pompey's general Gabinius, and then rebuilt very splendidly by Herod the Great. Upon the death of the latter it passed into the hands of Herod Antipas, and his relations with Nabatea doubtless made the place, strategically located in the direction of Nabatea, of special importance to him. In A.D. 72 the Roman commander Lucilius Bassus took Machaerus and, in connection with this event, Josephus (*War* VII 6, 1ff. §§164ff.) gives a description of the place. The site had great natural strength, being a rocky eminence entrenched on all sides within deep ravines. The valley on the west extends sixty stadia to Lake Asphaltitis, as Josephus calls the Dead Sea; the valley on the east falls away to a depth of a hundred cubits (150 feet). Particularly because of its proximity to Arabia, Herod the Great regarded the place as deserving the strongest fortification. He enclosed an extensive area with ramparts and towers and founded a city; on top of the mountain, surrounding the crest, he built a wall with corner towers each sixty cubits (90 feet) high, and in the center of this enclosure he built a magnificent palace. At convenient spots numerous cisterns were provided to collect rain water.

G. A. Smith in PEFQS 1905, pp. 229ff.; DB Supplément, "Machéronte," v, 613-618; E. Schürer, *Geschichte* 4th ed., *passim*, esp. I, 438 n. 135; *History* I, ii, 250f., n. 131. Archeological excavation was begun at Machaerus in 1968 by Jerry Vardaman of The Southern Baptist Theological Seminary, Louisville, Kentucky. Photograph: courtesy Jerry Vardaman.

15. The Church of John the Baptist at Samaria-Sebaste

While the death of John the Baptist probably took place at the remote and gloomy fortress of Machaerus (No. 14), it is stated in Mt 14:12 and Mk 6:29 that his disciples came and took his body and buried it. Therefore his grave was evidently in some place other than at Machaerus, and might well have been at some place outside of the jurisdiction of Herod Antipas. The fame of John the Baptist (cf. Ac 19:3, etc.) was such that he was remembered at many places. Possession of his head was claimed by several cities including Damascus and Constantinople; and in Aleppo, Baalbek, Beirut, Byblos, Gaza, Homs, and Tripoli the principal mosque or church is connected either with John or with his father Zechariah. The oldest available tradition, however, points to Samaria-Sebaste as the place of his tomb. Rufinus of Aquileia (d. 410) (*Ch. Hist.* II 28 MPL XXI, col. 536) and Theodoret of Cyrus (d. c. 466) (*Ch. Hist.* III 3 NPNFSS III, p. 96) relate that under Julian the Apostate (361-363) pagan rioters despoiled the tomb of John the Baptist at Sebaste, which makes it likely that it had already been a holy place for a long time. It is true that Eusebius does not mention the tomb

of John the Baptist when he lists Samaria (Σομερών) in the *Onomasticon* (p. 154), but he is only discussing the place in connection with Jos 12:20 and I K 16:24. Jerome, however, adds at this point in the *Onomasticon* that Samaria was where the remains of St. John the Baptist were buried. Likewise in his *Letter 108, 13 to Eustochium* (NPNFSS VI, p. 201) Jerome tells how Paula saw at Samaria-Sebaste the last resting places of the prophets Elisha and Obadiah and John the Baptist (cf. *Letter 46, 13 Paula and Eustochium to Marcella*, NPNFSS VI, p. 65), and also encountered many demonized persons who had evidently been brought to the holy tombs in the hope of healing (cf. II K 13:21). Recalling the probable connections that appear at the beginning of his work between John the Baptist and Elijah (cf. above No. 8), it may be judged not purely accidental if the disciples of John chose to inter him not beside Elijah, which would of course have been impossible according to II K 2:11, but in the place where rested the man who had inherited the spirit and mantle of Elijah, namely, Elisha. If the Obadiah in question here is the Obadiah of I K 18:3-16 who assisted the prophets in the days of Elijah, then he who fearlessly challenged Herod and Herodias, and was slain by them,

15

was given a resting place related to the remembrance of the courageous opponents of Ahab and Jezebel. In Samaria-Sebaste today the grave of John the Baptist, together with those of Elisha and Obadiah, is supposed to be just outside the Roman city wall at the east end of the village. A church was built over the grave at this place, probably in the fourth century, of which some stones may remain. The Crusaders found the earlier church in ruins and built a new cathedral in the second half of the twelfth century, and of this an arch and other portions are extant. Later a mosque was built here too. In the photograph the minaret of the mosque rises prominently above the walls which now surround the entire site. As for the tomb itself, it is described as of an ordinary Roman type of the third or second century if not earlier, i.e., it can be as early as the first century, which would be necessary if its traditional identification with the last resting place of John the Baptist is to be accepted.

R. W. Hamilton, *Guide to Samaria-Sebaste*. Amman: Hashemite Kingdom of Jordan Department of Antiquities, 1953, pp. 34-40; André Parrot, *Samaria*. Studies in Biblical Archaeology 7, 1958, pp. 122-126; Joachim Jeremias in ZNW 52 (1961), pp. 96-98. Photograph: The Matson Photo Service, Alhambra, Calif.

16. The Church of the Finding of the Head of John the Baptist at Samaria-Sebaste

On the acropolis at Samaria-Sebaste Herod the Great built a large temple in honor of the emperor Augustus. Running past the acropolis on the south was a broad columned street which was probably built at the end of the second century when Septimius Severus made Sebaste a Roman colony. Between the acropolis and the columned street is the small ruined church shown in this photograph. These ruins were found, almost by chance, by the Joint Expedition of Harvard University, the Palestine Exploration Fund, the Hebrew University, and the British School of Archaeology in Jerusalem, in their excavations at Samaria in 1931. The oldest building here may be of the sixth century. It was a small basilica, with nave and two aisles, projecting apse, and mosaic floor, of which some portions remain. This church was destroyed, but was replaced in the eleventh century by a church with a round dome carried on four granite columns; in the photograph three of the columns may be seen still standing, one fallen. This church was rebuilt once again, probably in the second half of the twelfth century at about the same time that the Latin cathedral was being built at the east end of the city (No. 15). The ruins correspond with a description by Phocas who visited Sebaste in 1185 (LPPTS V, p. 16). He mentions first a church which is evidently the cathedral at the east end of the city, and then writes: "In the midst of the upper part of the city stands a hill, upon which in ancient times stood Herod's palace, where the feast took place, and where that wicked damsel danced and received the sacred head of the Baptist as the reward of her dancing. At the present day, however, the place has become a Greek monastery. The church of this monastery is domed. On the left side of the altar is a little chapel in the middle of which is a marble circle lying over a very deep excavation wherein was made the discovery of the sacred head of the Forerunner, revered by angels, which had been buried in that place by Herodias."

Theodosius (530) says that Sebaste was the place where John the Baptist was beheaded (Geyer p. 137; LPPTS II, p. 7; CCSL CLXXV, p. 115), and the probability is that the ruins of the temple of Augustus on the acropolis had by then been taken for the remains of the palace of Herod Antipas where the famous events connected with the death of John had taken place. It was then natural to suppose that the head of John had been buried nearby by Herodias, and this legend led to the building of the church which, as we have seen, goes back to the sixth century and was so unmistakably described in the light of these assumed connections by Phocas in the twelfth century. In his day Burchard (1283) also saw two churches in honor of John the Baptist at Sebaste, one the cathedral on the side of the mountain, the other a building on the brow of the hill where the king's palace (as he also calls the ruins of Herod's temple to Augustus) once stood. At the second church the Greek monks showed him where John was imprisoned and beheaded, but Burchard rightly points out that this is not correct because better authorities, including Josephus, agree that John was beheaded at Machaerus beyond Jordan, and because Herod as tetrarch of Galilee and Perea had no authority in Samaria, which was in the jurisdiction of Pilate even as were Jerusalem and Judea (LPPTS XII, pp. 50-51).

J. W. Crowfoot, *Churches at Bosra and Samaria-Sebaste*. London: British School of Archaeology in Jerusalem, Supplementary Paper 4, 1937, pp. 24-39 and Pl. 13(a). Photograph: courtesy Department of Antiquities, Amman, Jordan.

The Life of Jesus

BETHLEHEM

17. The Terraced Slopes of Bethlehem

Mt 2:1 and Lk 2:4-7 state that Jesus was born in Bethlehem. The town of Bethlehem is on a ridge about 2,500 feet high some six miles south and slightly west of Jerusalem (cf. Eusebius, *Onomasticon,* p. 42). The photograph looks toward the southeastern end of the ridge, on the northern slope of which is the Church of the Nativity. The rocky hill, originally isolated from the village but now incorporated in it, contains caves and looks down on the fields steeply below to the east. In the fourteenth century B.C. Abdi-Heba, governor of Jerusalem, speaks of "the 'Apiru people" who are taking many places and mentions "a town of the land of Jerusalem, Bit-Lahmi by name" (ANET p. 489 and n. 21). This is an almost certain reference to Bethlehem, the latter part of the name perhaps being that of a Canaanite deity. In Hebrew, however, the name (בית לחם,

spelled Βηθλέεμ in Greek) was taken to mean "House of Bread." In OT history Bethlehem was the home of David (Ru 4:11; I Sam 16) and therefore the city of David (I Sam 20:6; Lk 2:4), but the famous king chose to make his capital at Jerusalem, and Bethlehem remained a "village" (κώμη) as it is called in Jn 7:42. The prophet Micah, however, thought of Bethlehem as of great potential importance when he wrote of it as the home of the future messianic ruler (Mic 5:2). This prophecy was quoted by Mt (2:5-6) in his narrative of the birth of Jesus, and Lk 2:7 states that the mother Mary laid the child in a manger because there was no place for them in the inn. The photograph also shows rising as a truncated cone against the horizon at the left the artificially heightened hill, four miles southeast of Bethlehem and now called Frank Mountain, on which was the Herodium, the fortress-palace and finally the tomb of Herod the Great (Josephus, *War* I 21, 10

18

§§419-421; 33, 9 §673), the king at whose grim threat Joseph and Mary fled with Jesus from Bethlehem (Mt 2:13ff.).

E. Jerry Vardaman, "The History of Herodium," in E. Jerry Vardaman and James L. Garrett, Jr., eds., *The Teacher's Yoke: Studies in Memory of Henry Trantham*. Waco, Texas: Baylor University Press, 1964, pp. 58-81. Photograph: JF.

18. Bethlehem from the South

This photograph of Bethlehem looks back at the town from the south. It also shows the olive groves of the countryside, and the rock walls which fence the fields.

Photograph: The Matson Photo Service, Alhambra, Calif.

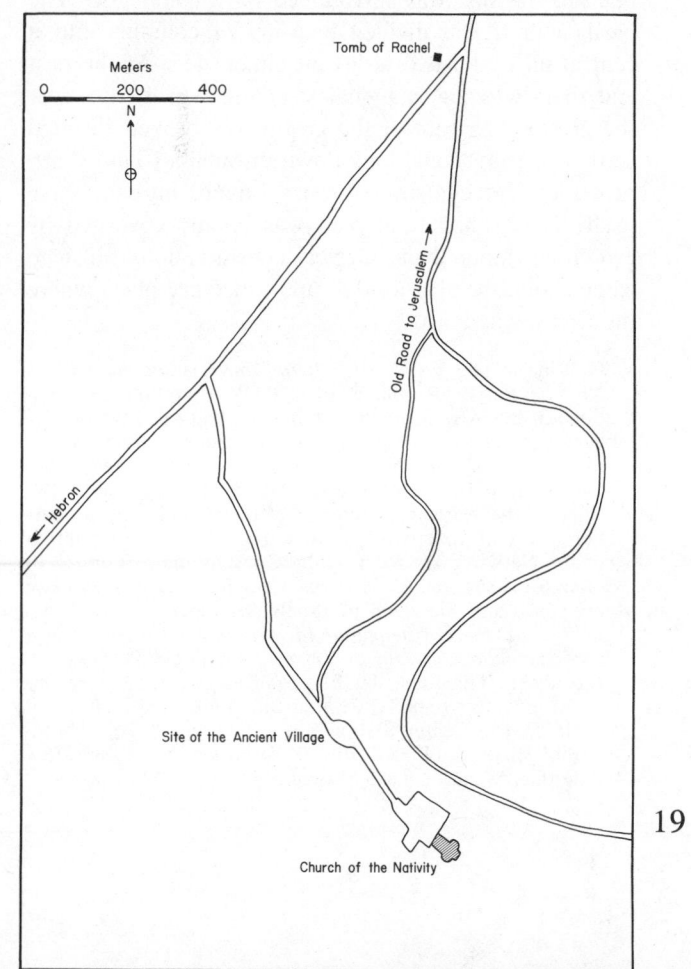

19. Plan of Bethlehem

This sketch plan shows the relation of the site of the ancient village of Bethlehem to the road from Jerusalem and the road to Hebron, and also its relation to the site of the Church of the Nativity.

Plan: JF, cf. *Les Guides Bleus: Moyen-Orient* (Paris: Librairie Hachette, 1956), p. 523.

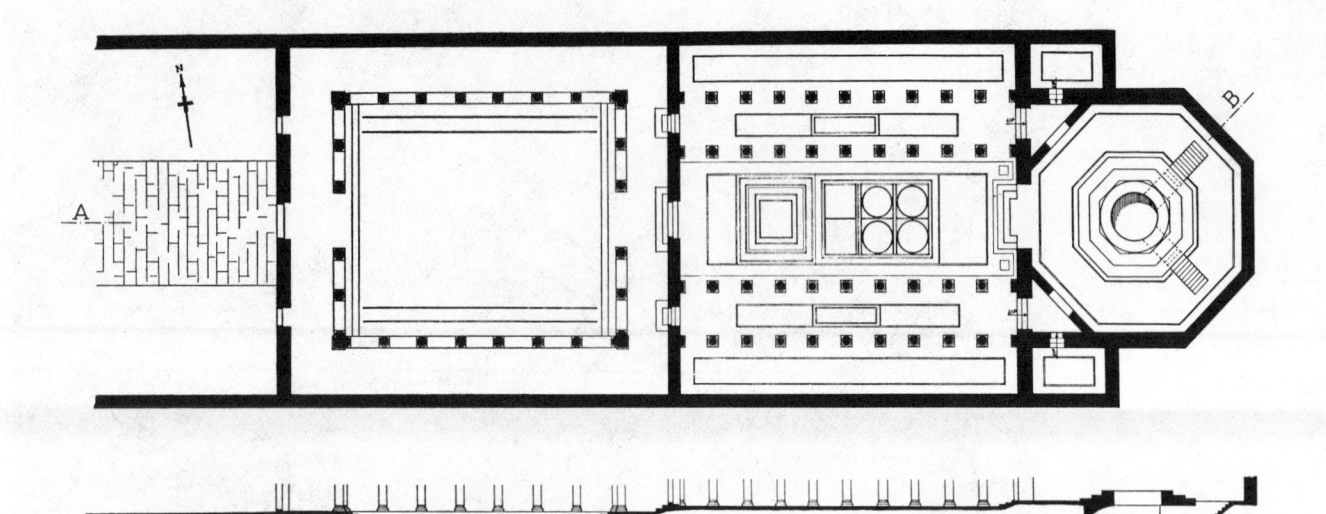

SECTION ON LINE A-B

20. Plan of the Constantinian Basilica at Bethlehem

Later tradition states that the place of the birth of Jesus in Bethlehem was a cave. In such tradition there was a recognizable tendency to localize events in caves, on the other hand caves have actually provided habitation and shelter for men and beasts in Palestine from ancient times until now. Justin Martyr, born soon after 100 in Neapolis and writing his *Dialogue with the Jew Trypho* shortly after the middle of the century, says (*Dialogue* 78): "But when the Child was born in Bethlehem, since Joseph could not find a lodging in that village, he took up his quarters in a certain cave near the village; and while they were there Mary brought forth the Christ and placed him in a manger, and here the Magi who came from Arabia found him."

Origen, who was in Palestine frequently from 215 onward and wrote *Against Celsus* about 248, reports what is evidently the same tradition as that given by Justin and speaks as if he himself were one of those to whom the cave had been shown (*Against Celsus* I 51): "In accordance with the narrative in the Gospel regarding his birth, there is pointed out at Bethlehem the cave where he was born, and the manger in the cave where he was wrapped in swaddling clothes. And this sight is greatly talked of in surrounding places, even among the enemies of the faith, it being said that in this cave was born that Jesus who is worshiped and reverenced by the Christians."

It was undoubtedly over this cave that a church was built by the emperor Constantine and dedicated by his mother, Helena, who visited Bethlehem on her trip to the eastern provinces shortly before her death, c. 327 at the age of eighty. Eusebius, writing the account, says (*The Life of Constantine* III 43) that the church was "at the grotto which had been the scene of the Savior's birth," and tells also of the rich gifts which both Helena and Constantine gave in order to beautify the sacred

cave. Only a few years later the Bordeaux Pilgrim (333) records concerning Bethlehem: "There a basilica has been built by order of Constantine" (Geyer p. 25; LPPTS I, p. 27; CCSL CLXXV, p. 20). The present Church of the Nativity in Bethlehem was examined by William Harvey in 1934 and by the Franciscan Custody of the Holy Land in 1948-1951. Beneath it are what are almost certainly the remains of the Constantinian basilica. The plan suggested by those remains is shown in the illustration. The basilica proper was almost square, about 27 meters on each side. There were three doors at the west end, and steps led up to them from a large atrium at a slightly lower level. The atrium, doubtless open to the sky, was surrounded by a colonnade. The basilica itself was divided by rows of columns into a central nave and two aisles on either side. At the east end there was an octagonal structure which rose over the grotto. The roof of the grotto was broken through so that pilgrims could look down through a round shaft, probably protected by a bronze screen, into the cave itself. The architectural plan was plainly governed by evidential rather than liturgical considerations: all who came should be able to look upon the very place where the Christ was born.

H. Vincent and F.-M. Abel, *Bethléem, Le sanctuaire de la Nativité*. Paris: J. Gabalda, 1914; R. W. Hamilton, "Excavations in the Atrium of the Church of the Nativity, Bethlehem," in QDAP 3 (1934), pp. 1-8; William Harvey, *Structural Survey of the Church of the Nativity, Bethlehem*. London: Oxford University Press, 1935; E. T. Richmond, "Basilica of the Nativity, Discovery of the Remains of an Earlier Church," in QDAP 5 (1936), pp. 75-81; "The Church of the Nativity, The Plan of the Constantinian Church," in QDAP 6 (1938), pp. 63-66; J. W. Crowfoot, *Early Churches*, pp. 22-30 and Fig. 2 on p. 18; Bellarmino Bagatti, *Gli antichi edifici sacri di Betlemme in seguito agli scavi e restauri praticati dalla Custodia di Terra Santa* (1948-51) PSBF 9. Jerusalem: Tipografia dei PP. Francescani, 1952; Gregory T. Armstrong, "Imperial Church Building in the Holy Land in the Fourth Century," in BA 30 (1967), pp. 90-102. Photograph: QDAP 6 (1938), Fig. 1 following p. 66, courtesy Palestine Archaeological Museum.

21. Interior of the Church of the Nativity at Bethlehem

In the examination of the Church of the Nativity, portions of floor mosaic were found in the nave and aisles at a level about 75 centimeters below the present floor, and other portions in what were the octagon and the atrium. Although attributed by some to the fifth century, they may probably be accepted from their position as belonging to the Constantinian basilica. This photograph shows the interior of the church at the time when the floor of the nave was broken through to expose the mosaics.

L.-H. Vincent in RB 45 (1936), pp. 544-574; Crowfoot, *Early Churches*, pp. 26, 120. Photograph: The Matson Photo Service, Alhambra, Calif.

22. Floor Mosaic in the Nave of the Church at Bethlehem

The pattern of the floor mosaics in the nave of the church consists of geometrical designs. The entire mosaic may be thought of as having been, in a way, like a great carpet covering the floor of the basilica.

Photograph: The Matson Photo Service, Alhambra, Calif.

23. Detail of Mosaic in the Church at Bethlehem

The considerable complexity of the geometrical designs may be seen in this more detailed photograph of another portion of the nave mosaics.

Photograph: The Matson Photo Service, Alhambra, Calif.

24. Floor Mosaic around the Grotto

At the east end of the nave in the Constantinian basilica steps led up into the octagon. On either side of the steps there was a small panel of mosaic. These were at a place where no one would ordinarily have walked and, in the panel on the left, there is to be seen, in addition to geometrical designs, the word ΙΧΘΥC, "Fish" (FLAP p. 535 and Fig. 193). Around the grotto itself, in the octagon, the mosaics were arranged to fit the floor plan.

A portion of what survives is shown in the photograph: an acanthus border, geometrical patterns, various flowers and fruits, a bird in one medallion and a cock in another.

In addition to these surviving fragments (Nos. 21-24) of the Constantinian basilica in Bethlehem, there exists in Rome what is probably to be recognized as a representation of the church from within the century in which it was built. As will be shown below (No. 184), there is in the Church of Santa Pudentiana a splendid apse mosaic. The original church is attributed to Pope Pius I in the middle of the second century; it was rebuilt by Pope Siricius (384-399), and the mosaic probably belongs to the time of the latter. Across the entire mosaic runs an arcade with tile roof. Above and behind the arcade are two sets of buildings. Those at the left are almost certainly a representation of the Church of the Holy Sepulcher in Jerusalem (see below Nos. 181ff.), and the buildings at the right are believed by many to compare closely enough with the plan of the Constantinian basilica at Bethlehem to be recognized as a representation of that structure. If this is correct, the long low building at the right is the atrium, the taller building next to it in the middle is the basilica proper, and the yet taller structure at the left end is the octagon.

Bagatti, *Gli antichi edifici sacri di Betlemme*, p. 2; Crowfoot, *Early Churches*, pp. 23-24, 120f. Photograph: *ibid.*, Pl. XI (Oxford University Press, 1941).

25. Statue of Jerome near the Church of the Nativity

In 385 Jerome moved to Bethlehem and lived there in a cave adjacent to the grotto of the Church of the Nativity until his death in 420. In his *Letter 58 to Paulinus* (NPNFSS VI, p. 120), written in 395, he refers to the fact that in Jerusalem from the time of Hadrian to that of Constantine the spot which had witnessed the

resurrection was occupied by a figure of Jupiter and the rock where the cross had stood bore a marble statue of Venus. Thus, he explains, the original persecutors "supposed that by polluting our holy places they would deprive us of our faith in the passion and in the resurrection." In a similar way he reports concerning Bethlehem: "Even my own Bethlehem, as it now is, that most venerable spot in the whole world of which the psalmist sings: 'the truth hath sprung out of the earth' (Ps 85: 11), was overshadowed by a grove of Tammuz, that is of Adonis; and in the very cave where the infant Christ had uttered his earliest cry lamentation was made for the paramour of Venus."

Tammuz was the Babylonian god who died and rose annually in the death and rebirth of vegetation. He was equated with Adonis who, in Greek mythology, was the lover of Aphrodite, i.e., Venus. The liturgical wailings of his worshipers are referred to in Ezk 8:14. This god was worshiped, according to Jerome's statement, in the grotto where Christ was born and in the grove of trees above it. The parallelism with pagan defilement of the places of the crucifixion and resurrection in Jerusalem shows that this spot in Bethlehem, to which Christian tradition had already attached special meaning, was also a deliberate choice. That this understanding of the meaning of Jerome is correct is confirmed by the probably independent and even more explicit statement of Paulinus of Nola (*Epistle* 31, 3 CSEL XXIX-XXX, p.

270): "For the emperor Hadrian, in the belief that he could destroy the Christian faith by the dishonoring of a place, dedicated a statue of Jupiter on the place of the passion, and Bethlehem was profaned by a grove of Adonis."

From both Jerome and Paulinus, then, we have evidence that the identification of the Bethlehem cave as the place of the birth of Jesus was already older than the time of Hadrian, i.e., it must go back into the first century. Adjacent to the grotto of the nativity and extending under the Franciscan Church of St. Catherine, which is beside the Church of the Nativity on the north, are several other subterranean chambers. The place where Jerome lived and worked, his tomb which the Anonymous of Piacenza (Geyer p. 178; LPPTS II, p. 23; CCSL CLXXV, p. 143) says Jerome carved out of the rock at the mouth of the cave where the Lord was born, and also the tombs of his friends Paula (d. 404, cf. Jerome, *Letter* 108, 34), Eustochium (d. 419), and Eusebius of Cremona (d. c. 423) are believed to be located in these chambers. Above ground in a cloister of the Church of St. Catherine the statue of Jerome shown in this photograph stands on a granite column. It is believed by some that the column derives from the Constantinian basilica.

Bagatti, *Gli antichi edifici sacri di Betlemme*, pp. 50, 195. Photograph: JF.

26. Plan of the Church of Justinian at Bethlehem

In his *Book of the Demonstration* (313, tr. Watt, I, p. 135) Eutychius speaks of the church at Bethlehem as bearing witness to the birth of Christ from Mary the Virgin, in a cave in that place, and in his *Annales* (MPG

111, col. 1070, 159f.) he tells of how the church was rebuilt by Justinian (527-565). The Bethlehem church was a small building, says Eutychius, and Justinian ordered his legate to pull it down and build another, large and beautiful, but was in the end displeased with what the legate accomplished. The new building must have been completed at least by 532, for Cyril of Scythopolis records that John Hesychastes prayed in the narthex of the church in that year (A. M. Schneider in RFAC II, col. 226). The examination of the Church of the Nativity by Harvey in 1934 (cf. above No. 20) showed that the present church is in plan that of Justinian. Like its predecessor the church built by Justinian had a nave and four aisles. To the west it was extended with a narthex and a new atrium, and to the east with a large apse and a transept with apses on either end. The grotto may have been roofed over at this time, and above it there was a semicircular stone structure of some sort.

E. T. Richmond, "The Church of the Nativity, The Alterations carried out by Justinian," in QDAP 6 (1938), pp. 67-72. Photograph: QDAP 6 (1938), Fig. 1 following p. 72, courtesy Palestine Archaeological Museum.

27. Column and Capital in the Church of the Nativity

This photograph shows the upper part and capital of one of over fifty columns which still stand in the Church of the Nativity, most of them in the two double rows which mark the central nave and the four side aisles. The columns are of the reddish limestone found in the country, and the capitals are of the Corinthian order, with acanthus leaves and curved scrolls at the top. Some think that the columns are Constantinian in date and that they were raised when Justinian raised the floor of the church, for they stand on blocks of stone which rest in turn upon longitudinal walls or stylobates, place having been made for the latter by cutting through the mosaics. Others believe that at least the capitals, or both the columns and the capitals, were first made for the

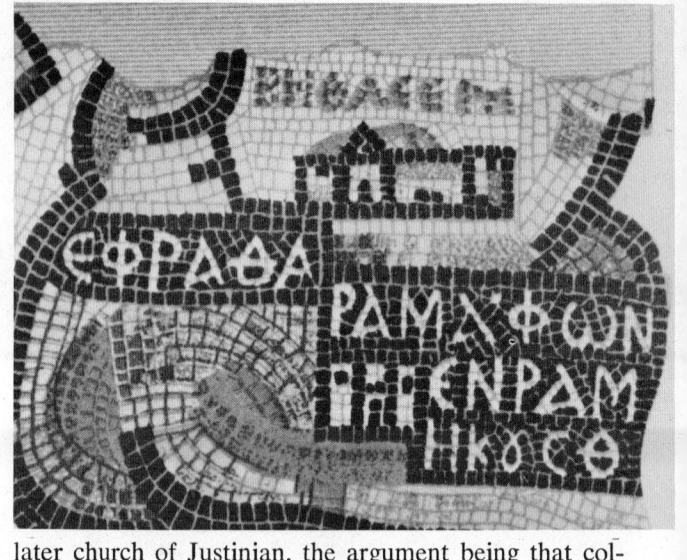

later church of Justinian, the argument being that columns and capitals are of the same workmanship and all are in the same state of excellent preservation; hence they were all made at the same time, and there are too many of them to have fitted into the Constantinian church. The paintings which are now to be seen on the columns are examples of medieval art, and show figures of various saints with names written in Greek and Latin.

E. T. Richmond in QDAP 6 (1938), p. 68; Crowfoot, *Early Churches*, p. 25 and n. 2, pp. 151-153; R. W. Hamilton in QDAP 13 (1948), p. 113 and n. 1; Bagatti, *Gli antichi edifici sacri di Betlemme*, pp. 48, 51-52. Photograph: courtesy École Biblique et Archéologique Française.

28. Bethlehem on the Madaba Mosaic Map

Bethlehem appears on the Madaba Mosaic Map south of Jerusalem (see also No. 185). The name is in red letters as used for important places: Βηθλέεμ, Bethlehem. The red-roofed building beneath the name is evidently the Church of the Nativity. Since the church must have been rebuilt by Justinian by 532 (No. 26) and since the Madaba Map dates about 560, it is presumably the church of Justinian that is represented. Correspondence of detail with the plan of Justinian's church (No. 26) is not altogether easy to see, but it may be taken that the attempt is made to show a basilica with three apses. Below the church are the legends: Ἐφραθᾶ, Ephrathah; and Ῥαμά. φωνὴ ἐν Ῥαμὰ ἠκούσθη, Ramah. A voice was heard in Ramah. This is a quotation of Jer 31:15, in connection with which the following explanation is necessary.

Gen 35:19 and 48:7 state that the burial place of Rachel was "on the way to Ephrath (that is, Bethlehem)." The wording suggests that Ephrath or Ephrathah was an older village which was absorbed into Bethlehem and in Mic 5:2 the two names are put together, Bethlehem Ephrathah. The traditional Tomb of Rachel, on the road just north of Bethlehem, is shown in No. 29. I Sam 10:2, however, places the tomb of Rachel in the territory of Benjamin, and the site of er-Ram five miles north of Jerusalem probably corresponds with a Ramah at this place. Indeed the Madaba Map shows another Ῥαμά, Ramah, north and slightly east of Jerusalem (this may be seen on Nos. 10 and 44). It was presumably to the northern Ramah that Nebuzaradan in 588 B.C. took Jeremiah and the captives of Jerusalem and Judah who were being exiled to Babylon (Jer 40:1). Rachel was the mother of Joseph and Benjamin, and Joseph's son Ephraim became synonymous with northern Israel (Jer 31:9). So Jeremiah (31:15) hears a voice in Ramah and it is

Rachel weeping for her children, perhaps with reference to the earlier deportation (722 B.C.) of the northern Israelites by the Assyrians (II K 18:11) as well as to the present carrying into exile by the Babylonians. Matthew in turn, evidently thinking of Ramah and Rachel's tomb as near Bethlehem, hears the lamentation of Rachel echoing in that of the mothers of Bethlehem at the time of the slaughter of the innocents by Herod the Great (Mt 2:18).

Bagatti, *Gli antichi edifici sacri di Betlemme*, pp. 2, 4. Photograph: courtesy Victor R. Gold.

29. The Tomb of Rachel

This is the traditional tomb of Rachel, referred to in the preceding section (No. 28), on the old road leading into Bethlehem from Jerusalem.

Photograph: JF.

30. View of the Church of the Nativity

Writing one of his *Anacreontics* in 603/04, Sophronius (LPPTS XI, p. 29) describes the church of Justinian with its three splendid apses (ἐκπρεποῦς τρικόγχου [κόγχος = anything like a mussel-shell]) and its paneled ceiling

which shone as if with the light of heavenly bodies (καλάθωσιν ἀστροφεγγῆ). When the Sasanian Persians under Chosroes II (590-628) invaded Palestine in 614 they destroyed the sanctuaries in Jerusalem and came on to Bethlehem. Although Justin Martyr (*Dialogue* 78, see No. 20 above) says that the Magi "came from Arabia," Clement of Alexandria (*Stromata* I 15, 71 ANF II, p. 316) attests the belief that the Magi were Persians. At the Bethlehem church the visit of the Magi to the Christ child (Mt 2:1) appears to have been depicted, probably in a mosaic, with the Magi in Persian costume. A Greek communication of the Synod of Jerusalem in 836 states that when the Persians arrived at Bethlehem they were amazed to see the figures of the Magi, observers of the stars and their own compatriots, and therefore they spared the church. When the Caliph 'Umar took Jerusalem in 638 he also came to Bethlehem and prayed in the south apse where he could face toward Mecca. Eutychius (*Annales*, MPG III, col. 1100) tells of this and in the same connection

mentions the mosaic work in the church. The Crusaders arrived in 1099 and Tancred raised his flag over the basilica; Baldwin was crowned king of the Latin Kingdom there on Christmas Day, 1100. On the north side of the church the Crusaders built a cloister and monastery which were given to the Canons of St. Augustine, and both the church and monastery were protected with a high wall and towers, making it a veritable fortress. Later the Franciscans received the basilica, established themselves in the deserted Augustinian monastery, and built the Church of St. Catherine which they still own. After repeated transfers of possession between the Latins and the Greeks, the latter held the basilica permanently and also built a monastery on the southeast side, while the Armenians established a monastery to the southwest. In the photograph, showing the church as it appears today, the rectangular paved square in front of the basilica occupies in part the area of the former atrium. The medieval façade of the church is directly ahead, a modern graveyard and the Franciscan convent are at the left, and the Armenian convent at the right.

Bagatti, *Gli antichi edifici sacri di Betlemme*, pp. 12-13. Photograph: The Matson Photo Service, Alhambra, Calif.

31. The Entrance to the Church of the Nativity

Of the three doors which gave access to the narthex, only the central one remains in use and, as seen in this photograph, it has long since been for the most part walled up in order to keep out animals and give protection in wartime. The rectangular doorway is the modern entrance. The arch is from the medieval period. The beam which runs straight across much higher up is the cornice and corbel of the great door of the once magnificent church of Justinian. The courses of stonework above are also medieval.

Bellarmino Bagatti, *L'archeologia cristiana in Palestina*. Civiltà orientali. Florence: G. C. Sansoni, 1962, p. 88 No. 6. Photograph: courtesy École Biblique et Archéologique Française.

NAZARETH

32. Nazareth

The town of Nazareth, a portion of which is shown in this photograph down a cactus-lined path, is in the hills of Galilee at an elevation of 1,150 feet. From the heights there is a view south across the Plain of Esdraelon, west to Mount Carmel, east to Mount Tabor, and north to Mount Hermon. In the OT Jos 19:10-15 gives a list of the towns of the tribe of Zebulun and (v. 13) names Japhia, which may be the Japha which is on a yet higher hill one and one-half miles southwest of Nazareth, but does not mention Nazareth. Josephus, who was responsible for military operations in this area in the Jewish War, settled at Japha (*Life* 52 §270) and fortified the place (*War* II 20, 6 §573), and also used Sepphoris, three miles north of Nazareth, as headquarters (*Life* 12 §63, etc.). In his writings he gives the names of forty-five towns in Galilee, but does not say anything about Nazareth. The Talmud also, although it refers to sixty-three Galilean towns, does not mention Nazareth. In spite of this silence of the OT, Josephus, and the Talmud, excavations shortly to be mentioned (No. 35) show that it was certainly a settled place at an early date. Lack of mention, therefore, does not suggest doubt that there was a city called Nazareth in Jesus' time (Cheyne in EB III, cols. 3358-3362), but only attests the relative insignificance of the city, which may also be reflected in the disparaging comment quoted in Jn 1:46. According to Lk 2:51 Jesus must have grown up in Nazareth; according to Mk 1:9 at his bap-

tism he came from Nazareth. He was therefore "the one from Nazareth" (ὁ ἀπὸ Ναζαρέθ) (Mt 21:11; Jn 1:45; Ac 10:38), "the Nazarene" (ὁ Ναζαρηνός) (Mk 1:24, etc.), or "the Nazoraean" (ὁ Ναζωραῖος) (Mt 2:23, etc.). Both of the last terms probably derive linguistically from Nazareth and mean "inhabitant of Nazareth."

In the light of recent archeological evidence (see No. 35 below) that Nazareth was an old established site long before the Early Roman period and during it, Vardaman remarks that there is little reason to question the Gospel record that Jesus grew up there. For representative older skepticism on this matter, he cites, besides Cheyne above, Champlin Burrage, *Nazareth and the Beginnings of Christianity*. Oxford: University Press, 1914, pp. 6f., 26, 27, 29, etc.; Arthur Drews, *The Christ Myth*. Chicago: Open Court Publishing Co., revised 3d ed. 1911, pp. 59-60; J. Z. Lauterbach, "Jesus in the Talmud," *Rabbinic Essays by Jacob Z. Lauterbach*. Cincinnati: Hebrew Union College Press, 1951, p. 483; and A. Powell Davies, *The Meaning of the Dead Sea Scrolls*. Signet Key Books. New York: New American Library, 1956, pp. 117ff. For the linguistic question see W. F. Albright, "The Names 'Nazareth' and 'Nazoraean,'" in JBL 65 (1946), pp. 397-401; Albrecht Alt, *Where Jesus Worked*. London: Epworth Press, 1961, pp. 15-16. Photograph: JF.

33. Plan of Nazareth

This sketch plan of Nazareth shows the chief places which will be mentioned in the following discussion.

Plan: JF, cf. B. Bagatti, "Ritrovamenti nella Nazaret evangelica," in LA 5 (1954-55), p. 7 Fig. 1; and in DB Supplément VI, cols. 319-320 Fig. 599.

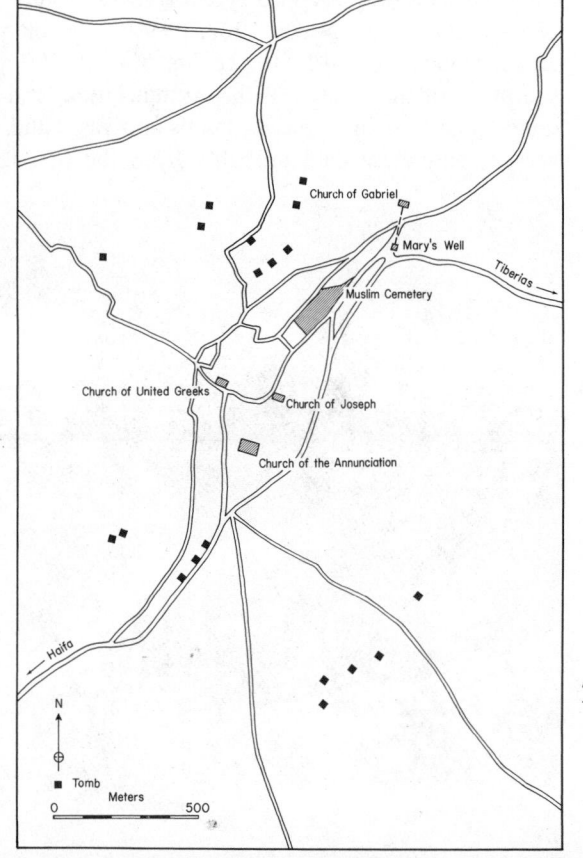

Church of Gabriel
Mary's Well
Tiberias
Muslim Cemetery
Church of United Greeks
Church of Joseph
Church of the Annunciation
Haifa
N
■ Tomb
Meters
0   500

34. Mary's Well at Nazareth

There is only one good spring in Nazareth, and it must have been the main source of water from the earliest times. The spring rises out of the ground above the Church of St. Gabriel, is conducted into the grounds of the church, and then piped down the hill to an outlet in the pictured enclosure, nearly 500 feet from the source and beside the road leading from Nazareth to Tiberias. Earlier designated by the name of the archangel Gabriel, from about the twelfth century the spring has been called Ain Maryam, or Mary's Well. The outlet was placed on the road to Tiberias in 1862.

Clemens Kopp in JPOS 19 (1939-40), pp. 253-258. Photograph: The Matson Photo Service, Alhambra, Calif.

35. An Ancient Grotto Habitation adjacent to the Church of the Annunciation

The oldest known human life in the region of Nazareth is attested by the skull found in 1934 by R. Neuville in a cave about one and one-half miles southeast of the city, a skull which may be older than that of Neandertal man. In Nazareth itself a complex of burial caves was found in the upper city in 1963, in which there was pottery of the first part of the Middle Bronze Age (RB 70 [1963], p. 563; 72 [1965], p. 547). Down in the area of the Latin Church of the Annunciation there was certainly an ancient village of long continuance. Archeological investigation in and around this church was conducted by B. Vlaminck in 1895, by Prosper Viaud in 1907-1909, and particularly by Bel-

larmino Bagatti in 1955 when the previously standing eighteenth-century (1730) church was demolished to make way for a new building. The area under and around the church, as well as at the Church of St. Joseph not far away, was plainly that of an agricultural village. There were numerous grottoes, silos for grain, cisterns for water and oil, presses for raisins and olives, and millstones. While the silos are of a type found at Tell Abu Matar as early as the Chalcolithic Age (IEJ 5 [1955], p. 23) the earliest pottery found in them here at Nazareth is of Iron II (900-600 B.C.). Vardaman calls attention to the characteristic large jar with a small "funnel" beside the mouth; this appendage, though designed like a funnel, is simply attached to the shoulder, and does not actually pierce the wall of the jar (for an illustration of this jar, see Bagatti in DB Supplément VI, col. 323, Fig. 601). Other pottery of the site comprises a little of the Hellenistic period, more of the Roman, and most of all of the Byzantine period. Of the numerous grottoes at least several had served for domestic use, and had even been modified architecturally for this purpose. One of these, where walls were built against a grotto to make a habitation, had already been found by Viaud under the convent adjoining the Church of the Annunciation and is shown in the photograph. Twenty-three tombs have also been found, most of them at a distance of something like 250 to 750 yards from the Church of the Annunciation to the north, the west, and the south. Since these must have been outside of the village proper, their emplacement gives some idea of the limits of the settlement. Eighteen of the tombs are of the kokim type, which was known in Palestine from about 200 B.C. (cf. No. 209), and became virtually the standard type of Jewish tomb. Two of the tombs, one (PEFQS 1923, p. 90) only 60 yards and the other (QDAP 1 [1932], pp. 53-55) 450 yards southwest of the Church of the Annunciation, still contained objects such as pottery lamps and vases and glass vessels, and these date probably from the first to the

third or fourth centuries of the Christian era. Four of the tombs were sealed with rolling stones, a type of closure typical of the late Jewish period (cf. Nos. 228, 235). From the tombs, therefore, it can be concluded that Nazareth was a strongly Jewish settlement in the Roman period.

R. Köppel, "Das Alter der neuentdeckten Schädel von Nazareth," in *Biblica* 16 (1935), pp. 58-73; Clemens Kopp in JPOS 18 (1938), pp. 191-207; Lagrange, pp. 14-15; B. Bagatti in DB Supplément VI, cols. 318-329. Photograph: courtesy École Biblique et Archéologique Française.

36. Inscription from Caesarea mentioning Nazareth

The findings in excavations already referred to (No. 35) provide positive evidence of the existence of a town at Nazareth in the time of Jesus. Fragments of an inscription found at Caesarea in 1962, in the excavations of the Hebrew University assisted by the Southern Baptist Theological Seminary, now provide the first known occurrence of the name Nazareth in an inscription and the earliest occurrence of the name in Hebrew. Two fragments were found at this time and a third, found some years previously, was recognized as evidently belonging with them. The first fragment, with which we are here specially concerned, shown in the photograph, is of dark gray marble, 153 x 124 mm. in size, and inscribed in square Hebrew characters with portions of four lines remaining. From the three fragments together and by comparison with materials in Talmudic and liturgical sources, it has been possible to show that the complete inscription was a list of the twenty-four priestly courses (cf. I Ch 24:7-19; Neh 12:1-21), giving the name of each course (or family) in its proper order and the name of the town or village in Galilee where it was settled. This transfer of the courses of priests to residences in Galilee must have taken place after the destruction of the Temple in Jerusalem in A.D. 70 and the subsequent expulsion of the Jews from the territory of Aelia Capitolina by Hadrian (cf. No. 146). The inscription fragments were found in the northern part of Caesarea where the Jewish synagogue

was located, and the whole stone tablet was probably once fixed on the synagogue wall. In the ruins of the Caesarea synagogue a hoard of 3,700 bronze coins was found which was apparently hidden in 355/356, and it is believed that the synagogue was built at the end of the third or beginning of the fourth century (cf. No. 96). The inscription is judged to be of about the same date. In the fragment shown in the photograph the name Nazareth (נצרת) is to be seen in Line 2; also in Line 4, assuming only that the initial Mem is missing, we have the name Migdal (מ[ג]דל), probably referring to Migdal Nunaiya or Magdala (No. 54).

M. Avi-Yonah, "A List of Priestly Courses from Caesarea," in IEJ 12 (1962), pp. 137-139; *Archaeology and Caesarea*. Louisville: The Southern Baptist Theological Seminary, p. 7; E. Jerry Vardaman, "Introduction to the Caesarea Inscription of the Twenty-four Priestly Courses," pp. 42-45, and M. Avi-Yonah, "The Caesarea Inscription of the Twenty-four Priestly Courses," pp. 46-57, in *The Teacher's Yoke: Studies in Memory of Henry Trantham*, ed. by E. Jerry Vardaman and James L. Garrett, Jr. Waco, Texas: Baylor University Press, 1964. Photograph: courtesy The Southern Baptist Theological Seminary.

37. Plan of the Church of the Annunciation at Nazareth

With respect to the possible remembrance of any particular location in Nazareth associated with the life of Jesus, it is important to recall that, according to positive evidence, members of the family of Jesus were still living in Palestine, some of them perhaps in Nazareth, until the end of the first century and the beginning of

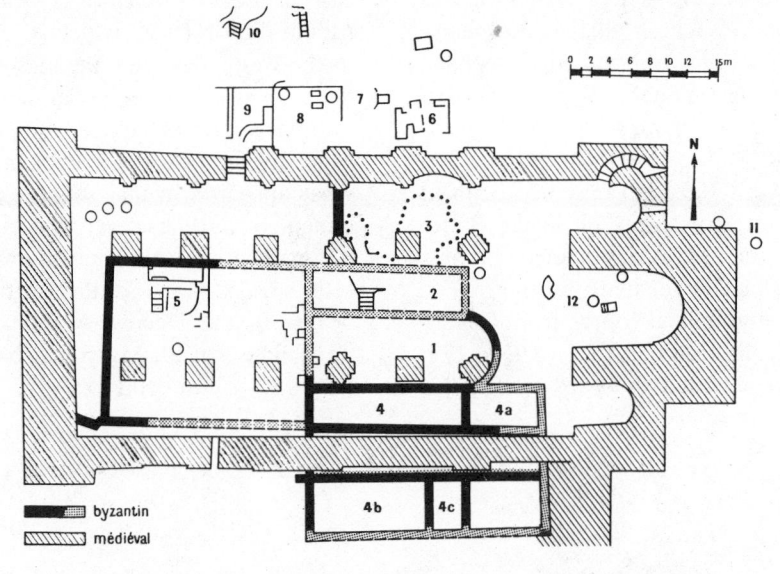

byzantin
médiéval

the second, and further descendants were probably there much longer than that. The Jewish Christian writer Hegesippus (c. 180), quoted by Eusebius (*Ch. Hist.* III, 11 and 32), says that Symeon (who succeeded James, the brother of the Lord, as head of the church in Jerusalem, and was himself a cousin of Jesus, being son of Clopas who was brother of Joseph) lived to the age of 120 and suffered martyrdom under Trajan (in the latter's tenth year of reign, i.e., 107, according to the *Chronicle* of Eusebius (ed. Helm p. 194); and (*Ch. Hist.* III, 20) that two grandsons of Jude, the brother of Jesus, were brought before Domitian (in his fifteenth year of reign, i.e., 96, according to Eusebius, *Ch. Hist.* III, 18) because of suspicion attaching to them as descendants of David, but were freed and lived on till the time of Trajan (98-117). In their examination before the emperor these two men admitted that they were indeed of the house of David, but declared possession between them of only a piece of land thirty-nine quarter-acres ($\pi\lambda\epsilon\theta\rho\omega\nu$ $\lambda\theta'$) in extent and worth 9,000 denarii, which they worked to pay their taxes and support themselves, and they confirmed their statement by showing their toil-calloused hands, so in the end the imperial suspicions were entirely allayed. They were, therefore, farmers and, since they were undoubtedly brought from Palestine to Rome for the examination, they may very well have been living at Nazareth, in an area the agricultural nature of which was abundantly demonstrated by the archeological finds cited above (No. 35). Upon release the two men also became leaders of the churches, both because they were witnesses ($\mu\acute{a}\rho\tau\upsilon\rho\alpha\varsigma$) and because they were relatives of the Lord. With such members of the family, and undoubtedly others after them, living on in Palestine and very probably in Nazareth itself, it is possible to believe that remembrance of at least some particular sites in the home town of Jesus would long be preserved.

It is true that the Caesarea inscription (No. 36), reporting the settlement of priests in Nazareth, suggests the strongly Jewish character of the town, and Africanus (c. 200), cited by Eusebius (*Ch. Hist.* I 7, 14), speaks of Nazareth and Cochaba as Jewish villages. Epiphanius (*Haer.* XXX 2, 16) mentions a place called Cochaba in Transjordan (cf. M. Avi-Yonah, *The Holy Land from the Persian to the Arab Conquests.* Grand Rapids: Baker, 1966, p. 168 and Map p. 169), but this Cochaba which is associated with Nazareth may be identified with modern Kaukab, north of Nazareth, in the Battof Valley (S. Liebermann and M. Avi-Yonah in QDAP 5 [1936], p. 171). Cochaba also seems to be referred to in a newly discovered geographical source from Cave 5 among the Dead Sea Scrolls (see DJD III, No. 9, p. 179, and other references there, cited by Vardaman). But in spite of speaking of Nazareth and Cochaba as Jewish villages, Africanus in the same passage also tells of the $\delta\epsilon\sigma\pi\acute{o}\sigma\upsilon\nu\upsilon\iota$, or relatives of the Lord, who come from both towns and keep the records of their descent with great care. Also a martyr named Conon, who died in Pamphylia under Decius (249-251), declared at his trial: "I belong to the city of Nazareth in Galilee, and am a relative of Christ whom I serve, as my forefathers have done" (Kopp, p. 90; SWDCB I, p. 621).

Later, Constantine authorized Joseph of Tiberias, a Jewish priest who had become a Christian and had the dignity of a count (SWDCB III, p. 460), to build churches in Galilee. In 359 Epiphanius met this man, then seventy years of age, in Scythopolis, and quotes (*Panarion haer.* XXX 11, 9f. GCS I, p. 347) Joseph as saying that no one had ever been able to build churches in the towns of Galilee (presumably he means before he himself did so), because no Greek or Samaritan or Christian was among them ($\check{\epsilon}\nu\theta\alpha$ $\tau\iota\varsigma$ $o\dot{v}\delta\acute{\epsilon}\pi o\tau\epsilon$ $\check{\iota}\sigma\chi\upsilon\sigma\epsilon\nu$ $o\dot{\iota}\kappa o\delta o\mu\hat{\eta}\sigma\alpha\iota$ $\dot{\epsilon}\kappa\kappa\lambda\eta\sigma\acute{\iota}\alpha\varsigma$, $\delta\iota\grave{\alpha}$ $\tau\grave{o}$ $\mu\acute{\eta}\tau\epsilon$ $\H{E}\lambda\lambda\eta\nu\alpha$, $\mu\acute{\eta}\tau\epsilon$ $\Sigma\alpha\mu\alpha\rho\epsilon\acute{\iota}\tau\eta\nu$, $\mu\acute{\eta}\tau\epsilon$ $X\rho\iota\sigma\tau\iota\alpha\nu\grave{o}\nu$ $\mu\acute{\epsilon}\sigma o\nu$ $\alpha\dot{v}\tau\hat{\omega}\nu$ $\epsilon\hat{\iota}\nu\alpha\iota$). That was specially true, Joseph added, in Tiberias and in Diocaesarea which is also called Sepphoris, and in Nazareth and in Capernaum, but in spite of the difficulties he himself, in his younger years, had built churches. Epiphanius reports that in Tiberias, where a pagan temple had been left unfinished since the time of Hadrian, Joseph rebuilt it into a church, and he also built churches in Sepphoris "and in other cities." Since Joseph first listed four places where it had not previously been possible to build churches, and since he is explicitly said to have built churches in the first two of these and in other places as well, it is probable that the next places in the list, namely, Nazareth and Capernaum, were also places where he did erect churches. If so, Joseph of Tiberias could have been the builder of the first Christian church in Nazareth.

It is some time, however, before a church is actually mentioned at Nazareth. In the *Onomasticon* (pp. 138-141) Eusebius locates Nazareth in Galilee fifteen miles east of Legio (which was near Megiddo) and near Mount Tabor (from which it is in fact only five miles to the west), and Jerome adds that it was a *viculus* or mere village, but neither author mentions a church at the place. The extant portions of the Madaba Mosaic Map do not extend far enough to show Nazareth, so what appeared in that source can no longer be ascertained. In 570, however, the Anonymous of Piacenza reports coming from Diocaesarea (Sepphoris) to Nazareth, speaks of the fertility of the region, refers to the beauty of the Hebrew women in the city, and says: "The house of St. Mary is a basilica" (Geyer p. 161; LPPTS II, p. 5; CCSL CLXXV, p. 131).

In the archeological investigation by Bagatti (cf. above No. 35) of the oldest remaining portions of the Church of the Annunciation, nothing was found that could be assigned to the time of Constantine and the church which may have been built by Joseph of Tiberias. But considerable portions are certainly Byzantine, probably of the first decades of the fifth century, hence certainly old enough to represent the basilica reported by the Anonymous of Piacenza, and it is possible that an earlier structure was torn down when the Byzantine church was built (Bagatti in LA 5 [1954-55], pp. 38-39). In the medieval period came a much larger church built by the Crusaders, and then the church of the eighteenth century (1730), which was never finished and was torn down to make way for the new church.

The Plan (No. 37) shows the outlines of the Byzantine church and of the much larger medieval church. The atrium of the Byzantine church was nearly 21 meters long and 16 meters wide. The central nave (1 in the Plan) was about 19 meters long and 8 meters wide, with an apse at the east end, and the two side aisles (2 and 4) were about 3 meters wide. On the south side there was also a sacristy (4a) and a monastery (4b and 4c). In

the central nave is a fragment of Byzantine mosaic with a cross-monogram (cf. below p. 234) encircled in a wreath (see Bagatti in DB Supplément VI, col. 330, Fig. 607); in the south aisle, sacristy, and monastery are fragments of mosaics with geometrical designs. From the side aisle on the north, rock-cut steps descend to subterranean grottoes (3 in the Plan). At the foot of the stairs is a floor mosaic of probably about the same date (fifth century) as those in the church above. An inscription on the mosaic (Kopp, Fig. 6) reads as follows when the first and third words, for which abbreviations are employed, are given in full: Παρα Κωνωνος Διακονου Ιεροσολυμων, "From Conon, deacon of Jerusalem." It may be wondered if the gift of the mosaic by this Conon of Jerusalem was in some way inspired by remembrance of the Conon of Nazareth, whose martyrdom under Decius has been mentioned above. Adjacent to the mosaic of Conon is the so-called Angel Chapel, which connects in turn with the grotto with the present-day Altar of the Annunciation. Again, immediately to the north of the Grotto of the Annunciation, is a large artificial cavern (6 in the Plan) which was an ancient wine press (Bagatti in DB Supplément VI, col. 325). Like many other such presses found in Palestine (Saller, Discoveries at St. John's, 'Ein Karim [PSBF 3], pp. 96-100), this is probably from the Roman period and is one of the remains of ancient agricultural Nazareth (cf. No. 35 above). Other remains are nearby, including an oven (8 in the Plan) and grain silos (10) (see Bagatti in DB Supplément VI, col. 326 and Fig. 604). Evidently the oldest accessible tradition supposed the home of Mary to have been in this vicinity.

Kopp in JPOS (1938), pp. 210-216; 19 (1939-40), pp. 82-116; Kopp, pp. 92-106; B. Bagatti, "Ritrovamenti nella Nazaret evangelica," in LA 5 (1954-55), pp. 5-44; and in DB Supplément VI, cols. 329-332. Photograph: Bagatti in DB Supplément VI, cols. 321-322, Fig. 600, courtesy Terra Santa.

38. The New Latin Church of the Annunciation at Nazareth

As stated above (Nos. 35, 37), the former Church of the Annunciation (1730) was torn down in 1955 to be replaced by a fine new church. In this view of Nazareth the new church appears in the center.

Photograph: courtesy Government Press Office, State of Israel.

39. The Church of St. Joseph in Nazareth

Other sites are also pointed out in Nazareth in connection with sacred history, but the earliest attestation of these is later than that for the Church of the Annunciation. Near the spring which is the source of Mary's Well (No. 34) is the Church of St. Gabriel. In 670 Arculf (Geyer p. 274; LPPTS III, pp. 83-84; CCSL CLXXV, p. 219) stated that there were two large churches in Nazareth, and described them as follows: "One in the middle of the city is founded on two vaults, where once there was the house in which the Lord was nourished in his infancy. This church . . . is raised on two mounds, with arches interposed, having down below among these mounds a very clear fountain, from which all the citizens draw their water in vessels by means of pulleys. There is another church, where the house was in which the angel came to Mary."

The first of the two churches, to which Arculf devotes more attention, was connected with the major spring to which the inhabitants came to draw water, and must therefore have been at or near the location of the present Church of St. Gabriel. In the time of Arculf

it was considered to stand on the site of the house where Jesus was nourished (*nutritus*) in his infancy, according to the mention of "Nazareth, where he had been brought up" in Lk 4:16, which reads in Latin, *Nazareth, ubi erat nutritus.* Hence, the church has been known as the Church of the Nutrition. But *The Protevangelium of James* (11:1ff.) said that Mary had taken a pitcher and gone forth to draw water at the time when the angel Gabriel (Lk 1:26ff.) spoke to her, hence it was easy in the course of time to connect this church with Gabriel and with the annunciation. In Arculf's time, however, it was the other church in Nazareth which was believed to mark the house where the angel came to Mary. As for the present Church of St. Gabriel, it was started in 1767.

Quaresmius (1626) (II 632 Kopp 113) wrote: "If you go from the Church of the Annunciation a stone's throw northward you will find the place which from long hence until today has been called the House and Workshop of Joseph." The present Church of St. Joseph, known also today as the Church of the Carpenter Shop, and shown in the photograph (No. 39), is in this location, north of the Latin Church of the Annunciation and the adjacent Franciscan monastery. It was completed in 1914 and rests upon Crusader ruins. As noted above (No. 35), this church, like the Church of the Annunciation, is in the area of early agricultural Nazareth, and immediately under the church is one of the ancient wine presses (Bagatti in DB Supplément VI, cols. 325-326, Figs. 602, B, and 603).

The synagogue in Nazareth (Mt. 13:54, etc.) was presumably destroyed in A.D. 67, as were other synagogues in Galilee, and perhaps rebuilt toward the end of the second century as were others also, including the synagogue at nearby Japha (RB 30 [1921], pp. 434-438; cf. below No. 60). In 570 the Anonymous of Piacenza (Geyer p. 161; LPPTS II, p. 5; CCSL CLXXV, pp. 130-131) visited the synagogue as well as the house of Mary (No. 37), while Peter the Deacon (1137) (Geyer p. 112) and Burchard of Mount Sion (1283) (LPPTS XII, p. 42) both say that the synagogue was made into a church. Quaresmius (II 632 Kopp 119) says: "If you go from the Church of St. Joseph farther northward you will come to a church which is dedicated to the Forty Martyrs, and farther beyond that to a spring and a church." Then, concerning the Church of the Forty Martyrs, he raises the question whether it was the place of the synagogue which the Lord formerly visited. In the Muslim cemetery in Nazareth, which is on the way north to Mary's Well, there is a small shrine still called the Place of the Forty (*maqam el-arba'in*), which may preserve remembrance of the church to which Quaresmius refers. And four gray granite columns, found here but now moved to another place in the city, may be remains of a Byzantine church on the site, since they are like others in the Church of the Annunciation. This site may have the best claim to be that of the synagogue, and is pointed to as such by the Orthodox Greeks. In modern times the Church of the United Greeks, which is nearer to the Church of the Annunciation, is accepted by some (Dalman) as marking the place of the synagogue. This church, in use since 1741, incorporates a room with a barrel-vaulted roof, which is probably the structure mentioned by Surius (1644) as being a portion of the synagogue and used in his time as a stall for camels. As a site for the synagogue, however, the place has no earlier attestation.

For the Church of St. Gabriel: Kopp in JPOS 19 (1939-40), pp. 258-277. For the House and Workshop of Joseph: Kopp in JPOS 19 (1939-40), pp. 277-285. For the Synagogue, the Place of the Forty, and the Church of the United Greeks: Kopp in JPOS 20 (1946), pp. 29-42; Dalman, *Sacred Sites*, p. 68. See also Donato Baldi, "Nazaret ed i suoi santuari," in LA 5 (1954-55), pp. 213-260. Photograph: The Matson Photo Service, Alhambra, Calif.

SAMARIA

40. The Landscape of Samaria

Jesus was born at Bethlehem (Nos. 17ff.), brought up at Nazareth (Nos. 32ff.), and baptized by John in the Jordan River (Nos. 8ff.). Afterward he worked repeatedly in Judea (Jn 2:13, etc.; cf. Mt 23:37; Lk 13:34) and intensively in Galilee (Nos. 51ff.). Between Judea and Galilee on the west side of the Jordan lay the territory of Samaria. Because of the hostility between Jews and Samaritans reflected in Jn 4:9, it is

probable that Jews ordinarily went around Samaria rather than through it on journeys between Judea and Galilee. On the occasion recorded in Jn 4:3-43, however, Jesus went from Judea to Galilee through Samaria. The territory is named for its city, on a prominent hill forty miles north of Jerusalem and capital of Israel for a time in the OT period (I K 16:24); in the NT period it was rebuilt and renamed Sebaste by Herod the Great (Josephus, *War* I 21, 2 §403). The territory itself varied in its boundaries at different times, but comprised mainly the hill country of the central highlands. The photograph shows the landscape of Samaria from the road north from Jerusalem.

André Parrot, *Samaria the Capital of the Kingdom of Israel.* Studies in Biblical Archaeology 7. London: SCM Press, Ltd., 1958. Photograph: JF.

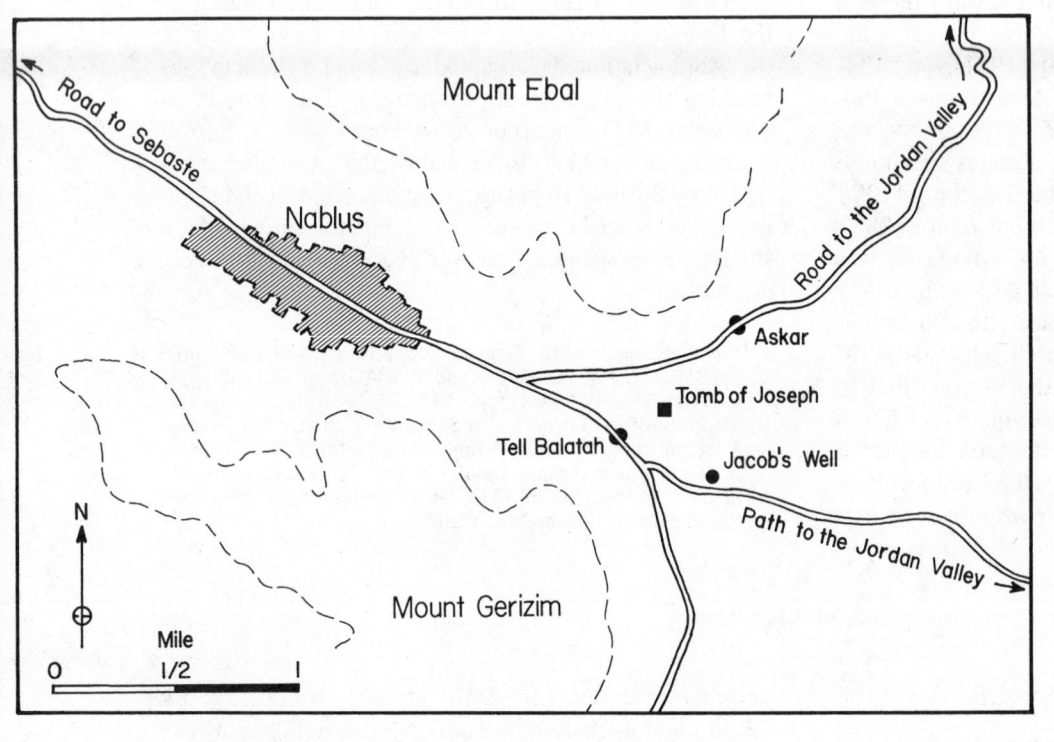

41. Map Showing Jacob's Well and Environs

42. Mount Gerizim

Thirty-five miles north of Jerusalem the road from Jerusalem to Samaria/Sebaste is joined by another road which comes up from the Jordan Valley past Corea and through Wadi Far'ah (Josephus, *War* IV 8, 1 §449; BASOR 62 [1936], p. 14), and the two proceed as one through the pass between Mounts Gerizim and Ebal and on another five miles to Samaria/Sebaste. Immediately prior to his journey from Judea to Galilee through Samaria (Jn 4:3-4) Jesus had been engaged in baptizing (Jn 4:1) and had had certain relationships with John the Baptist (Jn 3:25f.), therefore it is probable that he came up at this time from the Jordan Valley. The road just mentioned, or a path which took some shortcuts but followed a more or less parallel route, would have been the probable way. The sketch map shows where these routes converge in the vicinity of Jacob's well and proceed through the pass between Mounts Gerizim and Ebal.

Map: JF, cf. Kopp, p. 199.

Jesus (Jn 4:5-6) came to a city of Samaria called Sychar (Συχάρ, spelled Σιχάρ in a few manuscripts and Sichar in the Vulgate) or Shechem (in the Sinaitic and Curetonian Syriac manuscripts the name would correspond to Greek Συχέμ, i.e., שכם in Hebrew), which was near the field that Jacob gave to his son Joseph. Jacob's well (πηγή, literally "spring") was there and, as Jesus conversed beside it with a woman of Samaria, the latter referred to an adjacent mountain of which she said, "Our fathers worshiped on this mountain" (Jn 4:5-7, 20). The mountain on which the Samaritans had long worshiped and on which, indeed, their descendants worship until today, is Mount Gerizim (גרזים, LXX Γαριζίν, Dt 11:29, etc.), known in Arabic as Jebel et-Tor. It rises 2,890 feet above sea level and 700 feet above the narrow valley between it and Mount Ebal, the latter reaching 3,085 feet above sea level. At the time of the schism between the Samaritans and the Jews, Sanballat built on Mount Garizein (Γαριζείν or Γαριζίν) a temple like the one in Jerusalem, an event which Jo-

sephus (*Ant.* XI 8, 2 and 4 §§310, 324) puts in the time of Alexander the Great. It has hitherto been supposed that Josephus is in error in this dating, for the well-known Sanballat who is mentioned in the OT was a contemporary of Nehemiah (Neh. 4:1, etc.), and is also named in a letter dated in the seventeenth year of King Darius II, 408 B.C. (ANET p. 492); thus he lived something like a century earlier than Alexander. With the discovery of the Samaria Papyri in Wadi Daliyeh (Frank M. Cross, Jr., in BA XXVI, 4 Dec. 1963, pp. 110-121), however, it has become known that at least three different governors of Samaria bore the name of Sanballat, and Josephus may be quite correct as to the date of the Sanballat who built the Mount Gerizim temple (*ibid.*, p. 121 n. 27). Josephus (*Ant.* XIII 9, 1 §§255f.; cf. *War* I 2, 6 §63) also records that this temple was destroyed by John Hyrcanus (135-104 B.C.) at the same time that he destroyed Shechem. From recent excavations it appears that this destruction of Shechem took place in 108/107 B.C. (G. Ernest Wright, *Shechem.* 1964, pp. 183-184).

After A.D. 135 Hadrian built a temple of Jupiter on Mount Gerizim which appears on Roman coins from the Neapolis mint, beginning in the reign of Antoninus Pius (138-161) and continuing for nearly a century (BASOR 180 [Dec. 1965], p. 40). The coins show a colonnaded street at the foot of the mountain and a long stairway which leads up to the temple on the summit. It is evidently this stairway to which the Bordeaux Pilgrim (333) refers when he notes concerning Mount Gerizim (*mons Agazaren*) (Geyer p. 20; LPPTS I, p. 18; CCSL CLXXV, p. 13): "Here the Samaritans say that Abraham offered sacrifice, and one reaches the summit of the mountain by steps, three hundred in number." The reference can also suggest that the Samaritans were still using some part of the mountain top for worship at that time. In 484, however, the Samaritans fell upon the Christians in their church in Neapolis while they were celebrating Pentecost and wounded their bishop, Terebinthius (for the name cf. the terebinth in Gen 35:4); in response the Emperor Zeno (474-491) drove the Samaritans from the mountain and built on it an octagonal church dedicated to Mary as the Mother of God ($\theta\epsilon o\tau \acute{o}\kappa o\varsigma$), a church for which Justinian (527-565) contributed fortifications (Procopius, *Buildings* V 7, 7).

The ruins of the Theotokos church and its fortifications are on the higher southern peak of Mount Gerizim, were excavated by A. M. Schneider in 1928, and reported on by him in 1951 (*Beiträge zur biblischen Landes- und Altertumskunde hervorgegangen aus der* ZDPV 68 [1951], pp. 211-234). The ruins of the Hadrian temple are on a *tell* on the northern spur of the mountain known as Tell er-Ras. The temple was excavated by the Drew-McCormick expedition in 1966 (NTS 13 [1967], pp. 401-402), and the great stairway was traced down the mountain from the temple to the eastern edge of Neapolis in the valley below. Also under the temple were found the walls of another and different type of building, with which were associated fragments of Hellenistic pottery. This could have been the Samaritan temple of about the fourth century B.C. If this is correct then Hadrian chose, here as well as at Bethlehem (No. 25) and Jerusalem (Nos. 145, 181), to erect one of his temples on a site already held sacred. As for the Samaritans of the present day, they continue to offer their annual Passover sacrifice just to the west of the higher southern peak, where they also make their encampment (No. 43) during the seven days of the feast (RB 31 [1922], p. 435). This view is from the present village of 'Askar, probably ancient Sychar, on the slope of Mount Ebal, and shows Mount Gerizim and the Samaritan shrine on the summit.

J. Creten, "La pâque des Samaritains," in RB 31 (1922), pp. 434-442; Moses Gaster, *The Samaritans, Their History, Doctrines and Literature.* The Schweich Lectures, 1923. London: Oxford University Press, 1925; Joachim Jeremias, *Die Passahfeier der Samaritaner.* ZAW Beiheft 59. Giessen: Alfred Töpelmann, 1932; P. Antoine, "Garizim (Le Mont)," in DB Supplément III, cols. 535-561; A. M. Schneider, "Römische und Byzantinische Bauten auf dem Garizim," in *Beiträge zur biblischen Landes- und Altertumskunde hervorgegangen aus der* ZDPV 68 (1951), pp. 211-234; Harold H. Rowley, *Sanballat and the Samaritan Temple*, reprinted from BJRL 38 (1955), pp. 166-198; Robert J. Bull in BASOR 180 (Dec. 1965), pp. 37-41; Howard C. Kee, "Tell-er-Ras and the Samaritan Temple," in NTS 13 (1967), pp. 401-402; Robert J. Bull, "A Preliminary Excavation of an Hadrianic Temple at Tell er-Ras on Mount Gerizim," in AJA 71 (1967), pp. 387-393; "The Excavation of Tell er-Ras on Mt. Gerizim," in BA 31 (1968), pp. 58-72; and in RB 75 (1968), pp. 238-243. Photograph: The Matson Photo Service, Alhambra, Calif.

43. Encampment of the Samaritans on Mount Gerizim

The photograph shows an encampment of the Samaritans on Mount Gerizim in the area adjacent to the enclosure in which they conduct their Passover sacrifice, as mentioned in No. 42.

Photograph: The Matson Photo Service, Alhambra, Calif.

44. The Region of Jacob's Well on the Madaba Mosaic Map

The city of Samaria to which Jesus came in Jn 4:5 was near the field that Jacob gave to Joseph, and Jacob's well was there. When Jacob returned from Paddan-aram he came to the city of Shechem (שכם), camped before the city, and purchased for money the piece of land on which he had pitched his tent (Gen 33:18-19). About to die in Egypt, Jacob told Joseph that he had given him Shechem which he took with sword and bow (Gen 48:22), which sounds as if, at some point, an actual conquest had been involved. The passage just cited contains the word שכם, which may be taken as the name of the city (e.g., *An American Translation*: "I hereby give you Shechem"), or may be translated as a word meaning "shoulder" or "slope" (RSV: "I have given to you . . . one mountain slope"). This suggests that the city derived its name from its location on the slope of a mountain. According to Jg 9:7 this mountain would be Mount Gerizim. Ultimately the mummy of Joseph (Gen 50:26) was buried at Shechem in the portion of ground which his father had purchased (Jos 24:32). After playing an important part in many phases of OT history, Shechem was destroyed by John Hyrcanus in 129/128 B.C. at the same time that he destroyed the Samaritan temple on Mount Gerizim (Josephus, *Ant.* XIII 9, 1 §255; *War* I 2, 6 §63; cf. above No. 42). The new city which arose in this area was Flavia Neapo-

lis. Pliny (*Nat. Hist.* v 14, 69) mentions Neapolis and says it was formerly called Mamortha; Josephus (*War* IV 8, 1 §449) mentions it and gives the native name as Mabartha. Like the name Shechem which refers to the "shoulder" of Mount Gerizim, this old name probably comes from *ma'abarta* (מעברתא), meaning "pass" or "passage," and refers to the pass between Mounts Gerizim and Ebal. Justin Martyr, who was born here, says that his father and grandfather were natives of Flavia Neapolis in Syria Palestina (or Palestinian Syria) (ἀπὸ Φλαυίας Νέας πόλεως τῆς Συρίας Παλαιστίνης) (*Apology* I 1; cf. Eusebius, *Ch. Hist.* IV 12, 1), and this makes it probable that the city was founded by Vespasian (69-79), the founder of the Flavian dynasty. Coins put the epoch of the era of the city about A.D. 72 (SHJP I ii, p. 266). Neapolis is the modern Nablus, lying in the narrow valley between Gerizim and Ebal. Since Josephus (*Ant.* IV, 8 44 §305) says that Shechem (he spells the name Σίκιμον or Σίκιμα) is "between two mountains, the Garizaean on the right and that called 'Counsel' (the Hebrew Ebal [עיבל], Dt 11:29, etc., LXX Γαιβάλ, is here Hellenized as Βουλή) on the left," it might be thought that Shechem had occupied the same site as Flavia Neapolis and present-day Nablus, directly between the two mountains. Jerome (*Letter* 108, 13 NPNFSS VI, p. 201) also says that Shechem "is now called Neapolis." In the *Onomasticon* (pp. 158-159, 164-165), however, Eusebius says that Shechem (Συχέμ), where the bones of Joseph were buried, was near Neapolis (πλησίον Νέας πόλεως) rather than at it, and here Jerome repeats rather than changes the information (*iuxta Neapolim*). In the section of the Madaba Mosaic Map shown in the photograph, in the rather obscured area in the upper left-hand portion, but also visible on No. 10, Neapolis (Νεάπολις) appears plainly labeled and represented as a large city. From the eastern gate at the top, a colonnaded street runs westward. In the southern part of the city is a basilica, facing eastward, with red roof. Presumably this is the episcopal basilica attacked by the Samaritans in 484 (cf. No. 42), and the site is occupied today by the Main Mosque in Nablus. At the intersection of the east-west street with a north-south street is a dome on columns; this is where the en-Nasr Mosque is now. At the south end of the north-south street are semicircular steps, probably representing a nympheum at the Ain Qaryun spring where a Roman structure has been found. South of Neapolis is Tur Garizin (Τουρ Γαριζιν) and, across the valley to the east (with only the bottom of the legend visible at the extreme upper edge of this photograph), Tur Gobel (Τουρ Γωβηλ). These are Mounts Gerizim and Ebal with the names given in the Aramaic form, using Aramaic טור, *tur*, for "mountain" instead of Hebrew הר, *har*.

The section of the Madaba Mosaic Map shown in the present photograph (No. 44) overlaps with the bottom part of the section shown in No. 10, and in the latter place the names of both mountains can be read plainly, Τουρ Γαριζιν and Τουρ Γωβηλ. In the section in No. 10, however, we also see that the map made place for a second and evidently alternate tradition about the location of the two mountains. There, on the edge of the mountain range west of Archelais and the place (i.e., the spring) of Saint Elisha, and not far northwest of Jericho, are smaller size labels for the two mountains, using the form of their names as found in the Septuagint, Γεβαλ and Γαριζειν.

In the *Onomasticon* (pp. 64-65) Eusebius and Jerome also record the two traditions according to which the two mountains were either adjacent to Jericho (*iuxta Iericho*) or, as the Samaritans say, adjacent to Neapolis (*iuxta Neapolim*). Eusebius, followed by Jerome, thinks the Samaritan tradition unlikely because the two mountains at Neapolis are so far apart that the blessings and curses of Dt 11:29 could not have been heard back and forth. Actually, of course, the Samaritan tradition was correct and is verified by Josephus who mentions Sichem and Argarizin (Σίκιμα καὶ Ἀργαριζίν) together (*War* I 6 §63), and is recognized by the Bordeaux Pilgrim who, as we have seen (No. 42) cites what the Samaritans say about *mons Agazaren*, and also locates *Sechim* at the foot of the mountain (Geyer p. 20; LPPTS I, p. 18; CCSL CLXXV, p. 13). The rise of the Jericho tradition, on the other hand, was no doubt made possible by ambiguity in the language of Dt 11:30 and an exegesis thereof inspired by Jewish hostility to the Samaritans.

Between Tur Gobel and Tur Garizin on the map (No. 44) is Shechem. The label reads: Συχὲμ ἡ κ(αὶ) Σίκιμα κ(αὶ) Σαλήμ, Sichem which is also Sikima and Salem. The words are almost identical with the listing of Shechem in the *Onomasticon* (p. 150), where Eusebius writes: "Shechem which is also Sikima or also Salem (Συχὲμ ἡ καὶ Σίκιμα ἡ καὶ Σαλήμ). A city of Jacob now deserted (ἔρημος). The place is shown in the environs (ἐν προαστείοις = the space in front of a town) of Neapolis; there also the tomb of Joseph is shown."

As for the identification or association of the name Salem with Shechem, this is doubtless a reflection of the same tradition attested by Epiphanius when he writes, "But others say that the Salem of Melchizedek was opposite Shechem in Samaria, whose grounds are seen (lying) waste" (*On Weights and Measures* 74 [75a] ed. Dean p. 75); *Panarion haer.* 55, 2); and it agrees with the existence of ruins and a village east of Shechem to which the name Salim still attaches. As for Shechem itself, the site has been identified with almost complete certainty with Tell Balatah, beside the village of Balatah, and excavated by G. Ernest Wright beginning in 1956. The site is on the edge of the plain one and one-half miles southeast of Nablus, corresponding with the placement by Eusebius "in front of" Neapolis and with the location on the Madaba Map, and at the foot of Mount Gerizim, corresponding with the statement of the Pilgrim from Bordeaux and again with the location on the Madaba Map.

Just north of Shechem on the Madaba Mosaic is a building and the legend Τὸ τοῦ Ἰωσήφ, literally "The of Joseph." What is meant is quite certainly "The (monument, i.e., tomb) of Joseph." This is mentioned by Eusebius (as quoted above), and also by the Bordeaux Pilgrim who writes (Geyer p. 20; LPPTS I, p. 18; CCSL CLXXV, pp. 13-14): "At the foot of the mountain is the place which is named Sechim. Here is a tomb (*monumentum*) where Joseph is laid in the estate (*villa*) which Jacob his father gave him." Today the Tomb of Joseph is shown as a stone-built grave inside a domed Muslim building (*Maqam en-Nebi Yusuf*) on the northeastern outskirts of the village of Balatah.

East of the Tomb of Joseph on the Madaba Map is a village adjacent to Tur Gobel, and under it a partially effaced legend which is probably to be restored to read: [Συ]χαρ ἡ νῦν [Σ]υχωρα, Sychar which is now Sychora. This is no doubt the En Soker or "spring of Sychar" mentioned in the Mishna (*Menahoth* 10, 2 DM p. 505) and represented by the present-day village of ʿAskar which, with its spring, is on the slope of Mount Ebal a mile east of Nablus. South of Shechem, with its legend to the southeast, very plainly visible in the photograph, is a red-roofed church labeled: Ὅπου ἡ πηγὴ τοῦ Ἰακώβ, Here (is) the Well of Jacob. This corresponds with the deep well which is still today on the southeastern outskirts of the village of Balatah.

It has been noted above (No. 42) that in the Sinaitic and Curetonian Syriac manuscripts the city of Samaria in Jn 4:5 was Shechem. The excavation of Tell Balatah confirms that the city on the tell came to an end about the end of the second century B.C., in agreement with the literary evidence that Shechem was destroyed by John Hyrcanus in 108/107 B.C. (cf. above). The excavators believe, however, that a village probably continued to exist where the village of Balatah is now (Wright, p. 244 n. 6). This would allow the supposition that the city from which the woman of Samaria came out to draw water (Jn 4:7) and to which she went back (Jn 4:28) was none other than Shechem itself, in the form of a village which continued after the destruction of the city on the ancient tell. The distances involved would be very reasonable, for it is only some three hundred yards from the Tomb of Joseph on the northeastern edge of Balatah to the Well of Jacob on the southeastern edge. The name Sychar in Jn 4:5, in this case, would be a textual corruption of Sychem or Shechem which found its way into many of the manuscripts normally regarded as most dependable.

If, however, Sychar is the correct reading of Jn 4:5 then it must be supposed that the woman of Samaria came from the city now represented by the village of ʿAskar. In this case the distance is one kilometer south from ʿAskar to Jacob's Well. In spite of the greater distance, ancient writers as well as the major manuscripts tend to point to Sychar rather than to Shechem as the city connected with the event at the well. Eusebius (*Onomasticon* p. 164) gives this entry for Sychar: "Sychar (Συχάρ). In front of Neapolis near the field which Jacob gave to Joseph his son. In which Christ, according to John, conversed with the Samaritan woman at the well. And it is shown until now."

Likewise the Bordeaux Pilgrim, having spoken of Sichem and the tomb in which Joseph was laid, writes (Geyer p. 20; LPPTS 18-19; CCSL CLXXV, p. 14): "A thousand paces from there is the place which is named Sechar, from which the Samaritan woman came down (*descendit*) to the place where Jacob dug the well in order to draw water from it, and our Lord Jesus Christ talked with her; where there are plane trees which Jacob planted, and a bath (*balneus*, probably a baptistery, since the same word [*balneum*] is used a little later for the baptistery behind the Church of the Holy Sepulcher in Jerusalem [Geyer p. 23; LPPTS I, p. 24; CCSL CLXXV, p. 17]) which is filled from this well."

To complete consideration of the presently relevant portions of this part of the Madaba Mosaic Map it will suffice to notice the text written in red in the area otherwise blank on the west side of Tur Garizin. The text is:

·Ἰωσὴφ εὐλόγησέν σε
ὁ Θεὸς εὐλογίαν γῆς
ἐχούσης πάντα καὶ
πάλιν ἀπ᾽ εὐλογίας Κ(υρίο)υ
ἡ γῆ αὐτοῦ

Joseph "God blessed thee
with the blessing of the earth
possessing all things" and
again "Of the blessing of the Lord
is his land"

The two LXX quotations, separated by "and again," are from the blessings of Joseph by Jacob in Gen 49:25 and by Moses in Dt 33:13. The word "Lord" is abbreviated.

F.-M. Abel, "Naplouse, Essai de topographie," in RB 32 (1923), pp. 120-132; Albrecht Alt, "Salem," in PJ 25 (1929), pp. 52-54; Abel, *Géographie* I, pp. 360f., "Garizim et Ébal." Photograph: courtesy Victor R. Gold.

45. Jacob's Well

This shows the mouth of Jacob's well, and the manner of lowering a water vessel into its depths.

Photograph: The Matson Photo Service, Alhambra, Calif.

46. Tell Balatah

This view is from Mount Ebal and looks down upon Tell Balatah, site of the ancient city of Shechem, in the middle foreground. The modern village and refugee camp are just beyond. To the right can be seen the lower slope of Mount Gerizim.

For the excavation of Tell Balatah, see G. Ernest Wright, *Shechem, The Biography of a Biblical City*. New York and Toronto: McGraw-Hill Book Company, 1964. Photograph: Jerry Vardaman.

47. Sychar

This is a view of the village of 'Askar, probably ancient Sychar, on the lower slope of Mount Ebal.

Photograph: Jerry Vardaman.

48. Plan of the Church over Jacob's Well according to Arculf

As explained above (No. 44), the reference by the Pilgrim from Bordeaux (333) to a bath (*balneus*) which was filled with water from the Well of Jacob suggests that there was then already a baptistery at Jacob's Well. If the baptistery was associated with a church, this church would have been of Constantinian date. The Bordeaux Pilgrim does not mention a church, however, and neither does Eusebius when he tells about the well in the *Onomasticon* (p. 164). But in his description of the pilgrimage of Paula (386) Jerome (*Letter* 108, NPNFSS VI, p. 201) says that "she entered the church built upon the side of Mount Gerizim around Jacob's Well"; and in his translation of the *Onomasticon* (p. 165) he adds at the point of the mention of the well the words, "where now a church has been built." At least by around 380, therefore, there was a church at the well.

The account of the pilgrimage of Arculf (670), written by Adamnan, contains this passage (Geyer p. 270; LPPTS III, pp. 41-42; CCSL CLXXV, p. 216) concerning the site: "Arculf . . . passed through the district of Sa-

maria, and came to the city of that province which is called in Hebrew Sichem, but in Greek and Latin custom is named Sicima; it is also often called Sichar, however improperly. Near that city he saw a church (*ecclesiam*) built beyond the wall, which is four-armed, stretching towards the four cardinal points, like a cross, a plan of which is drawn below. In the middle of it is the Fountain of Jacob (*fons Iacob*). . . ."

Arculf also drank water from the well, and obtained a figure as to its depth. Using the Greek unit orgyia (ὄργυια) which was the length of the outstretched arms, or some six feet, he reported that the well had a depth of twice twenty orgyiae. The plan of the church which accompanied the description by Arculf is reproduced from Codex Parisinus (Latin 13048), a ninth-century manuscript of *De locis sanctis* preserved in the Bibliothèque Nationale, Paris. Since Arculf came to Palestine after the Persian invasion (614) and the Muslim conquest (638) it is possible that by then the upper church had been destroyed and what he saw and drew was only a cruciform crypt immediately over the well. His language, however, appears intended to say that the church itself was in existence and in this form at that time.

Photograph: Arculfus De Locis Sanctus, Codex Parisinus Lat. 13048, courtesy Bibliothèque Nationale, Paris.

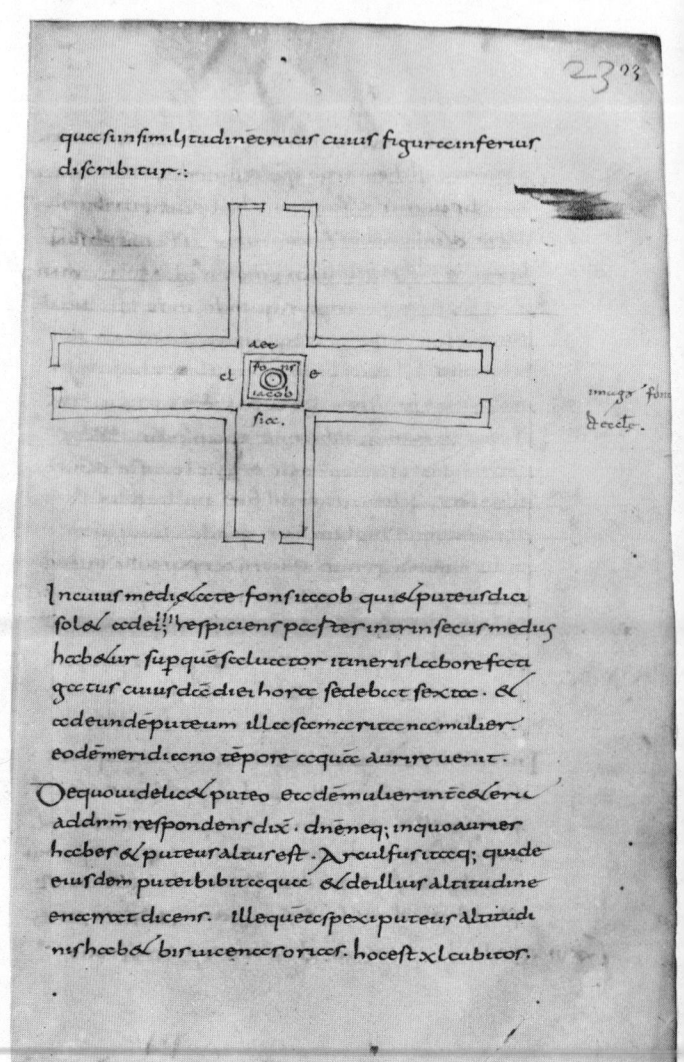

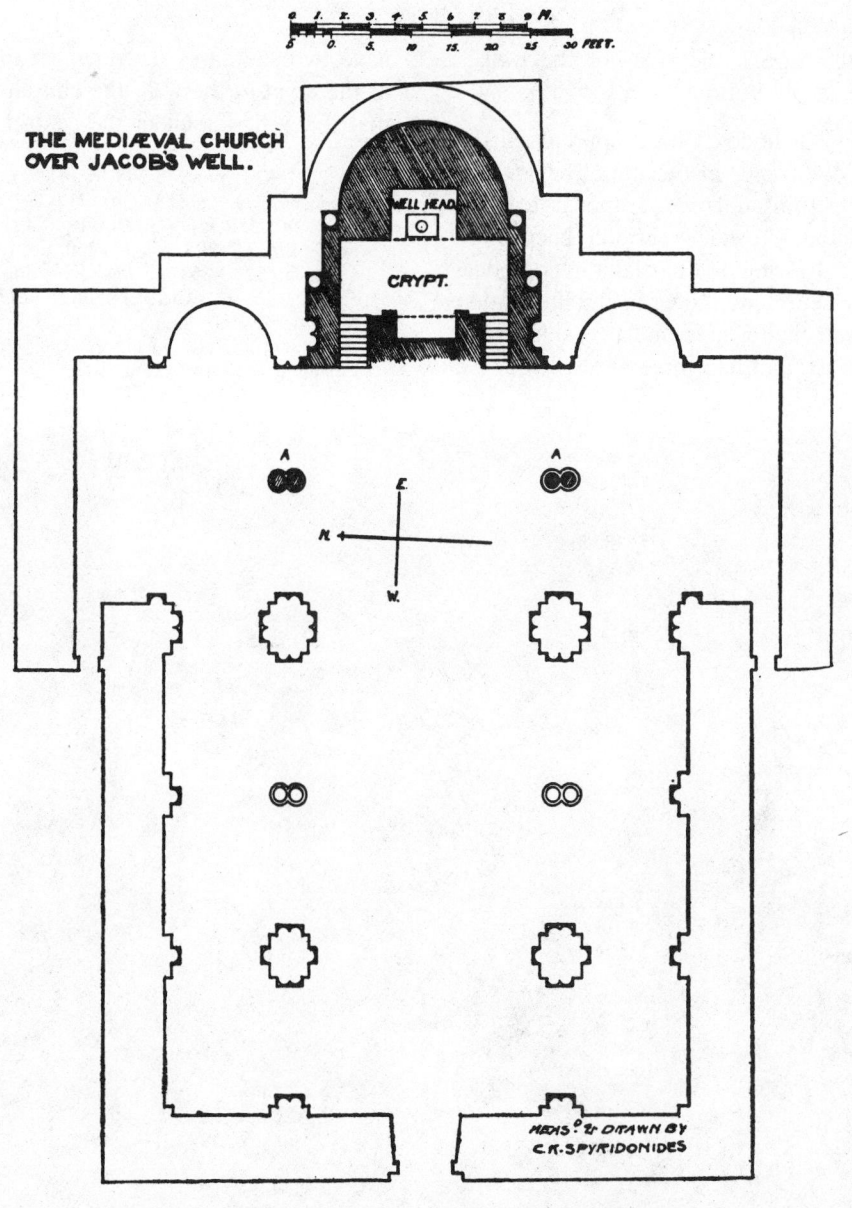

THE MEDIÆVAL CHURCH
OVER JACOB'S WELL.

WELL HEAD

CRYPT.

MEAS.º & DRAWN BY
C. K. SPYRIDONIDES

49. Plan of the Crusader Church over Jacob's Well

Before the Crusaders came the church at Jacob's Well was probably in ruins, at any rate they built a new church there. The Crusader church is attested as in existence around 1150, and was dedicated to the Savior of the world, in evident allusion to Jn 4:42. In this connection Vardaman suggests that it is of interest that a hoard of 35 Ptolemaic silver tetradrachmas was found in the 1960 excavations at Shechem. Many of these coins mention Ptolemy II as "Savior" (ΣΩΤΗΡΟΣ), which was used as a title for the emperor, Augustus, at a later period, of course (see Sellers, "The Coins of Shechem," in BA 25 [1962], pp. 90f.). The Crusader church at Jacob's Well was also ruined. In 1882 the *Memoirs* of *The Survey of Western Palestine* (II, pp. 172-178) describe only a broken vault and a massive stone of local white limestone with a round hole directly over the well, the stone deeply grooved from the ropes with which the water pots were drawn up. Concerning the well the *Memoirs* (pp. 174, 176) state:

The site is acknowledged by Jews, Moslems, and Christians. The existence of a well sunk to a great depth in a place where water-springs on the surface are abundant is sufficiently remarkable to give this well a peculiar history. It is remarkably characteristic of the prudence and forethought of the great Patriarch, who, having purchased a parcel of ground at the entrance of the vale [of Shechem], secured on his own property, by dint of great toil, a perennial supply of water at a time when the adjacent water-springs were in the hands of unfriendly, if not actually hostile, neighbours. . . . The well was undoubtedly sunk to a great depth for the purpose of securing, even in exceptionally dry seasons, a supply of water, which at great depths would

41

always be filtering through the sides of the well and would collect at the bottom.

In 1885 the Greek Orthodox Church purchased the property of Jacob's Well and, in due time, began certain excavations. The ruins uncovered appear to have been entirely from the Crusader period. They were sufficient to allow the drawing of a partially hypothetical plan of the Crusader church as shown in the illustration (No. 49). The church had a nave and two side aisles, was oriented to the east, and had three apses. From the nave two staircases ran down at the right and the left to the crypt at the well, the church being positioned so that the well was under the central apse.

RB 2 (1893), pp. 242-244; 4 (1895), pp. 619-622 (Paul-M. Séjourné); PEFQS 1881, pp. 212-214 (Charles W. Barclay); 1893, pp. 255-256 (G. Robinson Lees); 1894, pp. 108-112 (F. J. Bliss); 1895, p. 89; 1900, pp. 61-63 (Conrad Schick); 1908, pp. 248-253 (C. K. Spyridonidis); 42 (1933), pp. 384-402 (F.-M. Abel, "Le puits de Jacob et l'eglise Saint-Sauveur"). Photograph: C. K. Spyridonidis, "The Church over Jacob's Well," in PEFQS 1908, Plan on p. 252, courtesy Palestine Exploration Fund.

50. The Unfinished Greek Orthodox Basilica over Jacob's Well

In 1903 the Greek Orthodox Church began to build a new basilica over Jacob's Well and in 1959-1960 the structure stood at the point shown in this photograph.

The two small temporary shacks at the head of the nave give access to the two staircases which lead down to the crypt and the wellhead.

Photograph: JF.

GALILEE

51. The Southern End of the Sea of Galilee

The Hebrew name for Galilee, גָּלִיל, transliterated in Greek as Γαλιλαία, means "circle," hence signifies "region" or "district." Lying in the northern part of Palestine, Galilee was more exposed to foreign influences than the rest of the land and had a pagan as well as a Jewish population. Is 9:1 (Heb. 8:23) identifies the area as that of the tribes of Zebulun and Naphtali, and calls it "Galilee of the nations," equally well translatable as "the district of the nations." Mt 4:14-16 cites the passage in Isaiah in connection with the residence of Jesus at "Capernaum by the sea," and includes Is 9:2 (Heb. 9:1) as relevant to the effect of the work of Jesus: "the people who sat in darkness have seen a great light, and for those who sat in the region and shadow of death light has dawned." Josephus (*War* III 3, 1-2 §§35-43) delimits the area of Galilee as enveloped by Phoenicia and Syria on the west and north, and bounded by Samaria and the territory of Scythopolis on the south and the territory of Hippos, Gadara, and Gaulanitis on the east. He writes, perhaps not without exaggeration: ". . . the land is everywhere so rich in soil and pasturage and produces such variety of trees, that even the most indolent are tempted by these facilities to devote themselves to agriculture. In fact, every inch of the soil has been cultivated by the inhabitants; there is not a parcel of waste land. The towns, too, are thickly distributed, and even the villages, thanks to the fertility of the soil, are all so densely populated that the smallest of them contains above fifteen thousand inhabitants."

The large lake, which is an outstanding feature of Galilee, is called the Sea of Chinnereth or Chinneroth in the OT (Num 34:11; Jos 12:3; 13:27), Gennesar in I Macc 11:67 and Josephus, and the Lake of Gennesaret (Lk 5:1), the Sea of Tiberias (Jn 6:1; 21:1), and the Sea of Galilee (Jn 6:1, etc.) in the NT. It is approximately thirteen miles long and as much as seven miles across, and lies 696 feet below sea level. The Jordan River flows through it from north to south, and constantly renews the freshness of its waters, in which are said to be forty different species of fish. The photograph looks from west to east across the southern portion of the lake.

Photograph: JF.

43

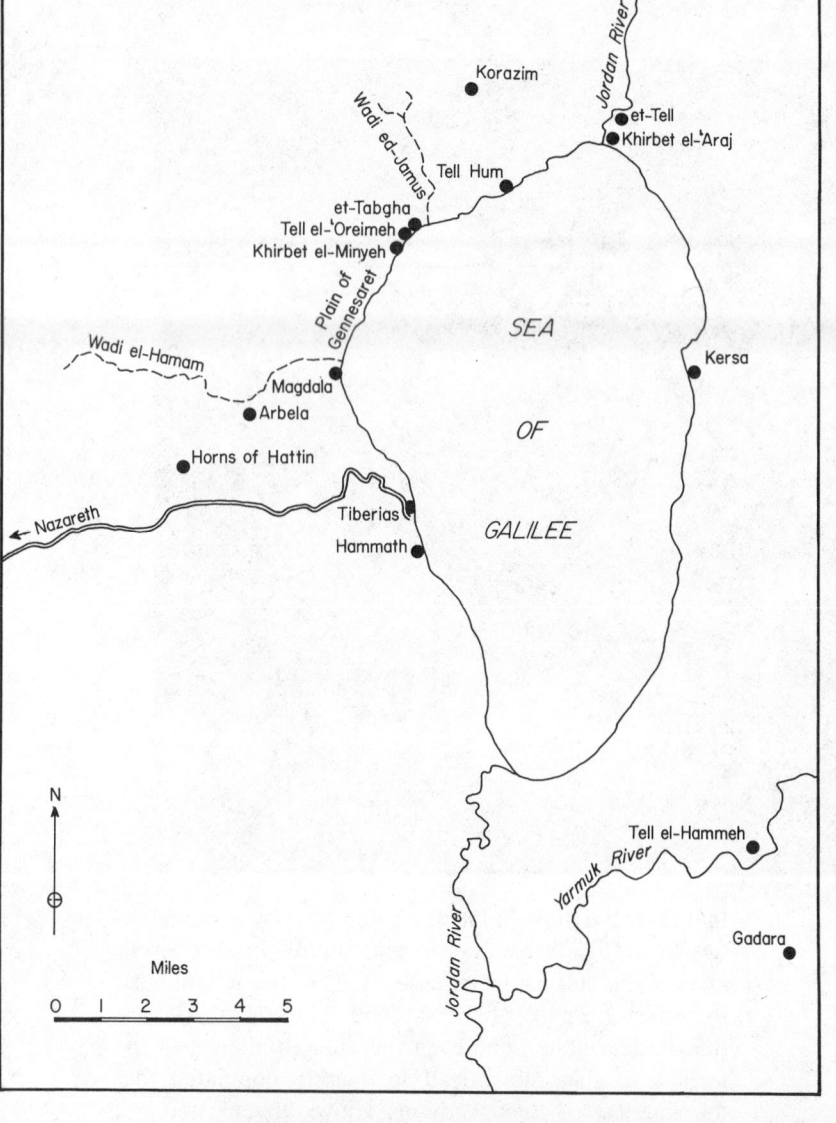

52. Map of the Sea of Galilee

This sketch map will locate the chief places on and near the Sea of Galilee which are to be mentioned in the following discussion.

Map: JF, cf. Dalman, *Sacred Sites*, pp 120, 132.

53. Tiberias on the Sea of Galilee

In 530 Theodosius (Geyer pp. 137-138; LPPTS II, p. 8; CCSL CLXXV, p. 115) came from Scythopolis, i.e., from the south, to the Sea of Tiberias and visited in succession Tiberias, Magdala, the Seven Springs (et-Tabgha, see No. 57), and Capernaum (Tell Hum, see No. 59). These were the sites of chief importance, enumerated in sequence from south to north, on the west side of the lake. Tiberias is about five miles north of the outlet of the Jordan, at the south end of the lake. Herod Antipas (4 B.C.-A.D. 39), who had resided at Sepphoris, built the city as a new capital and named it in honor of Tiberius (14-37). Since Josephus (*Ant.* XVIII 2, 3 §36) mentions the building of Tiberias by Herod the tetrach just after recording the coming of Pontius Pilate as procurator (probably A.D. 26), it has often been held that the city was built about that time. On the basis of coins and other evidence, however, Avi-Yonah (IEJ 1 [1950-51], pp. 160-169) has concluded that the foundation of the city was between the years 17 and 22 of the Christian era, and Spijkerman (LA 13 [1962-63], pp. 303-304) has narrowed the span to A.D. 17-20. Within these years, Avi-Yonah suggests A.D. 18 as the most likely, since the official foundation of Tiberias in that year would coincide with the sixtieth birthday of the emperor in whose honor the city was named.

In the NT the city is mentioned only in Jn 6:23. Jo-

sephus says that Herod built a palace for himself in Tiberias which contained representations of animals and had a roof partly of gold (*Life* 12 §65); also that there was a stadium there which was used for public assemblages (*War* II 21, 6 §618; III 10, 10 §539), and a synagogue (προσευχή, literally "place of prayer," the same word as in Ac 16:13, 16) which was a huge building and capable of accommodating a large crowd (*Life* 54 §277). Josephus also says that Tiberias was built on the site of tombs and was therefore a settlement contrary to the law and tradition of the Jews; hence it was difficult to obtain settlers and the king brought in a heterogeneous population of Galileans and others. While it might be thought that these were all Gentiles, the large synagogue speaks for the presence of many Jews too. In fact Tiberias became a strong center of Jewish life after A.D. 135, and the Sanhedrin or Beth Din which had been moved from Jerusalem to Jamnia (70-132) and to other places was at last brought here (cf. No. 236). Also the tombs of the famous Jewish leaders, Johanan ben Zakkai, establisher of the Beth Din at Jamnia, Rabbi Akiba, supporter of Bar Kokhba, Rabbi Meir, second-century scholar whose name means "giver of light," Maimonides, twelfth-century physician and philosopher, and others are at Tiberias. Five miles to the west and a little north are the Horns of Hattin, where the Crusaders were defeated by Saladin in 1187.

Not far from Tiberias was a hot spring and a village which Josephus (*Ant.* XVIII 2, 3 §36) calls Ammathus ('Αμμαθοῦς). The name, he says (*War* IV 1, 3 §11), may be interpreted as "warm baths" (θερμά), and the place was probably the Hammath (חמת, "hot spring") of Jos 19:35. The place indicated is undoubtedly to be identified with the hot springs on the lake shore about a mile and a half south of Tiberias. Excavations were conducted in the mound adjacent to the springs by N. Slousch in 1921 and by Moshe Dothan in 1961 and later. There are some remains of the southern gate of the city and of the baths of the Israelite period. Most notable is what Dothan calls Building II A. At least in part this building was probably used as early as the first century as a synagogue, and it certainly was a synagogue later.

At the end of the third or beginning of the fourth century it was provided with a splendid mosaic floor; in the fifth century it was transformed from a small rectangular room into a larger basilica with an apse. The mosaic just mentioned is perhaps the best early synagogue mosaic thus far known. At the top it has the ark of the law between two seven-armed lampstands, while the large central panel shows the signs of the zodiac and the seasons of the year. The mosaic contains a Hebrew inscription which refers to the peculiar formula, "Verily, verily" ("Amen, Amen"), just as we read in the Gospel according to John and the Manual of Discipline (Vardaman).

In the case of many Hellenistic towns in Palestine the name reverted in due time to an earlier Semitic form; Scythopolis, for example, became known again as Bethshean, Philadelphia as Amman, and so on, but since Tiberias did not displace any earlier Semitic name it has remained the name of the city until today. The hot springs at Hammath are called Hamei Tiberias. The photograph (No. 53) shows the city of Tiberias as it lies on the lake shore in what Josephus (*Ant.* XVIII 2, 3 §36) called the best region of Galilee.

M. Avi-Yonah, "The Foundation of Tiberias," in IEJ 1 (1950-51), pp. 160-169. Curiously enough, with respect to the proposed date of A.D. 18 for the foundation of Tiberias, and the mention of the city by Josephus just after mention of the coming of Pontius Pilate as procurator, there is independent evidence on the basis of which it has been argued that Pilate's term of office actually began in the fall of A.D. 18. See Robert Eisler, *The Messiah Jesus and John the Baptist according to Flavius Josephus' recently rediscovered 'Capture of Jerusalem' and the Other Jewish and Christian Sources.* New York: The Dial Press, 1931, pp. 18-19. L.-H. Vincent, "Les fouilles juives d'el-Hammam, a Tibériade," in RB 30 (1921), pp. 438-442; 31(1922), pp. 115-122; B. Lifshitz, "Die Entdeckung einer alten Synagoge bei Tiberias," in ZDPV 78 (1962), pp. 180-184; M. Dothan in IEJ 12 (1962), pp. 153-154; and in RB 70 (1963), pp. 588-590; A. Spijkerman, "Some Rare Jewish Coins," in LA 13 (1962-63), pp. 303-304; Pearlman and Yannai pp. 60-64. Photograph: JF.

54. Magdala

Proceeding northward from Tiberias along the lake shore, Theodosius (Geyer pp. 137-138; LPPTS II, p. 8;

CCSL CLXXV, p. 115) came next to Magdala, "where the lady Mary was born" (*ubi domna Maria nata est*). He gives the distance as two miles, but repeats the same figure for the distance from Magdala to the Seven Springs and from the Seven Springs to Capernaum, hence we may regard it as a round figure approximation. It is in fact somewhat less than three miles (4.50 km.) along the shore from Tiberias to the present-day village of Migdal (it was known in Arabic as Mejdel), which doubtless preserves the ancient name and probably also preserves substantially the ancient location of Magdala. This site is not only on the road from Tiberias but also at the junction therewith of the ancient road from Nazareth, which came down through the Wadi el-Hamam or Valley of Pigeons and past the great cliffs of Arbela to the lake. At Arbela the Jews fought against the Syrians (I Macc 9:2), in the grottoes in the mountainside Herod the Great trapped and slaughtered brigands, as Josephus calls them (*Ant.* XIV 15, 5 §§421-430; *War* I 16, 4 §§310-313), and in the war with Rome the village of the Cave of Arbela was one of the places in Lower Galilee, along with other villages and with the cities of Tarichea, Tiberias, and Sepphoris, which were fortified by Josephus (*Life* 37 §188; cf. 60 §311). Magdala itself, occupying this strategic junction, probably derived its name from *migdal* which is the Hebrew word for "tower" (מגדל), suggesting its place as a guard tower or fortress. As we have seen (No. 36), the name occurs in the Nazareth inscription from Caesarea. In the Talmud Migdal is mentioned as near Tiberias and is also given the fuller name of Migdal Nunaiya or "fish tower" (Pesahim 46a SBT II, 4, p. 219), appropriate to the good fishing here in the Sea of Galilee. The place which Josephus calls Tarichea, a name evidently derived from Greek τάριχος, meaning salted fish, was probably also the same as Magdala. Josephus (*War* III 9, 7-10, 5 §§443-502) gives a very detailed account of the conquest of Tarichea by Vespasian and Titus, which is not surprising since Tarichea was one of the Galilean cities which he himself had fortified. In the account he describes the Romans as moving up from Scythopolis to Tiberias, then advancing (προελθών) further and pitching camp between Tiberias and Tarichea, and finally taking the city; the sequence of the places and the description of the topography is entirely in accord with the identification of Tarichea and Magdala. Josephus also speaks of the Taricheans as numbering as many as 40,000—a perhaps exaggerated figure—and makes mention of their hippodrome, an indication of the Hellenistic character of the city (*War* II, 21, 3-4 §§599, 608). In the Gospels Magdala (Μαγδαλά) is mentioned in Mt 15:39 and Mk 8:10 in some manuscripts. Other manuscripts, and in fact the better ones, give Magadan in Mt 15:39 and Dalmanutha in Mk 8:10, while yet

other forms of the name also occur. Even so it is probable that all of these (with the possible exception of Dalmanutha which may require a different explanation) are variants of Magdala, related to Hebrew Migdal as explained above. For Magdala we have also the witness of the name of Mary Magdalene (Μαρία ἡ Μαγδαληνή), which occurs a number of times in all four Gospels (Mt 27:56, etc.), and which must mean "Mary, the one from Magdala." Although it is no longer identifiable, a Byzantine church must have been built at Magdala, for Eutychius (*The Book of the Demonstration*, ed. Watt, CSCO 193, p. 136), with obvious reference to Lk 8:2, writes: "The Church of Magdala near Tiberias bears witness that Christ here drove out the seven demons which were in Mary Magdalene." The photograph shows the village of Mejdel and the Plain of Gennesaret behind it.

W. F. Albright, "Contributions to the Historical Geography of Palestine: The Location of Taricheae," in AASOR 2-3 for 1921-22 (1923), pp. 29-46; Joseph Sickenberger, "Dalmanutha (Mk. 8, 10)," in ZDPV 57 (1934), pp. 281-285; Dalman, *Sacred Sites*, pp. 118-119, 126-128; Paul Thielscher, "Εις τα ορια Μαγδαλα," in ZDPV 59 (1936), pp. 128-132; Børge Hjerl-Hansen, "Dalmanutha (Marc, VIII, 10), Énigme géographique et linguistique dans l'Évangile de S. Marc," in RB 53 (1946), pp. 372-384; Clemens Kopp, "Christian Sites around the Sea of Galilee: IV. Magdala," in *Dominican Studies* 3 (1950), pp. 344-350. Photograph: courtesy École Biblique et Archéologique Française.

55. The Plain of Gennesaret

From the hills near Magdala northward along the lake shore to the hilly promontory on which are the ruins known as Khirbet el-Minyeh, which is a distance of

about three miles, and extending inland about a mile and a quarter, is a pleasant and fertile plain. After Vespasian and Titus took Tarichea or Magdala, as noted just above, they prepared rafts to pursue fugitives who had sailed out into the lake for refuge (*War* III 10, 6 §505), and at this point Josephus interrupts his narrative of the warlike events to give some account of the lake and of the land immediately adjacent to it. The lake, which he calls Gennesar (cf. No. 51), takes its name, he says (*War* III 10, 7 §506), from the adjacent territory, and he describes that territory as follows (*War* III 10, 8 §§516-521):

Skirting the lake of Gennesar, and also bearing that name, lies a region whose natural properties and beauty are very remarkable. There is not a plant which its fertile soil refuses to produce, and its cultivators in fact grow every species; the air is so well-tempered that it suits the most opposite varieties. The walnut, a tree which delights in the most wintry climate, here grows luxuriantly, beside palm trees, which thrive on heat, and figs and olives, which require a milder atmosphere. One might say that nature had taken pride in thus assembling, by a *tour de force* the most discordant species in a single spot, and that, by a happy rivalry, each of the seasons wished to claim this region for her own.

After some additional details, he says that this region extends along the border of the lake for a length of thirty stadia and inland to a depth of twenty. These are approximately the dimensions of the plain we have just delimited, and there is no doubt that this is the region which Josephus is describing. Thus we learn that the name of the plain was Gennesar, or Gennesaret as it is found in the Gospels (Mt 14:34, etc.). The photograph shows the Plain of Gennesaret in a view from the north. Toward the right in the distance is the mouth of Wadi el-Hamam, with the heights of Arbela above (cf. No. 54) and, against the horizon, the Horns of Hattin (cf. No. 53).

Photograph: The Matson Photo Service, Alhambra, Calif.

56. The Sea of Galilee from the Plain of Gennesaret

After the feeding of the five thousand Jesus and the disciples crossed over the Sea of Galilee by boat and came to land at Gennesaret or Gennesar, both spellings of the name being found in the various manuscripts (Mt 14:34; Mk 6:53); after the feeding of the four thousand they came by boat to Magdala, or Magadan, or Dalmanutha (for the various names cf. No. 54) (Mt 15:39; Mk 8:10). There is no doubt that the region indicated is the same as that described by Josephus on the northwest shore of the lake of Gennesar in the passage already quoted (No. 55). Since they crossed the lake to reach the landing point, the feeding must have been on the east side. A place somewhere between Bethsaida (Khirbet el-'Araj? see No. 75) in the north and a point more or less opposite Tiberias must be indicated, since Lk 9:10 localizes the feeding of the five thousand in connection with Bethsaida and Jn 6:23 refers to boats from Tiberias coming near the place afterward. That the disciples headed back from that place toward Bethsaida (Mk 6:45) or Capernaum (Jn 6:17) (Tell Hum, see No. 59) but landed at Gennesaret may not be surprising if one recalls the storm they encountered and if allowance is made for the strong current of the Jordan flowing from north to south through the lake. The photograph is a view of the Sea of Galilee from the Plain of Gennesaret.

Photograph: JF.

57. Mosaic of Loaves and Fishes in the Church of the Multiplying of the Loaves and Fishes

At the northern edge of the Plain of Gennesaret is the hilly promontory already referred to (No. 55) on which are the ruins called Khirbet el-Minyeh. This is a place visited by Saladin in 1187 and mentioned then under the Arabic name *minyeh*. Excavations begun here in 1932 by A. E. Mader uncovered an Arab palace of the seventh or eighth century, built in a square, with round towers at the corners, and a mosque on the southeastern side with mihrab indicating the direction of prayer toward Mecca. Three hundred yards to the north is a mound which slopes steeply to the lake shore, and is known in Arabic as Tell el-'Oreimeh. In 1929 A. Jirku found Late Bronze and Iron II pottery on the tell, and digging in 1932 by A. E. Mader and R. Köppel confirmed the existence of an important city which flour-

ished notably in the Late Bronze Age. This was probably the city of Chinneroth or Chinnereth which is mentioned in a list of Thutmose III (ANET p. 242) and in the OT (Dt 3:17; Jos 11:2; 19:35), and which gave its name to the lake when it was called the Sea of Chinnereth (Num 34:11, etc.; cf. above No. 51). Before a way was blasted along the shore it was not possible to pass on that side and the main road went through a hollow on the western side and was dominated by this mound. This road was the ancient Way of the Sea (דרן הים) mentioned by Is 9:1 (Heb 8:23) as passing through the land of Zebulun and of Naphtali, i.e., through Galilee of the nations (cf. above No. 51): it came from Mesopotamia by way of Damascus, crossed the Jordan, and sent a branch to Tyre and Sidon; the main route came on past Tell el-'Oreimeh and Khirbet el-Minyeh, followed the lake shore to Magdala, went through Wadi el-Hamam (cf. No. 54) and across the Plain of Esdraelon to the pass at Megiddo, thence to the coast of the Mediterranean and down this to Egypt. Whether the "sea" in the name of the road was the Sea of Galilee or the Mediterranean Sea, this route, with its branches, was an international highway of immemorial usage, undoubtedly thronged in the time of Jesus, and the famous *Via Maris* of the Middle Ages.

Somewhat more than half a mile farther northward along the lake shore from Tell el-'Oreimeh one comes to et-Tabgha, an Arabic corruption of the Greek name Heptapegon (Ἑπτάπηγον [χωρίον]), or place of the Seven Springs. Here there are indeed copious springs in a little plain built up by the silt from Wadi ed-Jamus which descends to the lake at this point. Josephus probably considered this small plain to be a part of the larger Plain of Gennesaret and, in fact, the spring waters were

led around to the vicinity of Khirbet Minyeh by channels. At any rate in his description of the district of Gennesar, Josephus says (*War* III 10, 8 §519) that "the country is watered by a highly fertilizing spring, called by the inhabitants Capharnaum (Καφαρναούμ)," which can hardly be other than one of the chief springs at Heptapegon. The fact that the spring was named after Capernaum is not surprising for the latter was almost certainly at Tell Hum (cf. below No. 59), only a mile and a quarter further along the lake shore, and et-Tabgha may easily have been associated in some way with Capernaum in ancient times. The powerful spring was imagined by some, Josephus adds, to be a branch of the Nile; this belief was encouraged by the fact that it produced a fish resembling the *coracin* found in the lake of Alexandria.

The accounts of the feeding of the five thousand and of the four thousand undoubtedly refer to the farther or eastern side of the Sea of Galilee, since afterward Jesus and the disciples came back by boat to Gennesaret (cf. above No. 56). Also we learn from Eutychius of Alexandria (*The Book of the Demonstration*, ed. Watt, CSCO 193, p. 137) that there was a church at Kursi, east of the sea of Tiberias, which was a witness to the feeding of the four thousand, and a witness as well to the healing of the demoniac from whom the demons went into the swine (cf. No. 76).

In the course of time, however, it became difficult for pilgrims to visit the far side of the lake and, probably for this reason, the traditional site was transferred to the west side and to the small plain of the Seven Springs, a region which undoubtedly had many actual associations with the Galilean ministry of Jesus, since nearby Capernaum was a center of that ministry. In 385 Aetheria, as quoted by Peter the Deacon (Geyer p. 113), speaks of the Sea of Tiberias, of Tiberias, and of Capernaum, and then gives this description:

> On the sea is a grassy field which has sufficient hay and many palm trees and nearby seven springs (*septem fontes*), each of which pours out abundant water, and in this field the Lord fed the people with five loaves and two fishes. Indeed the stone on which the Lord put the bread has been made into an altar, and from this stone those who come now break off pieces for their healing and it benefits all. Near the walls of this church (*ecclesia*) passes the public road where the apostle Matthew had his tax office (*theloneum* = τελώνιον). In the hill which is nearby is the eminence which the Savior ascended to speak the Beatitudes.

Here at et-Tabgha near the springs and at the foot of the hill which is still known as the Mount of the Beatitudes are the ruins of a mosaic-floored church which were investigated by Paul Karge in 1911 and excavated by A. E. Mader and A. M. Schneider in 1932. As brought to light in 1932 the church was a basilica in the form of an irregular quadrangle, facing east, 56 meters long and 24 meters wide at the eastern end and 33 meters wide at the western end. Of the total length the atrium occupies about 18 meters, and the narthex less than 5. The main portion of the basilica is divided into central nave and two side aisles, and has a broad transept and curving apse. In the apse, under the present small altar, is a rough piece of limestone, presumably the stone mentioned by Aetheria, or a part thereof.

The entire floor of the church was covered with mosaics of which considerable fragments have been preserved, most notably in the left transept and behind the altar. On the basis of the total floor space in the entire church and the average size of the cubes of which the remaining portions of mosaics are made, it is estimated that in its original form the entire mosaic contained seven million cubes. In 1936 Bernard Gauer was working on restoration of the mosaics and found at a deeper level the remains of an earlier chapel. The latter was a much smaller building, only about 18 meters in length including the apse, and 9.50 meters in width. It was oriented southeastward, but so that the sacred stone, in the identical position, was in the place of honor in front of the apse. The chapel has been thought to date about 350, which would be in the time of Joseph of Tiberias (cf. No. 37); the basilica obviously replaced the chapel at a later date, and its mosaics have been placed at the end of the fourth or beginning of the fifth century; there was probably some restoration, perhaps after earthquake damage, in the sixth century, but before long, perhaps in the Persian invasion in 614, the church was destroyed and not again rebuilt (Schneider p. 80; Gauer pp. 234, 245, 249).

The photograph (No. 57) shows the mosaic behind the altar. We see a basket full of loaves, two whole loaves and two halves showing on top, each marked with a cross. On either side is a fish. While loaves and fishes are shown frequently in early Christian art, and may be connected with the eucharist or the heavenly meal, in this case a specific connection with the miracle commemorated by this church may be assumed.

A. Jirku, "Durch Palästina und Syrien," in ZDPV 53 (1930), p. 148; A. E. Mader, "Die Ausgrabung eines römischen Kastells auf *Chirbet el-Minje* an der Via Maris bei et-Tābgha am See Gennesareth," in JPOS 13 (1933), pp. 209-220; Alfons M. Schneider, *The Church of the Multiplying of the Loaves and Fishes at Tabgha on the Lake of Gennesaret and Its Mosaics.* ed. A. A. Gordon, tr. Ernest Graf. London: Alexander Ouseley, Ltd., 1937; Bernhard Gauer, "Werkbericht über die Instandsetzung der Boden-Mosaiken von '*Heptapegon*' (Basilika der Brotvermehrung am See Tiberias)," in JPOS 18 (1938), pp. 233-253. Photograph: JF.

58. Mosaic of Waterfowl and Marsh Plants in the Church of the Multiplying of the Loaves and Fishes

The mosaics in the north and south transepts are the most remarkable. Beautifully executed in white and black, in violet, red, brown, and yellow, they represent the landscape at the lake, with an abundance of marsh plants and waterfowl. Among lotus, papyrus, oleander, and a thistlelike shrub, we see the duck, dove, heron, goose, cormorant, flamingo, and water snake. Also a few architectural features are included: in the north transept, a tower with a pyramidal top which may be a grave monument like the Tomb of Zechariah (No. 221) in the Kidron Valley; a city gate with two towers; and a pavilion; and in the south transept, a tower divided into stories marked with the Greek letters Vau, Zeta, Eta, Theta, and Iota, corresponding to the numbers 6, 7, 8, 9, and 10, probably a device like a Nilometer to measure the height of the water in the lake. Of the two the mosaic in the north transept is the better preserved. With its border of lotus blossoms it measures 5.50 by 6.50 meters. A small portion of its lower right-hand corner is shown in the present photograph. We see a heron dipping beak into a lotus bud, and a duck resting upon a lotus flower.

Photograph: JF.

59. The Sea of Galilee from Capernaum

A mile and a quarter farther along the lake shore from the Seven Springs, and some two miles short of the mouth of the Jordan River as it enters the lake,

is the site known as Tell Hum. The location accords with the best indications for the site of Capernaum, the city which was so important a center of the Galilean ministry of Jesus. Mt 4:13 places Capernaum by the sea and in the territory of Zebulun and Naphtali. According to the frontiers of these two tribes as given in Jos 19, Naphtali was immediately west of the Sea of Galilee, and Zebulun was west of that. Josephus suffered an accident near the mouth of the Jordan and was carried to a village called variously in the manuscripts Κεφαρνωκόν or Κεφαρνωμόν (*Life* 72 §403), which is undoubtedly Capernaum. Under the circumstances he would be taken to the nearest place for adequate help, which corresponds with the location of Capernaum at Tell Hum. Likewise, as already noted (No. 53), Theodosius coming from the south passed through Tiberias, Magdala, and the Seven Springs, before reaching Capernaum, and this accords with the same location. The name Capernaum (Καφαρναούμ) is doubtless derived from the Hebrew כפר נחום, Kefar Nahum, meaning Village of Nahum (although which Nahum is meant remains uncertain). The name appears in this form in the Midrash (Midrash Rabbah, Ecclesiastes, I 8; VII 26 SMR VIII, pp. 29, 210) where, interestingly enough, Capernaum is particularly associated with the *minim* or "sinners," i.e., the Christians. In one of these same passages (I 8 SMR VIII, p. 27) there is met upon the

main street of Sepphoris a man named Jacob (since he is a disciple of Jesus he may be James the son of Alphaeus [Mk 3:18, etc.] or the Less [Mk 15:40]) of Kefar Sekaniah, and his village illustrates the same kind of name. If, then, in the course of time Kefar meaning "village" became Tell referring to the mound of a deserted city, and if Nahum was shortened to Hum, the name of Tell Hum would itself preserve in that form the name of Capernaum. The photograph looks across the Sea of Galilee from the site of Tell Hum, toward Wadi el-Hamam, Arbela, and the Horns of Hattin (cf. Nos. 53, 54).

F.-M. Abel, "Le nom de Capharnaüm," in JPOS 8 (1928), pp. 24-34. Photograph: JF.

60. Plan of the Synagogue at Capernaum

At Capernaum Jesus taught in the synagogue (Mk 1:21), and also dealt with a centurion of whom the elders of the city said, "He built us our synagogue" (Lk 7:5). Aetheria (385), as quoted by Peter the Deacon (Geyer p. 113), reports concerning Capernaum: "There is the synagogue in which the Lord healed the demoniac. One goes up to it by many steps. This synagogue is built of quadrangular stones."

In his travels in Palestine in 1838 and 1852 Edward Robinson noted and described the site of Tell Hum and came to the conclusion that the chief ruins were those

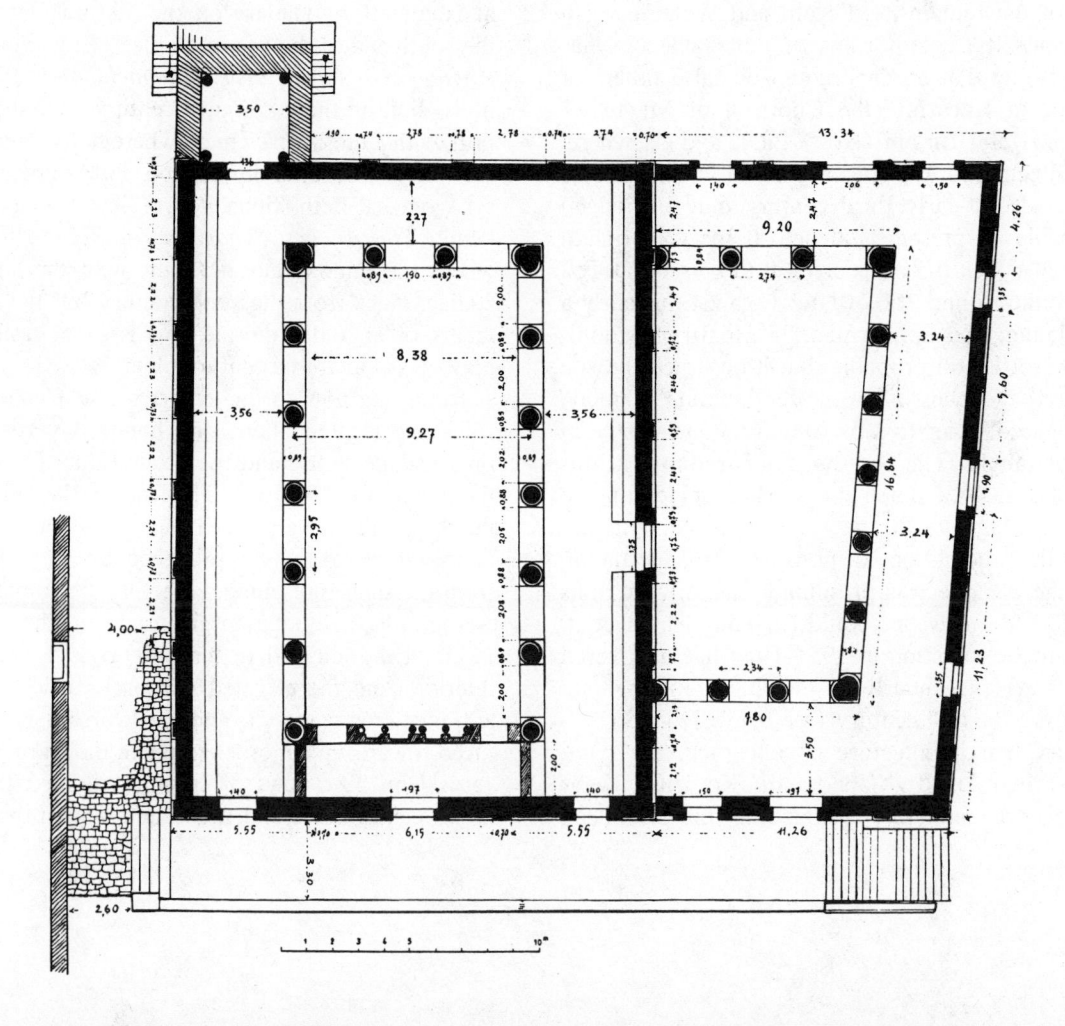

of a Jewish synagogue, although he did not believe that the place itself was Capernaum. Charles Wilson, however, came to the conclusion that Tell Hum was Capernaum, and made the first excavations there in 1865-1866. In 1894 the Franciscans acquired the site from the Turks and built a monastery near the synagogue ruins, but because of unsettled conditions covered the site over and planted it to keep it safe. In 1905 the synagogue was excavated by the *Deutsche Orient-Gesellschaft* under Heinrich Kohl and Carl Watzinger, and work was continued from 1905 to 1921 under the Franciscan Custody of the Holy Land; the results were published by Gaudence Orfali in the latter year.

Orfali (pp. 74-86) advanced a careful argument for considering the synagogue in its extant ruins to belong to the first century and prior to A.D. 70. The Jerusalem Talmud (Megillah III 1, BA 7 [Feb. 1944], p. 3), however, says that Vespasian destroyed 480 synagogues (an exaggerated figure, perhaps) in the city of Jerusalem, and it has generally been held probable that synagogues were destroyed throughout the land in the wars climaxing in A.D. 70 and 135. Another favorable time for the rebuilding of synagogues may have been after Septimius Severus made a journey through Palestine and Syria in 199: in his reign (193-211) and that of his son Caracalla (211-217) there was a more favorable attitude toward the Jews. These considerations, together with comparative analysis of the architectural and artistic character of the remains, led Kohl and Watzinger (p. 218) to place the extant ruins of the Galilean synagogues, not only that at Capernaum but also others of similar type at Korazim (the Chorazin of Mt 11:21 (Nos. 70f.), Kefar Bir'am (Nos. 72ff.), and elsewhere, in the third century (Watzinger II, p. 113), and a date in the late second-early third century may be judged most probable on present evidence. If the Capernaum synagogue of which the ruins are still to be seen at Tell Hum was built around 200 or later (against this early a date, Vardaman cites Spijkerman, "A Hoard of Antoniani," in LA), it is still probable that it occupied the site and followed the plan of an earlier building, namely, the synagogue of prior to A.D. 70 and the synagogue in which Jesus taught. The persistence of tradition in this regard is shown by a statement of Maimonides that in replacing a synagogue the new one must be built beside it and then the old one demolished. At Capernaum, however, the old one was presumably already in ruins and therefore the new one could be built right over it. In fact a small excavation in 1953-1954 has uncovered foundations which, underlying the later building, are probably from the first century (see below No. 63).

As far as their architecture is concerned, the synagogues just mentioned (Capernaum, Korazim, Kefar Bir'am, etc.) are commonly spoken of as of the Galilean type. They are built in the style of the Hellenistic assembly hall, the basilica, which was usually a rectangular building with the interior divided by rows of columns (Watzinger II, p. 108). As far as the synagogues are concerned, their ornamental façades faced toward Jerusalem and the people inside faced in the same direction (cf. Dan 6:10, etc.); a sacred enclosure, perhaps for the Torah, was evidently provided immediately in front of the main door. Since the basilica also became the prevailing type of early Christian church building, it is possible that the adaptation of this style of architecture for the synagogue prepared the way for the Christian usage (Goodenough I, pp. 183, 192). At Jerash (Gerasa) in Transjordan a synagogue was, in fact, turned into a church (C. H. Kraeling, *Gerasa*, 1938, pp. 234-241), even as at Eshtemoa, nine miles south of Hebron, one was made into a mosque (L. A. Mayer and A. Reifenberg in JPOS 19 [1939-40], pp. 314-326). From about the fourth century onward the Palestinian synagogues generally have their main entrance on the side away from Jerusalem and have an apse, for the Torah shrine, on the side toward Jerusalem. Some of these are of the broadhouse type, i.e., it is a long side of the rectangle of the building which is oriented toward Jerusalem, and some of them are characterized by the use of mosaic for floors. Outstanding examples are the synagogue at Hammath near Tiberias (above No. 53), with the signs of the zodiac in the mosaic; the synagogue at Hammath-by-Gadara on the Yarmuk River east of the south end of the Sea of Galilee (E. L. Sukenik, *The Ancient Synagogue of el-Hammeh.* 1935), a broadhouse built in the late fourth century or first half of the fifth, with a mosaic pavement where lions stand on either side of a memorial inscription in Aramaic; and the synagogue at Beth Alpha west of Scythopolis (E. L. Sukenik, *The Ancient Synagogue of Beth Alpha.* 1932) where the famous mosaic floor, with the signs of the zodiac, dates from the sixth century but lies over fragments of an older mosaic and is in a basilica which may be as much as a century older.

Returning now to the synagogue at Capernaum, the ruins are located about one hundred yards from the present lake shore, and the ground plan is as shown in the illustration (No. 60). The front of the building faces nearly south, toward the lake and toward Jerusalem. A raised platform is approached by steps leading up from the right, presumably the very steps mentioned by Aetheria in the quotation given above. The main building is at the left, where three doors give access to the interior from the elevated platform. Inside the central entrance was a screen, and the worshipers must have faced toward this in order to make their prayers toward Jerusalem. Two rows of columns divided the interior into a central nave and two side aisles, in the style of a basilica. The columns themselves supported a gallery which ran around the north, east, and west sides of the building, with access to the gallery by a stairway in an annex at the northwest corner. In the light of later custom it may be assumed that the gallery was intended for the women. Running around the walls on three sides on the ground floor are two benches, one built above the other, and these presumably provided seats for the men. Adjacent to the synagogue proper on the east side is a court of trapezoid shape entered by two doorways from the elevated platform in front. A colonnade ran around the three walls, and the central part of the court was left open to the sky. The probable use of an arch over the central doorway of the main building and of additional windows in the upper level of the façade appear in the model shown in No. 61, while Nos. 62ff. show more of the rich sculptural decoration of the synagogue.

Interestingly enough, a probable synagogue of the time of Herod the Great has now been found, built just inside the northwestern wall of Herod's fortress on the summit of the rock of Masada. In the first stage of its construction the building was oriented toward Jerusalem, had an anteroom, and a main room with columns along three sides. In a second stage, believed to be that of the time when the Zealots occupied Masada, the orientation was still toward Jerusalem, there was a small room in one corner, and the large room was enlarged and provided with benches along the walls as well as with a different arrangement of the columns. Even in this building of Herodian and Zealot times, the architectural plan with the columns and eventually the benches is already suggestive of what is found later in the synagogues at Capernaum and elsewhere in Galilee.

Edward Robinson, *Biblical Researches in Palestine, and in the Adjacent Regions.* Boston: Crocker and Brewster, 3 vols. 1856. II, pp. 406-407; III, p. 346; Charles W. Wilson in *The Recovery of Jerusalem.* New York: D. Appleton & Co., 1872, pp. 266, 292-301; and in *The Survey of Western Palestine,* Special Papers. London: The Committee of the Palestine Exploration Fund, 1881, pp. 298-299; Heinrich Kohl and Carl Watzinger, *Antike Synagogen in Galilaea.* Leipzig: J. C. Hinrichs, 1916; Gaudence Orfali, *Capharnaüm et ses ruines d'apres les fouilles accomplies a Tell-Houm par la Custodie Franciscaine de Terre Sainte (1905-1921).* Paris: Auguste Picard, 1922; Samuel Krauss, *Synagogale Altertümer.* Berlin-Wien: Benjamin Harz, 1922; E. L. Sukenik, *Ancient Synagogues in Palestine and Greece.* Schweich Lectures of the British Academy, 1930. London: Oxford University Press, 1934; Herbert G. May, "Synagogues in Palestine," in BA 7 (Feb. 1944), pp. 1-20; Goodenough pp. 178-267. Yigael Yadin, *Masada, Herod's Fortress and the Zealots' Last Stand.* London: Weidenfeld and Nicolson, 1966, pp. 181-187. Photograph: Orfali, *op.cit.*, Pl. III, courtesy A. & J. Picard, Paris.

61. Model of the Synagogue at Capernaum

This model represents the synagogue at Capernaum as seen from the southwest. Additional study of the extant remains of the building would indicate certain changes such as showing two doorways rather than one leading into the court at the right (cf. plan, No. 60), and the provision of additional doors or windows in the east wall of the court.

Photograph: Kohl and Watzinger, *Antike Synagogen in Galilaea,* Pl. v, courtesy J. C. Hinrichs Verlag, Leipzig.

62. Ruins of the Synagogue at Capernaum

This is a view of the main basilical hall, partly rebuilt by the Franciscans in 1925, looking northward toward the colonnade at the end and the north wall. The building is of white limestone, which was probably quarried in Wadi el-Hamam (No. 59).

Photograph: JF.

63. Southeast Corner of the Capernaum Synagogue

Here we see the steps which lead up to the platform in front of the synagogue. Kohl and Watzinger (p. 5) found these steps unique among all the synagogues they studied. Presumably they are the "many steps" mentioned by Aetheria (cf. above No. 60). The wall is also built of "quadrangular stones," just as Aetheria said. At the corner of the wall the results may be observed of the small additional excavation done in 1953-1954 (cf. above No. 60). Beneath the white limestone blocks of which the synagogue of c. 200 was built, are blocks of black basalt. The striking difference in material suggests that we have here, in fact, the foundation of the preceding synagogue, i.e., the synagogue of the first century and of the time of Jesus.

Photograph: JF.

64. Sculptured Capital at Capernaum

As shown in this example, the capitals of the columns in the Capernaum synagogue were elaborately sculptured in the Corinthian order.

Photograph: JF.

65. Ark of the Covenant at Capernaum

In the rich sculptured ornamentation of the Capernaum synagogue one of the most interesting items is that shown in this photograph. We see a chest with arched roof, double doors at the end, and columns along the side. Beneath also we see wheels, of which there were presumably four in all, on which the chest was transportable. The best theory to explain the nature of this object is that it represents the ark of the covenant.

Watzinger II, p. 113. Photograph: JF.

66. Menorah at Capernaum

This sculpture shows the seven-armed lampstand and, at the right, the shofar or ram's horn blown at festivals, at the left, the shovel used for incense (cf. No. 243).

Photograph: JF.

67. Star of David at Capernaum

This hexagram, used as a part of the sculptural ornamentation in the synagogue at Capernaum, was later known as the Shield or Star of David.

Photograph: JF.

68. Star of Solomon at Capernaum

This pentagram, shown here as sculptured at Capernaum, was later known as the Shield or Star of Solomon.

Photograph: JF.

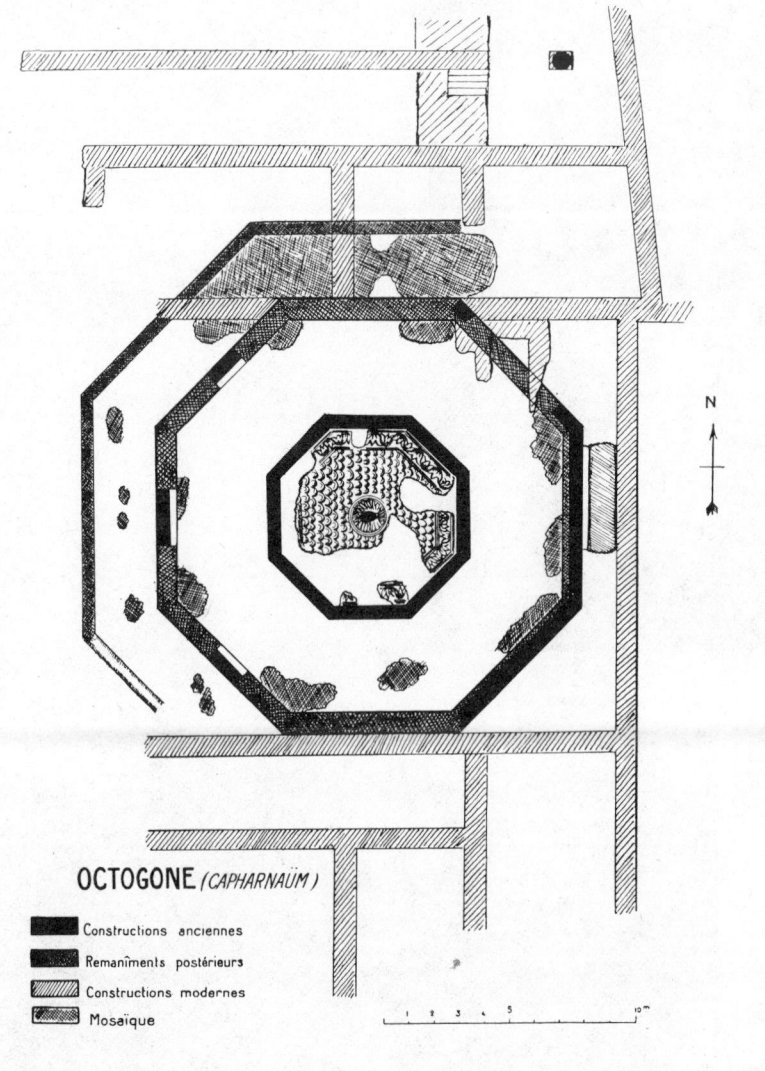

OCTOGONE *(CAPHARNAÜM)*

- ■ Constructions anciennes
- ■ Remaniments postérieurs
- ▨ Constructions modernes
- ▨ Mosaïque

69. Plan of the Octagon at Capernaum

According to the evidence of Epiphanius cited above (No. 37), it is possible that Joseph of Tiberias built a Christian church at Capernaum in the fourth century. In the record of her visit in 385 Aetheria, as quoted by Peter the Deacon (Geyer pp. 112-113), not only describes the synagogue (No. 60) but also writes: "In Capernaum out of the house of the first of the apostles a church was made, the walls of which stand until today as they once were. Here the Lord cured the paralytic." The last sentence by Aetheria evidently represents a traditional assumption that Jesus was "at home" (Mk 2:1) in Capernaum in the house of Peter (Mt 8:14; Mk 1:29; Lk 4:38). In 570 the Anonymous of Piacenza reports (Geyer p. 163; LPPTS II, p. 6; CCSL CLXXV, p. 159): "We came to Capernaum into the house of St. Peter, which is a basilica." This may suggest a rebuilt, larger church than that seen by Aetheria.

The octagon shown here is south of the synagogue, was cleared by Orfali in 1921, and excavated by Virgilio C. Corbo in 1968. Corbo reports (in IEJ 18 [1968], pp. 197-198) that this was the central octagon of a Byzantine church of probably the fifth century. Underneath were remains of a first century fishermen's quarter, with some rooms which were adapted, as colored ornamentation and graffiti showed, for Christian worship already in the second and third centuries and continued in such use through the fourth century. After that, the basilical church was built with its octagon directly over the earlier prayer room.

Orfali, *Capharnaüm et ses ruines*, pp. 103-109. Photograph: *ibid.*, Pl. XI, courtesy A. & J. Picard, Paris.

70. Ruins of the Synagogue at Chorazin

In the woe recorded in Mt 11:21-23 and Lk 10:13-15 Jesus linked two other cities with Capernaum, namely, Chorazin and Bethsaida. When Aetheria was at Capernaum (385) she mentioned but apparently did not visit the place. Her report, according to Peter the Deacon (Geyer p. 113), reads: "Not far from here is the synagogue over which the Savior pronounced a malediction; for when the Savior passed by and interrogated the Jews who were working on it and said: 'What are you doing?' they said: 'Nothing.' And the Lord said: 'Therefore if it is nothing that you are making, it will always be nothing.' So it remains until today."

In the *Onomasticon* (p. 174) Eusebius locates the place at two miles from Capernaum and describes it as abandoned and desolate (ἔρημος). Chorazin is almost certainly to be recognized at the site called Kerazeh or Korazim, which is some two miles up in the hills to the northwest of Tell Hum. The Anglican bishop Pococke, who visited Palestine in 1738 (see also Thomsen, *The Land and the Book* [Popular ed. 1908], II, p. 421), made the identification, although it was rejected by Edward Robinson (cf. Abel's criticism of Robinson on this point in JBL 58 [1939], p. 370). Charles Wilson, who conducted the first excavations at Tell Hum in 1865-1866 (cf. No. 60), visited the site and described the main ruins as those of a synagogue, built of very hard black basalt, with Corinthian capitals

and other ornaments. His description was repeated, and some additional details given, by H. H. Kitchener in *The Survey of Western Palestine* (I, 1881, pp. 400-402). Then a detailed investigation was made (1905) by Kohl and Watzinger. In striking contrast with the white limestone of the Capernaum synagogue, the synagogue at Chorazin was built, as Wilson observed, of the black basalt of the surrounding countryside. The basic plan was very much the same as at Capernaum, on a slightly smaller scale. The building faced south, the interior was like a basilica, with colonnades around the three walls, and there was an abundance of sculptural ornament. Since the synagogue had already been left desolate in the time of Eusebius, it must have been built at least as early as the preceding century, perhaps around 200. Like the companion building at Capernaum, it may well have had a predecessor of the first century.

In 1962 the Israel Department of Antiquities carried out excavations in the area surrounding the synagogue at Chorazin, Zeev Yeivin being in charge of the work. Three trenches were dug which ran up to the outside walls of the synagogue on the east, north, and west. The eastern trench revealed a large public building, 900 square meters in extent, adjoining the synagogue, so this was evidently the central quarter of the town. The northern trench uncovered additional structures, one perhaps a ritual bath, which were part of the synagogue. The western trench reached the edge of a residential quarter. Here the houses were built of basalt, and some of the walls were still preserved to a height of three meters. To the south at least two oil presses gave evidence of an industrial quarter. The town extended over fifteen acres, spread over the top and southern and western slopes of a small hill, with the synagogue and public buildings on the highest part. The major building period appears to have been in the second to fourth centuries of the Christian era, with destruction in the fourth century and additional construction in the fifth and sixth centuries. The photograph (No. 70) shows the ruins of the synagogue, and the rocky character of the surrounding countryside.

Wilson, *The Recovery of Jerusalem*, pp. 270f., and in *The Survey of Western Palestine*, Special Papers, p. 299; Kohl and Watzinger, *Antike Synagogen in Galilaea*, pp. 41-58; Sukenik, *Ancient Synagogues in Palestine and Greece*, pp. 21-24; Clemens Kopp, "Christian Sites around the Sea of Galilee: III. Chorazin," in *Dominican Studies* 3 (1950), pp. 275-284; Goodenough I, pp. 193-199; Z. Yeivin in IEJ 12 (1962), pp. 152-153; and in RB 70 (1963), pp. 587-588 and Pl. XXIV b; PEQ 1963, p. 3. Photograph: courtesy École Biblique et Archéologique Française.

71. Seat in the Synagogue at Chorazin

Perhaps the most interesting single object from the Chorazin synagogue is this large stone seat, now preserved in the Archaeological Museum in Jerusalem. It is 73 centimeters wide, 56 centimeters high and, at its maximum, as thick as it is high. On the seat back there is a rosette in a circle, and on the front an inscription in Aramaic in four lines, which is translated:

Remembered be for good Judah (literally, Judan)
  ben Ishmael
who made this stoa
and its staircase. As his reward may
he have a share with the righteous.

The word *stoa* in the second line is the Greek word transliterated into Aramaic. It was presumably judged applicable as a term descriptive of a synagogal hall. The word staircase in the third line may refer to steps which seem to have led up to the Torah shrine in many synagogues. Such an elaborate seat as this was probably occupied by the chief official in the synagogue, perhaps "the ruler of the synagogue" ($\dot{\alpha}\rho\chi\iota\sigma\upsilon\nu\dot{\alpha}\gamma\omega\gamma\sigma\varsigma$) of Mk 5: 38, etc. (cf. also No. 96). As such it was probably also the "Moses' seat" ($\dot{\eta}$ M$\omega\ddot{\upsilon}\sigma\dot{\epsilon}\omega\varsigma$ $\kappa\alpha\theta\dot{\epsilon}\delta\rho\alpha$) of Mt 23:2.

J. Ory, "An Inscription Newly Found in the Synagogue of Kerazeh," in PEFQS 1927, pp. 51-52; A. Marmorstein, "About the Inscription of Judah ben Ishmael," in PEFQS 1927, pp. 101-102; Sukenik, *Ancient Synagogues in Palestine and Greece*, pp. 57-61; A. Reifenberg, *Ancient Hebrew Arts*. New York: Schocken Books, 1950, p. 105. Photograph: courtesy École Biblique et Archéologique Française.

72. The Synagogue at Bir'am

Although it is not a NT site, mention may also be made of Kefar Bir'am, in the hills west of the Huleh Valley, because of its very well-preserved synagogue ruins, comparable in plan and probable date to the synagogues at Capernaum and Chorazin. The place was visited by Edward Robinson in 1852, and he noted the

ruins of two synagogues, as did also Charles Wilson who reported on them in *The Survey of Western Palestine* (1881). The smaller of the two has now disappeared completely, its stones no doubt having been carried off for building material. An inscription in square Hebrew characters which was written in one long line on the lintel of the main entrance is, however, preserved in the Louvre. It reads: "May there be peace (שלום) in this place and in all the places of Israel. Jose the Levite, the son of Levi, made this lintel. May blessing come upon his deeds." Lidzbarski (p. 117) assigned the inscription to the second-third century, which is in harmony with an assignment of the Kefar Bir'am synagogues to about the same time as those at Capernaum and Chorazin. The larger of the two synagogues was called by Wilson "the most perfect remain of the kind in Palestine" (*Survey* p. 297), and it still stands amazingly intact as may be seen in the photograph. The façade faces south, i.e., toward Jerusalem, and has a main doorway and two side doors. Before this façade was a porch with six columns in front and one on either end.

Robinson, *Biblical Researches in Palestine*, 1852, pp. 70-71; *The Survey of Western Palestine*, Special Papers (1881), p. 297 (Wilson); *Memoirs* I (1881), pp. 230-234 (Kitchener); Mark Lidzbarski, *Handbuch der nordsemitischen Epigraphik nebst ausgewählten Inschriften*. Weimar: Emil Felber, 1898. I. *Text*, pp. 117, 485 No. 5; II. *Tafeln*, Pl. XLIII No. 4; Kohl and Watzinger, *Antike Synagogen in Galilaea*, pp. 89-100; Goodenough I, pp. 201-203. Photograph: JF.

73. Arch over the Main Doorway of the Synagogue at Bir'am

The round decoration beneath the lintel is a crown of olive leaves. On the lintel is a grape vine with alternating bunches of grapes and leaves within its convolutions.

Photograph: JF.

74. Interior Hall of the Synagogue at Bir'am

As the photograph shows, the ground plan of the Bir'am synagogue was very much the same as that of the synagogues at Capernaum and Chorazin, i.e., it was essentially a basilica. There was a colonnade around the three sides, east, north, and west, and the columns probably carried a balcony above.

Photograph: JF.

75. The Jordan Flowing into the Sea of Galilee near the Probable Site of Bethsaida

Bethsaida, linked with Chorazin and Capernaum in Mt 11:21-23 and Lk 10:13-15 (cf. No. 70), was presumably the village which Philip the tetrarch (4 B.C.-A.D. 34) raised to the dignity of a city by reason of the number of its inhabitants and its size. He named it Julias in honor of Julia the daughter of Augustus, as Josephus relates (*Ant.* XVIII 2, 1 §28) and, since Julia was banished in 2 B.C., this must have taken place before that date. Josephus also locates Julias in lower Gaulanitis (*War* II 9, 1 §168), and says that "below the town of Julias" the river Jordan "cuts across the Lake of Gennesar" (*War* III 10, 7 §515). The place was, accordingly, on the east side of the Jordan and a little way above where the river enters the Sea of Galilee. Although the river was ordinarily considered the eastern border of Galilee, Bethsaida Julias may have been loosely considered as belonging to Galilee, for Jn 12:21 calls it "Bethsaida in Galilee," and Ptolemy (*Geography* V 15,

ed. Stevenson, p. 128) likewise reckoned Julias as belonging to Galilee. The air view shows the Jordan River at the point where it flows into the Sea of Galilee from the north. Two sites in the area have come under consideration with respect to the probable location of Bethsaida Julias. The first is Khirbet el-'Araj, only fifty yards from the lake shore; the second is a mound about a mile to the north known simply as et-Tell. On the basis of surface observations made in 1927-1928 W. F. Albright concluded that et-Tell was a Bronze Age site having nothing to do with Bethsaida, and that the latter was probably at the eastern end of the natural terrace of el-'Araj. Others have surmised that Julias was at el-Tell and Bethsaida, as a fishing village, was at et-'Araj on the lake shore. The name Bethsaida may be from the Aramaic and mean House of the Fisher.

W. F. Albright in BASOR 29 (1928), pp. 2, 7; Clemens Kopp, "Christian Sites around the Sea of Galilee: II. Bethsaida and el-Minyeh," in *Dominican Studies* 3 (1950), pp. 10-40; M. Avi-Yonah in IDB I, pp. 396-397. Photograph: The Matson Photo Service, Alhambra, Calif.

DECAPOLIS

76. Plan of Jerash

The Decapolis (Δεκάπολις) is mentioned only three times in the Gospels (Mt 4:25; Mk 5:20; 7:31) and only the last of these references speaks of Jesus as go-

ing there. Even in the last case the language is not un-ambiguous for ἀνὰ μέσον τῶν ὁρίων Δεκαπόλεως can be translated not only "through the region of the Decapolis" (RSV), but also "through the midst of the borders of Decapolis" (ASV), or even taken to mean "between"

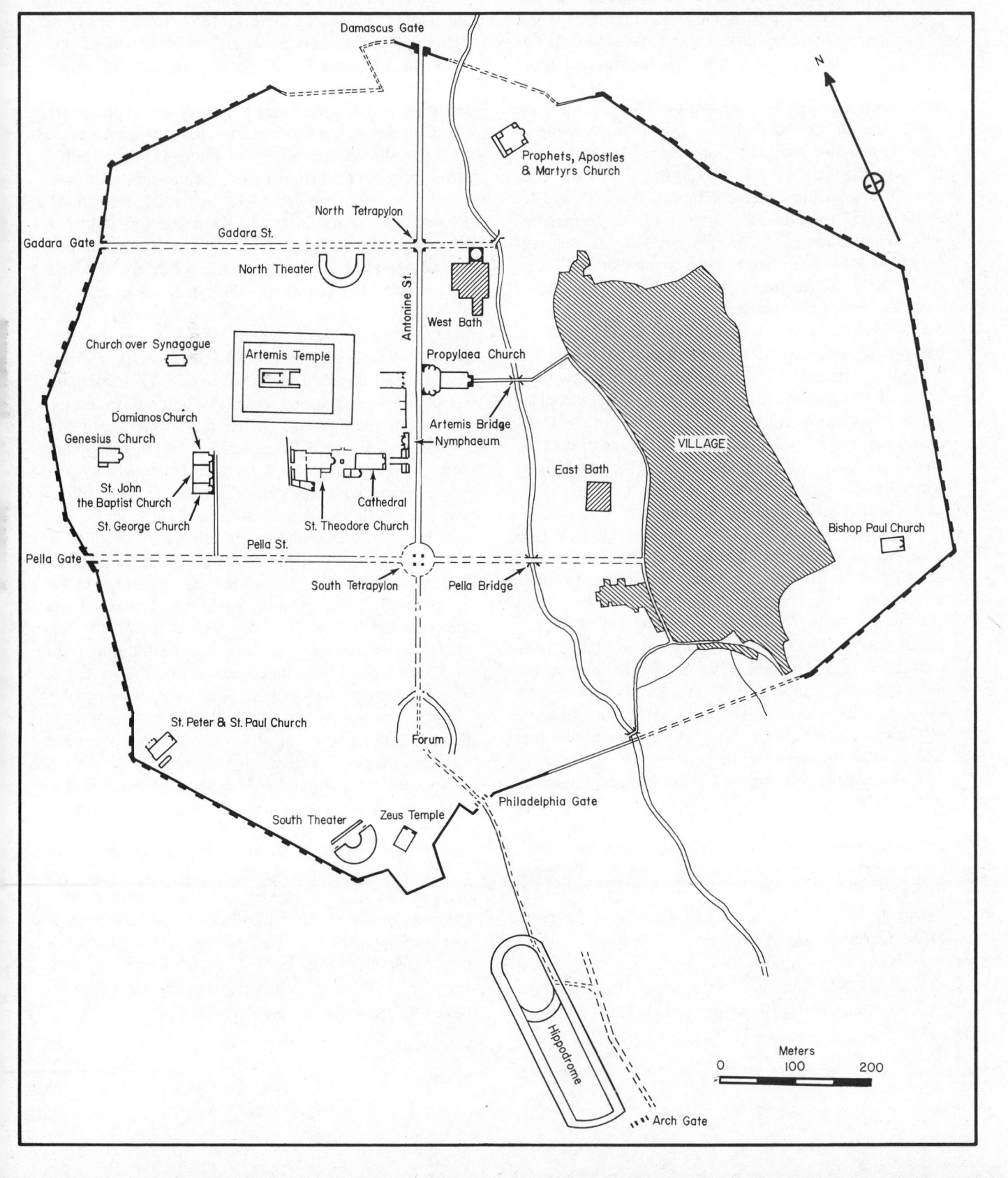

the political boundaries of the cities in the Decapolis league (cf. Sherman E. Johnson, Black's NT Commentaries, *Mark*, p. 139). As the name indicates, the Decapolis was a federation of "ten cities," although the actual number varied from time to time. Pliny, in the first century of the Christian era, names the cities in the league as Damascus, Philadelphia, Raphana, Scythopolis, Gadara, Hippo, Dion, Pella, Galasa, and Canatha (*Nat. Hist.* v 16, 74). Scythopolis was on the west side of the Jordan, the other cities on the east, and their territory as a whole, according to this list, formed a triangle from Scythopolis on the west to Damascus on the north and Philadelphia (present-day Amman) on the south. Galasa, in Pliny's list, is probably the same as Gerasa, and this city and Gadara are the two of the ten to which there are allusions in the text of the Gospels. In the narrative of the demoniac Mk 5:1 and Lk 8:26 and 37 refer to "the country of the Gerasenes" with "Gadarenes" and "Gergesenes" as textual variants, and Mt 8:28 refers to "the country of the Gadarenes" with "Gerasenes" and "Gergesenes" as textual variants. The word "Gergesenes" would imply a place called Gergesa, which may be found at Kersa on the east shore of the Sea of Galilee at a point where the hills plunge steeply to the lake as is implied in the narrative of the demoniac. This is undoubtedly the place where Eutychius of Alexandria (*The Book of the Demonstration*, ed. Watt, csco 193, p. 137) mentions "the church of Kursi, east of the sea of Tiberias," as bearing witness to the healing of the possessed man, as well as to the feeding of the four thousand (cf. No. 57).

The name "Gadarenes" will refer to Gadara (see map, No. 52), which is identified with the unexcavated site Umm Qeis five miles southeast of the Sea of Galilee and beyond the River Yarmuk. Likewise the name "Gerasenes" will refer to Gerasa, now called Jerash, which was yet farther south, more than thirty miles from the Sea of Galilee. In terms of proximity to the lake, Gergesa (probably = Kersa, Kursi) would seem the most likely location. Yet conceivably the "country" of Gadara or even of Gerasa could have been deemed to extend to the shore of the lake.

As Hellenistic cities in the Roman Empire, the towns of the Decapolis were characterized by such features as a main colonnaded street, forum, theater, temples, etc. Of the "ten cities" the one where the ruins have been best preserved and most thoroughly excavated is Gerasa or Jerash.

Gerasa is in the mountains of Gilead on a stream called Chrysorhoas, a tributary of the River Jabbok. With many of its ruins still visible above ground, the site attracted the attention of modern travelers from the early nineteenth century onward. J. L. Burckhardt,

for example, who was there briefly in 1812, was able to draw a plan showing town wall, temples, theaters, private habitations, colonnaded streets, and forum. The forum he found "enclosed by a magnificent semicircle of columns in a single row" (p. 256). Fifty-seven of these columns were still standing; in the ruins as a whole he enumerated 190 columns, and half again as many broken-off columns, all still standing (pp. 263f.). Guy Le Strange, who went there in 1884, found the ruins "Palmyra perhaps excepted, the most extensive and marvellous remains of the Graeco-Roman rule in Syria," and thought that as they stood out white and glaring in the noontime sun they had "that same appearance of recent desolation which is so striking a characteristic of the freshly cleared streets of Pompeii" (pp. 167f.). After more detailed studies by G. Schumacher who was there repeatedly between 1891 and 1902, and by O. Puchstein who came in 1902 for comparative studies in the course of his work (1898-1905) at Baalbek, repair and conservation work was begun in 1925 by the British School of Archaeology in Jerusalem under George Horsfield. The latter described the situation at that time: "The ruins were unapproachable except on foot; all was choked with earth and fallen stones, and the paved streets were lost under debris and fallen columns. Gardens encroached on monuments and cultivation extended into the theaters. The churches were hardly visible or even known." Large scale excavation was conducted from 1928 to 1934 by Yale University in conjunction first with the British School of Archaeology and later with the American School of Oriental Research in Jerusalem, and the results were published in 1938 under the editorship of Carl H. Kraeling.

The plan (No. 76) shows the chief features in the excavated city. The walls, ten feet in thickness and 3,500 meters in circumference, enclosed the slopes of the hills on both sides of the river which flowed through the middle of the city. The main ruins are on the west side, where the major north-south colonnaded street roughly parallels the stream. At the south end of the street is the great elliptical forum of the first century, the ruins of which Burckhardt admired. Not far away on the hill to the west are a temple of Zeus and the south theater. Proceeding north along the colonnaded street, there are tetrapylons at the intersections of two main east-west streets. Between these streets on the hill in the northwest is the chief temple, built in the second century and dedicated to Artemis, and beyond it the north theater. Outside the city walls to the south is the hippodrome, and the triumphal arch with its inscription welcoming the Emperor Hadrian on his visit to Gerasa in 130. Like the arch, many of the extant architectural remains belong to the second century rather than the first, yet presumably they preserve much of the plan of the city as it already existed in the first century. Between the fourth and the sixth century the fine Christian churches were built, eleven of which have been found. Many were in the area not far from the Artemis temple, and one replaced a synagogue which had been directly behind the temple.

John L. Burckhardt, *Travels in Syria and the Holy Land.* London: John Murray, 1822, pp. 251-264; Guy Le Strange, "Account of a Short Journey East of the Jordan," in PEFQS 1885, pp. 167-168; G. Schumacher, "Dscherasch," in ZDPV 25 (1902), pp. 109-177; Carl H. Kraeling, ed., *Gerasa, City of the Decapolis.* New Haven: American Schools of Oriental Research, 1938. Photograph: courtesy Palestine Institute.

77. The Triumphal Arch at Jerash

This photograph shows the triumphal arch mentioned in the preceding section (No. 76). In the excavation the arch was found preserved to this extent, and additional restoration has since been made. Located about 460 meters south of the ancient city, it is the first major monument seen upon approaching from the south. As excavated, the arch stands upon a rectangular piece of land over 37 meters long and 9 meters wide; the central structure is 25 meters long and, as reconstructed, 21.50 meters high. The arrangement is typical of triumphal arches in that period. In the center is a large arched passageway, 5.70 meters wide and 10.80 meters high; on either side is a smaller arched passage, 2.65 meters

wide and 5.20 meters high. Both façades of the arch are decorated with columns and niches. Over the central passageway on the north face was set a panel of some nineteen stones, in all over seven meters long, bearing an inscription which is now in the Palestine Archaeological Museum in Jerusalem. The inscription dedicates the gateway ($\pi \acute{\nu} \lambda \eta$) to the Emperor Hadrian and mentions among his honors the holding of the tribunician authority for the fourteenth time ($\delta \eta \mu \alpha \rho \chi \iota \kappa \hat{\eta}s$ $\dot{\epsilon} \xi o \nu \sigma \acute{\iota} \alpha s$ $\tau \grave{o}$ $\iota \delta'$), which gives the date A.D. 129/130 (Liebenam, *Fasti consulares*, KLT 41-43, p. 107).

Kraeling, *Gerasa*, pp. 73-83, 401-402 No. 58; W. F. Stinespring, "The Inscription of the Triumphal Arch at Jerash," in BASOR 56 (Dec. 1934), pp. 15-16; and in BASOR 57 (Feb. 1935), pp. 3-5 and Fig. 2. Photograph: Jerry Vardaman.

78. The Forum at Jerash

One enters this portion of the forum soon after passing into the area of the city. In extent the forum is over 80 meters wide and 90 meters long. The colonnades curve around it in unequal ellipses, the western one curving in more sharply toward the colonnaded street at the north, the eastern one (shown here) curving more gradually. The heavy paving blocks were laid on lines which follow the curve of the porticoes. The columns stand upon square bases, have Ionic capitals, and carry a continuous architrave. Certain architectural relationships of the forum led the Yale Expedition (Kraeling p. 157) to place its date in the first century.

Photograph: JF.

79. The North-South Colonnaded Street at Jerash

The main colonnaded street runs from the forum in the south some 800 meters to the north gate of the city in the north wall. Some of the columns of the porticoes are of the Corinthian order, as in the section shown here; some are of the Ionic order. The Ionic columns are probably of the middle of the first century, the Corinthian of the end of the second century. The heavy paving blocks show the ruts of ancient chariot wheels.

Photograph: JF.

80. Entranceway to the Cathedral at Jerash

If one proceeds northward on the main north-south colonnaded street (No. 79) to the South Tetrapylon and 120 meters beyond, there is on the left the imposing entranceway of which a portion is shown in this photograph. The portico stands on a terrace only a few feet above the street and gives access to a long flight of steps which leads up to a second terrace. On the second terrace are the imposing ruins of a church which the excavators regard as the cathedral of Gerasa (No. 81). Under the long flight of stairs were found the remains of an older staircase, and under the church the remains of a pagan temple, probably of the first century. While the temple was small (about 25 meters long by 10 meters wide) it was not far from the temple of Artemis

and may have been second in importance only to the latter.

J. W. Crowfoot, "Recent Work Round the Fountain Court at Jerash," in PEFQS 1931, pp. 143-154. Photograph: JF.

81. Plan of the Cathedral at Jerash

The church stood on the second terrace at the top of the long flight of stairs described in the preceding section (No. 80). It was a basilica over forty meters in length, with internal apse, and oriented to the east as usual, so that persons ascending the long staircase from the street approached the apse end of the building. Inside, two rows of twelve columns each, with Corinthian capitals, divided the side aisles from the central nave. The columns were probably all taken from some other

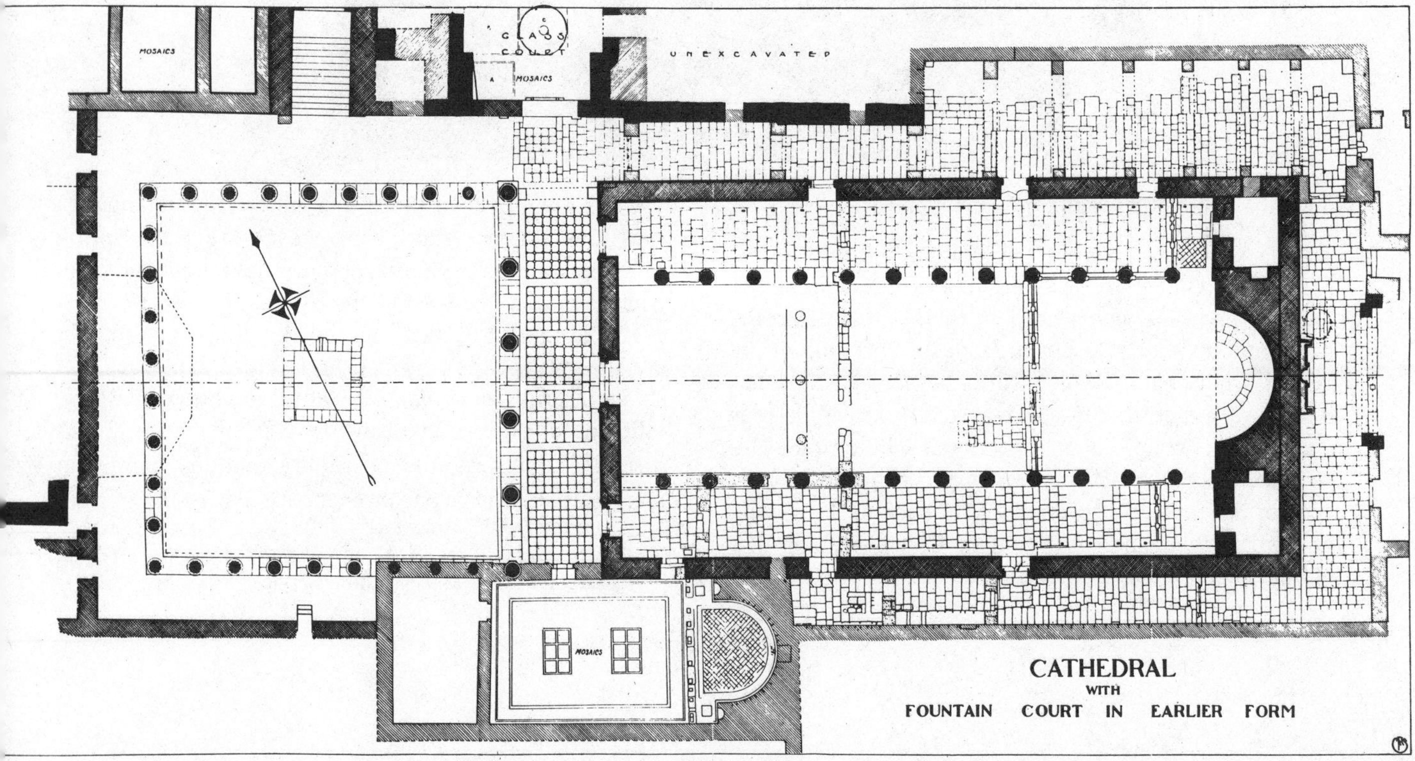

CATHEDRAL

WITH

FOUNTAIN COURT IN EARLIER FORM

building, perhaps the temple which was previously on the spot. Various considerations analyzed by the excavators lead to the conclusion that the Cathedral was built about 365 (Kraeling, *Gerasa*, p. 219). At the west end the atrium of the church was provided by the so-called Fountain Court (No. 82), twenty meters square and surrounded by colonnades. The portico on the east side of the court had six columns with Corinthian capi-

tals, dating probably at the end of the second century (Kraeling, *ibid.*, p. 210); the porticoes on the other three sides were lower and of the Ionic order. In the center of the court was a square tank to which water was brought, in a conduit coming in past the Temple of Artemis, from springs two miles away.

Photograph: Kraeling, *Gerasa*, Plan XXXI, courtesy American Schools of Oriental Research.

82. The Fountain Court at Jerash

This view looks across the Fountain Court to the northwest. Under the paving blocks the excavators found a lead pipe which ran into the fountain from the northwest corner of the court; from the east side of the tank a drain channel ran toward the northeast corner. At the west side of the court a small excavation was made under the apse of St. Theodore's Church (see No. 83) and a small patch of Roman mosaic found at the level of the court; this probably goes back to the second or third century and the Fountain Court must be that old or older. In 375 Epiphanius (*Panarion haer.* LI 30,

1-2 GCS XXXI, p. 301) refers to a martyrium and miraculous fountain in Gerasa, where every year the spring ran with wine on the anniversary of the miracle at Cana which was also the feast of the Epiphany. It seems most probable that the Cathedral and this adjacent fountain are the very places to which he referred. The fact that some inscriptions found at Jerash mention Dusares, "the god of Arabia," with whom a similar miracle was associated, suggests the possibility that the church in Gerasa took over a pagan event for its own.

J. W. Crowfoot in PEFQS 1929, pp. 31-35; 1931, pp. 153-154. Photograph: The Matson Photo Service, Alhambra, Calif.

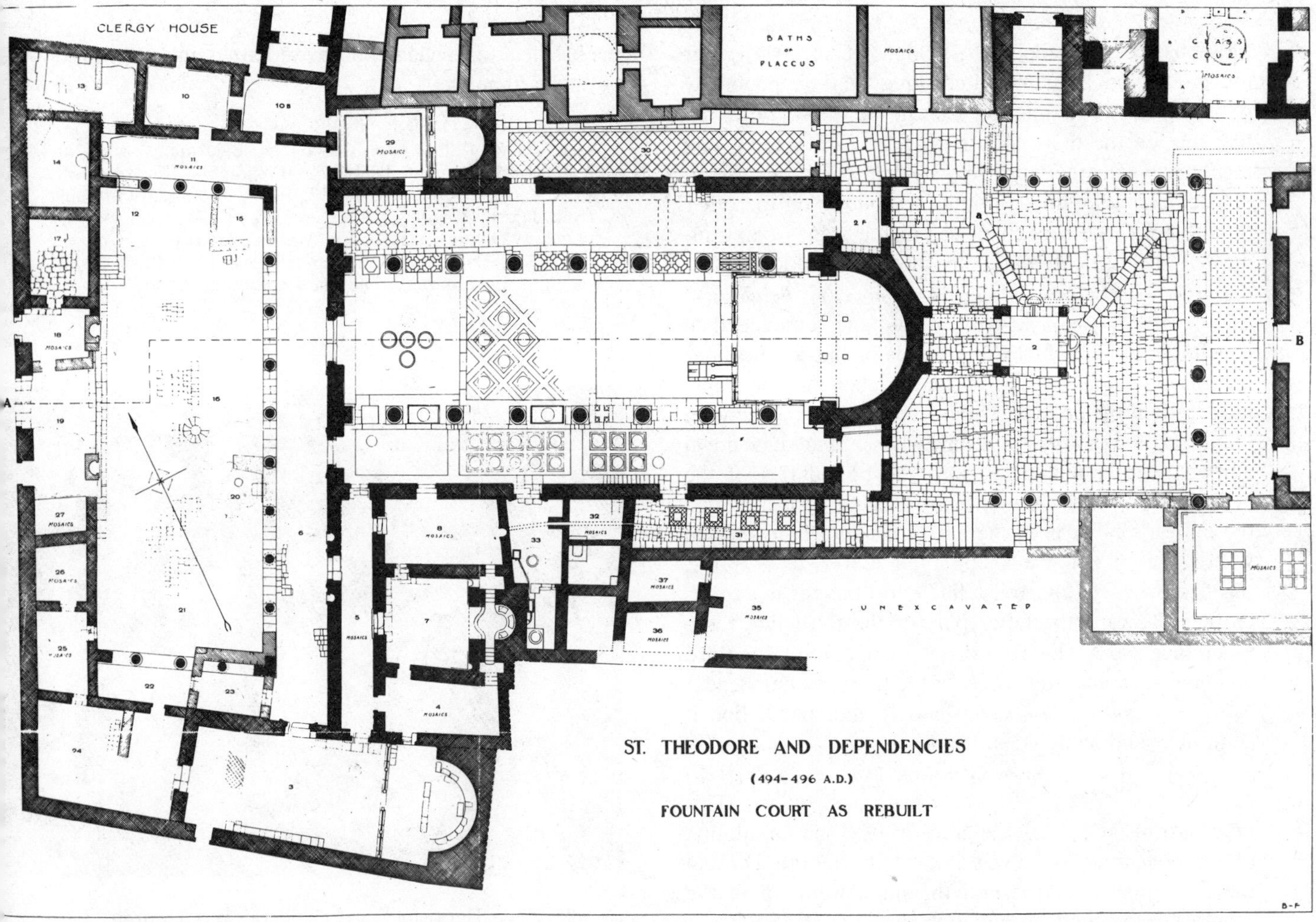

CLERGY HOUSE

BATHS OF PLACCUS

ST. THEODORE AND DEPENDENCIES

(494-496 A.D.)

FOUNTAIN COURT AS REBUILT

83. Plan of St. Theodore's Church at Jerash

On a third terrace (cf. Nos. 80, 81) west of the Cathedral and the Fountain Court was yet another great basilica. As shown in the plan, there was a large atrium on the west end, over 21 meters from west to east and 50 meters from north to south. An entrance hall gave access to an open court surrounded by colonnades on the north, east, and south. The columns had Ionic capitals, and the floor was paved with mosaics. From the east portico of the atrium three doorways led into the basilica, a building about forty meters in length, almost as long as the Cathedral. The nave and two side aisles were marked off by two rows of seven columns each, with Corinthian capitals, and the floor was laid out in patterns of colored stone and marble. The apse at the east end, polygonal on the exterior and vaulted with stone, was allowed to project into the area of the Fountain Court, where the earlier portico on the western side had been removed. The apse of the church was connected with the square tank of the fountain itself by two arches which supported a vault, and at the same time it appears that some kind of a vault was put up over the fountain tank itself. In addition to the three doors at the west end, the basilica had three doors on the north side, four on the south, and two at the east end of the aisles from which one could go on down into the Fountain Court.

J. W. Crowfoot, "The Church of S. Theodore at Jerash," in PEFQS 1929, pp. 17-36. Photograph: Kraeling, *Gerasa*, Plan XXXIII, courtesy American Schools of Oriental Research.

84. Broken Blocks with an Inscription from St. Theodore's Church

The lintel over the center doorway at the west end of the basilica (No. 83) carried an inscription, in a position to be read from the interior of the church. The lintel was made of four large blocks of stone. These were fallen and broken, and the left end of the first block, with the beginning of each line of the inscription, was missing. The missing piece was found later, and it was then possible to establish the correct reading of the initial portions of the lines (the earlier conjectural restorations were all shown to be incorrect). Altogether the inscription is in four long lines, and in poetically phrased Greek. As may be seen in the photograph, the first line on the first block is marked with a cross and then starts with the word Ἄχραντο[ς], which means undefiled. This long line continues as follows on the other three blocks, the broken places in the stones being indicated by vertical marks in the transcription: δόμος εἰμὶ ἀεθλοφόρου Θεοδώρου, μάρτυρος ἀθανάτ | ου, θεοειδέος οὗ κλέος ἔ | πτη ἐν χθονὶ κ(αὶ) πόντῳ, and the sentence then concludes with the first three words of the second line: καὶ τέρμασιν | ὠκεανοῖο. The entire sentence may be translated: "I am the undefiled house of victorious Theodore, immortal and godlike martyr, whose fame has flown abroad over land and sea and the boundaries of the ocean." In a second sentence it is stated that, although the martyr's body is in the earth, his soul is in heaven where it is a defense keeping off evil (ἀλεξίκακ[ο] | ν, the first word in the third line) for the town and its citizens. Toward the latter part of the third line there is another cross which marks the beginning of a third and final sentence. In the rest of the third line this reads: Χάριτι το | ῦ Θ(εο)ῦ ἐθεμελιώθη, and in the fourth line it continues and concludes: τὸ ἅγιο[ν μα] | ρτύριον μη(νὶ) Δίῳ τῆς [. . .] γ´ ἰνδ(ικτιῶνος) κ(αὶ) ἀνῆλθεν τὰ ὑπέ[ρ] | θυρα ἐν μη(νὶ) Δίῳ τῆς ε´ | [ἰν]δ(ικτιῶνος) τοῦ θνφ´ ἔτ(ους). This may be translated: "By the grace of God the foundation of the holy martyrium was laid in the month Dios in the . . . third indiction and the lintel went up in the month Dios in the fifth indiction in the year 559."

This inscription is of great value as giving both the name of the one to whom the church was dedicated and also the date of its building. The martyr Theodore is described as "victorious" (ἀθλοφόρος, which literally means bearing away the prize of a combat). He may very probably be identified with the young Syrian named Theodorus who was tortured at Antioch by Julian (361-363) and called by Theodoret (*Ch. Hist.* III 11, 3 ed. Parmentier 2d ed. GCS XLIV, p. 187) a "combatant of the truth" (ἀγωνιστὴς τῆς ἀληθείας, a phrase synonymous with ἀθλητὴς τῆς ἀληθείας). The lintel was raised in the month Dios (Δῖος), i.e., Oct/Nov (FHBC p. 68 Table 24), in the year 559 (θνφ´), and the foundation was laid two years before that in the very same month. If the era was that of Pompey, as seems generally to be the case in the inscriptions of Gerasa, with the epoch of that era from which we count falling in 63/62 B.C., then the year 559 given in the inscription as the date of the raising of the lintel would be equivalent to A.D. 496, and the date two years before that when the foundation of the church was laid would be equivalent to A.D. 494.

When excavated, the columns of the basilica and their capitals were all still lying where they had fallen;

the basilica was evidently destroyed at an unknown time by an earthquake.

R. P. Germer-Durand, "Exploration épigraphique de Gerasa," in RB (1895), pp. 374-400; F. Bleckmann, "Bericht über griechische und lateinische Epigraphik," in ZDPV 38 (1915), pp. 234-235; A. H. M. Jones, "Some Inscriptions from Jerash," in PEFQS 1928, p. 192; J. W. Crowfoot in PEFQS 1929, pp. 21-23; C. B. Welles in Kraeling, *Gerasa*, pp. 477-478 No. 300. Photograph: PEFQS 1928, Pl. II No. 2 facing p. 190, courtesy Palestine Exploration Fund.

85. The Baptistery at St. Theodore's Church

As the Plan (No. 83) of the Church of St. Theodore at Jerash shows, there were a number of additional buildings on both sides of the basilica and its atrium, probably chapels, residences for priests and visitors, etc. The most interesting of these buildings is the baptistery on the south side, which may have been a chapel of some sort before it was made into a baptistery. At the east end of the main room (7 on the Plan) was a semicircular apse, where the baptismal font was built. As shown in the photograph, steps led down into the baptismal tank from either end. In the semicircular apse a sort of bench, with three small bins, was installed. One hypothesis is that these may have had something to do with the ceremonies of anointing which accompanied the immersion. The steps descend into the font from very small chambers on either end, and beyond these on either side are large rooms (4 and 8) paved with mosaic floors, perhaps dressing rooms for use before and after the ceremonies. Behind the baptistery was a large cistern and some earthenware piping which evidently provided for filling the font with water.

Crowfoot in PEFQS 1929, p. 29; Kraeling, *Gerasa*, pp. 224-225. Photograph: Kraeling, *ibid.*, Pl. XLI, courtesy American Schools of Oriental Research.

86. A Christian Cross at Jerash

From the north side of the Fountain Court a flight of steps gave access to yet a fourth terrace (cf. Nos. 80, 81, 83), the highest in the entire series. In this area, which was between the Church of St. Theodore and the old court of the Artemis Temple, were public baths and what the excavators judge to have been ecclesiastical residences (not on plan, No. 76). The fragment of sculpture in this photograph was found in this area. It shows a Greek cross inside a wreath together with the Alpha and the Omega. Considering all the buildings on the four terraces, the first of which were pagan, the later Christian, they form a complex which extends 163 meters from east to west, and the buildings on the highest level at the west are 18 meters above the level of the main colonnaded street where the chief entranceway stood (No. 80). In the arrangement of the masses and the accommodation of the buildings to a site, this great complex may be compared with similar groupings of ecclesiastical structures at the famous pilgrimage centers of St. Simeon Stylites in North Syria, of St. Menas in Egypt, and of the Holy Sepulcher at Jerusalem. Of the Gerasa complex in comparison with that in Jerusalem, J. W. Crowfoot writes the following words (in Kraeling, *Gerasa*, p. 202, quoted courtesy American Schools of Oriental Research), which we quote particularly because we shall later be interested in a consideration of the buildings in Jerusalem:

. . . in disposition the completed group corresponds closely to the original disposition of the buildings round the Holy Sepulchre in Jerusalem. The portico on the street and the great stairway at Gerasa correspond with the propylaea and the eastern atrium at Jerusalem; the Cathedral with the Martyrium of Constantine; the Fountain Court with the second atrium and the Calvary, and St. Theodore's with the Anastasis. Even the baptisteries in the two places occupy approximately the same position. The configuration of the two sites was, of course, very different. At Jerusalem the

ground was more level on the whole and the rock was reduced more radically where it rose at the west end. At Gerasa it sloped gradually and a succession of levels was created with a moderate degree of scarping and terracing. But with this qualification the resemblance between the two dispositions is so close as to leave no doubt that in its final form the Gerasa plan was deliberately modeled on the Jerusalem pattern, and that it now shows better than any other extant group of structures what the buildings in Jerusalem once looked like.

Photograph: JF.

87. Floor Mosaic in the Church of SS. Cosmas and Damianus

Of all the other Christian churches (cf. No. 76) in Gerasa it is not necessary to speak here, although each is of great interest in and of itself (cf. FLAP p. 539). As a single example of their riches we show the floor mosaic in the Church of SS. Cosmas and Damianus, as this is the best preserved of the mosaic pavements in the Gerasa churches. One hundred and fifty meters westnorthwest of the atrium of St. Theodore's Church is a group of three churches (Kraeling, *Gerasa*, pp. 241-249) all of which open off a common atrium. On the left is a basilica dedicated to St. George in the year 592 = A.D. 529/530 (Inscription No. 309); in the center a round church with a baptistery in a room beside the apse, dedicated to St. John the Baptist and decorated with mosaics in 594 = A.D. 531 (Inscription No. 306); and at the right the basilica dedicated to SS. Cosmas and Damianus. In the floor immediately below the chancel step in the last church is a single line of

69

inscription which gives the dedication to the two famous martyrs and a date in 595 = A.D. 533. There follows below this (at the extreme top of the photograph) an inscription in ten lines. It speaks of the martyrs as victorious in combat (ἀθλοφόρων) (cf. No. 84), mentions a certain Bishop Paul as a shepherd and wise guide, and says that the name of the founder of the church will be learned to preserve the name of the Prodromos (πρόδρομος), the "forerunner," i.e., John (the Baptist). This is explained by a portrait of the donor, with the name Theodore, immediately at the left of the inscription. The Greek name Theodore, meaning "gift of God," was evidently considered the equivalent of John ('Ιωάνης, Hellenized form of 'Ιωανάν) because this was itself the equivalent not only of the Hebrew Johanan (יוחנן), "Yahweh has been gracious," but also of Jehonathan or Jonathan (יהונתן or יונתן), "Yahweh has given." In the corresponding position at the right of

the inscription, and visible in the photograph, is a portrait of Theodore's wife, Georgia, standing in the attitude of an *orant* (i.e., with arms outstretched in prayer, cf. below p. 231).

The rest of the mosaic covered much of the floor of the nave. As preserved it has a meander border and a field of squares and diamonds. In the first row of diamonds other donors are commemorated, namely, John son of Astricius who is shown in a portrait, the tribune Dagistheus who is named in an inscription (Inscription No. 311), and Calloeonistus who is shown in a portrait. The other diamonds exhibit a great variety of decorative patterns, while the squares contain representations of birds and animals, also in great variety and so arranged that both horizontally and vertically a row of birds alternates with a row of animals and so on.

F. M. Biebel in Kraeling, *Gerasa*, pp. 331-332. Photograph: JF.

CAESAREA

88. Aerial Photograph of Caesarea

Even though Caesarea is not mentioned in the Gospels it was the Roman capital of Palestine and hence of much importance in the time of Jesus. In the days of the early church it is mentioned frequently (Acts 8:40, etc.). A succinct history of the place is given by Pliny (*Nat. Hist.* V 14, 69) when he lists it as "the Tower of Strato, otherwise Caesarea, founded by King Herod,

but now the colony called Prima Flavia established by the Emperor Vespasian." Josephus (*Ant.* XIII 11, 2 §§312-313) mentions the place under the name of Straton's Tower. (Στράτωνος πύργος) in connection with the reign of Aristobulus (104/103 B.C.), and it may have been founded as a small harbor by the seafaring Phoenicians, for one or more of the last kings of Sidon had the name of Straton (SHJP II, i, p. 84). The 1962 excavation of The Hebrew University—Southern Baptist Seminary (see No. 96 below) was the first to discover this older Phoenician site. Professor Vardaman reports that Strato's Tower was located generally on the northern side of what later was Caesarea's town limit, and stretched at least from the synagogue area to the region around Herod's wall on the north. The Italian excavations uncovered some Hellenistic pottery in the lowest levels of clearing this wall in later seasons of work (see G. Dell'Amore, A. Calderini, L. Crema, A. Frova, *Scavi di Caesarea Maritima*. Rome: "L'Erma" di Bretschneider, 1966, p. 267, illustration 336).

Alexander Jannaeus (103-76 B.C.) took Strato's Tower from a local tyrant named Zoilus (*Ant.* XIII 12, 2 §§324-326), Pompey (63) set the town free and annexed it to the province of Syria (*Ant.* XIV 4, 4 §76), and Augustus gave it to Herod the Great (*Ant.* XV 7, 3 §217). Herod saw the possibilities in the place and set about building a splendid city there, as Josephus (*Ant.* XV 9, 6 §§331-332) tells us: "And when he observed that there was a place near the sea, formerly called Straton's Tower, which was very well suited to be the site of a city, he set about making a magnificent plan and put up buildings all over the city, not of ordinary material but of white stone. He also adorned it with a very costly palace, with civic halls and—what was greatest of all and required the most labor—with a well-protected harbor, of the size of the Piraeus, with landing-places and secondary anchorages inside."

The construction work of Herod at Caesarea occupied either twelve years (*Ant.* XV 9, 6 §341) or ten years (*Ant.* XVI 5, 1 §136) and was completed, according to the latter passage, in the twenty-eighth year of Herod's reign which fell in the one hundred and ninety-second Olympiad. If the twenty-eighth year of Herod's reign is counted from his taking of Jerusalem in the summer or fall of 37 B.C. it was equivalent to 10/9 B.C. and this corresponds with the third year of the one hundred and ninety-second Olympiad (FHBC pp. 114, 232), so the date of 10/9 B.C. is the probable date of the completion of the building of the city (against Avi-Yonah in IEJ 1 [1950-51], p. 169, who counts from 40 B.C. and reaches 13/12 B.C., which was the year before the first year of the one hundred and ninety-second Olympiad). The completion of the city was celebrated with a very great festival of dedication (*Ant.* XVI 5, 1 §137) and the institution of quinquennial games (πεντα-ετηρικοὺς ἀγῶνας). In honor of Augustus the city was named Caesarea (Καισάρεια) (*Ant.* XV 9, 6 §339) or Caesarea Sebaste (Καισάρεια Σεβαστή) (*Ant.* XVI 5, 1 §136), and the harbor was also called Sebastos (Σε-βαστὸς λιμήν). In addition to a palace and harbor, Josephus mentions (*Ant.* XV 9, 6 §§339, 341; *War* I 21, 7 §§414-415) a temple dedicated to Rome and Augustus which stood on an eminence facing the harbor mouth, a theater in the city, and an amphitheater on the south side of the harbor with a view to the sea (here Josephus probably reversed his terms for it is the theater [No. 97] rather than the amphitheater which has been found to the south of the harbor and with a fine view to the sea).

With Judea under Roman rule the procurators established their headquarters at Caesarea. This is indicated by various references in Josephus, e.g., where Pilate brought the Roman army from Caesarea to Jerusalem (*Ant.* XVIII 3, 1 §55), and where the Jews proceeded to Caesarea to present a request to Pilate (*War* II 9, 2 §171). In Caesarea the former palace of Herod the Great was no doubt taken by the procurators for their residence, and must be what is referred to in Ac 23:35 as "Herod's praetorium." The last word (πραιτώριον) is the Latin *praetorium*. It meant originally the tent of a *praetor* or general in an army camp, then the official residence of a governor in a province.

Herod Agrippa I, who ruled most of Palestine A.D. 41-44, visited Caesarea upon occasion (*Ant.* XIX 7, 4 §332) and, in fact, died there. According to Josephus (*Ant.* XIX 8, 2 §§343-352), he was present in Caesarea to celebrate spectacles in honor of Caesar (probably the quinquennial games instituted by Herod the Great), appeared in the theater in a garment woven completely of silver, was hailed by flatterers as a god, but was smitten by violent pain and died in a few days, probably in the spring or summer of 44 (FHBC pp. 302-303). This is clearly the same event cited in Ac 12:21-23.

At the outbreak of the Jewish War (66) 20,000 Jews were massacred in Caesarea (*War* II 18, 1 §457). In 67 Vespasian led his troops there from Ptolemais and in this connection Josephus remarks (*War* III 9, 1 §409) that the city was one of the largest of Judea, with a population consisting chiefly of Greeks. In the passage just cited Josephus says that Vespasian led his troops "to Caesarea-on-the-sea" (εἰς τὴν παράλιον . . . Καισά-ρειαν); on another occasion he tells (*War* VII 2, 1 §23) how Titus took his troops off "from Caesarea-on-the-sea" (ἀπὸ τῆς ἐπὶ θαλάττῃ Καισαρείας); and this manner of designation is reflected in the later much used Latin name, Caesarea Maritima (cf. Leo Kadman, *The Coins of Caesarea Maritima* [1957], p. 9). As not only the foregoing but also many other passages in Josephus show, Vespasian and Titus made Caesarea their headquarters throughout the Jewish War. After the fall of Jerusalem Titus planned to celebrate the triumph in Rome, but in October A.D. 70 held a victory celebration in Caesarea (on the birthday of his brother, Domitian, then eighteen years of age) with games in which 2,500 Jewish captives perished (*War* VII 3, 1 §§37-38). In the reorganization of the country Caesarea was made the sole capital of the province of Judea, and Tacitus (*His-*

tories II 78) says that it was the first city of Judea (*hoc Iudaeae caput est*). Vespasian also made Caesarea a Roman colony. As the first city to be honored in this way by the Flavian emperors it was called Colonia Prima Flavia Augusta Caesarea, and we have already noted above the brief reference by Pliny to this title.

With Origen, who lived there 230/231-253/254, and with Eusebius, who was probably born there within ten years of the death of Origen and was bishop from 313 until his death in 339/340, Caesarea became a famous Christian center. The Arabs took it in 639/640, the Crusaders in 1101, and the Sultan Baibars in 1265. Destroyed by the last named, Caesarea sank beneath the ever-shifting sand dunes of the coast, only to be settled again in the nineteenth century and excavated in the twentieth.

In the aerial photograph the arrow points to north, and the following points are identified by number: 1.

The ancient moles constructed by Herod. 2. The Crusader town. 3. The modern Jewish settlement of Sedot-Yam, "Fields of the Sea." 4. The ancient theater. 5. The ancient hippodrome. 6. The ancient amphitheater (?). 7. The semicircular Roman wall. 8. The low-level aqueduct. 9. The high-level aqueduct. To the left of Sedot-Yam (3 in the photograph) is a large suburban area with streets and blocks of buildings (*insulae*) clearly visible beneath the sand. Much Roman pottery found on the dunes in this area shows that this suburb already existed in Roman times.

C. R. Conder, *The Survey of Western Palestine, Memoirs* II. London: The Palestine Exploration Fund, 1882, pp. 13-29; A. Reifenberg, "Caesarea, A Study in the Decline of a Town," in IEJ 1 (1950-51), pp. 20-32; *Archaeology and Caesarea*, a booklet published by The Southern Baptist Theological Seminary, Louisville, Kentucky. Photograph: IEJ 1 (1950-51), Fig. 1, pls. viii-ix between pp. 16-17, courtesy Israel Exploration Society.

89. Crusader Moat and Walls at Caesarea

Coming into Caesarea one crosses the line of the Roman fortifications (7 in photograph No. 88) and has the ancient hippodrome on the left (5). Although the hippodrome is not yet excavated, the outline of its enclosure, approximately 320 meters long and 80 me-

ters wide, and the line of its *spina*, or central barrier (a low wall dividing the circus longitudinally), are plainly discernible. Along the line of the *spina* are still to be seen, fallen, a mighty obelisk and three conical columns, all of red granite. Also at the side of the running track is an enormous quadrangular block of red granite. In his description of a hippodrome (ἱππόδρομος), Pausanias

(*Description of Greece* VI—Elis II 20, 15-19 LCL III, pp. 124-129) says that a racecourse has one side longer than the other and, on the longer side which is a bank, there stands at the passage through the bank the object of fear to the horses which is called the Taraxippus (Ταράξιππος), the "horse frightener." Describing one example of this object as found at Nemea of the Argives, Pausanias writes: ". . . above the turning point of the chariots rose a rock, red in color, and the flash from it terrified the horses, just as though it had been fire." Presumably the purpose of the object was to increase, through fright, the speed of the running horses. The great red granite block, still lying in the Caesarea hippodrome, may be an example (and thus the only one known, certainly in Palestine) of such a Taraxippus. Beyond the hippodrome is a Byzantine ruin of the fifth-sixth centuries, uncovered accidentally in 1954. In it at the foot of a broad staircase are two large Roman statues, one of white marble from the second century and one of red porphyry from the third century. In a

mosaic floor is a Greek inscription which states that the mayor Flavius Stategius built the structure out of public funds. Obviously he brought in the ancient statues for adornment. Directly ahead from these ruins is the area of the Crusader town (2 on photograph No. 88). The excavation and restoration of this area was conducted by Avraham Negev of the Hebrew University in 1960 and later. The photograph (No. 89) shows the moated walls built by Louis IX of France in 1251, only a few years before the fall of the city to Baibars. The moat is 30 feet across, and the sloping embankment rises 30 to 45 feet from the bottom. These walls, running around the three landward sides of the town, enclose an area of 35 acres, but this is only about one-sixth of the area of the Roman city.

Joachim Jeremias, "Der Taraxippos im Hippodrom von Caesarea Palaestinae," in ZDPV 54 (1931), pp. 279-289; Baruch Lifshitz, "Inscriptions grecques de Césarée en Palestine (Caesarea Palaestinae)," in RB 68 (1961), pp. 121-123 No. 15; A. Negev in IEJ 10 (1960), pp. 127, 264-265. Photograph: courtesy Government Press Office, State of Israel.

90. Looking toward the Sea at Caesarea

Inside the Crusader walls at Caesarea one sees extensive ruins on a low hill facing toward the water. Here in contrast with the brown limestone of the Crusader masonry are many building blocks of white stone. Since Herod built Caesarea of white stone (Josephus, *Ant.* XV 9, 6 §331) and placed the temple of Caesar, with its statues of Augustus and of Rome, on an eminence facing the mouth of the harbor (*Ant.* XV i, 6 §339; *War* I 21, 7 §414; cf. above No. 88), it is probable that his temple of Rome and Augustus stood in this place. Identification of these ruins with that temple was suggested

in *The Survey of Western Palestine* (*Memoirs* II [1882], p. 18). Trial soundings by A. Negev in 1961 found preserved walls as much as seven meters high, with stones dressed in the typical Herodian manner, and with associated pottery not later than the end of the first century B.C. The excavator suggests that the remains may belong to a large podium on which the temple was erected, to make it the more conspicuous across the water. The photograph shows the view from within the Crusader town looking toward the waterfront; at the left is the minaret of a small Turkish mosque.

A. Negev in IEJ 11 (1961), pp. 81-82. Photograph: JF.

91. The Harbor at Caesarea

In his account of the works of Herod the Great at Caesarea, Josephus lays the greatest emphasis upon the construction of the harbor (*Ant.* xv 9, 6 §§332-338; *War* I 21, 5-7 §§409-413). The seacoast, he explains, was without a harbor all the way from Dora (10 miles to the north) to Joppa (35 miles to the south). Even these were only small towns with poor harbors, and the southwest wind beat upon them and drove sand upon the shore. Under the menace of that wind, ships bound coastwise for Egypt had to ride unsteadily at anchor in the open sea. To make a breakwater Herod lowered enormous blocks of stone, 50 feet in length, 10 or 18 feet in breadth, and 9 feet in depth, into 20 fathoms of water; upon this submarine foundation he built above the surface a mole 200 feet broad, of which the outer half broke the surge and the remainder supported a stone wall encircling the harbor. On the wall were towers, the largest named Drusion after Drusus, stepson of Caesar Augustus. The harbor entrance faced to the north, for the north wind was here the most favorable. On either side of the entrance were three colossal statues. These stood on columns and the columns in turn stood on a tower on the left side (as seen from a ship coming into the harbor), and on the other side on two upright blocks of stone which were clamped together and were even higher than the tower.

The ruins of Herod's splendid harbor are now fifteen or twenty feet beneath the surface of the sea at Caesarea, and were at least partially explored by the Link Marine Expedition to Israel in 1960. Using ship and underwater equipment designed and provided by Edwin A. Link, divers charted the circular breakwater of the ancient harbor and explored the entrance on the northern side. They found gigantic cut stones weighing as much as twenty to thirty tons. Under some of these blocks and beneath the shelter of a large wooden beam was found one intact Roman amphora of the second century. With an earthquake recorded in the Caesarea area about 130 (IEJ 1 [1950-51], p. 225), it is possible that Herod's harbor was at least partially destroyed and these things tumbled into the sea at that time. Among the finds particular interest attaches to a small medal or commemorative coin. On one side is a male figure with beard and dolphin tail. On the other side is the entrance of a port with round stone towers on either side surmounted by statues; two sailing vessels are coming in; and two letters, KA, are presumably the abbreviation for Caesarea (Καισάρεια). Almost certainly this is a contemporary representation, probably of the first or second century, of the ancient harbor.

Immanuel Ben-Dor, "A Marine Expedition to the Holy Land, Summer 1960," in AJA 65 (1961), p. 186; Charles T. Fritsch, "The Link Expedition to Israel, 1960," in BA 24 (1961), pp. 50-56; Vardaman cites *Israel Numismatic Bulletin* II for a detailed study of the medal by Ostreicher. Photograph: The Matson Photo Service, Alhambra, Calif.

92. Harbor Citadel at Caesarea

This point on the sea front at Caesarea is at the south end of the waterfront side of the Crusader town and corresponds to the more northerly of the two points indicated by 1 on the aerial photograph in No. 88 above. The ruins of a Crusader port tower stand here, with a later building above, while Roman columns of granite, which were used to buttress the tower, are in the water.

Photograph: The Matson Photo Service, Alhambra, Calif.

93. Byzantine Capital and Cross at Caesarea

When approaching Caesarea (see No. 89) there is a mound to the right of the road opposite the hippodrome. On the summit a fifth-sixth century mosaic floor, showing birds and animals, was found in 1957, evidently from a Byzantine church. Inside the Crusader town on the hill where it is believed Herod's temple of Rome and Augustus stood (cf. Nos. 88, 90) are the ruins of two Crusader buildings. One is an unfinished cathedral, built over a Roman vaulted warehouse. The cathedral, which was named in honor of Paul, has nave and two side aisles, and three apses at the eastern end. The other building was built around a large court. North of the Crusaders' cathedral the ruins of a very large Byzantine church were found in the course of the Hebrew University excavations in 1960. Impressive foundations and meager remains of marble and inlaid stone pavement were uncovered, also eight capitals, with a cross on the face of each. One is shown in the photograph.

The Survey of Western Palestine, Memoirs II (1882), pp. 27-28; A. Negev in IEJ 11 (1961), p. 82. Photograph: JF.

a large network of buildings, including a portico and many rooms and courtyards, with an apse at the western side facing the sea. Different layers of mosaic pavements were uncovered, indicating use of the buildings from the fourth to the seventh century. On the pavements are a number of Greek inscriptions, one of which quotes from Rom 13:3. Above the building was found this marble statue of the Good Shepherd carrying a lamb, a work of perhaps the fifth century. While the nature of these buildings is not yet elucidated it is clear that they have Christian connections and one cannot but wonder if the great school and library of Origen and Pamphilus and Eusebius were in this area.

A. Negev in IEJ 11 (1961), p. 82. For other Christian inscriptions from Caesarea see Baruch Lifshitz, "Inscriptions grecques de Césarée en Palestine (Caesarea Palaestinae)," in RB 68 (1961), pp. 115ff. Photograph: JF.

94. Statue of the Good Shepherd at Caesarea

Outside the Crusader wall and moat on the south side a small excavation in 1960 came upon the remains of

95. The High-Level Roman Aqueduct at Caesarea

As may be seen in the aerial photograph (No. 88 above, see 8 and 9), two aqueducts approach Caesarea from the north. The high-level aqueduct, which is the one nearest the sea at this point, originates at a spring at Ras en-Neba at the foot of the Carmel range about four and one-half miles northeast of Caesarea. It begins as a rock-cut channel, is carried over the River Zerqa on a low bridge, crosses a marsh in two branches each containing three earthenware pipes, tunnels through a sandstone ridge, turns south and runs along the shore to the city. The entire coastal stretch of the aqueduct was for a long time almost completely buried under the sand dunes but has now been cleared for a distance. The semicircular arches and conduit are very well preserved, but at this point, about 500 meters north of Caesarea, the aqueduct breaks off. The action of the waves has eroded the coast to the extent of an estimated 50,000 tons of soil and stone, and destroyed the aqueduct at the same time.

In 1927-1928 Zev Vilnay studied two Roman inscriptions which had been attached to the aqueduct in the area of the marsh mentioned above. On the first stone the inscription is cut into a plain rectangular area surrounded by a raised border. It reads:

IMP(ERATOR) CAESAR	Imperator Caesar
TRAIANVS	Traianus
HADRIANVS	Hadrianus
AVG(VSTVS) FECIT	Augustus has made (this aqueduct)
PER VEXILLATIONE(M)	by a detachment
LEG(IONIS) X FR(E)TEN(SIS)	of Legion X Fretensis

On the second stone a wreath is enclosed within an elaborate frame with triangles on either end, with Roman images on pedestals on either side, and the inscription is carved inside the wreath. It reads:

IMP(ERATOR) CAE(SAR)
Imperator Caesar
TR(AIANVS) HAD(RIANVS) AVG(VSTVS)
Traianus Hadrianus Augustus
VEXIL(LATIO) LEG(IONIS)
a detachment of Legion
VI FERR(ATAE)
VI Ferrata

The "Imperator Caesar Traianus Hadrianus Augustus" is the emperor Hadrian (117-138) (W. Liebenam, *Fasti Consulares*, KLT 41-43, p. 107), who visited Palestine in 130, suppressed the revolt of Bar-Kokhba a few years later, and during his reign supported various public building works in the land. In Caesarea itself a temple was built in his honor. It was called the Hadrianeion (τὸ Ἁδριανεῖον), and work on it is mentioned in a later Greek inscription (RB 4 [1895], pp. 75-76). Legion X Fretensis took part in the conquest of Jerusalem by Titus, had its headquarters there afterward (Josephus, *War* VII 1, 3 §17), and had detachments stationed at various places in Palestine. In the southwest corner of

the Old City of Jerusalem many fragments of tiles have been found, stamped with the abbreviation or initials of this legion, LEG X FR or LXF (PEFQS 1871, pp. 103-104; PEQ 1966, p. 88). Legion VI Ferrata was brought into Palestine from Syria by Hadrian in the course of his war with Bar-Kokhba (132-135) (PWRE 12:1, col. 1292). At Sebaste a limestone slab has been found, with a carved framework much like that on the Caesarea aqueduct stone but without the wreath, and with the inscription of the same legion:

VEXILLATIO
LEG VI FERR

(G. A. Reisner, C. S. Fisher, and D. G. Lyon, *Harvard Excavations at Samaria* [1924], I, p. 251 No. 1; II, Pl. 59, f). At Megiddo there is a village which has been known as el-Lejjun, obviously a corruption of "Legion," nearby are the remains of a Roman camp, and in an adjacent field was found a tile with the stamp LEGVIF, again the abbreviation for Legio VI Ferrata (G. Schumacher, *Tell el-Mutesellim* [1908], I, p. 175). It was, therefore, detachments of these two well-known Roman legions which, presumably after 132-135, built the great aqueduct to Caesarea. Since Josephus makes no mention of construction of any aqueduct by Herod the Great it may be presumed that the city of his time still depended upon cisterns and wells for its water supply.

As for the low-level aqueduct (8 in photograph No. 88), it was probably intended to provide additional water for agricultural purposes. There is a Roman dam across the Zerqa River about a mile and one-half inland from the sea and another dam, perhaps third century in date, across the adjacent swamp, to keep the impounded waters from spreading northward. Raised in this manner by several meters, the water was led southward in an open rock-cut channel. The distance to Caesarea is some three miles, and after somewhat more than one mile the low-level aqueduct crosses under the high-level aqueduct and comes to the city on the east side of the latter. The Muslims came in through the low-level aqueduct to take Caesarea from the Byzantines in 639/640. Later, perhaps still in early Arab times, much of the channel was vaulted to protect it against the encroachment of sand dunes.

The Survey of Western Palestine, Memoirs II (1882), pp. 18-23; Zev Vilnay, "A New Inscription from the Neighbourhood of Caesarea," in PEFQS 1928, pp. 45-47; "Another Roman Inscription from the Neighbourhood of Caesarea," *ibid.*, pp. 108-109; A. Reifenberg in IEJ 1 (1950-51), pp. 26-29; A. Negev, "The High Level Aqueduct at Caesarea," in IEJ 14 (1964), pp. 237-249; D. Barag, "An Inscription from the High Level Aqueduct of Caesarea—Reconsidered," in IEJ 14 (1964), pp. 250-252. Photograph: courtesy Don Fleming.

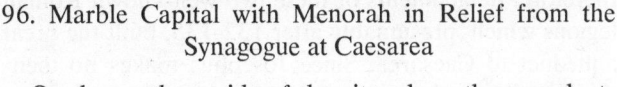

96. Marble Capital with Menorah in Relief from the
Synagogue at Caesarea

On the northern side of the city where the aqueducts
approach, outside the Crusader wall but within the Roman wall and not far from the seashore, synagogue remains were first reported in 1932, partly cleared in
1945, and further excavated in 1956 and 1962 by the
Department of Archaeology of Hebrew University under the direction of M. Avi-Yonah with the assistance
of A. Negev and, in 1962, of E. Jerry Vardaman. In
this area there was a Herodian building, part of which
was used later as a plastered pool and then filled with
a mixture of earth and debris. Over this filling was laid
the pavement of the synagogue. It was a building 18
meters long, from east to west, and 9 meters wide. In
it was found the hoard of 3,700 small bronze coins
already mentioned (No. 36) in connection with the
Nazareth Inscription also found in the general area,
but a few hundred feet to the east. Most of the coins
date from the time of Constantius II (337-361), there
are a few of Julianus Caesar. Since Julian became Caesar in 355 and Augustus in 360 (Liebenam, *Fasti Consulares*, KLT 41-43, p. 121) the date of 355/356 is suggested for the establishment of the cache. The synagogue
may have been built, then, at the end of the third or
beginning of the fourth century. Around the date given
of 355/356 it may have been destroyed, rebuilt in the
early fifth century, and again rebuilt in the sixth-seventh
century. Architectural fragments of the fourth or fifth
century synagogue include marble columns, one of
which has a dedicatory inscription reading, "The offering of Theodoros the son of Olympos for the salvation

of his daughter Matrona" (Rabinowitz Bulletin III
[1960], pp. 44-45); and marble capitals of debased Corinthian type, two of which carry the representation of
the menorah, one incised and one in relief (the latter
is shown in the photograph). In the later building is a
mosaic pavement with an inscription inlaid in Greek, the
type of letters suggesting the sixth century. Some of the
letters of the first line are damaged, but the whole inscription is probably to be transcribed, restored, and
translated as follows (Rabinowitz Bulletin III, p. 47):

BH . . ΛΛΟCΑΡΧΙCΥ
ΚΑΙ ΦΡΟΝΤΙCΤΗC
ΥΟC ΙΟΥΤΟΥ ΕΠΟΙ
ΗCΕ ΤΗΝ ΨΗΦΟ
ΘΕCΙΑΝ ΤΟΥ ΤΡΙ
ΚΛΙΝΟΥ ΤΩ ΙΔΙΩ

Βή[ρυ]λλος ἀρχισυ(ναγωγὸς)
καὶ φροντιστὴς
υ(ἱ)ὸς Ἰού(σ)του ἐποί-
ησε τὴν ψηφο-
θεσίαν τοῦ τρι-
κλίνου τῷ ἰδίῳ

Beryllos the head of the synagogue
and administrator,
the son of Iu(s)tus, made
the mosaic
work of the tri-
clinium from his own means.

If the last word in the first line is restored correctly this
is the title which is familiar in the NT (Mk 5:38, etc.)
where it is translated "ruler of the synagogue" (RSV)
(cf. No. 71).

As Vardaman also reports, the ruins of a large house
were found near the synagogue. Hellenistic pottery was
found (Rhodian jar handles, "fish plates," etc., most of
which dated about the middle of the second century
B.C.) in one corner of the house. Vast quantities of isolated fragments of "west slope" ware indicated a settlement there certainly before the end of the third century
B.C. The area was abandoned in the early first century
B.C., perhaps after the conquest of Strato's Tower by
Alexander Jannaeus. Thus the original town was doubtless in this area (cf. No. 88). Also a massive wall,
which may be a part of the harbor mole of Strato's
Tower, can be seen in the sea.

M. Avi-Yonah in IEJ 6 (1956), pp. 260-261; and "The Synagogue of Caesarea, Preliminary Report," in Louis B. Rabinowitz Fund for the Exploration of Ancient Synagogues, *Bulletin* III (Jerusalem, December 1960), pp. 44-48; M. Avi-
Yonah and A. Negev in IEJ 13 (1963), pp. 146-148; M.
Avi-Yonah in Vardaman and Garrett, eds., *The Teacher's
Yoke* (1964), p. 51 note 13. For other coins of Caesarea
see Leo Kadman, *The Coins of Caesarea Maritima*. Corpus
Nummorum Palaestinensium, II. Tel Aviv-Jerusalem: Schock-
en Publishing House, 1957. Photograph: courtesy Department of Archaeology, The Hebrew University of Jerusalem.

97. The Roman Theater at Caesarea

As we have seen (No. 88), Josephus mentions both a theater and an amphitheater at Caesarea, the amphitheater being said to be on the south side of the harbor with a view to the sea (*Ant.* xv 9, 6 §341; cf. *War* I 21, 8 §415). On the aerial photograph of Caesarea in No. 88 the theater is at 4, near the southwestern corner of the Roman city and just beyond the more southerly of the two projections into the water. It has a fine view out to sea. It corresponds, therefore, with what Josephus says about the location of the amphitheater; the ruins here, however, are of a theater rather than of an amphitheater, and it may be supposed that Josephus has simply reversed his terms. In 1882 *The Survey of Western Palestine* (*Memoirs* II, pp. 15-16) described the ruins at this spot as those of a Roman theater. Beginning in 1959 and continuing for a number of years the excavation and restoration of the theater were undertaken by an Italian archeological mission of the Istituto Lombardo of Milan, under the direction of Antonio Frova. As shown in the photograph, the theater was cut out of the cliff in a semicircle of many tiers, and had a magnificent view. There were frescoes on the floor of the orchestra, and oil lamps were found on the stage. The connection of the theater with NT history because of the appearance in it of Herod Agrippa I just before his death (Ac 12:21-23), has already been noted above (No. 88).

For a bibliography on Caesarea covering 1961-1963 and including the publications of the Italian expedition, see *'Atiqot*, Supplement to Vol. IV (Jerusalem, 1965), pp. 8-9; and now see specially Antonio Frova, *Scavi di Caesarea Maritima* (Rome, 1965). Photograph: courtesy Government Press Office, State of Israel.

98. The Pilate Inscription from Caesarea

During the work in the Roman theater (No. 97) in 1961 the Italian expedition found this inscription. The stone had been used to form a landing for a flight of steps at one of the entrances to the seats of the theater and was badly chipped away, probably at that time, on the left side. Originally the stone must have been embedded in the wall of the building for which it provided the dedicatory inscription. Four lines remain legible at least in part, though hard to see in the photograph. With restorations and translation they are as follows:

[CAESARIEN] S (IBUS)	To the people of Caesarea
TIBERIÉVM	Tiberieum
PON] TIVSPILATVS	Pontius Pilate
PRAEF] ECTVSIVDA[EA]E	Prefect of Judea

In the fifth line a diagonal accent mark may be recognizable and, like the one in Line 2, may have stood over an "e." Perhaps the word *dedit*, "has given," or *dedicavit*, "has dedicated," once stood there. The entire statement is therefore: "Pontius Pilate the prefect of Judea has dedicated to the people of Caesarea a temple in honor of Tiberius." The name of the dedicated building is written in Latin as Tiberieum. This is a temple to Tiberius with the name formed in the standard way, an example of which we have seen already (No. 95) in the Greek inscription at Caesarea which mentions the Hadrianeion ('Αδριανεῖον), or temple in honor of Hadrian. As is also standard practice, the Greek ει is reproduced in the Latin by é. The name Pontius Pilate is quite unmistakable and is of much importance as the first epigraphical documentation concerning Pontius Pilate, who governed Judea A.D. 26-36 according to the commonly accepted dates. In mentioning him Tacitus (*Annals* xv 44) and Josephus (*War* II 9, 2 §169) call him "Procurator" (Latin *procurator*, Greek ἐπίτροπος). This inscription uses the title "prefect" (Latin *praefectus*, to which the Greek ἔπαρχος corresponds). The latter term (ἔπαρχος) is used by Josephus for Valerius Gratus (15-26), the predecessor of Pontius Pilate (*Ant.* XVIII 2, 2 §33), and for Cuspius Fadus (44-46), who came after Herod Agrippa I. While the two terms are therefore broadly interchangeable, "prefect" seems to have been more of a military title and "procurator" to have carried more of the connotation of financial administration; also "prefect" seems to have been preferred in the time of Augustus, "procurator" to have become the prevailing title from Claudius (41-54) onward (SHJP I, ii, pp. 45-46). Perhaps there is a little evidence in this general development for dating this inscription earlier rather than later in the administration of Pontius Pilate. The Gospels call him only by the general term "governor" (ἡγεμών) (Mt 27:2, etc.).

Antonio Frova, "L'iscrizione di Ponzio Pilato a Cesarea," in *Rendiconti*. Milano: Istituto Lombardo, Accademia di Scienze e Lettere. 95 (1961), pp. 419-434; Jerry Vardaman, "A New Inscription which Mentions Pilate as 'Prefect,'" in JBL 81 (1962), pp. 70-71. For other, more recent bibliographical references, Vardaman cites Carla Brusa Gerra, "Le Iscrizióni," in *Scavi di Caesarea Maritima* (see above, No. 97), specially pp. 217-220. Gerra gives other alternate readings for Line 1 as: TIB(erio) CAES(are) AVG. V CONs(ule), and DIS AVGVSTI S. Photograph: courtesy Istituto Lombardo, Milan, and Department of Antiquities, Ministry of Education and Culture, State of Israel.

JERICHO

99. Air View of Jericho

The Synoptic Gospels indicate that on his journey to Jerusalem for the last time Jesus passed through Jericho (Mt 20:29; Mk 10:46; Lk 18:35), where he healed one (Mk 10:46-52; Lk 18:35-43) or two (Mt 20:29-34) blind men and was guest of Zacchaeus (Lk 19:1-10). Jericho was already a prominent city in OT times (Num 22:1, etc.), a city identified with a large mound on the west side of the Jordan Valley known as Tell es-Sultan. This has been excavated by Ernst Sellin and Carl Watzinger (1907ff.), John Garstang (1930ff.), and Kathleen M. Kenyon (1952ff.). According to the findings of the last-named archeologist the city had its beginnings as early as the seventh millennium B.C. (FLAP p. 141). In the air view the *tell* of this most ancient city is in the immediate foreground, modern Jericho is in the distance, and the Dead Sea and the mountains of the Moab are in the far distance. Also at the immediate base of the *tell*, about one-third of the way in from the right edge of the picture, and adjacent to a small building, is the double pool of the Spring of Elisha.

Photograph: The Matson Photo Service, Alhambra, Calif.

81

100. Looking from the Site of OT Jericho to Jebel Quarantal

It is not much more than a mile from Tell es-Sultan to the range of mountains which rises steeply on the western side of the Jordan Valley. These must be "the hills" to which the spies of Joshua fled from the house of Rahab (Jos 2:22). The picture looks westward from the *tell* toward these mountains, and toward the point called Jebel Quarantal which rises to a height of 1,200 feet above Jericho. The summit was probably the location of "the little stronghold called Dok" mentioned in I Macc 16:15 (cf. Josephus, *Ant.* XIII 7, 4-8, 1 §§228ff.) where Simon, the last of the Maccabees, was treacherously slain by his son-in-law Ptolemy (135 B.C.). Some of the ruins on the top probably belong to that stronghold, and a spring at the foot of the escarpment is still called Ain Duq. On the side of the mountain are numerous caves which attracted Christian hermits, including Chariton (340) and Palladius (386) and their pupils. In the *Life of Chariton* (MPG XCV, col. 912) there is mention of "Luke's Mountain," and in this name the Maccabean Duk is probably still to be recognized (Λουκâ

as an error for Δουκâ). The identification is also confirmed by an unpublished seventh-century Arabic manuscript in which Clermont-Ganneau (II, p. 21) found the name Jebel ed-Duq for the mountain from under which the spring of Elisha comes. The center of the Christian hermits was probably where the Greek monastery is now found, halfway up to the summit, and on the summit there are also ruins of a Byzantine church (Dalman, PJ 10 [1914], p. 16). It is possible that the church was connected with the tradition of the temptation of Jesus. At any rate with the Crusaders, who also built on the top, the temptation was located on the mountain and it was called Quarantana in memory of the forty days (*quadraginta diebus*, Mk 1:13, etc.). Today the place of the first temptation is shown at the Greek monastery halfway up the mountain, and of the third temptation (Mt 4:8) on the very summit. From the summit there is indeed a wide-ranging view from the mountains of Moab on the east to the Mount of Olives and the Judean highlands on the west.

Abel, *Géographie* II, p. 307; Dalman, *Sacred Sites*, p. 96; Kopp note 61 on pp. 147-150. Photograph: JF.

101. The Spring of Elisha

At OT Jericho there was a spring, the water of which was made wholesome when Elisha threw salt into it (II K 2:19-22). On the east side of Tell es-Sultan (cf. No. 99) and across the present-day road from it, is a copious spring known as Ain es-Sultan and also as the Spring or the Fountain of Elisha. Although in appearance, as shown here, it is only an unprepossessing double pool, it provides abundant water for a large and pleasant oasis. Already in the OT, Jericho was "the city of palm trees" (Dt 34:3; cf. Jg 1:16).

Photograph: The Matson Photo Service, Alhambra, Calif.

102. A *Tell* of NT Jericho

In Hellenistic and Roman times the city of Jericho was no longer on the original *tell* but was located on the plain and on both sides of Wadi el-Qelt, a mile or so to the south. It was through this Wadi (cf. No. 105), that the road to Jerusalem went. In Maccabean times Bacchides, commander of the Syrian army, built a fortress in Jericho (I Macc 9:50), undoubtedly to command this road. In 63 B.C. Pompey destroyed two forts there which were called Threx and Taurus (Strabo, *Geography* XVI 2, 40). When Gabinius, general of Pompey and proconsul of Syria (57-55 B.C.), divided Palestine into five districts he assigned the fourth to Jericho as its capital (*War* I 8, 6 §170; SHJP I i, pp. 372f.). Mark Antony gave the district of Jericho to Cleopatra (Josephus, *War* I 18, 5 §361), but Augustus gave it back to Herod the Great (*Ant.* XV 7, 3 §217; *War* I 20, 3 §396). At Jericho Herod did much building, making the city his winter capital, a position for which it was well suited because of its balmy winter climate. Above the town he built a citadel which he called Cypros after the name of his mother (*Ant.* XVI 5, 2 §143; *War* I 21, 4 and 9 §§ 407, 417). Other buildings were an amphitheater (*Ant.* XVII 6, 3 §161; 8, 2 §193; *War* I 33, 8 §666), a hippodrome (*Ant.* XVII 6, 5 §175; *War* I 33, 6 §659), and a royal palace. This palace was where Herod died (*War* I 33, 8 §666). After his death it was burned down by one of his former slaves named Simon (*Ant.* XVII 10, 6 §274); then it was splendidly rebuilt by Archelaus (*Ant.* XVII 13, 1 §340). Strabo (*Geography* XVI 2, 41) says that the plain and mountains at Hiericus, as he calls Jericho, gave the city a setting as if in a theater. The plain was watered with streams and full of dwellings, he says, and there were many fruitful trees, mostly palm trees. Pliny (*Nat. Hist.* V 15, 70) also remarks upon the numerous palm groves and springs of water. Josephus (*War* IV 8, 3 §§459-475) calls Jericho a "most favored spot," and describes the region in terms as glowing as those he used for the Plain of Gennesaret (cf. No. 55). The copious spring purified by Elisha irrigates a plain seventy stadia in length and twenty in breadth. Date palms are numerous in their varieties; the richer species, when pressed, emit honey not much inferior to that of the bees which are also abundant. The balsam, cypress, and myrobalanus also flourish. Indeed the warm air and wholesome water are beneficial to plants and human beings alike, and "the climate," Josephus concludes, "is so mild that the inhabitants wear linen when snow is falling throughout the rest of Judea."

The mounds which represent at least a portion of NT Jericho are found on either side of Wadi el-Qelt where this valley opens out onto the plain. They are called Tulul Abu el-'Alayiq. Excavation has been conducted here by the American School of Oriental Research in Jerusalem under James L. Kelso in 1950 and James B. Pritchard in the following year. In the mound on the south side of the Wadi, shown in the photograph (No. 102), were found the remains of an Arabic fortress of the ninth or eighth century; then a Roman building of concrete masonry; below that, Herodian masonry; and below that, a Hellenistic tower. This was probably the civic center of the Herodian city, with work done on it, in the masonry levels just referred to, first by Herod the Great and then by Archelaus. As for the Hellenistic tower, it may have been the fortress built originally by Bacchides, and perhaps also the Threx or Taurus taken by Pompey.

James L. Kelso, "The First Campaign of Excavation in New Testament Jericho," in BASOR 120 (Dec. 1950), pp. 11-22; and "New Testament Jericho," in BA 14 (1951), pp. 34-43; James M. Pritchard, "The 1951 Campaign at Herodian Jericho," in BASOR 123 (Oct. 1951), pp. 8-17; James L. Kelso, *Excavations at New Testament Jericho and Khirbet en-Nitla,* AASOR 29-30 (1949-51), 1955; James M. Pritchard, *The Excavations at Herodian Jericho, 1951,* AASOR 32-33 (1952-54), 1958. Photograph: JF.

103. A Façade at NT Jericho

At the foot of the *tell* just described (No. 102) there was a grand façade along the edge of the Wadi el-Qelt. As in the case of the Roman structure found in the *tell*, the masonry of the façade was lined with small, square-faced, pyramidal stones which give the impression of a net (*reticulum*), producing a type of work known as *opus reticulatum*. An example of this work appears in the photograph. The façade was also provided with semicircular benches and numerous niches. The appearance is somewhat that of an outdoor theater, but the finding of flower pots on the benches makes it perhaps more probable that this was a terraced garden instead. It has been suggested that the *opus reticulatum* work at Jericho reflects some of Herod's trips to Rome where he could have seen Augustus building in this fashion along the Tiber. At the same time the rather numerous coins of Archelaus found at Jericho tend to confirm the fact that he had an important part in the

building work here. Some soundings were also made in the *tell* on the north side of the Wadi, where a brick fortress and two stone buildings were found.

James L. Kelso in IDB II, pp. 838f. Photograph: JF.

104. A Sycamore Tree

With respect to the account concerning Jesus and Zacchaeus in Jericho (Lk 19:1-10), J. Wellhausen declared in 1904 (*Das Evangelium Lucae*, p. 103) that the statement in the opening verse that Jesus had entered Jericho and was passing through was contradicted by what followed because Jesus was then still outside the city, not within it, otherwise Zacchaeus would have climbed upon a roof and not up into a tree. Following this lead others have continued to question the localization of the incident in Jericho (e.g., Rudolf Bultmann, *Die Geschichte der synoptischen Tradition.* 1931, p. 69; S. MacL. Gilmour in IB VIII, p. 320). But the supposition implicit in Wellhausen's criticism is that Jericho was a city of tight-packed houses where roofs were indeed available for the ascent of Zacchaeus, but not trees. This conception would fit with the tightly-packed buildings which were found when OT Jericho was excavated in Tell es-Sultan. But it does not accord with the findings at Tulul Abu el-'Alayiq, where the excava-

tors draw their closest comparison with Roman cities such as Rome, Tivoli, and Pompeii. Like such cities NT Jericho undoubtedly had its parks and villas, avenues and public squares, where fine trees grew. The sycamore tree, in particular, grows in Palestine mainly on the coast and in the Jordan Valley. That it was well known in ancient Jericho is shown by the finding of precisely this timber as bonding in one of the Hellenistic forts. As for modern times, the sycamore tree may still be seen in a central square of present-day Jericho and in the surrounding area. In this photograph (No. 104) of the sycamore tree, the low spreading character of its branches may particularly be noted.

In his account of the *Jewish War* (IV 8, 1f. §§449ff.) Josephus dates the arrival of Vespasian at Jericho on the third day of the month Daisios (=May/June) in what is the year 68 of the Christian era. The city itself, he says, the Romans found deserted, for most of the population in the district had fled in fear. From evidence at Qumran seven miles to the south it appears that Vespasian destroyed that place at this time (FLAP p. 275), but with respect to Jericho Josephus (*War* IV 9, 1 §486) says only that he established a camp and placed a garrison there. In the *Onomasticon* (p. 104), however, Eusebius says that Jericho was destroyed at the time of the siege of Jerusalem and a third city built

in its place. He does not say when the last city was built, but states that it was to be seen in his time and that traces of its two predecessor cities were still preserved. In the time of Antoninus, son of Severus (193-211), Origen found an OT manuscript in a jar at Jericho (Eusebius, *Ch. Hist.* VI 16, 3) but it is not plain whether this implies a deserted or an inhabited city at the time. The Bordeaux Pilgrim (333) came down from Jerusalem to Jericho, i.e., to the third city described by Eusebius, and saw the sycamore tree, into which Zacchaeus climbed, before entering the city (Geyer p. 24; LPPTS I, p. 25; CCSL CLXXV, p. 18). Paula (386) also came down from Jerusalem to Jericho and was shown both the sycamore tree of Zacchaeus and the place by the wayside where the two blind men sat, who were healed by Jesus, before she entered the city (Jerome, *Letter* 108, 12 NPNFSS VI, p. 201). On the Madaba Mosaic Map (560), as noted above (No. 10), one sees the sanctuary of Saint Elisha which must mark the famous spring by the OT city, and a stream flowing from it southward to a large city labeled Jericho and set amidst palm trees. This also must be the Byzantine city, and it appears to be in the same place as the present town of Jericho, a mile or so east of the NT city. A little later the Anonymous of Piacenza (570) found the walls of the city destroyed by an earthquake, while not far away, proceeding in the direction of Jerusalem,

was the tree of Zacchaeus, enclosed in a chapel with an open roof (Geyer pp. 168-169; LPPTS II, pp. 12-13; CCSL CLXXV, pp. 136-137). At the time of the visit of Arculf (670) all three successive cities were in ruins (Geyer p. 263; LPPTS III, p. 35; CCSL CLXXV, p. 212). Under the Arabs, however, *erikha*, as they called Jericho, was again an important place, and a geographer of the ninth century says that it was the capital of the Ghor, i.e., the Lower Jordan Valley. The Crusaders also considered the district to be very valuable, but after their time Jericho became only the small village which it still was at the beginning of the twentieth century. Now, once again, it is a much larger town.

F. J. Bliss in HDB II, pp. 580-582; Kraeling, *Bible Atlas*, p. 395. Photograph: The Matson Photo Service, Alhambra, Calif.

105. Ruins of the Aqueduct of Herod the Great in Wadi el-Qelt

Going for the last time from Jericho (Mt 20:29 and parallels) to Jerusalem (Mt 21:1 and parallels), Jesus presumably took the usual main route to which he had doubtless also referred when he spoke in one of his parables about a man who went down from Jerusalem to Jericho (Lk 10:30). In connection with the siege of Jerusalem by Titus, Josephus (*War* v 2, 3 §§69-70) tells how the Roman Tenth Legion came up by way of Jericho and encamped at the Mount of Olives, and thus they presumably used the same road. In the course of time, perhaps for the most part after the Jewish War and the Second Revolt, the Romans paved the main roads in Palestine and marked them with milestones. The milestones, placed at intervals along the road, were normally inscribed with the name of the emperor and of the official who carried out the construction, and with the distance to or from some point of reference. From Jericho to Jerusalem some stretches of the Roman road can be traced and a few of its milestones have been found, thus giving an indication of the route of the older highway which the Roman road no doubt followed. The direct distance is scarcely twenty miles and in that distance the road climbed from Jericho at 770 feet below sea level to Jerusalem at 2,500 feet above sea level. Leaving Jericho, the route ran along the south wall of Wadi el-Qelt for more than three miles, then probably turned off to the southwest. The modern highway swings around farther south for the sake of a less precipitous ascent, but the road up along the wall of the Wadi is still usable. In the Wadi there were bridges and aqueducts of which ruins still remain, as may be seen in the photograph. By this system the water of three large springs in the Wadi was brought down to the pools

and palaces of Herodian Jericho and allowed to flow on out to enhance the irrigation of the plain.

The Survey of Western Palestine, Memoirs III (1883), p. 188 and map and drawing of aqueducts near Jericho between pp. 222-223; Peter Thomsen, "Die römischen Meilensteine der Provinzen Syria, Arabia und Palaestina," in ZDPV 40 (1917), pp. 1-103, specially pp. 78-79, and Map; G. Kuhl,

"Römische Strassen und Strassenstationen in der Umgebung von Jerusalem," in PJ 24 (1928), pp. 113-140; M. Avi-Yonah, *Map of Roman Palestine*. London: Oxford University Press, 1940, pp. 26-27 and Map; Stewart Perowne, *The Life and Times of Herod the Great*, p. 120; Anton Jirku, *Die Welt der Bibel*. Stuttgart: Gustav Kilpper Verlag, 2d ed. 1957, p. 251 Pl. 105. Photograph: Perowne, *ibid.*, Pl. facing p. 96 (London: Hodder and Stoughton Ltd., 1956).

106. Traditional Site of the Inn of the Good Samaritan

On the road just described (No. 105) running up from Jericho toward Jerusalem, there is a Roman milestone known locally as *dabbus el-'abd*, at a point somewhat more than three miles from Jericho. At a point more than a mile and one-half farther along, or about five miles from Jericho and twelve or thirteen miles short of Jerusalem, there is a pass which is 885 feet above sea level and 1,655 feet above Jericho. The Roman road probably went through here, as does the modern highway, because it is the shortest route between Jericho and Jerusalem. The name of the pass in Arabic is *tal'at ed-damm*, meaning Ascent of Blood. This corresponds with the Hebrew מעלה אדמים, Ascent of Adummim, in Jos 15:7; 18:17. Actually the Hebrew *adummim* means red objects, in this case probably red rocks, and the original reference was probably to the red marl of the pass. Where he lists the Adummim (Ἀδομμίμ) of Jos 15:7 in the *Onomasticon* (p. 24), Eu-

sebius says that the place is called Μαληδομνεῖ, which is a transliteration in Greek of the entire Hebrew phrase, and he declares that there is a castle (φρούριον) there. In his version of the *Onomasticon* (p. 25; cf. *Letter* 108, 12 NPNFSS VI, p. 201) Jerome renders the name as Maledomni, says that it is equivalent to Greek ἀνάβασις πυρρῶν and Latin *ascensus ruforum sive rubrantium*, i.e., Ascent of the Red, and explains that the name was given because of the blood which was repeatedly shed at this place by robbers. Also, Jerome suggests, it was of this blood-stained and sanguinary place that the Lord spoke in the parable of the man who was going down from Jerusalem to Jericho.

The Crusaders, who also had a castle on the hill above the pass, accepted this suggestion and Burchard of Mount Sion (LPPTS XII, p. 63), for example, writes: "Four leagues to the west of Jericho, on the road to Jerusalem, to the left of Quarentena, is the Castle of Adummim, the place where the man who went down from Jerusalem to Jericho fell among thieves. This has befallen many on the same spot in modern times, and the place has received its name from the frequent blood shed there. Of a truth it is horrible to behold, and exceeding dangerous, unless one travels with an escort." Because of its strategic location the pass is the site of a police station today and, in line with the opinion of

Jerome and the Crusaders, the spot is commonly considered as the location of the Inn of the Good Samaritan. The photograph looks west toward the highlands where Jerusalem is located.

Photograph: JF.

THE MOUNT OF OLIVES

107. Map of the Mount of Olives

As noted above (No. 105), when Titus brought the Tenth Legion up to Jerusalem they came by way of Jericho and encamped at the Mount of Olives (Josephus, *War* v 2, 3 §§69-70). Likewise when Jesus came to Jerusalem for the last days of his life we find

mention of arrival at the Mount of Olives (τὸ ὄρος τῶν ἐλαιῶν Mt 21:1; Mk 11:1, where ἐλαιῶν is the genitive plural of ἐλαία, "olive tree" or "olive," hence literally "the mountain of the olives," i.e., the Mount of Olives; for the slightly different form of the name in the parallel in Lk 19:29 see below under No. 116) and of descent (Lk 19:37) from there to the city. The Mount of Olives

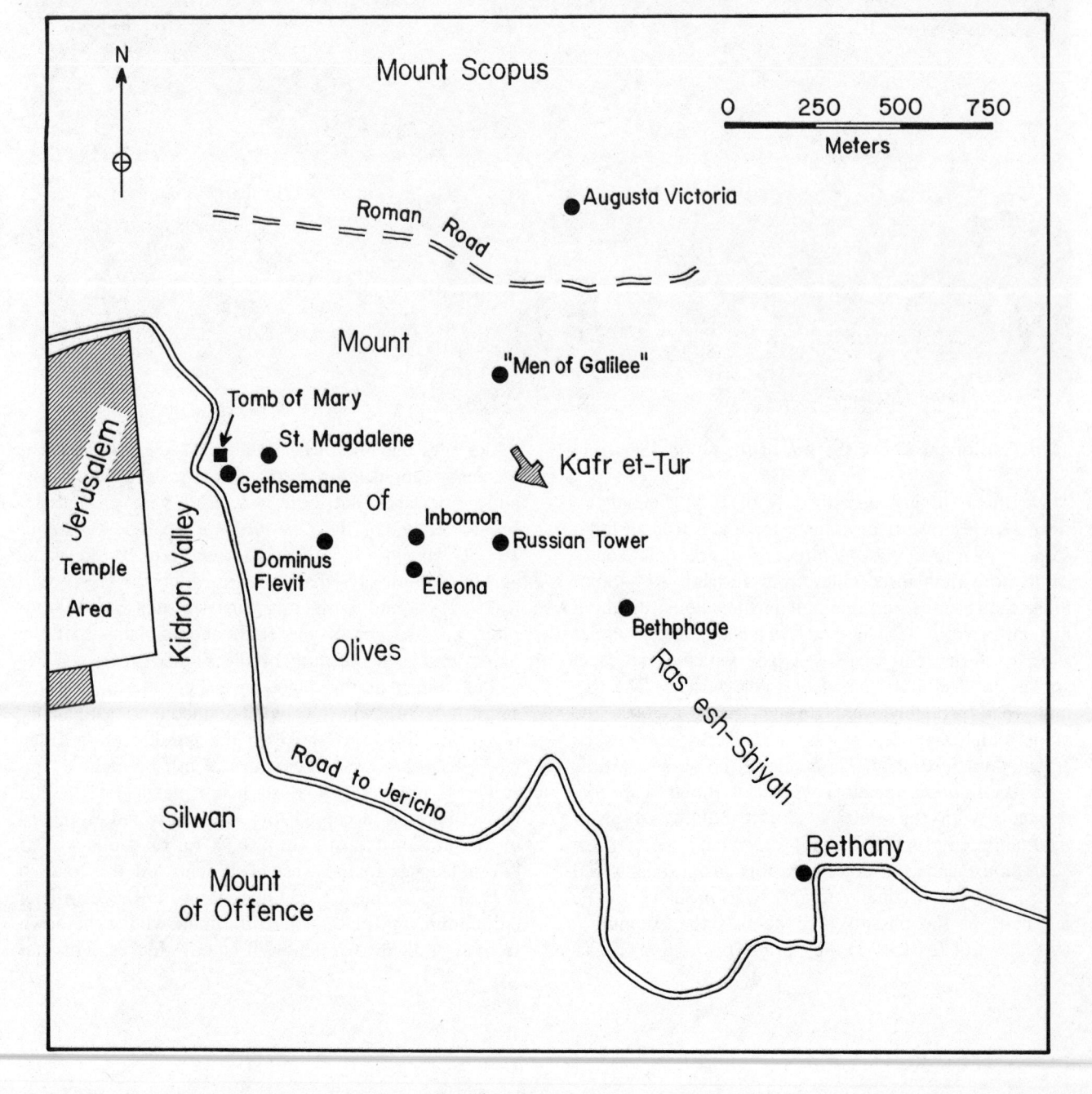

is part of a ridge of hills which overlooks Jerusalem across the Kidron Valley from the east, and is therefore encountered first by those approaching the city from the east. The ridge is some two and one-half miles long and has three main summits. The highest summit is at the north, is called Ras el-Mesharif, and is 2,690 feet above sea level. It is almost certainly the Mount Scopus where Titus placed his first camp while he considered the lay of the land, and determined how best to proceed with his attack on Jerusalem (PJ 12 [1916], p. 55). In telling of this Josephus (*War* v 2, 3 §67) explains that the Mount was appropriately so named (σκοπός = "one who looks out") because a person approaching from the north here obtained his first view of Jerusalem "and the grand pile of the temple gleaming afar." The second summit, 2,660 feet above sea level, is directly across the Kidron Valley east from the city and the Temple area, and is the Mount of Olives proper. The location corresponds, for example, with Zec 14:4 which states that the Mount of Olives lies "before" or "opposite" or "facing" Jerusalem on the east. The Arabic name is et-Tur, which means "the Mount," and the village on the top is called Kefar et-Tur. On the summit also are a Russian church and buildings with a high tower which is a prominent landmark from all directions. Running off to the southeast there is also a subsidiary ridge of the Mount with the separate designation of Ras esh-Shiyah. The present-day village of el-'Azariyeh (Bethany) is on the farther downslope of this ridge. The third main summit of the entire chain is farther south and somewhat lower than Mount Scopus and the Mount of Olives. It rises above the village of Silwan and is opposite the oldest part of Jerusalem south of the Temple area. This is probably the Mount of Corruption or Mount of Offence, where Solomon worshiped false gods (II K 23:13). The map shows the places which have just been mentioned and locates sites which will be discussed in what follows.

Map: JF, cf. Dalman, *Sacred Sites*, p. 260.

108. The Mount of Olives and Bethany from the South

The modern road from Jericho to Jerusalem comes past el-'Azariyeh (Bethany), between the Mount of Offence and the Mount of Olives, up the Kidron Valley, and around to the north side of the city (cf. Map No. 107). While this may have been an ancient route too, it is now known that the Roman road from Jericho to Jerusalem (cf. Nos. 105f.) came up over the ridge between Mount Scopus and the Mount of Olives proper. In this area the Empress Augusta Victoria Endowment (a German hospice, hospital, and church established in 1910) stands on the southern slope of Mount Scopus, the Greek chapel called Viri Galilaei (the name "Men of Galilee" reflects a traditional localization of the event in Ac 1:11 at this spot) is on the northern slope of the Mount of Olives, and the route of the Roman road passes between the two. Some of the paving of this road survived till modern times and one milestone stood not far from the entrance to the Augusta Victoria property, while a branch road running northward (to connect Jerusalem with Neapolis) was traceable through the garden of the same endowment (PJ 12 [1916], p. 75; ZDPV 40 [1917], p. 78 No. 277). From here the

Jericho-Jerusalem road must have proceeded down the western slope of the ridge and brought travelers to the Kidron Valley or allowed them to proceed to a gate on the north side of the city. The photograph is a view of the Mount of Olives from the south. The Russian Tower, mentioned above (No. 107), is visible on the summit. The village of el-'Azariyeh, ancient Bethany, is at the right on the lower slope of the ridge called Ras esh-Shiyah.

Photograph: JF.

109. The Franciscan Chapel at Bethphage

When Jesus and his disciples drew near to Jerusalem for what is commonly called the "triumphal entry" it is stated in Mt 21:1 that they came to (εἰς) Bethphage to (εἰς Codex Vaticanus) or toward (πρός Codex Sinaiticus) the Mount of Olives. In their parallel accounts Mk 11:1 and Lk 19:29 add to the name of Bethphage also the mention of Bethany and speak of coming to (εἰς) both places along with coming toward (πρός) the Mount of Olives. The instructions which follow immediately in all three Gospels to two disciples to go into "the village opposite" can obviously refer to only one village and therefore agree best with the mention in Mt of only Bethphage. Perhaps Bethany was added in Mk and Lk because it was the better known place and would help to locate Bethphage, and because it was familiar to come up the Jericho-Jerusalem road and turn to one side to Bethphage and Bethany. If, then, the tradition as preserved in Mt is basic to that found in Mk and Lk, the fact that both Mk and Lk speak of

going to (εἰς) Bethphage and Bethany along with movement toward (πρός) the Mount of Olives makes it probable that this was also the reading which was found first in Mt, as is preserved in Codex Sinaiticus where it is said that Jesus and the disciples came both to (εἰς) Bethphage and toward (πρός) the Mount of Olives. Used with the accusative as it is in these passages, the preposition πρός has this literal sense of toward and suggests a location up against. In this sense it well describes the situation of Bethany if Bethany is to be identified (as is virtually certain) with the village of el-'Azariyeh (cf. No. 110) and the vicinity thereof, as this location is up against the downslope of the southeastern ridge (Ras esh-Shiyah) of the Mount of Olives. These facts suggest, therefore, that Bethphage was somewhere between the Roman road and Bethany and probably, like Bethany, somewhere up against the southeastern ridge of the Mount of Olives. If it be supposed, however, that Jesus came up a route something like that of the modern highway which proceeds directly past Bethany (el-'Azariyeh) and on into Jerusalem, and if the references in Mk 11:1 and Lk 19:29 are taken to mean that on that route he came to Bethphage before Bethany, then a site for Bethphage would have to be sought somewhere east of Bethany. With this in view some have supposed that Bethphage was at the Arab village of Abu Dis, which is still farther down the southeastern ridge, to the southeast and across a ravine from el-'Azariyeh.

At any rate the village of Bethphage (Βηθφαγή) is surely to be identified with the place called Beth Page (בית פאגי) which is mentioned a number of times in

the Talmud. The Talmudic references occur particularly in connection with definition of the exact limits within which a sacred thing might be prepared or used. In the tractate *Menahoth* (78b GBT VIII, p. 680; SBT V, 2, pp. 468-469), for example, it is stated in the Mishnah passage that during the slaughtering of the thank offering, the bread of the thank offering must not be found "outside the wall." Then in the Gemara there is discussion of what this stipulation meant. One rabbi said that it meant "outside the wall of the Temple court," but Rabbi Johanan (third century) said it meant "outside the wall of Beth Page." From this we gather that Beth Page or Bethphage was a suburb of Jerusalem and probably located somewhere beyond the main outer wall of the Temple, i.e., the eastern wall, therefore probably somewhere on or over the Mount of Olives, which agrees with the deduction made in the preceding paragraph. Furthermore we learn here that the "wall" of Beth Page, which could have been an actual fortification of the village, or could have been simply a way of designating the extent of its territory, was considered to define the limits of Jerusalem. In the light of this fact it is particularly significant that Jesus now, by special arrangement, obtained a mount from Bethphage and rode on from that point. He who otherwise, as far as we know, had walked all over Palestine, including the long steep ascent from Jericho, chose to ride at last into Jerusalem precisely from the point which marked officially the entry point into the holy city. To this entry he obviously attached a very special significance.

Eusebius lists Bethphage in the *Onomasticon* (p. 58) but gives no more information than is already provided in the Gospels. It is a village, he says, at the Mount of Olives (πρὸς τῷ ὄρει τῶν ἐλαιῶν) to which the Lord Jesus came. Jerome (*Letter* 108, 12 NPNFSS VI, pp. 200-201)

says that Paula visited the tomb of Lazarus (at Bethany) as well as Bethphage and then "went straight on down the hill to Jericho." This could suggest that Bethphage was farther out from Jerusalem toward Jericho than Bethany, and could agree with some such location as that at Abu Dis mentioned above. The Jerusalem monk Epiphanius (750-800), however, said that the place where Christ mounted the ass was about one thousand paces from the Church of the Ascension (which was on the summit of the Mount of Olives, cf. No. 120) and that it was a like distance on to Bethany. The Crusaders accepted this as the location of Bethphage and here, about a half-mile east of the summit of the Mount of Olives, a stone with their frescoes and inscriptions was found in 1877. One picture showed the two disciples untying the ass and the colt. The stone is preserved in the Franciscan Chapel of Bethphage which is now at this site and shown in the photograph (No. 109). There has also been found on the Franciscan property a Christian tomb, marked with crosses and accompanied with fragments of mosaic, plainly of Byzantine date (A. Barrois in RB [1928], p. 262).

Photograph: courtesy Terra Santa.

110. The Village of Bethany

As for the village of Bethany (Βηθανία), Jn 11 recounts the raising of Lazarus at that place and states that this was a reason for which counsel was taken to put Jesus to death; Jn 12:1 says that Jesus was at Bethany six days before the final Passover, and Mt 21:17-18 and Mk 11:11-12 picture him as going there from Jerusalem for lodging at night. Neh 11:32 mentions Anathoth (which was at Anata three miles north of Jerusalem), Nob (which was on Mount Scopus), and

Ananiah in that order and the last place, which could well also have been called Bethananiah, may have been the town which the NT calls Bethany (W. F. Albright in AASOR 4 for 1922-23 [1924], pp. 158-160). Jn 11:18 places Bethany fifteen stadia from Jerusalem, and Eusebius (*Onomasticon* p. 58) says that it was at the second milestone from Aelia in a steep bank (ἐν κρημνῷ) of the Mount of Olives. The Bordeaux Pilgrim (Geyer p. 23; LPPTS I, p. 25; CCSL CLXXV, p. 18) puts the village of Bethany 1,500 paces eastward from the Mount of Olives and states that the crypt is there in which Lazarus was laid. Aetheria (Geyer pp. 77, 82; LPPTS I, pp. 51, 57; CCSL CLXXV, pp. 72, 76) gives Lazarium, obviously derived from the name of Lazarus, as the name of Bethany (*Lazarium autem, id est Bethania*), and places it at about 1,500 paces or at the second mile from the city. The distance of two Roman miles or fifteen stadia is equivalent to about three kilometers or something less than two English miles. This is the actual distance from Jerusalem to the present village of el-ʿAzariyeh and, as already stated (Nos. 107, 108), this village is on the lower slope of a ridge (Ras esh-Shiyah) of the Mount of Olives. It is also possible to see that the ancient name Lazarium, given by Aetheria, developed into the Arabic name, el-ʿAzariyeh, the initial letter of the Latin name probably being taken as the article (Kopp p. 333). The identification of this village with Bethany is therefore to be accepted.

The photograph (No. 110) shows the village as it appeared earlier in the present century. The hillside beyond the houses from one-third to one-half of the way from the left side of the picture was probably the location of the more ancient village. In this area, two or three hundred meters west of the present village, shaft tombs (cf. Nos. 202f.) were found in 1914 from the Canaanite period and other isolated finds gave evidence of habitation from 1500 B.C. to A.D. 100. In an olive grove owned by the Franciscans west of the ruined medieval tower (standing up prominently a third of the way from the right side of the photograph) and some eighty meters west of the abbey (cf. No. 115) there were new excavations in 1951-1953. Here the rock was virtually honeycombed with pits, caves, cisterns, and tombs. The objects found showed almost continuous occupation from about the sixth century B.C. to the fourteenth century of the Christian era. There were abundant small finds, including clay lamps and earthen vessels of many kinds, and coins, from the very period of Jesus as well as other periods. Among the coins was one of Herod the Great and another of the time of Pontius Pilate.

H. Vincent in RB 23 (1914), pp. 438-441; Sylvester J. Saller, *Excavations at Bethany (1949-1953)*. PSBF 12. Jerusalem: Franciscan Press, 1957, pp. 139-158 and 159ff. Photograph: courtesy École Biblique et Archéologique Française.

111. Plan of the Tomb of Lazarus and Adjacent Buildings

As we have just seen (No. 110) it was the tomb where Lazarus was laid that was naturally of greatest interest to Christian pilgrims to Bethany. In the *Ono-*

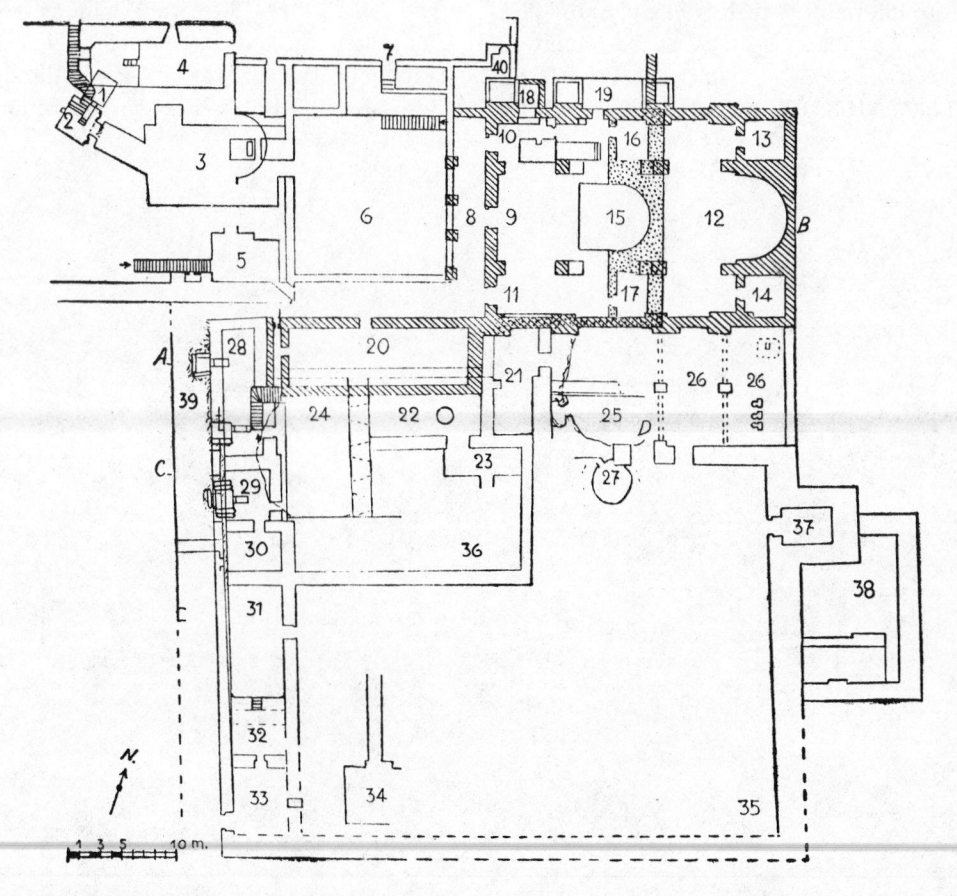

masticon (p. 58) Eusebius lists Bethany as the place where Christ raised Lazarus and says, "The place of Lazarus is still pointed out even until now" (δείκνυται εἰς ἔτι καὶ νῦν ὁ Λαζάρου τόπος). As was stated in connection with Origen as well as Eusebius (cf. p. xiv), the characteristic formula, "is pointed out," doubtless attests a tradition of very long standing. The location of the Tomb of Lazarus, as it is still pointed out in Bethany, is shown at 1-2 in the upper left-hand corner of the Plan.

Photograph: Sylvester J. Saller, *Excavations at Bethany (1949-1953)*, Fig. 2 on p. 6, courtesy Terra Santa.

112. Present Entrance to the Tomb of Lazarus

As shown in the Plan (No. 111) the present entrance to the Tomb of Lazarus is from the street on the north side. The exterior of this entrance is shown in the photograph. Inside this doorway twenty-two steps lead down into the vestibule of the tomb.

Photograph: JF.

113. The Tomb of Lazarus

This photograph shows the vestibule just mentioned (No. 112). From here two steps, as may be seen, descend into a narrow passage and the passage leads five feet into the vaulted inner chamber, about seven and one-half feet long and eight feet wide, of the tomb. On three sides of this chamber there are niches in the rock which widen out at the bottom to make slightly raised shelves for three burials. Jn 11:38 states that the tomb of Lazarus was a cave, "and a stone lay upon it." As may be seen in the picture, the stone to cover the entrance into this tomb would have been laid horizontally over the entrance steps.

Photograph: courtesy École Biblique et Archéologique Française.

114. Mosaic Pavement in the First Church at Bethany

As we have seen (No. 111) Eusebius said that "the place of Lazarus is still pointed out even until now" at Bethany. When Jerome revised the *Onomasticon* (p. 59) he changed this sentence to read as follows, adding the italicized words: *"a church which has now been erected there* points out his monument." From this it is evident that in the time after 330 when Eusebius composed the *Onomasticon* and before 390 when Jerome translated and revised it, a church was built at Bethany to mark the "monument," i.e., the tomb of Lazarus. While Jerome's word "now" suggests that the church was a relatively recent construction, it was probably built at least prior to the time of Aetheria who visited the Holy Land about 385. As we have seen (No. 110) she uses Lazarium as a name equivalent to Bethany. But in the case of Eleona, Aetheria uses this name as both the name of the Mount of Olives and also the name of the important church which stood on it, for she writes both "go up to the Mount of Olives, that is, to Eleona" (*ascendet in monte oliueti, id est in Eleona*, Geyer p. 83; LPPTS I, p. 58; CCSL CLXXV, p. 77), and also "services in Eleona, that is, in the very beautiful church on the Mount of Olives" (*in Eleona, id est in ecclesia, quae est in monte Oliueti, pulchra satis . . . celebrantur*, Geyer p. 77; LPPTS I, p. 51; CCSL CLXXV, p. 72). By analogy it seems probable, therefore, that Lazarium was the name both of the village and also of the church that was built there. Since Aetheria (Geyer pp. 71ff.; LPPTS I, pp. 45ff.; CCSL CLXXV, pp. 67ff.) describes elaborate services which were held at various times of the church year in various churches in and around Jerusalem, such as the Great Church in Golgotha, the Anastasis, and Eleona, and includes along with these "the Lazarium," it certainly seems most probable that this church was already in existence in her time.

In 1949-1953 prior to the erection of the new Church of St. Lazarus in Bethany the Franciscans were able to excavate and study much of the immediate area. This area has already been shown in the Plan in No. 111. As seen in this Plan the tomb of Lazarus (1-2) was at the west and the church was at the east with a courtyard providing connection between the two. In other words the plan was the same as found in other famous churches of the fourth century, e.g., in the Cathedral (c. 365) at Gerasa (No. 81) where the church was to the east of the celebrated fountain and connected with it. As seen in our Plan (No. 111) the oldest Bethany church had nave (9), two side aisles (10 and 11), and apse (15). The foundations of this church were partially uncovered at five different points in the Franciscan excavations, and the mosaic pavements in the nave and side aisles were cleared to a considerable extent. The photograph (No. 114) shows a portion of the mosaic in the nave. The panel at the right is a part of the main field of the mosaic, that at the left is a part of the border. The patterns are geometrical and there is no sign of any living being in them. Numer-

ous small crosses may be noted. The field mosaic has a close parallel in the mosaic pavement of a synagogue at Apamea on the Orontes which is dated by its inscriptions to the year 391 of the Christian Era (E. L. Sukenik in HUCA XXIII 2 [1950-51], pp. 541-551 and Plate VI). From the literary references, the plan, and the mosaics, the first church at Bethany may be dated, therefore, in the fourth century and probably after the middle of the century.

Sylvester J. Saller, *Excavations at Bethany (1949-1953)*. PSBF 12, 1957, pp. 9-33. Photograph: JF.

115. The New Church of St. Lazarus at Bethany

According to archeological excavations in Bethany, the first church at the tomb of Lazarus (No. 114) was probably destroyed by an earthquake and then replaced by a second church (Saller pp. 35-66). As shown in the Plan (No. 111) the apse (12) of the new structure was moved some thirteen meters eastward beyond that of its predecessor, but the basic plan remained the same. The second church also had a mosaic pavement, of which a large part was found intact. It was also geometric in pattern but, in contrast with the pavement of the first church, this mosaic contained no crosses whatever. This may point to a time after the year 427 when the emperor Theodosius prohibited the use of crosses in pavements (Saller p. 43). At the same time the continued absence of representations of animals and human beings points to a time prior to the sixth century when such representations became common. A known earthquake of 447, which was very strong at Jerusalem (D. H. Kallner-Amiran in IEJ 1 [1950-51], p. 225), could have damaged the first church and, if so, the second church may have been built about the middle of the fifth century.

In the twelfth century considerable modifications were made in the second church, leading the excavators to call this now the third church, but the basic plan was still unchanged and the apse (12) remained in the same place. About the same time the western end of the complex (3-5) was transformed into a distinct church which the excavators call the fourth church (Saller pp. 67-97). This church had a crypt which was connected with the tomb of Lazarus. In the Muslim period the crypt was converted into a mosque, however, and the entrance from it into the tomb was sealed off. Then the new entrance into the tomb from the north (No. 112) was constructed. This "fourth church" is still used as a mosque with the name of el-Uzeir. In 1955 it was provided with a new minaret.

South of the churches just described are the ruins of a large monastic establishment or abbey (20-38) (Saller pp. 99-130). Here many of the stones bear masons' marks, letters of the alphabet, crosses, etc., characteristic of the Crusaders. Between the abbey and the olive grove where remains of early Bethany were found are the ruins of the tower (cf. above No. 110) which protected the monastic institution. Both abbey and tower are described by the historian William of Tyre (1095-1184) (Saller p. 109).

By the middle of the fourteenth century the second and third churches described above were in ruins. After the archeological excavations in 1949-1953 a new Church of St. Lazarus was erected, and dedicated in 1954 (Saller pp. 131-137). It was built in the form of a Greek cross above the eastern part of the second and third churches and, where possible, utilized the ancient foundations. The apses of the two earliest churches were left visible within the new church, that of the first church in the western arm, that of the second church behind the altar in the eastern arm. In the western part of the church a portion of the mosaic pavement of the second church also remains visible; in the courtyard west of the church is a portion of the mosaic of the first church (No. 114). The photograph (No. 115), taken from within the beautiful garden, shows the east side of the new church, with the slender tower at the northeastern corner, and the cupola over the center.

Photograph: JF.

116. The Crypt of the Eleona Church

In his last days, according to Mt 24:3, Jesus sat on the Mount of Olives when he spoke to the disciples about the end of the world (συντέλεια τοῦ αἰῶνος; cf. τέλος in 24:6), and according to Mk 13:3 the spot was opposite the temple. After his resurrection, according to Lk 24:50 he led the disciples out "until *they were* over against (ἕως πρός) Bethany" (ASV) and parted from them; after he was taken out of their sight (Ac 1:9)

they returned to Jerusalem, according to Ac 1:12, "from the mount called Olivet (ἀπὸ ὄρους τοῦ καλουμένου ἐλαιῶνος, where ἐλαιών, "olive grove," is a proper noun and the phrase means literally, "from the mountain called Olive Grove," i.e., the Mount of Olives; cf. the Latin *mons oliveti*, "the mountain of the olive grove [*olivetum*]," i.e., the Mount of Olives, whence the English "Olivet"; so also in Lk 19:29; 21:37), which is near Jerusalem, a sabbath day's journey away." The sabbath day's journey, or distance that one could go without transgressing the commandment of Ex 16:29, was reckoned, on the basis of Num 35:5, at 2,000 cubits (*Erubin* IV 3; V 7 DM pp. 126, 128) or approximately 900 meters. Josephus gives almost exactly the same distance when he says that the Mount of Olives was five stadia (just over 3,000 feet) from the city (*Ant.* xx 8, 6 §169; in *War* v 2, 3 §70 the Tenth Legion encamped at the Mount of Olives at a distance of six stadia from Jerusalem, therefore presumably on the eastern side of the Mount on the way up from Jericho).

As is well known from the record provided by Eusebius in his *Life of Constantine* (III 25-43), the first Christian emperor built churches at three sites in Palestine which were of the greatest significance in Christian tradition, namely, at the sites which were pointed out as the places of the birth, the resurrection, and the ascension of Christ. With respect to the last two places particular credit for the building of the churches is given to Helena Augusta, the mother of Constantine, and with respect to the last of the places Eusebius (III 43) says: "The mother of the emperor raised a stately structure on the Mount of Olives also, in memory of his ascent to heaven who is the Savior of mankind, erecting a sacred church and temple on the very summit of the mount. And indeed authentic history informs us that

in this very cave the Savior imparted his secret revelations to his disciples."

The rhetorical language of Eusebius is slightly confusing, but from the excavations about to be mentioned it seems evident that Constantine built only one church on the Mount of Olives. It was over the cave where Jesus was believed to have taught the disciples about the end (Mt 24 and parallels), and it was near the summit of the mount where the ascension was believed to have taken place (Ac 1:9). The Bordeaux Pilgrim, who saw this church in 333, says explicitly that it was at the place "where before the Passion (*ante passionem*), the Lord taught the disciples" (Geyer p. 23; LPPTS I, pp. 24-25; CCSL CLXXV, p. 18). Aetheria (385) says with equal explicitness that "the cave in which the Lord used to teach is there" (Geyer p. 83; LPPTS I, p. 58; CCSL CLXXV, p. 77) and, as we have already seen (No. 114), uses Eleona as the name of the church as well as of the mount (Geyer p. 77; LPPTS I, p. 51; CCSL CLXXV, p. 72).

The ruins of the Eleona church have been identified and studied in excavations by the Dominicans beginning in 1910. The site is 70 meters south and slightly west of the absolute summit of the ridge where the Ascension Mosque (No. 121) stands. The photograph (No. 116) shows the uncovering of the crypt of the church, which was the cave mentioned in the tradition cited above.

Photograph: courtesy École Biblique et Archéologique Française.

117. Plan and Section of the Eleona Church

From the scanty remains of the Eleona church, including its foundation trenches cut in the rock, Vincent

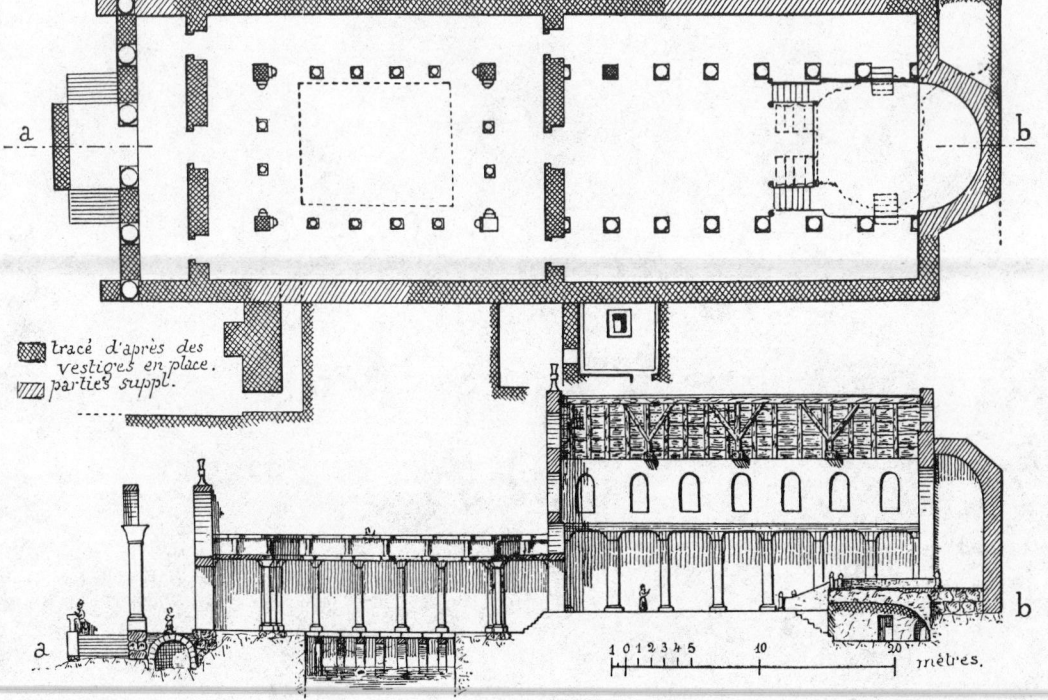

tracé d'après des vestiges en place. parties suppl.

1 0 1 2 3 4 5   10   50   mètres.

made the plan and section shown in this illustration. The entrance is thought to have been a portico of six columns. Three doors gave access to the atrium, under the center of which was a large cistern. Steps led up to the basilica proper which was on a higher level. It was about one hundred feet in length, and had nave, two side aisles, and inscribed apse. The orientation was such that the cave-crypt was beneath the eastern end of the apse. There are also small portions of mosaic pavement which remain in the south aisle and outside the south side of the church where there may have been a baptistery. The pattern is something like that in the Constantinian church at Bethlehem. Later buildings now obstruct the outlook to the west, but the spot must once have provided a splendid view toward Jerusalem and the temple (cf. Mk 13:3).

Vincent, *Jérusalem nouvelle*, pp. 337-360; Crowfoot, *Early Churches*, pp. 30-34; M. Avi-Yonah in QDAP 2 (1932), pp. 165-166 No. 113. Photograph: Crowfoot, *Early Churches*, p. 33 Fig. 5 (Oxford University Press, 1941).

118. The Church of the Lord's Prayer

Like other churches on the unprotected Mount of Olives, the Eleona was destroyed by the Neo-Persians in 614, but the tradition that Jesus taught in this vicinity persisted. In the Middle Ages a chapel marked the place where Jesus was supposed to have taught the disciples the Lord's Prayer, and another commemorated the spot where the Apostles were believed to have drawn up the Creed. In 1868 the site was purchased by the Princesse de la Tour d'Auvergne and the present Church of the Pater Noster and Church of the Creed date from that time. The ancient cave crypt and the east end of the Constantinian basilica of Eleona lie under the Pater Noster Church. In 1876 a convent of French Carmelite nuns was also built here. The group of structures is col-

lectively known as the Latin Buildings. The photograph shows the Church of the Lord's Prayer.

Photograph: The Matson Photo Service, Alhambra, Calif.

119. In the Church of the Lord's Prayer

This photograph shows a corridor in the present Church of the Pater Noster. The Lord's Prayer, believed by late tradition to have been taught at this place (cf. No. 118), is inscribed in panels in the walls of the church in forty-six different languages.

Photograph: JF.

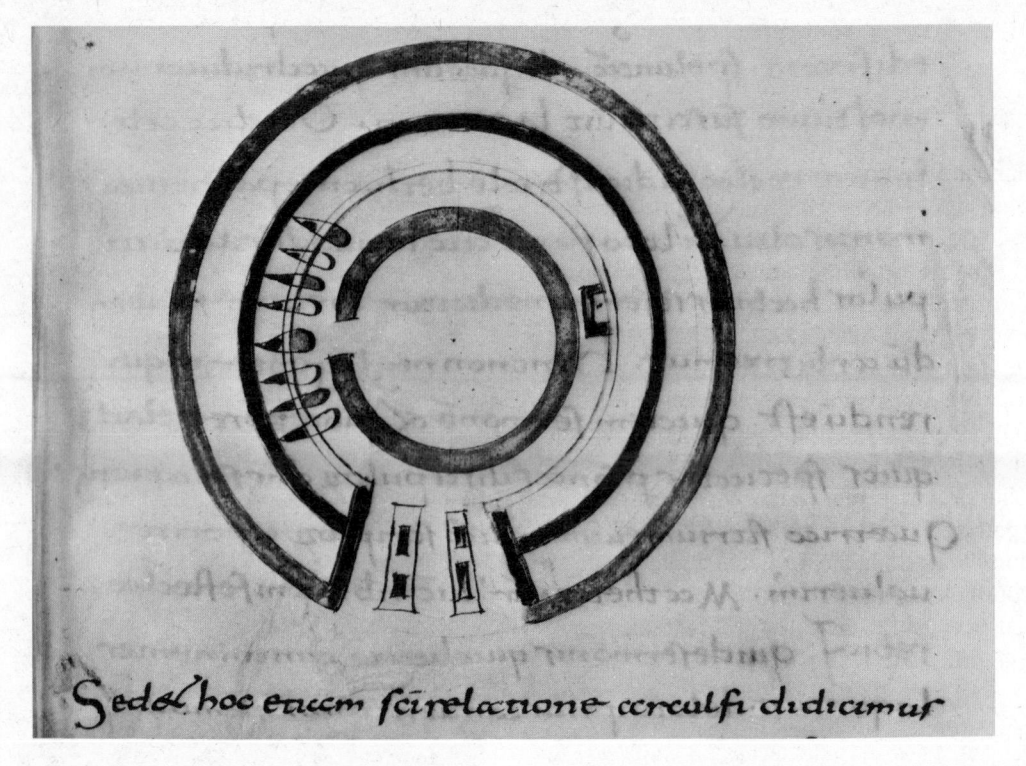

Sed & hoc etiam scire relatione cerculfi didicimus

120. Plan by Arculf of the Church of the Holy Ascension

In her description of the services that were held at Jerusalem on Palm Sunday, Aetheria (Geyer pp. 82-84; LPPTS I, pp. 58-59; CCSL CLXXV, pp. 76-78) says that the people go early to the Great Church at Golgotha, at the seventh hour go up to Eleona (cf. Nos. 114, 116), and then "when it begins to be the ninth hour they go up with hymns to the Inbomon—that is, to the place from which the Lord ascended into heaven." Finally at the eleventh hour "they go down on foot the whole way from the summit of the Mount of Olives" and proceed through the city back to the Cross and the Anastasis (cf. No. 184). The name Inbomon is explicable as a rendering in Latin of the Greek phrase ἐν βωμῷ which means "upon the height," βωμός being also a regular translation in the LXX of the Hebrew במה or "high place." At least by the time of Aetheria (385), then, the ascension was localized at a place of this name on the very summit of the Mount of Olives. That Inbomon was also already at that time an actual church is probable because Jerome (*Letter* 108, 12) makes Paula (386) say: "passing through Tekoa the home of Amos, I will look upon the glistening cross of Mount Olivet from which the Savior made his ascension to the Father." This cross was presumably lifted high above the Inbomon church on the uppermost ridge of the Mount of Olives and was hence visible as far away as Tekoa, ten miles south of Jerusalem. Confirmation of the foregoing deduction about the existence of the church is found when we come to Peter the Iberian (451), for he is authority for the statement that it was about 378 that "a very honorable and devout lady

named Pomnia (Poemenia) . . . built the Church of the Holy Ascension and surrounded it with buildings" (Raabe p. 35; Kopp p. 461).

Like the Eleona the Inbomon or Holy Ascension Church was destroyed by the Neo-Persians in 614, but whereas the Eleona was apparently left in ruins the Inbomon was soon rebuilt and from Arculf (670) we have both a description and a drawing of it. He says (Geyer pp. 246-251; LPPTS III, pp. 74-75; CCSL CLXXV, pp. 199-202) that there was a large round church (*ecclesia rotunda*) on the summit of the Mount of Olives, with three vaulted porticoes around it which were roofed over. The inner chamber (*interior domus*) of this church was without roof and without vault (*sine tecto et sine camera*) and open under heaven in the free air. In the center the last footprints of the Lord where he ascended were to be seen, and these were illumined by a great lamp which hung on a pulley and burned night and day. To the east of this innermost building was an altar under a narrow roof. In front of the innermost circle on the west side, above its entrance, eight lamps hung by ropes behind glass windows through which their light shone down as far as Jerusalem. The illustration (No. 120) reproduces the drawing with which Arculf accompanied his description, as given in the ninth-century Codex Parisinus Lat. 13048 in the Bibliothèque Nationale in Paris. The drawing clearly shows a main outer entrance which comes in from the south through the three circular porticoes, the inner circular chamber with its entrance on the west, the altar on the east, and the eight lamps on the west.

Photograph: Arculfus De Locis Sanctis, Codex Parisinus Lat. 13048, courtesy Bibliothèque Nationale, Paris.

98

121. The Mosque of the Ascension on the Mount of Olives

The Church of the Holy Ascension, described in the foregoing (No. 120) as it was seen by Arculf (670), was rebuilt by the Crusaders. The plan was the same as before except that the circular structure was now made octagonal. Like the innermost building it replaced, the chapel in the center was left open to the sky. This church was taken by Saladin in 1187 and converted into a mosque which it remains until today. An octagonal wall encloses a courtyard about one hundred feet in diameter. Near the center stands an octagonal building, twenty-one feet in diameter, surmounted by a cylindrical drum and a dome. This was the Crusader chapel, but the arches on the eight sides have now been walled in and the once-open roof covered with the cupola. Also there is a mihrab or niche showing the Muslim direction of prayer in the interior south wall. The use of this place for a mosque is appropriate from the Muslim point of view, for the statement in the Qur'an (Sura IV 158 cf. III 55 Abdullah Yusuf Ali, *The Holy Qur-an* [1946], I, p. 230 and note 664 cf. p. 137 and note 394) concerning Jesus that "God raised him up unto himself" provides a basis for Muslim belief in the ascension of Jesus.

Vincent, *Jérusalem nouvelle*, pp. 360-373. Photograph: courtesy École Biblique et Archéologique Française.

122. View of Jerusalem from the Summit of the Mount of Olives

From the summit of the Mount of Olives there is a splendid panorama in all directions. To the east the wilderness of Judea drops down to the Dead Sea, fifteen miles distant and 3,900 feet below, beyond which are the blue mountains of Moab. To the west, as seen in this photograph, one looks across the Kidron valley and upon the city of Jerusalem with the Dome of the Rock (No. 147) prominently visible in the Temple area.

Photograph: The Matson Photo Service, Alhambra, Calif.

123. The Franciscan Chapel at Dominus flevit

In his "triumphal" entry into Jerusalem Jesus came from the Mount of Olives (Mt 21:1; Mk 11:1; Lk 19:29), and Lk, who mentions the "descent" of the mount in 19:37, says in 19:41 that "when he drew near and saw the city he wept over it." If Bethphage (No. 109) was indeed on the heights of the Mount of Olives and perhaps about a half-mile east of the summit, then the most direct route to the city would have been right over the summit and straight down the slope to the west. This was a relatively steep descent and provided striking views of the city (cf. No. 128). The Inbomon and the Eleona were on this route at the top of the mount. As we have seen (No. 120), in her description of the Palm Sunday procession in her time (385) Aetheria (Geyer pp. 83-84; LPPTS I, pp. 58-59; CCSL CLXXV, pp. 77-78) says that the people and the bishop go up from the Great Church at Golgotha to the Eleona and to the Inbomon and then, at the eleventh hour, "they go down on foot the whole way from the summit of the Mount of Olives" (*de summo monte oliveti totum pedibus itur*). The people go before the bishop and sing, "Blessed be he who comes in the name of the Lord" (Mt 21:9), and the children hold branches of palm trees and of olive trees (*ramos tenentes alii palmarum, alii olivarum*). Thus they escort the bishop, singing in response, and thus, slowly and gently (*lente et lente*) lest the people be wearied, they come back to the city and through it to the Cross and the Anastasis (cf. No. 184). Since this was an obvious re-enactment of the triumphal entry it is presumable that what was at that time considered as the traditional route was followed, and since the account emphasizes the going by foot and slowly it is also probable that it was the steep descent down the west face of the Mount of Olives which was used. Whether this steep descent was also the most likely one for Jesus when he rode upon an animal and was accompanied by crowds (Mt 21:7f. and parallels) may perhaps be questioned. If it is questioned, then perhaps a more northerly route along the line of the Roman road (cf. No. 107) might be considered more likely (Kopp pp. 331-332). But the relatively old tradition attested by Aetheria is surely consonant with the idea of the more direct descent. The paths which go down there now mitigate the steepness by their zigzag course, which may be judged likely for the ancient way too.

About halfway down the direct descent on the west side from the summit of the Mount of Olives is the site known as *Dominus flevit*, the name embodying the tradition that this is the place where "the Lord wept" over Jerusalem (Lk 19:41). It is no doubt the area to which many pilgrims of the Middle Ages point, among others the Dominicans, Ricoldus de Monte Crucis (1294) (Kopp p. 330 n. 92) and Humbert de Dijon (1332) (RB 62 [1955], pp. 534-535). The latter, for example, says that there is a stone halfway up the mount where Jesus wept, and where he also dismounted from the foal, which was young and frisky (*pullus erat iuvenis et lascivus*), and mounted the ass. The last point may in some manner be dependent upon Jerome, who also speaks of the *pullus lasciviens* or frisky foal obtained from Bethphage (*Letter* 108, 12). At this place on the Mount the Franciscans have the striking chapel shown in the photograph (No. 123) and a monastery on the wall of which is a plaque with these words: *Locus, in quo Dominus videns civitatem flevit super illam*, "The place in which the Lord, when he saw the city, wept over it."

Photograph: JF.

100

124. Ossuaries *in situ* at Dominus flevit

The Franciscans began excavations in 1953 at Dominus flevit and found a very extensive ancient cemetery with many hundreds of graves. According to the accompanying materials which were discovered, including coins, pottery, and objects of glass and stone, the burials belonged to two distinct periods. The first period was 135 B.C.-A.D. 70 (or possibly 135), and the graves were of the kokim type (cf. No. 209). The second period was that of the third and fourth, especially the fourth, centuries, and the graves were characterized by arcosolia (cf. No. 210). In the graves were seven sarcophagi and 122 ossuaries, or fragments thereof. All of these were from the first period, which is in accordance with the otherwise supported opinion that ossuaries were used at Jerusalem only until A.D. 70 or 135 (cf. below p. 218). In the judgment of some scholars, some of the ossuary inscriptions and marks represent early Jewish Christianity, and they will be discussed in more detail later (Nos. 272ff.). This photograph shows a portion of the excavations, with ossuaries left in place in one of the chambers.

Other finds are preserved in the Museum of the Convent of the Flagellation in Jerusalem.

RB 61 (1954), pp. 568-570; P. B. Bagatti and J. T. Milik, *Gli scavi del "Dominus flevit" (Monte Oliveto—Gerusalemme)*, Part I, *La necropoli del periodo romano.* PSBF 13. Jerusalem: Tipografia dei PP. Francescani, 1958; reviews of the foregoing by J. van der Ploeg in JSS 5 (1960), pp. 81-82, and by M. Avi-Yonah in IEJ 11 (1961), pp. 91-94. Photograph: JF.

125. Byzantine Capital at Dominus flevit

In 1954 the ruins of a Byzantine church were found at Dominus flevit. The remains are preserved under and adjacent to the present Franciscan chapel (No. 123). In the garden is this capital. The church was no doubt one of the twenty-four churches which Theodosius (Geyer p. 140; LPPTS II, p. 10; CCSL CLXXV, p. 117) says were on the Mount of Olives in his time (530).

Photograph: JF.

126. Mosaic Pavement at Dominus flevit

This portion of mosaic pavement is also still intact from the Byzantine church at Dominus flevit.

Photograph: JF.

101

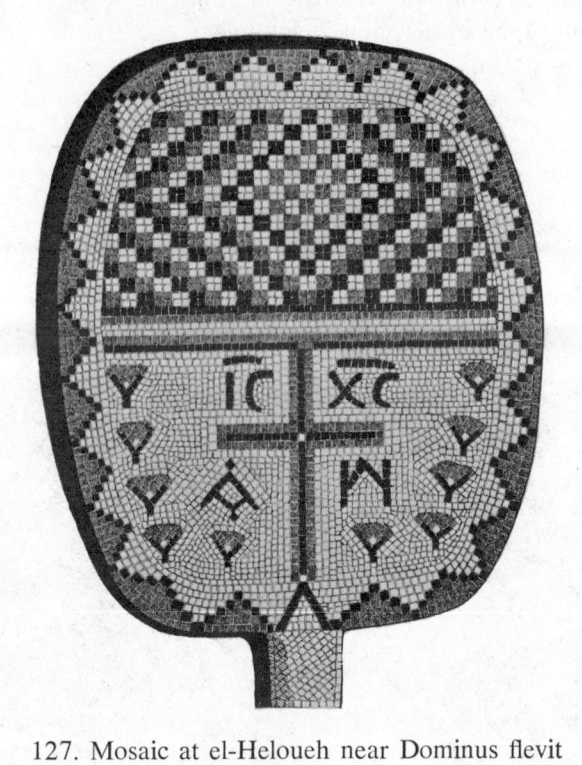

127. Mosaic at el-Heloueh near Dominus flevit

Opposite the Dominus flevit chapel there is a ruined mosque known as el-Mansuriya, built perhaps around

1500 (Vincent, *Jérusalem nouvelle*, p. 408). The place is also called el-Heloueh. Here there was found in 1907 an oval basin, 75 by 65 centimeters in size, paved in mosaic. As shown in the photograph, the upper register of the mosaic is a geometrical pattern in large cubes of red and white. In the lower register, surrounded by sprigs, is a large cross. Above the horizontal arms of the cross are the words I($\eta\sigma o\hat{v}$)C X($\rho\iota\sigma\tau\acute{o}$)C, below are the characters A and ω. The Latin form of the cross and the possible unfamiliarity with Greek shown in the strange shaping of the Omega suggest a relatively late date for this Christian inscription, but of course still prior to the building of the mosque.

H. Vincent, "Une mosaïque chrétienne au Mont des Oliviers," in RB 17 (1908), pp. 122-125; M. Avi-Yonah in QDAP 2 (1932), p. 165 No. 110. Photograph: RB 17 (1908), p. 123, courtesy École Biblique et Archéologique Française.

128. Panoramic View of Jerusalem from the Slope of the Mount of Olives

The Christian interest in the area now known as Dominus flevit, evidenced by the possibly Jewish-Christian burials in the cemetery (No. 124), the Byzantine church (Nos. 125-126), and the mosaic at el-Heloueh (No. 127), are at least not out of harmony with the traditional identification of this spot as being where

Jesus drew near and saw the city and wept over it. Certainly from almost anywhere on the western slope of the Mount of Olives there is a dramatic view of the Old City of Jerusalem. In this panorama in the temple area one can see from left to right the Mosque al-Aqsa, the Dome of the Rock, and the minaret at the northwest corner of the area, and in the background, between the Mosque and the Dome, the tower of the Lutheran Church and the domes of the Church of the Holy Sepulcher.

Photograph: courtesy Government Press Office, State of Israel.

129. The Mount of Olives from the Temple Area

This view is from within the temple area near the Dome of the Rock, eastward through an arcade to the Mount of Olives. Through the first arch at the left are seen the domes of the Russian Church of St. Mary Magdalene built by the Emperor Alexander III in 1888. Through the second arch is visible the tower at the Russian convent on the summit of the Mount of Olives. More details will be pointed out in the next photograph (No. 130).

Photograph: JF.

130. The Mount of Olives and the Gethsemane Church

When Jesus and the disciples went to the Mount of Olives after the Last Supper (Mt 26:30; Mk 14:26; Lk 22:39) they went to a place ($\chi\omega\rho\acute{\iota}o\nu$, a piece of land) called Gethsemane (Mt 26:36; Mk 14:32; cf. Lk 22:40) which was across the Kidron Valley where there was a garden ($\kappa\hat{\eta}\pi os$) (Jn 18:1). The name Gethsemane ($\Gamma\epsilon\theta\sigma\eta\mu\alpha\nu\acute{\iota}$) corresponds to the Hebrew גת שמני which designates an oil-press used for the making of olive oil, a type of installation naturally found at the mount which took its name from the abundant olive trees on its slopes.

Like No. 129, this photograph is taken from the temple area looking toward the Mount of Olives but from a point somewhat farther to the north, near the Golden Gate (No. 154), and at the extreme eastern edge of the area, looking through an aperture in the upper part of the eastern city wall. Again one sees on the summit of the mount the Russian tower. Not far to the right of it and somewhat nearer this way is the minaret at the Mosque of the Ascension (No. 121). Farther to the right and a little farther down the slope of the mount is the tower of the Carmelite convent at the site of the Eleona church (No. 118). In front of this is the large building of a Benedictine convent. Farther down the hill in the midst of many large trees is the Russian Church of St. Mary Magdalene (cf. No. 129). Now in view also, near the foot of the mount and across at the far edge of the Kidron valley, are the Franciscan Church and Garden of Gethsemane. Plainly visible to the left of the Garden of Gethsemane is the northern path which runs up the Mount of Olives from the Kidron Valley. To the left near the summit of the ridge is the site called Viri Galilaei. Yet farther left, i.e., to the north, was where the Roman road crossed the ridge between Viri Galilaei and the Augusta Victoria buildings (cf. No. 107). The middle and most direct and steepest path up the mount ascends from behind the Garden of Gethsemane, past the Church of St. Mary Magdalene, past Dominus flevit (No. 123), to the sites of the Eleona and the Inbomon. A third and southernmost path swings farther to the right, out of the scope of this picture, to circle around and come to the top of the mount.

The main path which descends past the north side of the Garden of Gethsemane joins the automobile road which runs in front of the Church of Gethsemane at a point which is just to the left, i.e., the north, of what is visible in our picture. Here, north of the path and east of the curve of the highway, is a large mass of rock. In the rock is a cave known as the Grotto of the Betrayal and immediately adjoining this on the west is the Church of the Tomb of Mary. From the grotto just mentioned to the Gethsemane Church is a distance of about one hundred yards.

Photograph: JF.

104

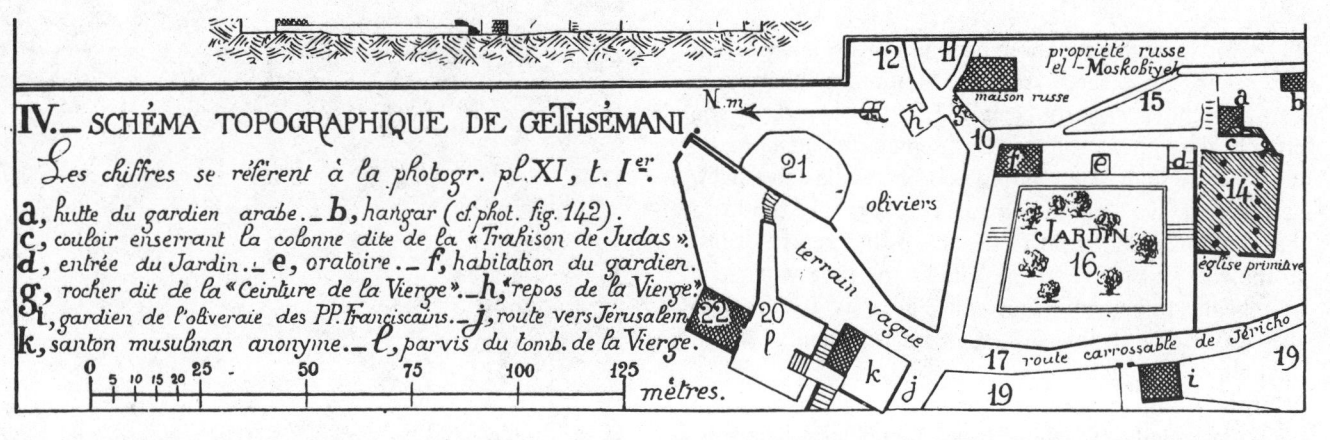

131. Plan of the Gethsemane Area

This plan shows details in the area just described (No. 130) where the Gethsemane Church and the Grotto of the Betrayal are located. Referring to the numbers in this plan, we see the early basilica above which the present Gethsemane Church stands (14), the adjacent garden (16), the Grotto of the Betrayal (21) with the passage leading to it (20), and the Tomb of Mary (22). The route to Jericho is shown which is the present highway (17), and there are olive trees in the area west of it (19) as well as in the garden (16) and in the area between the latter and the Grotto (21). The southern path up the Mount of Olives turns to the right at (10), the middle path is (11), and the northern path is (12). The Russian property is labeled on the plan, and the accompanying legend indicates certain other details.

Under the name Gethsemane (Γεθσιμανή) Eusebius says in the *Onomasticon* (p. 74) that this was the place (χωρίον as in Mt. 26:36 and Mk 14:32) where Christ prayed before the passion. It lies, he says, at the Mount of Olives (πρὸς τῷ ὄρει τῶν ἐλαιῶν), and the preposition πρός, used here with the dative and most simply translatable as "at," carries the sense of up against (cf. No. 109). In this place the faithful were zealous to make their prayers. This language sounds as if at this time (330) the spot indicated had long been identified as the Gethsemane where Jesus prayed, but it does not sound as if it had yet been marked by a church building.

About three years later (333) the Bordeaux Pilgrim (Geyer p. 23; LPPTS I, p. 24; CCSL CLXXV, pp. 17-18) went out from the city to the gate which is to the eastward (*contra oriente*) in order to ascend the Mount of Olives. This gate could have been the gate in the eastern city wall just north of the temple area later known as St. Mary's or St. Stephen's Gate (No. 197), or the so-called Golden Gate (No. 154) in the east wall of the temple area itself. Beyond the gate the Pilgrim mentions the "valley which is called Josaphat," which is the Kidron Valley (cf. No. 218). Now the Pilgrim is presumably proceeding southward down the valley and then turning eastward to ascend the main slope of the mount.

At this point he says: "On the left, where there are vineyards, is a rock where Judas Iscariot betrayed Christ; on the right is a palm tree from which the children broke off branches and strewed them when Christ came."

In this text the word for "rock" is *petra*, corresponding to the Greek πέτρα, which means a mass of living rock in distinction from πέτρος which means a detached stone or boulder. The "rock" is therefore probably the very mass of rock in which is found the so-called Grotto of the Betrayal (cf. No. 130). If the Pilgrim was at this point facing up the mount the palm tree on his right would probably have been beside the path descending steeply from the mount. Not far from there, he also says, about a stone's throw away, were the beautiful tombs of Isaiah (this one a monolith) and of Hezekiah. These are quite certainly two of the four large Hellenistic-Roman tombs which are still to be seen only a little way farther down the Kidron Valley (Nos. 218ff.), and the tomb of "Isaiah" is probably the tomb which is now called that of "Zechariah" which is indeed a monolith (No. 221). The Bordeaux Pilgrim was therefore quite plainly in the vicinity of what we know as the Grotto of the Betrayal and the Garden of Gethsemane when he saw the place which was considered to be that of the betrayal of Christ, an event (Mt 26:47 and parallels) which followed upon the prayer of Jesus in Gethsemane.

While neither Eusebius nor the Pilgrim from Bordeaux mentions a church at the area which he describes, later in the same century we find that a church existed there. In the account by Aetheria (385) of the services at Jerusalem during Holy Week she tells not only of the procession down the Mount of Olives on Palm Sunday (cf. No. 123) but also of the events of the Thursday of that week (Geyer pp. 85-87; LPPTS I, pp. 60-62; CCSL CLXXV, pp. 78-80). On Thursday evening and night the bishop and people are at the Eleona and the Inbomon churches (Nos. 116, 120). When the cocks begin to crow (but still deep in the night, as the subsequent narrative makes plain), "they descend from the Inbomon with hymns, and come to that place where the Lord prayed, as it is written in the Gospel [Lk 22:

105

41], 'And he withdrew about a stone's throw and prayed, etc.' " "In this place," Aetheria continues, "there is a fine church (*ecclesia elegans*)." After prayers in the church they move on to Gethsemane (*Gessamani*), where more than two hundred church candles give light, and the passage from the Gospel is read where the Lord was apprehended. From Gethsemane they return at last to the city and arrive at the gate at the time when one man begins to be able to recognize another. By the time they are back in front of the Cross it is becoming broad daylight.

From Aetheria we learn, then, that two spots were commemorated, one where Jesus prayed, one where he was taken captive. The spot where he prayed was marked by a fine church, the spot where he was apprehended was called Gethsemane. Coming down the mount the pilgrims reached the church first. Between mention of it and of Gethsemane Aetheria speaks of the weariness of the people from having to descend "so great a mountain," but this probably does not mean that the church was high up on the mountain but only that Aetheria is here making a resumptive reference to the entire nocturnal descent. As for the use of the name Gethsemane for the place of the betrayal and apprehension of Jesus, this is in accord with the Gospel record (Mt 26:36ff. and parallels) where Jesus and the disciples came to Gethsemane, and he went "a little farther" or "withdrew about a stone's throw" to pray, then returned to where the disciples were and was apprehended at that place. That the place a stone's throw away was outside the limits of "Gethsemane" is not, however, necessarily indicated and Eusebius (as cited just above) certainly used this as the name for the place where Jesus prayed.

Revising the *Onomasticon* of Eusebius in 390, Jerome also attests the existence of a church at this time in this area. He reproduces Eusebius' location of Gethsemane "at" the Mount of Olives with the somewhat more exact statement that it was "at the foot" (*ad radices*, literally, at the roots) of the mount, and then he replaces Eusebius' statement about the faithful who pray in the place with the statement, "Now a church (*ecclesia*) has been built over it" (*Onomasticon* p. 75). We conclude, then, that Gethsemane was considered, at least by this time, to include both the place of the betrayal of Jesus and the place of his prayer. The two spots were not far apart and it was the latter on which a church was actually built. These two traditional spots are marked on the plan (No. 131) with the numbers 21 (place of the betrayal) and 14 (place of the prayer and of the church) and, as noted above (No. 130), the distance between them is about one hundred yards.

Photograph: Vincent, *Jérusalem nouvelle*, p. 335 Fig. 147, courtesy École Biblique et Archéologique Française.

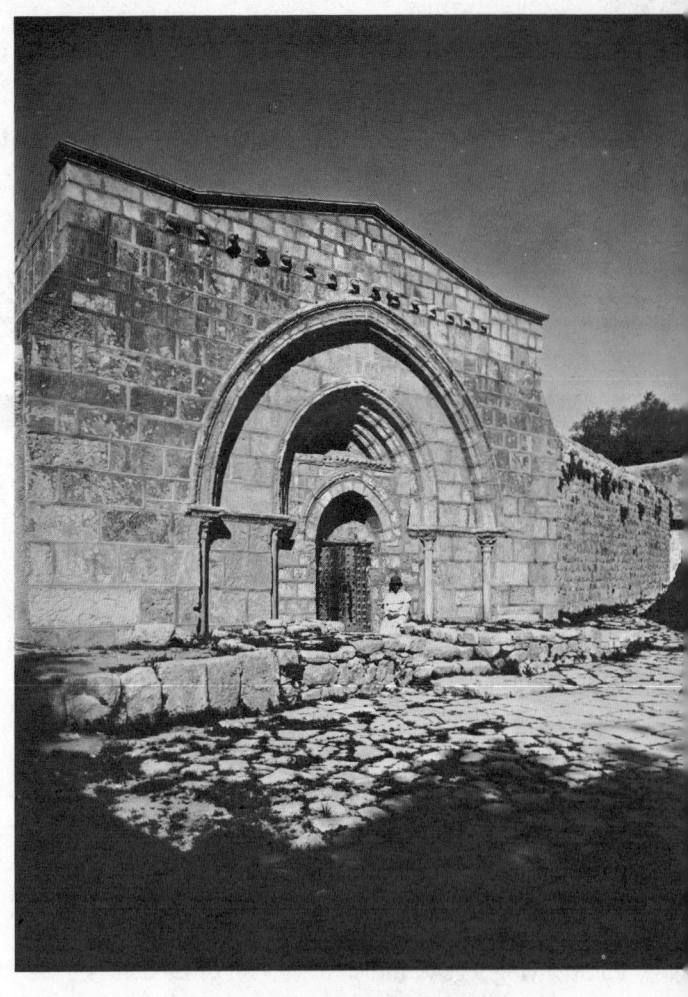

132. The Tomb of the Virgin

As for the Tomb of Mary (marked 22 in the Plan No. 131) the following explanation may be given. When Theodosius (530) (Geyer p. 142; LPPTS II, p. 11; CCSL CLXXV, p. 119) describes the Valley of Jehoshaphat he says that it is where Judas betrayed the Lord and also that there is there a church of St. Mary the mother of the Lord (*ecclesia domnae Mariae matris Domini*). The Anonymous of Piacenza (570) (Geyer p. 170; LLPTS II, p. 14; CCSL CLXXV, p. 137) came down the Mount of Olives into the Valley of Gethsemane, saw the place where the Lord was betrayed, and found in the same valley "a basilica of St. Mary which, they say, was her house in which she was taken from the body." Yet another source of the sixth century, the Jerusalem Breviary (Geyer p. 155), also mentions her sepulcher in connection with the basilica of St. Mary. Arculf (670) (Geyer p. 240; LPPTS III, p. 17; CCSL CLXXV, p. 195) describes the Church of St. Mary in the Valley of Josaphat as built in two stories, both round, in the lower of which is "the empty sepulcher of St. Mary in which for a time she rested after her burial." According to these references the church, with these traditions attaching to it, existed in the sixth and seventh centuries and must have

106

been built earlier, perhaps in the fifth century. This earlier Byzantine church was in ruins when the Crusaders came. They not only rebuilt the church but also built beside it a large monastery, the Abbey of St. Mary of the Valley of Jehoshaphat. The digging of trenches in this area in 1937 uncovered some mosaic floors and an inscription with crosses, reading "Tomb of Kasios and Adios," probably sixth century in date, and also later pavements and masonry of the time of the Crusader reconstruction of the church (C. N. Johns in ZDPV 8

[1939], pp. 117-136). The present church, shown in this photograph, is known as the Church of the Tomb of Mary or, simply, the Tomb of the Virgin. In it the underground crypt is still that of the church of the Abbey of St. Mary.

Vincent, *Jérusalem nouvelle*, pp. 805-831. For the alternate and probably later tradition of residence and death of Mary in Ephesus see Clemens Kopp, *Das Mariengrab, Jerusalem? —Ephesus?* Paderborn: Ferdinand Schöningh, 1955. Photograph: courtesy École Biblique et Archéologique Française.

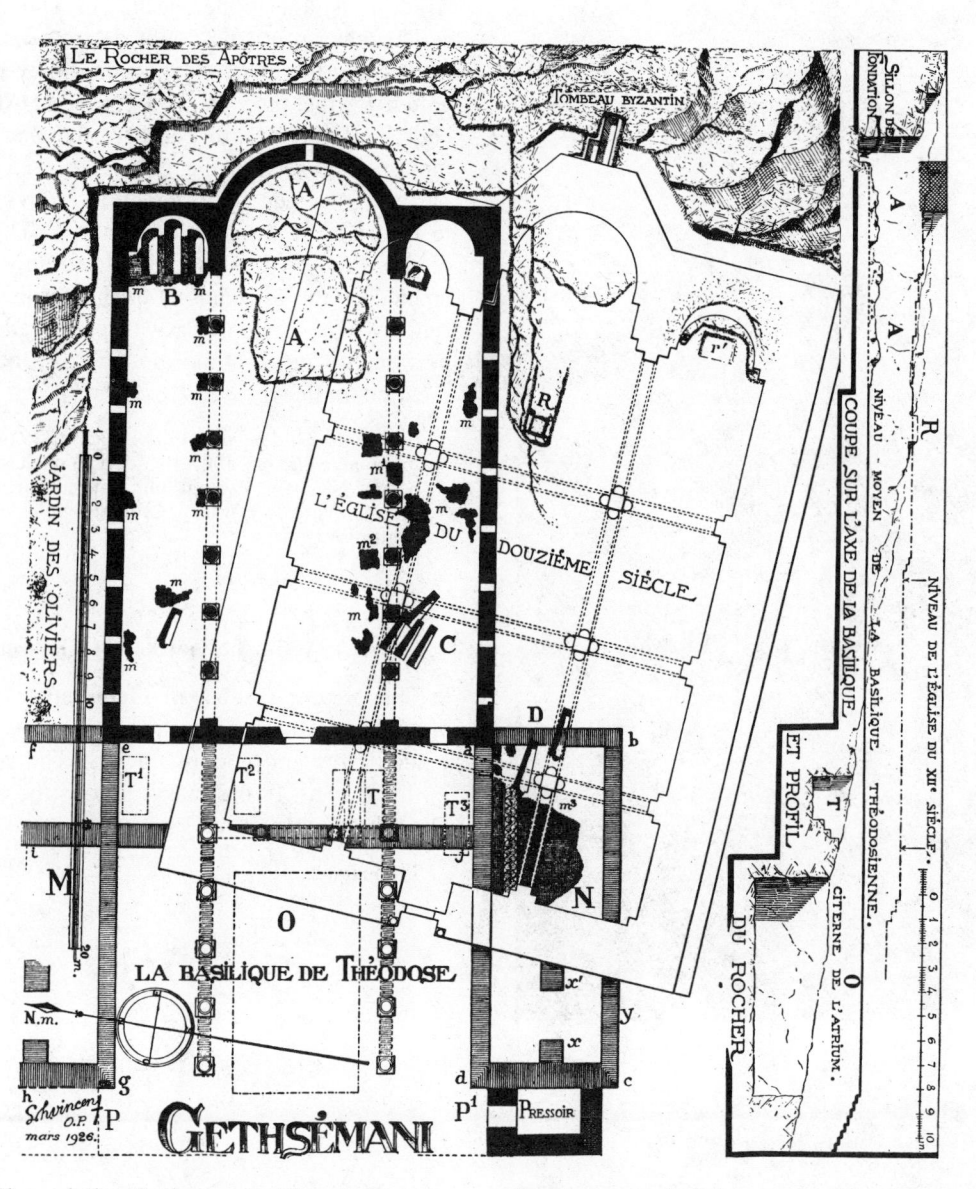

133. Plan of the Gethsemane Church

As indicated already (No. 130), the area of the present Gethsemane Garden and Church (see 16 and 14 in the Plan No. 131) belongs to the Franciscans. In 1919

they began to build a new basilica here and in the course of so doing uncovered and explored the remains of two earlier churches. The spot in question is shown as that of the primitive church (14) in Plan No. 131 above. In this Plan (No. 133) we see the superimposition of the two earlier churches. The oldest church is shown with the darkest outline: a basilica 20 meters long and 16 wide. It has a nave and two side aisles, and the aisles as well as the nave end in apses. The orientation is thirteen degrees to the north of east, and the purpose of this was evidently to allow a large mass of rock (marked in the plan with the letter A) to lie immediately in front of the central apse and the altar. Undoubtedly this was held to be the rock where Jesus prayed in Gethsemane. Some capitals, column bases, and portions of

geometrical floor mosaics (marked in the Plan with the letter m) remained. Since all indications are in harmony with a date in the latter part of the fourth century, this was almost certainly the church to which Jerome referred in 390 when he amended the statement of Eusebius about the place of prayer in Gethsemane to say, "Now a church has been built over it" (*Onomasticon* p. 75, cf. above No. 131). If, as the language may be taken to suggest, the church was built not long before these words were written, a date for the church under Theodosius I the Great (379-395) may be judged possible or probable and in the legend on the plan this structure is labeled the Basilica of Theodosius.

This church was no doubt destroyed by the Persians in 614 and the exact location of it may have been forgotten by the time of the Crusaders. At any rate the church of the twelfth century, the outlines of which may also be seen in the Plan (No. 133), was located partly to one side and oriented in a direction somewhat to the right of the primitive church. The new basilica of the Franciscans was completed in 1924 and was erected on the foundations of the basilica of the fourth century. The great rock was preserved in view, and portions of the early mosaic may also be seen beneath the modern floor.

G. Orfali, *Gethsémani*. Paris: Picard, 1924; Vincent, *Jérusalem nouvelle*, pp. 1007-1013; Avi-Yonah in QDAP 2 (1932), p. 164 No. 108. Photograph: Vincent, *Jérusalem nouvelle*, Pl. LXXXVIII, 1, courtesy École Biblique et Archéologique Française.

134. In the Garden of Gethsemane

The present Garden of Gethsemane contains many very large and very old olive trees, as well as carefully tended plots and pots of flowers. The picture is taken in this garden. In the background is the east wall of the Old City of Jerusalem.

Photograph: JF.

JERUSALEM

135. Plan of Jerusalem

The site of Jerusalem is, as a whole, a rocky quadrilateral plateau, about 2,500 feet above the level of the Mediterranean Sea. The area is bounded on the west and south by what the OT calls variously the valley of Hinnom (Jos 15:8), of the son of Hinnom (Jos 15:8), or of the sons of Hinnom (II K 23:10). In Jos 15:8 and elsewhere this depression is called by the Hebrew word גי which means a "valley" in the sense of a "gorge" (in distinction from an עמק which is a broad level valley or plain) and the entire resultant designation, גי-הנם, *Gehinnom*, although translatable in Greek as φάραγξ Ὀνόμ (Jos 15:8 LXX), was also rendered Γαίεννα (Jos 18:16 LXX) and hence resulted in the NT name γέεννα, Gehenna (Mt 5:29, etc.). From the horrible burning of children in this valley (Jer 7:31, etc.) the name became synonymous with hell (Mt 5:29, etc.). Today the valley of Hinnom is called Wadi er-Rababi.

On the east the physical boundary is provided by the Kidron. In the OT the Kidron is always called a נחל (II Sam 15:23, etc.) which means a winter torrent and, by implication, a narrow valley or ravine in which such a stream flows. In the RSV translation the designation is "the brook Kidron." The LXX translation of *nahal* is with the word χειμάρρους (from χεῖμα, "winter cold," and ῥέω, "to flow") which also designates a winter torrent and a ravine. This word is used with the name Kidron in Jn 18:1 and there the RSV translation is "the Kidron valley." That the Kidron Valley was ultimately identified as the valley of Jehoshaphat (Jl 3:2, 12) has already been noted (No. 131). Today it is also called Wadi en-Nar. With the Hinnom gorge on the west and south and the Kidron ravine on the east the whole area described was strongly protected on those three sides. On the north, however, it was relatively open and it was, in fact, from that side that came such a major conquest of Jerusalem as that by the Romans in A.D. 70.

Within the area described there is an eastern ridge and a western ridge with a valley between. The valley, which runs from north to south and is parallel with the Kidron Valley, is called the Valley of the Cheesemakers (ἡ τῶν τυροποιῶν φάραγξ) by Josephus (*War* V 4, 1 §140), from which designation we derive the name Tyropoeon. The word which Josephus uses for the valley means deep chasm or ravine. Although it presumably merited this designation at that time it has been so filled with debris, like many other low places in the city, that it is now scarcely more than a slight depression, known as el-Wad.

Of the two ridges the western is, as Josephus (*War* V 4, 1 §137) points out, the higher and straighter. The eastern ridge is lower and convex on each side, a point which Josephus makes by using for it the word (ἀμφίκυρτος) which describes the moon when it is "gibbous," i.e., between half-moon and full.

Each of the two ridges is also cut by one or more transverse valleys. In the case of the western ridge the transverse valley, sometimes called simply the Cross Valley, runs from west to east generally parallel to and on the north side of the present David Street and Street of the Chain, and runs into the Tyropoeon valley at a point nearly opposite the Gate of the Chain in the western side of the temple area. This divides the western ridge into two parts which, from the point of view of the whole area, may be called the northwestern hill and the southwestern hill. The Church of the Holy Sepulcher is on a part of the northwestern hill. While the hill continues to climb toward the northwest, this particular part amounts to a small promontory by itself and is sometimes designated by the term *ras* which means top or summit. It is about 755 meters or 2,477 feet above sea level.

The so-called Tomb of David and associated buildings stand on the southwestern hill. Here the plateau is about 771 meters or 2,529 feet above the Mediterranean, the highest part of the main city area. Josephus, accordingly, calls the city on this hill the "upper city" (*War* v 4, 1 §137). In the same passage Josephus also says that David called this hill the Stronghold (φρούριον), which sounds as if Josephus thought it was included in what David took from the Jebusites (II Sam 5:7). Another passage (*Ant.* VII 3, 2 §66) states that David enclosed the "upper" city, which gives the same impression, although in this case there is a variant reading which mentions the "lower city" instead. Although the meaning of Josephus is not unambiguous, early Christian tradition certainly considered the southwestern hill to be the Zion or Sion (LXX Σιών) of King David (II Sam 5:7). This is implied by the Bordeaux Pilgrim (Geyer p. 22; LPPTS I, p. 22; CCSL CLXXV, p. 16) who had been at the temple area and then came out of Jerusalem to go up Mount Sion (*exeuntibus Hierusalem, ut ascendas Sion*) and in doing so had the Pool of Siloam on the left hand. Likewise Eusebius says in the *Onomasticon* (p. 74) that Golgotha was to the north of the mount of Sion (πρὸς τοῖς βορείοις τοῦ Σιὼν ὄρους). No doubt this traditional identification of the southwestern hill with the Sion of David had something to do with the localization of the "tomb of David" in the church of the Last Supper, which became a Muslim mosque of the "prophet David" (Nos. 165ff.). From the southwestern hill a partly separate promontory extended eastward toward the Tyropoeon Valley, and this promontory was the site of the Palace of the Hasmoneans (*War* II 16, 3 §344; *Ant.* xx 8, 11 §190).

The eastern ridge may also be recognized as divided into a southeastern hill and a northeastern hill. It has now been established by excavation that the early Canaanite city of Jerusalem was on the southeastern hill above the spring Gihon (No. 138). This was accordingly the place which David took from the Jebusites, which was the stronghold of Zion and the city of David (II Sam 5:7). A portion of the hill was called Ophel (עֹפֶל) which means "hump" (Neh 3:26, etc.). This name was reproduced by Josephus (*War* v 4, 2 §145) in a Hellenized transcription of the Aramaic עׇפְלָא as Ὀφλᾶς, Ophlas. In 169/168 B.C. Antiochus IV Epiphanes took treasures from the temple in Jerusalem

(I Macc 1:20ff.) and two years later his commander came back with a large force and plundered the city (I Macc 1:29ff.). At that time the Syrians "fortified the city of David with a great strong wall and strong towers, and it became their citadel" (I Macc 1:33). The word used here is ἄκρα, *acra*, which means highest point and hence citadel. Since this citadel was made by fortifying the city of David it is probable that a whole fortified city-quarter is meant and it is evident that this was on the southeastern hill. Josephus also says that the "lower city" was on the hill which bore the name of Acra (*War* v 4, 1 §137), or that the lower portion of the town was itself known as Acra (*War* I 1, 4 §39).

The northeastern hill is the site of the temple area. Between the southeastern hill and the northeastern there was once, Josephus says (*War* v 4, 1 §139; cf. I 2, 2 §50; *Ant.* XIII 6, 7 §215), a broad ravine which the Hasmoneans filled in when they razed the Syrian Acra. At this time they not only demolished the citadel but also cut down the height of the hill which, according to Josephus, was once higher than the temple hill, a supposition which seems actually unlikely. The portion of the northeastern hill occupied by the temple area itself has an average elevation above the sea of about 737 meters or 2,418 feet. Toward the northeastern corner of what is the present temple area there was also at one time a small valley which ran diagonally into the Kidron. An upper reach of this valley can be recognized outside the present north city wall to the northeast of Herod's Gate and, inside the wall, to the northeast and east of the Church of St. Anne. The now filled-in reservoir called Birket Israin or Pool of Israel lay in this valley too, and it reached the edge of the Kidron Valley about one hundred meters south of St. Stephen's Gate.

Between St. Anne's Valley (if the valley just described may be so named) and the Kidron Valley on one side, and the Tyropoeon Valley on the other, the ridge of which we have been speaking continues to the north and northwest. This northern part of what we have called all together the northeastern hill, Josephus dignifies by designating as a separate hill. In his enumeration (*War* v 4, 1 §§137-138) the first hill is what we called the southwestern hill with the "upper city"; the second is our southeastern hill with the "lower city" and the Acra; the third is the temple hill; and the fourth is this northwestern extension of the temple hill. Of the last and fourth hill Josephus says (*War* v 5, 8 §246) that it was the highest of all the hills. If he means that it is the highest of the summits of the eastern ridge he is correct, but it is not as high as the summits of the western ridge, i.e., the northwestern and southwestern hills. This fourth hill, he also says (*War* v 4, 2 §149; v 5, 8 §246), was called Bezetha (Βεζεθά). The expanding population of Jerusalem made this a "recently built quarter" (*War* v 4, 2 §151) and as a city district it was called not only Bezetha from the hill but also New City (Καινόπολις).

Simons, *Jerusalem*, pp. 1-23 and especially p. 17, Fig. 4 and p. 24, Fig. 5 for elevations of rock levels, and Pl. VI facing p. 49 for relief map. For rock contours see also PEQ 1966, p. 134, Fig. 1. Plan: JF, cf. Kathleen M. Kenyon in PEQ 1966, p. 86 Fig. 4.

136. Air View of Jerusalem

This air view is taken from the east-southeast. Enclosed within the present-day wall is the Old City. Prominent in the foreground is the large rectangle of the temple area, with the Dome of the Rock near the center. To the left thereof is the site called Ophel on the southeastern ridge. Almost halfway to the top of the picture is the southwestern ridge. The cluster of buildings, one with a high tower, on this ridge, not far from the left margin of the picture and outside the present south wall of the city, is where "Sion" was later localized. At the angle about halfway along the western city wall is the Jaffa Gate and the Citadel with the "Tower of David." About halfway back across the city toward the temple area is the tall white tower of the Lutheran Church, and a short distance northeast of it are the domes of the Church of the Holy Sepulcher. About halfway along the course of the north wall is the Damascus Gate, halfway between it and the northeastern corner is Herod's Gate. In the eastern wall a short distance north of the temple area is St. Stephen's Gate, and a third of the way along the wall of the temple area itself is the Golden Gate, walled up. Around the northeastern corner of the city wall curves the road which descends into the Kidron Valley.

Photograph from Gustaf Dalman, *Hundert deutsche Fliegerbilder aus Palästina*. 1925, p. 13, Fig. 4. Photograph: courtesy C. Bertelsmann Verlag, Gütersloh.

137. The Access to the Gihon Spring

On the west side of the Kidron Valley at the foot of the southeastern hill and under the part thereof which is probably to be identified as Ophel, is a spring, the passageway leading down to which is shown in this photograph. This is undoubtedly the spring Gihon which is mentioned several times in the OT (I K 1:33, etc.). Its name (גיחון) is derived from a word (גיח) which means "to gush forth," and this may be connected with the fact that the spring is intermittent in action, gushing forth from its cave once or twice a day in the dry season and four or five times a day in the rainy season. In later times it has been known as Ain Sitti Maryam, the Spring of our Lady Mary, or the Virgin's Spring, or Umm ed-Daraj, "Mother of Steps," the last title referring to the thirty steps which lead down to it. The only other spring in the area is beyond the junction of the Kidron and the Hinnom valleys, 250 yards south of the southern end of the southeastern hill of which we have been speaking, and below the village of Silwan. This latter is almost certainly the spring which the OT calls En-rogel (Jos 15:7, etc.), known today as Bir Ayyub or Job's Well.

Simons, *Jerusalem*, pp. 45ff., 157ff. Photograph: JF.

1800 B.C., above it was some rebuilding which the excavator thought might date in the tenth century B.C. The photograph shows a portion of the massive wall, with rebuilding above. The boulder-built wall was evidently the east wall of the earliest town, the town of the Canaanite period. From the spring a tunnel ran west into the hill and connected with a shaft which came up inside the town walls. This gave the inhabitants protected access to the spring water from within the town, although they could also come to the mouth of the spring by a path down the hill and outside the wall.

Since the Egyptian execration texts of the nineteenth-eighteenth centuries (ANET p. 329) and the Amarna Letters of the fourteenth century (ANET pp. 487-489) mention the name of Jerusalem in the form Urushalim or Urusalim, the settlement behind the earliest wall just described may simply be called the earliest town of Jerusalem. In Jos 18:16 a tribal boundary is described which "goes down the valley of Hinnom, south of the shoulder of the Jebusites, and downward to En-rogel." The "shoulder" of the Jebusites must be the southeastern hill with which we have been dealing, and from this passage we learn that the inhabitants at this time were called Jebusites. The identification of the place is confirmed in Jos 15:8 where, after similar mention of "the southern shoulder of the Jebusite," a parenthetical notation adds, "that is, Jerusalem." From the name of the Jebusites their town was also called Jebus, as in Jg 19:10, "Jebus (that is, Jerusalem)." Similarly in I Ch 11:4 David and Israel went "to Jerusalem, that is Jebus, where the Jebusites were." Both II Sam 5:6-9 and I Ch 11:4-8 record the capture of the Jebusite town by David. At this point the place is also called "the stronghold of Zion," which is the first occurrence of the name Zion (ציון, Σιών) (II Sam 5:7; I Ch 11:5). The defensive strength of the stronghold was such that the Jebusites boasted that "the blind and the lame" could protect it

138. The Earliest Wall of Jerusalem above the Gihon Spring

The Gihon spring determined the location of the oldest settlement in the Jerusalem area. This was on the slope of the eastern ridge and the southeastern hill, above the spring. In excavations begun here in 1961 and 1962 Kathleen M. Kenyon found not far above the spring a massive wall, built of rough boulders. The date was established as early in Middle Bronze Age II, c.

(II Sam 5:6). David said: "Whoever would smite the Jebusites, let him get up the water shaft to attack 'the lame and the blind' " (II Sam 5:8). This suggests that the water tunnel and shaft described above in connection with the Gihon spring gave the attackers their initial access to the town. After the capture of the place by David it was called "the city of David" (II Sam 5:9;

I Ch 11:7). He and his successors probably used and re-used the old Jebusite wall for several centuries.

Kathleen M. Kenyon, "Excavations in Jerusalem," in PEQ 1962, pp. 72-89, especially pp. 76, 82; 1963, pp. 7-21, especially pp. 9-10 and Pl. III A; 1964, pp. 7-18; 1965, pp. 11-14; *Jerusalem*, p. 22 and Figs. 3-4 on pp. 20-21 (for the Jebusite water tunnel); pp. 24f. and Pls. 10-11 (for the Jebusite wall). Photograph: JF.

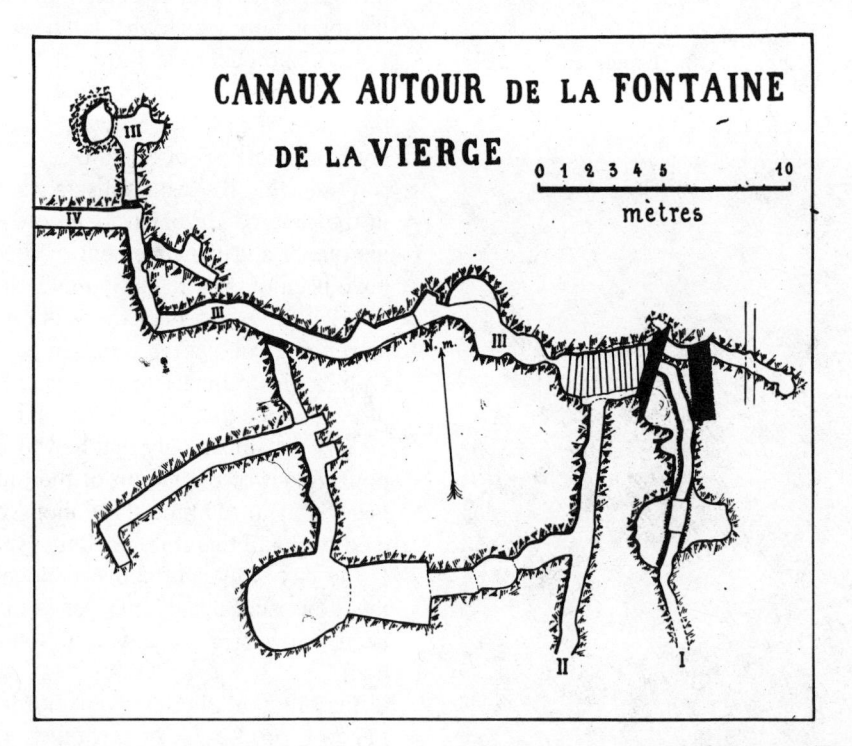

139. Plan of the Tunnels connected with the Gihon Spring

At the upper right-hand side of this plan are shown the steps which lead down to the Gihon Spring. Referring to the Roman numerals on the plan, Tunnel III leads from the spring westward under Ophel to a basin (the last number III), beside which is the bottom of the shaft which comes down from inside the earliest wall of Jerusalem, as described in the preceding section (No. 138). This was the water system of the Jebusites. Tunnels I and II start out from a reservoir which once existed underneath the modern steps to the spring. Tunnel I, the older of the two, has been followed for only a relatively short distance and its ultimate destination is not known. Tunnel II has been followed in most of its sections. This tunnel emerges on the side of the Kidron Valley and continues there as an open-air channel of gentle gradient. Some parts, however, were covered with flat stones and some parts went underground again because of the higher level of the rock. Apertures in the east side-wall of the channel made it possible to draw

water from it to irrigate the terraces of the western side of the Kidron. Finally this aqueduct led to the pool below the pool of Siloam now known as Birket el-Hamra, or Red Pool. The canal is probably referred to in Is 8:6 in the words about "the waters of Shiloah that flow gently," while the pool to which it led is probably the Pool of Shelah mentioned in Neh 3:15. The root from which these names are derived (שלח) means to send or consign and would be appropriate to an aqueduct in which water was sent to its destination.

Under the threat of the invasion of Sennacherib Hezekiah stopped "the water of the springs that were outside the city" (II Ch 32:3), which may mean that he obstructed the outlets of the aqueduct just mentioned. Also he "closed the upper outlet of the waters of Gihon and directed them down to the west side of the city of David" (II Ch 32:30), and he "made the pool (ברכה) and the conduit and brought water into the city" (II K 20:20). These references almost certainly describe the construction of what is known as "Hezekiah's tunnel." This tunnel turns off from channel III in the plan (No. 139) and proceeds as channel IV. All together it is an underground aqueduct winding through the rock 1,749 feet from the Gihon spring to the Pool of Siloam. In 1880 a Hebrew inscription was found on the wall of the tunnel about six meters in from the Siloam mouth, which told how it was dug by excavators who worked from both ends and finally met in the middle of the mountain. When they finished "the water started flowing from the source to the pool (ברכה), twelve hundred cubits."

H. Vincent, *Jérusalem sous terre*. London: Horace Cox, 1911; Simons, *Jerusalem*, pp. 175-188. Photograph: courtesy École Biblique et Archéologique Française.

140. Gihon Spring Cavern and Tunnel Opening

This photograph shows the cavern in which the Gihon spring was contained at a time when the water was diverted to facilitate exploration of the various canals which are connected with the spring (No. 139). In the far wall is the opening of the tunnel which, after the work of Hezekiah, led all the way to the Pool of Siloam.

Photograph: courtesy École Biblique et Archéologique Française.

141. The Pool of Siloam

The "pool" which is mentioned by the same Hebrew word in II K 20:20 and in the inscription found in Heze-

kiah's tunnel (No. 139) is the reservoir into which this aqueduct empties. When Jn 9:7 refers to the pool of Siloam (ἡ κολυμβήθρα τοῦ Σιλωάμ) the explanation is added that the name means "Sent." Since Shiloah has this meaning in Hebrew (cf. No. 139) and was transcribed in the LXX as Σιλωάμ (Is 8:6), it seems probable that the name of the earlier water channel on the edge of the Kidron Valley (cf. No. 139) was transferred to the water system of Hezekiah and used for the name of the pool into which the latter conduit emptied. The same name occurs in Latin in the forms Siloae, Silua, etc., and in Arabic as Selwan or Silwan, the latter being the name of the village directly across the Kidron Valley from the Pool of Siloam.

While this reservoir must have been inside the city in the time of Hezekiah to accord with the purpose of his tunnel and the statement of II K 20:20, it seems to have been outside the city in NT times: Josephus (*War* v 4, 2 §145) speaks of the wall on that side of the city as running "above the fountain of Siloam" and on past Ophlas (i.e., Ophel) to the eastern portico of the temple. The fact that he calls Siloam a fountain or spring (πηγή) may mean only that he was thinking of the water pouring out of the mouth of the tunnel, but it may also mean that in his time the Gihon spring itself was covered over and therefore possibly even unknown to many. If the city wall ran "above" Siloam, as Josephus says, the "tower in Siloam" mentioned in Lk 13:4 could have been a tower in the city wall somewhere "above" the pool.

In 333 the Pilgrim from Bordeaux (Geyer p. 22; LPPTS I, pp. 22-23; CCSL CLXXV, p. 16; cf. above No. 135) came out of Jerusalem to go up on Mount Sion (which by then was considered to be the southwestern hill rather than the southeastern) and saw "below in the valley beside the wall" a pool called Siloah (*Silua*).

It had a fourfold portico (*quadriporticus*), and there was another large pool outside it. Since Hadrian built a fourfold shrine to the Nymphs (τετρανύμφον) in Aelia Capitolina (*Chronicon Paschale* [631-641] MPG XCII, col. 613), and since a shrine to goddesses specially associated with springs might well have been at this pool, it has been surmised (Kopp p. 373) that the fourfold portico might have been the structure of Hadrian. As for the large pool farther outside, this probably corresponds with the Birket el-Hamra, or Red Pool, which is still recognizable farther down the valley. The Anonymous of Piacenza (570) (Geyer pp. 175-176; LPPTS II, pp. 20-21; CCSL CLXXV, p. 166) found a domed basilica (*basilica volubilis*) above Siloam (*super Siloa*). Beneath this, the Anonymous says, Siloam rises, with two marble baths, one for men and one for women. In these waters many cures have taken place, and even lepers have been cleansed. In front of the atrium of the church is a large pool, artificially constructed, in which people are constantly bathing. "For at certain hours the fountain (*fons*) of its own accord pours forth many waters (*aquas multas*) which run down through the valley of Gethsemane, which is also called Josaphat, as far as the Jordan. . . ." At that time, it is also stated in this record, the fountain of Siloam was included within the city walls because the Empress Eudocia (she was the estranged wife of the Emperor Theodosius II [408-450], lived at Jerusalem 444-460, and died there) had added the walls at this place to the city. In the Madaba Mosaic Map, which was probably executed only ten years before the coming of the Anonymous of Piacenza, there was shown at the extreme southeast corner of Jerusalem a building with an open dome (damage to the mosaic renders it scarcely recognizable any more, see the photograph in No. 185). The location and the architecture, which would fit a building over a watering place, make it probable that this was a representation of the church which the Anonymous saw.

This church was presumably destroyed by the Persians only a few years later (614), and may not have been rebuilt. In 1897 F. J. Bliss and A. C. Dickie of the Palestine Exploration Fund found and excavated the ruins of a Byzantine church on the hill just above the Pool of of Siloam, and this must be the church of which we have been speaking. It was a basilica with nave and two side aisles. The bases of four large piers indicated that it was domed. At the eastern end the apse of the church was directly over the mouth of the water tunnel. In the nave and side aisles some portions of floor mosaic were still preserved. The excavations also uncovered an almost square court about seventy-two feet across, which was surrounded by a probably covered arcade. In the center was the large pool into which the tunnel emptied, and the structure was surely the *quadriporticus*

which the Bordeaux Pilgrim mentioned, which may go back, as surmised, to Hadrian.

After the excavations the people of Silwan erected a small mosque at the northwest corner of the original pool, the minaret of which still rises above the present pool. The photograph (No. 141) shows the mouth of the water tunnel and the pool of Siloam as they are today. Although the arch of the tunnel exit is more recent, the stumps of ancient columns may be seen. The tank itself, to which one descends by eighteen steps, is about fifty feet long and fifteen feet wide, much smaller than the ancient pool surrounded by the rectangular arcade. Here persons come to do their washing from the southern districts of Jerusalem and from the village of Silwan on the eastern side of the Kidron Valley. As the etymology explained above shows, the village derives its name from the pool and the inhabitants, in the same manner as Josephus (above), call the waters a spring, Ain Silwan.

Frederick J. Bliss and Archibald C. Dickie, *Excavations at Jerusalem, 1894-1897*. London: The Committee of the Palestine Exploration Fund, 1898, pp. 154-159, 178-230; Avi-Yonah in QDAP 2 (1932), p. 164 No. 107; Simons, *Jerusalem*, pp. 189-192. Photograph: JF.

142. The Great Rock beneath the Dome of the Rock

As established above (No. 138), "the city of David" was on the southeastern hill at Jerusalem above the Gihon spring. When the prophet Gad instructed David to make an offering to avert a plague from Israel, he told him to "go up" and erect an altar on the threshing

floor of Araunah the Jebusite (by which the destroying angel had been standing), and Araunah saw the king and his servants coming toward him when he "looked down" from where he was (II Sam 24:18ff.). The threshing floor was therefore probably in the relatively free, open land to the north of and higher than the "city of David" on the southeastern hill, i.e., it was on the northeastern hill and in the region which is now recognized as the temple area (see Nos. 135, 136). Near the center of this area from north to south and to the west of the center from east to west is a large outcropping of natural rock which forms the highest point of the entire hill. The rock (es-Sakhra in Arabic) is about 58 feet long, 51 feet across, and from 4 to 6½ feet high. It is shown here as now enclosed beneath the Dome of the Rock (Qubbet es-Sakhra) (No. 147) and surrounded immediately by a high wooden screen. As may be seen, there are channels and holes in the surface of the rock; there is also a hole at one side which communicates with a cave underneath. As a high and therefore breezy place the rock itself may have provided the threshing floor for Araunah, and thus the altar of David may have been erected directly upon it (FLAP pp. 179f.).

According to II Ch 3:1 the threshing floor of Ornan (a variant of the name Araunah), which was connected with David in the manner we have just seen, was on Mount Moriah. The name is the same as that of the land of Moriah, on one of the mountains of which Abraham was to offer Isaac but did not (Gen 22:2ff.). Whether the three-days' journey of Abraham from Beersheba on that occasion was actually to this site at Jerusalem, or to some other place as some believe (Nelson Glueck, *Rivers in the Desert, A History of the Negev.* New York: Farrar, Straus and Cudahy, 1959, pp. 62-64), the name Mount Moriah, at least from the time of the Chronicler on, was attached to the hill north of the "city of David" and to the area of the great rock which we have just described. On this mount, we are told in the same passage in II Ch 3:1, Solomon built the house of the Lord. The probability would seem to be that the altar of this temple, like the altar of David before it (cf. above), was on the sacred rock and, in this case, the sanctuary itself probably rose behind the rock, i.e., to the west (FLAP pp. 180, 326f.). This first temple or temple of Solomon was burned by the Chaldeans (II K 25:8f.; Jer 52:12f.), probably in 587 B.C. (FHBC §§323, 325).

In 539 Cyrus the Persian took Babylon and decreed the rebuilding of the temple (II Ch 36:23; Ezr 1:2-3; 6:3-5). At the urging of Haggai (1:2ff.) and Zechariah (4:9f.), and under Zerubbabel, grandson of Jehoiachin (Mt 1:12) and governor of Judah (Hag 1:1), this work was undertaken and, with the support of a fresh decree by Darius (Ezr 6:7-8), finished in the sixth year of the latter king (Ezr 6:15), 515 B.C. (FLAP p. 234). In comparison with the first temple of Solomon this second temple or temple of Zerubbabel may have been more modest, for its state, at least during construction, seems to have elicited unfavorable comparisons by those who remembered the first house (Ezr 3:12; Hag 2:3). Also the Talmud (Yoma 21b SBT II 5, p. 94 cf. JE XII, p. 96) says that it lacked five things which were in Solomon's temple, namely, the ark, the fire, the Shekinah or divine manifestation, the Holy Spirit, and the Urim and Thummim.

Josephus tells us that the temple was also restored (*War* I 21, 1 §401) or built (*Ant.* XV 11, 1 §380) by Herod the Great. In the two passages just cited apparently contradictory statements are made as to when this work was begun. Upon analysis, the date indicated was probably the nineteenth regnal year of Herod which began in the spring of 19 B.C. (FHBC §§430-432). Besides the reasons given in FHBC, Professor Vardaman suggests that this date is further supported when it is remembered (see Josephus, *Ant.* XV 10, 4) that the year 20/19 B.C. was a drought year, and thus it would be natural for Herod the Great to use in temple construction the labor of his subjects, whose taxes he had to remit in large part. Perhaps the wine shipments to Herod from Italy (which are dated to this very year), were sent by Augustus to help alleviate this drought and famine (see Y. Yadin, *Masada.* London: Weidenfeld and Nicolson, 1966, p. 189).

On account of Jewish religious sensibilities the temple proper or sanctuary (ναός) was built by the labor of priests only, and it was completed in a year and six months; Herod occupied himself with the porticoes and outer courts (τὰς στοὰς καὶ τοὺς ἔξω περιβόλους), and these were finished in eight years (*Ant.* XV 11, 5-6 §§420-421). Jn 2:20 can mean that other work was still being done on the temple in the time of Jesus. In *War* V 1, 5 §36 Josephus says that Herod Agrippa II (who was in charge of the temple although the various territories over which he reigned did not include Judea [FLAP p. 262 n. 42]) brought beams from Lebanon to underprop the sanctuary, and in *Ant.* XX 9, 7 §219 he reports that the whole temple precinct (τὸ ἱερόν) was completed in the time of the procurator Albinus (62-64). In A.D. 70, only a few years later, this third temple or temple of Herod was burned by the Romans, and both Josephus (*War* VI 4, 5 and 8 §§250, 268) and the Rabbis (FLAP p. 328 n. 4) say that this was done on the very month and day (the ninth day of Ab = Jul/Aug) when, long before, the first temple was burned by the Babylonians.

E. T. Richmond, *The Dome of the Rock in Jerusalem.* Oxford: Clarendon Press, 1924. Photograph: The Matson Photo Service, Alhambra, Calif.

116

JERUSALEM

143. Plan of the Temple of Herod

With respect to Herod's temple the chief literary sources of information are Josephus, particularly in *Ant.* xv 11 §§380ff. and *War* v 5 §§184ff., and the tractate *Middoth* ("Measurements") in the Mishna (SBT v 6; DM pp. 589-598), a work written probably

in the middle of the second century. As Vardaman observes, a new Dead Sea Scroll, known as the "Temple Scroll," has just been announced at the time of this writing, which promises to add some useful information concerning other temple aspirations of an Essenic nature around the time of Herod the Great (see *New York Times*, Oct. 23, 1967, pp. 1c and 4c; and *ibid.*,

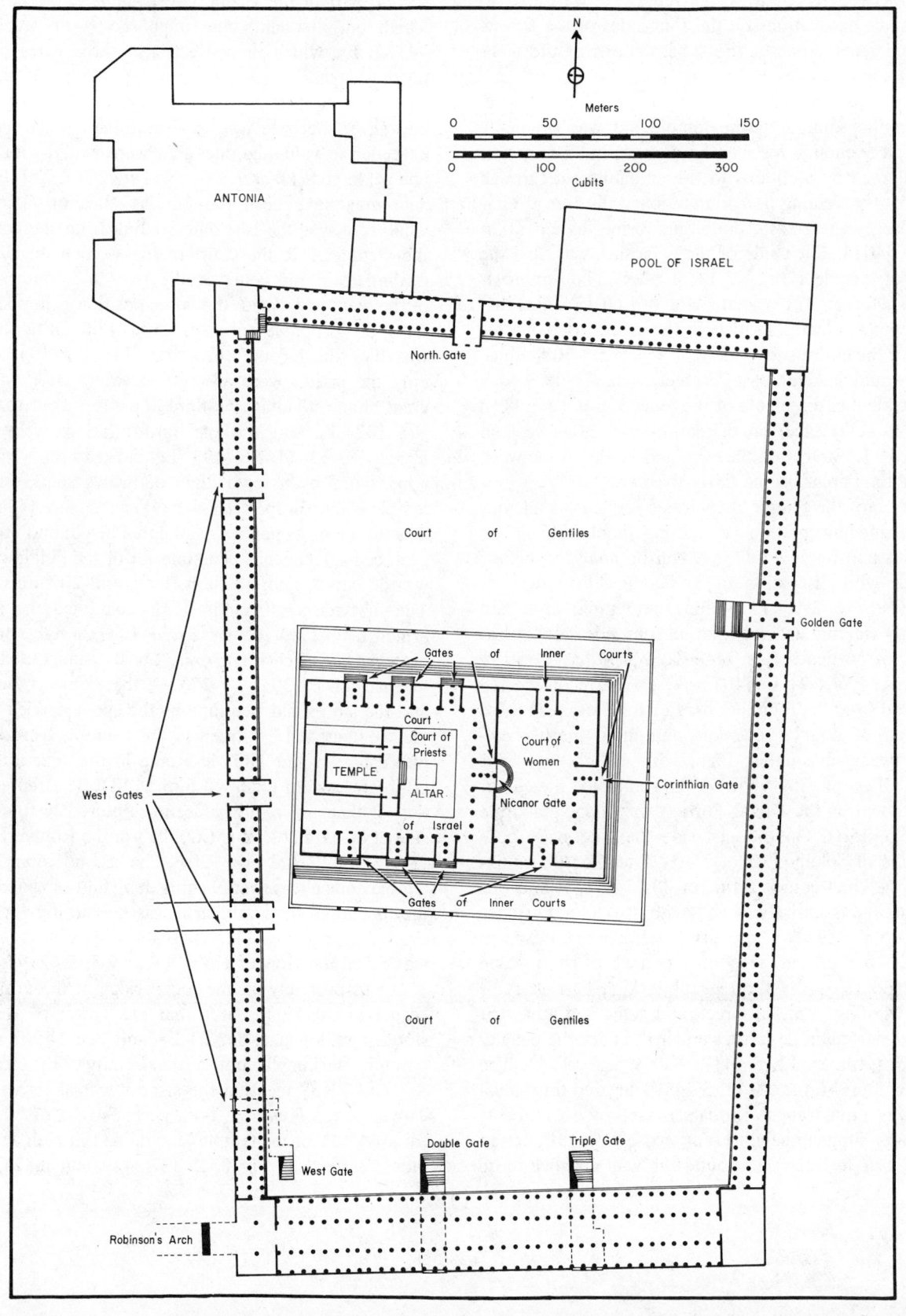

Nov. 11, 1967, pp. 1c and 10c; *Time*, Nov. 3, 1967, p. 83; *American Schools of Oriental Research Newsletter* 7 [Nov. 13, 1967], pp. 1-10).

As far as archeological exploration is concerned, very little of this has been possible inasmuch as the temple area has long been a sacred place of the Muslim religion. Probably the most important work is that done in 1867-1870 by Charles Warren, who was able to make some excavations on the four sides of the temple area and reach some of the substructures of the walls by shafts and tunnels.

Josephus (*War* v 5, 1 §§184ff.) says that the level area on the summit of the temple hill was originally barely large enough for shrine and altar, but was gradually enlarged by additions to the embankment through the ages. By erecting new foundation walls Herod himself enlarged the area to double its former extent (*War* I 21, 1 §401). Each side of the enclosure was now the length of a stade (*Ant.* xv 11, 3 §400), i.e., approximately 600 feet. The tractate *Middoth* (II 1) states that the "temple mount" (which is the name used in this work for the entire enclosed area) measured 500 cubits, which would make at least 750 feet on each side. Today the outside measurements of the temple area have been reckoned at 929 feet on the south side, 1,041 feet on the north, 1,556 feet on the east, and 1,596 on the west, and the total area is some thirty-five acres.

Entry into the temple area was by gates on all four sides. Some information concerning them is given by Josephus and by *Middoth* and will be analyzed below, together with discussion of archeological vestiges of them (Nos. 152-154). Within the temple area and evidently running around it on all four sides were great "stoas" or porticoes (μεγάλαι στοαὶ περὶ τὸ ἱερόν) which, Josephus (*War* I 21, 1 §401) says, were reconstructed by Herod from the foundations. For the most part these consisted of double rows of monolithic marble columns, twenty-five cubits high, with ceilings of cedar panels (*War* v 5, 2 §190). On the south side the colonnade known as the Royal Portico was more elaborate still (No. 150). On the east side the colonnade bore the name of Solomon (No. 154). These porticoes enclosed the "first court" (*Ant.* xv 11, 5 §417), and this large area was entirely paved with varicolored stones (*War* v 5, 2 §192). The court was freely open even to Gentiles, but at the edge of the next court a stone balustrade (δρύφακτος) three cubits high carried slabs giving warning, some in Greek and some in Latin, that no foreigner might go farther under threat of the penalty of death (*Ant.* xv 11, 5 §417; *War* v 5, 2 §194). The "second court" (*Ant.* xv 11, 5 §417) beyond this balustrade was a quadrangular area screened by a wall of its own, forty cubits in height (*War* v 5, 2 §196). Fourteen steps led up to a terrace around the wall and five more

steps ascended to the gates in the wall. The first part of this entire second court was walled off to make a special place into which all Jewish women, whether natives of the country or visitors from abroad, were allowed to go. Access was through a gate on the north side, a gate on the south, and a gate on the east. Opposite the last gate another gate allowed access to the second part of the second court, namely, the part into which only Israelite men might go (*Ant.* xv 11, 5 §418), for which there were also three gates on the north side and three gates on the south. Of the ten gates now accounted for, nine were overlaid with gold and silver, but one was of Corinthian bronze and far exceeded in value the ones that were plated with silver and set in gold (*War* v 5, 2-3 §§198, 201). This bronze gate may have been the famous Nicanor Gate, but whether it was the east gate leading from the court of the Gentiles into the court of the women, or the one leading from the court of the women into the court of the men, is debated, the latter position being perhaps the more probable (cf. No. 154). Still farther within was the "third court" (*Ant.* xv 11, 5 §419), which only the priests were allowed to enter. Here was the great altar (standing, we think, on the sacred rock, cf. No. 142) on which whole burnt-offerings were sacrificed (*Ant.* xv 11, 5 §419). Behind it to the west, and approached by its own flight of twelve steps, was the temple edifice proper (ὁ ναός) (*War* v 5, 4-5 §§207ff.). The façade of its porch was of equal height and breadth, each being 100 cubits. The interior of the building itself was 60 cubits high, 60 cubits long, and 20 cubits wide. The first room, 40 cubits long, contained the seven-armed lampstand (cf. Ex 25:31-40), the table for the bread of presence (cf. Ex 25:23-30), and the altar of incense (cf. Ex 30:1-10, 27). Of these objects the table and the lampstand were among the spoils carried off by the Romans and exhibited in the triumphal procession of Vespasian and Titus in Rome in the year after the fall of Jerusalem (*War* VII 5, 5 §148). The representation of them may still be seen sculptured on the inner side of the Arch of Titus (A.D. 81) in the Roman Forum (FLAP p. 329 and Fig. 120). The second room of the temple edifice was twenty cubits long and screened from the first room by a veil. In it was no furniture whatsoever. "Unapproachable, inviolable, invisible to all, it was called the Holy of Holy" (*War* v 5, 5 §219).

It was probably on the rocky ridge at the northwest corner of the temple area that the Tower of Hananel stood, mentioned in Jer 31:38 and Zec 14:10 as apparently marking the northern extremity of the city. Neh 3:1 and 12:39 mention the same tower along with the Tower of the Hundred, both perhaps part of "the fortress (בירה) of the temple" mentioned in Neh 2:8 (Simons, *Jerusalem*, pp. 231, 327, 429 and n. 2). This tower or fortress probably became the citadel which Josephus (*Ant.* xv 11, 4 §403) says the Hasmoneans built and called Baris (βᾶρις), a name perhaps derived from the Hebrew word for "fortress" seen in Neh 2:8. Herod, in turn, made the Baris stronger for the safety and protection of the temple and, to please his friend Mark Antony, called it Antonia (*Ant.* xv 11, 4 §409). Josephus (*War* v 5, 8 §§238ff.) says the Antonia, the work of King Herod, was built upon a rock 50 cubits high, precipitous on all sides, and covered with smooth flagstones to make it unclimbable. The edifice itself rose to a height of 40 cubits and had towers at its four corners, three of these 50 cubits high, the one at the southeast angle 70 cubits high to command a view of the whole area of the temple. Inside the Antonia resembled a palace in spaciousness and appointments. Broad courtyards provided accommodation for troops, and a Roman cohort was quartered there permanently. Particularly at festivals the soldiers kept watch on the people in the temple area to repress any insurrectionary movement. Stairs led down at the point where the fortress impinged on the temple area porticoes, so that the soldiers could descend rapidly. The tribune and his soldiers and centurions ran down these steps to apprehend Paul (Ac 21:32) and from them Paul addressed the people (Ac 21:35). Also there was a secret underground passage from the Antonia to the eastern gate of the inner sacred court (*Ant.* xv 11, 7 §424). Including the Antonia and the porticoes, the entire circuit of the temple precinct was six stades (*War* v 5, 2 §192).

The plan (No. 143) corresponds with the preceding description of the temple of Herod. Letters and numbers indicate the following features which have been mentioned already or will be mentioned in later sections: A, the temple edifice proper; B, the altar of burnt-offerings; C, the court of the priests; D, the court of the Israelite men; E, gate, probably the Nicanor Gate; F, the court of the women; G, gate, possibly the Nicanor Gate; H-H, the court of the Gentiles; I¹, opening of a western gate; I² and I³, openings of the Double and the Triple Gates; J, Robinson's arch; K, L, M, and N, western gates; O, northern gate; P, Golden Gate; 1-10, gates of the inner courts. Enclosing the area are the porticoes: on the east is Solomon's, on the south the Royal Portico. At the northwest corner is the Antonia, at the northeast a onetime pool known as Birket Israin. Note also that the scale for measurements indicates cubits as well as meters.

F. J. Hollis, *The Archaeology of Herod's Temple, with a Commentary on the Tractate "Middoth."* 1934; Watzinger II, pp. 35-45; Galling, *Reallexikon*, cols. 518-519; André Parrot, *The Temple of Jerusalem* (Studies in Biblical Archaeology 5). New York: Philosophical Library, 1955; Vincent, *Jérusalem*, pp. 711-713. Photograph: Vincent, *Jérusalem*, pl. CII, courtesy École Biblique et Archéologique Française.

144. Fragment of a Warning Inscription from Herod's Temple

As we have just seen (No. 143), Josephus says that there were warning inscriptions in Greek and in Latin on the balustrade between the court of the Gentiles and the next more inward court of the temple area, "prohibiting the entrance of a foreigner (ἀλλοεθνῆ) under threat of the penalty of death" (*Ant.* xv 11, 5 §417). One of these stone slabs with a complete inscription in Greek was found by Clermont-Ganneau and published in 1871 (FLAP p. 325 and Fig. 118). The text reads:

ΜΗΘΕΝΑΑΛΛΟΓΕΝΗΕΙΣΠΟ
ΡΕΥΕΣΘΑΙΕΝΤΟΣΤΟΥΠΕ
ΡΙΤΟΙΕΡΟΝΤΡΥΦΑΚΤΟΥΚΑΙ
ΠΕΡΙΒΟΛΟΥΟΣΔΑΝΛΗ
ΦΘΗΕΑΥΤΩΑΙΤΙΟΣΕΣ
ΤΑΙΔΙΑΤΟΕΞΑΚΟΛΟΥ
ΘΕΙΝΘΑΝΑΤΟΝ

μηθένα ἀλλογενῆ εἰσπο-
ρεύεσθαι ἐντὸς τοῦ πε-
ρὶ τὸ ἱερὸν τρυφάκτου καὶ
περιβόλου. ὃς δ' ἂν λη-
φθῇ ἑαυτῷ αἴτιος ἔσ-
ται διὰ τὸ ἐξακολου-
θεῖν θάνατον.

No foreigner is to en-
ter within the balus-
trade and enclosure around
the temple area. Whoever is
caught will have himself to
blame for his death which
will follow.

The fragment of a second stone with a portion of the
same Greek inscription was found outside St. Stephen's
Gate (No. 197) and published in 1938. This stone is
shown in the illustration (No. 144). In this case the
inscription was arranged in six lines rather than seven.
The words at least partly preserved are the following,
and from them it would appear that the wording of the
entire inscription was identical (except for αὐτῷ instead
of ἑαυτῷ) with the complete example above:

MH]ΘΕΝΑΑΛΛ[ΟΓΕΝΗ
ΕΝ]ΤΟΣΤΟΥΠ[ΕΡΙ . . . . ΤΡΥ
ΦΑΚ]ΤΟΥΚΑΙ[
Λ]ΗΦΘΗΑΥ[ΤΩΙ
Δ]ΙΑΤΟΕΞ[ΑΚΟΛΟΥΘΕΙΝ
ΘΑΝΑΤΟΝ

μη]θένα ἀλλ[ογενῆ
ἐν]τὸς τοῦ π[ερὶ . . . . τρυ-
φάκ]του καὶ[
λ]ηφθῇ αὐ[τῷ
δ]ιὰ τὸ ἐξ[ακολουθεῖν
θάνατ[ον.

Interestingly enough, in this case at least, the letters of
the inscription were painted red and, when the stone
was found, the incised marks still retained much of the
red paint with which they were filled.

Charles Clermont-Ganneau in PEF 1871, p. 132; *Une stèle
du temple de Jérusalem.* Paris, 1872; L.-H. Vincent in RB
30 (1921), p. 263 and n. 1 and Pl. IV; J. H. Iliffe, "The
ΘΑΝΑΤΟΣ Inscription from Herod's Temple, Fragment of
a Second Copy," in QDAP 6 (1938), pp. 1-3 and Pl. I. Photograph: Palestine Archaeological Museum.

145. Latin Inscription of Hadrian on Stone built into Southern Temple Enclosure Wall

When Jerusalem was captured by the Romans in
A.D. 70 the temple and almost the whole city were razed
to the ground. Afterward, to have custody of Jerusalem,
the tenth legion (Fretensis) was left as a local garrison
(*War* VII 1, 1-3 §§1-17). In A.D. 130 (SHJP I ii p. 295
n. 76) Hadrian traveled in the East, went from Syria
to Egypt and back again, and visited Jerusalem twice.
In his *Weights and Measures* (14 [54c], ed. Dean, p.
30) Epiphanius gives an account of what must be this
journey even though he dates it erroneously only forty-
seven years after the destruction of Jerusalem, i.e., in
117. He calls Hadrian "a man who loved to see places,"
and writes:

And he went up to Jerusalem, the famous and
illustrious city which Titus, the son of Vespasian,
overthrew in the second year of his reign [the second year of Vespasian's reign began on July 1,
A.D. 70]. And he found the temple of God trodden
down and the whole city devastated save for a few
houses and the church of God, which was small,
where the disciples, when they had returned after
the Savior had ascended from the Mount of Olives,
went to the upper room. For there it had been built,
that is, in that portion of Zion which escaped destruction, together with blocks of houses in the
neighborhood of Zion and the seven synagogues
which alone remained standing in Zion, like solitary huts, one of which remained until the time of
Maximona the bishop and Constantine the king,
"like a booth in a vineyard," as it is written [Is 1:
8]. Therefore Hadrian made up his mind to (re)-
build the city, but not the temple. . . . And he
gave to the city that was being built his own name
and the appellation of the royal title. For as he
was named Aelius Hadrian, so he also named the
city Aelia.

Dio (A.D. 229) gives an account of the same journey
of Hadrian in his *Roman History* (LXIX 12), and writes:
"At Jerusalem he founded a city in place of the one
which had been razed to the ground, naming it Aelia

Capitolina, and on the site of the temple of the god he raised a new temple to Jupiter." Dio continues to explain that this brought on a war, because the Jews felt it was intolerable for foreign races to be settled in their city and foreign religious rites planted there. As long as Hadrian was still close by in Egypt and again in Syria they remained quiet, but when he went farther away they revolted openly. This was of course the uprising which was led by Bar Kokhba and lasted from 132 to 135.

From Epiphanius we derive a vivid picture of the desolation of Jerusalem and the temple area after the destruction by Titus. From Dio we understand that it was Hadrian's projected building of a new pagan city and a new pagan temple which provoked the revolt of Bar Kokhba. Presumably only after that revolt was quelled was the full project carried out. The two sources appear to differ, however, as to whether Hadrian built a temple at Jerusalem. But perhaps Epiphanius only means to say that Hadrian did not propose to rebuild the Jewish temple. If that is his meaning it would not necessarily exclude the building of a pagan temple, which Dio says Hadrian did. That a pagan sanctuary was actually established on the former site of the Jewish temple is confirmed by other writers including Jerome, who says (*Commentary on Isaiah* I ii 9 CCSL LXXIII, p. 33): "Where once were the temple and the religion of God, there a statue of Hadrian and an idol of Jupiter are set up together." The fact that the Bordeaux Pilgrim (Geyer p. 22; LPPTS I, p. 22; CCSL CLXXV, p. 16) mentions two statues of Hadrian in the temple area probably can be explained by supposing that the statues were so similar in appearance that he mistakenly took the statue of Jupiter to be a second statue of the emperor.

Interestingly enough there is now built into the south enclosure wall of the temple area, just east of the Double Gate (No. 152), a block of stone which must have been the base of this statue of Hadrian. Although the stone is built into the wall with the inscription upside down, we have inverted the drawing of it in the illustration (No. 145), and the text is easily read, as follows:

TITO AEL HADRIANO
ANTONINO AUG PIO
PP PONTIF AUGUR
D D

In the inscription PP abbreviates *pater patriae*, and DD abbreviates *decreto decurionum*, the *decuriones* being the members of the senate of a Roman colony. The whole text is:

To Titus Aelius Hadrianus
Antoninus Augustus Pius,
the father of his country, pontifex, augur.
By decree of the decurions.

Other archeological witness to the history recounted above is provided by the coins of Aelia. They give the official name of the city as *Col(onia) Ael(ia) Cap(itolina)*, and most often show the figure of Jupiter (SHJP I ii, pp. 315-317 and n. 130). From Jerome in his Latin version of the *Chronicle of Eusebius* (ed. Helm, 2d ed. 1956, p. 201) we learn that as a final sign of the subjection of the Jews to the Roman power a swine was sculptured in the marble of the gate through which one went out of Aelia toward Bethlehem. Such a sculptured stone has not, however, been found.

Simons, *Jerusalem*, pp. 358-359 and Fig. 51; Vincent, *Jérusalem*, pp. 753-782; *Jérusalem nouvelle*, pp. 1-39; Leo Kadman, *The Coins of Aelia Capitolina*. Corpus Nummorum Palaestinensium, I. Jerusalem: Universitas Publishers, 1956. Photograph: courtesy Palestine Archaeological Museum.

146. General View of the Temple Area from the Air

When Hadrian rebuilt Jerusalem as the pagan city of Aelia Capitolina he not only settled foreign races there, as Dio said (cf. No. 145), but also prohibited the Jews from coming there. In this connection Eusebius (*Ch. Hist.* IV 6, 3) cites the Jewish Christian Ariston of Pella as his source, and states that after the Jew-

ish rebellion was crushed Hadrian commanded by a legal decree that the whole Jewish nation "should be absolutely prevented from entering from thenceforth even the district round Jerusalem, so that not even from a distance could it see its fatherland (πατρῷον)." From Justin (*Apology* I 47; cf. *Dialogue with Trypho* 16 and 92) we learn that the prohibition was enforced by the death penalty. From Tertullian (*An Answer to the Jews* 13 ANF III, p. 169) we gather that the interdict extended in geographical scope to include Bethlehem. And from Eusebius in another work (*Theophany* IV 20 ed. Gressmann p. 197) we obtain the impression that the edict was still in effect in his time; he speaks as if of a contemporary situation when he says that it is only the Jews who may not set foot in Jerusalem and may not even see the land of their fathers from afar.

When the Bordeaux Pilgrim (333) came to Jerusalem, however, we learn that at least in his time there was in effect a sort of annual amnesty for the Jews which permitted them to enter Jerusalem for a visit on a special occasion. After his mention, noted above (No. 145), of the two statues in the temple area which he took to be those of Hadrian, this pilgrim writes (Geyer p. 22; LPPTS I, p. 22; CCSL CLXXV, p. 16): ". . . and not far from the statues there is a perforated stone (*lapis pertusus*), to which the Jews come every year and anoint it, bewail themselves with groans, rend their garments, and so depart."

Since Hadrian's statues (actually one of himself and one of Jupiter, as we have seen) were presumably erected on the site of the former Jewish sanctuary, it is probable that the stone mentioned by the Bordeaux Pilgrim was the sacred rock itself, and his description of it as "perforated" will accord with the fact that various holes are still to be seen in that rock (No. 142). So there was an annual lamentation by the Jews for their destroyed temple, conducted at the rock in the temple area, and obviously permitted by the Romans. Whether this was first allowed in the time of the Bordeaux Pilgrim, i.e., under the Emperor Constantine, or had already been a practice for a longer time, is not clear. Jerome (*Commentary on Zephaniah* I 15-16; SHJP I ii, pp. 320-321) also, in the latter part of the fourth century, describes this annual visit of the Jews to weep for the temple and makes it plain that this was done on the very anniversary of the destruction, i.e., on the ninth day of Ab (No. 142).

Although the traveler from Bordeaux certainly appears to have included the temple area in the itinerary of his pilgrimage, that area had remained in ruins ever since the Roman destruction. At about the same time Eusebius (*Demonstratio Evangelica* VIII 3, 12 ed. Heikel p. 393) says that it is a sad spectacle to see with the eyes the stones of the temple area and even of the

formerly inaccessible sanctuary taken away to be used for the temple precincts of idols, or for the erection of places for public pageants. He also comments (*Theophany* IV 18 ed. Gressmann p. 193), with only slight exaggeration, that in his time the desolation of the temple had already lasted more than four times as long as the seventy years of ruin in the time of the Baylonians. This long-continued desolation was nothing other, Eusebius declares, than a fulfillment of the words of Jesus, for when Jesus said, "Behold, your house is left unto you desolate" (Mt 23:38), he meant by "house" nothing other than the temple, and when the disciples were impressed by the mighty buildings of the temple area he spoke plainly of this area and said, "There shall not be left here one stone upon another, that shall not be thrown down" (Mt 24:2). The example of the Bordeaux Pilgrim shows that Christians continued to visit the site of the temple, and the fact that the statues of Hadrian and Jupiter are no longer mentioned after Jerome (cf. No. 145) may mean that these evidences of paganism were removed from the site because of Christian influence. But Eutychius (940), who quotes the same two Gospel passages as Eusebius (Mt 23:38; 24: 2), makes it evident that the Christians considered these words as a curse upon the temple area, and says explicitly: "On this account the Christians left it desolate, and built no church upon it" (*Annales* II; MPG 111, cols. 1099-1100; LPPTS XI, p. 67).

Such was evidently the desolate state of the temple area when the Muslims came. In A.H. 17 = A.D. 638 Jerusalem fell to the conqueror 'Umar (634-644), second successor (*khalifah*) of Muhammad. According to Eutychius in the record just cited 'Umar himself cleared the sacred stone (No. 142) in the temple area of much accumulated filth. Some then proposed to build a temple and use the stone to mark the direction of prayer (*qibla*). 'Umar, however, said that the temple should be built so that the stone was in the back of it. The Byzantine chronographer Theophanes (751-818) says that 'Umar began to build the temple in Jerusalem in the year of the world 6135 which would correspond, in the Alexandrian system, to A.D. 643 = A.H. 22/23 (MPG 108, col. 700; Vincent, *Jérusalem nouvelle*, p. 413), but other sources would make the date a few years earlier (CEMA I, p. 25). Theophanes also says in the same passage that when 'Umar experienced difficulty in the collapse of his building, the Jews persuaded him that he could not succeed unless he took down the cross which was above on the summit of the Mount of Olives (on the Church of the Ascension, No. 120), and 'Umar did remove the cross. Although Eutychius and Theophanes speak of 'Umar as erecting a "temple," it may be assumed that any building which he put up in the temple area, and in the orientation of which the *qibla* or direction of prayer was a factor, was in fact a mosque. This is confirmed by Arculf (670), who was in Jerusalem within thirty years of the date of 'Umar's work, for he explicitly uses for the building he describes in the temple area the term "house of prayer" which corresponds to the Arabic *masjid* or "mosque," meaning literally a place of prostration (FAWR p. 508). Arculf's record reads as follows (Geyer pp. 226-227; LPPTS III, pp. 4-5; CCSL CLXXV, p. 186):

> But in that renowned place where once the temple had been magnificently constructed, placed in the neighborhood of the wall from the east (*in vicinia muri ab oriente locatum*), the Saracens now frequent a quadrangular house of prayer (*quadrangulam orationis domum*), which they have built rudely, constructing it by raising planks and great beams on some remains of ruins (*super quasdam ruinarum reliquias*); which house, it is said, can hold three thousand men at once.

If the "wall from the east" may be taken to mean the enclosure wall running from the southeastern angle along the south side of the temple area, then the "remains of ruins" on which the planks and beams of the new structure were placed may have been what remained at that time of the colonnades of the famous Royal Portico (No. 150). If the mosque was placed thus at the southern side of the temple area it would indeed leave the sacred stone to the back of it, i.e., to the north, as 'Umar said. This would also place the building in more or less the same position as the present al-Aqsa mosque (No. 148). In the latter building the mihrab, or niche marking the direction of prayer (No. 149), is in the south wall, and a line drawn from it and perpendicular to the wall will pass directly through the center of the sacred stone (CEMA I, p. 25).

From this time on, then, the temple area was in the hands of the Muslims. As such it has been known as the Haram esh-Sherif or Noble Sanctuary. This photograph (No. 146) is a general view of the area from the air.

Vincent, *Jérusalem nouvelle*, pp. 875-1006. Photograph: courtesy Palestine Archaeological Museum.

147. Windows in the Dome of the Rock

It was the Umayyad Caliph of Damascus, 'Abd al-Malik (685-705), who erected a building over the sacred rock (No. 142) itself. This was not a mosque but a shrine or "place of witness" (*mashhad*) and is known today simply as the Dome of the Rock (Qubbet es-Sakhra) (FAWR pp. 511-513). In architecture it is essentially a circle of four masonry piers and twelve marble columns around the rock, upholding a drum and dome, and around this circle an octagonal colonnade and outer octagonal wall. In each face of the wall are five windows and in the drum above sixteen windows. A Kufic inscription in the interior of the building still shows the date, "in the year two and seventy" (A.H. 72 = A.D. 691), which falls in the reign of 'Abd al-Malik and substantiates the attribution of the building to that Caliph. It is thus the oldest existing monument of Muslim architecture. Extensive mosaic decorations still remaining in the interior enhance the beauty of the building; they derive also in large part from the seventh century. In the inscription just mentioned the name of the 'Abbasid Caliph al-Ma'mun (813-833) has been inserted—he probably made restorations on the structure. In A.H. 407 = A.D. 1016 the wooden dome fell and was reconstructed soon after, to be replaced recently by a new aluminum dome. In 1189 Saladin put slabs of marble on the walls of the building. On the lower windows is the name of Soliman the Magnificent, sultan of Turkey, and the date A.H. 935 = A.D. 1528; the beautiful tile work in blue and white and green around the windows was added by this ruler in 1561. The windows have perforations filled with colored glass in a variety of designs. Above are passages from the Qur'an, in beautifully interwoven characters, running around the building like a frieze. The photograph looks up at a pair of the windows from the outside, and also shows a portion of the inscription above.

CEMA I, pp. 42-94, and pp. 147-228 (by Marguerite van Berchem on the mosaics). Photograph: JF.

148. The Mosque al-Aqsa

As we have seen (No. 146), the first Muslim mosque in the Jerusalem temple area was probably built by the Caliph 'Umar soon after the taking of Jerusalem in A.H. 17 = A.D. 638. From the description by Arculf (670), we think that it was built in the ruins of the former Royal Portico on the south side of the area, and we learn that it was "rudely" constructed. This first mosque was replaced by a second and no doubt better structure, erected by the Umayyad Caliph al-Walid (705-715), son of 'Abd al-Malik, builder of the Dome of the Rock; he himself was also the builder of the Great Mosque at Damascus (FAWR pp. 513-514). Confirmation of the enterprise at this time is found in the dated contemporary Aphrodito papyri (CEMA II, p. 119), which record the sending of laborers from Egypt to work on "the mosque of Jerusalem" (μασγιδα Ἱεροσο-λύμων). In the course of time the mosque was frequently damaged by earthquakes and there is evidence for repeated rebuildings by several more Caliphs: the third mosque was built by al-Mansur perhaps in A.H. 154 = A.D. 771, the fourth by al-Mahdi perhaps in A.H. 163 = A.D. 780, and the fifth by az-Zahir in A.H. 426 = A.D. 1035. While there is also work by the Crusaders to the east and west of the nave, in quite large part the mosque as it still stands is the work of az-Zahir, and his plan was probably much the same as that of al-Mahdi. From the description of the mosque of al-Mahdi by Muqaddasi (985) (LPPTS III, pp. 41-42) and the portions of masonry which remain probably from the mosque of az-Zahir and earlier ones (CEMA II, p. 123 Fig. 119),

it appears that the plan of that time had a central nave and seven aisles on either side (four more on each side than in the present mosque). On the north end of the building was the great central doorway, opposite the mihrab, with seven more doors to the right of it and seven to the left. Inside the aisles were marked out with rows of columns and of round piers. Over the central part of the building was a mighty gable roof with a magnificent dome rising behind it.

In the Qur'an (Sura XVII 1 tr. A. Yusuf Ali p. 693) it is related that Muhammad was taken for "a journey by night" (the famous Mi'raj on which he went on through the seven heavens) from the Sacred Mosque, i.e., the Ka'bah at Mecca, to the Farthest Mosque. This name, Masjid al-Aqsa or the Farthest Mosque, designated the temple site in Jerusalem as the farthest west place of worship known to the Arabs in that time. Thus it became the name of the mosque built in the temple area and is so used, for example, by Muqaddasi in his description (cited above) of the mosque which stood there in his time.

Today the Aqsa Mosque stands perpendicularly against the south wall of the temple enclosure, and occupies an area eighty-eight yards long and sixty yards wide not including the various annexes on either side. On the north the entrance is through a porch consisting of seven arcades. The porch was constructed by Melik el-Mu'azzam 'Isa (who died in 1227), and has been restored since. The photograph shows this north end of the mosque, with the seven arcades of the porch.

CEMA II, pp. 119-126. Photograph: JF.

149. Minbar and Corner of Mihrab in the Aqsa Mosque

At the south end of the Aqsa Mosque, marking the direction of prayer toward Mecca, is the niche known as the mihrab and, beside it, the minbar or pulpit. The pulpit, carved in wood and inlaid with ivory and mother-of-pearl, was made in A.H. 564 = A.D. 1168 by an artist of Aleppo. The prayer niche, flanked by marble columns, is a part of a restoration in this end of the mosque by Saladin in A.H. 583 = A.D. 1187. The photograph, taken over the heads of worshipers kneeling on prayer rugs in front of the niche, shows the upper side of the mihrab and most of the minbar.

Photograph: JF.

150. The Pinnacle of the Temple

As Josephus said (*War* I 21, 1 §401; cf. above No. 143), in order to enlarge the temple area Herod had to erect new foundation walls. In another passage (*War* V 5, 1 §188) the same author says that where the foundations were lowest the walls were built up from a depth of three hundred cubits or even more, a depth which was not fully apparent, however, since the ravines

were in considerable part filled up. It is evident that these foundation walls must have been set well down the slopes of the Kidron Valley on the east and the Tyropoeon on the west, and that is where the present walls of the temple area are found. At the southeastern corner the level of the temple area is now about forty feet above the ground outside but the slope of the valley has been built up a great deal in the course of time. Warren (*Recovery of Jerusalem*, p. 117) sank a shaft here outside the wall and then drove a gallery in until he struck the enclosure wall at a point thirty-two feet to the north of the southeastern angle; at this point he was at a level of 2,312 feet above the sea, or 106 feet below the average level of the temple area above (cf. No. 135). Inside the walls it was then necessary to build up a level area. This was probably done not only by the filling of the former ravines to which Josephus referred (above) but also by the building of extensive substructures. At any rate Josephus says (*War* V 3, 1 §102) that during the siege of Jerusalem by the Romans people took refuge in the temple vaults (εἰς τοὺς ὑπονόμους τοῦ ἱεροῦ), i.e., in underground passages beneath the temple area, and (*War* VI 9, 3 §§429-430) that when the city fell the victors found more than two thousand dead down there (ἐν τοῖς ὑπονόμοις). Actually the south side of the temple area rests almost entirely upon massive and vaulted substructures. Those under the southwest corner are inaccessible, but those in the middle are reached by a flight of eighteen steps which descends east of the entrance of the al-Aqsa mosque, and those in the southeast corner are similarly accessible from that part of the area. These last are known as Solomon's Stables, a name used by the Crusaders who probably rebuilt this structure and used it for their horses and camels. Here there are 13 rows of vaults 30 feet high with 88 piers, and the floor of the hall is over 40 feet below the surface of the temple area above. From the angle of the enclosure the structure extends more than 260 feet to the west and 200 feet to the north. Herodian masonry may still be seen in the lower part of some of the piers; the upper part represents the rebuilding of the Crusader period.

Above ground here on the south end of the temple area there was, according to Josephus (*Ant.* xv 11, 4 §§411ff.), a Royal Portico (ἡ βασίλειος στοά) of four rows of columns and three aisles, stretching from the eastern to the western ravine, i.e., from the Kidron to the Tyropoeon. Josephus says that if one went up on the high rooftop of this portico and looked down into the ravine, doubtless meaning the Kidron Valley on the east, "he would become dizzy and his vision would be unable to reach the end of so measureless a depth." In Mt 4:5 and Lk 4:9 there is mention of "the pinnacle of the temple" (τὸ πτερύγιον τοῦ ἱεροῦ). Here the word used for "temple" is that which refers to the entire area, and the word "pinnacle" is literally a "little wing," a term used for the tip or extremity of anything, hence the edge or the summit. It is a probable supposition, therefore, that the point referred to was precisely that described by Josephus at the southeastern corner of the temple area, high above the Kidron. The photograph (No. 150) looks up from the south toward the southeastern angle of the temple enclosure wall which, according to the reasoning just presented, was the "pinnacle" of the temple. At this corner, Herodian masonry

survives to within about twenty feet of the top of the wall.

Charles Warren, *The Recovery of Jerusalem.* New York: D. Appleton & Company, 1872; *Underground Jerusalem.* London: Richard Bentley and Son, 1876; Charles Warren and C. L. Conder, *The Survey of Western Palestine,* v, *Jerusalem.* London, 1884. Kenyon, *Jerusalem,* Pls. 60-62, 64. Photograph: JF.

151. The Wailing Wall

In the southern section of the east wall of the temple enclosure (cf. No. 150) and also in the south wall and in the west wall the lower courses of stone are all of the same style. This style is characterized by the use of very large blocks of what is now called drafted stone. When Edward Robinson observed this stonework in 1838 (*Biblical Researches,* I, p. 286) he spoke of the stones as beveled and described them as having the whole face first hewn and squared, then a narrow strip cut along the edge a quarter or half an inch lower than the rest of the surface. In some cases the stone has a depressed plane surface of this sort around the margin and a plane surface in the center too, in other cases there are rough projections in the center and these blocks may perhaps have been intended to be hidden underground. A synonymous expression also in use for a drafted stone is a bordered stone. Masonry of the sort just described is found not only here in lower courses of the temple area enclosure wall but also in lower courses of the so-called Tower of David in the Citadel in Jerusalem (QDAP 14 [1950], pp. 140ff., Plate XLVII, 3), and in the great enclosure wall known as the Haram el-Khalil at the traditional Cave of Machpelah in Hebron (L. H. Vincent and E. J. H. Mackay, *Hébron, le Ḥaram el-Khalîl.* 1923, pp. 99f., 102f., 108f.). In the Tower of David we undoubtedly have the surviving base of Herod's tower called Phasael (No. 158), the masonry of Hebron is most probably Herodian even though Josephus does not speak of building work there by Herod, and the masonry just described in the east, south, and west walls of the temple enclosure at Jerusalem is most probably Herodian too (Simons, *Jerusalem,* pp. 270, 324 n. 1, 384-391, 412, 422f.).

At the southwest angle of the temple enclosure the Tyropoeon Valley runs diagonally under the corner of the temple area. At a place one hundred yards north of the angle there is a depression where relatively low courses of the enclosure wall may readily be seen. We have already quoted (No. 146) the statement of the Bordeaux Pilgrim (Geyer p. 22; LPPTS I, p. 22; CCSL CLXXV, p. 16) concerning the "perforated stone" near the statues of Hadrian, to which the Jews came every year to make lamentation for the destroyed temple, and have judged that this stone was none other than the great

sacred rock itself (No. 142). In the course of time, however, the place of Jewish lamentation came to be on the outside of the stretch of wall on the west side of the temple enclosure which we have just described. A small portion of this wall is shown in the photograph (No. 151). In speaking of the foundation walls of the temple enclosure Josephus (*War* v 5, 1 §189) mentions stones which measured forty cubits. Elsewhere he speaks of the temple building proper as built of stones which were twenty-five (*Ant.* xv 11, 1 §392) or even forty-five (*War* v 5, 6 §224) cubits in length. While all of these figures are probably exaggerations, the stones before us in the first five or six courses in the Wailing Wall are certainly very large, mostly around fifteen feet long and three to four feet high. Also they are smooth-faced marginally drafted blocks, of the kind we have described as probably typical of the work of Herod the Great. Above these courses are four courses of smooth undrafted stones which are probably of the Roman or Byzantine period, and above these are smaller stones representing Arabic and Turkish work.

At the exterior base of the south wall of the temple area, Israeli archeologists began new excavations in 1968. In press reports in the summer of that year they were reported to have exposed about twelve yards of the Temple wall which had not been visible before. Also sample trenches dug at various points near the southern wall gave evidence that there had been a large formal square in front of the temple area on that side. Visitors would move across this square and through the Double Gate (No. 152), which served as the main entrance to the temple. In front of the Double Gate a small fragment of a stone utensil was found, with the Hebrew word *corban* (cf. Mk 7:11 Greek κορβάν for Hebrew קָרְבָּן), meaning offering or sacrifice, which makes it probable that this was an actual instrument used in the Herodian temple and, if so, the first such ever found (for the ossuaries found in the same excavations, see below No. 263).

Simons, *Jerusalem*, p. 361 and note 1; *The New York Times* July 11, 1968, p. 18c; August 15, 1968, p. 14c (newspaper references by Vardaman). Photograph: JF.

152. The Double Gate

In the enclosure wall of the temple area, as described by Josephus and *Middoth*, there were a number of gates. Josephus describes four gates on the west side (*Ant.* xv 11, 5 §410), says that there were "gates in the middle" on the south side (*ibid.*) and, in telling about the Roman attack, speaks of a gate on the north side of the temple area (*War* II 19, 5 §537; VI 4, 1 §222). The fact that he does not mention a gate on the east side is probably only an inadvertent omission, for in

his basic description he speaks of the north side of the temple area (*Ant.* xv 11, 4 §403) and of the west side (xv 11, 5 §410), and then of the fourth front facing south (xv §411) without having accounted for a third side at all. *Middoth* (I 1 and 3) states that there were five gates to the temple mount, two Huldah Gates on the south, the Kiponus Gate on the west, the Tadi Gate on the north, and the Eastern Gate on which was portrayed the Palace of Shushan.

On the south side of the temple enclosure may be seen two gates which are about seventy meters apart and now walled up. They are known as the Double Gate and the Triple Gate. From their position they are most probably to be identified with the gates in the middle on the south side mentioned by Josephus, and with the two Huldah Gates mentioned in *Middoth*. Assuming this identification we may call them the Western and the Eastern Huldah Gates. The photograph (No. 152) shows in its present state the Double Gate or the Western Huldah Gate. An extraneous building encroaches on the left, and the ornamental archivolt is from a reconstruction possibly in the sixth or seventh century. Behind and above the archivolt, however, may be seen part of an enormous lintel stone, five and one-half meters long and nearly two meters thick, with drafted margins. This and other large stones notably visible in the lower right-hand corner are surely Herodian. Inside this double gate is a double vaulted vestibule and a tunnel-like passage which rises in inclines to an opening on the main level of the temple area above. Presumably it became necessary to construct this subterranean connection when the temple area was filled in above and when Herod's Royal Portico (cf. No. 150) was built. In the vestibule and passageway Herodian masonry is still extant. Today the passage runs under the al-Aqsa mosque, a little to the east of its central aisle, and comes out in front of the mosque.

Watzinger II, pp. 35-38; Spencer Corbett, "Some Observations on the Gateways to the Herodian Temple in Jerusalem," in PEQ 1952, pp. 7-14 and especially Pl. I. Photograph: courtesy Palestine Archaeological Museum.

153. The Triple Gate

In accordance with the evidence given in the preceding section (No. 152), this gate, seventy meters east of the Double Gate, is almost surely the site of the Eastern Huldah Gate of Herod's temple. The triple arches, now walled up, are from a medieval alteration. Originally the gate probably had the same plan as the Western Huldah Gate, i.e., was a double gate with vaulted passages behind it leading up into the temple area above. In the photograph there can still be seen near the lower left-hand corner a portion of an immense jamb stone which probably survives from the Herodian structure. If these gates, the Double and the Triple, with their tunnel-like passages to the temple area, are as we believe the Huldah Gates of *Middoth*, it makes plausible the hypothesis (C. Schick in ZDPV 22 [1899], pp. 94-97) that explains their name from the Hebrew word חלדה, which means "mole" as well as "weasel" (in Lev 11:29 the related חלד is translated "weasel" in RSV, but "mole" in the New Translation of the Torah by The Jewish Publication Society of America [1962]). There was also a prophetess by the name of Huldah (perhaps from the same root), mentioned in II K 22:14; II Ch 34:22, and there could have been some historical connection between this personage and these gates but, if so, we do not know what it was.

Photograph: courtesy École Biblique et Archéologique Française.

154. The Golden Gate

As far as the east side of the temple area is concerned, Josephus (*Ant.* xx 9, 7 §§220-221) mentions an east portico (στοά) which he attributes to Solomon (cf. No. 143, no doubt the Solomon's Portico of Jn 10: 23; Ac 3:11; 5:12) but (probably by inadvertence, as we think, cf. No. 152) does not mention any gate. *Middoth* I 3, however, speaks of "the Eastern Gate on which was portrayed the Palace of Shushan" (cf. No. 152). Shushan, or Susa, was a capital of the Persian Empire (Est 1:2; Dan 8:2, etc.) and representation of the Shushan palace on the Jerusalem gate was intended, according to a Rabbinical tradition (*Menahoth* 98a SBT V 2, p. 599), to make the people "ever mindful whence they came," and presumably therewith to commemorate the permission granted by the kings of Persia for the rebuilding of the temple (cf. No. 142). We may therefore call the east gate of the temple area the Shushan Gate.

In Ac 3:2, 10 there is mention of the Beautiful Gate (ἡ θύρα ἡ ὡραία and ἡ ὡραία πύλη) of the temple. In the narrative a lame man was laid at this gate so that he would be in position to ask alms "of those who entered the temple" (Ac 3:2). Here he also saw Peter and John when they were "about to go into the temple" (Ac 3:3) and, being made able to walk, he "entered the temple with them" (Ac 3:8). The word used for "temple" in all three of these statements is not the word which designates the sanctuary or temple building proper (ναός) but is the word which is normally used to designate the entire temple area (ἱερόν).* Therefore the gate at which the man was laid was probably a gate in the outer enclosure wall through which people came into the temple area. After his healing the man went on with Peter and John into the temple area. At this point "all the people ran together to them in the portico called Solomon's" (Ac 3:11). Since this was the portico on the east side, as Josephus tells us (above), the gate from which the apostles and the formerly lame man had just come must also have been on the east side. If this is correct the Beautiful Gate of Ac 3:2, 10 must have been the Shushan Gate. It is true that in Ac 3:11 there is a reading in Codex Bezae (D) different from that of the other major manuscripts from which we have just quoted a portion of this verse. The reading in Codex Bezae describes the action of the healed man and of the people at the point of verse 11 as follows: "But when Peter and John were going out he went with them holding on to them, and they [the people], astonished, stood in the portico called Solomon's." This can simply

* Yet, as Professor Vardaman points out, the use of ἱερόν is also to be noted at the Nabatean temple at Si'a in Syria. There the term is equivalent to the Aramaic *birtha* (בירתא), both of which terms refer to the sanctuary (to Baal Shamayin) proper. This Nabatean temple at Si'a was in the territory of Herod and the temple was constructed at the same time Herod's temple at Jerusalem was built. See M. de Vogüé, *Syria Centrale*, p. 38; CIL II, No. 163; Enno Littmann, *Princeton Expedition to Syria, Semitic Inscriptions*, pp. 85-90, for a fuller form of the Nabatean text. See also, for ἱερόν, Gerhard Kittel, *Theologisches Wörterbuch zum Neuen Testament*, Vol. Θ-Κ, 232ff. (Eng. ed.).

mean that the man who was healed at the eastern gate and then went on into the temple area with the apostles was now going back out with them and was the object of this excited attention in Solomon's portico. But it can mean that the healing had taken place at a different gate farther within the temple area, from which the apostles and the man were now returning. In this case the guess frequently accepted is that the Beautiful Gate was the Nicanor Gate. Josephus (*War* II 17, 3 §411) refers to "the bronze gate—that of the inner temple (τοῦ ἔνδον ἱεροῦ) facing eastward," and (*War* v 5, 3 §201) says that it was of Corinthian bronze and exceeded in value the other gates that were plated with silver and set in gold (cf. No. 143). *Middoth* II 3 gives the name Nicanor Gate (cf. No. 263) for what is probably the same gate of bronze. As to the location of this gate, it has commonly been held that the references in Josephus imply that it gave access from the east from the court of the Gentiles to the court of the women, but that the Mishna puts it between the court of the women and the court of the men; it is quite possible, however, that both sources are actually in agreement and that this gate gave access from the east from the court of the women to the court of the men (E. Stauffer in ZNW 44 [1952-53], pp. 44-66). So, it is held, Ac 3:11 in Codex Bezae supposes that the healing took place at the Nicanor Gate, the apostles and the lame man went on within and then, when they "were going out," and had reached Solomon's portico at the east side of the temple area the crowd stood there astonished. In fact, however, the reading of Ac 3:11 in Codex Bezae seems less likely than the reading in the other major manuscripts. Both readings agree that there was intense exictement (ἔκθαμβοι in B etc.; θαμβήθεντες in D) over the healing of the lame man. Surely it is more likely that this excitement arose immediately. This agrees with the supposition that the healing took place at the Shushan Gate and the crowd gathered around in their astonishment as soon as the lame man had stood up and walked on with Peter and John into the immediately adjacent portico called Solomon's.

The identification of the Beautiful Gate of Ac 3:2, 10 with the gate at the east side of the temple area, i.e., with the Shushan Gate, is affirmed by early Christian tradition. The Anonymous of Piacenza (Geyer pp. 170-171; LPPTS II, pp. 14-15; CCSL CLXXV, p. 163) tells of ascending by many steps from Gethsemane to the Gate of Jerusalem, and says: "This is the gate of the city which is connected with what was once the Beautiful Gate of the temple (*porta civitatis, quae cohaerit portae speciosae, quae fuit templi*), of which the threshold and floor still stand." Likewise Peter the Deacon (Geyer p. 108) says that below the temple to the east was the

Beautiful Gate where Peter healed the lame man, and where the Lord entered, seated upon the colt of the ass.

The references just given surely point to the part of the eastern temple area enclosure wall opposite the Garden of Gethsemane, where the so-called Golden Gate now stands. While the name of the Beautiful Gate is rendered correctly in the Latin text of Ac 3:2, 10 and also in the Anonymous of Piacenza and Peter the Deacon as Porta Speciosa, in the course of time the Greek word ὡραία ("beautiful") evidently suggested the Latin word *aurea* and gave rise to the name Porta Aurea or Golden Gate.

In Herod's temple this eastern gate was probably of the same plan as the two Huldah Gates (Nos. 152, 153), i.e., twin doorways led into a double vaulted vestibule from which there was access on up into the temple area. Like the Western Huldah Gate (No. 152) this gate was also rebuilt, perhaps in the sixth or seventh century, and like both the Double and the Triple Gate it is now completely walled up on the outside. On either side of the great double gateway, however, there are still in place two immense jamb stones which probably remain from the structure of Herod, i.e., the Shushan Gate which was probably also the Gate Beautiful. The photograph (No. 154) is taken from within the temple area and shows the vaulted vestibule inside the gate.

C. Schick, "Durch welches Thor ist Jesus am Palmsonntag in Jerusalem eingezogen?" in ZDPV 22 (1899), pp. 94-101; Spencer Corbett, "Some Observations on the Gateways to the Herodian Temple in Jerusalem," in PEQ 1952, pp. 7-14 and specially Fig. 2 on p. 10. Photograph: JF.

155. Robinson's Arch

Concerning the western side of the temple area Josephus writes (*Ant.* XV 11, 5 §410): "In the western part of the court there were four gates. The first led to the palace by a passage over the intervening ravine, two others led to the suburb, and the last led to the other part of the city, from which it was separated by many steps going down to the ravine and from here up again to the hill."

Middoth (I 3) mentions only one gate on the west side, presumably the most important of the four specified by Josephus, and says that it was called Kiponus, a name which some think could have been derived from the name of Coponius, the first Roman procurator of Judea (Simons, *Jerusalem*, p. 405, note 3). The passage which led over the ravine and to the palace, according to the quotation from Josephus just given, is presumably the same as the bridge which connected the temple area with the Xystus (probably the gymnasium built by Jason [II Macc 4:9]), and the same as the bridge which connected the temple area with the upper city which the same author mentions in *War* II 16, 3 §344 and VI 6, 2 §325. In two other passages (*Ant.* XIV 4, 2 §58; *War* I 7, 2 §143) Josephus mentions the bridge which connected the temple area with the city as in existence in the time of Pompey, therefore some such bridge was a feature of the approach to the temple even before the rebuilding by Herod.

The gate from which this bridge led was no doubt the most important on the west side of the temple area, and therefore probably the same as the Kiponus gate of *Middoth*. As the most important gate, Josephus (in the passage quoted above) mentions it first. The two other gates which "led to the suburb" would have been farther north in the western enclosure wall to give access to the new northern suburb. The last gate, Josephus says, led to "the other part of the city." In distinction from the northern suburb and the western area with the royal palace, this must have been the southwestern region of the city, and this last gate was therefore somewhere to the south of the main gate (Simons, *Jerusalem*, p. 424).

In 1838 Edward Robinson found several courses of stone projecting from the western temple enclosure wall at a point twelve meters north of the southwestern angle. As shown in the photograph (No. 155), these appear to be part of an ancient arch and they have been known ever since as "Robinson's Arch." The stones are twenty or more feet in length and about five feet in thickness. They are an integral part of the ancient wall, in contrast with the later stonework above. Measured along the wall the arch was over 15 meters long. From the curve of the arch its span, if complete, has been estimated at 12.80 meters. Robinson supposed the arch to have belonged to the bridge of which Josephus speaks in the passages cited above. Charles Warren dug shafts and galleries in a line west of the fragment and found a pier at the point to which the calculated span of the arch would reach, but beyond that found no evidence of further arches. It appears probable, therefore, that the bridge mentioned by Josephus was not at this point, and that "Robinson's Arch" in fact supported only

some kind of porch or balcony at the west end of the Royal Portico (cf. Nos. 143, 150).

Edward Robinson, *Biblical Researches in Palestine* (1856), I, pp. 287-289; Charles Warren, *Underground Jerusalem* (1876), pp. 310-316; Simons, *Jerusalem*, pp. 362-364, 424-425. Photograph: courtesy Palestine Archaeological Museum.

156. Wilson's Arch

In the western temple area enclosure wall 82 meters north of the southwestern angle is "Barclay's Gate," named after the American who discovered it in 1848. Here there is an enormous lintel 7.50 meters in length and over two meters in height (Simons, *Jerusalem*, p. 364). The gateway of which it was a part is now walled in and extends deep underground. Behind it is a passage, only partly accessible, which undoubtedly once led up into the temple area. A part of this passage has been made into a mosque called al-Buraq, the name coming from the traditional belief that here Muhammad tethered the horse al-Buraq on which he made his "night journey" (cf. No. 148) through the heavens (A. J. Wensinck, *A Handbook of Early Muhammadan Tradition* [1960], p. 40). From the same connections the gate is also called the Gate of the Prophet. Above it is a present-day portal in the enclosure wall of the Haram esh-Sherif, called Bab el-Mugharibeh or Gate of the Moors. In location and relationships it would seem as if Barclay's Gate could well have been the fourth gate mentioned by Josephus in the quotation above (No. 155), namely, the gate which gave access to "the other part of the city," i.e., probably the southwestern region, and from which many steps went down into the Tyropoeon, and from there up again to the hill (Simons, *Jerusalem*, p. 424).

Just north of Barclay's Gate is the stretch of ancient temple enclosure wall known as the Wailing Wall (No. 151) and beyond that, at a total distance of 100 meters from the southwestern angle of the temple enclosure, is "Wilson's Arch." At this point on the ground level above is the main entrance to the temple area from the west, a double gate called Bab es-Salam or the Gate of Peace, and Bab es-Silsileh or the Gate of the Chain, the latter providing also the name of the main west-east street which reaches the temple enclosure here, namely, the Street of the Gate of the Chain. Below ground under the Gate of the Chain is the ancient arch which has been called by his name ever since it was found in 1864 by Charles Wilson. In 1867 and later Charles Warren explored the arch and other subterranean vaults, passages, and chambers which are associated with it. He found that the bedrock of the Tyropoeon Valley was here at a depth of 80 feet beneath the present level of the Street of the Chain, and the top of Wilson's Arch is itself about 10 feet beneath the street level. The arch is 13.40 meters or 43 feet wide and has a span of 12.80 meters or 42 feet, the same span calculated for Robinson's Arch (No. 155). Wilson (*The Recovery of Jerusalem*, p. 13) judged the arch to be of the same age as the wall at the Wailing Place, which would mean that it was a part of the Herodian temple area. Probably because the arch is so perfectly preserved, Warren (*ibid.*, p. 64) was inclined to attribute it to the fifth or sixth century. One large chamber associated with the arch which Warren, himself a member of the Masonic order, called the Masonic Hall, he thought (*ibid.*, p. 68) to be perhaps as old as the temple enclosure walls. This chamber is built of well-joined, square stones and at each corner there were pilasters with capitals, the one at the northeast angle being fairly well preserved.

The first scientific investigation of Wilson's Arch since Warren's work was conducted by William F. Stinespring in 1963, 1965, and 1966. He found that the arch, built entirely of undrafted stones, was an integral part of the ancient enclosure wall of the temple area. Therefore it was probably built by Herod and was a part of the bridge which Josephus (cf. above No. 155) describes as connecting the temple area with the upper city including the Xystus and the palace. Since Josephus also mentions a bridge here in the time of Pompey, Herod's bridge probably replaced a smaller Maccabean bridge at this same location. As for the so-called Masonic Hall, the preliminary opinion is that this large chamber existed as far back as the Hellenistic period, perhaps in the time of Antiochus IV.

In the photograph (No. 156) the under side of the arch is shown, looking toward the north. In the curve of the arch at the right are rectangular indentations which may have held timber supports when the arch was being built. The far end is blocked by the wall of a cistern, so that only 27 feet of the total width of 43 feet can be seen. At the right is the opening of a shaft dug by Warren.

Wilson and Warren, *The Recovery of Jerusalem* (1872), pp. 13, 58-72; William F. Stinespring, "Wilson's Arch Revisited," in BA 29 (1966), pp. 27-36; "Wilson's Arch and the Masonic Hall, Summer 1966," in BA 30 (1967), pp. 27-31. Photograph: courtesy Palestine Archaeological Museum.

157. Looking toward the Northwestern Corner of the Temple Area

As for the north side of the temple area, we have seen (No. 152) that Josephus (*War* II 19, 5 §537; VI 4, 1 §222) says that there was a gate there, and that *Middoth* (I 3) gives the name of the portal on the north side as the Tadi Gate, a name the meaning of which is unknown. In the absence of any ancient architectural

remains which can be identified with such a gate, other evidence must be sought. Other than Josephus it is Nehemiah who gives the most detailed information on the topography of Jerusalem. Nehemiah came to Jerusalem to rebuild the walls in the twentieth year of Artaxerxes (Neh 2:1) and, assuming that this was Artaxerxes I (FLAP p. 238), the date was 445/444 B.C. The account of the rebuilding in Neh 3 begins and ends with the Sheep Gate. As we near the end of the circuit with Nehemiah we are obviously coming north from Ophel (3:27) and we encounter the East Gate (3:29), then the Hammiphkad Gate, translated Muster Gate in the RSV, and then "the upper chamber of the corner" (3:31). The "corner" mentioned in this sequence must be the northeast corner of the city wall. After that the next point specified is the Sheep Gate (3:32). Beyond the Sheep Gate, i.e., farther westward, in Nehemiah's description we come "as far as the Tower of the Hundred, as far as the Tower of Hananel" (3:1), after which we come to the Fish Gate (3:3). Likewise in Neh 12:39 the reverse sequence, i.e., from west to east, is the Fish Gate, the Tower of Hananel, the Tower of the Hundred, and the Sheep Gate. The sequence makes it most probable that the Fish Gate was in the north wall and this is at least in harmony with the fact that the fish merchants in Jerusalem at the time were men of Tyre (Neh 13:16), a city to the north. So the Sheep Gate was between the northeastern angle of the city wall and certain points farther west along the northern city wall, accordingly it was probably only a little way west of the northeastern angle. Perhaps, then, there was some correspondence between the Tadi Gate on the north side of the temple enclosure and this Sheep Gate.

By the same reasoning the Tower of the Hundred and the Tower of Hananel could well have been somewhere in the vicinity of the northwestern corner of the temple area. At least the first of these names has a probable military connotation, and it is a reasonable surmise (Simons, *Jerusalem*, p. 429 n. 2) that the two towers were the eastern and western towers of a fortification overlooking the temple which Neh 2:8 calls "the castle (בירה) which appertaineth to the house" (ASV), i.e., "the fortress of the temple" (RSV). As we have already observed (No. 143), this fortress was evidently replaced by the Hasmonean citadel called Baris (from the Hebrew *birah*) and then by the famous Antonia of Herod (Josephus, *Ant.* xv 11, 4 §§403, 409).

In the northwestern corner of the temple area there is still evidence of how the terrain rose in that direction toward the hill on which the Antonia stood. The photograph (No. 157) looks toward that corner of the area and shows the minaret (el-Gawanimeh) at the extreme northwestern angle and the large Muslim school building to the east of it. In that area the native rock rises

to the surface and slopes upward toward the angle, while vertical scarps are cut in it both to the east and to the south of the minaret. Concerning vestiges of the Antonia itself which have been found beyond, more will be said later (Nos. 174ff.).

Simons, *Jerusalem*, pp. 342f., 347, 429ff. Photograph: JF.

158. The Tower of David

As we have seen (No. 135), the southwestern hill of Jerusalem is the highest of the city's hills, and is separated by a cross valley from the northwestern hill. The point at the northwestern corner of the southwestern hill, which commands the saddle made by the cross valley between the southwestern hill and the northwestern hill, was obviously of great strategic importance. It is undoubtedly to this commanding high point that Josephus refers when he speaks (*War* v 4, 4 §173) of the crest of a lofty hill on which Herod the Great erected three mighty towers (*War* v 4, 3 §§161-171). One tower was called Hippicus after a friend of Herod who is otherwise unmentioned but was evidently deceased by this time. This tower had a quadrangular base which measured 25 cubits on each side and was solid throughout to a height of 30 cubits. Above this were a reservoir, a double-roofed chamber, and turrets and battlements, making the total height of the tower 80 cubits. The second tower was named for Herod's brother Phasael, who fell prisoner to the Parthians and took his own life (*War* I 13, 10 §271). This tower was 40 cubits in length and breadth, and 40 cubits also in the height of its solid base. Above this were sumptuous apartments, and the tower as a whole had the appearance of a palace. Its total height was about 90 cubits, and Josephus even compared it with the Pharos tower at Alexandria (cf. *War* IV 10, 5 §613). The third tower bore the name of Mariamme, a loved wife whom Herod put to death (*War* I 22, 5 §§443-444; *Ant.* xv 7, 4ff. §§218ff.). This tower was only 20 cubits in length and breadth and 55 cubits in height, but in its residential quarters was the most luxuriously appointed of all. The stones of these towers, Josephus says (*War* v 4, 4 §§174-175), were cut of white marble, each block 20 cubits long, 10 cubits broad, and 5 cubits deep, all so well joined together that each tower seemed like one natural rock.

Josephus came to his description of the three towers, from which we have excerpted the preceding information, from mention (*War* v 4, 3 §159) of a tower called Psephinus which was at the northwestern angle of the "third wall" (cf. No. 161), therefore he probably lists the towers from west to east, Hippicus, Phasael, and Mariamme. He also says (*War* v §§161, 173) that they were all three built into what he calls "the old wall." To the south of the towers Herod built his palace (*War* v 4, 4 §§176-183). This was enclosed within a wall of its own, had banquet halls and guest chambers, cloisters and gardens. So Herod secured his control of Jerusalem by the two palace-fortresses which we have now described, his palace with the adjacent three great towers here on the hill dominating the city, and the Antonia overlooking and commanding the temple area (*War* v 5, 8 §245; *Ant.* xv 8, 5 §292). When Titus took Jerusalem (A.D. 70) he razed Antonia (*War* VI 2, 1 §93) but left standing the loftiest of the towers, Phasaël, Hippicus, and Mariamme (which Josephus names here in the order of their height), as well as the portion of the wall enclosing the city on the west (*War* VII 1, 1 §§1-2). The towers were to show to posterity the kind of formidable defenses the Romans had overcome, the wall was to provide an encampment for the garrison that was to remain, namely, the Tenth Legion, called Fretensis (cf. No. 95).

Not only the Romans but also the Arabs, the Crusaders, and the Mamluke and Turkish governors continued to use the site of Herod's palace as the seat of government in Jerusalem, and the place is still known today as the Citadel of the city. Excavations in the Citadel were conducted from 1934 to 1948 by C. N. Johns. As it stands the present castle is mainly Mamluke work of the fourteenth century, but its plan follows that of the Crusader castle of the twelfth century. Among the several towers of this castle the most imposing is the one in the northeastern angle which has been known, at least since the time of the Crusaders, as the Tower of David. In fact, Arculf (670) already calls the adjacent gate the Gate of David (Geyer pp. 224, 242; LPPTS III, pp. 2, 19; CCSL CLXXV, pp. 185, 197), so the identification probably goes back that far or farther. The photograph (No. 158) shows the northwestern angle of this tower. The lower courses of stonework, which have been followed further underground by excavation, are of large drafted blocks like the stones in the ancient enclosure wall of the temple area (No. 151) and, like those, are almost surely of Herodian origin. The material is limestone which was white when it was cut and could easily have been called white marble by Josephus. The jointing is very close, which also accords with the statement of Josephus. The figures given by Josephus for the size of the stones in the towers are equivalent to approximately 9 by 4 by 2 meters, but he has probably exaggerated as is often the case. The largest of these stones are only about half that size, but they are not small, for the largest ones weigh 10 tons and the average weight is 5 tons. As revealed by the excavation the substructure of the Tower of David consists of sixteen courses in all. The total height of these courses is 19.70 meters, which is only a little less than the 40 cubits or 21 meters which Josephus gives as the height of the solid base of the Phasael tower. The base measurement of the Tower of David, 22 by 17 meters, is also not far from the same figure of 40 cubits given by Josephus for the length and breadth of Phasael. From these correspondences it is probable that the substructure of the Tower of David is actually the remaining base of Phasael. Hippicus, then, stood to the west of it, probably close to the present Jaffa Gate, and Mariamme must have been to the east. In the excavations Johns found that the base of the Tower of David was set into an older Jewish wall, which agrees with the statement of Josephus that all three towers were built into "the old wall."

C. N. Johns in PEQ 1940, pp. 36-56; and in QDAP 5 (1936), pp. 127-131; 6 (1938), p. 214; 9 (1942), pp. 207-209; 13 (1948), pp. 170-171; 14 (1950), pp. 121-190; Simons, *Jerusalem*, pp. 265-271; R. Pearce S. Hubbard in PEQ 1966, p. 133. Photograph: courtesy École Biblique et Archéologique Française.

159. Ancient Walls in the Russian Alexander Hospice

The foregoing discussion (Nos. 142ff.) has provided positive information concerning the temple area and the adjacent Antonia, and the palace of Herod with the three great towers nearby, Hippicus, Phasael, and Mariamme. Of temple, Antonia, and palace Josephus wrote (*War* v 5, 8 §245): "If the temple lay as a fortress over the city, Antonia dominated the temple, and the occupants of that post were the guards of all three; the upper town had its own fortress—Herod's palace." These points also provide the reference points from which to understand what Josephus says (*War* v 4, 1-3 §§136ff.) about the walls of the city.

There were, in the time of Josephus, three walls. The first and oldest wall (*War* v 4, 2 §§142-145), which Josephus attributes to David and Solomon and the kings after them, began at Hippicus, extended to the Xystus, joined the council-chamber, and terminated at the western portico of the temple. We have already seen (No. 158) that the tower of Hippicus probably stood near the present Jaffa Gate, and that the adjacent tower of Phasael is probably the present Tower of David. Also we have noted the statement of Josephus (*War* v 4, 3 §§161, 173) that the three towers, Hippicus, Phasael, and Mariamme, were all built by King Herod into "the old wall," which must be this same "first wall," and that portions of an old Jewish wall have in fact been found at the base of the Tower of David. This gives virtually positive identification, therefore, for the beginning point of the

first wall as described by Josephus. The Xystus was the gymnasium connected by bridge with the temple area (*War* II 16, 3 §344), therefore it lay somewhere westward across the Tyropoeon from the main west gate of the temple area, and the latter was probably about at the present Gate of the Chain (cf. Nos. 155f.). The council-chamber ($\beta o \nu \lambda \dot{\eta}$), not encountered previously, was probably the usual meeting place of the Sanhedrin, called in the Mishna by a name usually translated as the Chamber of Hewn Stone, but perhaps rather to be rendered the Chamber beside the Xystus (SHJP II i, pp. 190-191). *Middoth* v 4 places this chamber to the south in the temple court, but the description by Josephus sounds more as if it were between the Xystus and the temple area enclosure wall. The western portico of the temple is, of course, the colonnaded porch along the western side of the temple area. Therewith we are given a reasonably plain indication of the route of the first wall. It began at Hippicus, i.e., in the vicinity of the present Jaffa Gate, ran eastward along the north edge of the southwestern hill, parallel to the cross valley and probably not far from the present David Street and Street of the Chain, passed and enclosed the Xystus and the council-chamber, and reached the western enclosure wall and western colonnade of the temple area probably not far from the present Gate of the Chain. From the same point of the Hippicus tower this first wall also ran southward along the edge of the Hinnom Valley, swung above the Pool of Siloam and past Ophlas (by which Josephus must mean Ophel; cf. No. 135),

135

and finally joined the eastern portico of the temple area. With the problems of tracing this southern course of the first wall more precisely we are not, for our present purposes, particularly concerned. The southern line shown on our Plan, No. 135, corresponds with that in Kathleen M. Kenyon's "Provisional plan of Herodian Jerusalem" in PEQ 1966, p. 86 Fig. 4. A line farther south is shown by R. Pearce S. Hubbard in his plan of Jerusalem in the time of Herod the Great in PEQ 1966, p. 148 Fig. 7.

In the present context Josephus describes the second wall in a single sentence (*War* v 4, 2 §146): "The second wall started from the gate in the first wall which they called Gennath, and, enclosing only the northern district of the town, went up as far as Antonia." A little later (*War* v 4, 3 §158) he states that this "middle wall" (as he here calls it) had fourteen towers, which compares with sixty in the old wall and ninety in the third wall. Both the mention of "only" one district of Jerusalem as enclosed by the second wall, and the enumeration of a relatively small number of towers in it, suggest that the second wall was of relatively short length. Although Josephus does not say who built the second wall, it was obviously later than the first one since it began from a gate in that wall. It was also obviously earlier than the third wall, which was built by King Agrippa c. A.D. 41 (see No. 161), therefore must have been in existence in the time of Jesus. Probably both this wall and the first wall constituted the fortifications for the restoration of which Julius Caesar issued a decree of permission in 44 B.C. (*Ant.* XIV 10, 5 §200). The gate called Gennath is not mentioned elsewhere by Josephus, and is otherwise unknown too. Since Josephus says plainly that it was in the first wall, and that the second wall which started from it went on up to Antonia, the gate must have been somewhere in the northern stretch of the first wall, i.e., somewhere in the wall's more or less direct line between Hippicus and the temple area. Since Josephus otherwise describes both the first wall and the third wall as beginning at the tower Hippicus, it is not likely that the second wall began at or near Hippicus or Phasael or Mariamme; in that case he would surely have been more likely again to use one of the great and frequently mentioned towers as the point of reference. Therefore the gate in question must have been a considerable distance east of the towers.

In the attempt to find a likely location for the Gennath Gate in terms of the requirements worked out in the preceding paragraph, we may ask if there is any other or earlier evidence for a corresponding gate, even if known earlier under a different name. We have already seen (No. 157) that in Nehemiah's survey of the north wall of Jerusalem, which must have been more or less the first wall of Josephus, the Tower of the Hundred and the Tower of Hananel must have corresponded more or less with the later Antonia, and that the next point westward was the Fish Gate (Neh 3:1-3). Beyond that, still going westward, Nehemiah mentions the Old Gate (3:6), the Broad Wall (3:8), and the Tower of the Ovens (3:11). Coming back in the reverse direction in Neh 12:38-39 he lists the Tower of the Furnaces, the Broad Wall, the Gate of Ephraim, the Old Gate, and the Fish Gate. With respect to a yet earlier time, namely, the time of Jehoash king of Israel, II K 14:13 and II Ch 25:23 give a distance of 400 cubits from the Ephraim Gate to the Corner Gate, and II Ch 26:9 says that Uzziah king of Judah built a tower at the Corner Gate. When these sequences are compared it looks as if the Corner Gate could have been the site of the Tower of the Furnaces, and the latter have been the predecessor of one of Herod's towers, perhaps of Hippicus (Simons, *Jerusalem*, pp. 233-234). Coming eastward from the Corner Gate, the first gate mentioned is the Ephraim Gate, the name of which is appropriate to a gate in the north wall through which people went to and from the northern territories of Israel. This gate, we have seen, was 400 cubits from the Corner Gate. Assuming that the Corner Gate (and the Tower of the Furnaces) was approximately where the Citadel now is, and measuring eastward 400 cubits, i.e., about 200 meters or 650 feet, we come to a point in the first wall approximately where we have shown the point of origin of the second wall in our Plan, No. 135. A wall starting from this point and following some such course as shown on our Plan would indeed enclose a "northern district" of Jerusalem, as required by the statement of Josephus about the second wall. It would also follow a course that is reasonable from the point of view of topographical and defense considerations (C. T. Norris in PEQ 1946, pp. 19-37, against N. P. Clarke in PEQ 1944, pp. 199-212). The gate from which the wall started would remain a gate in the first wall and would give access to the countryside outside both walls. That there was indeed an unbuilt area outside the Ephraim Gate is shown by the fact that Neh 8:16 mentions "the square at the Gate of Ephraim." Also the name of the wall just beyond the Ephraim Gate to the west, which is called the Broad Wall in the usual text (Neh 12:38 and 3:8 RSV), may have been originally "the wall of the square" (RB 1 [1904], pp. 62, 67). The argument just followed, then, assumes that the Ephraim Gate of the older references had become known, at least by the time of Josephus, as the Gennath Gate (Simons, *Jerusalem*, pp. 300f.). Interestingly enough, the Greek name of the gate ($\Gamma\epsilon\nu\nu\acute{a}\theta$), which Josephus uses, may well be derived from the Hebrew word for "garden" which appears, for example, in the form גנת in Est 1:5, etc. From the name, then, the gate probably opened out to an area of gardens, and this should agree precisely with the location we have judged probable for the Gennath Gate.

It is natural to ask if there are any ancient architectural remains along more or less the line we have indicated as probable, on the above evidence, for the second wall in its course from the Gennath Gate to the Antonia. In this connection we shall have to refer to the Muristan and to certain present-day buildings in the vicinity of the Church of the Holy Sepulcher. The Muristan is a large relatively open area, to the south of the Church of the Holy Sepulcher, about 170 yards long and 150 yards wide. In the Middle Ages there were pilgrim inns and hospitals in this space, particularly institutions of the Knights of St. John (Hospitalers). Later under the Muslims one hospital was called by the Arabic-Persian name Muristan, and this name was eventually applied to the whole plot of ground. In the northeast corner of the area was the Church of Santa Maria Latina, built in 1030. This was replaced in 1898 by the German Lutheran *Erlöserkirche* or Church of the Redeemer, built along the lines of the original church, with a high tower which is a prominent landmark in present-day Jerusalem (cf. No. 136). Outside of the Muristan but not very far to the north and east of the Church of the Redeemer is the Russian Alexander Hospice, and north and west of it is a Coptic Convent. The Russian Hospice is perhaps 500 feet southeast of the present Church of the Holy Sepulcher, the Coptic Convent is yet closer to the Church of the Holy Sepulcher on the northeast.

In 1844 certain remains of ancient walls and columns were found at the point 500 feet southeast of the Church of the Holy Sepulcher where the Russian Alexander Hospice now stands, were excavated and investigated in following years, and are now carefully preserved in their original position inside the Hospice. There are portions of two walls, built of large plain stone blocks. One runs north and south, the other east and west, and the two meet at a right angle. The photograph (No. 159) shows this angle of intersection of the two walls in a view taken from the northeast. In the line of an eastward continuation of the east-west wall are two stone slabs worn as if from many footsteps and with depressions which could have had to do with the support of a gate (Vincent, *Jérusalem nouvelle*, p. 63, Fig. 32). This could be the threshold of a side entrance into a gate passage. That the region outside, i.e., to the west of, a north-south wall in this location was in fact at an earlier time a region outside of the inhabited city is shown by the discovery in 1885 of ancient rock-hewn tombs under the Coptic Convent to the northwest of the Russian Hospice (C. Schick in PEFQS 1887, pp. 154-155 and accompanying plans; and in PEFQS 1893, p. 192). If, then, Jesus came from condemnation by Pilate at the Antonia (Nos. 174ff.) to Golgotha, and if

the latter were where the Church of the Holy Sepulcher now is (Nos. 181ff.), he might indeed have gone "outside the gate" (Heb 13:12) at this very place still marked by ancient stonework in the Russian Alexander Hospice.

Vincent, *Jérusalem nouvelle*, pp. 40-88; and in DB Supplément 4, cols. 926-935; Simons, *Jerusalem*, pp. 319-324; *The Threshold of the Judgment Gate on the Place of the Russian Excavations in Jerusalem*, compiled upon works of Archimandrite Antonine, B. P. Mansourov and V. N. Khitrovo. Jerusalem: Greek Convent Press, 1959. Photograph: courtesy École Biblique et Archéologique Française.

160. Ancient Arch in the Russian Alexander Hospice

Associated with the walls just described in the Russian Alexander Hospice (No. 159) and standing a short distance southward on the line of the north-south wall is a portion of an arch with a Corinthian capital built into it, as shown in the photograph. With this type of capital we may probably have here Roman work rather than Jewish, as in the case of the plainer walls not far away. In fact this is probably only a portion of the side arch of a great triple-arched Roman gateway (Vincent, *Jérusalem nouvelle*, p. 75 Fig. 42), and in that case likely to be part of Hadrian's work. From Eusebius (*Life of Constantine* III 26 NPNFSS I, p. 527) we know that Hadrian buried the traditional sepulcher of Christ and covered the whole area with a large quantity of earth, then laid a stone pavement over everything, upon which he erected a shrine of Venus. This probably means that here, in the area which may have been "the square at the Gate of Ephraim" in the time of Nehemiah (8:16) and was probably an area of gardens outside the Garden Gate in the time of Jesus (cf. No. 159), Hadrian built the forum of Aelia Capitolina (Simons, *Jerusalem*, p. 318; Vincent, *Jérusalem nouvelle*, Planches II, Pl. I). If all of this is correct, the arch in the Russian

Alexander Hospice may well be a part of the great three-fold arch which was the entrance from the east to the Roman forum. When Constantine built the Church of the Holy Sepulcher he of course demolished the pagan shrines which had polluted the place, as Eusebius relates in the passage already cited, but he may well have utilized other architecture in the area as part of the new layout and surroundings of the church, and this arch may have been preserved in that connection.

Photograph: JF.

161. Ancient Wall and Arch beside the Damascus Gate

Along with the evidence of the walls, threshold, and arch in the Russian Alexander Hospice (Nos. 159-160), there is available now an additional and very important item of evidence which also points to the fact that the "second wall" of Jerusalem, as Josephus calls it (*War* v 4, 2 §146; cf. No. 159), did run from a Gennath Gate situated some two hundred meters east of the Citadel and did run past the east side of the area where the Church of the Holy Sepulcher now is. In 1961 and later Kathleen M. Kenyon excavated in a small area in the Muristan (cf. No. 159), belonging to the Order of St. John and due south of the Church of the Holy Sepulcher. A deep pit was dug here which reached bed rock at a depth of fifteen meters. At the bottom of the pit there was a rock quarry, with pottery of the seventh century B.C. Above this was a large fill containing pottery most of which was of the first century of the Christian era, with a little which was probably later, i.e., of the beginning of the second century. This fill can well

be explained as a part of the work of Hadrian, leveling up the area in the course of building Aelia Capitolina. Since a quarry would naturally not be inside a city, this site must have been outside the seventh century B.C. town. Since there are no buildings or occupation layers between the pottery and the large fill, the area must have remained vacant until the construction of Aelia Capitolina. And since the site is directly south of the Church of the Holy Sepulcher, the site of the church must also have been outside the city. From this evidence also, it is probable that the second wall in this area was on a line running north and south past what is now the east side of the Church of the Holy Sepulcher. This is the line shown in our Plan, No. 135, and it agrees with the location of the same wall in the plan of Jerusalem in the time of Herod the Great given by Kathleen M. Kenyon in PEQ 1966, p. 86 Fig. 4 and in *Jerusalem*, p. 145 Fig. 14 (for the excavations in the Muristan see PEQ 1964, pp. 14-16; 1966, p. 87; *Jerusalem*, pp. 151-154 and Pls. 70-72).

Josephus describes yet a third wall of Jerusalem (*War*

v 4, 2 §147). He says it was built by Agrippa, i.e., King Herod Agrippa I (A.D. 41-44), but also states that after the king had laid only the foundations he desisted from the project because he feared that Claudius (A.D. 41-54) might suspect that he had revolutionary designs. Another passage (*Ant.* XIX 7, 2 §§326-327) states that Claudius, for the same reason, ordered him to stop. Still another passage (*War* II 11, 6 §219) says Agrippa died at Caesarea (A.D. 44) before his work reached its projected height. In the first passage cited Josephus goes on (*War* v 4, 2 §155) to say that the Jews subsequently completed the work which Agrippa had not finished. Since he says that at that time the wall was "hurriedly erected by the Jews," it seems likely that this was not done until the great war with the Romans was imminent and under the pressure of that emergency. As thus completed the wall rose to a height of twenty cubits with battlements of two cubits and bulwarks of three cubits, making a total height of twenty-five cubits. When Titus attacked Jerusalem, coming from the north, he therefore confronted a series of three walls. At this point, in his narrative of how Titus selected a spot against which to direct his attack, Josephus (*War* v 6, §§259-260) mentions all three walls, but speaks of them now in reverse order—the first, second, and third from the point of view of Titus: "Baffled at all other points, the ravines rendering access impossible, while beyond them the first wall seemed too solid for his engines, he decided to make the assault opposite the tomb of John the high priest; for here the first line of ramparts was on lower ground, and the second was disconnected with it, the builders having neglected to fortify the sparsely populated portions of the new town, while there was an easy approach to the third wall, through which his intention was to capture the upper town and so, by way of Antonia, the temple."

In his formal description of the third wall Josephus (*War* v 4, 2 §147) states that it began at the tower Hippicus, ran northward to the tower Psephinus, descended opposite the monuments of Queen Helena of Adiabene, proceeded past the royal caverns, bent around a corner tower over against the so-called Fuller's tomb and, joining the ancient rampart, terminated at the Kidron Valley. From the other quotation from Josephus in our immediately preceding paragraph we know also that at one place this wall was opposite the tomb of John the high priest.

Of the points just mentioned from which we may hope to get an idea of the course of the third wall, the tower of Hippicus at one end and the Kidron Valley at the other are of course well known. Proceeding from Hippicus the next point mentioned is the tower Psephinus. According to another reference in Josephus (*War* v 4, 3 §§159-160) this tower was at the northwest an-

gle of the third wall and Titus placed his camp opposite it; the tower was octagonal in form, seventy cubits high, and from it one could see both Arabia and the utmost limits of Hebrew territory as far as the sea. The northwest corner of the present north wall of Jerusalem is indeed on the high point of the northwestern hill and at a likely place for a high tower with a far-reaching view, even if this view were not quite as extensive as that described by Josephus. At this place just inside the wall there are some ancient ruins which used to be known as Qasr Jalud or the Castle of Goliath, and are now in the basement of the buildings of the Collège des Frères. These consist of some pilasters built of large blocks of drafted stone, like the ancient masonry at the southwest angle of the temple area (cf. No. 151), and they may therefore be of Herodian date. As such, they could be part of the structures of the tower of Psephinus, to which Herod Agrippa brought the third wall from the tower of Hippicus (Vincent in RB 22 [1913], pp. 88-96; 36 [1927], pp. 525-532; Simons, *Jerusalem*, pp. 486-491).

The last point mentioned before the third wall reached the Kidron Valley was a corner tower which was over against the so-called Fuller's tomb. On the Fuller's tomb we have no other information, but if the third wall "bent around" a corner tower at about the place where the present wall turns south on the edge of the Kidron Valley to run down to the northeast angle of the temple area, the monument in question could have been on the knoll called Karm esh-Sheikh where the Palestine Archaeological Museum now is (Vincent in RB 36 [1927], p. 547 n. 1; Simons, *Jerusalem*, p. 482 n. 1).

Between the points thus far provisionally identified there are mentioned the monuments of Queen Helena of Adiabene and the royal caverns: the wall descended opposite the monuments of Helena and proceeded past the royal caverns. The monuments of Helena are quite certainly identified with the so-called "Tombs of the Kings" (Nos. 229ff.) which are on the Nablus Road about 700 meters in a direct line north of the present north wall of Jerusalem. The royal caverns are likewise quite certainly the so-called Solomon's Quarry, the entrance to which is 100 yards east of the Damascus Gate. These are subterranean caverns, 100 by 200 meters in extent, from which much of the building stone of ancient Jerusalem was probably obtained. Across the road to the north is another quarry known as the Grotto of Jeremiah. This was probably connected originally with the Quarry of Solomon but the connecting portion has been cut away. The statement that the third wall was "opposite" (ἀντικρύ) the monuments of Helena can allow a considerable intervening distance, for the camp of Titus, for example, was "opposite" Psephinus but also about two stadia from the ramparts (*War* v 3, 5

§133). In fact Josephus elsewhere (*Ant.* xx 4, 3 §95) states that the tomb of Helena was three stadia from the city. If the north wall of the time of Josephus, i.e., the third wall which we are discussing, ran on the line of the present north wall of the city, Josephus has estimated the distance from it to the monuments of Queen Helena at not much less than the actual measurement of about 700 meters between the two points today. The statement that the third wall ran past the royal caverns uses in fact the phrase διὰ σπηλαίων βασιλικῶν and should strictly be translated, "through the royal caverns." This is exactly true of a wall on the line of the present north wall of Jerusalem, for this wall has broken into the roof of Solomon's Quarry and runs between that cavern and the Grotto of Jeremiah on the north side of the road, the latter once having been part of the same set of caverns (Simons, *Jerusalem*, pp. 461-463, 478-481).

As for the tomb of John the high priest, mentioned in *War* v 6, 2 §259 (see above), it is mentioned again (*War* v 7, 3 §304; cf. v 9, 2 §356) in the fighting after Titus had shifted his camp within the outer wall. This monument, which was probably that of John Hyrcanus (135-105 B.C.), was therefore probably somewhere inside the third wall but outside the second wall and outside the first wall, and one suggestion places it at the site of the Byzantine and medieval Church of St. John the Baptist at the southwest corner of the Muristan (Simons, *Jerusalem*, p. 299 n. 5).

The line of the third wall thus described by Josephus (*War* v 4, 2 §147) running from Hippicus to Psephinus, opposite the monuments of Helena and through the royal caverns, around a corner tower, and to the Kidron Valley, appears then to correspond very closely with the line of the present north wall of Jerusalem (cf. Vincent in RB 36 [1927], p. 523 Fig. 1).

In 1937-1938 R. W. Hamilton made soundings at the Damascus Gate in the present north wall, and in 1966 J. B. Hennessy excavated much more fully, and a new bridge was built to carry foot traffic to the gate above the level of the earlier remains. As shown in the photograph (No. 161), to the east side of the present Damascus Gate and at a lower level there is the base of a massive wall and the arch of a gate. In the immediate area the most ancient remains were of the first half of the first century of the Christian era. Some burials, including an infant burial in a jar of the beginning of the first century, showed that at that time this area was outside the city. Other pottery, of the end of the first century B.C. and the beginning of the first century of the Christian era, and coins of the procurators were found. After that, the massive wall was built, and it may therefore in all probability be considered to be the work of Herod Agrippa I in about A.D. 41-42. To the west side of the Damascus Gate and at a similar lower level there

are also some massive blocks which probably belong to this same period (QDAP 10 [1940], p. 6). The lower part of the arch associated with the wall to the east of the Damascus Gate is also probably the work of Herod Agrippa. The upper part of the arch is of different masonry, and in the first course of stones above it there is a stone on which, although most of its face has been chiseled away, a few letters of an inscription still remain. In the second line from the bottom one letter remains, and in the bottom line are these letters: CO AEL CAP D D, i.e., Colonia Aelia Capitolina Decurionum Decreto. Thus the inscription refers to a decree of the decurions (cf. No. 145), and gives the name of Jerusalem as the Colony Aelia Capitolina. The date of the inscription is probably in the time of Hadrian (QDAP *ibid.*, pp. 22-23 and Fig. 12). As seen in our illustration, then, the archway probably represents the rebuilding or the completion by Hadrian of the earlier arch of Herod Agrippa, to serve as part of the main north gateway of Aelia Capitolina. That entire gateway was presumably triple-arched, like the other great gateways of Hadrian (Nos. 160, 180, cf. 77), and this arch was the eastern passageway for foot traffic alongside the higher, central passageway.

The Islamic rulers of Jerusalem, including the Mamlukes and the Turks, also did work on the walls of the city. The major restoration was carried out in A.D. 1537-1541 by Soliman I (sometimes styled Soliman II) the Magnificent (1494-1566), sultan of Turkey. While even later repairs may be seen on upper parts of the walls, the main lower parts of the existing walls in almost their entire circuit of the Old City are his masonry, and the present Damascus Gate appears much as it did in his day. The work of Soliman is attested by no less than eleven inscriptions which are still in place on the walls; one of these is at the Damascus Gate, and gives a date for the gate corresponding to A.D. 1537. Since there is evidence (Kenyon, *Jerusalem*, p. 197) that the wall of Soliman corresponds at key points on the south as well as on the north with the walls of Hadrian, the present outlines of the Old City may be seen to reflect the configuration of Aelia Capitolina. Only on the south the city extended for a time in the Byzantine period farther down toward the Hinnom Valley (cf. Nos. 141, 185).

Vincent, "La troisième enceinte de Jérusalem," in RB 36 (1927), pp. 516-548; 37 (1928), pp. 80-100; R. W. Hamilton, "Excavations against the North Wall of Jerusalem, 1937-8," in QDAP 10 (1940), pp. 1-54; Vincent, "Encore la troisième enceinte de Jérusalem," RB 54 (1947), pp. 90-126; Simons, *Jerusalem*, pp. 459-503; Kenyon, *Jerusalem*, pp. 162-163, 188, 196-197, Pls. 76-78; J. B. Hennessy in RB 75 (1968), pp. 250-253. Photograph: RB 75 (1968), Pl. XXVIII, courtesy École Biblique et Archéologique Française.

162. South Face of a Wall North of the
Old City of Jerusalem

One other line of wall is represented by considerable remains on the north side of Jerusalem. In the course of street repair at the intersection of Nablus Road and Richard Coeur de Lion Street a large block of drafted stone was found which was similar to the stones in the temple enclosure (cf. No. 151). Thereupon in 1925-1928 E. L. Sukenik and L. A. Mayer excavated and found other portions of wall or traces thereof, from perhaps as far west as the Swedish Girls' School (where they thought it could be seen that a wall had rested) to Saladin Road in front of the American School of Oriental Research, and in 1940 found two other portions east of the latter school. In publication Sukenik and Mayer presented these finds as parts of the "third wall" of Jerusalem. The line does not, however, correspond with what Josephus describes (No. 161), for it is only about 250 meters from the tomb of Queen Helena of Adiabene and Josephus says (*Ant.* xx 4, 3 §95) that the distance from that monument to the city was three stadia (a much greater distance), nor does the line go "through" any known "royal caverns." Also Josephus (*War* v 4, 2 §153) says that Agrippa began the wall with stones "twenty cubits long and ten broad, so closely joined that they could scarcely have been undermined with tools of iron or shaken by engines." Here, however, the portions of wall which have been uncovered were not well built. While there were some relatively large and well-finished blocks of stone like the one first discovered, there were other roughly made square blocks and unhewn boulders, and often all of them were put together irregularly, with poor jointing and poor foun-

dation. In 1965 Kathleen M. Kenyon, with E. W. Hamrick as site supervisor, conducted further excavation at a portion of the wall between Nablus Road and Saladin Street. Kenyon reports that the wall "certainly faced south and not north," and therefore certainly could not be the north wall of Herod Agrippa's city (PEQ 1966, p. 87). Hamrick thinks it faced north, but "the incredibly poor and haphazard masonry" would not be from Agrippa (BASOR 183 [Oct. 1966], pp. 24-25; 192 [Dec. 1968], pp. 23f.). Two coins of procurators were found in association with the wall, one of the fourteenth year of Claudius (A.D. 54), one of the fifth year of Nero (A.D. 58-59), and this also indicates that the wall is of later date than Agrippa. Probably, then, as Kenyon suggests, this was part of the wall which, according to Josephus (*War* v 12, 1-2 §§499-511), Titus put around the city in the siege, or, as Hamrick suggests, part of an outwork put up by the Jews early in the war. That the wall was associated with the headquarters of the Tenth Legion Fretensis which Titus left to guard Jerusalem after the war was over (cf. Nos. 95 and 145) is less likely, since these headquarters were probably in the southwestern corner of the city where many tiles bearing the stamp LEG.X.FR., or a variant thereof, have been found (Kenyon in PEQ 1966, p. 88; *Jerusalem*, p. 168). The photograph shows the south face of one portion of the wall.

E. L. Sukenik and L. A. Mayer, *The Third Wall of Jerusalem, An Account of Excavations.* Jerusalem, 1930; and "A New Section of the Third Wall, Jerusalem," in PEQ 1944, pp. 145-151; Simons, *Jerusalem*, pp. 470-481; Kathleen M. Kenyon, "Excavations in Jerusalem, 1965," in PEQ 1966, pp. 87-88; E. W. Hamrick, "New Excavations at Sukenik's 'Third Wall,'" in BASOR 183 (Oct. 1966), pp. 19-26. Kenyon, *Jerusalem*, pp. 162, 166-168 Pl. 86. Photograph: courtesy École Biblique et Archéologique Française.

163. The Church of St. Anne

An event of interest in the earlier ministry of Jesus in Jerusalem, connected with a specific place in the city, is recorded in the fifth chapter of the Gospel according to John. This was the healing of the man ill for thirty-eight years to whom Jesus said, "Rise, take up your pallet, and walk" (5:8). Because it was the sabbath the objection was raised that it was not lawful for the man to carry his pallet, and the event became one in a series of circumstances which led finally to the death of Jesus in the same city.

The place where the healing of this man took place is described in Jn 5:2 in a Greek sentence which appears in different forms in different manuscripts. All agree that the sentence begins, "Now there is in Jerusalem." After that it is a question of how to connect and interpret the Greek word, *probatike*, which is an adjective meaning "of sheep." The oldest manuscript presently available which contains this text is P⁶⁶ or Papyrus Bodmer II, about A.D. 200 in date. On numbered Page 25 (ΚΕ) of this codex and in Lines 18-19 (ed. Victor Martin and J. W. B. Barns, 1962) the words are: ΕΠΙ ΤΗ ΠΡΟΒΑΤΙΚΗ · ΚΟΛΥΜΒΗΘΡΑ · . The same Greek text, but not necessarily with the same punctuation marks, is found also in P⁷⁵ (Papyrus Bodmer XV, early third century), Codex Vaticanus, and many manuscripts of the Koine text, and also in D and other Western manu-

scripts except that in the latter ἐπί is replaced by ἐν without any real change of meaning. The fact that the word *probatike* is here preceded by the preposition ἐπί meaning "at" or "by" or "near" (or by ἐν, "in"), indicates that it must be taken as a dative, ἐπὶ (ἐν) τῇ προβατικῇ, "at the sheep. . . ." In and of itself the last word in the sequence from Papyrus Bodmer II, which means "pool," could also be taken as a dative, but that would complicate the grammar with respect to the continuation of the sentence, so it probably is to be taken as a nominative, κολυμβήθρα. This also appears to have been the understanding of the scribe who wrote P⁶⁶ for, as shown above, the word is set off in this manuscript between punctuation dots. Accordingly we have, literally, "at the *probatike* a pool." What the *probatike* was must be surmised, and it is at least a reasonable guess that the reference is to a sheep market or a sheep gate. Both of these meanings could of course be related, for the holding of a sheep market outside a certain gate would lead naturally to the designation of that portal as a sheep gate. If this is correct, then a suitable English translation can be, "Now there is at Jerusalem by the sheep market a pool" (KJV), or "Now there is in Jerusalem by the sheep *gate* a pool" (ASV), or "Now there is in Jerusalem by the sheep gate a pool" (RSV).

Codex Sinaiticus, however, reads simply, "Now there is in Jerusalem a sheep pool" (προβατικὴ κολυμβήθρα). Since this does simplify the text as compared with the

142

preceding reading, it may be judged to be secondary. At the same time, whether because of the existence of this reading or simply because of the proximity of the pool to the sheep market and/or the sheep gate, it would appear that the pool was, at least in due time, known as the sheep pool. In the *Onomasticon* (pp. 58-59) Eusebius speaks of "a pool in Jerusalem which is the Probatike," and Jerome repeats and adds, "a pool in Jerusalem which is called Probatike, which can be interpreted by us as 'belonging to cattle'" (*piscina in Ierusalem quae vocobatur* προβατική, *et a nobis interpretari potest pecualis*).

We have reference, then, to a pool which was near a certain place associated with sheep, probably a sheep market and/or a sheep gate, a pool which was itself, at least later, also naturally enough called the sheep pool. Now we have already noted (No. 157) that there was in fact a Sheep Gate which is mentioned by Nehemiah (3:1; 12:39) and that, according to his references, this was probably in the north city wall on the north side of the temple area, between the "corner" on the northeast and the Tower of the Hundred and Tower of Hananel, the latter probably predecessors of the Antonia, on the northwest. The fact that this gate was built by Eliashib the high priest and his brethren the priests (Neh 3:1) confirms its close association with the temple area, and it may have been the same as the Tadi Gate mentioned by Middoth I 3 as the portal on the north side of the temple area (cf. No. 152). Since the pool in question was "by" this gate we have thereby established its approximate location.

The text in Jn 5:2 continues, "Now there is in Jerusalem by the sheep gate a pool, in Hebrew called. . . ." At this point the name of the pool is given, but again there is a problem for different manuscripts give different names. The manuscripts which were found probably the most accurate in the earlier part of the sentence now give, with some variation in spelling, the name Bethsaida. P⁶⁶ reads Βηδσαϊδά and P⁷⁵, Codex Vaticanus, and other manuscripts have Βηθσαϊδά. Jerome also changes the *Onomasticon* (p. 59) at this point to read Bethsaida. As we have seen (No. 75) this name probably means House of the Fisher and is the name of a town on the Sea of Galilee. With reference to this place, which was the city of Andrew and Peter as well as of Philip, the name has already occurred in Jn 1:44. Appropriate as the name is to a fishing village, it seems that it would be less appropriate to a pool in the city of Jerusalem. Therefore in spite of the early and wide attestation of the name in sources just cited, it may be judged probable that this name is due to a scribe who wrongly wrote here what was really the name of a well-known town.

In Codex Alexandrinus and Codex Ephraemi re-

scriptus, both of the fifth century, and in other manuscripts including the majority of the Byzantine manuscripts, the name Bethesda (Βηθεσδά) is found, and this is the reading adopted in the KJV and ASV. In Hebrew בית means "house" and אשד means "pour," and the related form in Aramaic, בית אשדא, can lie back of the Greek name, thus giving some such meaning as House of Outpouring or House of Poured-out Water. Interestingly enough this can recall the statement in the fourth-century parchment from Oxyrhynchus (OP 840 Lines 25, 32-33 FHRJ §262) about the Pharisee who said that he had washed in the pool of David (ἐν τῇ λίμνῃ τοῦ Δ(αυεί)δ), to whom the Savior said that he had washed "in these poured-out waters" (τοῖς χεομένοις ὕ[δ]ασιν). Perhaps this last expression, which otherwise appears lacking in any particular significance, is actually a reference to the pool of Bethesda. In this case the pool of David of the Oxyrhynchus parchment, which is otherwise unidentified, can be identified with the pool of Bethesda.

In the Old Syriac version, found as early as the fifth-century Curetonian manuscript, the name is given as Byt hsd', i.e., Bethhesda. Back of this form must be the Hebrew בית "house" and חסד "mercy," and the related Aramaic בית חסדא, giving the meaning, House of Mercy. This name was certainly appropriate in view of the healing performed by Jesus, but probably appropriate earlier, in view of the healings which were evidently already associated with the pool.

That there was a place called Bethesda, with a pool or pools, in Jerusalem is now confirmed in the Hebrew text of the Copper Scroll from Qumran (3Q 15 DJD III p. 297, cf. pp. 271-272; J. T. Milik in RB 66 [1959], pp. 328, 345, 347-348; J. M. Allegro, *The Treasure of the Copper Scroll*, 2d ed. 1964, p. 84), a work written probably between A.D. 25 and 68 (F. M. Cross, Jr. in DJD III pp. 217, 219). Here in Column XI Lines 12-13 and in a list of places at Jerusalem we read: "At Beth Eshdathayin (בית {א}אשדתין), in the pool where you enter its small(er) reservoir. . . ." This is a writing of the name Bethesda which agrees with the etymology suggested in the second paragraph above, but with two **interesting additional features. The first is the simple fact that the initial Aleph in the second word has been written twice, no doubt the result of a familiar type of error in the copying of manuscripts known as dittography. The second is the important fact that the word is written with the Hebrew dual ending. In view of the latter fact and if we may now take the phrase "poured-out water," which was explained above, in the broad sense of "pool," we may understand the name, as written here, to mean the House of the Twin Pools.**

At this point we may note the remaining significant variant in the name, which is the reading Bethzatha

(Βηθζαθά). This reading is found in Codex Sinaiticus. Also in the *Onomasticon* (p. 58) Eusebius omits one letter of the same name and writes Βηζαθά. The Western text in Codex Bezae and several manuscripts of the Itala has Βελζεθά, and this is also no doubt only an orthographic variation. We have then simply to account for the name Bethzatha. In the Copper Scroll we have seen the Hebrew dual form, Beth Eshdathayin. If we suppose that this name was reproduced in Aramaic, we have to remember that in Palestinian Aramaic the dual ending was largely lost (Franz Rosenthal, *A Grammar of Biblical Aramaic*, 1961, p. 24 No. 45). If in this case the Hebrew dual was replaced by the feminine plural, the Aramaic form of the name would have been בית אשדתא, Beth Eshdatha. Then we can explain the name Bethzatha as a Greek transcription of the Aramaic which does not reproduce the Aleph, and which represents the Shin and the Daleth together by Zeta, as may be paralleled for example in the Greek Ἄζωτος which renders the Hebrew אשדוד, Ashdod.

We have just observed that in writing the name Bethzatha in Greek the first Theta could be omitted and the name be given as Bezatha (Βηζαθά), as Eusebius did. In this form the name is very similar to the name Bezetha (Βεζεθά) which is found in Josephus. In his description of the "third wall" of Jerusalem, built by King Herod Agrippa I (No. 161), Josephus says (*War* v 4, 2 §§148-151) that this wall was built to enclose later additions to the city which were in a district north of the temple. Here there was a hill, opposite Antonia, called Bezetha; the recently built quarter was also called in the vernacular Bezetha which, Josephus says, might be translated into Greek as New City (cf. No. 135). New City is not actually a translation of Bezetha, and in another passage (*War* ii 19, 4 §530) Josephus says more accurately that the district was known as Bezetha and also as New City (τὴν τε Βεζεθὰν . . . τὴν καὶ Καινόπολιν). The name Bezetha is then in all probability the same as the name Bethzatha, and the area to which it applies as the name of a city district, namely, the area north of the temple, is the area within which we have already suggested that the Bethesda/Bethzatha pool was located. Accordingly it is a reasonable surmise that the pool gave its name to the expanded city district.

From this survey of the most important variants in the manuscript evidence we conclude that the name Bethsaida is a scribal alteration which erroneously introduces the name of a well-known town, but that otherwise the tradition is essentially consistent and homogenous, i.e., Bethesda and Bethzatha (and the variant spellings of these two names) represent respectively the Hebrew and the Aramaic forms of the name of the pool. Furthermore, comparing the tradition with the item in the Copper Scroll from Qumran, we have evidence (in a Hebrew dual ending) that the pool was in fact a twin or double pool.

Eusebius, we have noted, uses the name Bezatha in the *Onomasticon* (p. 58), where he gives the oldest description of the pool after the NT. Eusebius writes: "Bezatha. A pool in Jerusalem, which is the Sheep Pool (ἡ προβατική), which formerly had five porticoes (ε´ στοάς). And now it is shown in the twin pools which are there, each of which is filled by the yearly rains, but one of which paradoxically exhibits water colored purple-red (πεφοινιγμένον), a trace, it is said, of the sacrificial animals formerly washed in it. That is also why it is called Sheep Pool (προβατική), on account of the sacrifices." From this we learn that the place was pointed out in Jerusalem, and we are told explicitly that it had twin pools. The tradition of connection with sacrifices implies proximity to the temple area.

In a description of Jerusalem in the vicinity of the temple the Bordeaux Pilgrim (Geyer p. 21; LPPTS I, p. 20; CCSL CLXXV, p. 15) mentions the same double pool: "Farther in the city are twin pools (*piscinae gemellares*), having five porticoes, which are called Bethsaida. There those who have been sick for many years are cured. The pools contain water which is red when it is disturbed (*in modum coccini turbatam*)." Here the additional item is the reference to the disturbance of the water which evidently took place from time to time (cf. Jn 5:7).

In a sermon on the healing of the ill man at the pool, Cyril of Jerusalem says (MPG 33, col. 1133): "For in Jerusalem there was a Sheep Pool (προβατικὴ κολυμβήθρα), having five porticoes, four of which ran around it, but the fifth ran through the middle, in which [i.e., in the portico in the middle] lay a multitude of the sick." Knowing from the other references that the pool was in fact a twin pool, i.e., really two pools, we can picture the four porticoes as surrounding both, and the fifth portico as running between the two pools.

Next we learn that a church was built here. Peter the Iberian (Raabe p. 94), who came to Jerusalem in 451, on his way from the Church of the Holy Sepulcher to Gethsemane, went "into the (Church) of the Lame Man." Eutychius of Alexandria (ed. Watt CSCO 193, p. 139) also speaks of "the church which is called the Place of the Sheep in Jerusalem," and describes it as bearing witness to the healing by Christ of the man paralyzed for thirty-eight years. The church was therefore evidently known as the Church of the Lame Man, or the Church of the Sheep Place (Probatike).

Interestingly enough the place of the pool was also associated with commemoration of the birth of Mary the mother of Jesus. First we learn that there was a

Church of St. Mary at the pool. Theodosius mentions it in 530, saying only that it was near the pool. Speaking of the Sheep Pool, he writes (Geyer p. 142; LPPTS II, p. 11; CCSL CLXXV, pp. 118-119): "There the Lord Christ healed the paralytic, whose bed is still there. There near the Sheep Pool is the church of St. Mary (*Iuxta piscinam probaticam ibi est ecclesia domnae Mariae*)." And the Anonymous of Piacenza (570) locates the church in relation to the pool more precisely in the statement (Geyer p. 177; LPPTS II, p. 22; CCSL CLXXV, p. 143): "Returning to the city we came to a swimming pool (*piscina natatoria*) which has five porticoes, one of which has the basilica of St. Mary." From this we gather that the church was built right into a stoa of the pool, therefore it was probably the same as, or a replacement of, the Church of the Lame Man which was presumably also closely related to the pool. The pool itself was now choked with filth, according to the Anonymous, and the relic to be seen there was no longer the bed of the healed man but rather the iron chain with which Judas had hanged himself.

From these references we still do not know the particular connection of the church here with the name of Mary, but we learn the answer when we find that the place was believed to have been the place of the birth of Mary. Concerning "the church which is called the Place of the Sheep in Jerusalem," Eutychius of Alexandria not only says, as noted just above, that it marked the place where Christ healed the man, but he also writes (ed. Watt CSCO 193, p. 139): "That church also bears witness that the birth of Mary, the mother of Christ, took place there, her father being Joachim son of Binthir of the sons of David of the tribe of Judah, the tribe of the king, and her mother being Anne of the daughters of Aaron of the tribe of Levi, the tribe of the priesthood." Eutychius then continues with a brief account not only of the birth of Mary but also of how Joachim and Anne, in accordance with a vow, placed Mary in the temple in the charge of Zacharias, where she also received food from the hands of an angel. This account corresponds generally with the fuller narrative in the apocryphal work of the middle of the second century known as *The Protevangelium of James* (HSNTA I, pp. 374ff.), and with the brief summary in the Qur'an (Surah III, 35-37). In the *Protevangelium* the connection of events with the temple could lead one to the surmise that Joachim and Anne were living in the vicinity; also Joachim is represented as a shepherd, and therefore it could be appropriate to suppose that his residence was near the Sheep Gate. These factors were perhaps influential in fixing upon the place at the Sheep Pool for the home of Joachim and Anne and the birthplace of Mary.

When the Persians took Jerusalem in May 614 the church at the pool was no doubt among the buildings they destroyed, but afterward a small chapel was built there in its place. When the Crusaders took Jerusalem on July 15, 1099, the chapel was probably in ruins. They built a new basilica of St. Anne, the existence of which is attested by Saewulf in 1102. He writes (LPPTS IV, p. 17; Vincent, *Jérusalem nouvelle*, p. 681): "From the temple of the Lord you go towards the north to the Church of St. Anne, the mother of blessed Mary, where she lived with her husband, and where she brought forth her most beloved daughter Mary, the savior of all the faithful. Near there is the Probatica Pool which is called in Hebrew Bethsayda, having five porches." An account of the Crusader conquest called *Deeds of the Franconians Conquering Jerusalem* (1108) states that the Crusaders found "in front of" the church the vestiges of the old pool with five porticoes (Jeremias, *The Rediscovery of Bethesda*, p. 22), therefore the new Church of St. Anne must have been to the east of the Pool of Bethesda where the present-day church stands. Underneath is a grotto which was taken to be the very place where Mary was born. In addition to this church, however, the Crusaders also built a chapel over the ruins of the chapel and the Byzantine church at the pool. This is mentioned by the French pilgrim Ernoul in 1231, who calls it a *moustier*, literally a monastery (Vincent, *Jérusalem nouvelle*, p. 681).

In 1192 Saladin turned the Church of St. Anne into a Muslim college. The ancient double pool had evidently long since been filled with debris, and even the Crusader chapel disappeared below the rising level of the ground. At the end of the Crimean War in 1856 the Sultan of Turkey gave the basilica of St. Anne to Napoleon III of France. In 1871 the French architect C. Mauss, restoring the church, found thirty meters to the northwest a vaulted cistern and surmised that this was a part of the ancient pool. Five years later heavy rain removed more of the debris and over the cistern was found a structure which was part of the Byzantine church of the fifth century, with ruins of the Crusader chapel over it. Finally in 1878 the French government gave the property of St. Anne's Church to the White Fathers, and modern excavations became possible (see No. 164).

The photograph (No. 163) shows the modern Church of St. Anne, corresponding to the Crusader basilica east of the Pool of Bethesda.

Vincent, *Jérusalem nouvelle*, pp. 669-742; Joachim Jeremias, *The Rediscovery of Bethesda*, NTAM 1, 1966; D. J. Wieand, "John V.2 and the Pool of Bethesda," in NTS 12 (1966), pp. 392-404. Photograph: courtesy École Biblique et Archéologique Française.

164. Excavations at the Pool of Bethesda

Modern excavations by the White Fathers, which are still continuing, have established that the cistern already mentioned (cf. No. 163), and another cistern found later, occupied only a small part of the south side of the entire area of the northern of two very large pools. These pools were in the small valley running off diagonally from the Kidron, which has already been mentioned and called St. Anne's Valley (No. 135). In part the pools were cut in the rock and in part they were built of large well-dressed blocks of stone. The two pools were separated by a dike of stone over six meters in width. Since the pools extend far underground and in part under heavily built-up sections of the city it has not yet been possible to trace them fully. They appear to have been generally rectangular in shape, but of irregular proportions. Provisional estimates make the northern pool 174 feet on its south side, 131 feet on the east and west sides, and 164 feet on the north side, and the southern pool 189 feet on its north side, 162 feet and 157 feet on the east and west sides respectively, and 215 feet on the south side. Such dimensions would mean a water surface in the two pools in excess of 5,000 square yards.

The first cistern mentioned above, in the southeast corner of the northern pool, is a vaulted chamber about 16 meters in length from east to west, and 6 meters in breadth from north to south. As early as 1888 it was observed (C. Schick in PEFQS 1888, pp. 115-124, especially p. 119) that while this cistern was cut out of the

rock on its west, south, and east sides, its north side was a built-up wall. The lowest part of this wall is now recognized as Roman work, so it is a possible guess that the cistern was part of their effort to preserve drinkable water, free from contamination by the rest of the pool. As to the source of water for the two large pools, their location in the valley as already mentioned undoubtedly meant that they were in a good place for the collection of rain water. Perhaps there was also a spring in the valley, at least in ancient times. It may be surmised that some feature of the connecting channels for the water, or even the existence of an intermittent spring like the Gihon spring (No. 137), accounted for the occasional troubling of the water mentioned by Jn 5:7 and the Bordeaux Pilgrim (cf. No. 163).

In the excavations many fragments of columns, including capitals, bases, and cylinders, have been found. From these it has been estimated that the columns around the pools were 7 meters high, and that the total height of the porticoes was about 8.50 meters. For the portico which ran crossways between the two pools a width of 6.50 meters is indicated.

A tunnel was dug along the south wall of the southern pool and in 1932 a graffito in Hebrew characters was observed on this wall. Such a graffito would be unlikely after Hadrian excluded the Jews from Jerusalem, therefore a date before the time of Hadrian is indicated. The evident magnificence of the porticoes makes one think of the magnificence of Herod's work on the nearby temple, and it is highly probable that these structures were the work of that king.

In 1866 a broken marble foot was found in the debris in the vaults of the Church of St. Anne. On the top was this inscription in Greek:

ΠΟΝΠΗ
ΙΑ ΛΟΥΚΙ
ΛΙΑ ΑΝΕΘΗ
ΚΕΝ

i.e., Πονπηία Λουκιλία ἀνέθηκεν, "Pompeia Lucilia dedicated (this as a votive gift)" (Vincent, *Jérusalem nouvelle*, pp. 694-695). The donor, a Roman lady to judge by her name, had certainly visited the place and left a sign of her visit; it could be that the foot commemorates a healing. Paleographically the inscription may be from the second century. At that time the Pool of Bethesda may have been a pagan healing sanctuary. In 1962 an underground vaulted gallery was found just east of the pools, in which were badly damaged paintings, and this may also have been a part of the pagan sanctuary.

In the Curetonian Syriac version of Jn 5:2, where the Aramaic form of the name Bethhesda is so plainly recognizable (cf. No. 163), the text runs, ". . . there was in Jerusalem a baptistery. . . ." This makes it likely that in some periods the Pool of Bethesda was used as a place of Christian baptism, a fact likely enough in and of itself in view of the paucity of places of abundant water in Jerusalem (Jeremias, *The Rediscovery of Bethesda*, pp. 33-34).

When it became possible the Christians no doubt wished to build a church here, both to supplant the pagan sanctuary and to commemorate the healing by Christ of the ill man. As we have seen (No. 163), Peter the Iberian in 451 refers to a Church of the Lame Man, a church which was undoubtedly at this location. The excavations have uncovered the ruins of a Byzantine church which was probably built in the fifth century. In its western part the center of this church and its main entrance were on the rock dike between the two pools, while the north side was supported on the Roman structure of the cistern and the south side was carried by a system of arches. To the east of the pools the underground Roman sanctuary was destroyed and filled in, and the eastern part of the church was built out to its termination in three apses. From fragmentary remains the narthex appears to have had a mosaic floor, and the rest of the church to have been paved with slabs of marble.

The church just described was probably destroyed by the Persians (614) and then replaced by a small chapel erected above the north aisle of the basilica, a chapel which was itself in ruins when the Crusaders came. The Crusaders built the new basilica of St. Anne to the east of the pools (cf. No. 163), and also worked very extensively at the pools. These were filled in, but a number of cisterns were preserved. A whole quarter of buildings was erected, and some of these had mosaic floors for which cubes from the Byzantine mosaics were used. Over the Roman cistern in the southeast corner of the north pool the chapel was constructed which, as we have seen (No. 163), was known as the Moustier. A stairway running under a Byzantine vault was built to lead down into the cistern, and this stairway gives access to the cistern today.

The photograph (No. 164) shows the excavations at the stage they had reached in 1968. The ruins of the apse of the Crusader chapel rise above the Byzantine ruins and over the Roman cistern. Extending far underground are the ancient twin pools of Bethesda.

J.-M. Rousée in RB 69 (1962), pp. 107-109. Photograph: JF.

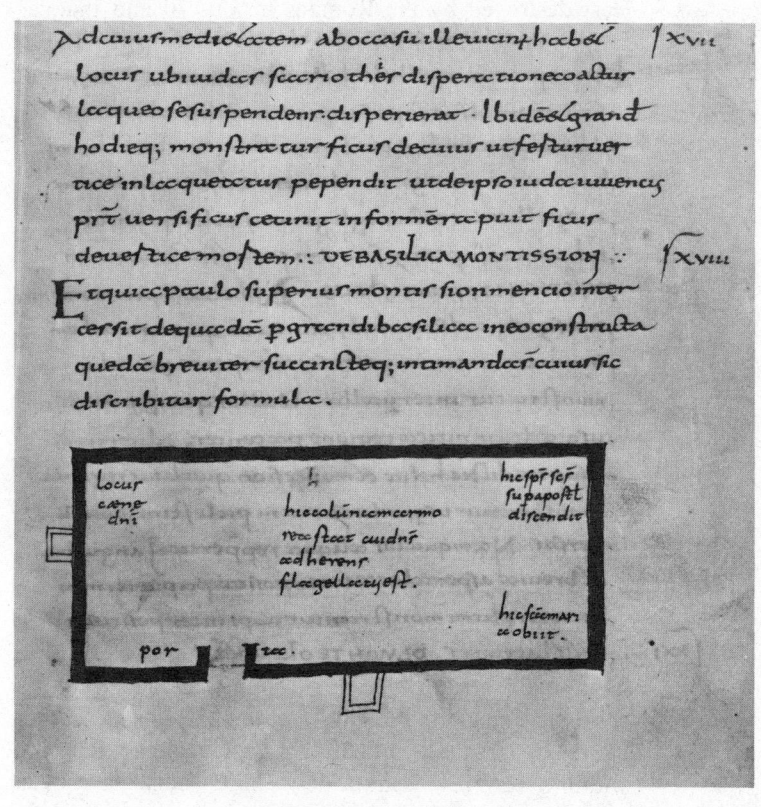

165. Plan of the Church on Mount Sion
according to Arculf

According to Mk 14:15 and Lk 22:12 the last supper of Jesus with his disciples was in an "upper room" (ἀνάγαιον). According to Ac 1:13 the disciples were staying, after the ascension, in an "upper room" (ὑπερῷον). Although two different Greek words are used in these passages they both designate a room upstairs, and in his Latin translation Jerome rendered both by the same word, *cenaculum*. This word, also spelled *coenaculum*, means a dining room and, since such a room was usually in an upper story, it means also an upper room. No doubt the use of *cenaculum* for the upper room of the last supper and also for the upper room of the time after the ascension furthered the supposition that one and the same room was in question. Although that supposition is not fully demonstrable it is not impossible. That the same room was still the center of the disciples on the day of Pentecost (Ac 2:1) is also at least possible. Still later, many of the disciples were gathered together in the house of Mary, the mother of John Mark (Ac 12:12), and the further supposition that this was the house of the "upper room" is likewise not impossible although not fully demonstrable.

It will be remembered (No. 135) that the southwestern hill of Jerusalem was the highest hill in the city and came to be called Zion or Sion. It will also be remembered (No. 145) that this portion of the city was the least destroyed by the Romans in A.D. 70 and that, as Epiphanius tells us (*Weights and Measures* 14 [54c], ed. Dean, p. 30), when Hadrian came in 130 he found in Zion "the church of God, which was small, where the disciples, when they had returned after the Savior had ascended from the Mount of Olives, went to the upper room," and also "the seven synagogues which alone remained standing in Zion, like solitary huts, one of which remained until the time of Maximona the bishop and Constantine the king, 'like a booth in a vineyard,' as it is written [Is 1:8]."

The Bordeaux Pilgrim (333) ascended Sion and found that of the seven synagogues which once were there only one remained and the rest were "ploughed over and sown upon, as Isaiah the prophet [Is 1:8 cf. Mic 3:12] said" (Geyer p. 22; LPPTS I, p. 23; CCSL CLXXV p. 16), but he says nothing about a Christian church in the place, unless this "synagogue" itself was a Jewish-Christian church. Even if this was not the case and if the small church which Hadrian saw had by then disappeared, the fact that the Pilgrim included Sion in his itinerary makes it probable that Christian tradition continued to attach there. In fact the place of the earlier church was in all probability well remembered and within a very few years a new church must have been built there, for Cyril of Jerusalem makes unmistakable reference to such a church in his time.

In 348 Cyril delivered catechetical lectures in the Church of the Holy Sepulcher and devoted Lecture XVI to the subject of the Holy Spirit. Here he remarked (XVI, 4 NPNFSS VII, p. 116) that, just as it was appropriate to discourse concerning Christ and Golgotha in the church right there at Golgotha, so it would be appropriate to speak concerning the Holy Spirit "in the Upper Church" (ἐν τῇ ἀνωτέρᾳ ἐκκλησίᾳ). But, he reflected further, the One who descended there (i.e., the Holy Spirit) partakes jointly of the glory of him who was crucified here (i.e., Jesus Christ), therefore it was in fact not inappropriate to speak here (i.e., at Golgotha) also of him who descended there (i.e., at the site of the Upper Church). The "upper church" which marked the place where the Holy Spirit came upon the disciples must have been the church on Sion, by this time no doubt a larger and more splendid basilica than the church which Hadrian saw, "which was small."

Theodosius (530) calls the church Holy Sion (*sancta Sion*), describes it as "the mother of all churches" (*mater omnium ecclesiarum*), says that it was the house of St. Mark the Evangelist, and locates it at 200 paces from Golgotha (Geyer p. 141; LPPTS II, p. 10; CCSL CLXXV, p. 118). Also Eutychius of Alexandria (940), drawing upon the source from which his information about the sanctuaries in Jerusalem came, writes (ed. Watt, CSCO 193, p. 142): "The church of the holy Mount Zion bears witness that Christ ate the passover of the Law in the upper room there on the day of the passover of the Jews."

These references indicate that all of the connections rendered possible by the scripture passages cited at the beginning of this section were brought into play. The church on Mount Sion commemorated the upper room of the Last Supper and the upper room of the early disciples after the ascension and their gathering place at Pentecost, being in fact a room in the house of Mary, the mother of John Mark the writer of the Second Gospel.

As a church of such importance, we are not surprised to find the Madaba Mosaic Map (560) (see No. 185) representing what must be this very church as a very large basilica, with red roof and yellow doors, near the southwest corner of the city. The other red-roofed building attached to the basilica may have been a service building (*diaconicon*).

Arculf (670) also spoke of the church on Mount Sion as a "great basilica" (Geyer p. 243; LPPTS III, p. 20; CCSL CLXXV, p. 197), and accompanied his reference to it with a drawing. From the legends in the drawing we learn that two other traditions had become attached to this site, namely, the column where Jesus was scourged was believed to be preserved here, and the place was said to be that where Mary, the mother of Jesus, died. Arculf's drawing is reproduced here (No. 165) from a page of the ninth-century manuscript of *De locis sanctis* known as Codex Parisinus (Latin 13048), preserved in the Bibliothèque Nationale. From the lower left and around to the lower right the legends in the drawing read: Entrance, Site of the Lord's Supper, Here the column to which the Lord was bound when he was scourged, Here the Holy Spirit descended on the apostles, and Here St. Mary died.

E. Power, "Cénacle," in DB Supplément I, cols. 1064-1084. Photograph: Arculfus De Locis Sanctis, Codex Parisinus Lat. 13048, courtesy Bibliothèque Nationale, Paris.

166. Mount Sion as Seen from Abu Tur

The site described in the preceding section (No. 165) is today outside the south wall of the Old City of Jerusalem. A whole complex of buildings is now located there, namely, the Dormition Church and Monastery of the Benedictines, the supposed place of the *dormitio sanctae Mariae*, the sleep of death of St. Mary; the traditional Tomb of David which has also been used as the Mosque of the Prophet David; and, in the second story of the Tomb of David building, the supposed hall of the Last Supper. The photograph (No. 166) is taken from the south, from the village of Abu Tur which was, until 1967, divided by the line of partition between Jordan and Israel. The large buildings at the left are those of the Dormition, and the small dome not far to the right of them is above the Tomb of David and the Hall of the Last Supper. The dome at the extreme right is that of the Dome of the Rock in the Temple area.

Photograph: JF.

167. The Tomb of David on Mount Sion

Here, in a closer view, the Tomb of David is the building under the black dome. The minaret of the adjacent mosque rises at the right.

Photograph: The Matson Photo Service, Alhambra, Calif.

persistent on this site, and since an early Christian assembly-place, particularly a Jewish-Christian one, can be called a "synagogue" (συναγωγή) (Jas 2:2), one wonders if this "synagogue" on Mount Sion, and even others of the seven of which we hear earlier, could perhaps have been Jewish-Christian churches (cf. No. 165).

As to the other parts of the hall, the west wall appears to have been built in the Arab period, and the dividing wall between the two rooms in the late Turkish period. Opposite the apse in the north wall a small niche was made in the south wall to serve as a mihrab and indicate the direction of prayer toward Mecca. The large plain cenotaph in the hall, adorned on the front with a rosette of acanthus leaves, is Crusader work.

J. Pinkerfeld, " 'David's Tomb,' Notes on the History of the Building," in the Hebrew University Department of Archaeology, Louis M. Rabinowitz Fund for the Exploration of Ancient Synagogues, *Bulletin* III (1960), pp. 41-43. Photograph: courtesy École Biblique et Archéologique Française.

168. The South Wall of the Tomb of David on Mount Sion

In the building which contains the supposed Tomb of David the burial hall is a long rectangular hall divided into two rooms. In the inner room, to the north, a large stone cenotaph stands in front of an apse. In 1951 J. Pinkerfeld removed the plaster in this apse and found a well-built wall of squared stones which he judged to belong to the late Roman period. The same masonry was found in the eastern part of the north wall of the building, in the east wall, and in the eastern part of the south wall. The photograph shows the south wall from the outside, and the large squared stones may be seen at the right and in the lower part of the picture.

Since the hall and the apse point actually several degrees to the east of north and in fact directly toward the temple mount, Pinkerfeld concluded that we have here the remains of a synagogue from the first centuries after the destruction of the temple. Since seven synagogues stood in Zion when Hadrian came in 130, and one of these still remained when the Bordeaux Pilgrim came in 333, one wonders if there is a connection between these remains of the Roman period and that history. Moreover, since the Christian traditions are so

169. Column from the Ancient Church on Mount Sion

In 1898 the German Emperor Wilhelm II obtained and presented to the German Catholic Society of the Holy Land the plot of ground northwest of the Tomb of David (No. 167) which was specially associated with the Dormitio Sanctae Mariae, and here the Dormition Church, properly known as the Marien-Kirche or Church of the Virgin, was built in Romanesque style in 1901-1910 by the architect Heinrich Renard. On the south side of the church is also the Zion Convent of the Dormitio, a monastery of the Benedictines from Beuron. In 1899, prior to building, Renard conducted a small excavation and brought to light remains of a Byzantine church, doubtless the church on Mount Sion which is attested, as we have seen (No. 165), in the fourth century. This was, according to Renard, a basilica 60 meters long and 40 meters wide, but whether it had three or five aisles and how it was related to the traditional room of the Last Supper which it was supposed to commemorate are still debatable points. One of the ancient columns which stands in the garden at this place is shown in the photograph.

Above (No. 165) we have assumed that the words *sancta Sion* in Theodosius were the name of this church, and this is confirmed by finding the same name, in Greek, in inscriptions in a number of rock-hewn tombs in the nearby Valley of Hinnom (Wadi er-Rababi). Beside the road which leads southward from the Tomb of David there is a tomb with three chambers (PEFQS 1900, pp. 226-227). Over the entrance to the tomb, and accompanied by two crosses which have been defaced, is this inscription:

THC AΓIAC
CIωN

Over the doorway which leads from the first chamber in the tomb to the second, and also accompanied by the sign of the cross, is this inscription:

MNH[MA] THC
AΓ[IAC C]IωN

Similar inscriptions are found in a number of other tombs in the area. What we have, then, are readings, τῆς ἁγίας Σιών, "of Holy Sion," μνῆμα τῆς ἁγίας Σιών, "tomb of Holy Sion," and the like. In other words these burial places were in the possession of the church on the hill above, and the name of that church was Hagia Sion, the Church of Holy Sion.

R. A. Stewart Macalister, "The Rock-Cut Tombs in Wâdy er-Rababi, Jerusalem," in PEFQS 1900, pp. 225-248; 1901, pp. 145-158, 215-226; Vincent, *Jérusalem nouvelle*, pp. 421-481, especially pp. 431-440; Kopp, p. 386 n. 45. Photograph: JF.

170. The Cenacle in the Franciscan Restoration of the Fourteenth Century

Hagia Sion was presumably destroyed by the Persians in 614, then built again as the "great basilica" of which Arculf (670) spoke and of which he made a drawing (No. 165). In ruins again when the Crusaders came (1099), the church was rebuilt by them as the Church of Zion or of St. Mary. In the lower story was the Tomb of David and an altar at the spot where Mary died, in the upper story the place of the Last Supper. In 1335 the site came into the possession of the Franciscans. In the second story of the building they gave the Cenacle or Hall of the Last Supper the form which it has today.

As shown in this photograph, there are two columns in the middle of the room, and half-pillars built into the walls, and these carry a pointed vaulting. So the hall which commemorates the holding of the Last Supper

and the coming of the Holy Spirit exists in the form of a Gothic chapel.

Photograph: The Matson Photo Service, Alhambra, Calif.

171. The Church of St. Peter in Gallicantu

After Jesus was apprehended in Gethsemane (Nos. 130ff.) he was taken to Annas (Jn 18:13) and to Caiaphas (Jn 18:24). Annas had been high priest A.D. 6-15 and his son-in-law Caiaphas held the office A.D. 18-36. The scribes and elders gathered with Caiaphas (Mt 26:57; Mk 14:53), i.e., in the high priest's house (Lk 22:54), and there ensued the trial and condemnation of Jesus and the denial of Peter.

In A.D. 66, as Josephus tells us (*War* II 17, 6 §426), revolutionists went into the upper city and burned the house of Ananias the high priest (appointed by Herod of Chalcis [d. in the eighth year of Claudius = A.D. 48], predecessor of Herod Agrippa II [*Ant.* XX 5, 2 §§103-104], Ananias figures in Ac 23:2 and 24:1 and was slain by the brigands in 66 [*War* II 17, 9 §441]) as well as the palaces of Agrippa and Bernice. The palaces were probably additions of Agrippa II to the former palace

of the Hasmoneans (*Ant.* XX 8, 11 §189) on the western slope of the Tyropoeon, and the house of Ananias must also have been somewhere on the southwestern hill which was the site of the upper city (cf. No. 135). If the house of the high priest went with the office this house which Ananias occupied could have been that formerly used by Caiaphas (and perhaps Annas, his father-in-law, at the same time). Even if this was not the case, it probably gives a clue as to the area in which the high priest would be likely to reside.

When the Bordeaux Pilgrim came (333) it was in fact up on Mount Sion that he was shown "where the house of Caiaphas the priest was" (*ubi fuit domus Caifae sacerdotis*) (Geyer p. 22; LPPTS I, p. 23; CCSL CLXXV, p. 16). The perfect tense suggests that the house was in ruins, although still well known, and this is confirmed some years later by Cyril who also knew it well and describes it as ruined and desolate. "The house of Caiaphas will arraign thee," says Cyril (*Catechetical*

Lectures XIII, 38 NPNFSS VII, p. 92), "showing by its present desolation the power of him who was formerly judged there." Evidently in the Christian thought of the time it was deemed appropriate that the place be left lying in its ruins as a visible sign of judgment.

Theodosius (530) gives at least a rough indication of how far the house was from the Cenacle (but not, unfortunately, in what direction), and also gives the information that it had by then been converted into a church named after Peter. Having just referred to the Church of Holy Sion as the mother of all churches (cf. No. 165), Theodosius says (Geyer p. 141; LPPTS II, p. 10; CCSL CLXXV, p. 118): "From holy Sion to the house of Caiaphas, now the Church of St. Peter, it is 50 paces more or less" (*De sancta Sion ad domum Caiphae, quae est modo ecclesia sancti Petri, sunt plus minus passi numero L*).

Fifty meters north of the Cenacle and across a narrow street from the Dormition is the present Armenian chapel, which is held to mark the site of the house of Caiaphas. The chapel is from the fifteenth century, but the few excavations which have been made show that there was a church here in the sixth century. A piece of Byzantine mosaic pavement 4 to 5 meters long and 2.50 meters wide has been found, and a threshold farther west; taken together, these remains may indicate a church some 30 to 35 meters in length. This may have been the Church of Peter.

The monk Epiphanius (780-800) also refers to the place of the Last Supper as the place where the disciples gathered after the ascension at Hagia Sion (MPG CXX col. 209), and puts the house of Caiaphas and thus the place where Peter denied Jesus nearby (MPG CXX col. 261). But with respect to the statement in the Gospels that after his denial Peter "went out and wept bitterly" (Mt 26:75; cf. Mk 14:72; Lk 22:62), Epiphanius indicates a different place for this event and points to another church which marked it. The description he gives seems to be written from the standpoint of one on Mount Sion, inside the city wall, and facing northward. He says: "To the right outside the city and near the wall there is a church where Peter, when he went out, wept bitterly; and to the right from the church, approximately three bowshots distant, is the Pool of Siloah" (MPG CXX col. 264 Kopp pp. 406-407). In distinction, then, from the Church of Peter which was at the house of Caiaphas and near Hagia Sion, the location of this church is eastward down the slope of Mount Sion and perhaps halfway to the Pool of Siloam, and while the former was really a Church of the Denial of Peter this one was a Church of the Repentance or of the Tears of Peter.

Also the monk Bernard (870), having visited Hagia Sion, says: "Directly to the east is a church built in honor of St. Peter, in the place where he denied the Lord" (Tobler-Molinier, *Itinera Hierosolymitana* I 2, p. 316; RB 23 [1914], p. 78; *Biblica* 9 [1928], p. 172). The church must be the one indicated by Epiphanius but here the distinction is not drawn between one place of denial and another place of repentance.

In the time of the Crusaders the church commemorating the Repentance is mentioned repeatedly and in particular connection with the Gospel statement (Mt 26:74 and parallels) that it was when "the cock crowed" (*gallus cantavit*) that Peter remembered the prediction by Jesus of his denial and went out and wept bitterly. Saewulf (1102) speaks of Hagia Sion, which he calls the Church of the Holy Spirit and locates on Mount Sion outside the city wall a bowshot to the south, and a little later writes (LPPTS IV, pp. 19, 21; Vincent, *Jérusalem nouvelle*, p. 494): "Under the wall of the city outside, on the declivity of Mount Sion, is the Church of St. Peter which is called Gallicantus (*ecclesia sancti Petri quae Gallicanus* [sic] *vocatur*), where he hid himself in a very deep cave, which may still be seen, after his denial of our Lord, and there wept over his crime most bitterly." Daniel (1106), having mentioned Mount Sion, writes (LPPTS IV, p. 37): "Not far off, on the eastern slope of the mountain, there is a deep cavern to which one descends by thirty-two steps. It is there that Peter wept bitterly (after) his denial. A church is built above this cave and named after the holy Apostle Peter." And Anonymous VII (1145), to cite one more witness where the church is brought into connection with the Latin phrase about the cock-crowing, writes (LPPTS VI, p. 73): "Beyond Mount Sion is a church where Peter fled when he denied the Lord at the crowing of the cock (*in galli cantu*)."

On the eastern slope of Mount Sion, 250 meters east of the Cenacle, is an area which corresponds to the place indicated in the foregoing quotations and which belongs to the Assumptionist Fathers. Excavations were begun here in 1888, and in 1911 the ruins of an ancient church were found. Original construction toward the end of the fifth century was indicated by coins from Theodosius II (408-450) to Leo I (457-474), and restoration on a smaller scale (no doubt after destruction by the Persians in 614) in the first half of the seventh century by coins of Phocas (602-610) and Heraclius I (610-642). To judge from the citations given above, this was the Church of St. Peter in Gallicantu, marking the supposed place to which the apostle went to weep in repentance after the cock crowed. In 1931 a new church of the same name was dedicated here by the Assumptionists.

The situation of the church just described appears plainly in the photograph (No. 171). This is a telephoto view, looking westward from above Siloam. At the upper right is a portion of the present south wall of the

Old City. Outside the wall, on the summit of Mount Sion, are the buildings and high tower of the Dormition Church and Monastery. To the right of the high tower is the small black dome over the Cenacle and the Tomb of David. Coming down the hill, the large, domed building nearest the camera is the present Church of St. Peter in Gallicantu.

Under this church there are certain rock-hewn chambers. One was probably originally a tomb chamber. Steps lead down into it on the east side but stop abruptly halfway down, showing that it was artificially deepened at a later time. In this room there are galleries surrounding a central court, and rings high up on the walls. On the south side there is a step from which one can look through an aperture in the stone wall and down into the other chamber which is itself a very deep pit. On the inner walls and roof of this pit are fourteen Byzantine cross marks, eleven painted on the walls and three incised in the roof.

On the basis of these finds the theory has been advanced that the house of Caiaphas was actually here rather than near the Cenacle, and that the rock-hewn chambers were the prison associated with that palace. The upper chamber, it is suggested, was a guard chamber and the rings in the walls were used to tie prisoners for flagellation; the lower pit was the place of incarceration and the aperture in the wall allowed the guards to watch those below. That Christ himself was confined here during the night of his trial before Caiaphas is then also surmised.

One other line of argument is also held to favor the location of the house of Caiaphas here at St. Peter's in Gallicantu. If the Cenacle is indeed the place where the disciples gathered after the ascension, it would seem strange that they would so soon meet in a place as close to the residence of Caiaphas as would be the case if that house was at the Armenian site as described above. But if the house of Caiaphas was far down the slope

of the hill at this latter place the difficulty would not arise.

On the other hand the most natural reading of the earlier witnesses, as followed above, would seem to locate the house of Caiaphas in proximity to Hagia Sion, and this makes it most natural to recognize here, farther down the hill, only the church marking the supposed place of Peter's repentance. As for the rock-hewn chambers under the church, some simpler explanation may account for them and some hold, in fact, that the deep pit is only an ancient cistern.

J. Germer-Durand, "La maison de Caiphe et l'église Saint-Pierre a Jérusalem," in RB 23 (1914), pp. 71-94, 222-246; E. Power, "The Church of St. Peter at Jerusalem, Its Relation to the House of Caiaphas and Sancta Sion," in *Biblica* 9 (1928), pp. 167-186; 10 (1929), pp. 116-125, 275-303, 394-416; Vincent, *Jérusalem nouvelle*, pp. 482-515; and "Saint-Pierre en Gallicante," in RB 39 (1930), pp. 226-256; Kopp pp. 405-408. Photograph: The Matson Photo Service, Alhambra, Calif.

172. Ancient Walk with Steps by the Church of St. Peter in Gallicantu

In the vicinity of the Church of St. Peter in Gallicantu are the clear traces of a number of paths or streets, probably representing routes through the city in Jewish and Roman as well as Byzantine times. One of these runs from the vicinity of the Cenacle to the Pool of Siloam and passes directly beside the Church of St. Peter in Gallicantu. A portion of this way beside the church is shown in the photograph, with stone steps to mitigate the steepness of the descent. This path is believed to be from the Jewish period and if, when Jesus went from the Last Supper to Gethsemane (Jn 18:1), he went from Mount Sion to the Kidron he could have walked upon these very steps.

Germer-Durand in RB 23 (1914), pp. 244-245 and Pl. I and III; Lagrange Pl. XXVII facing p. 584. Photograph: JF.

173. The Traditional Site of Akeldama in the
Valley of Hinnom

According to Mt 27:3-10 when Judas returned to the
chief priests the money he had received for betraying
Jesus, they purchased with the money the potter's field
to bury strangers in. Therefore the field was called the
Field of Blood (ἀγρὸς αἵματος, v. 8). Ac 1:19 explains
that in the language of Jerusalem this name (χωρίον
αἵματος) is Ἀκελδαμάχ, Akeldama (RSV), probably corresponding to Aramaic חקל דמא.

In the *Onomasticon* (p. 38) Eusebius gives this listing for the place: "Akeldama. 'Field of Blood.' In the
Gospels. It is shown until now in Aelia north of Mount
Sion (ἐν βορείοις τοῦ Σιὼν ὄρους)." Jerome (*ibid.*, p. 39)
corrects this statement to read "south" (*ad australem*)
rather than north.

Akeldama is also mentioned in the *Onomasticon* (p.
102) in connection with the listing of Topheth. According to Jer 7:31f. the high place of Topheth was in the
valley of the son of Hinnom, and was where sons and
daughters were burned in the fire (cf. No. 135). Eusebius writes: "Topheth. Altar of Topheth in Jeremiah.
The place thus called is shown until now in the suburbs
of Aelia. The Pool of the Fuller and the Field Akeldama
lie beside it." According to this, Akeldama was in the
Valley of Hinnom and in the vicinity of the Pool of the
Fuller. The Pool of the Fuller is probably the same as

Enrogel, the Spring of the Fuller, which in Jos 15:7
and 18:16 appears to be located near the junction of
the valley of the son of Hinnom with the valley of the
Kidron. This location makes it probable that the spring
is to be identified with what is today called Bir Ayyub
or Job's Well, which is below the village of Silwan on
the left bank of the Wadi en-Nar, or Kidron Valley,
shortly after its junction with the Wadi er-Rababi, or
Valley of Hinnom. Accordingly Akeldama should be
sought somewhere toward the east end of the Valley of
Hinnom.

The Anonymous of Piacenza (570) (Geyer p. 177;
LPPTS II, p. 22; CCSL CLXXV, p. 167) went from Siloam
to Akeldama; Arculf (670) (Geyer pp. 243, 245; LPPTS
III, p. 21; CCSL CLXXV, p. 198), who visited Akeldama
often, said that it was situated toward the southern region of Mount Sion (*ad australem montis Sion plagam
situm*).

The traditional site, which corresponds with the above
indications, is on the south slope of the Valley of Hinnom toward its eastern end. A view of the region is
shown in the photograph (No. 173). Looking across to
the south side of the valley, we see at the left the enclosure and buildings of the Greek Monastery of St.
Onuphrius. To the west and above, the ruins mark the
traditional site of Akeldama.

Kopp pp. 408-411. Photograph: courtesy École Biblique et
Archéologique Française.

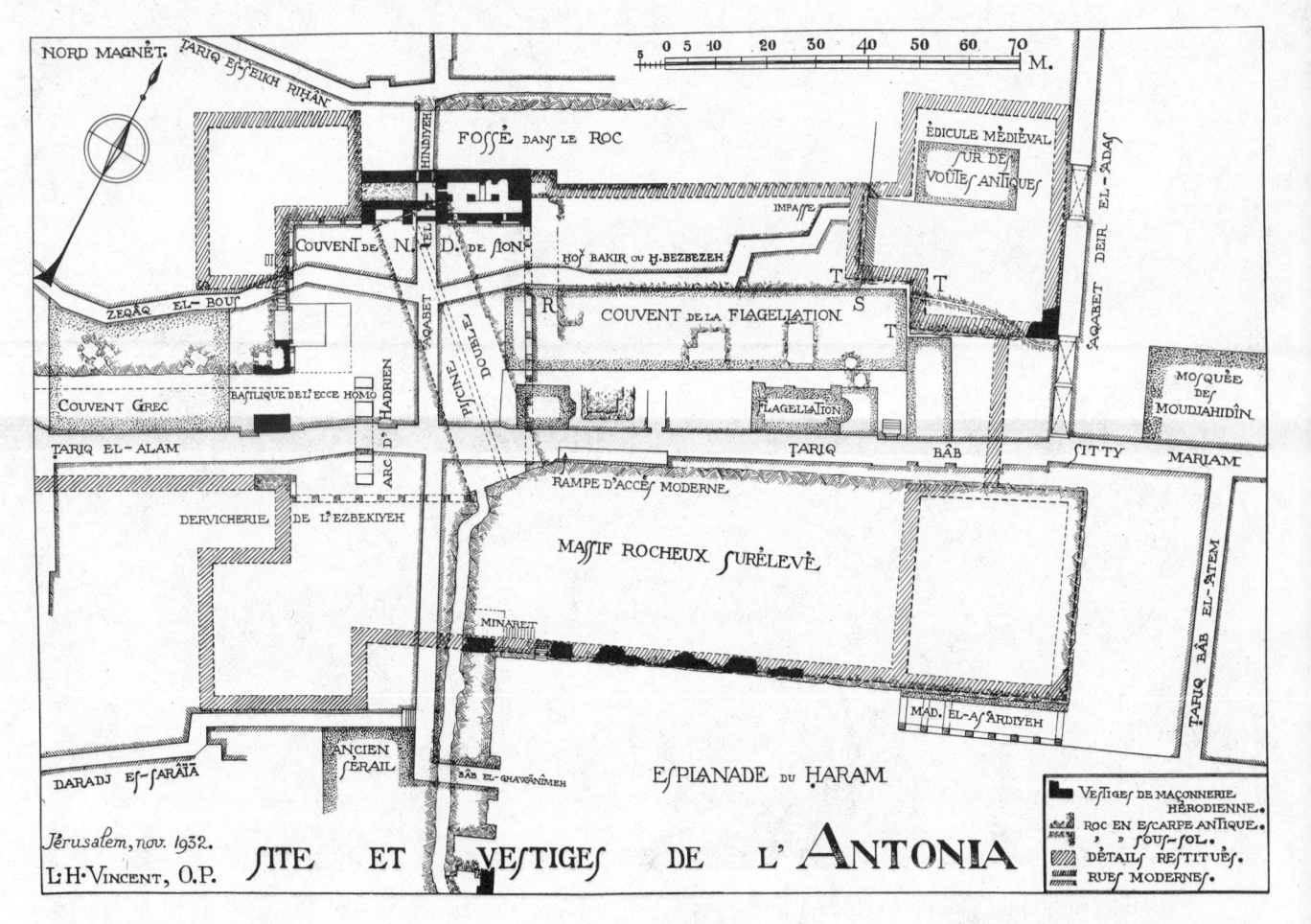

Within the map image, visible labels include: NORD MAGNÉT., ȚARIQ EŞ-ȘEIKH RIḤAN, FOSSÉ DANS LE ROC, ÉDICULE MÉDIÉVAL SUR DE VOÛTES ANTIQUES, AQABET DEIR EL-ADAȘ, COUVENT DE N. D. DE ȘION, HOȘ BAKIR OU Ḥ. BEZBEZEH, IMPAȘȘE, ZEQAQ EL-BOU, COUVENT DE LA FLAGELLATION, ARC D'HADRIEN, PIȘCINE DOUBLE, AQABET, BAȘILIQUE DE L'ECCE HOMO, COUVENT GREC, FLAGELLATION, MOSQUÉE DEȘ MOUDJAHIDÎN, ȚARIQ EL-ALAM, ȚARIQ, BÂB, ȘITTY MARIAM, DERVICHERIE DE L'EZBEKIYEH, RAMPE D'ACCÈS MODERNE, ȚARIQ BÂB EL-ATEM, MINARET, MAȘȘIF ROCHEUX ȘURÉLEVÉ, DARADJ EȘ-ȘARAÏA, ANCIEN ȘÉRAIL, BÂB EL-GHAWÂNIMEH, EȘPLANADE DU ḤARAM, MAD. EL-AȘ'ARDIYEH, Jérusalem, nov. 1932. L. H. VINCENT, O.P. ȘITE ET VEȘTIGEȘ DE L'ANTONIA. Legend: VEȘTIGEȘ DE MAÇONNERIE HÉRODIENNE, ROC EN EȘCARPE ANTIQUE, " SOUS-SOL, DÉTAILȘ REȘTITUÉȘ, RUEȘ MODERNEȘ.

174. Plan Showing the Site and Vestiges of the Antonia

The trial of Jesus before the Roman governor Pilate, procurator of Judea probably in A.D. 26-36 (cf. No. 98), was held at a building, or palace (αὐλή, literally "courtyard" and hence "palace," Mk 15:16), in Jerusalem which is called the praetorium (the Greek πραιτώριον is a loanword from the Latin *praetorium*) in Mt 27:27, Mk 15:16, and Jn 18:28, 33; 19:9. Here Pilate sat on the judgment seat (βῆμα) (Mt 27:19; Jn 19:13) which, as the last reference states, was at a place called Lithostroton, i.e., The Pavement and, in Hebrew, Gabbatha (Λιθόστρωτον, Ἑβραϊστὶ δὲ Γαββαθά). The adjective λιθόστρωτος is derived from λίθος, "stone," and στρώννυμι, "spread," hence means "paved with blocks of stone," and the substantive τὸ λιθόστρωτον means a "stone pavement." As for the equivalent word Γαββαθά, this is the Greek transliteration of an Aramaic word, but one of which the etymological derivation is still uncertain.

At Caesarea in the time of the governor Felix (for his date see FHBC pp. 322f.) we hear of "Herod's praetorium" (Ac 23:35) and surmise, as mentioned above (No. 88), that this was the former palace of Herod the Great which the procurators had taken over for their official residence. In Jerusalem also it may be assumed that the Roman governors appropriated the buildings of Herod for their own use. Here there were two chief buildings, as we have seen, the palace of Herod on the northwestern corner of the southwestern hill of the city (No. 158) and the Antonia at the northwestern corner of the temple area (No. 143). Although Josephus calls the former building a palace (αὐλή) (*War* v 4, 4 §176) and the latter a tower (πύργος) (*War* v 5, 8 §240), both were really fortress-palaces. The palace had banquet halls and guest rooms but was adjacent to the mighty towers of Hippicus, Phasael, and Mariamme, and of it Josephus (*War* v 5, 8 §245) says that the palace of Herod (τὰ Ἡρώδου βασίλεια) was the fortress (φρούριον) of the upper city. The Antonia was a fortress (φρούριον) (*Ant.* xv 8, 5 §292) the whole appearance of which was that of a tower (πυργοειδής) (*War* v 5, 8 §242), but Josephus also compares it with a palace and gives details which show that it fully deserved that comparison. He writes (*War* v 5, 8 §241): "The interior resembled a palace (βασιλείων) in its spaciousness and appointments, being divided into apartments of every description and for every purpose, including cloisters, baths, and broad courtyards for the accommodation of troops (στρατοπέδων αὐλαῖς πλατείαις); so that from its possession of all conveniences it seemed a town (πόλις), from its magnificence a palace (βασίλειον)."

In the thirteenth year of Herod's reign (*Ant.* xv 9, 1 §299), i.e., 25/24 B.C. (cf. FHBC p. 232), there was a famine, and around that time he sent some forces to

156

reinforce the expedition of Aelius Gallus in Arabia (*Ant.* xv 9, 3 §317) which took place in 25-24 (SHJP I i, p. 407); then, when Herod's affairs were in good order and prosperous he built the palace in the upper city (*Ant.* xv 9, 3 §318), so the palace must have been built in 24 or 23. After that Herod built the Herodeion (*Ant.* xv 9, 4 §323) and then started the construction of Caesarea (*Ant.* xv 9, 6 §331), probably in 22/21 since it was probably completed in 10/9 after twelve years of work (cf. No. 88), which also confirms the approximate date given for the building of the palace. While it was only in the eighteenth year of his reign (*Ant.* xv 11, 1 §380), 20/19 (or perhaps the nineteenth, 19/18, FHBC p. 277), that Herod began to build the temple, he must have built the Antonia much earlier, for he presumably needed such a place as soon as possible after he succeeded in taking possession of Jerusalem (37 B.C.), and the giving of the name in honor of his friend Mark Antony (*Ant.* xv 11, 4 §409) must surely have taken place before Antony was defeated (31 B.C.) and Herod transferred his loyalty to Octavian (*Ant.* xv 6, 6 §§187-193; Plutarch, *Antony* 71). Therefore the Antonia must undoubtedly have served as the actual palace of Herod for many years in the earlier part of his reign, and it deserves the designation of a palace as well as a fortress just as much as does the palace-fortress in the upper city.

For the use of the palace in the upper city by the procurators there is adequate evidence. Philo (*The Embassy to Gaius* XXXVIII 299; XXXIX 306; LCL X, pp. 150f., 154f.) relates that on one occasion Pilate, to the annoyance of the Jews, put up golden shields in the palace of Herod; in this connection he also calls Herod's palace the residence of the procurators (οἰκία τῶν ἐπιτρόπων, using the same word ἐπίτροπος by which Josephus [*War* II 9, 2 §169] designates Pilate as procurator). Josephus (*War* II 14, 8 §301) tells how the procurator Florus (64-66) came from Caesarea and lodged at the palace, and this palace is later (*War* II 16, 5 §328) clearly distinguished from the fortress Antonia. Florus also had his judgment seat (βῆμα) placed in front of the building, and took his seat upon it to receive the chief priests and others who came before him.

There is also evidence which makes it likely that upon occasion the procurators were in residence in the Antonia. As noted (No. 143), Josephus (*War* V 5, 8 §244) says that a Roman cohort was permanently quartered there. Particularly at the festivals, he adds, the armed soldiers took up positions around the temple porticoes to watch the people and repress any insurrectionary movement. Particularly at such times also, it seems probable, the procurator might wish to be in residence as close by as possible, i.e., in the Antonia. The apparently swift action of Pilate, who mingled the blood of certain Galileans with that of their sacrifices, according to Lk 13:1, would suggest that at the time he was close at hand. Later, as Josephus relates (*War* II 12, 1 §§224-227; *Ant.* xx 5, 3 §§106-112), when the Feast of Passover was at hand the procurator Ventidius Cumanus (48-52) put troops on the porticoes of the temple. A soldier gave crude offense to the people, and they began to throw stones. Cumanus, fearing an attack upon himself, sent for reinforcements. Again the incident suggests that the procurator was immediately at hand, i.e., in the Antonia.

Since the trial of Jesus before Pilate took place at Passover time (Jn 18:28) the observations in the preceding paragraph constitute an argument for the probability that Pilate was then in the Antonia. A very interesting item of correspondence also exists in the literary references in the fact that Jn 19:13 states that Pilate sat on his judgment seat at a place called the Lithostroton, i.e., a place where stones were spread out in a pavement, and that Josephus (*War* V 5, 8 §241) particularly mentions the "broad courtyards," doubtless paved ones, inside the Antonia. As will be shown shortly, such a large paved courtyard is an impressive part of the remains of the Antonia as found by archeological research.

Turning now to the reports of the early pilgrims we find that, although not always altogether unambiguous, they point generally toward the area where the Antonia stood for the site of the praetorium of Pilate. The Bordeaux Pilgrim (333) (Geyer p. 22; LPPTS I, p. 23; CCSL CLXXV, pp. 16-17) came past the Pool of Siloam, went up on Mount Sion, and went on inside the wall of Sion where he saw the place where David's palace was. Here he was undoubtedly looking at the site where the towers Hippicus, Phasael, and Mariamme still stood, and was assuming that this was the site of David's palace, even as the remains of the tower of Phasael are today called the Tower of David. After that the pilgrim went toward the gate of Neapolis (*ad portam Neapolitanam*). This gate, from which one took the road to Neapolis (cf. No. 44) in the north, was obviously in the north city wall. Facing and moving toward that gate, the Bordeaux Pilgrim writes (*ibid.*): ". . . towards the right (*ad partem dextram*), below in the valley, are walls, where was the house or praetorium of Pontius Pilate (*ubi domus fuit sive praetorium Pontii Pilati*); here the Lord was tried before he suffered. On the left hand is the little hill of Golgotha (*a sinistra autem parte est monticulus Golgotha*) where the Lord was crucified." It seems to be perfectly plain that the Bordeaux Pilgrim had no thought whatsoever that the praetorium was where Herod's palace was in the vicinity of Hippicus, Phasael, and Mariamme, and that he did look toward the praetorium site as somewhere toward the northwest corner of the temple area, i.e., in the area where the Antonia had stood.

In 451 Peter the Iberian (Raabe p. 99) came from the north. He came first to the martyrium of St. Stephen. This was the site north of the Damascus Gate where the Empress Eudocia (444-460) built a basilica in honor of the martyr (Ac 7:60), and where the present St. Stephen's Church now stands with the Dominican Monastery and the École Biblique et Archéologique Française (see No. 193). From there Peter came to Golgotha. From there he descended to the church which is called after Pilate. From there he came to the Church of the Paralytic (i.e., at the Pool of Bethesda), and from there he came to Gethsemane. The church which was called after Pilate was plainly in the area of the Antonia.

Theodosius (530) put the house of Caiaphas at 50 paces more or less from Hagia Sion, as we have seen (No. 171), and then he says (Geyer pp. 141-142; LPPTS II, pp. 10-11; CCSL CLXXV, pp. 118-119): "From the house of Caiphas to the praetorium of Pilate (*De domo Caiphae ad praetorium Pilati*) it is 100 paces more or less. There is the Church of Holy Wisdom (*ecclesia sanctae Sophiae*). . . . From the house of Pilate to the Sheep Pool (*De domo Pilati usque ad piscinam probaticam*) is 100 paces more or less." It seems evident that the distances given by Theodosius are somewhat arbitrary and approximate. At any rate the sequence of places—going from the house of Caiaphas, evidently on Mount Sion, to the praetorium of Pilate and then 100 paces more or less farther to the Pool of Bethesda —is in agreement with a location of the praetorium at the Antonia. If this is correct then the Church of the Holy Wisdom is doubtless the same as the church called after Pilate, mentioned by Peter the Iberian. That a church first designated by its relationship to a place connected with Pilate would not be given the permanent name of the Church of Pilate, but a different name, is very understandable.

The Anonymous of Piacenza (570) says (Geyer p. 175; LPPTS II, pp. 19-20; CCSL CLXXV, p. 141): "And we prayed in the praetorium where the Lord was tried, where there is the basilica of Holy Wisdom in front of the ruins of the temple of Solomon, on a place which extends to the fountain of Siloam beside the portico of Solomon." Again the place indicated fits with the location of the Antonia.

It is true that later pilgrim reports put the praetorium of Pilate on Mount Sion. For a single example, Anonymous Pilgrim VIII (1185) (LPPTS VI, p. 76) speaks of coming to Jerusalem from Nazareth, i.e., from the north. Outside the walls, he says, you will find the place where St. Stephen was stoned. In the midst of the city you will come to the Church of the Holy Sepulcher. Then he writes: "After this we come to Mount Sion, where is St. Savior's Chapel, which is called the judgment hall of Pilate. Here our Lord was crowned, bound, spat upon, and judged by Pilate."

Beyond that he speaks of the place where the Virgin Mary passed away, and the place of the Lord's Supper, and the place where the Holy Spirit descended on the Day of Pentecost, etc., i.e., of Hagia Sion, and beyond that of the place where Peter hid himself when he had denied Christ, and of the fountain of Siloam. The routing is plain and the praetorium, commemorated by a church named St. Savior's, is on Mount Sion a little short, coming from the north, of Hagia Sion. The vestiges of the ancient Church of St. Savior, including a portion of mosaic still in place, are in fact just north of the supposed house of Caiaphas in the Armenian holding on Mount Sion (Vincent, *Jérusalem nouvelle*, p. 489 Fig. 181). Thus the tradition represented by the Anonymous VIII and others of the later period is not the survival of an ancient tradition which put the praetorium where Jesus was tried at the palace of Herod; rather, in general, it simply demonstrates the increasing tendency to localize many traditional events on Mount Sion, and, in particular, it reflects what probably became necessary or desirable after the Muslim occupation of the former temple area, namely, a moving away from that vicinity of a place of Christian pilgrimage.

Both factors, then, the correlation of the situation described in the Gospels with the known circumstances of the time, and the weight of early pilgrim tradition, agree in pointing to the Antonia as the probable praetorium of Pilate at the time of the trial of Jesus.

The illustration (No. 174) shows the site of the Antonia and the vestiges that remain of that fortress-palace. As has already been noted (No. 157) and as is shown on this plan, in the northwestern corner of the temple area and in the vicinity of the minaret known as el-Gawanimeh, there are outcroppings of rock which have been cut down vertically. These and other similar rock scarps, in some cases accompanied by fragments of what appears to be Herodian masonry, mark out a roughly rectangular rock platform which measures about 150 meters from east to west and 90 meters from south to north, say about 13,500 square meters in all. This was the platform on which the Antonia was built.

Vincent, *Jérusalem nouvelle*, pp. 562-586; "L'Antonia, palais primitif d'Hérode," in RB 61 (1954), pp. 87-107; Soeur Marie Aline de Sion, *La forteresse Antonia à Jérusalem et la question du prétoire*. Ex Typis PP. Franciscalium, 1955. For the view that the palace of Herod rather than the Antonia was the praetorium see Pierre Benoit, "Prétoire, Lithostroton et Gabbatha," in RB 59 (1952), pp. 531-550; Eduard Lohse, "Die römischen Statthalter in Jerusalem," in ZDPV 74 (1958), pp. 69-78; Josef Blinzler, *The Trial of Jesus*. Cork: The Mercier Press Ltd., 1959, pp. 173-176. Photograph: courtesy École Biblique et Archéologique Française.

175. View from the Courtyard of the Convent of the Flagellation

The narrow street which runs from east to west into the city from what is now called St. Stephen's Gate, but was earlier called St. Mary's Gate (cf. Nos. 131, 197), has been known as the Tariq Bab Sitty Mariam, and it roughly parallels the northern side of the temple area. On the north side of this street are, from east to west, the Franciscan Convent of the Flagellation, the Convent of Our Lady of Sion also called the Ecce Homo Orphanage, and the Greek Orthodox Convent. Under these buildings explorations and excavations have been possible, chiefly the excavations of M. Godeleine and L.-H. Vincent in 1931-1937 under the Convent of Our Lady of Sion, and of the Franciscans in 1955 under the Convent of the Flagellation. The illustration is a view from the courtyard of the Convent of the Flagellation looking up toward the minaret already mentioned (Nos. 157, 174), which is at the northwest corner of the temple area.

L.-H. Vincent, "L'Antonia et le prétoire," in RB 42 (1933), pp. 83-113; "Autour du prétoire," in RB 46 (1937), pp. 563-570; *Jérusalem*, I (1954), pp. 193-221. Photograph: JF.

176. Cistern Belonging to the Antonia

Underground in the area just described (Nos. 174-175) are the cisterns and basins of an extensive water supply system, a part of which is shown in the photograph. The main element in this system is a very large underground basin extending from northwest to southeast, 52 meters long, 14 meters wide, and as much as 10 meters deep. This is vaulted in such fashion that it looks much like a great double tunnel. On the Plan in No. 174 it is labeled "piscine double." The construction is integral with that of the very large paved courtyard above, of which we will speak in the next section (No. 177). With such cisterns the Antonia was evidently well provided for in respect to its water supply, a provision naturally of great importance, especially in the event of siege.

The further question which arises is whether the large basin just described is to be equated with the pool called Struthion which is mentioned by Josephus. In describing the attack of Titus upon Jerusalem he tells of four earthwork embankments which the Romans erected. Of these one was at the Antonia, and concerning it Josephus writes (*War* v 11, 4 §467): "Of the first two, that at Antonia was thrown up by the fifth legion over against the middle of the pool called Struthion (κατὰ μέσον τῆς Στρουθίου καλουμένης κολυμβήθρας)." The embankment which was erected to facilitate the attack against the Antonia was naturally built at some point outside the Antonia. That point is here identified (if the foregoing translation of the Greek is correct) as over against the middle of the Struthion pool, and the pool is presumably a part of the Antonia, hence may be in fact the large pool described above. Conceivably, however, the translation of the Greek should be to the effect that the embankment was put up "in the middle of the pool called Struthion." In that case the pool would have to be pictured as outside the Antonia, presumably somewhere on the north side, but such a pool has not been identified in that area. Therefore the first

translation and the conclusion that the large water basin in the Antonia was the Struthion pool remain the more likely.

Vincent in RB 42 (1933), pp. 96-102; *Jérusalem*, pp. 203-207; Aline, *La forteresse Antonia*, pp. 64-87; Christian Maurer, "Der Struthionteich und die Burg Antonia," in ZDPV 80 (1964), pp. 137-149. Photograph: JF.

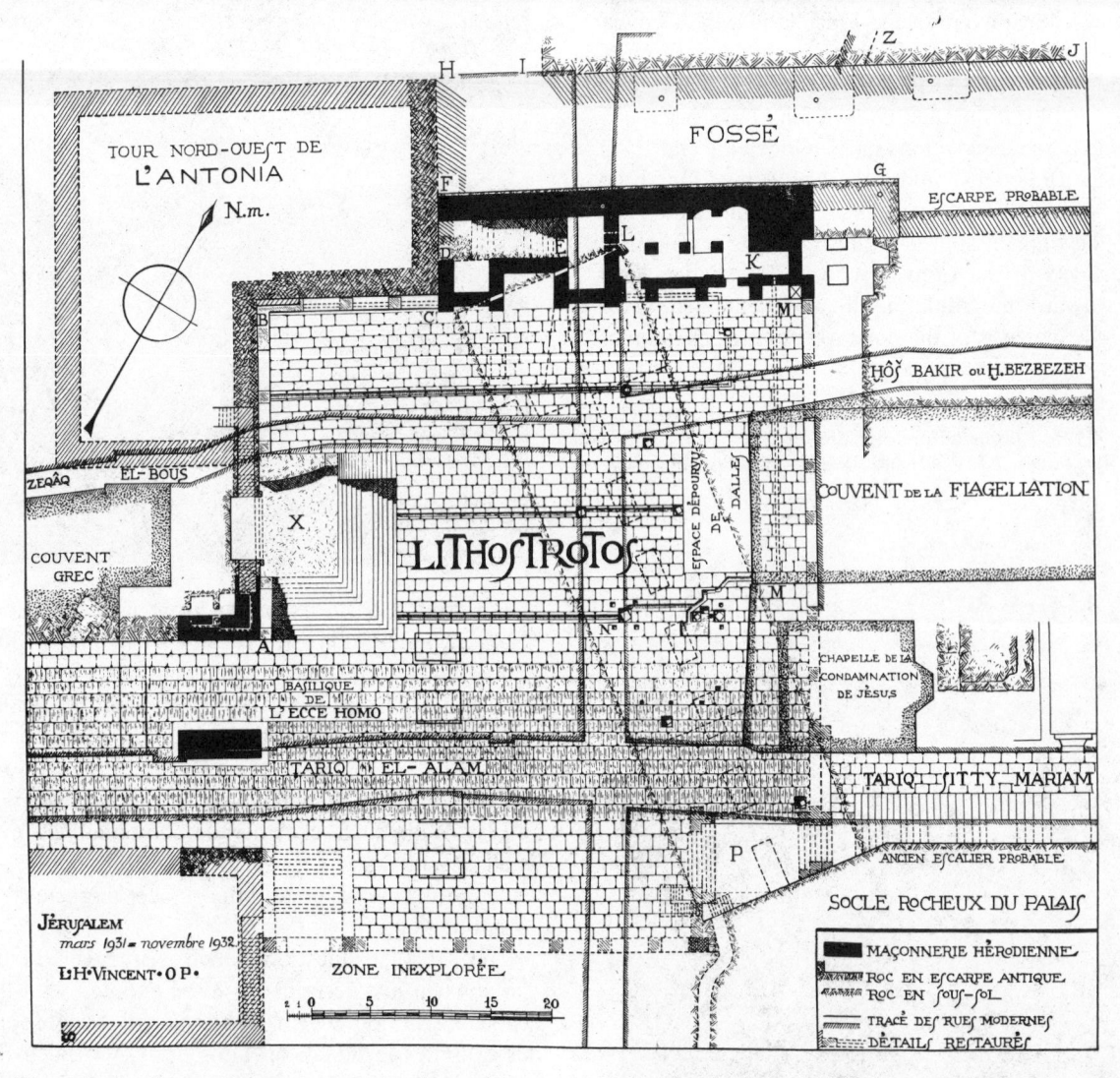

177. Plan of the Stone Pavement of the Antonia

This plan shows the relation of the underground double basin described in the preceding section (No. 176) to the large stone pavement (Lithostrotos), extensive portions of which have been found under the Convent of the Flagellation, the Convent of Our Lady of Sion, and the Greek Orthodox Convent. The pavement extended over an area some 32 meters from west to east, and 48 meters from north to south, thus covering an area of over 1,500 square meters. Architectural remains around the area show that this was an impressive courtyard surrounded by galleries. The paving stones are slabs of limestone, some square and some rectangular, as much as a meter on a side, sometimes as much as two meters or more. Some channels are cut out into the stones for the drainage of rain water.

L.-H. Vincent, "Le Lithostrotos évangélique," in RB 59 (1952), pp. 513-530; *Jérusalem*, pp. 207-214, 216-221; Aline, *La forteresse Antonia*, pp. 88-94, 107-118; W. F. Albright in *The Background of the New Testament and Its Eschatology*, edited by W. D. Davies and D. Daube in honour of Charles Harold Dodd. Cambridge: University Press, 1956, pp. 158-159. Photograph: courtesy École Biblique et Archéologique Française.

178. Striated Paving Stones of the Antonia Courtyard

Toward the south side of this court there is a transverse zone of the paving stones, running from west to east, where the slabs are grooved or striated. The striations run from north to south. Thus it is plain that there was a roadway here running across the court from west to east, and the stones were grooved to prevent the horses' hoofs from slipping. Some of the striated stones appear in the photograph. By following the line of the roadway it was possible to identify the location of the fortified portal at the west side of the Antonia.

Aline, *La forteresse Antonia*, pp. 95-106. Photograph: JF.

179. A Game Board on a Paving Stone of the Antonia

On some of the stones of the Antonia courtyard there were also patterns incised, such as appear in this picture. Such a pattern is recognized as a playing board (*lusoria tabula*), doubtless for the games of the Roman soldiers quartered in the Antonia.

The finding of such an interesting and impressive pavement on the site of the Antonia, coupled with the line of argument in preceding sections (Nos. 174ff.) as to the probable location of the praetorium of Pilate, makes probable the identification of this pavement with the Lithostroton or Gabbatha of Jn 19:13.

For the *lusoriae tabulae* see Aline, *La forteresse Antonia*, pp. 119-142. Photograph: The Matson Photo Service, Alhambra, Calif.

180. The Ecce Homo Arch

In the narrow street in front of the Convent of our Lady of Sion (Ecce Homo Orphanage) is to be seen this arch, a portion of the central arch of a great Roman gateway. The rest of the main arch seen here extends on northward within the walls of the Basilica of the Ecce Homo which is a part of the Convent of our Lady of Sion, while the northern side arch of the same gateway stands behind the altar in the same basilica. The southern side arch of the gateway has been lost on the other side of the street. Within the Ecce Homo Basilica the bases of the arches rest upon the great pavement already described (Nos. 177-179).

Josephus tells us that when Titus took Jerusalem and destroyed the temple (cf. No. 145) he razed the foundations of the Antonia (*War* VI 2, 1 §93), and Josephus also speaks explicitly of "the demolition of Antonia"

(τὴν καθαίρεσιν τῆς Ἀντωνίας) (*War* VI 5, 4 §311). After that we know that Hadrian built the new city of Aelia Capitolina, and we have recognized, in the arch preserved in the Russian Alexander Hospice (No. 160), what is probably the remains of a great gateway leading into the forum of Hadrian's city. The most probable reconstruction of that gateway is a monumental structure with three passages, a larger arch in the center and two smaller ones on the sides. Here we have preserved more extensive portions of another gateway of exactly the same type (see the reconstructions of the two gateways in Vincent, *Jérusalem nouvelle*, p. 31 Fig. 13 for the gateway in the Russian Alexander Hospice; p. 25 Fig. 6 for the gateway here at the Ecce Homo Basilica). Still another gateway of the same type, which is even better preserved and of which the date is certainly known, is the triumphal arch at the southern approach to the city of Gerasa, dating from the time of the

162

visit of Hadrian (129/130) (No. 77). It may be concluded, then, that the arch set down upon the earlier pavement of the Antonia is also an arch of Hadrian and that it marked in a monumental way the eastern entrance to Aelia Capitolina. Other fragments of columns, capitals, etc., found in the area of the Antonia appear to be in part from the time of Herod, in part from that of Hadrian, and it is not always possible to decide clearly between the two periods (ZDPV 80 [1964], p. 148). This situation agrees with the rest of the evidence, which all shows that we may have at the site under consideration the remains of the Herodian An-

tonia and also remains of the work of Hadrian.

The arch just discussed, and the mass of ruins to the north of it, were acquired in 1857 for the Convent of Our Lady of Sion. At that time the arch was supposed to have been the place where Pilate said, "Behold the man!" (*Ecce homo*) (Jn 19:5), and the popular designation of it has continued to be the Ecce Homo Arch.

Vincent, *Jérusalem nouvelle*, pp. 24-31; Aline, *La forteresse Antonia*, pp. 36-38. Photograph: The Matson Photo Service, Alhambra, Calif.

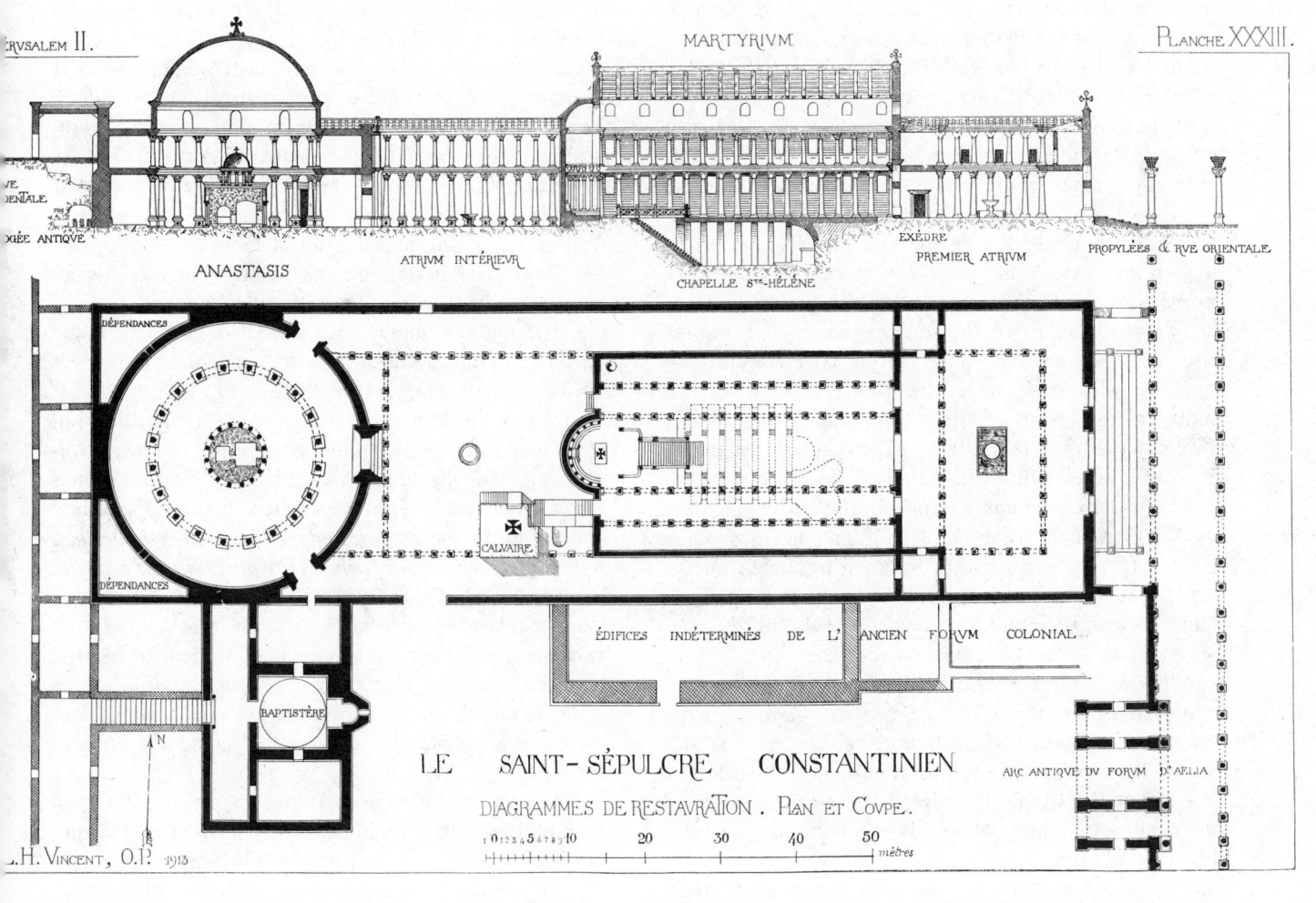

181. Plan and Section of the Constantinian Church of the Holy Sepulcher

The place where Jesus was crucified was called Golgotha. Where they use this name Mt 27:33 and Mk 15:22 explain parenthetically that it means the place of a skull (κρανίου τόπος), and Lk 23:33, omitting the Semitic name, simply calls the place The Skull (Κρανίον). Jn 19:17 also calls the place the place of a skull, and explains that Ἑβραϊστί, i.e., "in Hebrew," as the word means literally and as it probably means actually in Rev 9:11 and perhaps also in Rev 16:16, or "in Aramaic," as the word probably means actually here and elsewhere in Jn, the name is Golgotha. This name is in fact Aramaic, גלגלתא, corresponding to Hebrew, גלגלת, which is translated by κρανίον in Jg 9:53 LXX, etc. In Latin the word for skull is *calva*, and in Jerome's Latin translation of the NT the name of the place is *Calvariae locus* in Mt 27:33, Mk 15:22, and Jn 19:17, and *Calvariae* in Lk 23:33, hence Calvary in English. This place was "near the city" according to Jn 19:20, and "outside the gate" according to Heb 13:12, a place outside the city certainly being normal for execution as well as for burial in both Jewish and Roman custom. In the place there was a garden, and in the garden a new tomb (Jn 19:41), which became the tomb of Jesus.

The remembrance of the place of Golgotha and of the tomb of Jesus on the part of the early Christians in Jerusalem is highly probable. Even when the Jewish Christians fled to Pella on the eve of the Jewish War (Eusebius, *Ch. Hist.* III 5, 3) they were only fifty miles away, and when Jews were forbidden entry into Jerusalem by Hadrian (cf. No. 146) there were Gentile Christians in Jerusalem under a series of bishops, of whom Marcus was the first (Eusebius, *Ch. Hist.* IV 6), to continue the traditions.

As we have seen (No. 145), both Dio and Jerome tell us that Hadrian put a pagan sanctuary of Jupiter on the site of the former Jewish temple. Likewise Jerome (see No. 25) compares the pollution of the birthplace of Jesus in Bethlehem with the fact that from Hadrian onward there was a marble statue of Venus (cf. No. 3) on the rock where the cross had stood, and a figure of Jupiter at the place of the resurrection; and Eusebius (see No. 160) tells us that Hadrian covered the holy sepulcher with earth, paved the whole area (which we think was the forum of Aelia Capitolina), and built a shrine of Venus there. So it is evident that Hadrian carried out a systematic profanation of the shrines of the Jews and the Christians (perhaps not even distinguishing the Christians from the Jews), and he must have selected the place of Calvary for such treatment on the basis of a traditional identification which long antedated his own time and thus reached back into the earliest periods of the Christian movement.

When we continue with the report of Eusebius concerning these events in *The Life of Constantine* (written after the death of Constantine in 337 [IV 64] and before the death of Eusebius in 340), we learn (III 26ff.) that the Emperor ordered the clearing away of the Venus shrine and, while this was being done (326/327), "contrary to all expectation" a tomb came to light in a manner which was a similitude of Christ's own return to life. This was evidently the only tomb on the immediate site, so it was understood to be the sepulcher of Christ. Thereupon Constantine instructed Bishop Macarius to build a church (the term used in the Emperor's letter [III 31] is βασιλική, "basilica," and this word appears here for the first time in literature in reference to a Christian church [FLAP pp. 506, 527]) upon the site and this was done. Constantine's architect was Zenobius (the name is given by Theophanes under

A.M. 5828 = A.D. 328, Crowfoot, *Early Churches*, p. 21 n. 1) and the dedication of the church was in 335 (which was also the thirtieth year [*tricennalia*] of the reign of Constantine), when a large synod of bishops was convened in Jerusalem for the services of consecration (Socrates, *Ch. Hist.* I 28; Sozomen, *Ch. Hist.* II 26). In honor of the occasion Eusebius afterward delivered in Constantinople an oration on the sepulcher of the Savior (ἀμφὶ τοῦ σωτηρίου μνήματος λόγος), as well as an oration in praise of Constantine. He proposed to append both orations to his *Life of Constantine* (IV 33, 40); the latter is found in this position (NPNFSS I, pp. 581ff.) but the former is no longer extant.

While in the foregoing context Eusebius speaks only of the tomb, i.e., of the place of the resurrection, in the *Onomasticon* (p. 74) he lists Golgotha with the notation: " 'Place of a skull,' where Christ was crucified. It is pointed out in Aelia to the north of Mount Sion." This general statement of location is in agreement with what we hear from the Bordeaux Pilgrim (333). As we have already seen (No. 174), he came from Mount Sion and went toward the Neapolis Gate in the north wall of Jerusalem, and the hill of Golgotha was on his left hand. The passage in the itinerary of the Pilgrim from Bordeaux, beginning with the statement just alluded to and continuing with a brief description of the basilica of Constantine which was at that time not yet finished, reads (Geyer pp. 22-23; LPPTS pp. 23-24; CCSL CLXXV p. 17): "On the left hand is the little hill of Golgotha (*a sinistra autem parte est monticulus Golgotha*) where the Lord was crucified. About a stone's throw from thence is a crypt where his body was laid and the third day was raised (*Inde quasi ad lapidem missum est cripta, ubi corpus eius positum fuit et tertia die resurrexit*). There by the command of the Emperor Constantine a basilica has been built, that is, a church (*basilica . . . id est dominicum*), of wonderful beauty, having at the side reservoirs (*excepturia*) from which water is raised, and a bath behind in which infants are washed [i.e. baptized] (*balneum a tergo, ubi infantes lavantur*)."

The location of Golgotha and the tomb of Christ thus indicated by Eusebius and the Bordeaux Pilgrim, north of Mount Sion and on the left hand as one proceeds toward the Neapolis Gate in the north wall of Jerusalem, corresponds with the location of the present Church of the Holy Sepulcher. Although it was inside the third wall of Jerusalem, which corresponded with Hadrian's wall and the present wall of the city on the north side, it was outside the second wall, i.e., the wall of the time of Jesus, according to the evidence presented above (Nos. 159ff.), and in the area of an old quarry which had been utilized as a cemetery (Nos. 159, 161, 183; cf. BA 30 [1967], p. 83); thus it may be accepted as the correct site in accordance with the earliest Christian tradition.

When Eusebius wrote *The Life of Constantine* between 337 and 340 the church had been finished but a short time, and Eusebius gives a description (III 33-40) of it in some detail. This description and some architectural remains are the chief basis for the Plan (No. 181). We follow the description by Eusebius in reverse order and move through the Plan from right to left, i.e., from east to west.

Entrance from the square in front was through monumental propylaea ($\pi\rho o\pi\acute{v}\lambda\alpha\iota\alpha$) or entrance gates. The remains of this portico are north of the Russian Alexander Hospice within which are remains of what was probably the entrance arch to the forum of Aelia Capitolina, as well as remains of the still earlier wall of the city (Nos. 159-160). The portico was nearly 10 meters in depth and 50 meters long.

Next, and several steps higher up, was the first atrium, an open court, entered by three doorways and surrounded by porticoes. It was about 23 meters across from east to west. Beyond this was the main basilica, also entered by three doors. It was probably about 39 meters square, with nave and two aisles on either side. Eusebius says that it was floored with marble slabs of various colors, and roofed with lead on the outside for protection against the winter rains. At the west end of the basilica was a hemisphere ($\acute{\eta}\mu\iota\sigma\phi\alpha\acute{\iota}\rho\iota o\nu$) which rose to the very summit of the church, which may be a way of referring to the apse of the basilica, with a handsome half-dome. Here there were twelve columns, with their capitals adorned with large silver bowls presented by the emperor himself.

Beyond the basilica to the west was the second atrium, a large open space, paved with finely polished stone, and enclosed on three sides (i.e., the north, west, and south, since the basilica was at the east) with long porticoes. Although Eusebius does not mention it at this point, the rock of Calvary was in the southeast corner of this court. The rock was evidently cut away on the sides and left standing to a height of about 4.5 meters, as it still is.

Finally at the west end was the holy sepulcher itself. The tomb was evidently cut free from the hill and "as the chief part of the whole" it was "beautified with rare columns, and profusely enriched with the most splendid decorations of every kind."

Although Eusebius does not mention it, we know that there was also at this time a baptistery which was already a part of the complex of buildings. This was mentioned by the Bordeaux Pilgrim, as quoted just above, and he puts it behind (*a tergo*) the church. The actual place was probably to the south of the tomb, as shown on the Plan (No. 181). At Jerash the baptistery (No. 85)

adjoining the church of St. Theodore is in an analogous position, and we have already noted (No. 86) that the entire cathedral complex at Gerasa was probably a reflection of the arrangement of buildings in the complex at the holy sepulcher in Jerusalem. As for a precedent, it may be added that the Constantinian Martyrion is much like the Severan basilica at Leptis Magna in Tripolitania (Conant p. 8).

Vincent, *Jérusalem nouvelle*, pp. 89-300 and specially Pl. XXXIII; Joachim Jeremias, *Golgotha*. ΑΓΓΕΛΟΣ, Archiv für neutestamentliche Zeitgeschichte und Kulturkunde, Beiheft 1, 1926; Crowfoot, *Early Churches*, pp. 9-21; J. G. Davies, "Eusebius' Description of the Martyrium at Jerusalem," in AJA 61 (1957), pp. 171-173; André Parrot, *Golgotha and the Church of the Holy Sepulchre*. Studies in Biblical Archaeology 6. New York: Philosophical Library, 1957; Kenneth J. Conant and Glanville Downey, "The Original Buildings at the Holy Sepulchre in Jerusalem," in *Speculum* 31 (1956), pp. 11-48 and specially p. 19, Pl. IV for a plan with some modifications from that in our No. 273 (this article is cited in the present context as Conant); P. Testini, "L'Anastasis alla luce delle recenti indagini," in *Oriens Antiquus* 3 (1964), pp. 263-292; Robert H. Smith, "The Tomb of Jesus," in BA 30 (1967), pp. 74-90. Photograph: courtesy École Biblique et Archéologique Française.

182. Ancient Masonry under the Church
of the Holy Sepulcher

In the description from which we have just quoted (No. 181) Eusebius says that Constantine put beautiful columns and other decorations at the tomb of Jesus, but does not make it plain in this passage whether an actual building was erected over the sepulcher or not. In the *Oration in Praise of Constantine*, delivered in 335, however, he speaks of "the hallowed edifices and consecrated temples which you have raised as trophies ($\tau\rho\acute{o}\pi\alpha\iota\alpha$) of his victory over death; and those lofty and noble structures, imperial monuments of an imperial spirit, which you have erected in honor of the everlasting memory of the Savior's tomb" (XI 2). Here the plural certainly sounds as if more than just the Martyrion basilica were referred to, and one interpretation would make the "consecrated temples" the buildings of the Martyrion and the baptistery, and the "hallowed edifices" those of the tomb and its porticoes (Conant p. 44). If this is correct, Constantine had probably already built an actual building around the tomb. At any rate, such a building surely existed only a few years later, when Cyril gave lectures in it (see below No. 183). Far underground, beneath the portion of the Church of the Holy Sepulcher now known as the Rotunda, where the traditional tomb is, there are some sections of ancient masonry forming part of a curving wall. Here, in the light of the evidence just given, we probably have a portion of the structure which Constantine himself built around the tomb. The photograph shows a section of this masonry at a point immediately opposite two ancient *kokim* graves, known as the family tomb of Nicodemus.

Photograph: JF.

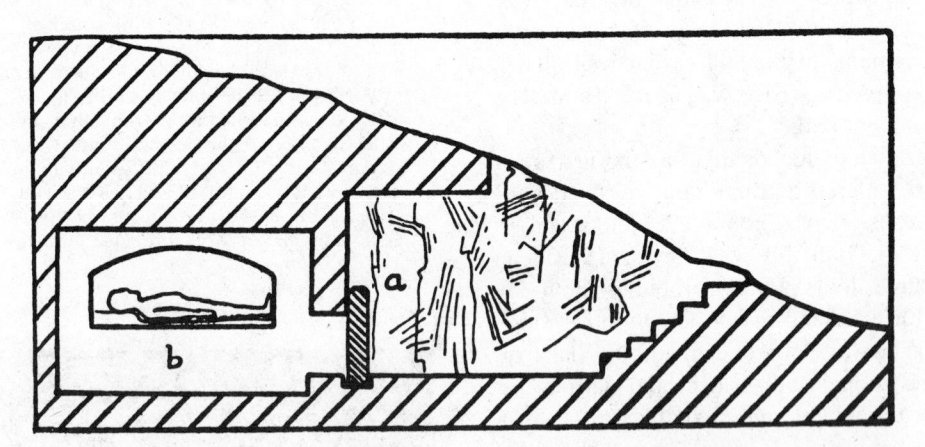

183. Hypothetical Reconstruction of the Tomb of Jesus

The Church of the Holy Sepulcher was seen, evidently still under construction, by the Bordeaux Pilgrim in 333, it was completed in 335, and it was described in detail (see No. 182) by Eusebius soon after 337. In 348, only ten to fifteen years later, in the season leading up to Easter (Sozomen, *Ch. Hist.* VII 19, says that the interval before the festival of the resurrection, called Quadragesima, consisted of six weeks in Palestine, although seven at Constantinople), Cyril of Jerusalem gave his famous series of *Catechetical Lectures* in this church. We can discern that the introductory lecture was delivered in the basilica proper, i.e., the Martyrion, before the whole congregation, with the catechumens present, because we hear Cyril ask them (*Procatechesis* 4 NPNFSS VII, p. 2) if they behold the venerable constitution of the church, and if they view her order and discipline, the reading of Scriptures, etc. For the third lecture, which dealt with baptism, it is possible that the catechumens were assembled in front of the baptistery, for Cyril says (*Catechetical Lectures* III 2) to them that they are now meanwhile standing outside the door. In several later lectures mention is made of looking at the rock of Calvary. The Martyrion may well have been so arranged, as the Plan (No. 181) shows, that a view of the rock was possible for at least some of the congregation from inside the basilica. But it is also very possible that for these lectures the group was assembled in the second atrium. There Cyril could have lectured in one of the porticoes, as the Greek philosophers did in the stoas, and the rock would have been visible to all. That this was the case is the more probable because in *Lecture* IV 10 he speaks of "this blessed Golgotha, in which we are now assembled," and goes on to say that Jesus was crucified "on Golgotha here" (IV 14) and "in Golgotha" (XIII 23). Again he speaks of Golgotha as "the holy hill standing above us here" (X 19) and uses such phrases as "here is Golgotha" (XIII 4), "this most holy Golgotha" (XIII 22), "in this Golgotha" (XIII 26), and "this holy Golgotha, which stands high above us" (XIII 39). On one occasion he even asks his hearers if they see the spot of Golgotha, and they answer with a shout of praise (XIII 23).

In Lecture XVIII Cyril speaks to the catechumens when they have been "wearied by the prolongation of the fast of the Preparation [i.e., Friday], and by the watchings" (XVIII 17), and when they are about, on Easter eve, to receive baptism (XVIII 32 cf. NPNFSS VII p. xlv). After baptism and after celebration of the church service on Easter Sunday, the newly initiated ones are to come on the second day of the week (i.e., on Monday) and for four more days to hear of the "spiritual and heavenly mysteries" (XIX 1), i.e., the doctrines which may be taught only to fully-admitted church members, doctrines which are set forth by Cyril in his so-called Mystagogical Lectures (XIX-XXIII). As he instructs his hearers about attendance at these post-Easter lectures Cyril says that they are to come "into the holy place of the resurrection" (ἅγιον τῆς ἀναστάσεως τόπον). This must assuredly mean that there was a building around and over the tomb, and a building of proportions sufficient for such a meeting as Cyril was announcing. At a later date the same thing is attested when Epiphanius Bishop of Salamis visited Jerusalem in 394, and delivered an address to clergy and people in the presence of John the Bishop "in front of the Lord's tomb," as Jerome reports (*To Pammachius against John of Jerusalem* 11 NPNFSS VI, p. 430, cf. VII p. 142 n. 3).

In the *Catechetical Lectures* Cyril not only appeals to Golgotha and the Holy Sepulcher as bearing witness to Christ, but also speaks of the wooden Cross in the same way. He says, for example (X 19 cf. IV 10; XIII 4): "The holy wood of the Cross bears witness, seen among us to this day, and from this place now almost filling the whole world, by means of those who in faith take portions from it." Here there must be an allusion to the discovery of what was believed to be the cross on which Jesus was put to death, a discovery made, according to Socrates (*Ch. Hist.* I 17) and Sozomen (*Ch. Hist.* II 1), by Helena the mother of Constantine. According to the narrative of these fifth-century church historians, three crosses were found and the cross of Jesus was identified by a miracle. Eusebius himself, however, although he tells of the visit of Helena to Palestine (*The Life of Constantine* III 41-47) does not mention her finding of the cross. It is uncertain, therefore, if the Chapel of St. Helena shown under the Martyrion in the Plan of the Constantinian buildings (No. 181) was actually a part of the Constantinian structure or was added at a later time. In the sixth century the Jerusalem Breviary (Geyer p. 153; LPPTS II, p. 13; CCSL CLXXV, p. 109; Conant p. 11) states that when one enters the church of Constantine there is at the west (*ab occidente*) a vault where the three crosses were found and, above (*desuper*) this vault a place at a higher level with an altar supported by nine columns. Today the latter and higher crypt is called the Chapel of St. Helena and the lower sub-crypt is the Chapel of the Invention (i.e., of the finding) of the Holy Cross.

Most interesting of all, perhaps, in the *Lectures* of Cyril is what he has to say about the original tomb itself. In this connection it may be remembered that Cyril was probably born in Jerusalem c. 315 and therefore could very well have seen the tomb as it was before the changes made by Constantine's workmen, as well as after. As to the location of the tomb, it was stated in Jn 19:41 to be in a garden, and Cyril says (XIV 5) that, although the place had by then been so much adorned with royal gifts, "yet formerly it was a garden, and the signs and the remnants of this remain." As to the type of construction of the original tomb and the nature of the changes made in the course of Constantine's constructions, Cyril says (XIV 9) that there was formerly a cave before the door of the Savior's sepulcher, but this outer cave was cut away for the sake of the present adornment. Presumably this means that the cutting away of the outer cave was to make room for the "rare columns" and "splendid decorations" which, as we have seen (No. 182), Eusebius (*Life of Constantine* III 34) says were put around the tomb, as well as for such building as was erected above it. There was also a stone which closed the door of the tomb, and Cyril says that this was rolled away and was still "lying there to this day" (XIII 39; XIV 22).

What Cyril says suggests that this tomb was a normal Jewish tomb as known from other examples in the Herodian period (cf. Nos. 209-210). In its simplest form and as shown in the drawing (No. 183), such a tomb consisted of an antechamber (a) which was cut out of the rock and entered perhaps by some steps, then a low doorway closed by a stone door or by a rolling stone (cf. Nos. 228, 235), and a passageway leading into a generally rectangular tomb chamber (b). In the tomb chamber the graves were usually of either the kokim or the arcosolia type. The kok was a horizontal shaft driven back into the vertical rock face, into which the body was placed lengthwise. The arcosolium provided a ledge cut laterally into the rock with a vaulted arch over it. In either case the body, wrapped in a winding-sheet, was usually laid on the bare rock. Occasionally a sarcophagus was used. The drawing is intended to represent a rolling stone at the doorway and an arcosolium grave in the tomb chamber. That the arcosolium is shown as recessed into a side wall is only a matter of simplicity in the drawing; it might as well have been in the back wall. The antechamber or vestibule in front with its projecting ledge of rock for a partial roof would constitute what Constantine's workmen cut away to isolate and beautify the tomb proper.

The reconstruction corresponds not only with the allusions by Cyril but also with the details of the Gospel narratives. The tomb of Joseph of Arimathea was hewn in the rock (Mt 27:60; Mk 15:46; Lk 23:53), and was closed by a rolling stone (Mt 28:2; Mk 16:4; Lk 24:2; cf. Jn 20:1). There was probably an antechamber into which one could go without entering the tomb chamber proper; standing in this vestibule one had to stoop down to look into the tomb chamber itself (Jn 20:5). The actual burial place was probably a shelf or ledge, no doubt with an arch above, i.e., it was an arcosolium rather than a kok, for there was place to sit where the body was (Mk 16:5; Jn 20:12).

That the Anastasis stood in an area associated with burials is shown by the existence of a rock-hewn tomb with three kokim on each of three sides of the tomb chamber, found under the foundations of the Rotunda of the Church of the Holy Sepulcher on the west side (Kopp p. 425), as well as by the rock tombs found under the Coptic Convent just to the northeast of the Church of the Holy Sepulcher (see No. 159).

Vincent, *Jérusalem nouvelle*, pp. 93-96, with Fig. 53 giving the reconstruction of a tomb essentially the same as we have shown but slightly more elaborate; Conant p. 3; Parrot, *Golgotha and the Church of the Holy Sepulchre*, pp. 43-48. Photograph: Parrot, *op.cit.*, p. 45 Fig. IX, courtesy Philosophical Library, New York.

184. Apse Mosaic in Santa Pudentiana

From the pilgrim Aetheria (385) we learn the names by which, at least in her time, the buildings at the rock of Calvary and over the tomb of Jesus were known. In the account of her pilgrimage she reports on the church services which were held at Jerusalem. These were held on every day (LPPTS I, p. 45), on the Lord's day (*ibid.*, p. 47), on several festivals (*ibid.*, pp. 50f., 69ff.), and during the period prior to Easter (which she says was of eight weeks duration rather than the six reported by Sozomen [cf. No. 183]) (*ibid.*, pp. 52ff.). From her account of what transpired on Palm Sunday we have already quoted (Nos. 120, 123). Finally Aetheria refers to an eight-day festival called the "days of dedication" (*dies enceniarum* = Greek τὰ ἐγκαίνια), which we recognize to be the same as the festival of the same length described by Sozomen (*Ch. Hist.* II 26) in which the anniversary of the consecration of the "temple" (as she calls it) at Golgotha was celebrated by the church of Jerusalem. The record of Aetheria is (Geyer p. 100; LPPTS I, p. 76; CCSL CLXXV p. 89): "Those days are called the days of dedication, on which the holy church in Golgotha, called the Martyrium (Latin *martyrium* = Greek μαρτύριον), and the holy church at the Anastasis (Latin *anastase* = Greek ἀνάστασις), where the Lord rose again after his passion, were on that day (*ea die*) consecrated to God."

Here we have for Constantine's basilica the name Martyrion, which means "witness" or "testimony" and may be taken as meaning something to the effect that this church was a witness to the place of the martyrdom of Christ and thus a monument testifying to his own witness to the world in his crucifixion. Likewise the name of the church at the tomb is Anastasis, meaning "resurrection," and thus this building was intended to stand as witness to this event. Furthermore we gather from the most natural reading of the statement that both of these churches had been dedicated in a double ceremony on a single day, hence had been built at the same time, i.e., both by Constantine as we have already thought probable (cf. No. 182).

In the account by Aetheria we also read with interest of the services which were held on the Friday of the Easter week, particularly those which extended from the sixth to the ninth hour of that day. At this point Aetheria speaks of what we have called the second atrium of the Constantinian complex, namely, the "atrium, very large and beautiful, situated between the Cross and the Anastasis," and says that in this place "a chair (*cathedra*) is placed for the bishop in front of the cross" and there readings take place during the solemn hours just mentioned (Geyer p. 89; LPPTS I, p. 64; CCSL CLXXV, p. 81).

This passage is of particular interest because it is practically a description of much of the scene in the apse mosaic of the Church of Santa Pudentiana in Rome. This mosaic, shown in the illustration (No. 184), has already been cited in No. 24 where it was explained that it probably dates from Pope Siricius (384-399), and is therefore approximately contemporary with Aetheria (385). Central in the background in the mosaic is what is surely the rock of Calvary, and this is surmounted by a jeweled cross. The arcade with tiled roof which runs across the picture may be intended to represent the porticoes of the second atrium in the complex of Constantinian buildings at Jerusalem. In front of the rock Christ is seated upon a throne, and on either side of him are the apostles. These were once

twelve in number but the outermost figure on each side has been lost in later alterations of the apse. As was customary in Roman tradition at that time (FLAP p. 522 and p. 524 n. 47) Peter stands at the viewer's right at the left hand of Christ, and Paul at the viewer's left. Over the heads of these two men two women, representing perhaps the Jewish Church and the Gentile Church, hold wreaths of laurel, the symbols of victory for the two great martyrs. Above in the sky, partly destroyed, are the winged symbols of the four evangelists, the man, lion, ox, and eagle from Ezk 1:10; 10:14; Rev 4:7, standing for Matthew, Mark, Luke, and John respectively (FLAP p. 525). The buildings behind the arcade at the right probably represent those erected by Constantine in Bethlehem (No. 24); the buildings at the left are probably those of Constantine at the rock of Calvary and the tomb of Jesus in Jerusalem, and the round, domed building is presumably to be identified as the Anastasis.

Photograph: cf. FLAP Fig. 187.

185. Jerusalem on the Madaba Mosaic Map

On the Madaba Mosaic Map (560) we have a representation of Jerusalem at the height of the Byzantine period and the most prominent of all the city's monuments is unmistakably recognizable as the Church of the Holy Sepulcher. The Madaba Mosaic pictures the city as enclosed in an oval wall. Above at the left is the label, ἡ ἁγία πόλις Ιερουσα[λημ], "the holy city Jerusalem." Through the city from north to south runs a great colonnaded street which, in a Roman city such as Aelia Capitolina, would be the *cardo maximus*. At the north end of this street is an oval place, with a large column,

and in the wall an important gate. As the principal gate on the north this will be the Gate of Neapolis (*porta Neapolitana*) of the Bordeaux Pilgrim (333) (Geyer p. 22; LPPTS I, p. 23; CCSL CLXXV, p. 16; cf. Nos. 174, 181). Theodosius (530) (Geyer pp. 141-142; LPPTS II, p. 11; CCSL CLXXV, p. 118) calls the gate on the north the Galilean Gate (*porta Galilaeae*), and says that outside it was the church built by Eudocia (444-460) in memory of the stoning of Stephen. Because of this connection the gate was also known as St. Stephen's Gate (*porta sancti Stephani*), as it is called by Arculf (670) (Geyer p. 224; LPPTS III, p. 2; CCSL CLXXV, p. 185). Today it is the Damascus Gate, and the Arabic name for it is Bab el 'Amud or Gate of the Column, an obvious reference to the great column which once stood in the plaza and is shown on the Mosaic Map.

At the south end the main colonnaded street ends at a small gate which corresponds to the present Zion Gate of the Old City of Jerusalem. The south wall of the city on the Mosaic Map swings out farther south than the Zion Gate and surrounds the area of Mount Sion where we have already recognized (No. 165) the large building (indeed the second largest building in the whole city) that represents the basilica of Hagia Sion. The same south wall evidently continues on eastward to enclose the Pool of Siloam. We have already seen (No. 141) that the Anonymous of Piacenza (570) (Geyer p. 176; LPPTS II, p. 21; CCSL CLXXV, p. 166) says that Eudocia added to the city these walls which enclosed Siloam, so this entire southern extension of the city wall is probably the work of that empress. Given a southern wall, then, enclosing Mount Sion and the Pool of Siloam in this fashion, it is evident that the gate at the south end of the *cardo maximus* was no longer a gate in the south wall but a gate which was left in the interior of the city. In this connection it may be recalled that the Bordeaux Pilgrim found Sion outside the wall (No. 174), but the monk Epiphanius (750-800) spoke of Sion as inside the wall (No. 171),

while Saewulf (1102) again found Sion outside as it is today (No. 171).

Another colonnaded street runs from the southeastern corner of the plaza and more or less parallels the *cardo maximus* to the east. This probably follows the course of the Tyropoeon Valley, between the temple area and the upper city, and corresponds to the street called Tariq el-Wad in modern times. At about the middle of this street, a shorter street runs eastward to a gate. These correspond to the street called Tariq Bab Sitty Mariam and the gate known as St. Stephen's Gate in the east wall of the city (cf. No. 175).

In the west city wall about one-third of the way from the Church of the Holy Sepulcher to the southwest corner of the city is a gate with a tower behind it and a street running eastward from it. The gate corresponds to the modern Jaffa Gate, and the tower must be the Tower of David. The street would be the *decumanus* of the Roman city, the street running through it from west to east. Although there was not room on the mosaic to show its continuation, it probably continued across the *cardo* to the temple area and thus was equivalent to the modern David Street and Street of the Gate of the Chain.

Now we come to the Church of the Holy Sepulcher. In the middle of the *cardo* the colonnade on the west side is broken by four steps which lead up to three doors. These give access to a basilica which has a triangular pediment and a red sloping roof indicated by criss-cross lines. This must be the Martyrion. Beyond, i.e., west of this is a court shown in black cubes, which must be the second atrium of the Calvary. And further west is a great dome which must be the Anastasis.

South of the church in line with the three doors is an open area which is probably the forum of Aelia Capitolina, where the Russian Alexander Hospice, Lutheran Church, and Muristan are now (cf. No. 159). On the west side of this area and on the south side of the basilica is another building with a red roof, the criss-cross lines of which are probably intended to represent a dome. This will probably be the baptistery attached to the Church of the Holy Sepulcher.

Vincent, *Jérusalem nouvelle*, pp. 922-925; Peter Thomsen, "Das Stadtbild Jerusalems auf der Mosaikkarte von Madeba," in ZDPV 52 (1929), pp. 149-174; 192-219 and specially Pl. 6 facing p. 184; Avi-Yonah, *Madaba Mosaic*, pp. 50-60; R. T. O'Callaghan in DB Supplément V, cols. 656-666. Photograph: courtesy Victor R. Gold.

186. Plan of the Church of the Holy Sepulcher according to Arculf

In the month of May in the year 614 the Persians broke into the city of Jerusalem, burned the Christian sanctuaries, massacred many persons who had taken

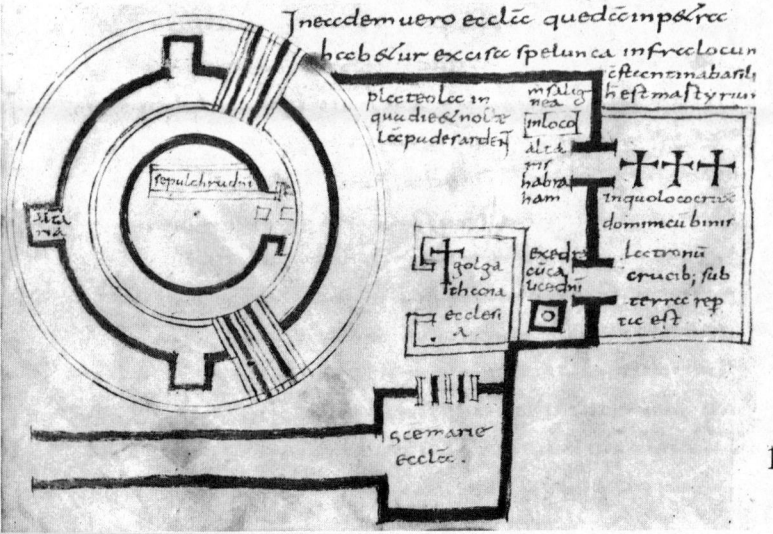

refuge in them and carried others off captive, including Zacharias the patriarch. Afterward Heraclius (575-642) appointed Modestus to serve as vicar in place of the captive bishop, and provided funds for the rebuilding of the sanctuaries. These works of reconstruction were carried out by Modestus, like "a second Bezaleel, or a new Jerubbabel," as Eutychius (940) says, who relates these events and also describes the rebuilt Church of Golgotha and of the Resurrection as still standing in his day (*Annales* MPG 111, cols. 1083f., 1091; LPPTS XI, pp. 36-38, 47-48; SWDCB III, p. 929). As rebuilt, the church was no doubt simpler than the splendid structures of Constantine, but was laid out along essentially the same lines (Vincent, *Jérusalem nouvelle*, p. 218). By way of comparison, it is probable that the roughly contemporary Church of St. Demetrius in Thessalonica was much like this basilica (Conant p. 8).

Eutychius (MPG 111, col. 1099; LPPTS XI, pp. 65-66; CEMA I, pp. 25-26) also tells what happened when the Muslims took Jerusalem in 638, and as far as the Church of the Holy Sepulcher is concerned the story is a happier one than that when the Persians came. Upon entering the city the conquering Caliph 'Umar came and sat down in the *sahn* (court) of the Ἀνάστασις, i.e., probably in the atrium in front of the Church of the Resurrection. When the time of prayer came he said to the Patriarch Sophronius, who had surrendered the city to him, "I wish to pray." Sophronius said, "O Commander of the Faithful, pray where you are," but 'Umar replied, "I will not pray here." The patriarch then took the caliph to the basilica of Constantine, i.e., the Martyrion, but 'Umar said, "I will not pray here either." Then the caliph went out to the steps which are at the door of Constantine's church, at the east end, and prayed there alone upon the steps. He explained that if he had prayed within the church the Muslims would have considered that a ground for seizing the church, and he gave Sophronius a charter forbidding Muslims to be called together in that place for prayers by the voice of the muezzin.

Arculf came not many years later (670) and tells us how this "very great church" appeared to him (Geyer pp. 227ff.; LPPTS III, pp. 5ff.; CCSL CLXXV, pp. 186ff.). Also he made a drawing of the church which is reproduced here (No. 186) from the ninth-century manuscript of his *De locis sanctis* known as Codex Parisinus (Latin 13048) (cf. Testini in *Oriens Antiquus* 3 [1964], pp. 272f.). Reading his description and looking at his drawing, we find that he describes a large round church over the sepulcher, supported by twelve stone columns (not shown in his drawing), with entrances from the northeast and southeast, and with altars in recesses in the walls on the north, west, and south. Next, moving eastward, there is a four-sided church on the site of Golgotha. Opposite this, on the north side of the court, is a small square in which, the legend on the Plan says, by day and night lamps burn. Beside this is another place where, also according to the legend, Abraham built an altar, namely, the altar on which it was proposed to sacrifice Isaac. On to the east is the basilica known as the Martyrium. Under this was found the cross of Christ, with the two crosses of the robbers. Between the basilica of Golgotha and the Martyrium is an exedra, i.e., a small chamber or chapel, in which, it was said, was the cup which the Lord gave to the apostles at the Last Supper. Finally, adjoining the four-sided Church of Golgotha on the south side is the four-sided Church of St. Mary, the mother of the Lord, a building evidently somewhat to the east of the baptistery in the Constantinian complex (No. 181).

> Vincent, *Jérusalem nouvelle*, pp. 218-247. Photograph: Arculfus De Locis Sanctis, Codex Parisinus Lat. 13048, courtesy Bibliothèque Nationale, Paris.

187. Bell Tower at the Church of the Holy Sepulcher

In 1009 the famous church was destroyed by the Fatimid Caliph al-Hakim, but was later rebuilt by the Byzantine emperor Constantine IX Monomachus (1042-1054). At the capture of Jerusalem by the

Crusaders in 1099 the timber-domed rotunda of Constantine Monomachus still rose above the holy sepulcher, and the rock of Calvary stood to the height "of a lance" in the south side of the court to the east. The Martyrion was in ruins, but the crypt of St. Helena under it still existed.

The Crusaders then built a church which enclosed under one roof both the rock of Calvary and the court which had adjoined it, and they connected this church with the rotunda over the tomb by a triumphal arch. From the same church a stairway descended into the crypt of St. Helena, made into a chapel. The east-west direction of the Constantinian complex was given up, and the entrance was across a court, marked by a bell tower, on the south side of the Rotunda. With some repairs and modifications through the centuries, this church of the Crusaders has continued to exist until today.

In 1935 a structural survey revealed the great dilapidation of the building, and iron scaffolding was provided to prevent complete collapse. In 1963 the Greek Orthodox, Roman Catholic, and Armenian churches began works of repair and renovation expected to continue for five years and intended to make the church once again resemble in almost every particular that built by the Crusaders in the twelfth century.

The photograph is taken from the court on the south side and shows the Crusaders' bell tower at the left of the main entrance. The tower is held together with iron bands, and some of the iron scaffolding supporting the walls of the church is visible at the right. Behind the bell tower the dome of the Rotunda may be glimpsed.

Vincent, *Jérusalem nouvelle*, pp. 248-300; William Harvey, *Church of the Holy Sepulchre, Jerusalem, Structural Survey, Final Report*, 1935. Photograph: JF.

188. The Church of the Holy Sepulcher from the Tower of the Lutheran Church

This view of the Church of the Holy Sepulcher is taken, looking northwest, from the high tower of the German Lutheran Church of the Redeemer at the northeast corner of the area known as the Muristan, where once was the forum of Aelia Capitolina (No. 159). At the left is the bell tower (No. 187), and beside it the portal of the church. The large dome rises over the tomb. The small dome is above the Choir of the Greeks, at the east side of which steps lead down into the Chapel of St. Helena. The small terrace on this side of the domes is over the rock of Golgotha.

Photograph: JF.

189. Looking East from the Tower of the Lutheran Church

This additional view, also taken from the tower of the Lutheran Church, helps to bring out the relationship of the Muristan and Holy Sepulcher area to the rest of Jerusalem. Looking across the rooftops of the city we see at a distance the Dome of the Rock in the temple area and, beyond that, the Mount of Olives with the Russian Tower on the high summit.

Photograph: JF.

172

190. The Rocky Hill known as Gordon's Calvary

From the foregoing (Nos. 181ff.) it is abundantly
evident that the appearance of the site of Golgotha and
the Holy Sepulcher is very different now from what
it was in the time of Jesus. At that time, if the above
analysis is correct, the area was a garden area outside
the city wall, and now the area is within the city wall
and densely packed with buildings. Also the modifications introduced by Hadrian in the building of the
forum of Aelia Capitolina, and by the workmen of
Constantine as they cut away large parts of the rock
of Calvary and of the tomb, have very largely altered
the appearance of what does remain of the natural
and ancient features of the first century, while the
church of the Crusaders is different in many ways from

the Martyrion and Anastasis of the fourth century.
For this reason a rocky hill and adjacent garden tomb
outside the present north wall of Jerusalem have seemed
to some visitors a better place in which to try to visualize Golgotha and the tomb of Christ.

It has already been noted (No. 161) that there is
an ancient quarry under the present north wall of
Jerusalem some one hundred yards east of the Damascus Gate, known as Solomon's Quarry; another
quarry, known as the Grotto of Jeremiah, lies across
the road to the north, and the two have probably been
separated by a cutting away of the rock in between.
The rocky hill above the Grotto of Jeremiah is called
el-heidemiyeh, and in 1842 Otto Thenius (in ZHT
1842, pp. 16ff.) suggested that this was the real hill
of Golgotha. In 1867 a rock-hewn tomb was found in
the northwestern slope of this hill. In 1883-1884
Charles G. Gordon visited Jerusalem and accepted the
view originally proposed by Thenius (Gordon in PEFQS
1885, pp. 79f.). After that the hill became known
as "Gordon's Calvary" and the tomb as "Gordon's
Tomb" or, more recently, the Garden Tomb (No.
191).

The rocky hill in question is shown in this photograph, which is a view taken from the north wall of
the Old City. On the top of the hill is a Muslim cemetery.

Gustaf Dalman, "Golgotha und das Grab Christi," in PJ 9
(1913), pp. 98-123; L.-H. Vincent, "Garden Tomb, Histoire
d'un mythe," in RB 34 (1925), pp. 401-431; Simons, Jerusalem, pp. 287-290; C. C. Dobson, The Garden Tomb, Jerusalem, and the Resurrection. London: George Pulman and
Sons Ltd., 1958. Photograph: The Matson Photo Service,
Alhambra, Calif.

191. The Garden Tomb

This photograph shows the tomb just mentioned
(No. 190) cut into the rock in the lower slope of the
hill which some have believed to be the hill of Calvary.
From the entrance one descends one step into an antechamber, then turns right to enter the tomb chamber
proper. The small window above and to the right of
the entrance admits light to this chamber, in which are
ledges on three sides. The one on the left hand, i.e., on
the north side, is the best finished. It provides a trough
burial place, a type of arrangement most characteristic
of the Byzantine period (cf. Nos. 211-212). When the
tomb was first discovered in 1867 there were two Byzantine crosses painted in red on the east wall of the
tomb chamber. The fact that there are other Byzantine
tombs in the neighborhood (No. 196) also tends to
point to a Byzantine date for this tomb.

Photograph: JF.

192. At the Entrance to the Garden Tomb

Here the entrance doorway of the Garden Tomb (No. 191) appears at the right and we also see the rock-cut trough which runs along the whole front of the tomb at ground level. The trough does not appear adequate to provide for a rolling stone closure of the tomb such as may be seen in certain other Jerusalem

tombs (Nos. 228, 235), and probably its purpose was simply to carry away rain water from the cliff above (Dobson, *The Garden Tomb*, p. 20).

Photograph: JF.

193. Excavations at the Basilica of St. Stephen

It will be remembered that in 451 Peter the Iberian came to Jerusalem from the north and saw the martyrium of St. Stephen before he came on into the city and to Golgotha (No. 174); that in 530 Theodosius says that outside the north gate of the city, which he calls the Galilean Gate, was the church which was built in memory of the stoning of Stephen by Eudocia (No. 185); and that Arculf calls the north gate St. Stephen's Gate (No. 185). The Anonymous of Piacenza (570) (Geyer p. 176; LPPTS II, p. 21; CCSL CLXXV p. 166) also tells us that Eudocia (444-460), who extended the southern walls of Jerusalem so that they enclosed the fountain of Siloam (Nos. 141, 185), herself built the basilica and tomb of St. Stephen, and placed her own tomb next to the tomb of St. Stephen.

The site which best corresponds to these indications is about 320 meters north of the Damascus Gate on the Nablus Road, and about 150 meters northwest of the Garden Tomb, the latter being reached from a side street off from the Nablus Road. Certain ancient ruins were found here in 1881, and in the next year the site was acquired by the French Dominicans. In 1885 the latter inaugurated serious excavations which were continued for many years.

In these excavations were found the remains of a basilica of the fifth century which is doubtless that built by Eudocia. Under the atrium was a large cistern. The basilica had nave, two side aisles, and apse, oriented to the east (Vincent, *Jérusalem nouvelle*, Pl. LXXVII). Many fragments of columns and capitals were found, and considerable portions of mosaic pavement, also of the fifth century (QDAP 2 [1932], pp. 176-177). The photograph (No. 193) shows these excavations while they were still in progress. The view is from the north-northwest and looks toward the hill of Bezetha in the distance. The cistern in the atrium and debris of the basilica are to be seen.

Vincent, *Jérusalem nouvelle,* pp. 766-804. Photograph: courtesy École Biblique et Archéologique Française.

194. The Basilica of St. Stephen

In its exposed position on the north side of Jerusalem the basilica of Eudocia (No. 193) was no doubt quickly destroyed by the Persians in 614. At the end of the century a new chapel was built in the atrium of the former basilica, and this chapel was restored by the Crusaders. The remains of these building operations were also uncovered in the excavations (No. 193). In 1900 the modern Basilica of St. Stephen, built upon the foundations of the church of Eudocia, was consecrated, and this photograph shows its façade. Adjacent to the basilica are the Dominican Monastery and the École Biblique et Archéologique Française.

Photograph: JF.

195. In the Atrium of the Basilica of St. Stephen

This picture shows the atrium of the modern basilica, which is built over the atrium of the church of the fifth century. In the center stands a portion of a column of the ancient church.

Photograph: JF.

196. Inscription of the Deacon Nonnus

In the grounds of the Basilica of St. Stephen a number of rock-hewn tombs have been found, extending in the direction of the Garden Tomb (No. 191) not far away (cf. No. 193). One large tomb may have been of the Herodian period and appears to have been converted into a burial place of the Byzantine type about the middle of the fifth century. In the north gallery of the basilica is another Byzantine tomb which was covered by a large stone with an inscription in Greek. The inscription begins with a cross, and reads as follows:

ΘΗΚΔΙΑ
ΦΕΡΝΟΝ
ΝΟΥΔΙΑ
ΚΟΝΙϹ
ΤΗϹΑΓΤ
ΟΥΧΥΑϹΚ
ΤΗϹΜΑΥΤΗ
Ϲ

Θήκ(η) διαφέρ(ουσα) Νοννοῦ διακ(όνου) Ὀνισ(ίμου)
τῆς ἁγ(ίας) τοῦ Χ(ριστο)ῦ Ἀ(ναστάσεω)ς κ(αὶ)
τῆς μο(νῆς) αὐτῆς

Private tomb of the deacon Nonnus Onesimus,
of the holy Anastasis of Christ, and
of this monastery.

This says, then, that this particular monk, Nonnus Onesimus, had been attached during his lifetime to the

Anastasis, i.e., to the Church of the Holy Sepulcher, and had been a member of the monastery of St. Stephen's, where he was now buried.

Considering all the foregoing, the inscription just quoted of course does not mean that the Anastasis of Constantine was to be found at the site of the Basilica of St. Stephen, which would place it near to the Garden Tomb. Rather the existence of these various tombs of Byzantine date in connection with the Basilica of St. Stephen suggests that the Garden Tomb, not far away, may well have been another of the same group, or at any rate of a similar date, i.e., of the Byzantine period (cf. No. 191).

Vincent in RB 34 (1925), pp. 408-409; *Jérusalem nouvelle*, p. 802; Simons, *Jerusalem*, pp. 288-289. Photograph: courtesy École Biblique et Archéologique Française.

197. St. Stephen's Gate

As we have just seen (No. 193), the earliest tradition places the place of death (Ac 7:60) and the martyrium of Stephen outside the north gate of Jerusalem, this gate being called St. Stephen's Gate by Arculf and corresponding to the Damascus Gate today. By the ninth century other tradition began to speak of a chapel dedicated to St. Stephen in the Valley of Josaphat, i.e., the Valley of the Kidron (No. 131), doubtless in line with the tendency to associate a number of martyrs with that valley (Vincent, *Jérusalem nouvelle*, p. 758). In the same way the place of the stoning of Stephen was later thought by some to have been outside an east gate of Jerusalem, and thus the name, Gate of St. Stephen, was attached to the gate in the east wall not far north of the temple area. Earlier, however, this was

176

known as the Gate of St. Mary, with reference to her tomb in the Kidron Valley below (No. 132), and the street leading into the city from the gate was called the Tariq Bab Sitty Mariam (No. 175), which means the Street of the Gate of St. Mary. The photograph shows St. Stephen's Gate, as it is now called. Like the Damascus Gate, it was probably restored by Soliman in the sixteenth century (cf. No. 161).

Photograph: JF.

EMMAUS

198. Air View of el-Qubeibeh, A Possible Site of Emmaus

With respect to the resurrection appearances of Christ, the specific place that is mentioned in addition to Jerusalem and its environs and Galilee is on the road to Emmaus (Lk 24:13-35). Here (Lk 24:13) Emmaus (Ἐμμαοῦς) is said to be at a distance of 60 stadia (σταδίους ἑξήκοντα) (about "seven miles" RSV) from Jerusalem, according to Papyrus Bodmer XIV (P75 of the early third century), Codex Vaticanus, and many other manuscripts, but 160 stadia (ἑκατον ἑξήκοντα) (about eighteen miles) according to Codex Sinaiticus and some other manuscripts, including the Palestinian Syriac.

Corresponding to the two distances given in these variant readings, there are two main sites which have been thought to represent the ancient Emmaus, namely, el-Qubeibeh and 'Amwas. The modern village of el-Qubeibeh is beyond Nebi Samwil on the road which runs northwest from Jerusalem, and is at a distance of seven miles from the city which agrees with the sixty stadia of Papyrus Bodmer XIV, Codex Vaticanus, and the other manuscripts. Although the Arabic name means only the Little Dome, the Crusaders in 1099 found a Roman fort here which was called Castellum Emmaus. In 1852 the Franciscans noted church ruins, in 1861 purchased the site, and in 1902 erected above the ruins of the older church the church which still stands. According to their excavations the older church, which was used as a foundation for the new building, was a basilica of the Crusaders. Within its enclosure were the remains of a more ancient structure, which might have been a Byzantine church, but which some think was a house of the Roman period, and even the very house of Cleopas. Additional excavation in 1943 confirmed the existence of a village of the time of Christ very near the church. The air view (No. 198) looks eastward in the direction of Jerusalem, shows the village of el-Qubeibeh, and just beyond it the Franciscan church and monastery on the site just described.

Eugene Hoade, *Guide to the Holy Land*. Jerusalem: Franciscan Press, 1946, pp. 387-391; Kopp, pp. 449-450. Photograph: The Matson Photo Service, Alhambra, Calif.

199. Mosaic of the Roman Villa at 'Amwas,
Ancient Emmaus

The town of 'Amwas is on the main ancient road which ran west-northwest from Jerusalem to Jaffa. The site is about twenty miles from Jerusalem, which is not much more than the 160 stadia mentioned in Lk 24: 13 according to Codex Sinaiticus and the Palestinian Syriac. Preserving as it does in Arabic form the very name of Emmaus, there is little doubt that this was the ancient town of that name which is mentioned frequently in I Macc (I Macc 3:40, etc.) and in Josephus (*War* II 5, 1 §71 Ἀμμαοῦς; *Ant.* XVII 10, 7 §282 Ἐμμαοῦς, etc.). It is true that in one instance (*War* VII 6, 6 §217) Josephus mentions an Emmaus which cannot be identified with this 'Amwas for it was, he says, only thirty stadia (about three and one-half miles) from Jerusalem. At this place, so near to Jerusalem, Vespasian in A.D. 75 settled 800 army veterans. Since there is a place called Qaloniyeh, which could be derived from Latin Colonia, about four miles west of Jerusalem, this could be the site of the Emmaus mentioned by Josephus in the one instance. This can hardly be the Emmaus of Lk 24:13, however, since the distance given there is at least twice as great (60 stadia), if not much more (160 stadia).

Returning to the Emmaus probably identical with present-day 'Amwas, Josephus (*War* II 5, 1 §71; *Ant.* XVII 10, 9 §291) relates that the place was burned down by Varus, Roman governor of Syria (6-4 B.C.). Sozomen (*Ch. Hist.* V 21), in turn, reports that after the conquest of Jerusalem by the Romans, Emmaus was given the name of Nicopolis. Finally Eusebius identifies this well-known Emmaus as the Emmaus of Lk 24:13, for in the *Onomasticon* (p. 90) he says that Emmaus "is now Nicopolis, a famous city of Palestine." Likewise the Bordeaux Pilgrim (Geyer p. 25; LPPTS I, p. 28; CCSL CLXXV, p. 20) mentions a city by the name of Nicopolis, and places it at twenty-two Roman miles from Jerusalem. While this distance of 'Amwas from Jerusalem has often been urged as an argument against the identification of the place with the Emmaus of Lk 24:13, it agrees well, as we have noted, with the 160 stadia of the text in Codex Sinaiticus and the Palestinian Syriac (probably representing Palestinian tradition), and F.-M. Abel and J. W. Crowfoot (PEFQS 1935, p. 43) agree that no one who is acquainted with the country and the habits of the people of Palestine will have any difficulty in believing that Cleopas and his companion could have walked from Jerusalem to 'Amwas and back on the same day.

At 'Amwas excavations were begun in 1875 and completed in 1924-1930 by the Dominicans of the École Biblique in Jerusalem. On the main site five buildings of considerable magnitude were distinguished. The first was a small church which L.-H. Vincent assigns to the first half of the twelfth century, i.e., to the period of the Crusaders. Under this was an earlier and

178

much larger church, a basilica with nave and two aisles, and with three apses, oriented toward the southeast. The floor of this basilica was 70 centimeters below the floor of the Crusaders' church. In turn, under the northwest corner of the basilica were the remains of a house which was partially destroyed when the basilica was built. Part of the west wall of the basilica coincided with one of the house walls, and some of the floor mosaics of the house were re-used as floor mosaics of the church. The house had extended farther to the north and there, against one of its walls, and separated from the larger basilica by a small court, was built another and smaller basilica. At the southeast end of the latter basilica was a baptistery. These are the five buildings, the Crusaders' church, the larger and the smaller basilicas, the baptistery, and the house.

Vincent (*Emmaüs*, Pl. VIII) attributed the mosaics of the house, presumably part of a fine Roman villa, to the Severan epoch, i.e., the late second and early third century, and put the large basilica, in which the mosaics were re-used, in the third century. The smaller basilica was only built in the sixth century, he thought, after the great church had fallen. Watzinger (II, p. 126) thinks the house was built in the third or fourth cen-

tury, and the large basilica after that. Crowfoot (PEFQS 1935, pp. 45-47) puts the house not earlier than the end of the fifth century, and the large basilica not earlier than the middle of the sixth century. The smaller basilica could possibly have been in existence, he thinks, while the house with the mosaics was still standing. A section of the house mosaics, re-used in the large basilica, featuring birds and plants, is shown in this photograph (No. 199).

L.-H. Vincent and F.-M. Abel, *Emmaüs, sa basilique et son histoire*. Paris: Ernest Leroux, 1932; Review by J. W. Crowfoot in PEFQS 1935, pp. 40-47; Vincent in RB 35 (1926), pp. 117-121; and "Autour du groupe monumental d' 'Amwas," in RB 45 (1936), pp. 403-415; Kopp, pp. 445-449; *Bible et Terre Sainte* (March 1961), pp. 1-13. Photograph: courtesy École Biblique et Archéologique Française.

200. Plan of the Basilica at 'Amwas

The plan and restoration show the large basilica with its nave, two aisles, and three apses, as described above (No. 199). The dimensions of the church are 46 meters in length and 24 meters in width.

Photograph: courtesy École Biblique et Archéologique Française.

201. The Baptistery at 'Amwas

With about six meters between their respective walls, the smaller basilica was located parallel to the larger basilica on the north side. At its southeast end, directly in line with the three apses of the principal basilica, was a small enclosure with the baptismal basin. This view is taken from the southwest side in the angle of the modern shelter which is over the baptistery. In the left wall near the corner are the openings of the canals which brought water to the baptistery from an adjacent reservoir. The baptismal basin itself is in the shape of a quatrefoil, like a flower with four leaves.

As to places associated with the Ascension of Christ, these have been dealt with in connection with earlier consideration of sites on the Mount of Olives (Nos. 116ff.).

Photograph: courtesy École Biblique et Archéologique Française.

Tombs

In a preceding section (No. 183) a hypothetical reconstruction of the tomb of Jesus has been presented, based upon knowledge of contemporary Jewish tombs and comparison with references in the Gospels. In order to substantiate what was said there briefly about the tombs of that time a survey will now be made of the evolution of Jewish tombs, and this will also prepare for what follows when we look at some marks and signs which have been found in burial places, some of which are possibly and some certainly connected with early Christianity.

It may be presumed that from the earliest times the great mass of burials in Palestine were simple interments in the earth which have long since been irrevocably lost. In pre-pottery Neolithic Jericho burials were made in pits under the floors of the houses. At Teleilat Ghassul in the Chalcolithic period there is a child burial in a house in a pottery jar surrounded by stones. Where the burial pit is lined and covered with stones, as is often the case, it is customary to speak of a cist burial (from Greek κίστη and Latin *cista*, "box"). Natural caves as well as excavated pits also served as burial places, and could also of course be more or less modified for this purpose.

Kathleen M. Kenyon, *Digging Up Jericho.* New York: Frederick A. Praeger, 1957, pp. 63f.; Alexis Mallon, Robert Koeppel, and René Neuville, *Teleilat Ghassul,* I, *Compte rendu des fouilles de l'Institut Biblique Pontifical 1929-1932.* Scripta Pontificii Instituti Biblici. Rome: Piazza della Pilotta, 35, 1934, p. 49 and Pl. 24, Fig. 5; *Tell en-Nasbeh* I, pp. 68-76, 77-83; Galling, "Nekropole," p. 80; Joseph A. Callaway, "Burials in Ancient Palestine: From the Stone Age to Abraham," in BA 26 (Sept. 1963), pp. 74-91.

More elaborate tombs were cut in the rock. Because they were more elaborate and more difficult to make it may be assumed that these were usually the property of the minority better able to afford them. At Jerusalem there are approximately 500 ancient rock tombs known and, it has been estimated, these would have provided for less than 5 per cent of the burials which must be assumed for a city of that size during the period in which those tombs were used. The historical development of the chief types of rock-hewn tombs will be illustrated (Nos. 202-212) and then some specific tombs of the NT period (Nos. 213-235).

DEVELOPMENT OF EARLY TOMBS

Shaft Tombs

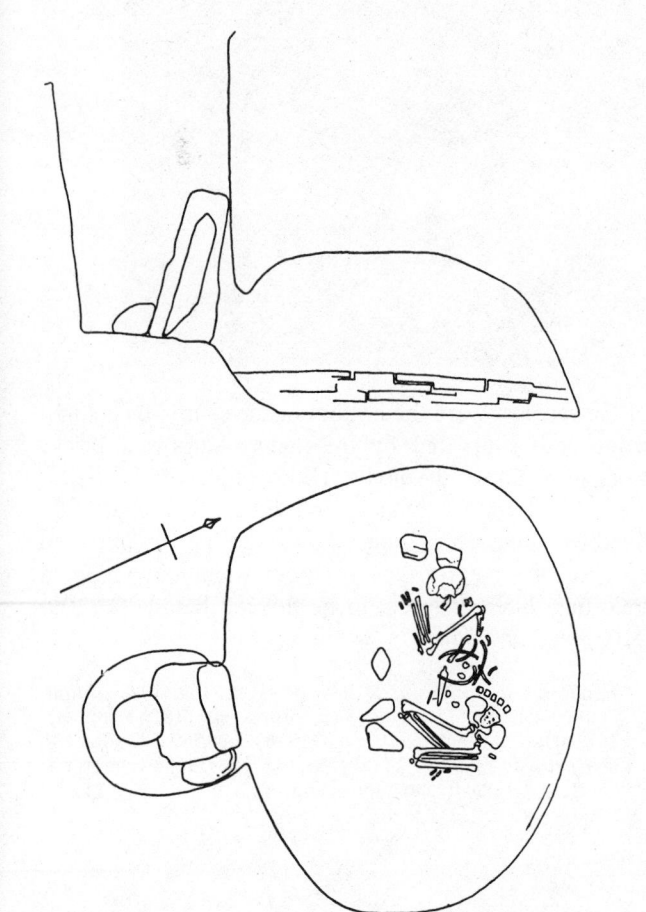

METRES

202. Section and Plan of Tomb A 111 at Jericho

At Jericho from the second half of the fourth millennium down into the Iron Age hundreds of tombs were cut into the rock in the area north and northwest of the *tell* of the ancient city. Except for the Iron Age burials which were made in the side of a steep slope with an almost horizontal approach, most of these tombs consisted of a vertical shaft at the bottom of which a small opening, closed by a stone or stones, gave access to the burial chamber. The arrangement of such a shaft tomb is shown in this section and plan. In the excavations at Jericho this grave was designated as Tomb A 111. It belongs to the Intermediate Early Bronze—Middle Bronze period.

Kenyon, *Digging Up Jericho*, p. 196, Fig. 10; *Excavations at Jericho,* I, *The Tombs Excavated in 1952-54.* Jerusalem: The British School of Archaeology, 1960, p. 188, Fig. 69. Photograph: courtesy Jericho Excavation Fund.

181

203. The Shaft of Tomb A 3 at Jericho

This shaft tomb is also of the Intermediate Early Bronze—Middle Bronze period. The view looks down into the shaft and shows the large stone which closes the entrance into the burial chamber.

Kenyon, *Digging Up Jericho*, pl. 38, Fig. B; *Excavations at Jericho*, I, pl. IX, Fig. 3. Photograph: courtesy Jericho Excavation Fund.

204. Burial in Tomb A 23 at Jericho

This burial was found intact in the inner chamber of another shaft tomb at Jericho, known as Tomb A 23. The body was placed in a contracted position at the back of the chamber, with the head to the west, and a dagger was laid between the arms and the chest. The date is in the Intermediate Early Bronze—Middle Bronze period. Shaft tombs are found at many other places besides Jericho.

Interestingly enough a quite similar type of burial was still in use at the end of the pre-Christian and the beginning of the Christian era at the famous site of Qumran, not many miles from Jericho. Here there is an extensive cemetery to the east of the main settlement, with two smaller cemeteries to the north and south of the larger one, containing in all perhaps 1,200 graves. One of these tombs was excavated by Charles Clermont-Ganneau in 1873, more than forty by R. de Vaux between 1949 and 1955, and one more by S. H. Steckoll in 1966. These consisted of a shaft some four to six feet deep, at the bottom of which was a recess in the side wall for the burial place proper. On the side of the recess toward the bottom of the shaft was a slight ledge and, supported by this ledge, sun-dried bricks were piled above the body. The opening of the recess was closed by flat stones, and finally the shaft was filled with soil. Thus Qumran seems to have maintained the use of an early type of tomb when elsewhere in Palestine different types, to be noticed below (§§209-210), were in vogue.

Kenyon, *Excavations at Jericho*, I, pl. IX, Fig. 1; Clermont-Ganneau II pp. 15-16; de Vaux in RB 60 (1953), pp. 95, 102-103; 61 (1954), p. 207; 63 (1956), pp. 569-572; *Steckoll* in *Revue de Qumran* 23 (1968), pp. 323-336. Photograph: courtesy Jericho Excavation Fund.

Chamber Tombs

205. The Entrance to Tomb 77 at Megiddo

In the case of a normal shaft tomb the distinctive feature of design is the vertical shaft, which ordinarily leads to a burial chamber or chambers. Where the emphasis falls upon the inner room or rooms, more or less carefully hewn out of the rock, and access is by any one of several ways other than a vertical shaft, such as a direct doorway, or horizontal or sloping passageway,

or stairs, we may speak of a chamber tomb. At Megiddo in the many Bronze Age burials which have been explored the predominant form is still that of the normal shaft tomb (some, such as Tomb 84, with numerous chambers), but in the Late Bronze Age we find examples of the chamber tomb. The entrance to one of these tombs is shown in this photograph.

P. L. O. Guy, *Megiddo Tombs.* OIP XXXIII. Chicago: The University of Chicago Press, 1938, p. 83, Fig. 96. Photograph: courtesy The Oriental Institute, University of Chicago.

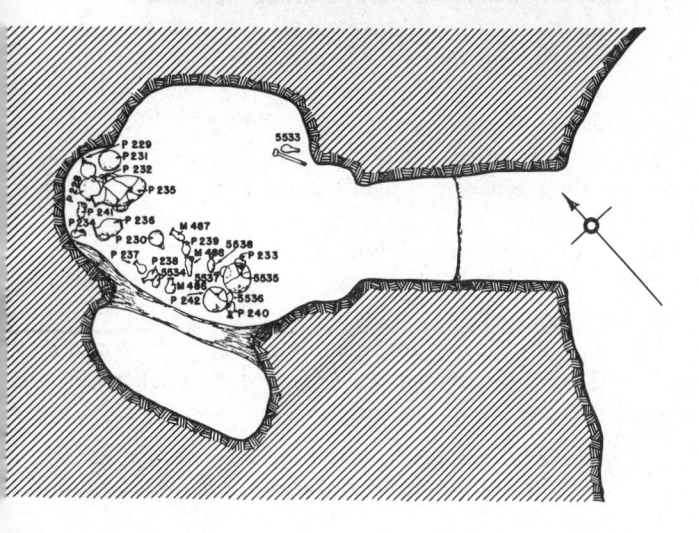

206. Plan of Tomb 77 at Megiddo

This is the plan of the Late Bronze Age tomb of which the entrance was shown in No. 205. The tomb consists of a short passageway and an inner rock-hewn chamber. Within, on the southwest side, there is a recess, separated by a raised place from the main chamber, which is large enough for a full-length adult burial and was probably used for such, although the bones and pottery which remained in the tomb were, when found, all on the floor of the main chamber. Chamber tombs are found at many other places besides Megiddo.

Guy, *Megiddo Tombs*, p. 84, Fig. 98. Photograph: courtesy The Oriental Institute, University of Chicago.

Chamber Tombs with Ledges

207. Plan and Section of Tomb 5 at Tell en-Nasbeh

A distinctive form of chamber tomb was developed when, instead of placing the burial on the floor or even in a recess, as in the preceding plan, place was provided for the body on a rock ledge, shelf, bench, or divan, as the arrangement is variously called. This plan and section represent an excellent example of such an arrangement as found in Tomb 5 in the north cemetery at Tell en-Nasbeh. According to the pottery found in it, the tomb was in use in Iron I and Iron II, probably beginning in the tenth century and continuing through the eighth century. In Palestine in general this type of tomb is known from the Late Bronze Age, is predominant in the ninth century and later, is gradually replaced by new styles in the Hellenistic period, but is still found in some examples in Roman times.

Galling, *Reallexikon* I, col. 244, No. 8; Nötscher p. 100; *Tell en-Nasbeh* I, p. 84, Fig. 8. Photograph: courtesy Palestine Institute.

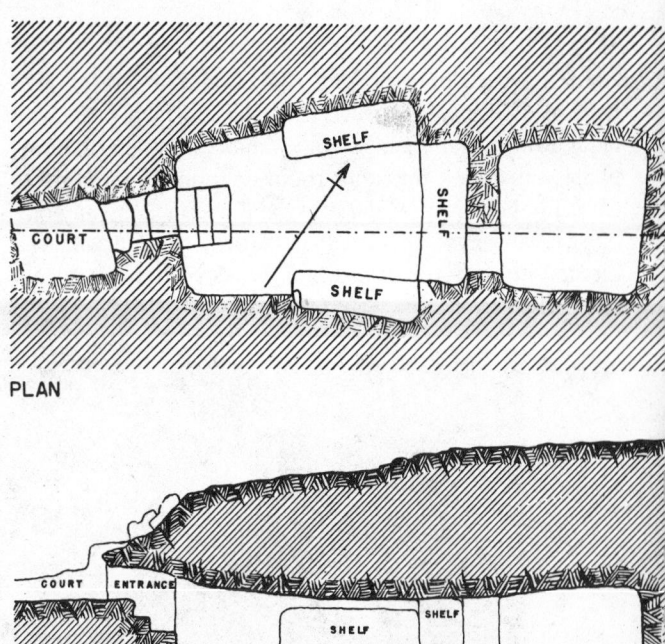

PLAN

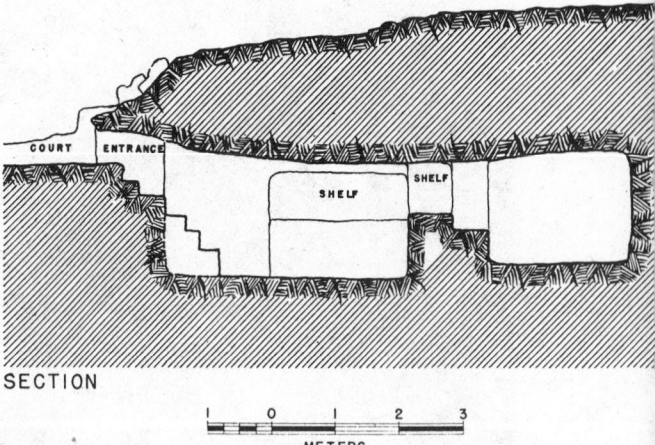

SECTION

208. Model of Tomb 5 at Tell en-Nasbeh

In addition to the plan and section in No. 207, this "exploded" model makes it possible to visualize Tomb 5 at Tell en-Nasbeh. There was an exterior court, then a small square entrance, and then five steps which led down into a rectangular room. In the rear half of this room on each side and against the back wall a stone ledge or shelf had been left in the excavation. At the right end of the back shelf there was another small square entranceway, with one broad step down, which gave access to a plain inner chamber almost cubical in dimensions. Like most tombs this one had been plundered long ago and what was left in it, meager skeletal remains and much pottery, was thrown together into the large chamber. It seems evident, however, that originally the bodies of the deceased were placed on the ledges in the large chamber; when room was needed on these ledges for new burials, the bones of the older ones were probably collected in the smaller chamber at the back. From numerous examples we learn that this type of chamber tomb with burial ledges was in use in Palestine throughout the time of the Israelite kings and into the Persian period.

Badè, *Tombs*, pp. 18-33, 48-63; *Tell en-Nasbeh* I, pp. 83 f., 99. Photograph: courtesy Palestine Institute.

Chamber Tombs with Kokim

209. Plan and Section of Tomb 4 at Tell en-Nasbeh

Another development of the chamber tomb was that in which the burial places in the inner chamber or chambers consisted of horizontal shafts or niches driven

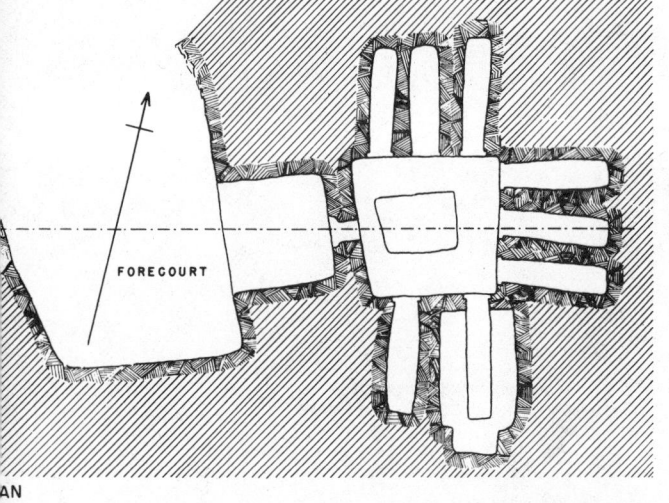

straight back into the walls. Such a shaft was ordinarily quadrangular or perhaps vaulted, and of such dimensions as to accommodate a body put into it lengthwise and probably head first. A good example of a tomb of this type is found in Tomb 4 in the north cemetery at Tell en-Nasbeh, the plan and section of which are shown here. There was a large sunken forecourt with a covered vestibule and a small entrance, no doubt once closed with a movable stone. The main chamber

was roughly square, with a squarish pit in the center of the floor, presumably a place for the collection of skeletal remains. The broad floor space which remained around the four sides of this pit provided a passageway adjacent to the walls of the chamber. On this floor level and into the walls of the chamber were cut horizontal burial shafts, three on the north side, three on the east, and two on the south. One shaft on the south side was bordered on three sides by a broad ledge, and was probably intended for a person of special importance such as the head of the family. The pottery in the tomb was Hellenistic-Roman, and one bronze coin of Herod Archelaus was found which probably dates the tomb in his reign (4 B.C.-A.D. 6).

The type of tomb illustrated here (No. 209) may have originated in Egypt and become known in Palestine through Phoenician influence. The underground room or hall, with rows of horizontal burial shafts extending off from it, is especially common in the necropolis of Alexandria and is known in the cities of Phoenicia as well as elsewhere in the Hellenistic world. In Palestine it is already found at Marissa (Nos. 213ff.), a Phoenician colony in existence around 200 B.C. At Jerusalem the great majority of ancient tombs are of this type, and date approximately from 150 B.C. to A.D. 150. It may fairly be said that this type of tomb virtually became the canonical form of the Jewish family grave.

With respect to such tombs in the Hellenistic world it is customary to designate the horizontal burial shafts or niches of which we have been speaking as *loculi*, singular *loculus*, literally "a little place." In Palestine, however, it is customary to use the late Hebrew word by which the Rabbis called the burial shafts, namely, כוכים, *kokim*, singular *kok*. Using this term for the niches and employing the customary Hebrew designations of length where 6 handbreadths = 1 cubit = approximately 18 inches, the Mishna (Baba Bathra VI 8 fol. 100b-101a GBT VI 1211f. SBT IV 3, 421ff. DM 375) explains the construction of a family tomb: "The central space of the grotto must have [an area of] four cubits by six, and eight burial niches (*kokim*) are to open out into it, three on this side, three on that side, and two opposite [the doorway]. The niches (*kokim*) must be four cubits long, seven handbreadths high, and six wide." Varying opinions of various Rabbis follow, and in the accompanying Gemara different plans and dimensions are discussed in detail.

Badè, *Tombs*, pp. 33-38; *Tell en-Nasbeh* I, pp. 103-104 and Fig. 12; Galling, "Nekropole," p. 76; Nötscher p. 100. Photograph: courtesy Palestine Institute.

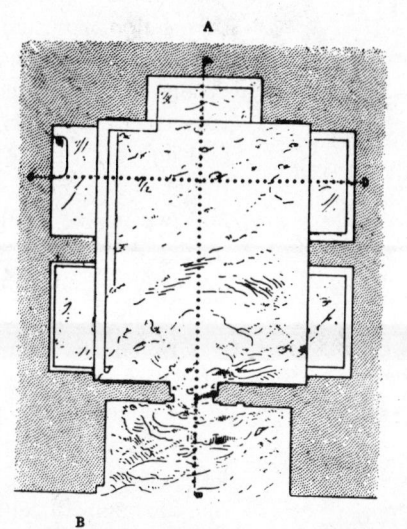

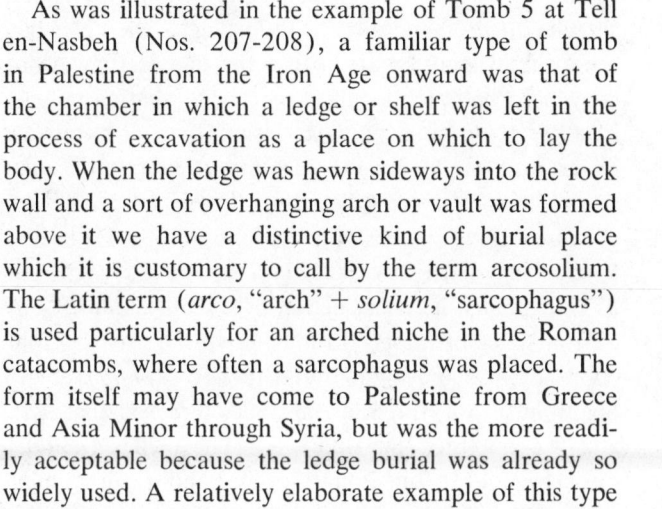

Chamber Tombs with Arcosolia

210. Plan and Sections of a Tomb at Tell ez-Zakariyeh

As was illustrated in the example of Tomb 5 at Tell en-Nasbeh (Nos. 207-208), a familiar type of tomb in Palestine from the Iron Age onward was that of the chamber in which a ledge or shelf was left in the process of excavation as a place on which to lay the body. When the ledge was hewn sideways into the rock wall and a sort of overhanging arch or vault was formed above it we have a distinctive kind of burial place which it is customary to call by the term arcosolium. The Latin term (*arco*, "arch" + *solium*, "sarcophagus") is used particularly for an arched niche in the Roman catacombs, where often a sarcophagus was placed. The form itself may have come to Palestine from Greece and Asia Minor through Syria, but was the more readily acceptable because the ledge burial was already so widely used. A relatively elaborate example of this type of tomb construction, with five arcosolia, is represented in the plan and sections shown here. This tomb is at Tell ez-Zakariyeh, probably biblical Azekah, in the Shephelah. The date is probably in the Late Hellenistic period. In the illustration A is the plan of the entire tomb, B is a section on the long axis in A, and C a section on the short axis. As the example in the next illustration (No. 211) shows, the arcosolium type tomb

was still being used in Palestine in the fourth century of the Christian era.

Clermont-Ganneau II, pp. 353-355; Watzinger II, p. 71. Photograph: courtesy Palestine Exploration Fund.

Chamber Tombs with Sunk Graves

211. Arcosolium and Sunk Grave in Tomb 33 at Tell en-Nasbeh

The burial ledge beneath an arcosolium (cf. No. 210) might be a simple shelf, or it might be provided with a raised margin at the front edge and a raised place at the head end, or be deepened into a whole trough

186

or sunk grave to receive the body. Tomb 33 in the west cemetery at Tell en-Nasbeh provides an example of the combination of the arcosolium and the sunk grave. In this tomb an oblong shaft leads to a small square entrance, closed with a stone of unusual shape, which gives access to a rectangular chamber. On the wall to the left of the entrance are three kokim, on the back wall three more, but on the wall to the right is an arcosolium with a grave sunk in its shelf, as shown in our illustration. This grave had a profusion of glass beads, bracelets, and other objects. In the tomb were numerous lamps, some decorated with pillars and arches and with as many as seven holes for wicks. Half a dozen lamps were decorated with crosses, so the tomb was ultimately, even if not originally, used by Christians. A date in the early part of the Byzantine period, perhaps in the fourth century, is probable.

Tell en-Nasbeh I, pp. 112-116, Pl. 23 No. 5; Galling, "Nekropole," p. 90. Photograph: courtesy Palestine Institute.

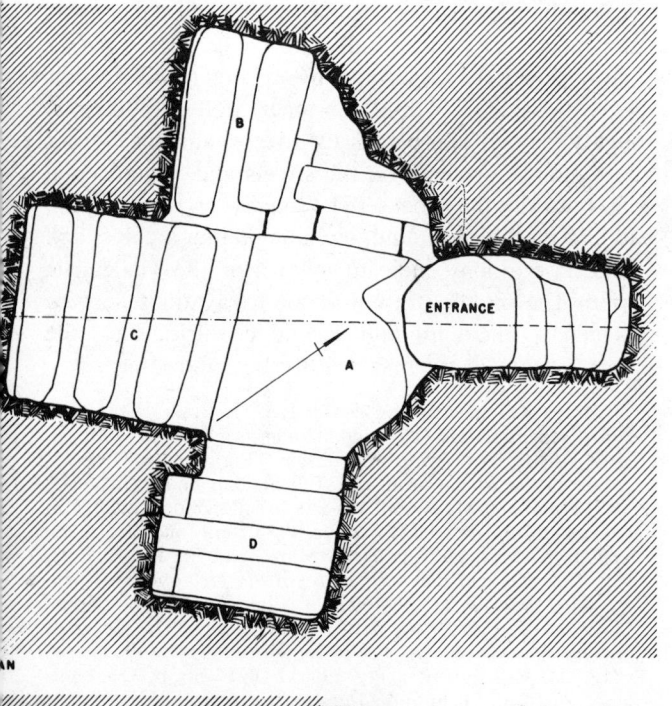

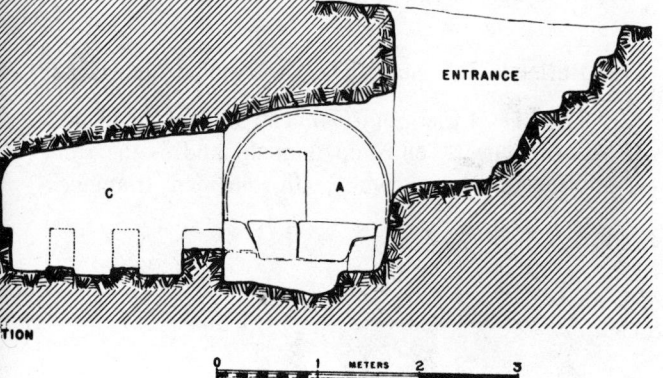

212. Plan and Section of Tomb 19 at Tell en-Nasbeh

Tomb 19 is in the west cemetery at Tell en-Nasbeh. The original tomb was probably a simple chamber, perhaps provided with rock shelves for burial places as in Tomb 5 (No. 208), and other tombs at Tell en-Nasbeh. The original tomb was probably as old as the period of the Exile, since the famous seal of Jaazaniah (cf. II K 25:23; Jer 40:8; FLAP pp. 176-177) was found in it. Later, however, the tomb was enlarged with large barrel-vaulted recesses containing sunk graves as shown in this plan and section. While a little of the pottery in the tomb, and the Jaazaniah seal, belong to the Middle Iron Age, the rest of the pottery, especially numerous lamps, belongs to the fourth to the sixth centuries of the Christian era. Indeed more than one-third of the lamps are explicitly Christian, since they are ornamented with crosses and one has, in a garbled form, the inscription φῶς Χριστοῦ, "light of Christ." Many other examples also show that the period of wide use of the vaulted chamber tomb with sunk or trough graves was from the fourth to the sixth centuries, and this type has been called the essentially Christian form of tomb in the Byzantine period.

Tell en-Nasbeh I, pp. 118-122, Fig. 18; Galling, "Nekropole," pp. 79, 90. Photograph: courtesy Palestine Institute.

DECORATED HELLENISTIC-PERIOD TOMBS AT MARISSA

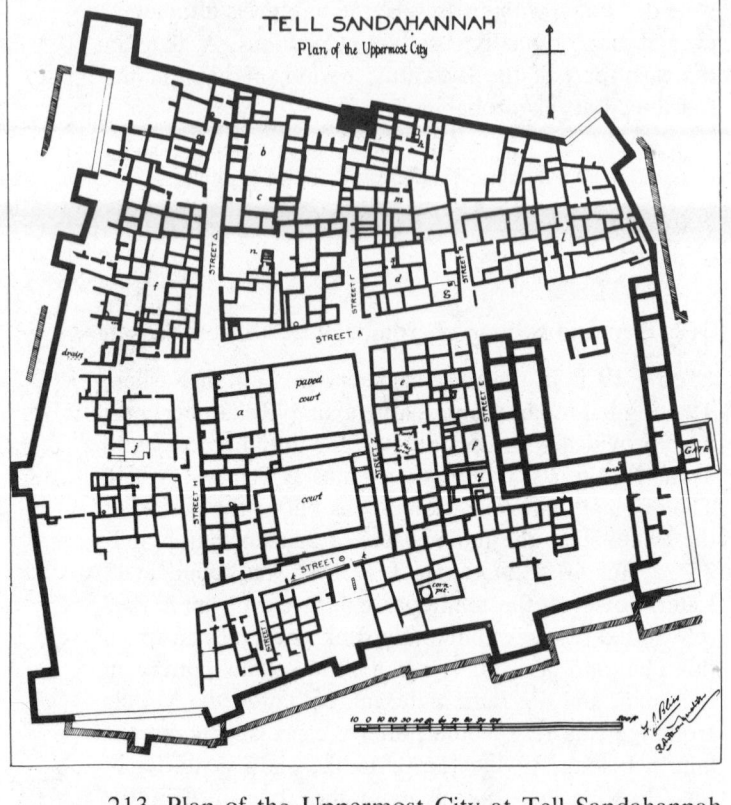

213. Plan of the Uppermost City at Tell Sandahannah

Tell Sandahannah is two kilometers south of Beit Guvrin (Eleutheropolis) in the Shephelah. The Arabic name is a corruption from the nearby Church of St. Anna, a twelfth-century Crusader building over a Byzantine basilica. The *tell* is probably to be identified with the OT city of Mareshah, known as Marissa in Greek. This was originally a Canaanite city (Jos 15:44 LXX Μαρησά); it was fortified by Rehoboam (II Ch

11:8 LXX Μαρεισάν), captured from the Idumeans by John Hyrcanus c. 110 B.C. (Josephus, *Ant.* XIII 9, 1 §257 Μάρισα; Μάρισσα according to some manuscript evidence in *Ant.* XII 8, 6 §353), and destroyed by the Parthians in 40 B.C. (*Ant.* XIV 13, 9 §364). The ancient town on top of the *tell* was excavated by the Palestine Exploration Fund in 1900, and examined again by Eliezer Oren in 1961-1963. The town area, roughly five hundred feet square in maximum dimensions, was surrounded by an inner wall on the edge of the *tell* or slightly down the slope, and by an outer wall farther down the slope. Within the inner wall the town is roughly divided into blocks by streets, and the houses and buildings are built on the streets and around open courts within the blocks. The relatively regular plan and also the objects found, including pottery, coins, and Greek inscriptions, indicate a town of the Hellenistic period. The middle stratum of the excavations may be assigned to the third and second centuries B.C., the upper stratum to the first century B.C. and later.

Clermont-Ganneau II, pp. 445-447; F. J. Bliss, "Report on the Excavations at Tell Sandahannah," in PEFQS 1900, pp. 319-338; R. A. Stewart Macalister, "Preliminary Observations on the Rock-Cuttings of Tell Sandahannah," in PEFQS 1900, pp. 338-341; and "'Es-Suk,' Tell Sandahannah," in PEFQS 1901, pp. 11-19; John P. Peters and Hermann Thiersch, "The Necropolis of Mareshah," in PEFQS 1902, pp. 393-397; and *Painted Tombs in the Necropolis of Marissa (Marêshah)*. London: Palestine Exploration Fund, 1905; RB 11 (1902), pp. 438f.; Eliezer Oren, "The Caves of the Palestinian Shephelah," in *Archaeology* 18 (1965), pp. 218-224. Photograph: PEFQS 1900, Plan facing p. 326, courtesy Palestine Exploration Fund.

214. Burial Loculi and Niches in Tomb D at Marissa

In 1873-1874 Clermont-Ganneau studied the Church of St. Anna near Tell Sandahannah, and in the same vicinity examined a tomb with nineteen triangular-

topped loculi and noticed a second tomb of the same type. In 1902 Peters and Thiersch investigated four more tombs of this type a quarter of a mile to the south. In 1961-1963 Oren examined no less than fifty-two tombs, including those already known, in the region around Tell Sandahannah. All the tombs were cut into the rock in the same way, with the same basic plan. On top there are remnants of structures which were probably pyramids. Steps lead through a stone door to an entrance hall. From the entrance hall there is access to a central burial hall, with burial chambers branching off from it. In the latter are the loculi or kokim with triangular tops. These were sealed with stone slabs and clay. Above the recess the name of the deceased, and sometimes the date of his death, are written with red paint, clay, or charcoal. The inscriptions are in Greek, Nabatean, and Aramaic, and extend in date from the beginning of the third century to the first century B.C. In the ledge beneath the kokim are smaller niches which may have been used for the keeping of bones from previous burials. The illustration shows Tomb D, as it is designated by Oren, with its gabled loculi and small niches below.

Eliezer Oren in *Archaeology* 18 (1965), pp. 218-224. Photograph: courtesy E. Oren, Beit-Jibrin Survey.

215. Plan and Sections of Tomb I at Marissa

Of the tombs at Marissa, that which Peters and Thiersch designated as Tomb I is the best known and in many ways still the most interesting. As seen in plan and sections in the present illustration, the entrance of the tomb gives access to a flat-roofed antechamber (A). On either side is an oblong barrel-vaulted chamber (B and C), while ahead is the flat-roofed main chamber (D), with a niche-like extension (E). There is a ledge or shelf around the edges of the chambers and above it, cut at right angles into the walls, are the triangular-topped loculi, forty-one in number. Opening out of the extension (E) at the east end of the main

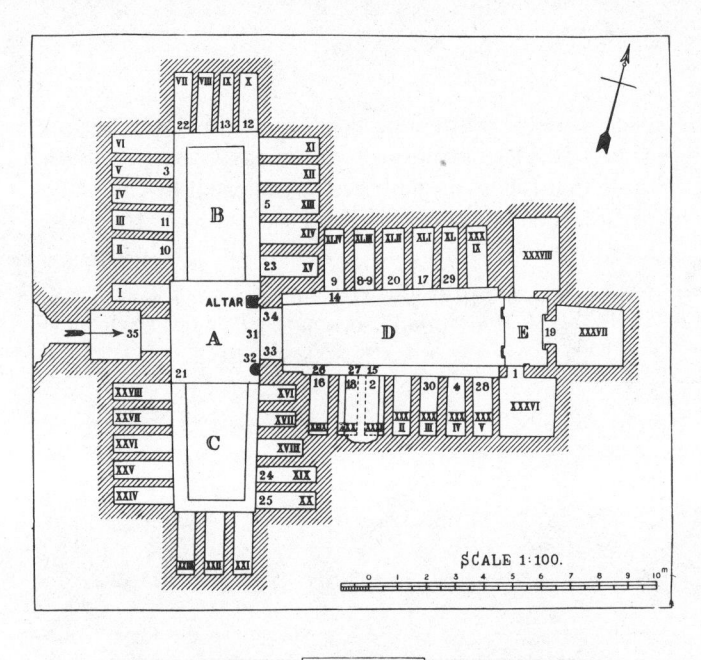

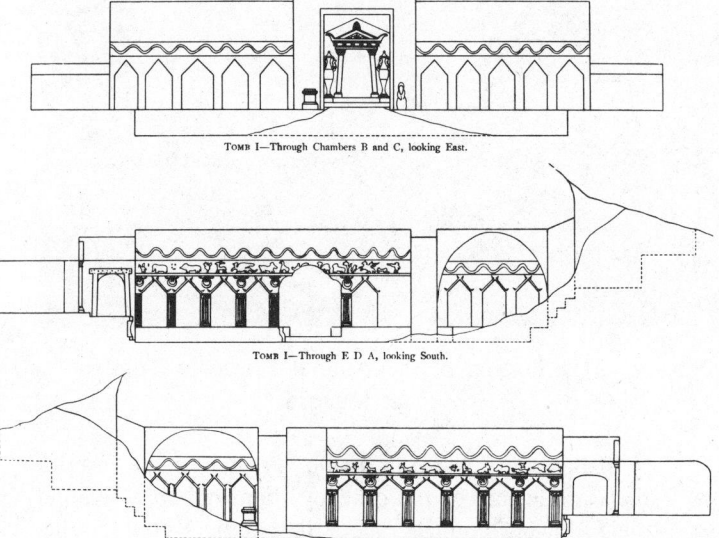

TOMB I—Through Chambers B and C, looking East.

TOMB I—Through E D A, looking South.

TOMB I—Through A D E, looking North.

chamber are three burial chambers probably meant for sarcophagi and intended for the chief persons buried in the tomb.

Photograph: Peters and Thiersch, *Painted Tombs in the Necropolis of Marissa*, pp. 16-17, Figs. 1, 2, courtesy Palestine Exploration Fund.

216. Hunting Scene in Tomb I at Marissa

Tomb I at Marissa is most remarkable for the paintings of its main chamber (D in No. 215). On either side of the entrance to this chamber is a painted cock, and on the right-hand jamb a three-headed jackal-like dog, the Cerberus of Greek and Roman mythology who guards the lower regions. Inside on the wall just over the kokim is an animal frieze which begins in the southwest corner and ends near the opposite northwest corner. The first portion of this frieze is shown here. While a man blows a long trumpet, a hunter on horse-

back, assisted by hunting dogs, raises his lance against a leopard. The identity of this animal, as well as of those that follow in the frieze, is indicated by the name written above in Greek, in this case ΠΑΡΔΑΛΟΣ, "leopard."

Photograph: Peters and Thiersch, *Painted Tombs in the Necropolis of Marissa*, Pl. VI, courtesy Palestine Exploration Fund.

217. Portion of the Animal Frieze in Tomb I at Marissa

In the entire frieze in Tomb I, as far as the inscriptions are legible or the drawings unmistakable, we find the following animals: leopard, panther, bull, giraffe, boar, griffin, oryx, rhinoceros, elephant, crocodile, ibis, hippopotamus, wild ass, porcupine, and lynx. The illustration shows the last portion of the frieze on the south side. The animals are a bulky rhinoceros (ΡΙΝΟΚΕΡѠϹ) painted reddish-brown, and a grayish-black elephant (ΕΛΕΦΑϹ).

In addition to the inscriptions above the animals which give their identity and were presumably written at the time the paintings were made, there are also graffiti in more or less similar script just over the entrances to many of the loculi. In the photograph (No. 217), for example, we see at the right in the triangular area between the sloping line of the right top of the entrance to the loculus and the base of the animal frieze the inscription

ΔΗΜΗΤΡΙΟΥ ΤΟΥ
ΜΕΕΡΒΑΛΟΥ

which means, "(Grave) of Demetrios, son of Meerbal." Demetrios is a common Hellenistic name; Meerbal is

a Greek form of the common Phoenician name, Maherbaal, "gift of Baal." In similar script there is a long graffito over the entrance to the sarcophagus chamber on the south side of the extension (E) (see the Plan in No. 215) of the main chamber of the tomb. It reads:

Ἀπολλοφάνης Σεσμαίου ἄρξας τῶν ἐν Μαρίσῃ Σιδωνίων ἔτη τριάκοντα καὶ τρία καὶ νομσθεὶς | πάντων τῶν καθ' αὐτὸν χρηστότατος καὶ φιλοικειότατος ἀπέθανεν δὲ βιώσας ἔτη | ἑβδομήκοντα καὶ τέσσαρα ἐτ.

"Apollophanes, son of Sesmaios, was the ruler of the Sidonians in Marise for thirty-three years, and he was recognized as the kindest and most household-loving of all those of his time, and he died having lived seventy-four years."

At the end the writer started to repeat the word ἔτη again and then, recognizing his mistake, desisted. The importance of this inscription is evident, for it confirms the name of Marissa (in the spelling Μαρίσῃ) for this place, shows that a colony of Phoenicians from Sidon was settled here, and gives the name of the ruler who was their chief for a third of a century.

Still other burial inscriptions are painted above the loculi, usually in the animal frieze itself, and since they are sometimes written across the animal figures and damage them in that way they are evidently later in date. An example of these painted superscriptions also shows in the photograph. It begins with the angular sign for a year and the letter Beta corresponding to the numeral two, and reads:

LB ΔΥϹΤΡΟΥ
ϹΑΒΟΥϹ   ΤΗϹ
ΚΟϹΝΑΤΑΝΟΥ

In the second year in the month Dystros. (Grave) of Sabo, the daughter of Kosnatanos.

Kosnatanos is an Idumean name, meaning "Kos has given." It may be compared with the name of the Idumean Kostobaros (or Kosgobaros), whom Josephus mentions (*Ant.* XV 7, 9 §§253-254) as married to Salome, the sister of Herod the Great. In the same connection Josephus says that the ancestors of Kostobaros had been priests of the Idumean god Koze (Κωζέ). Dystros is a month-name (usually corresponding to February/March) in the Macedonian calendar which was used in varying forms throughout the ancient Middle East (FHBC §§117ff.).

In comparison with the date "in the second year" (Beta) in the foregoing inscription there may be noted also the date "in the first year" (Alpha) in another painted superscription and the date "in the fifth year" (Epsilon) in a graffito which paleographically is one of the latest inscriptions in the tomb. These three dates are presumably stated in terms of some era which had only recently been established and come into use at Marissa. Since there is inscriptional evidence for a local era of the nearby city of Eleutheropolis (RB 11 [1902], pp. 438f.), an era which perhaps began about the birth of Christ or earlier, the dates may be in terms of this era. Otherwise the rather numerous dates in Tomb I and in the other three tombs of this necropolis comprise a consistent series extending from the 117th to the 194th year. If these dates are stated in terms of the widely used Seleucid era, according to the Macedonian calendar (FHBC §193), they correspond to dates extending from 196/195 to 119/118 B.C.

The other tombs in this necropolis at Marissa need be mentioned only briefly. Tomb II was constructed on a plan much the same as that of Tomb I. In general it was simpler in its arrangements and contained fewer

inscriptions and paintings. Of the paintings the best preserved represents two musicians, a man and a woman, both in colorful striped garments. Likewise Tombs III and IV were of the same general arrangement. In all, then, this necropolis at Marissa represents a community of the Hellenistic period. It was in Idumean territory, and an Idumean divine name appears in personal names in the inscriptions. The region was under the Ptolemies until 198 B.C., and the fauna of the animal frieze are primarily Egyptian. After 198 B.C. the area was under the Seleucids, and the majority of the dates are Seleucidan. At Marissa a Sidonian colony was settled, and its chief, Apollophanes, and others of his family were evidently buried here.

Photograph: Peters and Thiersch, *Painted Tombs in the Necropolis of Marissa*, Pl. x, courtesy Palestine Exploration Fund.

HELLENISTIC AND ROMAN TOMBS IN THE KIDRON VALLEY

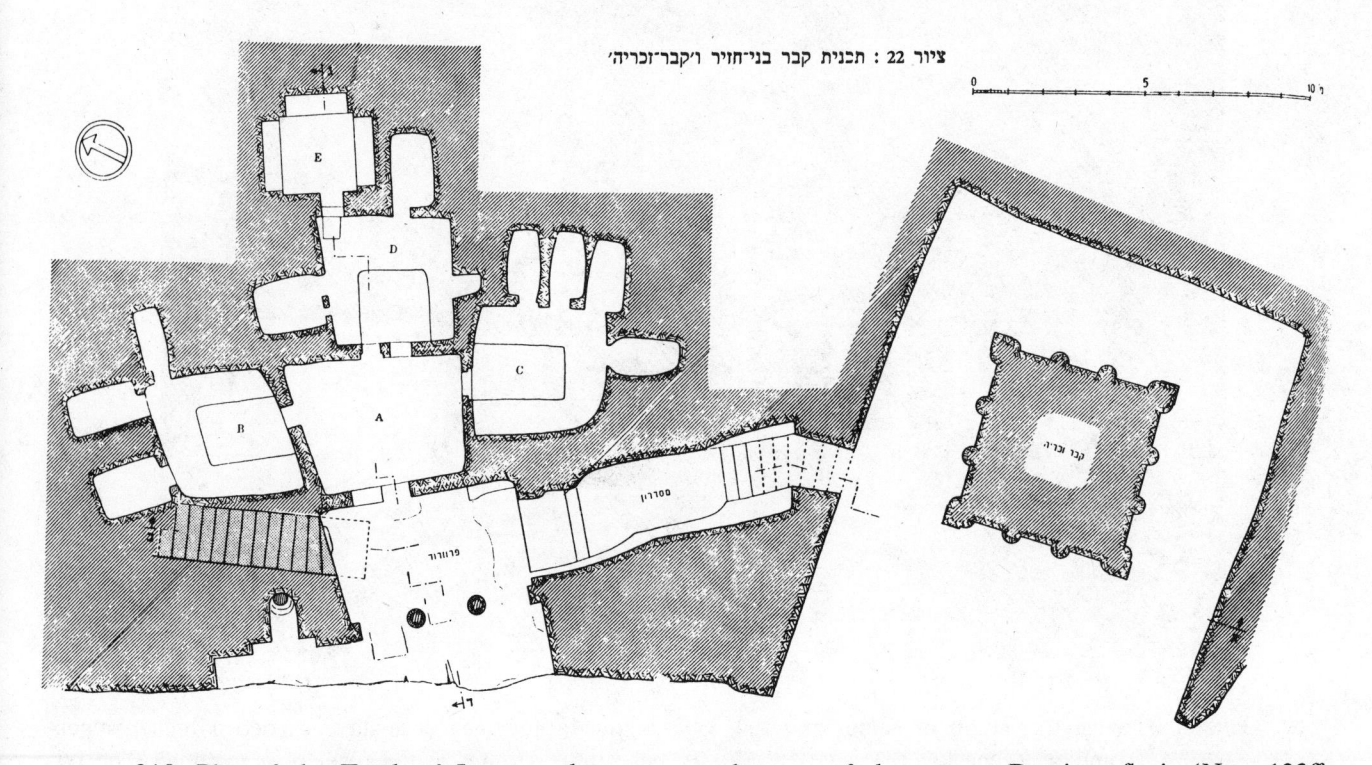

218. Plan of the Tomb of James and the Tomb of Zechariah

It has been noted (No. 138) that the ancient or Jebusite city of Jerusalem was on the west side of the Kidron valley above the Gihon spring. Across the valley on the west slope of the Mount of Olives and in the area of the present Dominus flevit (Nos. 123ff., 272ff.) was the Jebusite burial place, a necropolis that was in use from the end of the Middle Bronze Age into the Late Bronze Age or approximately from the sixteenth to the thirteenth century. Jl 3:2 speaks of the valley of Jehoshaphat ("Yaweh judges") as the place where the Lord will hold judgment on the nations, and it is located by the Bordeaux Pilgrim (cf. No. 131) and by Eusebius and Jerome (*Onomasticon* pp. 118-119) as lying between Jerusalem and the Mount of Olives, i.e., as being identical with the ravine of the Kidron. So the fact that there were burials on the slopes of this valley from an early time and the fact that the prophet's words were taken as pointing to the valley as the place of the last judgment worked together to make it a much used burial place through many centuries, for Jews, possibly for Christians (No. 279), and for Muslims. Of the great number of tombs in the valley four which are particularly notable and belong to Hellenistic and Roman times will be discussed, namely, the tombs popularly known as those of James, of Zechariah, of Absalom, and of Jehoshaphat.

In the plan (No. 218) the Tomb of James is at the left and the Tomb of Zechariah at the right. The portico of the Tomb of James is actually high up on the side of a cliff (see No. 219), and the porch behind is entered by two passages, the one on the north coming from the open, the one on the south connecting with the enclosure around the Tomb of Zechariah. Through the porch there is access to a large chamber (A) which in turn connects with a number of tomb chambers (B, C, D, E) in which are both kokim and arcosolia.

Sylvester J. Saller, *The Excavations at Dominus Flevit (Mount Olivet, Jerusalem)*, II, *The Jebusite Burial Place*. PSBF 13. Jerusalem: The Franciscan Press, 1964; Theodore Reinach, "Les fouilles de M. Nahoum Schlouszch dans la Vallée du Cedron," in CRAI 1924, pp. 144-146; Watzinger II, pp. 63-64; Simons, *Jerusalem*, pp. 10, 14; Vincent, *Jérusalem*, 1:1, pp. 331-342; N. Avigad, *Ancient Monuments in the Kidron Valley* (in Hebrew, with summary in English). Jerusalem: Bialik Institute, 1954; Howard E. Stutchbury, "Excavations in the Kidron Valley," in PEQ 1961, pp. 101-113. Photograph: Avigad, *op.cit.*, p. 37, Fig. 22, courtesy The Bialik Institute, Jerusalem.

219. General View of the Tomb of James and the Tomb of Zechariah

The Tomb of James is again at the left and the Tomb of Zechariah at the right. The portico of the Tomb of James is marked by two Doric columns and two corner pilasters supporting an entablature above. At the left is a smooth face of rock with an open doorway which leads only a short distance into the rock. This portion of the façade may once have carried a higher superstructure, perhaps in the form of a pyramid. The hypothesis that this was so is strengthened by comparison with examples of funerary structures in Egypt which combine colonnade with pyramid. On the basis of its architecture the tomb is judged to belong to the latter half of the second century B.C.

Photograph: courtesy Palestine Archaeological Museum.

220. Inscription on the Tomb of James

This inscription is found on the architrave immediately above the two Doric columns of the porch of the "Tomb of James." It is written in square Hebrew characters judged paleographically to belong to the first half of the first century of the Christian era, i.e., perhaps two generations after the tomb was first prepared. It is transcribed and translated as follows: זה קבר והנפש שלאלעזר חניה יועזר יהודה שמעון יוחנן | בני יוספ בן עובד יוספ ואלעזר בני חניה | כהנים מבני הזיר.

This is the tomb and the *nephesh* of Eleazar, Haniah, Jo'azar, Iehudah, Shime'on, Iohannan, (the) sons of Joseph son of 'Obed (and also) of Joseph and Eleazar (the) sons of Haniah, priests (of the family) of the sons of Hezir.

The tomb was, accordingly, the burial place of a family of priests, the Bene Hezir (בני חזיר) or the "sons of Hezir." The genealogical table implied by the inscription is:

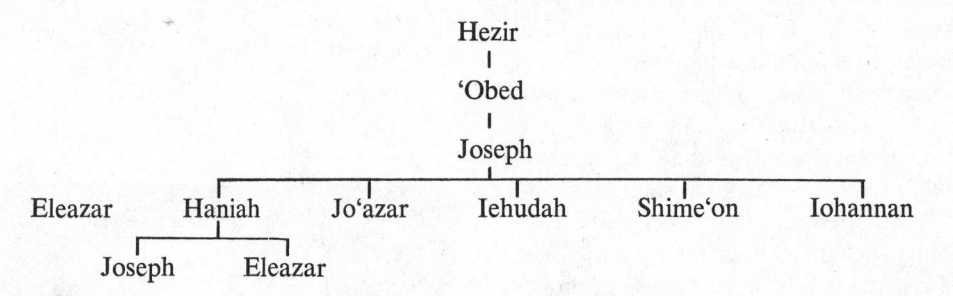

In the OT the name Hezir appears as that of the head of a priestly house in I Ch 24:15, and of a person associated with Nehemiah in Neh 10:20.

At the beginning of the inscription the monument which it identifies is described as "the tomb and the *nephesh*" (קבד והנפש) of the persons buried there. The word *nephesh* ordinarily means "life," "soul," or "self," but is used on occasion to refer to a tomb or to a sepulchral monument. Here, since the word is used in addition to the word "tomb," it must mean a "sepulchral monument." Accordingly some feature of the entire arrangement must be the "monument" in distinction from the tomb proper. If there was in fact originally a pyramidal superstructure at the left that was probably the "monument" or *nephesh*. Another possibility is to identify the *nephesh* of the burial place of the Bene Hezir with the Tomb of Zechariah (No. 221). The latter is not far away and a passage leads from the porch of the Tomb of James to the enclosure around it.

While the burial place just described was that of the

Bene Hezir, as the inscription shows, tradition has called it the Tomb of James. The head of the early Christian church in Jerusalem was James the brother of the Lord (Gal 1:19). Hegesippus relates (according to Eusebius, *Ch. Hist.* II 23) that he was martyred by being cast down from the pinnacle (πτερύγιον) of the temple, and that he was buried on the spot, by the temple, where his monument still remains. If the "pinnacle" (cf. Mt 4:5; Lk 4:9) of the temple was the southeast corner of the enclosure wall which was so high above the Kidron ravine that "one who looked down grew dizzy" (Josephus, *Ant.* xv 11, 5 §412) (cf. No. 150), then James might have fallen into the valley at a point approximately opposite the tomb of the Bene Hezir. Later it would not have been difficult to imagine that that tomb was the monument of James.

Frey II, pp. 324-325 No. 1394. Photograph: Avigad, *Ancient Monuments in the Kidron Valley*, p. 60 Fig. 35, courtesy The Bialik Institute, Jerusalem.

193

221. The Tomb of Zechariah

The plan in No. 218 and the photograph in No. 219 have already shown the relationship of the Tomb of Zechariah to the Tomb of James; this is another view of the western front of the Tomb of Zechariah. The monument is cut out of the cliff as a monolith 9 meters high and 5.20 meters wide. The sides are adorned with pilasters and columns with Ionic capitals, and the top is a large pyramid. Architecturally a date is suggested in the second half of the first century B.C. Since no opening is to be found anywhere this is probably a sepulchral monument (*nephesh*) rather than a tomb. The passage leading from the porch of the Tomb of James to the enclosure around the Tomb of Zechariah makes it possible to think that the latter monument is the *nephesh* associated with the tomb of the Bene Hezir. If that *nephesh* was, however, a pyramidal superstructure once existing immediately beside the tomb of the Bene Hezir (cf. No. 219), then the Tomb of Zechariah is presumably the *nephesh* of another burial complex and the tombs associated with it may be hidden somewhere in the adjacent hill.

The traditional attribution of this monument to Zechariah presumably refers to Zechariah the son of Jehoiada the priest, who was stoned under King Joash in the court of the house of the Lord (II Ch 24:20-22). In Mt 23:35 most manuscripts mention Zechariah the son of Barachiah, presumably thinking of the well-known prophet whose father was Berechiah (Zec 1:1), but there is no other information about such a murder of this prophet. Actually Codex Sinaiticus mentions only Zechariah here, without any father's name, and the Gospel according to the Hebrews reads "son of Joiada." Therefore the original reference in Mt 23:35

was undoubtedly to the martyr of II Ch 24:20-22. Since he was slain "between the sanctuary and the altar," it was natural to look for his monument not too far away from the temple.

Vincent, *Jérusalem*, 1:1, pp. 335-337; 1:2, pl. LXXIX. Photograph: JF.

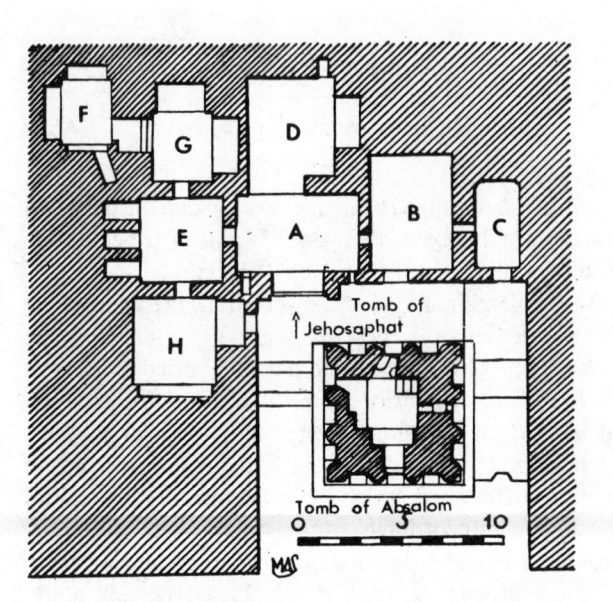

222. Plan of the Tomb of Absalom and the Tomb of Jehoshaphat

This shows the arrangement and relationship of the Tomb of Absalom and the Tomb of Jehoshaphat.

Vincent, *Jérusalem* 1:1, pp. 332-335. Photograph: *ibid.*, p. 333, Fig. 90, courtesy École Biblique et Archéologique Française.

223. The Tomb of Absalom

Like the Tomb of Zechariah (No. 221), the Tomb of Absalom is also, in its lower part, a monolith cut out of the side of the cliff. This part of the monument is 6.00 meters wide and 6.50 meters high. It is adorned with corner pilasters and Ionic columns, which support an entablature with architrave, frieze, and cornice. On this is a square structure of large stone blocks. On the south side above the cornice is the opening of a stair-

case which leads down to a small interior burial chamber with two arcosolia. Thus far the monument was therefore a tomb. Above the square structure there is a superstructure with a cylindrical body and a conical tower which brings the total height of the monument to 16.50 meters. Architecturally this is like the *tholos* found in Hellenistic and Roman sepulchral monuments, except that the columns which there lift the conical portion above the cylindrical part and provide a place for statues of the dead are here, understandably in a Jewish environment, omitted. In effect, then, the superstructure constitutes a *nephesh* (cf. No. 220) for the tomb below. The date of the tomb may be at the beginning of the first century of the Christian era. As for the connection of the monument with Absalom, this tradition undoubtedly embodies the idea that this is the pillar (LXX στήλη) which Absalom set up for himself in the King's Valley (II Sam 18:18), a name which probably designates the Kidron.

Vincent, *Jérusalem*, 1:2, Pl. LXXII. Photograph: JF.

224. The Pediment of the Tomb of Jehoshaphat

The Tomb of Jehoshaphat is behind the Tomb of Absalom (see Plan, No. 222) and is reached by a flight of steps and through a doorway eight feet wide. The illustration shows the triangular pediment over this doorway. It is ornamented with an acanthus and with oranges, lemons, grapes, and olive branches. Through the doorway one enters a large oblong chamber and from it, in turn, there is access to a complex of tomb chambers (A to H in the plan). One tomb chamber (E) has kokim graves, several of the others have arcosolia. The connection of this burial complex with the Tomb of Absalom suggests that both are of the same date, i.e., at the beginning of the first century of the Christian era. The Tomb of Absalom may also be a burial monument to mark the entire burial place behind it. Since this relatively large burial place and its

prominent *nephesh* (if the Tomb of Absalom may be considered as such) were located in the Valley of Jehoshaphat, it may have been natural enough for tradition to identify it as the Tomb of Jehoshaphat.

If the dates given above for the four "tombs" which have just been described are correct, all of these monuments existed in the Kidron Valley in the time of Jesus. When he crossed that valley (Jn 18:1) he would have

seen them; when he spoke of those who hypocritically "build the tombs of the prophets and adorn the monuments of the righteous" (Mt 23:29) he could have had these very objects in mind.

Vincent, *Jérusalem*, 1:2, Pl. LXXVI upper; Parrot, *Golgotha and the Church of the Holy Sepulchre*, pp. 94-95. Photograph: courtesy École Biblique et Archéologique Française.

THE SANHEDRIYYA TOMBS

225. Plan and Sections of Tomb XIV of the Sanhedriyya Tombs

The so-called Sanhedriyya Tombs, also previously known as the Tombs of the Judges, are located in a northern suburb of Jerusalem, off from Samuel Street

(Rehov Shemuel Hannavi). When the tombs were discovered at the beginning of the seventeenth century it was reckoned that there were seventy burial places. Like the seventy elders appointed by Moses (Num 11:24), the Sanhedrin had seventy members (*Sanhedrin* I 6 DM 383) with the high priest as president (Mt 26:57

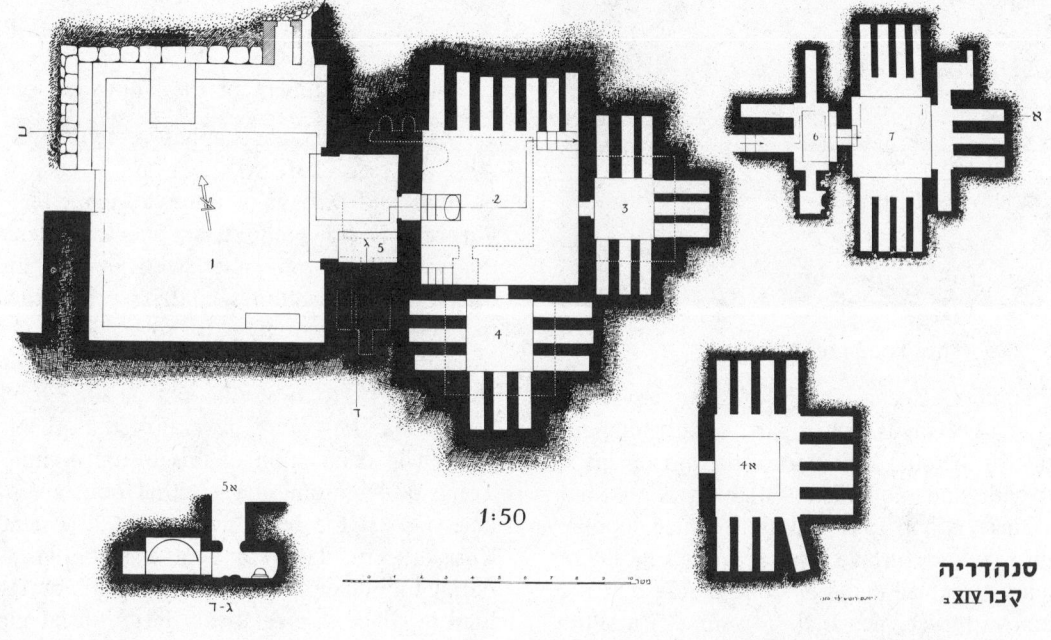

1:50

סנהדריה
קברXIV ב

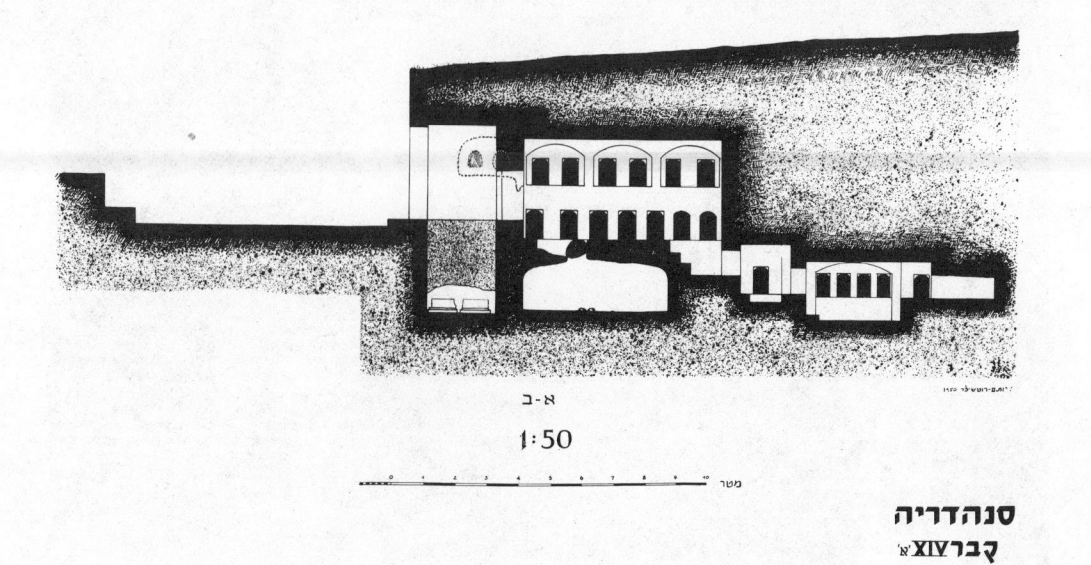

1:50

סנהדריה
קברXIVא

and parallels; Josephus, *Ant.* xx 9, 1 §200), so the idea arose that this was the burial place of those seventy personages. There is no reason to suppose, however, that the members of the Sanhedrin were buried otherwise than in their own family tombs. This is the normal Jewish custom, attested by the OT phrases, "was gathered to his people" (Gen 25:8, etc.), "lie with my fathers" (Gen 47:30, etc.), and "sleep with your fathers" (Dt 31:16), and by the passage in *Sanhedrin* VI (DM 391; SBT IV 5, 305) where "buried in their proper place" can hardly mean anything but in the family burying-place. Also when Julius Jotham-Rothschild counted the tombs carefully he found only fifty-five *kokim*, four *arcosolia*, and two caves used to contain ossuaries, rather than the supposed seventy. The tombs are indeed large and fine and must have belonged to wealthy families, so individual members of the Sanhedrin might have been buried in some of them, but as a whole this is not to be considered the mass burial ground of the Sanhedrin. In plan the Sanhedriyya Tombs consist of a forecourt, a vestibule, and a main chamber with adjoining side chambers. The burial places are kokim, arcosolia, and rock benches or shelves. Also nearly all of the tombs have separate small chambers which may be for the collection of bones or the reception of ossuaries. The one known as Tomb XIV is outstanding architecturally, and it is shown here in plan and sections.

Julius Jotham-Rothschild, "The Tombs of Sanhedria," in PEQ 1952, pp. 23-38; L. Y. Rahmani, "Jewish Rock-Cut Tombs in Jerusalem," in *'Atiqot* 3 (1961), pp. 93-104, and Fig. 4. Photograph: courtesy Department of Antiquities, State of Israel.

226. Entrance to Tomb XIV of the Sanhedriyya Tombs

The forecourt of Tomb XIV of the Sanhedriyya Tombs, shown here, is 9.90 meters in breadth and 9.30 meters in length, second in size only to the forecourt of the Tombs of the Kings (No. 231). On three sides are almost perfectly preserved benches, cut from the rock, on which the people would presumably sit during the last rites. At the entrance to the vestibule of the tomb is a fine façade, and the pediment is carved with acanthus leaves, pomegranates, and citrons. The tomb chambers within are arranged in three descending stories, as seen in the sections (No. 225).

The pottery found in the Sanhedriyya Tombs is important for the establishment of their date. Numerous jars are of a type common between the middle of the first century B.C. and the year 70 of the Christian era. Pyriform or pear-shaped bottles, used to contain costly oils or wine, are like those found in Herodian Jericho. Lamps are of the round, closed type with the nozzle shaped like a spatula, such as are also found in Jericho together with coins belonging to the early years of the reign of Herod. So the use of these tombs evidently extended from about 37 B.C. when Herod began his reign in fact (FHBC §363), to the time of the fall of Jerusalem in A.D. 70. Other important objects found from this period were fragments of sarcophagi and possibly of ossuaries. Some later material including fragments of glazed ware and glass indicates use of the tombs, probably as dwellings, in the thirteenth to fifteenth centuries, when the Arabs probably had a cara-

vanserai in the forecourt of Tomb XIV.

Jotham-Rothschild in PEQ 1952, pl. IX, Fig. 2. Photograph: courtesy Government Press Office, State of Israel.

THE HERODIAN FAMILY TOMB

227. Plan and Sections of the Herodian Family Tomb

One of the landmarks at Jerusalem to which Josephus refers in his account of the Jewish War (*War* v 12, 2 §507) is the memorial monument or tomb of Herod (τὸ Ἡρώδου μνημεῖον). In one passage (*War* v 3, 2 §108), using the plural, he speaks of the tombs of Herod as near the Serpent's Pool. West of the Old City of Jerusalem, near the King David Hotel and off from King David Road, is the subterranean burial place of which the plan and sections are shown here. This tomb is cut out of the solid rock, and its corridors and chambers are also walled with fine, large blocks of limestone. There are no kokim or arcosolia in the tomb-chambers, and the manner of burial was presumably by the use of sarcophagi. Two sarcophagi were, in fact, still in the longest tomb-chamber (F) (see No. 250). The impressive architecture of this tomb which probably also had a superstructure now lost, agrees well with its identification as the tomb of Herod mentioned by Josephus. If the identification is correct then the Serpent's Pool which Josephus described as near the tomb of Herod may perhaps be identified with the nearby Mamilla Pool which goes back at least to Roman times. Herod the Great himself, however, was not buried in this tomb, but at the Herodium four miles southeast of Bethlehem (No. 17). His oldest son, Antipater, was buried at Hyrcania, probably to be identified with Khirbet Mird five miles southwest of Qumran (FLAP p. 280), and two other sons, Alexander and Aristobulus, in the Alexandrium seventeen miles north of Jericho. It remains possible that other members of the family rested in the

tomb at Jerusalem.

F.-M. Abel, "Exils et tombeaux des Herodes," in RB 53 (1946), pp. 56-74; Vincent, *Jérusalem*, 1:1, pp. 342-346; Smith, *Jerusalem*, I, p. 114; Dalman, *Jerusalem*, pp. 202f. Photograph: Vincent, *Jérusalem*, 1:2, Pl. LXXXII, courtesy École Biblique et Archéologique Française.

228. Rolling Stone in the Herodian Family Tomb

The Herodian family tomb is notable for one of the two examples (the other is in the Tomb of Queen Helena of Adiabene, No. 235) still to be seen at Jerusalem of a "rolling stone" used to close the entrance of a place of burial. On the plan of the Herodian family tomb (No. 227) the main entrance is at the point labeled A. Here there is a side channel in which the great stone stands on its edge and from which it can be rolled forward to close the doorway. This photograph shows that the stone is an enormous disk like a millstone, 1.60 meters in diameter and .80 meters in thickness, and almost perfectly preserved.

F.-M. Abel in RB 34 (1925), pp. 278-279. Photograph: courtesy École Biblique et Archéologique Française de Jerusalem.

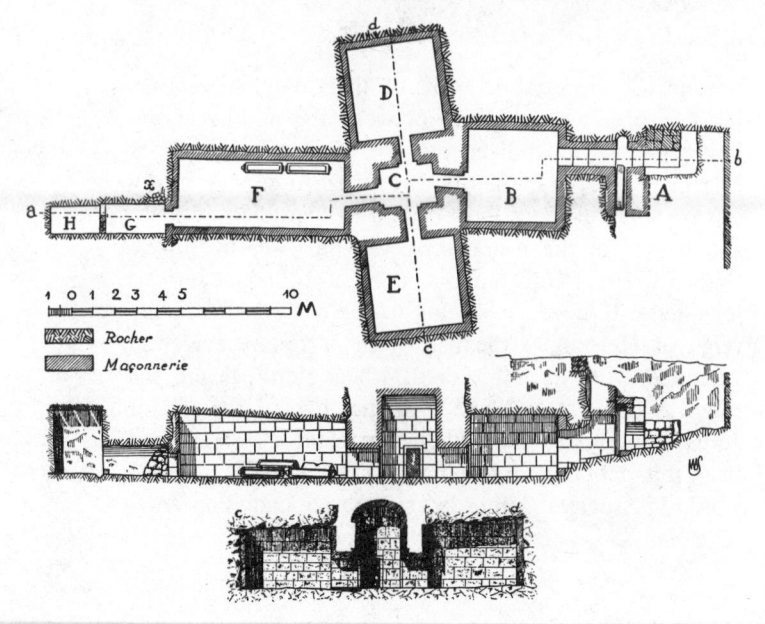

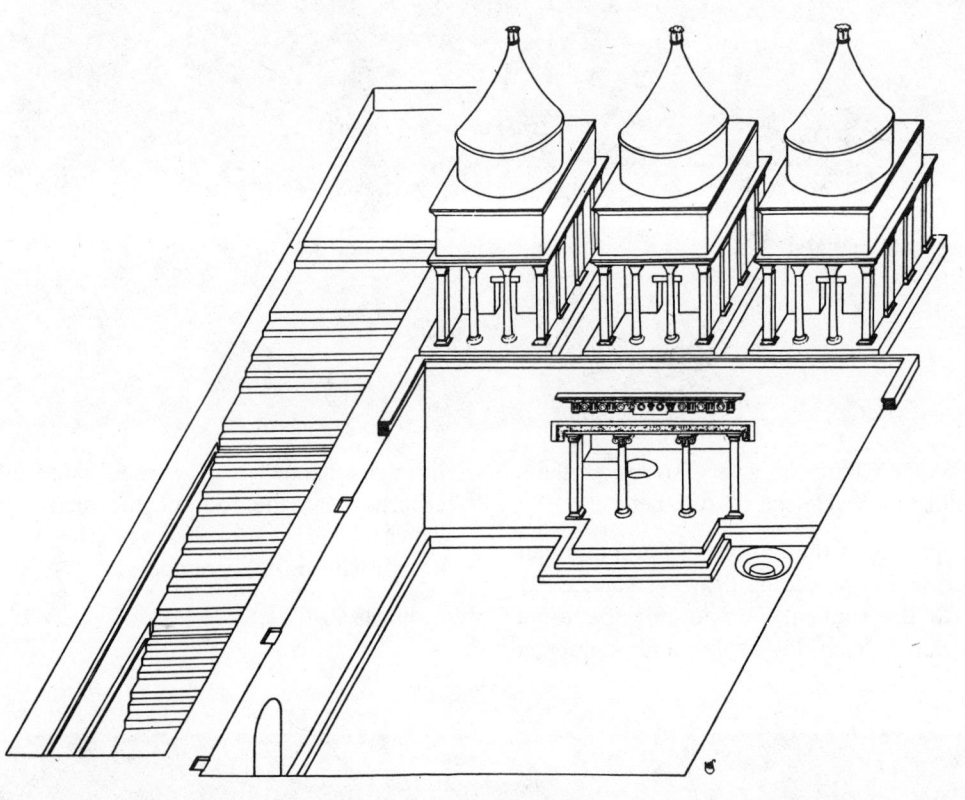

229. Restoration in Perspective of the Tomb of Queen Helena of Adiabene

This tomb is north of the Old City of Jerusalem on the Nablus Road, a short distance beyond St. George's Cathedral and just beyond the intersection of Saladin Road with Nablus Road. When L. F. Caignart de Saulcy excavated at the spot in 1863 he believed that these were the tombs of the kings of Judah, and they have continued to be known popularly as the Tombs of the Kings. There is reason to believe, however, that the tombs are the burial place established by Queen Helena of Adiabene, which was a district on the upper Tigris (Pliny, *Nat. Hist.* v 13, 66; vi 16, 41-42). Josephus relates (*Ant.* xx 2-5 §§17-117) that Helena and her son Izates were both converted to Judaism. She made a journey to Jerusalem in order to worship in the temple there, and she also procured food from Alexandria and Cyprus for the people, since there was a great famine. This famine took place when Tiberius Alexander was procurator (A.D. 46-48), and is probably the same as that mentioned in Ac 11:28 as coming to pass in the days of Claudius (A.D. 41-54). Upon his death Izates was succeeded by his older brother, Monobazus II.

Helena died soon after, and Josephus (*Ant.* xx 4, 3 §95) reports: "But Monobazus sent her bones and those of his brother to Jerusalem and ordered that they should be buried at the pyramids, three in number, which the mother had erected three stadia from the city of Jerusalem" (cf. above No. 161). Elsewhere Josephus also makes mention of the monuments or tomb of Helena (τῶν Ἑλένης μνημείων) as a well-known landmark at Jerusalem (*War* v 2, 2 §55; 3, 3 §119; 4, 2 §147). Pausanias (viii 16, 4-5) compares this grave in Jerusalem with the tomb of Mausolus at Halicarnassus; and Eusebius (*Ch. Hist.* ii 12, 3) says that the splendid monuments (στῆλαι διαφανεῖς) of Queen Helena were still shown in his time in the suburbs of Aelia, as Jerusalem was then called. The three pyramids mentioned by Josephus no longer exist. They may have had somewhat the appearance of the Tomb of Absalom (No. 223), and are included in the hypothetical restoration in this drawing.

L. F. Caignart de Saulcy, *Carnets de voyage en Orient (1845-1869), publiés avec une introduction, des notes critiques et des appendices par Fernande Bassan.* Paris: Presses Universitaires de France, 1955, pp. 29, 167f., 185; Vincent, *Jérusalem,* 1:1, pp. 346-363. Photograph: *ibid.,* 1:2, Pl. xcvii, courtesy École Biblique et Archéologique Française.

230. Steps, Water Channels, and Cisterns at the Tomb of Queen Helena of Adiabene

This photograph shows the bottom of the monumental stairway seen in the preceding drawing (No. 229). It leads down to the sunken courtyard of the tomb. Water was collected from the stairs and conducted through channels in the rock side-wall to two large cisterns near the foot of the steps, an arrangement which evidently provided water for the ablutions connected with burial ceremonies.

Photograph: JF.

231. In the Courtyard of the Tomb of Queen Helena of Adiabene

The courtyard of the tomb, to which the steps shown in the preceding illustration (No. 230) lead, is sunk to a depth of eight or nine meters below the top of the rock cliff and is about 26.50 meters square. This photograph looks toward the vestibule at the west side of the court, through which one passes to the burial chambers.

Photograph: JF.

232. The Entablature of the Tomb of
     Queen Helena of Adiabene

Photograph: courtesy École Biblique et Archéologique Française.

The doorway to the vestibule of the tomb, shown in the preceding photograph (No. 231), is twelve meters wide. Two columns, now missing, supported the entablature, the center and right-hand portions of which are shown here. On the architrave is a bas-relief with thick foliage, pomegranates, and pine cones. The frieze above has triglyphs and circular ornaments, and in the center is a bunch of grapes with a crown and triple palm on either side of it. The cornice consists of projecting ledges.

233. Plan of the Tomb of Queen Helena of Adiabene

From the vestibule of the tomb a passage at the left leads to a large antechamber (A) about six meters square. From this, other passages lead to the tomb chambers with their kokim and arcosolia. Also sarcophagi were used for some of the burials. The tomb chambers were closed with stone doors which turned on hinges.

Photograph: Vincent, *Jérusalem*, 1:2, Pl. LXXXIX, courtesy École Biblique et Archéologique Française.

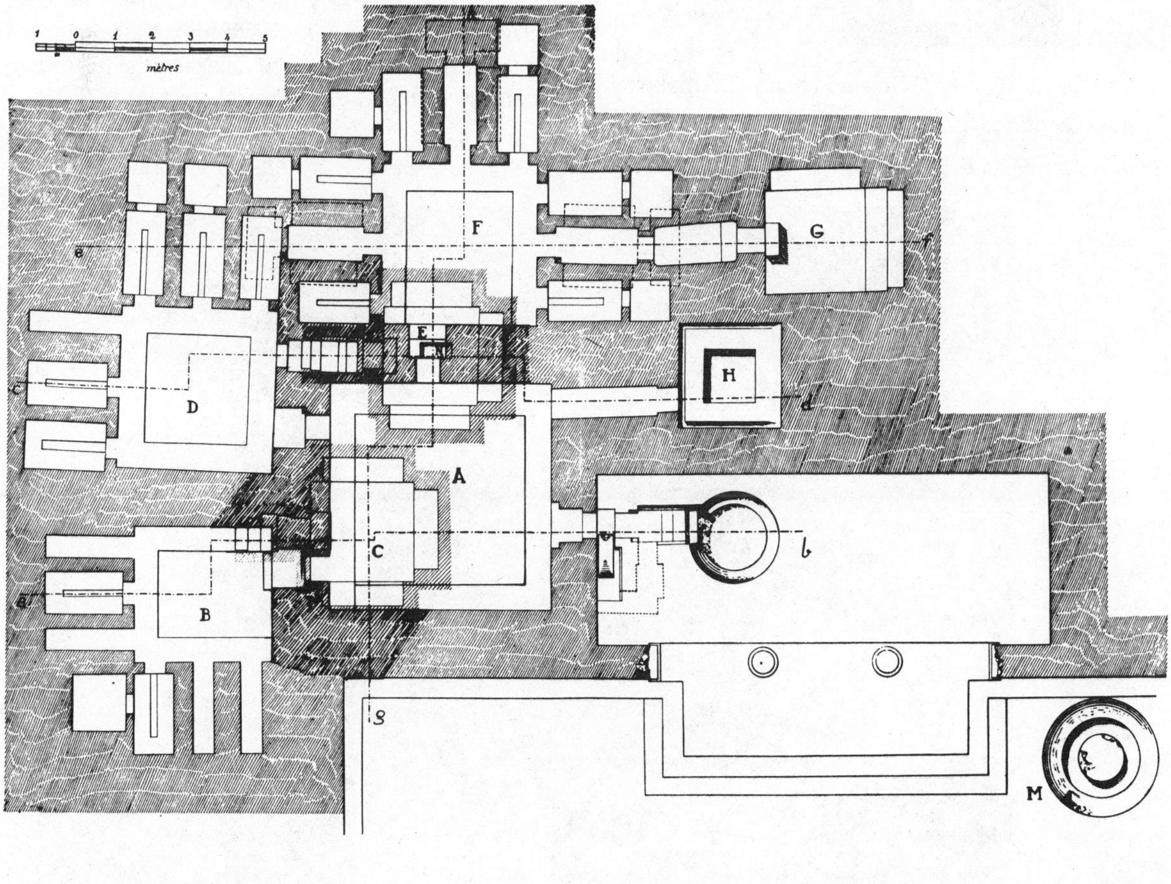

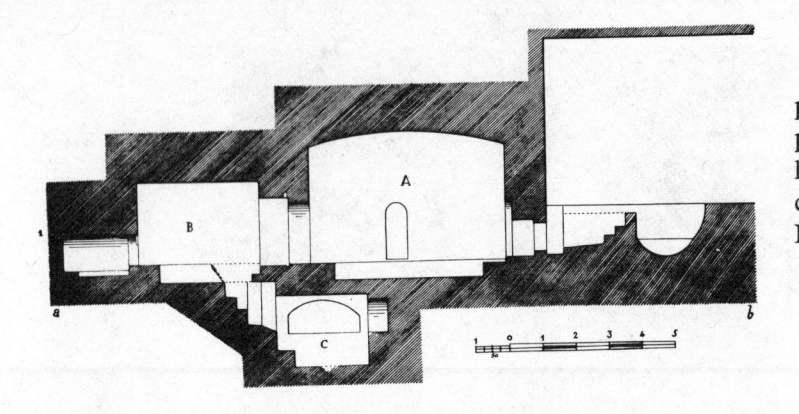

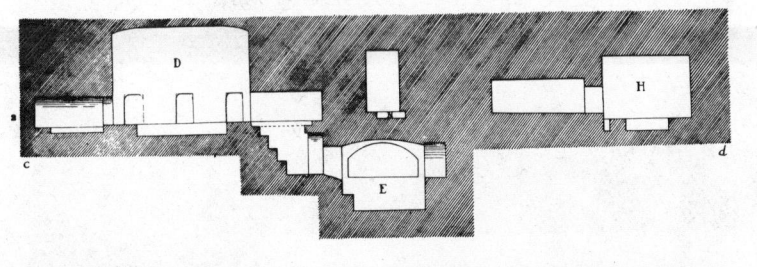

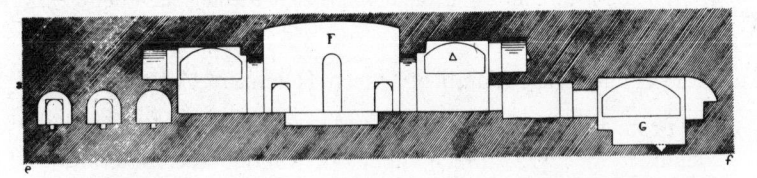

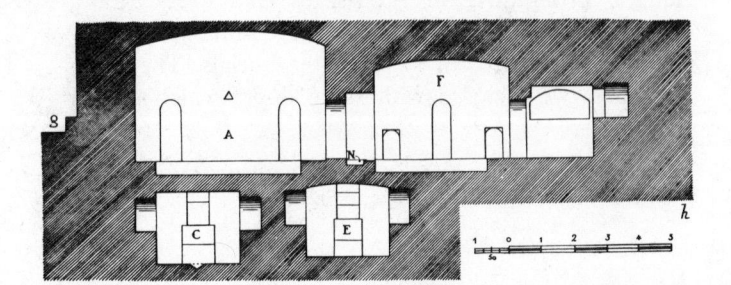

234. Sections of the Tomb of Queen Helena of Adiabene

The ramifications of the tomb chambers suggest that the preparation of them continued over quite a long period of time. Also two chambers (C and E in the plan and sections) were placed on a lower level. In one lower chamber, which had not been plundered, a sarcophagus still contained the dust of the deceased (see No. 252).

Photograph: Vincent, *Jérusalem*, 1:2, Pl. xc, courtesy École Biblique et Archéologique Française.

235. Rolling Stone at the Entrance of the Tomb of Queen Helena of Adiabene

The entrance to all the subterranean chambers of the tomb is through a passageway at the left end of the vestibule (cf. Plan No. 233). This photograph shows the arrangement for closing that entrance, consisting of a large rolling stone set in a deep transverse channel. Behind the stone is a small chamber just large enough to admit the men who would push the stone forward across the doorway. In his account of this tomb, and probably referring to this stone, Pausanias (VIII 16, 5) reports that at a fixed time on one certain day of the year a mechanism would, unaided, open the door and then, after a short interval, shut it. While this is obviously only a legend which was believed in the second century, the great rolling stone itself is very tangible. It and the similar stone at the Herodian family tomb (No. 228) are the two examples still to be seen at Jerusalem of the type of tomb closure referred to in the Gospels (Mt 27:60, etc.) in connection with the burial place of Jesus. Judging by these examples at Jerusalem, and a very few others elsewhere in Palestine (notably at Abu Ghosh, northwest of Jerusalem), this manner of tomb closure with a rolling stone seems to have been characteristic Jewish practice only in the Roman period up to A.D. 70.

Vincent, *Jérusalem*, 1:1, p. 349 Fig. 97. Photograph: The Matson Photo Service, Alhambra, Calif.

BETH SHE'ARIM

236. General View of Beth She'arim

Under certain circumstances Jewish tombs were expanded into the form known as catacombs (cf. FLAP pp. 469f.). These are subterranean cemeteries consisting of galleries and rooms (*cubicula*) in the walls of which are burial niches in the form of simple loculi or more elaborate arched arcosolia. In Palestine the most remarkable Jewish catacomb is at Beth She'arim.

As we have noted (No. 159), the Jewish law court known as the Sanhedrin (סנהדרין, συνέδριον) met in Jerusalem in a place the name of which is usually translated as Chamber of Hewn Stone, but which may actually have meant Chamber beside the Xystus. After the destruction of Jerusalem (A.D. 70) the court of course had to move elsewhere. In the Talmud (Rosh Hashanah 31a-b SBT II, 7, p. 149) Rabbi Johanan (d. 279) reports the tradition that "the Sanhedrin

wandered to ten places of banishment." We list the original location of the Sanhedrin and the ten places to which it moved, with a few explanatory notes: Chamber of Hewn Stone (or, Chamber beside the Xystus; in or near the temple area). 1) Hanuth (perhaps the chamber of the sons of Hanan, a priestly family, Jer 35:4; the place to which the Sanhedrin moved when it ceased to judge capital cases). 2) Jerusalem (since the two preceding locations were in Jerusalem it is not clear what is meant here). 3) Jabneh (also called Jabneel or Jamnia, a town on the western border of Judea, nine miles northeast of Ashdod and only four miles from the Mediterranean; when Jerusalem fell Rabbi Johanan ben Zakkai took the court here and it, now called the Beth-Din, remained at Jamnia until the beginning of the Second Revolt in 132). 4) Usha (a town in Galilee; this was in the time of Rabban Gamaliel II). 5) Jabneh (back there from Usha, according to Johanan). 6) Usha (back there again from Jabneh).

7) Shefar'am (also a town in Galilee; the last three were in the time of Rabbi Simeon ben Gamaliel). 8) Beth She'arim. 9) Sepphoris. 10) Tiberias ("and Tiberias is the lowest-lying of them all," a figurative way of saying that at Tiberias [the city itself being on the shore of the Sea of Galilee, 696 feet below the level of the Mediterranean, cf. No. 53] the authority of the Sanhedrin was reduced to its lowest level).

With respect to Beth She'arim, in which we are presently interested, it is known from many references in the Talmud (cf. JE VII, pp. 333-337) that it was the Patriarch Judah I, usually called Rabbi Judah ha-Nasi (i.e., "the Prince"), who moved the court and the center of Jewish studies to this place. Judah is famed as the great redactor of the Mishnah, in which are many of his own statements, introduced by the words, "Rabbi says," and with respect to his time it was said that to follow justice meant to follow Rabbi to Beth She'arim (Sanhedrin 32b SBT IV 5, p. 205). Along with his Hebrew studies Judah also took a liberal attitude toward Hellenistic culture, and was the author of the saying (Sotah 49b SBT III 6, p. 269): "Why use the Syrian language (i.e., Aramaic, spoken generally by the unlearned) in the land of Israel? Either use the holy tongue (i.e., Hebrew) or Greek!" After illness during which he moved to Sepphoris for its higher ground and more salubrious air, the patriarch died at the age of eighty-five in about the year 220, and was buried in a place reserved for him at Beth She'arim (Kethuboth 103b SBT III 4, p. 663). Before his death he distributed his various functions with the sentence (Kethuboth 103b SBT III 4, p. 658): "My son Simeon is Hakam (i.e., "wise"), my son Gamaliel Nasi (i.e., the "prince" in succession to his father), and Hanina ben Hama shall preside (i.e., over the Sanhedrin)."

In Hebrew the name of Beth She'arim means House of Gates. In Josephus the name appears in Greek in the form Βησάρα, Besara (Life 24 §§118-119). In view of the great prominence of Beth She'arim, as shown in the foregoing references and particularly those of the Talmud, it is surprising that the place was utterly lost. This was the case, however, and later it was even supposed (IEJ 5 [1955], p. 237) that the tomb of Rabbi Judah ha-Nasi was at Sepphoris, the town where he did in fact die but not where he was actually buried. Then in 1936 the accidental discovery of a tomb led to the explorations and excavations which have brought to light a town and a number of very large catacombs, which almost certainly represent the long lost Beth She'arim.

The site was in the vicinity of an Arab village called Sheikh Abreiq after a local holy man whose white domed tomb is on a small hill. In 1936 a Jewish youth group settled here and made the initial discoveries;

these were followed by the excavations of the Israel Exploration Society under Benjamin Maisler (Mazar) in 1936-1940 and Nahman Avigad and others from 1953 onward.

Josephus said that Besara was twenty stadia from Gaba (Life 24 §118). The latter was the Gaba Hippeum (Γάβα, πόλις ἱππέων) or "city of cavalry" where Herod the Great settled his discharged cavalrymen, and was adjacent to Carmel (War III 3, 1 §§35-36). The indicated location of Besara agrees with the location of Sheik Abreiq, which is beside the high road between Haifa and Nazareth. Furthermore, in the early excavations, the very name Βεσάρα was found in a Greek inscription on a marble slab at Sheikh Abreiq (Maisler, Beth She'arim, p. 3).

According to the excavators, the city on the mound at Beth She'arim was probably built originally in the second century B.C., was at its height in the third and early fourth centuries of the Christian era, and was destroyed in the fourth century, probably in A.D. 351 when Gallus, the brother-in-law of Constantius II, suppressed a Jewish revolt in Galilee (IEJ 10 [1960], p. 264). Excavations have uncovered a large synagogue (something like the one at Capernaum), a basilica, public buildings, dwelling houses, a glass factory with a slab of glass weighing nearly nine tons still in place (IEJ 15 [1965], pp. 261-262; Archaeology 20 [1967], pp. 88-95), an olive press and, of course, the catacombs, of which more than twenty have been found so far.

In this general view of Beth She'arim (No. 236), the entrances of Catacombs No. 20 and No. 14 may be seen at the left and the right, respectively, just above the center of the picture. Above each catacomb may be recognized an open-air structure also cut back into the hillside and obviously planned as an integral part of the structure (see also No. 238). These are provided with stone benches and evidently were a place of assembly for mourning and anniversary services (IEJ 9 [1960], pp. 212-214).

N. Avigad, "Excavations at Beth She'arim," in IEJ 4 (1954), pp. 88-107; 5 (1955), pp. 205-239; 7 (1957), pp. 73-92, 239-255; 9 (1959) pp. 205-220; 10 (1960), p. 264; Benjamin Maisler, Beth She'arim, Report on the Excavations during 1936-1940. Jerusalem: Israel Exploration Society, Vol. I, English Summary, 1950; Benjamin Mazar (Maisler), Beth She'arim, Report on the Excavations during 1936-40 (in Hebrew). Jerusalem: Israel Exploration Society, Vol. I, The Catacombs I-IV (with English summary), 2d ed. 1957; Vol. II, The Greek Inscriptions (with French summary), 1967; cf. Norman Bentwich, The New-Old Land of Israel: London: George Allen & Unwin Ltd., 1960, pp. 109-114; Robert Payne, The Splendor of Israel. New York: Harper & Row, 1963, pp. 111-117; Moshe Pearlman and Yaacov Yannai, Historical Sites in Israel. Tel Aviv: Massadah-P.E.C. Press Ltd., 1964, pp. 86-93. Photograph: courtesy Government Press Office, State of Israel.

237. Burial Chambers in the Beth She'arim Catacombs

In general, each of the Beth She'arim catacombs is approached through an open courtyard cut into the hill, with entrances on the three sides of the court. These entrances are closed with large stone doors, which move on hinges and are decorated with panels and knobs, to make them look like wooden doors. Within, as seen in this photograph, are long halls with arched openings into the burial chambers.

Photograph: courtesy Government Press Office, State of Israel.

238. Entrance of Catacomb No. 14

Of all the catacombs at Beth She'arim, perhaps the greatest interest has attached to No. 14, with its triple-arched main façade, and the open-air stone benches of the assembly place above (cf. above No. 236). This catacomb was judged to be one of the oldest at Beth She'arim and to date from the end of the second century of the Christian era, although its façade was perhaps added only in the first half of the third century (IEJ 4 [1954], p. 106; 5 [1955], pp. 225-226).

Inside, there are two large rooms, with connecting corridors. As usual there are various tombs cut in the walls, and smaller niches perhaps for the collection of bones, but in the farther large room there is also one built tomb. In a long burial niche at the end of the left-hand wall of the first large room part of a vertical slab is still in place (IEJ 4 [1954], Pl. 9 c). On it, painted in large red letters, is the name רבי שמעון, Rabbi Simeon (ibid., p. 104 Fig. 6). Above the first loculus on the right side of the passage which leads to the room with the built tomb there is a bilingual inscription written in black letters. It reads in Hebrew: זו של רבי גמליאל מ, "This is (the tomb) of Rabbi Gamaliel M"; and in Greek: ΡΑΒΙ ΓΑΜΑΛΙΗΛ, "Rabbi Gamaliel" (ibid., p. 104 Fig. 7). Not far from the Tomb of Simeon there is another grave cut in the wall at ground-level, and above the opening there is an inscription in Hebrew which reads: אנינא הקטן, "Anina ha-Qatan," i.e., "Anina the Little" (IEJ 5 [1955], p. 222 Fig. 9).

Interestingly enough, the names in the inscriptions just cited are precisely those of the two sons of Rabbi Judah ha-Nasi, namely, Simeon and Gamaliel, while Anina is equivalent to Hanina, the name of the man whom Judah designated to preside over the Sanhedrin after his own death (cf. No. 236). While identification is of course not guaranteed, it is at least possible that these were the same persons and that this was none other than the family tomb of Rabbi Judah ha-Nasi. As for the obviously most important tomb in the whole catacomb, namely, the built grave, the question has

naturally been raised as to whether this may be the tomb of the patriarch himself. But the grave carries no inscription whatsoever, and the identification remains uncertain.

IEJ 4 (1954), pp. 99-107; 5 (1955), pp. 218-226, 236-239. Photograph: courtesy Government Press Office, State of Israel.

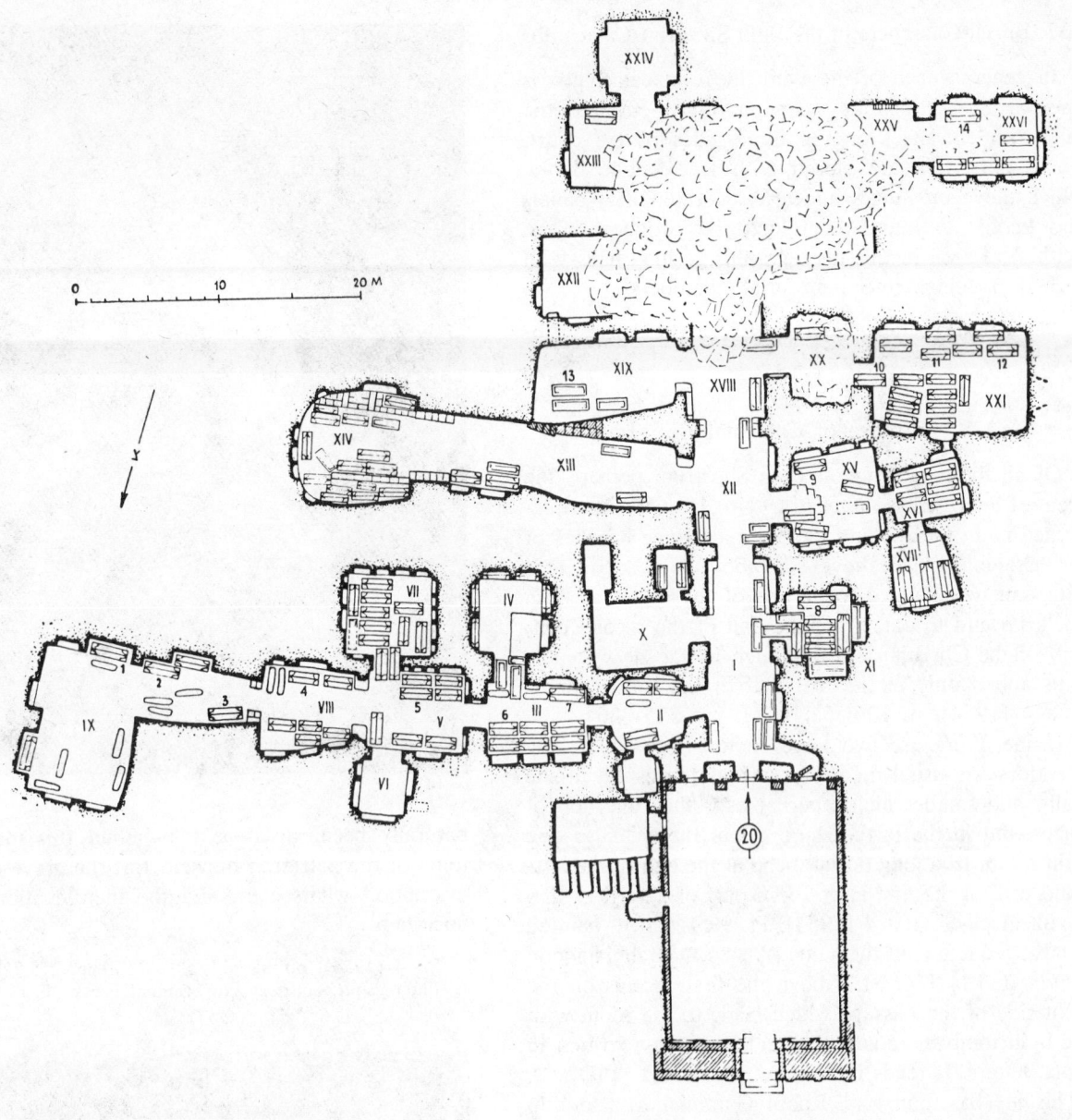

239. Plan of Catacomb No. 20

Catacomb No. 20 at Beth She'arim has also been of much interest. Its façade is visible in the general view (No. 236), and this sketch plan shows the entire complex. The entrance gives access to a long central hall which runs north and south, with rooms and chambers branching off on either side. At the far end, collapse of the rock has destroyed several rooms. In most of the rooms there were arcosolia in the walls, and also small niches closed with perpendicular stone slabs, the latter perhaps for the collection of bones (IEJ 7 [1957], p. 81), as in Catacomb No. 14 (No. 238). In some rooms graves were also cut in the floor.

In most of the Beth She'arim tombs burial was without any coffin, but particularly in this catacomb, in addition to scanty remains of burials in coffins of wood,

lead, and pottery, there were many sarcophagi of stone and marble. Sometimes these were placed in recesses in the walls, but in most cases they stood inside the rooms as shown in numerous examples in the Plan (No. 239). Among these burial chests those that were found intact or partly intact were all of limestone and numbered approximately 130. Most were made smooth and without ornamentation, but not a few were adorned with various reliefs in patterns taken from animal or still-life. Among the representations are lions (No. 254), bulls' heads, an eagle, a lion in pursuit of a gazelle, and the head or mask of a bearded man, as well as rosettes, shells, acanthus, a gate with flanking columns, and a menorah or seven-branched lampstand (cf. No. 240).

IEJ 7 (1957), pp. 77-92. Photograph: ibid., Fig. 4 facing p. 81, courtesy Israel Exploration Society.

240. Menorah in Catacomb No. 3

In addition to the menorah on a sarcophagus (cf. above No. 239), this symbol is also carved on the wall of one room (No. XXIII) in Catacomb No. 20. In other catacombs at Beth She'arim the menorah is found very frequently on the walls. The fine example shown in this photograph is in Hall E in Catacomb No. 3.

As is well known, the menorah or seven-armed lamp-stand goes back to Ex 25:31-39; 37:17-24, and was found not only in the temple at Jerusalem (FLAP p. 329) but also in synagogues and homes everywhere. It was thus a symbol of Judaism (FLAP p. 455) and, in a funerary context, it may have been thought of as a provision for the afterlife and thus have been specially associated with the thought of immortality (Wirgin).

W. Wirgin, "The *Menorah* as Symbol of After-Life," in IEJ 14 (1964), pp. 102-104. Photograph: Benjamin Maisler, *Beth She'arim* (1950), Pl. XXVI, courtesy Israel Exploration Society.

241. Epitaph of Marinos and His Wife in Catacomb No. 13

It will be remembered (No. 236) that Rabbi Judah ha-Nasi commended the use of the Hebrew and Greek languages rather than Aramaic. In most of the cata-combs at Beth She'arim the language of the inscriptions is predominantly Greek, but in Nos. 14 and 20 it is predominantly Hebrew which accords well with the supposition that these two catacombs in particular are for the burial of rabbinical families. In the examples already given (No. 238) from Catacomb No. 14 we saw inscriptions in Hebrew and, bilingually, in Hebrew and Greek.

This photograph (No. 241) shows a Greek inscription on a marble slab found in Catacomb No. 13 at Beth She'arim (see *The Greek Inscriptions*, by Schwabe and Lifshitz, p. 64 No. 149). The slab measures 18 by 37 centimeters. It is carved with a menorah (cf. No. 240), shofar (ram's horn blown at festivals, cf. Ps 81:3), *lulab* (palm branch used in the Feast of Tabernacles, cf. Lev 23:40), and shovel (used at the altar, perhaps for incense, cf. Ex 27:3; 38:3; Num 4:14). The inscription is in seven lines and reads: Τόπος Μαρινου καὶ Ειουσστας γυνεκὸς αὐτοῦ. Place (i.e., Tomb) of Marinos and his wife Justa.

In addition to identifying the person or persons buried in a given tomb, as in the foregoing example, the inscriptions sometimes express a malediction upon anyone who might molest the burial, this being a common means of attempting to prevent tomb robberies. For example in Catacomb No. 12, which dates probably in the second half of the third century, there is this inscription above Arcosolium No. 3 in Room No. III: "Anyone who shall open this burial upon whoever is inside shall die of an evil end" (IEJ 4 [1954], p. 95). But in spite of the maledictions all of the tombs found at Beth She'arim were plundered long ago.

Another interesting inscription is one of the six in Greek found in Catacomb No. 20. It is a graffito written in three lines, as follows (IEJ 7 [1957], p. 247):

ΕΥΤΥΧΩС
ΤΗ ΥΜΩΝ
ΑΝΑϹΤΑϹΙ

εὐτυχῶς

τῇ ὑμῶν

ἀνάστασι

Good fortune

in your

resurrection

Thus along with the idea of immortality (if the menorah stands for that), belief in resurrection is also attested at Beth She'arim.

IEJ 5 (1955), p. 217; 7 (1957), pp. 239-255. Photograph: IEJ 5 (1955), Pl. 26 c, courtesy Israel Exploration Society.

ROME

Since the most numerous and earliest Jewish catacombs are those found at Rome, it is necessary, in order to complete the survey of Jewish burial places more or less contemporary with the life of Jesus and the early church, to consider them also. At Rome the underlying volcanic tufa lent itself particularly well to the construction of this type of burial place, and no less than six Jewish catacombs have been found there. The first was discovered in 1602 by Antonio Bosio. It was on the Via Portuensis in Monteverde about a mile outside the Porta Portese on the west side of the Tiber. It was afterward lost again, then accidentally rediscovered in 1904, at which time Nikolaus Müller began its partial excavation. Inscriptions taken from the catacomb at that time and others obtained in 1913 were placed in a *Sala Giudaica* in the *Museo Cristiano Lateranense* in Rome. The second Jewish catacomb was found in 1859 in the Vigna Randanini, on the Via Appia outside the Porta San Sebastiano and near the side road called the Via Appia Pignatelli. This catacomb was explored, and many of its inscriptions published, by Raffaele Garrucci. The third was discovered in 1867 by Giovanni Battista de Rossi in the Vigna Cimarra, which was also on the Via Appia outside the Porta San Sebastiano. The fourth was found accidentally in 1882 in the Vigna Apolloni, on the Via Labicana over a mile outside the Porta Maggiore, and was explored by Orazio Marucchi. The fifth was found in 1885 by Nikolaus Müller on the Via Appia Pignatelli near the cemetery already mentioned in the Vigna Randanini. Finally the sixth Jewish catacomb was discovered accidentally in 1919 in the Villa Torlonia on the Via Nomentana, about a half mile outside the Porta Pia. It was excavated by Agostino Valente, and investigated by Roberto Paribeni and later by Hermann W. Beyer and Hans Lietzmann.

In location the Jewish catacomb in Monteverde corresponds with the statement of Philo (*The Embassy to Gaius* XXIII 155) that the Jews inhabited a great section of Rome on the other side of the Tiber; and the three catacombs on the Via Appia agree with the mention by Juvenal (*Satire* III 10-15) of Jews in the vicinity of the old Porta Capena which was on the Appian Way. Many stamped bricks are found in the catacombs with formulas which provide indications of date. The bricks found in Monteverde show that its first burial galleries could have been dug in the first century before the Christian era, that it was certainly in use in the first century of the Christian era and most widely employed in the second and third centuries, but was abandoned in the fourth century. In the catacomb of the Villa Torlonia the bricks belong to the first and second centuries of the Christian era and show that the catacomb was established not later than the second and third centuries. In the catacomb in the Vigna Randanini the stamped bricks belong to the second century of the Christian era. The inscriptions in the Jewish catacombs therefore probably extend over a period of two or three hundred years. In all approximately five hundred inscriptions are known. They contain mention of nearly a dozen synagogues in Rome and confirm the existence of a relatively large Jewish population at that time, estimates of which have run from 20,000 to 60,000. A count of the inscriptions with respect to language shows 366 or 74 per cent in Greek, 120 or 24.4 per cent in Latin, and 8 or 1.6 per cent in Hebrew or Aramaic. The Jews of Rome were therefore predominantly Greek-speaking, while the more Romanized ones used Latin too, but the Semitic languages were relatively little known. In the personal names of over 500 individuals named in the inscriptions, however, 40 per cent are purely Latin names, 32 per cent are Greek, 13 per cent are Hebrew names, and the rest are combinations of Latin and Greek or Latin and Hebrew. The largest proportion of Hebrew names (17 per cent) is found in the catacomb in Monteverde; in the catacomb in Villa Torlonia there are more Greek names (43 per cent) than Latin names (37 per cent); and in the three catacombs on the Via Appia there is the largest proportion of Latin names (50 per cent). Accordingly, if any distinction is to be made, it may be supposed that the most conservative community was on the other side of the Tiber; the most Hellenized in the northeast (Villa Torlonia); and the most Romanized on the Via Appia. And, in fact, the painted catacomb rooms found on the Via Appia reveal such allegorical symbols of paganism as a winged Victory, the goddess Fortuna with a cornucopia, and the genii of the seasons; the paintings in the rooms at the Villa Torlonia are Hellenistic in style but emphasize symbols of the Jewish faith; but the catacomb in Monteverde, as far as is known, has no such paintings.

Harry J. Leon, "The Jewish Catacombs and Inscriptions of Rome: An Account of Their Discovery and Subsequent History," in HUCA 5 (1928), pp. 299-314; "New Material about the Jews of Ancient Rome," in JQR 20 (1929-30), pp. 301-312; *The Jews of Ancient Rome*. Philadelphia: The Jewish Publication Society of America, 1960, *passim*; and in *The Teacher's Yoke* (see above No. 17), pp. 154-165.

simply, "Annia, wife of Bar-Calabria." Accordingly, as usual in grave inscriptions, the name of the deceased is given, and some indication of family relationship.

Nikolaus Müller, *Die jüdische Katakombe am Monteverde zu Rom, der älteste bisher bekannt gewordene jüdische Friedhof des Abendlandes*. Schriften herausgegeben von der Gesellschaft zur Förderung der Wissenschaft des Judentums. Leipzig: Gustav Fock, 1912; Giorgio Graziosi, "La nuova Sala Giudaica nel Museo cristiano Lateranense," in NBAC 21 (1915), pp. 13-56 and Pl. II No. 3; Umberto Cassuto, "Un 'iscrizione giudeo-aramaica conservata nel Museo cristiano Lateranense," in NBAC 22 (1916), pp. 193-198; Müller-Bees pp. 129-131 No. 142; DACL 8:2, col. 1872 No. 7; Frey I, pp. 228-229 No. 290. Photograph: courtesy Museo Cristiano Lateranense.

242. An Aramaic Inscription from the Jewish Catacomb in Monteverde

243. A Greek Inscription from the Jewish Catacomb in Monteverde

Although the Jewish Catacomb in Monteverde has long since fallen again into ruins, many inscriptions from it are preserved in the *Museo Cristiano Lateranense* in Rome. In that Museum the marble plaque shown here is No. 21 in the *Sala Giudaica*. The first word in the text is probably the personal name Annia, comparable to the Hebrew חניה, Hania or Ḥanniya, and perhaps influenced in form by the Greek 'Αννία. After that, interpretations of the text vary, but the second word in the first line can contain the Aramaic possessive pronoun and mean "the wife of him." The second line then repeats "of" (ד) and gives the name of the husband. This name employs the Aramaic *bar*, equivalent of Hebrew *ben*, meaning "son" or "son of," and apparently uses the man's country of origin, Calabria in South Italy, as a part of his name. If these interpretations are correct, the translation is literally, "Annia, the wife of him, of Bar-Calabria," or more

This marble plaque from the catacomb is No. 28 in the Jewish Hall in the Lateran Museum. While the spellings employed are frequent enough in that time, it would more normally be written as follows: ἐνθάδε κεῖται Ἰούδας ἱερεύς. The translation is: Here lies Judas, a priest. The first two words, "here lies," are a standard formula in the grave inscriptions.

Along with the text are shown three objects. In the center is a menorah or seven-armed lampstand (cf. No. 240). At the left is a vase, probably thought of as containing the olive oil necessary for the lamps on the lampstand (Ex 27:20; 35:14). At the right is probably an ivy leaf, of the sort usually identified with the genus of vines known as Hedera. Such an ivy leaf is used in Latin inscriptions, and is also taken over in Greek inscriptions, to separate words, mark abbreviations, etc. (Cagnat p. 28; Avi-Yonah, *Abbreviations*, p. 38).

Here it is presumably used, therefore, simply as a conventional decoration accompanying an inscription. Insofar as the leaf was recognized as belonging to a type of vine, however, one wonders if its use with a Jewish inscription could have anything to do with the conception of Israel as a vine (e.g., Ps 80:8). It must be said also that it is not always possible to distinguish the drawing of the ivy leaf from the drawing of the *ethrog*. The latter at any rate is a specifically Jewish symbol. It is the citron which was used along with the *lulab* or palm branch (cf. No. 241) in the Feast of Tabernacles (Lev 23:40), and *ethrog* and *lulab* are often shown together as symbols. Other fruits also are shown, e.g., the pomegranate, and exact identification is sometimes not easy.

Schneider Graziosi in NBAC 21 (1915), p. 15 No. 2; Müller-Bees p. 88 No. 98; DACL 8:2, col. 1871 No. 2; Frey I, p. 271 No. 346; Goodenough II, pp. 6-7, III, No. 713; cf. J. B. Frey, "Inscriptions inedites des catacombes juives de Rome," in RAC 5 (1928), pp. 281-282 for the most frequent formulas, and 7 (1930), pp. 248-250, 259-260 for the most usual symbols. Photograph: courtesy Museo Cristiano Lateranense.

244. A Latin Inscription from the Jewish Catacomb in Monteverde

This marble plaque, No. 32 in the Jewish Hall of the Lateran Museum, is broken into three pieces, with a portion completely missing. The menorah is in the upper left-hand corner, and the last letter in the first line has been traced in double outline. To judge from the available space, the first word in the fourth line may have been abbreviated and is to be read, *an(nos)*. In the last line the first part of the word [*die*]*s* was probably in the space now broken away. The translation is therefore: "Flavius Constantius, who lived 23 years, 14 days."

Schneider Graziosi in NBAC 21 (1915), p. 47 No. 107; Müller-Bees, p. 117 No. 128; Frey I, pp. 341-342 No. 463. Photograph: courtesy Museo Cristiano Lateranense.

245. A Greek Inscription in the Jewish Catacomb in the Vigna Randanini

This marble plaque which is still in the catacomb contains a text in four lines and a representation of the menorah. It would now be written: Ἐνθάδε κεῖται νήπιος Μαρκέλλος. Ἐν εἰρήνῃ ἡ κοίμησις σου.

The text uses a standard phrase with which we are already familiar (above No. 243) in the first line, and another phrase also very customary in Jewish burial inscriptions (cf. Ps 4:8) in the last two lines, and reads: Here lies a child, Marcellus. May your sleep be in peace.

Orazio Marucchi, *Le catacombe romane*. Rome: La Libreria dello Stato, 1932, pp. 676-678; Frey I, p. 97 No 138. Photograph: courtesy Pontificio Istituto di Archeologia Cristiana.

mo). Deuteros is a Greek name corresponding to the Latin name Secundus; *dulcis* is a frequently found abbreviation of the superlative adjective, *dulcissimo*. The inscription may be translated: To Deuteros, a scribe well meriting it, most sweet.

Beneath the text, in the center, is the menorah. To the left is the *ethrog*. Along with the *ethrog* the *lulab* is also often shown, but if the latter was once on this plaque it is no longer visible. To the right are a scroll of the law and an ivy leaf (cf. No. 243).

Frey I, pp. 160-161 No. 225; Leon, *The Jews of Ancient Rome*, p. 296 No. 225. Photograph: courtesy Pontificio Istituto di Archeologia Cristiana.

246. A Latin Inscription in the Jewish Catacomb in the Vigna Randanini

This marble plaque is also still in the catacomb. The text reads: *Deutero gramateo bene merenti dulcis(si-*

247. Plan of the Jewish Catacomb in the Villa Torlonia

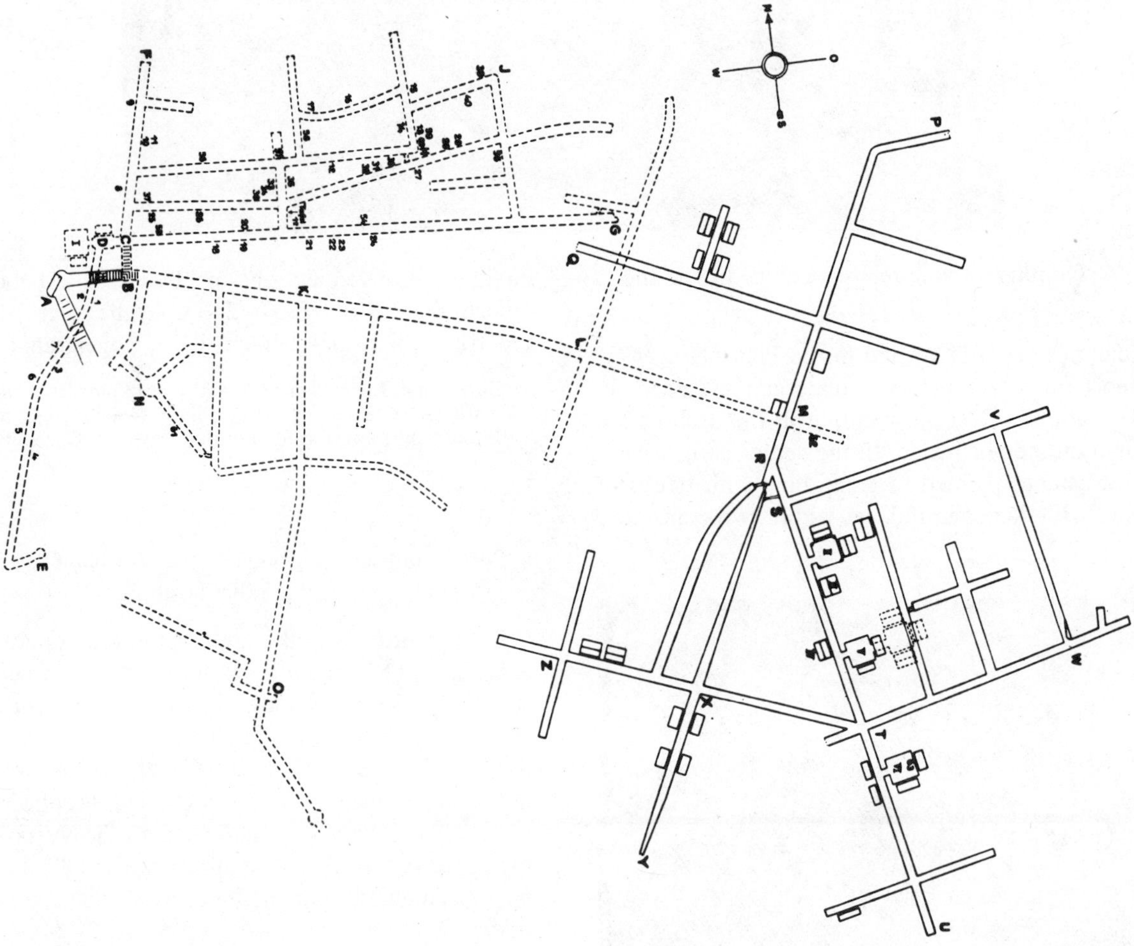

The galleries of this catacomb lie on two levels, and in the plan the outlines of the higher level are drawn in solid lines, those of the lower level in dotted lines. Points of reference are marked with capital letters, the more important *cubicula* and arcosolia with Roman numerals, and the inscriptions with Arabic numbers. Entrance to the lower level is at the west at the point marked A. At the crossing marked M it is possible to climb up to the higher level. Originally, however, there must have been separate access to the higher level, perhaps at the east beyond the present end of the corridor marked P. The higher and the lower catacombs were actually, therefore, separate complexes. The stamped bricks already mentioned (above p. 208) belong to the northern area of the lower level and suggest that this may have been laid

out in the second century or beginning of the third, while the separate higher level will not be later than the third century. As the legends on the plan show, it is in the northern area of the lower level that most of the inscriptions have been preserved; in the larger *cubicula* of the higher level are the paintings.

Hermann W. Beyer and Hans Lietzmann, *Die jüdische Katakombe der Villa Torlonia in Rom*. Studiën zur spätantiken Kunstgeschichte 4, Jüdische Denkmäler I. Berlin and Leipzig: Walter de Gruyter & Co., 1930, Pl. 31. Photograph: courtesy Walter de Gruyter & Co., Berlin.

248. A Painting in the Jewish Catacomb in the Villa Torlonia

Cubiculum II, as it is labeled in the Plan (No. 247), is the most fully decorated chamber in the catacomb. This photograph shows the painting in the arch of the arcosolium on the north side. In the center is the seven-armed lampstand, painted in green-blue with daubs of black, and with flames in red, set within two concentric circles, one of red and one of blue-green. At the left is a horn, the shofar (cf. No. 243). At the right is a round red fruit which looks much like a pomegranate.

Beyer and Lietzmann, *Die jüdische Katakombe der Villa Torlonia in Rom*, pp. 10f., Pl. 6; Goodenough II, p. 37. Photograph: courtesy Walter de Gruyter & Co., Berlin.

249. Another Painting in the Jewish Catacomb in the Villa Torlonia

This painting is in the arch of the arcosolium on the east side in Cubiculum II. Again the seven-armed lampstand, with its red flames, is in the center, and on the left is the red fruit. On the right, however, is a scroll of the Torah or Law. Both ends of the scroll are shown at the same time, and it is represented as rolled around a rod, whose knobs are indicated by heavy points. At the upper end there is a small triangular tab; this would have been glued to the roll and would have carried the title.

Beyer and Lietzmann, *Die jüdische Katakombe der Villa Torlonia in Rom*, pp. 12, 21, Pl. 4: FLAP p. 455, Fig. 155; Goodenough p. 38. Photograph: courtesy Walter de Gruyter & Co., Berlin.

250. Sarcophagi in the Herodian Family Tomb

In the preceding survey of representative types of tombs (Nos. 202ff.) we have seen that the body of the deceased was often placed in the tomb in a simple way such as being laid on a ledge or pushed into a loculus. In these cases the earlier custom was probably to wrap the corpse in the garment which the person wore when alive, as is reflected when the medium at En-dor sees Samuel coming up as an old man "covered with a mantle" (I Sam 28:14); and the later custom was to wrap the body in a linen shroud, as is stated in respect to the burial of Jesus (Mt 27:59 and parallels) (cf. above No. 183). The latter custom is also evidently reflected when the Talmud says of Rabban Gamaliel II (fl. A.D. c. 140-165) that "they carried him out in garments of linen, and [then] all the people followed his example and carried out [the dead for burial] in garments of linen" (Kethuboth 8b SBT III 3, 43; cf. Moed Katan 27b SBT II 8, 178). The use of a chest or coffin for the reception of the corpse was also familiar, however, among the Egyptians, Greeks, and Romans, and so also in due time

among the Jews. The first of these burial chests were probably made of wood, and a Rabbinic source (Pal. M. K. 1, 5, 80c ap. Rahmani in 'Atiqot 3 [1961], p. 102 note 48) refers to the bodies or bones of the deceased and says, "They were buried in cedars," i.e., in boxes of cedar wood. When such a coffin is made of stone, particularly of limestone, it is called a sarcophagus. In Greek and Latin the words σαρκοφάγος and sarcophagus mean "flesh-eating" and were used adjectivally to describe a kind of limestone which, because it quickly consumed the flesh of corpses, was widely used for coffins (Pliny, Nat. Hist. XXXVI 27). Used substantively the same words denoted a coffin, and hence passed into English as "sarcophagus." Since these great stone chests, often elaborately carved, must have been not inexpensive, they usually occur in tombs which also otherwise appear to have belonged to the wealthy. Thus in the Herodian family tomb, in the longest tomb-chamber (F in the Plan in No. 227), there were still two sarcophagi, as shown here.

Vincent, *Jérusalem,* Pl. LXXXIV, 1. Photograph: courtesy École Biblique et Archéologique Française.

251. Ornamentation of a Sarcophagus in the Herodian Family Tomb

This shows the front of one of the two sarcophagi just mentioned (No. 250) in the Herodian family tomb. In the center an acanthus rises above a vase-shaped object, and scrolls with leaves extend on either side, while rosettes are placed in the curves of the scroll.

The rosette, which is a frequent symbol in funerary art, looks like a conventionalized drawing derived ultimately from the representation of a star with several points, and star and rosette are very widespread symbols in the ancient Middle East, from early Mesopotamia onward. In Sumerian pictographs a star is the sign for "heaven" and "god." Thus the rosette could come to symbolize God as the source of light and life, and could express the hope for life in him and in heaven. But in particular the rosette could well be derived from the star of the goddess Inanna or Ishtar, who was often identified with the planet Venus. This star, shown with eight points, appears, for example, on boundary stones of the Kassite period soon after Hammurabi (ANEP No. 518) and on a stela of Bel-harran-bel-usur, a chamberlain under Tiglath-pileser III (744-727 B.C.) (ANEP

No. 453), where Inanna is called "shining goddess of the stars" (ARAB I, §824). Also it may be noted that in later Jewish thought stars represent angels (e.g., II En 30:14) and angels carry the deceased to heaven (Lk 16:22) and are there in charge of their souls, as Enoch saw on his visit to the sixth heaven (II En 19:5). Along this line of thought the rosette would be a very appropriate symbol in a funerary context.

Vincent, *Jérusalem*, 1:2, Pl. LXXXIV, 2; Goodenough VII, pp. 179-198. Photograph: courtesy École Biblique et Archéologique Française.

252. Sarcophagus of Queen Saddan

This sarcophagus, now in the Louvre Museum, was found in an arcosolium in an unopened lower chamber of the Tomb of Queen Helena of Adiabene at Jerusalem (cf. No. 234). When the cover was removed the contents had long since been reduced to dust. The inscription on the front side reads in Aramaic צדן מלכתא, *Saddan malakta'*, and in Hebrew צדה מלכתה, *Saddah malaktah*, i.e., the Queen Saddan or Saddah. In accordance with the widespread custom among the Jews in the Hellenistic era of using both a Semitic and a

Greek name, it is quite possible that the famous Queen of Adiabene was known by this Semitic name as well as by the Greek name, Helena ('Ελένη), which Josephus uses regularly. If this is correct, this is the sarcophagus of Queen Helena of Adiabene to whom the entire tomb

is attributed.

Vincent, *Jérusalem*, 1:1, p. 351, Fig. 98, pp. 352f., 355f.; Frey II, p. 320 No. 1388; André Parrot, *Le Musée du Louvre et la Bible*. Neuchatel and Paris: Delachaux & Niestlé S. A., 1957, pp. 139-140. Cliché du Service de Documentation Photographique des Musées Nationaux.

253. Sarcophagus from the Tomb of Queen Helena of Adiabene

This large sarcophagus, also in the Louvre Museum, probably also comes from the Tomb of Queen Helena of Adiabene at Jerusalem. It is adorned with floral designs in the form of large rosettes (cf. No. 251).

Vincent, *Jérusalem*, 1:2, Pl. XCIII, 2; Parrot, *Le Musée du Louvre et la Bible*, p. 140. Cliché du Service de Documentation Photographique des Musées Nationaux.

254. The Lion Sarcophagus at Beth She'arim

Sarcophagi were also used, we have noted (No. 239), at Beth She'arim and in particularly large numbers in Catacomb No. 20 (IEJ 7 [1957], pp. 82-92). The sarcophagus shown in this photograph was found still in its recess in the wall in this catacomb. In the relief carvings of the front panel we see a twisted column at either end, and a sort of twisted cord decoration across the top. A lion on the left and a lioness on the right face each other with a vessel between, from which they are perhaps about to drink. Primitive as is the execution, the impression of strength and fierceness is unmistakable. Elsewhere in the Palestinian tombs and synagogues of the Hellenistic and Roman periods the lion is not uncommon in the decorations (cf. Goodenough I, pp. 68, 95, 185, 195, 199, 207, etc.).

IEJ 7 (1957), pp. 82-84. Photograph: courtesy Government Press Office, State of Israel.

255. A Lead Coffin from Beth She'arim

On the slope of the hill above Catacomb No. 20 (cf. above No. 236) at Beth She'arim was a group of surface graves. Burials may have been made here after the town was destroyed in the middle of the fourth century and the digging of catacombs stopped. In one of these graves was the lead coffin of which one end is shown in this picture. The coffin is 1.94 meters long and about 0.3 meters wide and high, with a cover which had been welded on at eight points around the edges. While the dimensions are sufficient for this to have been a container for a complete body, the excavators believe that only the bones of the deceased were interred in it (IEJ 9 [1959], pp. 215, 217), as in the case of ossuaries next to be discussed (see below pp. 216ff.). In decoration, the lead coffin is ornamented on the cover and long sides with vines, birds drinking from a bowl, human heads, and small *menorot*. On the narrow sides, the other end is plain, but on this end is an arch supported by two columns with Corinthian capitals, and in the archway a menorah. The lampstand has three legs, and the central leg has three prongs. On the right are a shofar and an incense shovel, on the left are a *lulab* and *ethrog* (cf. No. 243). Interestingly enough, the coffin is virtually identical with another lead coffin discovered in the nineteenth century at Sidon in Phoenicia, save that in the latter there is an arch on either end and, in the archway, on one end the standing figure of a man, presumably the deceased, and on the other end a Christ-monogram (cf. p. 234) with the letters of the word ΙΧΘΥC, "Fish" (cf. No. 22) written around it in the interstices of the monogram (Goodenough V, p. 56 and Fig. 59). Thus on similar coffins the symbols of Judaism and of Christianity respectively were employed in accordance with the faith of the deceased. That the coffin at Beth She'arim belonged to a Jew from Sidon is probable, for the epitaphs show that many Sidonian Jews were buried in this place.

IEJ 8 (1958), p. 276; 9 (1959), pp. 214-218. Photograph: IEJ 9 (1959), Pl. 24 A, courtesy Israel Exploration Society.

OSSUARIES

The ossuary is a small chest, usually of wood or stone, and usually 50 to 80 centimeters (20 to 32 inches) in length, 28 to 50 centimeters (11 to 20 inches) in width, and 25 to 40 centimeters (10 to 16 inches) in height, i.e., just of the size to contain the bones of a burial. When such a container is made of stone, and particularly of limestone as is usually the case, the Greek word ὀστοφάγος, meaning "bone-eating" (cf. Strabo XVI 4, 17), is applied to it in analogy with the word "sarcophagus" (cf. No. 250). In Latin it is called an *ossuarium* (from *os, ossis*, "a bone"), and from this we have the English word "ossuary."

The ossuary is used for a secondary disposition of the bones. While sometimes a sarcophagus was employed for burial (cf. No. 250) and presumably served as the permanent resting place of the remains, in a great many cases the body was simply placed on a ledge or in a loculus or kok. It could be possible, then, that the same place would later be needed for another deposition. To make room, the dry bones which finally remained could be collected and put in some available place or in some receptacle. In Tomb 5 at Tell en-Nasbeh (Nos. 207-208), with its ledge burials, there was a small chamber at the back which is thought to have been used for such a collection of bones. In Tomb 4 at Tell en-Nasbeh (No. 209), with its kokim burials, there was a pit in the floor of the main chamber which is supposed to have been used in the same way. In the tombs at Marissa (No. 214) there are niches beneath the burial loculi, and these probably served in the same fashion. From this custom doubtless came the practice of using ossuaries, as described above. In the Sanhedriyya tombs certain small chambers may have been places for such receptacles, and some of the stone fragments found in these tombs are probably fragments of ossuaries as well as of sarcophagi (No. 225). At Beth

She'arim there were a few skeletons without coffins, and sarcophagi of wood and stone were used, but there were smaller niches probably used for the collection of bones. The lead coffin described above (No. 255) was probably employed just for bones, and there were many fragments found, the excavators report, of stone and wooden ossuaries. They say that the practice of secondary burial was evidently the rule, i.e., the bones were transported to Beth She'arim, or they were gathered there, in ossuaries which were placed in the arcosolia and the kokim (*Beth She'arim*, Vol. I by Mazar [Maisler], English summary, 1st ed. p. 7, 2d ed. p. viii). In fact one Greek inscription has this very interesting reading (*Beth She'arim*, Vol. II by Schwabe and Lifshitz, p. 25 No. 78):

ΜΑΓΝΑ
ΓΛΟΣΟ
ΚΟΜΩ ΚΙΤΕ

i.e., Μαγνα γλοσοκόμῳ κῖτε. In Greek the word γλωσσόκομος or γλωσσόκομον properly designates "a case for the mouthpiece" of a flute, and then is used generally for a casket, and also for a coffin or sarcophagus. In this case there seems to be no doubt that the word means an ossuary, and the excavators translate: "Magna lies in the ossuary."

This practice of secondary burial is also attested in the Mishnah. One passage which has already been cited (No. 225) for the fact that "proper place" means the family burying-place, reads: "When the flesh was completely decomposed, the bones were gathered and buried in their proper place" (Sanhedrin VI 6 DM p. 391 SBT IV 5, p. 305). In a discussion of activities which were deemed permissible during the middle days of the Feasts of Passover and of Tabernacles, Rabbi Meir (fl. A.D. c. 140-165) said: "A man may gather together the bones of his father or his mother, since this is to him an occasion for rejoicing" (Moed Katan I 5 DM p. 208; cf. Pesahim VIII 8 DM p. 148). A reason why the gathering of the bones was deemed an occasion for rejoicing may lie in the fact that the process of decay of the flesh was considered to be a means of expiation, and only when this was complete was atonement accomplished. In the Talmudic discussion of the first Mishnaic passage quoted just above, it is stated that in the case of a criminal both death by execution and burial in the criminal's graveyard are necessary for forgiveness, but even more than that is required, it is said, for "the decay of the flesh too is necessary" (Sanhedrin 47b SBT IV 5, p. 314). Yet the righteous also are in need of the same expiation, for "there is not a righteous man on earth who does good and never sins" (Ec 7:20) (Sanhedrin 46b SBT IV 5, p. 308).

It may also be supposed that where belief in the resurrection was held, this could be favorable to the use of the ossuaries. While such belief was denied by the Sadducees who held that "souls die with the bodies" (Josephus, *Ant.* XVIII 1, 4 §16; cf. Mt 22:23 and parallels), it was affirmed by the Pharisees (Ac 23:8) and was held by many to be as much a fundamental of the Jewish faith as belief in the Law (Sanhedrin X 1 DM p. 397). In Ezk 37 the figure of resurrection applied to the return of the community of Israel to Palestine involved a picture of dry bones which came together again, were clothed with flesh, and made to live. While the nation was referred to here in a symbolic way, in Is 26:19 there was almost certainly thought of a literal resurrection of individuals and, where this passage says that their bodies shall rise, the Targum adds, "the bones of their dead bodies." Given such conceptions, it is possible that the gathering and keeping of the bones in an ossuary would seem especially appropriate.

It is true that some aspects of Jewish thought might seem to militate against any practice which went beyond the original burial procedure. There was, for example, a very strong feeling in Judaism against coming into any kind of contact with the remains of the dead. Num 19:16 states that to touch a dead body, or a bone of a man, or a grave, makes a person unclean (cf. Num 6:6). Mt 23:27 describes the "whitewashed tombs" which were "full of dead men's bones and all uncleanness," and Lk 11:44 makes it likely that the plain marking of the tombs was to prevent coming upon them inadvertently. Such marking of graves is confirmed in the Mishnah, where it is said that a grave must be marked "by whiting mingled with water and poured over the grave" (Maaser Sheni V 1 DM p. 80), and it is stated that this is done, evidently annually, on the 15th of Adar (Shekalim I 1 DM p. 152; cf. Moed Katan I 2 DM p. 208). We have also noted (No. 241) a concrete example of the kind of malediction which was expressed against any disturbance of a completed burial. Again, we have a case where it was desired to exhume a body to ascertain age by a *post mortem*, and Rabbi Akiba refused to permit this act of dishonor (Baba Bathra 154a SBT IV 4, p. 669). Nevertheless these considerations were evidently not powerful enough to preclude the practice of secondary burial and the use of ossuaries, for which there is abundant evidence as indicated above.

It also seems quite possible that early Christians, as well as Jews, could have made use of ossuaries. Among at least many of the early Christians there was a less strict regard for all the details of the Law, and there was also an increased emphasis upon the resurrection. At any rate we have various references to the preservation of the bones of the deceased by the early Christians. After Ignatius was thrown to the beasts in Rome (A.D. c. 110), "only the harder portions of his holy remains were left," and these were carried back to be kept by his home church at Antioch (*The Martyrdom of Ignatius* 6 ANF I, p. 131). Likewise when Polycarp was burned to death at Smyrna (A.D. 156), his companions "took up his bones, as being more valuable than jewels and more precious than gold, and deposited them in a suitable place, to gather together there every year on the anniversary [literally, the birthday] of his death" (*The Martyrdom of Polycarp* 18 ANF I, p. 43). If then we actually find on the ossuaries signs, markings, names, etc., which can with some probability be connected with early Christianity, there is no real reason for denying the possibility of such a connection and perhaps even real reason for affirming it.

As to the date of the ossuaries, fragments of them were found in the Sanhedriyya Tombs (No. 225), and these tombs are quite definitely dated by other contents to the period from the beginning of the reign of Herod (37 B.C.) to the fall of Jerusalem (A.D. 70). In many other tombs at Jerusalem the situation is much the same, and the use of ossuaries is indicated for a period beginning not much earlier than 50 B.C. and continuing up to the year 70 of the Christian era (Rahmani in *'Atiqot* 3 [1961], p. 116 and note 4). Many ossuaries have also been found in the cemetery at Dominus flevit (Nos. 272ff.), in tombs which were in use up to A.D. 70 and possibly to A.D. 135 (W. F. Albright in BASOR 159 Oct. [1960], p. 37). That the use of ossuaries at Jerusalem ceased with the fall of the city in A.D. 70, or at any rate with the exclusion of Jews (and Jewish Christians) from the area by Hadrian in A.D. 135, is understandable. Elsewhere, however, there is evidence that they were in use over a much longer period of time. Many ossuaries were found in the "Maccabean" cemetery at Gezer (R. A. S. Macalister in PEFQS 1904, pp. 340-343), so they must have come into use in Hellenistic times, say around 150 B.C. (Goodenough I, pp. 114-115) or 200 B.C. (Vincent in RB 43 [1934], pp. 564-567). While Goodenough and Vincent also think that the custom continued to around A.D. 150 or 200, the evidence from Beth She'arim cited above shows that ossuaries were still in use there into the third and fourth centuries, and the Greek inscription quoted with explicit mention of an ossuary must belong to the first half of the fourth century (BASOR 189 Feb. 1968, p. 54). For Jerusalem, however, the most probable dates are from about 50 B.C. to A.D. 70 or 135 (cf. above No. 124).

On the ossuaries the most common decoration is the rosette (see e.g., No. 256), a symbol of which we have already spoken (No. 251). In many cases the ossuaries have inscriptions, scratched, carved, drawn with charcoal, or painted. These are usually names, and it may be presumed that these were normally the names of those whose bones were contained within.

Samuel Krauss, "La double inhumation chez les Juifs," in REJ 97 (1934), pp. 1-34; L.-H. Vincent, "Sur la date des ossuaries juifs," in RB 43 (1934), pp. 564-567; P. B. Bagatti, "Resti Cristiani in Palestina anteriori a Constantino?" in RAC 25 (1949), pp. 117-131; L. Y. Rahmani, "Jewish Rock-Cut Tombs in Jerusalem," in *'Atiqot* 3 (1961), pp. 116-117; Testa pp. 446-474; R. A. Mastin, "Chalcolithic Ossuaries and 'Houses for the Dead,'" in PEQ 1965, pp. 153-160; Saul Lieberman, "Some Aspects of After Life in Early Rabbinic Literature," in *Harry Austryn Wolfson Jubilee Volume*. Jerusalem: American Academy for Jewish Research, 1965, English Section, II, pp. 495-532; Arthur D. Nock, "The Synagogue Murals of Dura-Europos," *ibid.*, pp. 638f.

256. Ossuary from Tomb 14 at Tell en-Nasbeh

This ossuary was found in Tomb 14 in the west cemetery at Tell en-Nasbeh, a tomb which was probably in use from the Iron Age and into the Roman period, as late as the third century. The chest is 71 centimeters (23½ inches) long, 28 centimeters (11¼ inches) wide, and 34 centimeters (13½ inches) high. The lid on the top is shaped like a barrel vault, with a projecting beveled edge. The front of the chest is ornamented with two large rosettes, between which is a short pillar set on a three-staged plinth and supporting a large capital. The back is carved to look like a wall of regularly laid blocks, and three rosettes are drawn thereon. Another rosette is still to be seen on the left end of the chest, and similar decoration may once have existed on the other end as well as on the lid. The significance of the rosette has already been spoken of (No. 251). As for the carving of the back side to look like a wall of stone blocks, this also is a familiar decoration of the ossuaries. Since this appears to represent the wall of a house, it may be taken as symbolic of the בית עלם, οἶκος αἰῶνος, *domus aeterna*, or house of eternity (Ec 12:5), the last resting place of mortal man.

Tell en-Nasbeh, I, p. 124 and Pl. 43; Goodenough, I, pp. 75, 116. Photograph: courtesy Palestine Institute.

257. Ossuary Inscriptions from a Tomb in the Kidron Valley

In 1934 a simple tomb was found by the Archaeological Department of the Hebrew University in the Kidron Valley near Beit Sahur el-'Atiqa. It consisted of a single chamber, partly cut out of the rock and partly built of layers of stone. The few pottery fragments suggested the Herodian period. Five ossuaries were in the chamber, most of them broken by the collapse of the roof of the tomb. Three had inscriptions, as shown in the illustration. The first inscribed ossuary was 67 centimeters in length, 30 centimeters in width, and 39 centimeters high. It stood on four small feet, and was covered with a flat lid. On the back, cut in the soft stone with a sharp tool, was the inscription numbered 1. It may be transcribed as follows, and recognized as Aramaic: חניה א בר אלכשה. The first word is doubtless one possible spelling of the name Onias ('Ονίας), a name which is familiar in the books of the Maccabees and in Josephus. The single letter, Aleph, which follows, was probably written by mistake as the initial letter of the last name, and then it was recalled that *bar*, "son (of)," should be inserted first. In the last name the characters Kaph and Shin can transliterate the Greek letter Xi, and the name can be a hypocoristic form of Alexander ('Αλέξανδρος), or a slightly shortened form of Alexas ('Αλεξᾶς), both of which names are well known in Josephus (e.g., *Ant.* XVIII 5, 4 §138). In this case the inscription may be translated: Onias, son of Alexa.

The second inscribed ossuary was of unknown length, since it had been broken, but was 26 centimeters wide and 29 centimeters high, and had a rounded lid. On the fragments of a long side was an inscription in Greek, of which this much can be read (3 in the illustration): ΑΠΦΙΑΣ ΑΘ.

Scratched somewhat more hastily on an end of the same chest, but preserved completely, is a Hebrew graffito which may be recognized as a transcription of the foregoing Greek. It reads (2 in the illustration): אפיחם בת אתנגרש. The first name is the same as the 'Απφία in Phm 2, but written here in the genitive case, meaning the ossuary "of Apphia." Although not actually necessary in the Hebrew, the Sigma of the Greek genitive has been reproduced by what is probably a Samekh in the Hebrew transcription. The Hebrew also supplies next the word *bath*, "daughter (of)," making

1.

2.

3.

4.

it plain that the first name is that of the daughter of the person identified by the second name. The complete Hebrew of the second name makes it possible also to recognize that this was probably the Greek name 'Αθηναγόρας in the genitive form, 'Αθηναγόρου. The translation of this inscription is, therefore: (Of) Apphia, daughter of Athenagoras.

The third inscribed ossuary was a plain chest, but scratched on its back side was this graffito (4 in the illustration): ΟΣΤΟΦΑΓΟΣ ΟΣ[Τ]ΟΦΑΓΟΣ. This, twice repeated, is the word ὀστοφάγος, *ostophagus*, "bone-eating," which, as already explained (p. 216), was the term for an ossuary, analogous to the term *sarcophagus*, or "flesh-eating."

Other ossuaries will be dealt with in what follows (Nos. 263ff.) where we will note some marks and names which may possibly be connected with early Christianity and may involve reference back to Jesus. It is chiefly with the mark of the cross that we shall be concerned.

E. L. Sukenik, "A Jewish Tomb in the Kedron Valley," in PEFQS 1937-38, pp. 126-130 and Pl. v. Photograph: courtesy Palestine Exploration Fund.

The Cross

258. Painted Pebbles with Cross Marks from
Tell Abu Matar

In the sense of a figure formed by the intersection of two more or less straight lines, a cross is one of the most elemental marks which it is possible to make. At Tell Abu Matar, 1.50 kilometers southeast of Beersheba,

a small settlement of the Chalcolithic Age was excavated in 1952-1954. The two lowest levels consisted of underground houses, connected in groups by tunnels, a type of dwelling useful for protection from sun and sandstorms and still employed by Bedouin in the Central Negev. Here in the lowest level and on the earliest floor of House 127 was a group of "painted pebbles." Fourteen in number, these flat stones were arranged in a crescent shape and each was marked with red ocher which had been applied with the fingers after the pebbles were in place. Most of the marks are in the form of a cross. Since these pebbles were found in their original place and were connected stratigraphically with the setting up of the dwelling, the guess may be hazarded that the cruciform mark was intended as a sign which would avert evil and give protection. Similar marks are indeed found widely in the whole history of religions, and a similar protective significance may often be surmised for them. The photograph shows these cross-marked pebbles as they are displayed in their original arrangement in the Negev Museum in Beersheba.

J. Perrot, "The Excavations at Tell Abu Matar, near Beersheba," in IEJ 5 (1955), 17-40, 73-84, 167-189, and specially p. 168 Fig. 17 and Pl. 21 A. Photograph: JF.

HISTORY OF THE CROSS MARK

The Cross Mark as a Character of the Semitic Alphabet

The simple mark of a cross also became a character of the alphabet in Semitic languages including Canaanite, Phoenician, Hebrew, and Aramaic. In 1905 W. M. Flinders Petrie discovered at Serabit el-Khadem in the Peninsula of Sinai the so-called proto-Sinaitic inscriptions. As he recognized at the time, these date about 1500 B.C. The inscriptions were composed of characters which appeared to depict or at least represent specific objects. An oxhead, for example, was quite plainly recognizable, and there was a rectangle, sometimes with an opening into it, which could be the drawing of the plan of a house. Several times there occurred a certain sequence of characters, and these appeared to be, in sequence, a house, an eye, an oxgoad, and a cross. The order in which these signs were to be read was established by the fact that they sometimes occurred in vertical columns which were no doubt to be read from top to bottom, while in horizontal lines they gave the same order when read from left to right. In 1915 Alan Gardiner suggested that these characters were acrophonic in

nature, which means that a given character stands for the initial sound of the name of the object which it depicts, and he identified the sequence of characters just mentioned as corresponding to the Semitic letters which are called in Hebrew Beth, 'Ayin, Lamedh, and Taw. Therewith he read the sequence of characters as giving the name Ba'alat, which means "the female Ba'al." Since the Canaanite goddess, Ba'alat, was called Hathor by the Egyptians, as is shown by an inscription (No. 259) which will be mentioned shortly, and since Hathor was recognized as the goddess of the turquoise mines at Serabit el-Khadem, as the inscription also shows, this identification made very good sense. Accepting this explanation of the signs as correct, we have in the proto-Sinaitic inscriptions an early form of the Semitic alphabet. This early alphabetic writing contains an oxhead, and in Hebrew the first letter of the alphabet is 'Aleph, which is a word (אלף, occurring in the OT only in the plural, אלפים, e.g., Pr 14:4) which means ox. Another character is a house, and in Hebrew the second letter is Beth, which is a word (בית, e.g., Ex 12:30) which means house. In the course of time the

220

drawing of the characters was increasingly conventionalized and so we have finally in Hebrew for the oxhead the letter א and for the house the letter ב. Yet another character is a simple cross mark, and in Hebrew the twenty-second and last letter of the alphabet is Taw which is a word (תו, e.g., Ezk 9:4) which means mark or sign. Inasmuch as the characters we have been discussing are essentially little pictures they remind us of the picture writing of Egyptian hieroglyphics and suggest that this manner of writing arose under Egyptian influence, either directly or indirectly. Inasmuch as the pictographs are employed according to the acrophonic principle, however, they are the characters of a true alphabet and thus, in that respect, they represent a new invention. In view of the area in which this alphabet was widely used, as examples to be given shortly will show, it may be supposed that its origins are to be sought somewhere in Syria-Palestine. Indeed it is now considered that the language of the proto-Sinaitic inscriptions is Canaanite and that the script is the normal alphabetic Canaanite of its period, i.e., of the early fifteenth century B.C. (FLAP pp. 148-149).

259. Sandstone Statue from Serabit el-Khadem with proto-Sinaitic Inscription

This statue is now in the Egyptian Museum in Cairo. The squatting figure of a man is a familiar Egyptian type. The inscription (No. 346 in the series) is in

proto-Sinaitic, and the main line of writing, running from left to right and sloping somewhat downward across the front of the statue, consists of a sequence of characters which, according to Gardiner's explanation, correspond to Lamedh, Beth, 'Ayin, Lamedh, and Taw. This, then, means "belonging to Ba'alat." As for the character with which we are presently concerned, it is the last one at the right, namely, a cross mark, serving as a letter of the alphabet and corresponding to the Hebrew Taw. Of the several other examples where the same sequence of characters, spelling "Ba'alat," occurs, it will suffice to mention the inscription on the left side of the base of a sandstone sphinx from Serabit el-Khadem which is now in the British Museum (No. 41748). This is of special interest because on the right shoulder of the sphinx is a hieroglyphic inscription reading, "Beloved of Hathor, [lady of] the turquoise" (No. 345 in the series), thus confirming the identification of Ba'alat and Hathor. The character in which we are particularly interested, namely, the simple mark of the cross, is, in fact, the most common sign in the proto-Sinaitic inscriptions, occurring more than thirty-five times.

W. M. Flinders Petrie, *Researches in Sinai*. London: John Murray, 1906, 129 and Figs. 138, 139, 141; Alan H. Gardiner, "The Egyptian Origin of the Semitic Alphabet," in JEA 3 (1916), 1-16 and Pl. III, No. 345, Pl. IV, No. 346; Romain F. Butin, "The Protosinaitic Inscriptions," in HTR 25 (1932), 130-203 and Pl. X, No. 345, Pl. XI, No. 346; W. F. Albright, "The Early Alphabetic Inscriptions from Sinai and Their Decipherment," in BASOR 110 (Apr. 1948), 6-22; *The Inscriptions of Sinai* by Alan H. Gardiner and T. Eric Peet, 2d ed. rev. by Jaroslav Černý. London: Egypt Exploration Society, Pt. I, 1952, Pt. II, 1955. I, 202, No. 345; II, Pl. LXXXII, No. 345; Frank M. Cross, Jr., "The Evolution of the Proto-Canaanite Alphabet," in BASOR 134 (1954), 15-24. Photograph: HTR 25 (1932), Pl. XI, No. 346 front, courtesy Egyptian Museum, Cairo.

There are many more inscriptions and texts which illustrate the evolution of the alphabet in which the Semitic languages are written. In these, for a millennium and a half, we continue to find the cross mark as an alphabetic character. As examples, this mark may be seen in the following: In Canaanite: in the inscriptions on the bronze javelin heads which come from el-Khadr, five kilometers west of Bethlehem, dating about 1100 B.C. (the last character in each inscription, reading from top to bottom). In Phoenician: in the temple inscription of King Yehimilk (see below No. 260) which was found at Byblos (No. 1141), dating c. 950 B.C. (the second character in the first line, reading from right to left, and a number of other occurrences in the balance of the text). In Aramaic: in the Bir-Hadad stela, a votive stone set up c. 850 B.C. by Ben-Hadad I of Damascus in honor of, and with a carved representation of, the god Melqart (the first character, reading from right to left, in Line 4). In Hebrew (reading from right to left): in the Gezer Calendar in what has been called "perfect classical Hebrew," c. 925 B.C. (at the end of Line 3); in the Lachish ostraca, c. 588 B.C. (e.g., in Letter II, in the second line, the sixth letter); and in several parchment manuscripts from Qumran, namely, in a large scroll with much of the Book of Exodus from Cave 4 (4QEx^a), c. 225-175 B.C. (e.g., on the page containing Ex 32:10-30, in the seventh line, the eighth character); in a fragment of the Book of Genesis from Cave 6 (6Q1), probably from the second half of the second century B.C. (the second character in the second readily legible line, and a number of other instances); and in fragments of the Book of Leviticus from Caves 1 and 2 (1Q3 and 2Q5), c. 125-75 B.C. (in 1Q3, Fragment 2, Line 5, the second character; in 2Q5, Line 3, the fifth character, and Line 5, the fourth character).

El-Khadr: J. T. Milik and Frank M. Cross, Jr., "Inscribed Javelin-Heads from the Period of the Judges: A Recent Discovery in Palestine," in BASOR 134 (Apr. 1954), 5-15 and Fig. 1 on p. 7. Yehimilk: Maurice Dunand, "Nouvelle inscription Phénicienne archaïque," in RB 39 (1930), 321-331 and Pl. xv; and Fouilles de Byblos. Paris: Paul Geuthner, I, Atlas, 1937, Pl. XXXI, 2; Texte, 1939, 30, No. 1141; W. F. Albright, "The Phoenician Inscriptions of the Tenth Century B.C. from Byblus," in JAOS 67 (1947), 153-160. Bir-Hadad: W. F. Albright, "A Votive Stele Erected by Ben-Hadad I of Damascus to the God Melcarth," in BASOR 87 (Oct. 1942), 23-29, Figs. 1, 2; Frank M. Cross, Jr. and David N. Freedman, Early Hebrew Orthography. New Haven: American Oriental Society, 1952, 23-24. Gezer Calendar: W. F. Albright, "The Gezer Calendar," in BASOR 92 (1943), 16-26; Sabatino Moscati, L'Epigrafia ebraica antica 1935-1950. Rome: Pontificio Istituto Biblico, 1951, 8-26, Pl. VII, 1. Lachish Ostraca: Harry Torczyner, Lachish I (Tell ed Duweir), The Lachish Letters. London: Oxford University Press, 1938, 34ff. 4QEx^a: Patrick W. Skehan, "Exodus in the Samaritan Recension from Qumran," in JBL 74 (1955), 182-187 and Fig. fac. p. 185. 6Q1: DJD III Textes 105-106 No. 1, Planches XX No. 1. 1Q3: DJD I, 51-53 and Pl. VIII, No. 3. 2Q5: DJD III Textes 56f. No. 5, Planches XII No. 5. Solomon A. Birnbaum, "The Leviticus Fragments from the Cave," in BASOR 118 (Apr. 1950), 20-27, Fig. 1; S. Yeivin, "The Date and Attribution of the Leviticus Fragments from the Cache in the Judaean Desert," in BASOR 118 (Apr. 1950), 28-30. Richard S. Hanson, "Paleo-Hebrew Scripts in the Hasmonean Age," in BASOR 175 (Oct. 1964), 26-42.

260. The Inscription of Yehimilk, King of Byblos

From the inscriptions carved on the rocks of Serabit el-Khadem in the fifteenth century B.C. to the texts penned on the parchments at Qumran in the second and first centuries B.C., the documents which have just been cited extend over a period of nearly 1,500 years. They also extend from the lapidary script with which inscriptions were cut into stone to the cursive script with which texts were written on ostraca and parchment. But the alphabetic character we are discussing continued to be formed essentially as a simple cross mark. The major difference in the way in which it is written consists in whether it stands erect with a vertical and a horizontal bar or whether it is shifted sideways to produce an X form. In the inscriptions from Serabit el-Khadem (c. 1500 B.C.) in the example on the squatting figure (Inscription No. 346, our illustration No. 259), except for the slanting of the entire line of text, the character stands quite erect and symmetrical; in the text on the sphinx (Inscription No. 345), however, the vertical line of the character is shifted considerably sideways. In the el-Khadr inscriptions (c. 1100 B.C.) the cross is quite firmly upright and symmetrical, although in one case the horizontal bar slopes considerably; but in the Yehimilk inscription from Byblos (c. 950 B.C.), which we illustrate here, the character is shifted fully sideways to the X position. In this last text the sign may be seen frequently, beginning with the second character (reading from right to left) in the first line, where it is the second letter in the word בת, *beth*, "house," in this case meaning temple. In Albright's translation, and in lines corresponding to those on the stone, the text reads:

The temple which Yehimilk, king of Byblus, built—
it was he who restored the ruins of these temples.
May Baal-shamem and Baal(ath)-Gebal
and the assembly of the holy gods of Byblus
prolong the days of Yehimilk and his years
over Byblus as a rightful king and a true
king before the h[oly] gods of Byblus!

Dunand in RB 39 (1930), Pl. xv fac. p. 322; and *Fouilles de Byblos*, I, Atlas, Pl. XXXI, 2; Albright in JAOS 67 (1947), 156-157. Photograph: RB 39 (1930), Pl. xv fac. p. 322, courtesy École Biblique et Archéologique Française.

In addition to the major difference as to whether the cross mark is formed in an upright position or shifted sideways, there are also other differences. These include the lengthening of the horizontal stroke in the Gezer Calendar, the lengthening of the vertical stroke in the Bir-Hadad stela, the thickening of the main stroke in the Lachish ostraca, and the thickening and curving of the main stroke in the Qumran fragments.

As far as texts in the Hebrew language are concerned, the script we have been discussing is commonly called Phoenician Hebrew, Paleo-Hebrew, or Old Hebrew. The conclusion at this point may be stated simply. In Old Hebrew script the letter Taw was written as a cross mark. This stood erect like what we ordinarily mean by a "cross," or it tilted sideways like an X, or it was formed with intermediate variations, but it was still essentially a cross mark. The examples we have noted of the use of this mark extend from the inscriptions at Serabit el-Khadem in the fifteenth century B.C. to the

fragments at Qumran dating in the second and first centuries B.C. In fact Jerome (*In Hiezechielem* III 9, 4 CCSL LXXV 106) states that the ancient Hebrew letters, including the Taw which was similar to a cross, were still in use in his day among the Samaritans.

In the pen-and-ink texts of the ostraca from Lachish and the fragments cited from Qumran there is a decided tendency to curve the main stroke of the character, and in other manuscripts written on parchment or papyrus there was developing, meanwhile, a cursive script which was considerably modified from the lapidary script of the old stone inscriptions. This development may be seen in the Aramaic papyri of the fifth century from Elephantine, in the Nash Papyrus, a Hebrew document of c. 165-37 B.C., and in the majority of the Dead Sea Scrolls. The final result is the so-called square character which is still considered the standard script in Hebrew. Here the Taw is less and less obviously a cross mark and is ultimately transformed into the character as we know it today (ת).

Frank M. Cross, Jr., "Epigraphic Notes on Hebrew Documents of the Eighth-Sixth Centuries B.C.," in BASOR 163 (Oct. 1961), 12-14; 165 (Feb. 1962), 34-46; 168 (Dec. 1962), 18-23; and "The Development of the Jewish Scripts," in *The Bible and the Ancient Near East, Essays in honor of William Foxwell Albright*, ed. by G. Ernest Wright. Garden City: Doubleday & Company, Inc., 1961, Anchor Books edition, 1965, 170-264.

The Hebrew Taw and Its Equivalents

In Hebrew, then, the word Taw both signified a "mark" and was also the name of the last letter of the alphabet, a letter which, in the Old Hebrew script, was still written in the elemental form of a cross down at least to the eve of the NT period, or even into that period. In the further evolution of the alphabet the Semitic Taw became the Tau (ταῦ) of the Greek alphabet and the T of the Latin. The Greek letter Chi (χῖ) was also recognized as an equivalent of the Taw. This was the more readily possible because, on the one hand, in early Greek the Chi was often written as an erect cross mark, and because, on the other hand, the Taw itself was often written in the sideways position, so that it was already like the later more usual form of the Chi (χ) and like the Latin X. However, since the Taw was the last letter of the Hebrew alphabet, it was sometimes considered that the last letter of the Greek alphabet, the Omega (ὦ μέγα), was also its equivalent. Examples of all of these equivalences will appear in what follows.

Leonard Whibley, *A Companion to Greek Studies*. Cambridge: University Press, 3d. ed. 1916, p. 690, Epigraphy, Table of Phoenician and early Greek local alphabets.

The Sign of Deliverance

In the OT the word *taw* occurs in two very interesting passages in both of which it can very well mean "mark" not only in a general sense but also in the specific sense of the cross mark which was also the alphabetic character. The first passage is in Jb 31:35, where Job says, "Here is my signature!" (RSV), and the Hebrew is literally, "Here is my mark (*taw*)." Thus Job probably made his mark, at least figuratively, in the form of a cross mark, erect or like an X, just as a person may make an X as a legal signature today.

The second passage is Ezk 9:4-6. In 9:4 the man clothed in linen is instructed to go through the city of Jerusalem and put a mark (*taw*) upon the foreheads of the men who sigh and groan over the abominations that are committed in the city. In 9:6 the destroyers are told to touch no one upon whom is this mark (*taw*). As to the significance of the mark (*taw*), it is evident that it designates those who are faithful to the Lord, and it puts them under his protection for deliverance. With respect to this meaning of the mark, we may recall the protective significance surmised for the cross marks on the painted pebbles at Tell Abu Metar (No. 258), as well as elsewhere in the history of religions. As for the mark on the forehead, this was often a preferred place for ritual marks as the history of religions also abundantly shows. And as to the form of the mark in this case, it is probable that it was nothing other than the cross mark which was also the alphabetic character, Taw, and this will be substantiated by the evidence which follows in the next two paragraphs.

In the Cairo Document of the Damascus Covenanters (CD), known more briefly as the Damascus Document or also as the Zadokite Document, a work which doubtless represents in general the same movement as that of the Qumran community, there is a significant reference to the passage in Ezekiel. At this point in the text there is an introductory reference to the prophecy of Zechariah about the smiting of the shepherd and the scattering of the sheep (Zec 13:7), and then the passage in which we are interested continues, including an allusion to Zec 11:11 and an explicit quotation of Ezk 9:4, as follows (Manuscript B, VII [XIX] 9-12 Rabin 30): "And 'they that give heed unto Him' are 'the poor of the flock.' These shall escape in the time of the visitation, but they that hesitate shall be given over to the sword when the Messiah of Aaron and Israel shall come. As it happened in the epoch of the visitation of the forefathers, which He said by the hand of Ezekiel: 'to set the mark upon the foreheads of such as sigh and groan.' "

The argument of this passage is extremely interesting. As other statements in the Damascus Document

(VII 9; VIII 2-3 Rabin 28, 32) make plain, the time of visitation is the Last Judgment. When that time comes and the Messiah appears, the circumstances of the destruction of Jerusalem as described by Ezekiel will be repeated, i.e., only those marked with the Taw on their foreheads will be saved. While the statement may be only figurative, it is at least possible that the Taw mark was literally put upon the foreheads of the members of this community, perhaps at the time of their initiatory baptism, as a sign to guarantee their salvation in the final Judgment. It may also be noticed that in the Masoretic text of Ezk 9:4 we have the simple word תו, *taw*, "a mark," but in the quotation here in the Damascus Document we have the same word written with the definite article, התיו, "the Taw." Therefore, as we have already surmised, the form of the mark in Ezk 9:4 was almost certainly that of the cross mark which was the alphabetic character, Taw.

This understanding of the *taw* in Ezk 9:4 as the alphabetic character in the form of the cross mark is also represented by some of the Greek translations of the passage. The LXX indeed simply translates the Hebrew *taw* here with σημεῖον, meaning "mark" or "sign," but Origen (*Selecta in Ezechielem* 9 MPG XIII 800) states that Aquila and Theodotion translated the passage to read that the mark of the Tau (τοῦ Θαῦ) was to be put upon the foreheads of the faithful, and the use of the name with the definite article surely points to the alphabetic character we are discussing. Tertullian (*Against Marcion* III 22 ANF III 340) also was familiar with a similar form of the text, for he quotes it thus: "Go through the gate, through the midst of Jerusalem, and set the mark Tau upon the foreheads of the men." In all probability, then, in its original meaning, and certainly in the understanding of these Greek translations and of the Damascus Document, Ezk 9:4 refers to a mark (*taw*) which is nothing other than the alphabetic character, Taw, a mark in the form of a cross, standing for protection, deliverance, and salvation.

The influence of the passage in Ezekiel may also be noted in the Psalms of Solomon, a work of the middle of the first century B.C., now found in Greek and Syriac but doubtless originally written in Hebrew. In this work in 15:8, 10 it is said that "the mark of God is upon the righteous that they may be saved," but concerning the sinners it is declared that "the mark of destruction is upon their forehead." The allusion to Ezk 9:4-6 is unmistakable, but now the sinners are marked for destruction and the righteous for salvation. For "mark" the Greek has in both statements the word σημεῖον. For the righteous the mark is undoubtedly the Taw, meaning deliverance; for the sinners it may even be the same mark, but if so it is certainly with the opposite connotation of destruction. In explicit connection with Ezk 9:4 the Talmud (*Shabbath* 55a SBT II 1, 253-254) also tells of two Taws, and distinguishes between them as "a *taw* of ink upon the foreheads of the righteous," and "a *taw* of blood upon the foreheads of the wicked." In the same context Rab (third century) is quoted in the explanation: "*Taw* [stands for] תחיה [thou shalt live], *taw* [stands for] תמות [thou shalt die]."

It may also be mentioned here that in the discussion of Ezekiel to which we have referred above, Origen (*Selecta in Ezechielem* 9 MPG XIII 800-801) tells how he asked among the Jews about the teachings which had been handed down on the subject of the Taw. The answers which he received are included in the following passage, which may be quoted in its entirety because some of the opinions stated are relevant to the further course of our investigation.

Upon inquiring of the Jews whether they can relate any traditional teaching regarding the Taw (τοῦ Θαῦ), I heard the following. One of them said that in the order of the Hebrew letters the Taw is the last of the twenty-two consonantal sounds. The last consonant is therefore taken as proof of the perfection of those who, because of their virtue, moan and groan over the sinners among the people and suffer together with the transgressors. Another said that the Taw symbolizes the observers of the Law. Since the Law, which is called Tora by the Jews, begins [its name] with the consonant Taw, it is a symbol of those who live according to the Law. A third [Jew], one of those who believe in Christ, said the form of the Taw in the old [Hebrew], script resembles the cross (τοῦ σταυροῦ), and it predicts the mark which is to be placed on the foreheads of the Christians.

Saul Liebermann, *Greek in Jewish Palestine*. New York: The Jewish Theological Seminary of America, 1942, 185-191.

The Phylacteries and the Sign of the Name of God

It has been noted thus far that the wearing of a ritual sign on the forehead is a custom widely attested in the history of religions, and that in the particular case in Ezk 9:4 the Taw on the foreheads of the faithful signified that they belonged to the Lord and were under his protection for salvation. We have even thought that the literal placing of such a mark upon the forehead could possibly have been a practice of the people of the Qumran community and its related groups. Another adaptation of the basic idea of a ritual sign on the fore-

head is to be seen in the wearing of phylacteries, as they are called in Mt 23:5. With respect to the feast of unleavened bread Ex 13:9 and 16 state that "it shall be to you as a sign on your hand and as a memorial between your eyes"; and with respect to the commandments of the Lord Dt 6:8 and 11:18 say, "you shall bind them as a sign upon your hand, and they shall be as frontlets between your eyes." Whether these statements were meant in the first instance figuratively or literally, they became the basis of a literal practice. A small box containing portions of Scripture was tied upon the forehead, and another such upon the hand or arm. Such a box was called a תפלה, *tefillah*, "a prayer," in Hebrew and a φυλακτήριον, phylactery, "a safeguard," in Greek. In the Talmud there are numerous references to the *tefillin*, with a particularly extended description in *Menahoth* 34a-37b (SBT V 2, 215-232). The hand *tefillah* was worn on the left hand and more exactly on the left forearm or, according to one authority, on the biceps muscle; for the head *tefillah* the Scriptural place "between your eyes" was interpreted to mean not between the eyebrows but upon the brow of the head (*Menahoth* 37a-37b SBT V 2, 228-230). To wear the head phylactery too low down, or the other one on the palm of the hand, was in the manner of heresy (*Megillah* 24b SBT II 8, 148). The *tefillah* worn on the forehead has the letter Shin (שׁ) on each side, while the strap holding it is tied in a knot in the shape of the letter Daleth (ד). Also the *tefillah* worn on the arm is tied on with a knot in the shape of the letter Yodh (י). Together these letters form the divine name שדי, Shaddai (*Menahoth* 35b V 2, 222 note 3), a word which was often rendered παντοκράτωρ in the LXX (e.g., Jb 5:17, etc.) and hence is now usually translated "Almighty." So the faithful Jew wore the divine name upon his forehead in the form of an abbreviation consisting of the first letter (Shin) of that name or, if the knot be counted as making a Daleth, an abbreviation consisting of the first two letters of the name, while the knot on the arm could be considered as completing the spelling of the name.

Since the Shin on the box on the forehead stood for the name of the Almighty and signified that the bearer belonged to him, we wonder if the Taw which signified that its bearer was faithful to the Lord and under his protection, as we have already established, did not itself also stand for the very name of the Lord. In the quotation from Origen given above, it was stated that one opinion in Jewish tradition was that the Taw, as the twenty-second and last letter of the Hebrew alphabet, stood for perfection. As the last letter of the alphabet it could also be connected with the statement of the Lord in Is 44:6 and 48:12, "I am the first and I am the last." This statement might indeed suggest that both Aleph, the first character, and Taw, the last, could stand together for the name of the Lord. Indeed in the Midrash *Rabbah* on Genesis (81, 2 SMR II 747) it is stated, with explicit citation of Is 44:6, that the seal of God consists of the three letters, Aleph, Mem, and Taw, the first, the middle, and the last of the alphabet, which together form the word אמת, *'emeth*, meaning "truth." Of these letters special importance attaches to the last and final one, and the Talmud (*Shabbath* 55a SBT II 1, 254) says with respect to the same seal of God, "*Taw* is the end of the seal of the Holy One." Taken together, the Hebrew Aleph and Taw correspond to the Greek Alpha and Omega, and in the collocation of the two characters we probably have the Hebrew expression upon which is based the statement of God in Rev 1:8 and 21:6, and of Christ in Rev 22:13, "I am the Alpha and the Omega." Furthermore in the Book of Revelation, even as in the Psalms of Solomon (15:8, 10) cited above, both the righteous and the sinners are marked. The followers of the beast are marked on the right hand or the forehead (Rev 13:16) or, more probably, on both (Rev 20:4). The position of these marks reflects the Jewish phylacteries, which we have described above, but the manner of the followers of the beast is a travesty of the Jewish custom, for here the one mark is on the right hand, not the left, and the other mark is on (ἐπί) the brow, not over the brow. The one hundred and forty-four thousand servants of God are sealed on their foreheads (Rev 7:3; 9:4; 14:1), and this plainly reflects Ezk 9:4. In Ezk 9:4 the mark on the foreheads of the faithful showed that they belonged to the Lord. Here what presumably was the very same mark is plainly stated in Rev 14:1 and 22:4 to represent the name of God. Therefore it is a reasonable conclusion that already in Jewish thought, as well as certainly here in Christian application, the Taw stood for the name of God as well as marking the one upon whom it was placed, literally or figuratively, for protection and salvation.

The Sign of the Anointed One

The *taw*-sign stood for deliverance and for the name of God. Since, however, the name of God stood for the manifestation of God in the world (see, e.g., Dt 12:11, where his name is made to dwell in the temple), it was easy for the early Christians to think of the divine name as manifest in Jesus Christ (see, e.g., Jn 17:6, where Christ has manifested the name of the Father). That this mode of thought was prevalent already in Jewish Christian circles, and that the Name was there a designation of Christ, is made most probable by Jas 2:7, where "the honorable name which was

called upon you" (ASV margin; cf. Ac 15:17) is probably the name of Christ, or includes the name of Christ; and by the *Gospel of Truth* (cf. No. 291), a Gnostic work of the second century with strong elements of Jewish Christian theology, which says flatly, "But the Name of the Father is the Son" (ed. Malinine, Puech, and Quispel, *Evangelium Veritatis*, folio XIX *verso*, p. 38, Lines 6-7; cf. Daniélou, *The Theology of Jewish Christianity*, pp. 147-163; *Primitive Christian Symbols*, pp. 141-142). Therefore the *taw*-sign, which stood for the name of God in Jewish thought, probably also stood for the name of Christ in Jewish Christian thought. In fact in Rev. 22:4, where it is said that "his name shall be on their foreheads," it may be noted that the reference in the immediately preceding verse was not only to God but also to the Lamb.

Where the Greek language was known it was almost inevitable, for another reason, that the Taw would come to stand for the name of Christ. Particularly when it was written in its sideways position, the Taw was immediately identifiable with the Greek Chi, and Chi is the first letter of the Greek word χριστός, *Christos*, Christ. This word is, of course, the usual translation in the LXX and elsewhere of the Hebrew word "anointed," or Messiah, and it is of interest to find that in connection with the "anointed one" there was also a characteristic application of a mark to the forehead. In the OT both the king (I Sam 10:1) and the high priest were anointed in consecration to office. The pattern for the anointing of the high priest was set when Moses anointed Aaron, as is recorded in Lev 8:12, "And he poured some of the anointing oil on Aaron's head, and anointed him, to consecrate him." In the Talmud (*Horayoth* 12a SBT IV 7, 86; cf. *Kerithoth* 5b SBT V 6, 36) this passage is taken to imply two acts corresponding to the two words "poured" and "anointed." In practice the pouring evidently consisted of pouring oil upon the head, and the anointing was the application of some oil on the forehead and specifically between the eyelids. The discussion here turns upon which should be done first, and is not of consequence to us, but in the same connection there is a very interesting statement as to the shape in which the oil was traced upon the forehead in the anointing. "Our Rabbis taught: How were the kings anointed?—In the shape of a wreath. And the priests?—In the shape of a Chi. What is meant by 'the shape of a Chi'? R. Menashya b. Gadda replied: In the shape of a Greek χ."

The oil mark on the forehead of the anointed priest must, therefore, have been the old letter Taw, probably written with the sideways orientation which made it immediately identifiable with the Greek Chi, and so the initial letter of Greek *Christos*, "anointed."

261. Column XXXV of the Isaiah Scroll from Cave 1 at Qumran

Another example of the use of the Taw mark with reference to the "anointed," the Messiah, is possibly to be recognized in the Qumran literature. In the Isaiah Scroll from Cave 1 (1QIsᵃ) there is a whole series of signs marked in the margins of the manuscript. One of these is a cross mark which can be the Taw, written sideways like a Chi, and it appears eleven times, namely, in columns XXVI, XXXV twice, XXXVI, XXXVIII, XLI, XLV, XLVI twice, XLVIII, and LIII. In each case it looks as if it were intended to mark the passage to its left, with the exception of the example on column XLV where the placement of the mark may more probably relate it to the text on its right. If this is correct, the passages to which attention is called by the cross marks are Is 32: 1ff.; 42:1ff. and 42:5ff.; 42:19ff.; 44:28; 49:5-7; 55: 3-4; 56:1-2 and 56:3ff.; 58:13ff.; 66:5ff. In general these may be recognized as passages having to do in one way or another with messianic expectation, an expectation which we know otherwise was a subject of much interest in the Qumran community. In column XXVI the mark stands to the left of a seam in the parch-

ment and there seems no question but that it must refer to the passage at its left. This passage is the beginning of chapter 32 in the Book of Isaiah, "Behold, a king will reign in righteousness. . . ." In column XXXV, illustrated here, the mark is seen twice in the right-hand margin. The text to the left of the first mark is the beginning of chapter 42, "Behold, my servant, whom I uphold . . ."; the text to the left of the second mark is 42:5ff., where the Lord is continuing to address his "servant." The same mark in the left-hand margin near the top of the column doubtless refers to the passage at its left, in column XXXVI, and here in the first three lines, in 42:19ff., the Lord is also speaking about the "servant." It may also be noted that in the lower part of the right-hand margin there is another sign, this one consisting essentially of a loop which is on top of a straight line and which tends to extend in a single stroke below that line. In fact if the vertical stroke extended farther downward we would have something very much like the ankh sign of ancient Egypt which became a form of the cross among the Coptic Christians, as we will illustrate below (Nos. 291ff.). In this case the sign may appear to be more closely related to the text at its right, in column XXXIV, which consists of Is 41: 17ff., an eschatological passage about the transformation of nature in the end time.

With these signs in the Isaiah Scroll we may compare a list of signs given by Epiphanius in *On Weights and Measures*, a work written in A.D. 392, the first part of which is extant in late Greek manuscripts, and the whole in Syriac translation in two manuscripts of the seventh and ninth centuries. Near the beginning of this work Epiphanius lists a number of signs which are employed, he says, in the prophetic writings. One of these signs appears in the Greek manuscripts (MPG 43, 237) as an upright, symmetrical cross mark, and in the Syriac manuscripts (ed. Dean, 15) as a cross mark written in the sideways position, in other words it is precisely the Taw in the two positions with which we are familiar. This sign, Epiphanius says, is for the Messiah or the Christ, i.e., it is used to mark passages of messianic import. It is precisely this sign, in form like a Chi, which marks messianic passages in the Isaiah Scroll of the Qumran community. Therefore the later custom of Christian scribes, attested by Epiphanius, may have had its antecedent in the markings used by Jewish scribes, as illustrated here in the Jewish sectarian community. In this Jewish and later Christian tradition of markings, the Taw = Chi was a mark for passages which had to do with the Messiah. The continuity of tradition in the signs in the Isaiah Scroll and in Epiphanius appears to be confirmed also in the case of the other sign we have noticed in the Isaiah manuscript, namely, the one which bears some resemblance to the ankh. In the Isaiah manuscript this sign appears in columns XXVIII, XXXII, XXXIV, XXXVIII, XLIII, and XLIX, and seems to refer to Is 36:1ff.; 40:1ff.; 41:17ff.; 45:1ff.; 52:7ff.; 60:1ff. Like the example we see here in column XXXIV, which refers to Is 41:17ff., all of these passages may be considered eschatological. Turning again to Epiphanius, we find that the last of the several signs he lists was one probably very similar to this ankh-like one. In the Greek manuscripts, indeed, it is not recognizable as such, but the sign that is reproduced in these manuscripts at this point is virtually the same as another sign which occurs earlier in the list, therefore is probably not correctly reproduced at all. In the Syriac manuscripts, however, we find at this point a sign which, except that the loop is formed in a rectangular manner, is probably the same as the one we see in the Isaiah manuscript. As to the significance of this sign, the text of Epiphanius says in both the Greek and the Syriac that it is for the foretelling of future events. This is precisely the nature of the passages marked by this sign in the Isaiah Scroll. Almost all are obviously eschatological in character, and even the first one which appears to be purely historical may be supposed to have had some eschatological interpretation. The congruity of what Epiphanius says with the evidence in the Isaiah Scroll, therefore, justifies us in taking the Christian signs as a heritage from Jewish scribes, and in recognizing the cross marks in the Isaiah manuscript as the Taw = Chi alphabetic character which was used to single out passages of messianic import, just as the other sign, possibly related to the ankh-cross, marked those of eschatological character.

John C. Trever, "Preliminary Observations on the Jerusalem Scrolls," in BASOR 111 (Oct. 1948), 8f., cf. 12, 14; Millar Burrows, *The Dead Sea Scrolls of St. Mark's Monastery*, I, *The Isaiah Manuscript and the Habakkuk Commentary*. New Haven: The American Schools of Oriental Research, 1950; J. L. Teicher, "Material Evidence of the Christian Origin of the Dead Sea Scrolls," in JJS 3 (1952), 128-130; Isaiah Sonne, "The X-Sign in the Isaiah Scroll," in VT 4 (1954), 90-94; J. L. Teicher, "The Christian Interpretation of the Sign X in the Isaiah Scroll," in VT 5 (1955), 189-198. Photograph: Burrows, *The Dead Sea Scrolls of St. Mark's Monastery*, I, Pl. XXXV, courtesy American Schools of Oriental Research.

The evidence cited above shows that the cross mark which was called *taw*, and the alphabetic character which consisted of that mark and was named the Taw, already stood in Jewish thought for deliverance and eschatological salvation, and probably also for the name of God and for the Messiah. The sign was written either + or X, and the one who, literally or figuratively, bore this sign was distinguished as belonging to the Lord and was marked for deliverance at the end time.

The Cross Mark in Jewish Christianity

It could have been from this background that the cross mark passed into use in early Christianity. We must speak first of Jewish Christianity, including the eschatological community in Palestine prior to A.D. 70 and the Jewish Christianity known in Syria and elsewhere after that date. Writers and written sources in which Christianity is expressed in the thought forms of later Judaism, which are therefore witnesses to the Jewish Christianity of which we speak, include the following. The Shepherd of Hermas was probably written at Rome between A.D. 90 and 140, and shows strong influence of Jewish apocalyptic. Ignatius, bishop of Antioch, died in Rome under Trajan about A.D. 110; although his name is Latin, as was common enough, his style is very Semitic and his thought is an expression of Syrian Christianity. The Letter of Barnabas was written between A.D. 70 and 132, perhaps about 120, and perhaps in Egypt; it employs typological and allegorical exegesis of Scripture. The Odes of Solomon were probably written in Greek in Syria about the middle of the second century, and are extant in Syriac. The Acts of John may have been written in Syria or Asia Minor, perhaps in the latter part of the second century. The Acts of Thomas were probably written in Syria in the early part of the third century. The Sibylline Oracles are of various dates, some are Jewish, some Jewish Christian. All of these sources will be cited in what follows.

In the quotation given above from Origen (*Selecta in Ezechielem* 9 MPG XIII 801) we saw that one of the Jews who was a believer in Christ, i.e., a Jewish Christian, told Origen that the Taw in the Old Hebrew script predicted the mark which was to be placed on the foreheads of the Christians. Therefore the conception existed in Jewish Christianity of a cross mark, either literal or figurative, on the forehead, and this mark no doubt signified, as the antecedent history of the sign suggests, that the person so marked belonged to the Lord and was marked for salvation. Since that mark in its earlier history may have already stood for the name of the Lord or the Messiah, it may stand here also for the name of God or Christ. There is probably a direct reference to this mark, therefore, in the Shepherd of Hermas IX 13, 2 in the phrase, "bear the name," and in the Odes of Solomon 8:15 (Harris and Mingana II 254) in the statement, "And on their faces I set my seal." In both cases the thought of baptism is almost certainly implied. In the Shepherd of Hermas VIII 6, 3 Christian believers are ones who have received the seal, and in IX 16, 3ff. the seal is received in baptism. In the Acts of Thomas 120-121 (AAA II 2, 229-231; Klijn 129-130) Mygdonia requests, "Give me the sign of Jesus the Messiah" (Δός μοι τὴν σφραγῖδα Ἰησοῦ Χριστοῦ), and the apostle proceeds to put oil on her head and to baptize her; and in another passage (157 AAA II 2, 266-267; Klijn 149) the anointing and baptism of a group are described: "And after he had anointed them, he made them go down into the water in the name of the Father and the Son and the Spirit of holiness" (cf. also chaps. 25, 27, 49, 132). In Greek the sign or seal is a σφραγίς, and this word means first of all an actual seal with which to mark anything. Therefore the above references probably mean that at baptism the candidate was actually marked with a sign on the forehead which stood for the name of God or of Christ. Since this was done in a ceremony of anointing it was done with oil. Since it was done in connection with baptism, the word *sphragis* or "seal" became a term for baptism itself. Since this custom of the seal or the mark was widespread in Jewish Christianity in the time of the documents cited, and since there was a comparable reference at Qumran, either figurative or literal, to the Taw on the forehead, it seems very possible that in the intervening time and place, i.e., in the Jewish Christianity of Palestine prior to A.D. 70, a mark was used which stood for the name of God or Christ and conveyed the assurance of salvation, and that this mark was the Taw.

The conception just observed in Jewish Christian writings is found also among the Valentinian Gnostics, and it is evident that Gnosticism preserved many elements from Jewish Christianity. In the Excerpts which Clement of Alexandria gives from the Valentinian teacher, Theodotus, there is a discussion of baptism (77-86 GCS Clemens Alexandrinus III 131-133; Casey 86-91). Here too it is spoken of in connection with being "sealed (σφραγισθείς) by Father, Son and Holy Spirit" (80, 3). Then (86, 1-2) the saying of Jesus about the coin with Caesar's superscription (ἐπιγραφή) is recalled, and it is said: "So likewise the faithful; he has the name of God through Christ as a superscription. . . . And dumb animals show by a seal (διὰ σφραγῖδος) whose property each is, and are claimed from the seal. Thus also the faithful soul receives the seal of truth and bears about 'the marks (στίγματα) of Christ.' " Like the mark of ownership on an animal, the believer has a mark which shows whose property he is. Literally or figuratively he is marked with the name of God through Christ and, insofar as this mark is visualized or made actual, it must still be the Taw of the early Jewish Christians. (Could this reference and allusion possibly be the "seal" which Jesus had in mind in John

6:27; cf. 3:33, "him hath God the Father sealed"? asks Professor Vardaman.)

In the foregoing quotations we have met not only the noun σφραγίς, meaning "seal," but also the verb σφραγίζω, meaning "mark with a seal." In other passages, too, we find the same verb but without the connection with baptism which was characteristic of the preceding quotations. In the Acts of John 115 the action of the apostle immediately prior to his death is described in these words: "And having sealed himself wholly (σφραγισάμενος ἑαυτὸν ὅλον), he stood and said: 'Thou art with me, O Lord Jesus Christ.' " Here the verb must mean that John marked the seal upon himself and indeed upon every part of his body, either literally or more probably figuratively in the sense of a gesture which traced the pattern of the seal. In other words "to seal" meant to make the sign that constituted the seal and, in accordance with what has been set forth hitherto, it meant to make a sign corresponding to a cross mark, i.e., to the Taw. That such action was well known from the days of the earliest Jewish Christian church is, in fact, affirmed by Basil of Caesarea; he says in his work *On the Spirit* (27 NPNFSS VIII 41) (A.D. 375) that "to sign with the sign of the cross those who have trusted in the name of our Lord Jesus Christ" is one of the practices in the Church which derive from unwritten tradition going back to the apostles.

The Cross as Representation of the Stauros

In the foregoing we have evidence of the use of the cross mark as a "seal" in baptism and as a gesture of faith in Jewish Christianity, and of its probable employment in the primitive community in Palestine. The mark is still essentially the Taw of the Semitic alphabet and of the passage in Ezk 9:4. It stands for the divine name and the eschatological salvation. In the quotation from Origen (*Selecta in Ezechielem* 9 MPG III 801) cited above (p. 225), however, his Jewish Christian informant told him not only that the Old Hebrew Taw predicted the mark which would be placed on the foreheads of the Christians, but also that it resembled the cross (σταυρός). The *stauros* was an instrument of execution in the form of an upright stake often with a crosspiece at or near the top (Artemidorus, *Onirocriticon* II 53 Pack 183), and was the instrument of the death of Jesus (Mt 27:32, etc.). The statement of Origen's informant that the Taw resembled the *stauros* is obviously correct, and the fact that this resemblance was noted in Jewish Christian thought is confirmed by allusions in various Jewish Christian writings. In the Jewish Christian Sibylline Oracles VIII 217-250 (Geffcken 153-157), for example, there is an elaboration of the famous early Christian acrostic, Ἰησοῦς Χριστὸς Θεοῦ Υἱὸς Σωτήρ, "Jesus Christ, God's Son, Savior," the initial letters of which words in Greek spell ἰχθύς, "fish." Here in the Oracles the word Σταυρός, "cross," is added to the formula, and then the letters in this entire sequence of words (the second word being spelled Χρειστός) were made the initial letters of the thirty-four lines of an acrostic poem. The last seven lines, corresponding to the word *stauros* may be rendered roughly in English as follows:

> Sign (σῆμα) then for all mortals, distinguished seal (σφρηγίς),
> The wood (ξύλον) shall be for all believers, the desired horn (κέρας),
> And life of devout men, but occasion of stumbling of the world,
> Ultimate illumination (φωτίζον) for the elect in the waters by means of twelve springs,
> Rod of iron, which will shepherd and rule.
> Our God, now portrayed and written above (προγραφείς) in the acrostics (ἀκροστιχίοις), is this one,
> Savior immortal, king, the one who suffers for our sake.

In the multifarious allusions of this passage we hear again of the *sphragis* (in a slightly variant Greek spelling) or "seal," and of baptism (called φωτίζον, "illumination," in accordance with a widespread usage, e.g., Justin *Apology* I 61, 14 ANF I 183), and together with these we hear of the "wood" or "tree" (ξύλον, cf. Dt 21:22, Ac 5:30, etc.) which is the cross in the sense of the *stauros*. The *stauros* is also referred to as a "horn" (κέρας). Here comparison may be made with Justin, *Dialogue with Trypho* 91, 2 (ANF I 245), who sees in "the horns of unicorns" in Dt 33:17 (KJV) a type of the *stauros*. In form the cross has horns; in significance it is a manifestation of power, as the "horn" was a symbol of power in the OT. Concerning the form of the cross Justin writes: "For the one beam is placed upright, from which the highest extremity is raised up into a horn, when the other beam is fitted on to it, and the ends appear on both sides as horns joined on to the one horn. And the part which is fixed in the center, on which are suspended those who are crucified, also stands out like a horn; and it also looks like a horn conjoined and fixed with the other horns."

Also in the word προγραφείς the writer may mean not only to refer to what he has "written above" (cf. Eph 3:3, προέγραψα, "I have written above") in the entire acrostic, but also to allude to Gal 3:1 which speaks of how Christ "was portrayed on the cross" (προεγράφη ἐσταυρωμένος). This passage in the Sibylline

Oracles is quoted, it may be added, by Eusebius (*Oration of Constantine* 18 NPNFSS I 574f.) in full, and by Augustine (*City of God* XVIII 23 NPNF II 372f.) with the omission of the last part about the *stauros* but with explanation of the acrostic "fish" which is left intact with that omission.

The Letter of Barnabas is another example of a writing emanating from a Jewish Christian atmosphere in which there is a statement about the *stauros*. The letter was written in Greek, and now it is not the Semitic Taw but the Greek Tau which is spoken of as representing the cross. Here (IX 8) Scripture is quoted as saying, "And Abraham circumcised from his household eighteen men and three hundred," which is a brief statement of the information provided by Gen 14:14 and 17:26-27. The eighteen is then explained as comprised of the Greek letters Iota (= ten) and Eta (= eight), which are the two first letters of the name of Jesus. As for the three hundred, it is the numerical value of Tau, and therewith the cross is symbolized. "So he indicates Jesus in the two letters and the cross (σταυρός) in the other."

The Cross in the Hellenistic Church

When Christianity moved into the area of Greek and Latin thought and language there was no doubt a certain shift in emphasis. The meaning of the Semitic *taw* and therewith the original understanding of Ezk 9:4 would naturally tend to fade out. Yet the idea of a ritual mark on the forehead, an idea so ancient and widespread in the history of religions, was of course known in the Gentile world too. Tertullian (*On Prescription against Heretics* 40 ANF III 262), for example, speaks of how in the kingdom of Satan, as he calls it, "Mithra . . . sets his marks on the foreheads of his soldiers." Here the concept may not be that of sealing eschatologically, as in Ezk 9:4, but the mark no doubt signifies belonging to the deity and being therewith under his protection. Tertullian himself, as we have already seen (p. 224), quotes Ezk 9:4, where "the mark Tau" was to be set upon the foreheads of the men of Jerusalem, and in respect to this quotation he continues immediately (*Against Marcion* III 22 ANF III 340f.): "Now the Greek letter Tau and our own letter T is the very form of the cross, which he predicted would be the sign on our foreheads in the true catholic Jerusalem." So the mark is still on the foreheads of Christians, literally or figuratively, but here in the Greco-Roman world it is not the Semitic Taw but the Greek Tau or the Latin T, and it has especially to do with the cross, i.e., the instrument on which Jesus died. In fact, this mark, which Tertullian elsewhere calls simply "the sign," was evidently traced upon the forehead, at least in a gesture, by the Gentile Christians upon every possible occasion. "At every forward step and movement," writes Tertullian (*The Chaplet* 3 ANF III 94f.), "at every going in and out, when we put on our clothes and shoes, when we bathe, when we sit at table, when we light the lamps, on couch, on seat, in all the ordinary actions of daily life, we trace upon the forehead the sign." Likewise Cyril says in his *Catechetical Lectures* delivered in Jerusalem in A.D. 348 (XIII 36 NPNFSS VII 92): "Let us not then be ashamed to confess the Crucified. Be the Cross our seal made with boldness by our fingers on our brow, and on everything: over the bread we eat, and the cups we drink; in our comings in, and goings out; before our sleep, when we lie down and when we rise up; when we are in the way, and when we are still. Great is that phylactery (μέγα τὸ φυλακτήριον). . . . It is the sign of the faithful, and the dread of devils."

Like the Jewish Christians the Gentile Christians also found many types of the cross in the OT Scriptures, e.g., as Justin (*Dialogue with Trypho* 112 ANF I 255) and Tertullian (*An Answer to the Jews* 10 ANF III 165f.) tell us, in the outstretched hands of Moses (Ex 17:12), and in the brazen serpent on a standard (Num 21:9). They also recognized the cross in many objects in the world about them and Tertullian (*ibid.*) refers in this respect, for example, to the mast and the yard of a ship. Minucius Felix (A.D. 166) writes this (*The Octavius* 29 ANF IV 191): "We assuredly see the sign of a cross, naturally, in the ship when it is carried along with swelling sails, when it glides forward with expanded oars; and when the military yoke is lifted up, it is the sign of a cross; and when a man adores God with a pure mind, with hands outstretched."

The final comparison given by Minucius Felix may be compared with the statement of St. Nilus, a famous ascetic in Sinai at the end of the fourth century (SWDCB IV, pp. 43f.), who also explains (MPG LXXIX, Epp. I 86, 87 cf. III 132) that standing at prayer with arms outstretched is a figure of the cross as well as a testimony to the resurrection. Since the cross was compared, then, with a ship's mast and yard and with a person with hands outstretched in prayer, it is plain that the form of the cross was recognized not only in the T but also where the vertical member extended above the crossarm.

In summary to this point, we have seen that the Semitic Taw, written + or X, was a sign of salvation in the OT and Judaism, and also in Jewish Christianity. In Jewish Christianity already and also particularly in Hellenistic Christianity the same sign was connected with the instrument on which Jesus died (the *stauros*) and in such connection was used still in the form of the Taw, +, but also in the form of the equivalent Tau, T, and likewise in the form †. The Semitic Taw also stood for the name of the Lord and of the Messiah. Written either erect or sideways it was recognized that the Greek Chi was its equivalent, and indeed the latter was itself written both erect like a symmetrical cross mark and also in the more familiar form X. Chi was of course the initial letter of the Greek word which translated "Messiah," namely, Χριστός, *Christos*. Therefore it was natural that, particularly in the Hellenistic church, the cross mark, written as a Chi, was taken as standing for the name of Christ. As an example which almost certainly means this, we have the case cited by Eusebius (*Martyrs of Palestine* VIII 7 NPNFSS I 349 Schwartz GCS II 2, 926) of the martyr Valentina. When she was dragged into the midst of the court before the judge, she wrote on the honorable name of the Savior (καὶ τὸ σεβάσμιον τοῦ σωτῆρος ἐπιγραψαμένη ὄνομα), which must mean that she inscribed the name on herself, probably on her forehead. Further, this must have been done by tracing a mark on herself, at least in a gesture, and this can hardly have been anything other than the cross mark understood as the letter Chi and the initial letter and abbreviation of the name of Christ.

The Forms of the Cross

The forms of the cross mark considered in this survey of the literary evidence are, therefore: the equilateral cross, which is essentially the Semitic Taw in upright position, which was still used widely in the Hellenistic church and is commonly known as the Greek cross; the Tau cross (*crux commissa*), which corresponds in shape to the Greek letter Tau and the Latin letter T, the letters which were the first equivalents in those languages of the Hebrew Taw; the Latin cross (*crux immissa*), which is like a Greek cross but with the lower arm longer than the other three; and the cross which is like the Taw written sideways, the Greek Chi, and the Latin X or "ten," hence is known as the *crux decussata*. Originally this cross mark signified salvation and the divine name; even when the mark was connected with the instrument of the execution of Jesus it continued to express the saving power which works through his death.

Two other cross forms will also be encountered. One is the *crux gammata* or "gammadion," in which to each arm of an equilateral cross a further arm is attached at right angles, turning either to the left or to the right, until the whole can be described as like four Greek capital letters Gamma joined at right angles. This is found widely in the history of religions, and is usually thought to have been originally a solar symbol or a sign of life or blessing. In India it is called *swastika* (from *su,* "well," and *asti,* "it is") when the outer arms are turned to the right, and *sauvastika* when they are turned to the left. The other form is the *crux ansata* or handled cross. This looks like a Tau cross surmounted by a handle in the form of a loop. This is essentially the form of the Egyptian ankh, which may have been first of all a knotted amulet, and is found in the hieroglyphic writing as a sign meaning life and prosperity (cf. Nos. 291f.). Both of these forms, the *crux gammata* and the *crux ansata,* were adopted as forms of the Christian cross.

Goblet d'Alviella, "Cross," in HERE IV, pp. 324-329; John J. Collins, "The Archaeology of the Crucifixion," in CBQ 1 (1939), pp. 154-159; G. W. H. Lampe, *The Seal of the Spirit.* London: Longmans, Green and Co., 1951; Hugo Rahner, "Das mystische Tau," in ZKT 75 (1935), pp. 385-410; Maria Cramer, *Das altägyptische Lebenszeichen im christlichen koptischen Ägypten.* Wiesbaden: Otto Harrassowitz, 3d ed. 1955; Franz J. Dölger, "Beiträge zur Geschichte des Kreuzzeichens," in JAC 1 (1958), pp. 5-19; 2 (1959), pp. 15-29; 3 (1960), pp. 5-16; 4 (1961), pp. 5-17; 5 (1962) pp. 5-22; 6 (1963), pp. 7-34; Erich Dinkler, "Kreuzzeichen und Kreuz," in JAC 5 (1962), pp. 93-112; P. E. Testa, *Il simbolismo dei Giudeo-Cristiani.* Jerusalem: Tipografia dei PP. Francescani, 1962; Jean Daniélou, *Primitive Christian Symbols.* Baltimore: Helicon Press, 1964, pp. 136-145; and *The Theology of Jewish Christianity.* London: Darton, Longman & Todd, 1964.

Abbreviations and Monograms

In the writing of inscriptions and manuscripts, abbreviations were already employed in the last centuries before the Christian era, and increasingly in the Christian era (see Avi-Yonah, *Abbreviations,* for Greek abbreviations, and Cagnat pp. 399-473 for Latin abbreviations). A statistical tabulation of dated abbreviations by centuries shows the highest proportion of abbreviations to inscriptions in the second and third centuries of the Christian era and again in the sixth and seventh (Avi-Yonah, *Abbreviations,* p. 17). Abbreviation is usually accomplished by dropping some of the letters of a word so that one or more letters remain to stand for the whole word. Such abbreviations may then be indicated by adding a conventional mark, such as a horizontal line drawn over or through or under one or more of the letters, or by changing the position or shape of one or more of the letters. A special form of the last procedure consists in linking two or more letters so that a single compound character results. This is called a ligature or, as the representation of a name, a monogram.

With respect to the figure 318 in Gen 14:14, we have already noted (above p. 230) that the Letter of Barnabas (IX 8) says that the three hundred, which is expressed by the letter Tau in Greek, discloses the cross, and says that in the ten and the eight, expressed by I and H, "you have Jesus (ἔχεις Ἰησοῦν)," i.e., you have the abbreviation of his name. Therefore this abbreviation, consisting of the first two letters of the name of Jesus in Greek, was familiar in the Jewish Christian circles represented by the Letter of Barnabas in the time in which it was written (probably between A.D. 70 and 132) and doubtless earlier too. If the Iota and the Eta, constituting this abbreviation, were written together, a simple monogram (H) could result. At the same time this design could be considered to contain a plain equilateral cross standing erect between two vertical lines. This symbol may be seen in an inscription from Anatolia which is probably of pre-Constantinian date (W. M. Calder in ASR pp. 88-89 No. 10; see also Dölger I, p. 263).

The initial letters of the name Jesus and the title Christ, i.e., Iota and Chi, could also be written together. This would be essentially the combination of a cross mark and a vertical stroke and, in its simplest form, would look like a six-pointed star (✳). This could be the abbreviation, in a ligature, of the name and title, Jesus Christ. But the Chi could be considered as the mark of the cross, and the vertical mark as the initial and abbreviation of the name of Jesus. An example is found in an inscription, probably of pre-Constantinian date, from Eumeneia in Phrygia (Ramsay, *Phrygia,* pp. 526-527 No. 371). In a passage preserved in two fifteenth-century manuscripts (Cod. 26 of Merton College and Har. 3049), Jerome mentions a monogram which appears to be composed of a cross and a Hebrew letter Waw. Save that the vertical stroke is thus somewhat curved, the appearance of this symbol is much the same as that just mentioned. The Waw, however, has the value of six in the Hebrew system of numerals. Since there are six letters in the Greek spelling of the name of Jesus (Ἰησοῦς), the Waw can stand as a sign of that name. In that light this monogram expresses the idea of Jesus and the cross. It is also possible that the Waw and the cross could be reminiscent of the brazen serpent on the standard in the wilderness in which Justin (*Dialogue with Trypho* 112 ANF I 255) saw a type of Jesus crucified (cf. p. 231).

That a numerical interpretation, such as that just suggested for the Waw, is not far-fetched and could have been made even at an early period is shown by the numerical understanding set forth in the Letter of Barnabas (IX 8), as cited above (p. 230). Irenaeus (*Against Heresies* I 14-15) also mentions several numerical values which were connected with the name of Jesus Christ by the Marcosian Gnostics. Although this is a later reference than that in Barnabas, and the numerology is related to far-ranging Gnostic speculations, the Gnostics appear to have derived not a few elements of which they made use from Jewish Christianity, and it is possible that some of these other numerical observations come from that source too. Just as it was remarked in the preceding paragraph that the Hebrew Waw ($= 6$) could stand for the name of Jesus, so here in what Irenaeus reports it is observed that the name of Jesus consists of six letters and therefore the Greek character Vau ($= 6$) can stand for it. Like the other archaic characters, Koppa ($= 90$) and Sampi ($= 900$), which were used in the numerical system along with the twenty-four characters of the regular Greek alphabet, the Vau was called an Episemon (τὸ ἐπίσημον, distinguishing mark or device [Herodotus I 195], from ἐπίσημος, having a mark, notable [cf. Rom 16:7]). So, Irenaeus tells us, in the usage of the Marcosian Gnostics, Vau was the "Episemon number" and as such a sign for the name of Jesus. It is also observed here that the name Christ (evidently with the spelling Χρειστός) contains eight letters, and this would point to the possibility of its representation by the Greek letter Eta, which has the numerical value of eight. Yet other observations reported by Irenaeus in the same passage include the following: When Christ is called the Alpha and the Omega (cf. Rev 22:13) the number 801 is reached ($A=1 + \Omega=800 = 801$). The same may be symbolized by the dove since the sum of the letters of this word is the same ($\pi = 80 + \epsilon = 5 + \rho = 100 + \iota = 10 + \sigma = 200 + \tau = 300 + \epsilon = 5 + \rho = 100 + a = 1 = 801$). Also if the numerical value of all the letters of the name of Jesus is reckoned the total is 888 ($I = 10 + \eta = 8 + \sigma = 200 + o = 70 + v = 400 + s = 200 = 888$).

In addition to the initial letter, Chi, as an abbreviation for Christ, the first two letters, Chi and Rho, could be used and could also readily be written together in the form of a monogram. The same two letters of course begin many other words too, and were written in monogram fashion as an abbreviation of other words. The Chi-Rho monogram, with the Rho written vertically through the cross mark of the Chi, is found, for example, as the abbreviation of χ(ιλιά)ρ(χης), which means "commander of a thousand men" and is used as the translation of the Roman *tribunus militum* or "military tribune"; of χρ(ήσιμον), which means "useful"; and of χρ(όνος), which means "time" (Avi-Yonah, *Abbreviations*, p. 112). Accordingly the significance of the monogram, particularly if it appears in isolation, cannot always be ascertained.

In other cases, however, this monogram occurs in contexts which are unmistakably Christian. This may be seen in the inscriptions on two funeral stelae found in the district of Eumeneia in Phrygia. The rather long inscription of a certain Gaius is now judged to show plainly from its language that the author was a Christian. The date is probably around A.D. 200. In the last line on the front (A 11) of the monument we have the word Θ(εο)ῦ, "of God," written in the abbreviation of a monogram and, immediately after it, the monogram of which we are speaking, which must stand for Χρ(ιστοῦ), "of Christ" (JRS 16 [1926], pp. 61-64 No. 183). The less extended epitaph of a certain Glyconides, an inscription dating probably in the latter half of the third century, identifies him (in the first line on the shaft of the stela) as Εὐμενεὺς Χρ(ιστιανὸς) ἐπίσκοπος. Here, where the monogram occurs between the words which indicate that Glyconides was a citizen of Eumeneia and a bishop, it must be taken as an abbreviation for "Christian" (JRS 16 [1926], pp. 73-74 No. 200).

Other clues also may demonstrate the Christian significance of the monogram. At Dura-Europos (YCS 14 [1955], p. 194 No. 216) it is found as a graffito on a broken sherd of pottery, which is probably of the third century in date. Immediately beside the monogram at the left is a large capital letter Alpha. This suggests the Alpha and Omega which are frequently written along with the Chi-Rho monogram (and also with the cross-monogram which will be mentioned later). There are also other examples of the placing of the Alpha alone alongside the monogram (DACL 1:1, cols. 11-12). Standing alone with the monogram the Alpha could also have the significance of the initial letter of Ἀ(ρχή), "the beginning" (Testa pp. 365-366 No. 22, p. 403 No. 1). "The Alpha and the Omega" (τὸ ἄλφα καὶ τὸ ὦ) derive of course from Rev 1:8; 21:6; and 22:13. In the last two passages "the beginning and the end" (ἡ ἀρχὴ καὶ τὸ τέλος) stand in parallel with "the Alpha and the Omega"; and in the first passage (Rev 1:8) "the beginning and the end" is the reading of Codex Sinaiticus instead of "the Alpha and the Omega."

Since context and accompanying clues do demonstrate in such cases as these just cited the almost certainly Christian usage of the symbol in the time before Constantine, even when the monogram stands alone and even in the pre-Constantinian period the possibility of its Christian significance may often be considered.

In addition to the understanding of the Chi and the Rho as the beginning letters of the names Christ and Christian, other possibilities of interpretation arise in the light of the numerical understanding of alphabetic characters to which we have referred above. In the Greek system of numerals the character Rho has the value of one hundred. Since Abraham was one hundred years old when he received the promise of the birth of

Isaac to Sarah and himself (Gen 21:5; Rom 4:19f.), the combination of Rho and Chi (or also of Rho and Tau) could stand for the fulfillment of the promise in the Cross. Ephraem the Syrian (d. 373) attests another interpretation. He says (ed. Assemani III p. 477c) that when the letter Rho is put above the cross it signifies (literally, "shows by a sign") help, which is reckoned as one hundred (σημαίνει βοήθεια ψηφιζόμενον ἑκατόν). The word βοήθεια, which means "help," was also written βοήθια, which may be a popular spelling corresponding to its actual pronunciation. In numerical value the letters of this word total one hundred ($\beta = 2 + o = 70 + \eta = 8 + \theta = 9 + \iota = 10 + a = 1 = 100$). Accordingly, as Ephraem leads us to see, when Rho was written with the cross (which could be with either Chi or Tau) it was affirmed that "the cross (is our) help" (RAE VI, pp. 84-85).

Another combination of Greek letters which resulted in a monogram somewhat similar to the foregoing was that achieved by the ligature of Tau and Rho to make the sign ⳨. This occurs as an abbreviation of various words in pagan inscriptions, e.g., of τρ(ιακάς) (Avi-Yonah, *Abbreviations*, p. 105), which means the number thirty and also the thirtieth day of the month. This sign is even found on coins of Herod the Great dated to his third year (see the discussion of this monogram on Herod's coins in BA 26 [May 1963], pp. 48ff. [Vardaman]). But the combination of the two letters could also have Christian significance. When the word σταυρός, "cross," was written in the abbreviated form, σ̄τ̄ρ̄ο̄ς̄, it was readily possible to make the usual combination of the Tau and the Rho and thus have the abbreviation σ⳨ος. This is actually found in Christian manuscripts as early as A.D. 200 (see below Nos. 288f.). At the same time the Tau itself was recognized as a form of the Christian cross (see above p. 230), and with this recognition it was possible to see the combination of the Tau and the Rho as constituting a cross-monogram (⳨), as we may call it in distinction from the Christ-monogram (☧) which was constituted by the combination of the letters Chi and Rho. That the cross-monogram had some similarity to, and might have been influenced by the Egyptian ankh will be spoken of further at a later point (Nos. 291f.).

With respect to the cross-monogram an epitaph found at Rome provides a relatively early example. This inscription was connected with a burial loculus found in the area between the Via Appia and the Via Latina and inside the Aurelian Wall. Since burial was prohibited within the walls of the city, this interment must have been made before the time when Aurelian (A.D. 270-275) built the wall which bears his name. The grave is that of a certain Beratio Nicatora, whose name is given in the first line of the inscription (BHPA-TIOYC NIKATOPAC). Beneath the inscription, which

is in mixed Greek and Latin, the cross-monogram occurs twice, and beneath that are certain representations, namely, of Jonah, the Good Shepherd, an anchor, and a lion. The style of lettering agrees with the place of discovery in pointing to a date in the third century (Orazio Marucchi in BAC 1886, pp. 15-17).

According to a well-known account (Lactantius, *Of the Manner in Which the Persecutors Died*, 44; Eusebius, *Life of Constantine*, I, 28-31), Constantine saw a certain sign in a dream or vision and inscribed it on the shields of his soldiers or fashioned it into a labarum or imperial standard, before his victory at the Milvian bridge (A.D. 312). Lactantius describes this sign as consisting of the letter X, with a perpendicular line drawn through it and turned around at the top, thus making the sign of Christ. The most natural understanding of this description would see the resulting sign as the equivalent of what we have called the Christ-monogram. From this time on this sign may therefore also be spoken of as the "Constantinian monogram." Not long after the date of Constantine's vision, the sign appears in a Roman funerary inscription (Diehl No. 3257) which is definitely dated *Severo et Rufino conss.*, i.e., when Severus and Rufinus were consuls, the year 323 (*Fasti consulares imperii*, ed. Willy Liebenam, KLT 41-43, p. 35). From then on it occurs frequently. But the evidence cited above shows that both the Christ-monogram and the cross-monogram must have had a long history before the time of Constantine.

All together, then, and already in the centuries before Constantine, we find the cross mark and the letters Iota, Eta, Chi, Tau, and Rho used as abbreviations of Christian significance, and we find combinations of these forming monograms, notably ⧾, ✳, ⳨, and ☧ (cf. Dölger I, p. 386).

Germain Morin, "Hieronymus de Monogrammate," in *Revue Bénédictine* 20 (1903), pp. 225-236; H. Leclercq, "Monogramme," in DACL XI 2, cols. 2369-2392; Max Sulzberger, "Le symbole de la Croix (et les monogrammes de Jésus) chez les premiers chrétiens," in *Byzantion* 2 (1925), pp. 393-448; W. H. Buckler, W. M. Calder, and C. W. M. Cox, "Monuments from Central Phrygia," in JRS 16 (1926), pp. 61-74; Dölger I, pp. 353-386; M. Burzachechi, "Sull'uso pre-costantiniano del monogramma greco di Cristo," in *Atti della Pontificia Accademia Romana di archeologia* (*serie* III), *Rendiconti* XXVIII (1954-55), pp. 197-211; R. N. Frye, J. F. Gilliam, H. Ingholt, and C. B. Welles, "Inscriptions from Dura-Europos," in YCS 14 (1955), pp. 123-213.

The Cross Mark in Relation to Funerary Customs, Jewish and Christian

In the foregoing discussion it has been established that the Taw mark in the basic passage, Ezk 9:4, stands for deliverance and salvation in the end time. Furthermore, as also documented above, quotation of and allusion to this passage in Jewish (e.g., Damascus Document), Jewish Christian (e.g., Odes of Solomon), and Gentile Christian (e.g., Tertullian) sources show that understanding of the underlying eschatological significance of this sign lived on in all these areas, while specific connections with the cross of Jesus and the name of Christ were also introduced in Jewish Christian and Gentile Christian thought. Since the sign stood for salvation in the Last Judgment, it is evident that it was a mark particularly appropriate for use in connection with places of burial, and this could have been already true for Jews as well as later for Jewish Christians and Gentile Christians.

As for putting a mark or sign on a grave in Jewish custom we can cite the Assumption of Moses, probably the work of a Pharisaic author between A.D. 7 and 29. Here (11:1-6 CAP II, p. 423), Joshua is grieved that Moses is to die, and he asks: "What place shall receive thee? Or what shall be the sign that marks (thy) sepulcher?" As to what the sign would be which would be used to mark a Jewish sepulcher, the appropriateness of the Taw mark to which we have called attention just above makes it entirely possible that it would be so employed. Actually, however, in the many Jewish tombs already surveyed where decorations were employed (Nos. 213ff.) it was not this sign but others such as the menorah (No. 240), shofar, lulab (No. 241), ethrog (No. 243), etc., which were characteristically used. Therefore the use of the Taw sign may have been more of a Jewish Christian and later development than we might otherwise have supposed.

For the custom of putting a mark or sign on a grave in Jewish Christian circles we can cite a reference in the first two chapters of II Ezra (IV Esdras), a portion of that work which was probably written soon after A.D. 150. Here (2:23) the Latin text of the Vulgate reads: *Mortuos ubi inveneris, signans commenda sepulcro, et dabo tibi primam sessionem in resurrectione*

mea. The word *signans* can be referred to the *mortuos*, and this translation be made: "Wheresoever thou findest the dead, set a sign upon them and commit them to the grave, and I will give thee the first place in my resurrection" (Oesterley 11). Or, and with greater intrinsic probability, the word *signans* can be related to the *sepulcro*, and this translation be given: "When you find any who are dead, commit them to the grave and mark (or, seal) it, and I will give you the first place in my resurrection" (RSV). With respect to the connotation of *signans*, translated "mark," "seal," or "set a sign on," there can be little doubt that it refers to the mark of the cross (cf. above p. 229).

Another and even more explicit illustration in the same respect, still in the area of Jewish Christianity, is found in the account by Eusebius (*Ch. Hist.* II 23) of the martyrdom of James, the brother of the Lord, and the head of the church in Jerusalem (A.D. 61/62, cf. GCS *Eusebius* VII 182f.; Josephus, *Ant.* xx 9). James was thrown down from the pinnacle of the temple. "And they buried him on the spot," Eusebius writes (II 23, 18), "by the temple, and his monument (στήλη) still remains by the temple." At this point there is an additional note in one early Greek manuscript of the *Church History* (MPG XX 203, note 12), which reads: "This monument (στήλη) was an unshaped stone (λίθος . . . ἄμορφος), having as an inscription (ἐπιγραφήν) the name of the interred James. From which (example) even until now the Christians set up stones in their tombs, and they either write letters (γράμματα) on them, or they cut in the sign of the cross (τὸ σημεῖον τοῦ σταυροῦ)." According to this evidence, from the time of James on the customary marking on a tomb monument included the "letters" of the name of the deceased and the "sign" of the cross mark.

ILLUSTRATIONS OF THE CROSS MARK

We proceed now to a series of illustrations of objects with the cross mark, together with occasional illustrations of related objects which are needed for explanation of some details. In the light of the references which have been given just above it may be expected that the monuments on which the cross mark appears will often be those of a funerary character and this will be found to be the case. We begin, however, with examples where the cross mark appears to be only a conventional sign of purely secular significance. After that we look for examples of the cross mark in contexts where, particularly because of funerary relationships, some of the religious significance elucidated above may be believed to attach to the sign. According to the theoretical understanding worked out above, some of these may be Jewish if other factors in the situation point to that fact, but some of them may be Jewish

Christian if circumstances point in that direction. If we do have examples of Jewish Christian cross marks in Palestine these will presumably be the earliest archeological evidences of the earliest Christian Church. Likewise a cross mark at Herculaneum, if it is indeed a Christian sign, may hold a similar position of priority in the area of the Gentile Christian Church. Finally, of course, we come to examples of the cross mark which are unmistakably Christian, and the survey is rounded out by noticing some of these and their most notable variations in Rome and in Egypt. Since in many of the earlier cases now to be cited we will be concerned with ossuaries at Jerusalem, it may be recalled (see above p. 218) that the use of ossuaries in and around Jerusalem is probably to be placed in the period from about 50 B.C. to A.D. 70 or possibly 135.

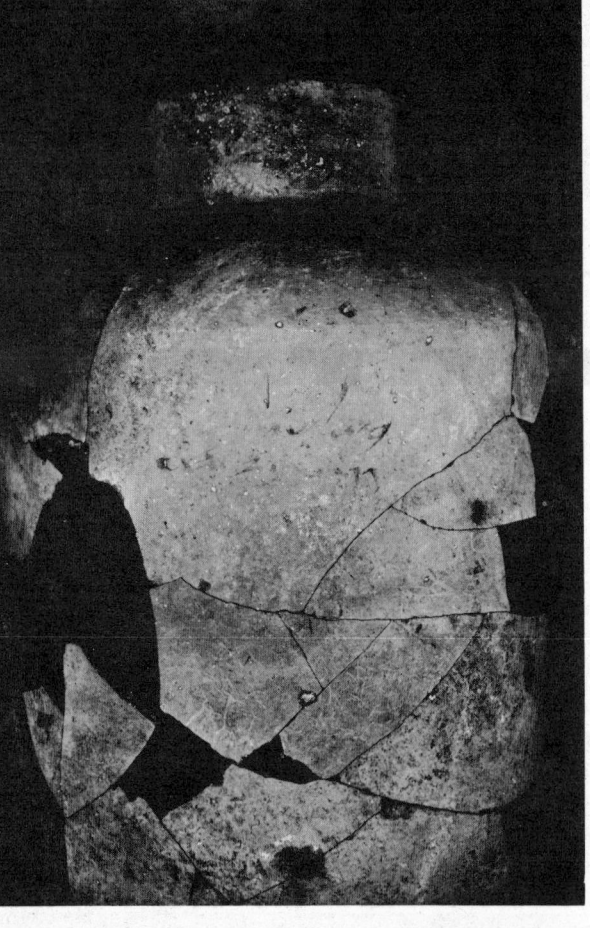

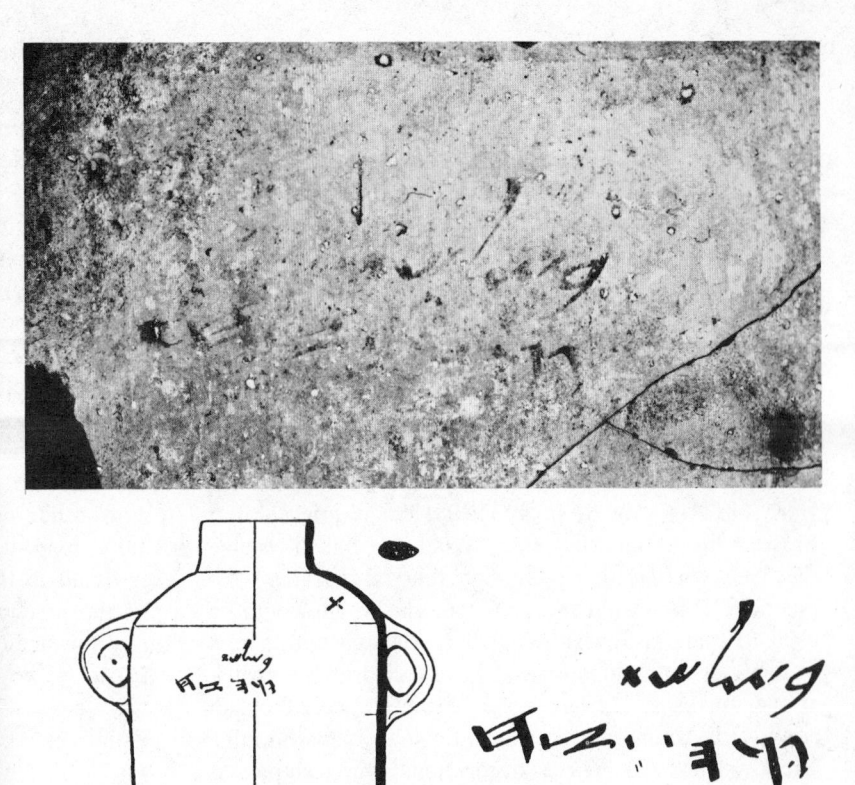

The Tel Arad Jar

262. Jar from Tel Arad with Hebrew Inscription and *Taw* Mark

The *taw* appears both as a letter of the alphabet in the inscription, and as a separate mark on the shoulder of this jar, which was found in 1962 in the excavation of Tel Arad, a large *tell* in the eastern Negev. The jar was on the floor of a room in a house in Stratum VI, which is dated to about the seventh century B.C. The inscription in two lines on the side, written in black ink in early Hebrew characters, probably reads as follows:

בשלשת	*bslst*	In the third (year),
ירח צח	*yraḥ ṣḥ*	the month Ṣaḥ.

If this is the correct transcription and interpretation of the inscription, the *yeraḥ Ṣaḥ* is a previously unrecognized month in the Israelite calendar. It may also be mentioned in Is 18:4, where it could be translated "like the heat of the month of Ṣaḥ," and must be a summer month. A guess as to the significance of the inscription is that the jar was for storage of perfume and the date is that on which the jar was filled. The alphabetic character *taw*, written as a cross mark in

the sideways position, is the last letter at the left end of the first line of the inscription. The *taw* mark, again written as a cross mark in the sideways position, in black ink, and in larger size, also appears on the curve of the jar below the neck and near the handle. The significance of the latter mark is not evident but it provides an example of the use of the cross presumably as a merely conventional mark and of only secular significance.

Similar examples of the Taw mark, written in ink and in charcoal, may be seen on storage jars found in the excavation of the storerooms of the fortress of Herod the Great on the rock of Masada. In this case the excavator, Yigael Yadin, interprets the mark as an abbreviation for the Hebrew word תרומה, *truma*, which is the "heave offering" and the priests' portion (cf. RSV) in Ex 29:27, etc. He draws the conclusion that the defenders of Masada were not only Zealots but also rigid adherents of the Law, adhering strictly to such commandments as tithing, in spite of the difficult conditions of life on Masada.

PEQ Jan.-Jun. 1963, pp. 3-4; Y. Aharoni and Ruth Amiran, "Excavations at Tel Arad," in IEJ 14 (1964), pp. 142-143; Yadin, *Masada*, p. 96. Photographs: courtesy Arad Expedition.

263. Inscription and Cross Mark on the Nicanor Ossuary

At a site on the north end of the Mount of Olives, where there is a view directly across to the temple area, an elaborate tomb with four independent groups of chambers was found in 1902. Seven ossuaries were obtained from the tomb, and the one dealt with here is now in the British Museum. It has painted red ornamentation in the form of rosettes on the front and zigzag lines on the back and lid and one end. On the other end is the inscription here shown. This is begun with some care but apparently executed with increasing haste and carelessness as it proceeds. The first three lines are in Greek, the fourth in Hebrew, as follows:

OCTATΩNTOYNEIKA
NOPOCΑΛΕΞΑΝΔΡΕΩC
ΠΟΙΗCΑΝΤΟCΤΑCΘΥΡΑC
נקנר אלכסא

The first two lines may be read as: Ὀστᾶ τῶν τοῦ Νεικά- νορος Ἀλεξανδρέως. Here it is possible that we have in the first word the plural contracted form of the Greek word for "bones" (ὀστέα), and that between the second and third words we should supply an understood word such as "sons," "descendants," or "family." If this is correct the translation will be: "Bones of the (sons) of Nicanor the Alexandrian." It is also possible, however, that the first seven letters of the first line constitute a single word, namely, ὀστατῶν. Although it is not otherwise known, this word could be understood to mean a "receptacle for bones," and therewith be an equivalent of ὀστοφάγος (cf. above p. 386). In this case we would translate: "Ossuary of Nicanor the Alexandrian."

Confirmation that the latter is the correct interpretation may be seen in the Hebrew portion of the inscription. The first Hebrew word is *nqnr*, which is a Hebrew spelling of Nicanor, otherwise found also as ניקנור, *nyqnwr*. The second word is *'lks'*, which could be spelled out as Aleksa. This could be the Hebrew equivalent of Ἀλεξᾶς, which in turn could be a contraction of Ἀλεξ- ανδρεύς, meaning "the Alexandrian." Thus the Hebrew probably simply gives the name of "Nicanor the Alexandrian," and thus tends to confirm the fact that this is indeed the ossuary of that person.

Concerning this Nicanor the third line of the Greek identifies him as the one

ποιήσαντος τὰς θύρας
who made the gates

In the Talmud (*Yoma* 19a SBT II, 5, p. 82) there is mention of the Nicanor Gate which was on the east of the Temple court, probably between the Court of the Women and the Court of the Israelites (see above No. 154). In contrast with the other gates, which were of gold (*Middoth* II, 3 SBT V, 6, p. 7), this one was of Corinthian bronze (*Yoma* 38a SBT II, 5, p. 175) and is doubtless the same one that is singled out by Josephus in these words (*War* V, 5, 3 §201): "Of the gates nine were completely overlaid with gold and silver, as were also their doorposts and lintels; but one, that outside the sanctuary, was of Corinthian bronze, and far exceeded in value those plated with silver and set in gold." Concerning the doors of this gate the Talmud (*Yoma* 38a SBT II, 5, p. 174) also states explicitly that Nicanor brought them from Alexandria of Egypt. The fact that certain miracles are also narrated here, with respect to the doors and their transport, at least attests the attention that was directed toward them. The conclusion seems entirely likely, therefore, that "Nicanor the Alexandrian who made the gates," according to the ossuary inscription, is this same Nicanor. That this man was buried across the valley on the Mount of Olives, at a place in full view of his famous gate, was very appropriate.

Interestingly enough, in the 1968 excavations at the

south wall of the temple area (cf. above No. 151) some five burial caves were uncovered, three of which contained ossuaries, and on one ossuary there was a Hebrew inscription appearing twice which reads, "Simon, the builder of the temple." In addition to Nicanor, this is the only other man associated with the construction of Herod's temple whose personal remains have been found.

PEFQS 1903, pp. 93, 125-131 (Clermont-Ganneau, "The 'Gate of Nicanor' in the Temple of Jerusalem"), 326-332 (Gladys Dickson, "The Tomb of Nicanor of Alexandria"); 1905, pp. 253-257 (R. A. Stewart Macalister, "Further Observations on the Ossuary of Nicanor of Alexandria"); Frey II, pp. 261-262 No. 1256; Goodenough I, pp. 130-131; Erich Dinkler in JAC 5 (1962), p. 109 and Pl. 5, b; *Biblical Museums Bulletin Eisenberg Issue* (Louisville: Southern Baptist Theological Seminary), Fall 1962, pp. 4-5, with additional bibliography. Photograph: courtesy the Trustees of the British Museum.

264. Cross Mark on the Lid of the Nicanor Ossuary

As may be seen in the preceding illustration (No. 263), there is on the end of the Nicanor ossuary, be-

neath the lines of Greek text and to the left of the line of Hebrew text, a relatively large and rather irregular cross mark cut into the stone in a sideways position. In this photograph (No. 264) it may be seen that there is a very similar cross mark cut into the top of the lid of the ossuary very near one end. It is perhaps possible to hold that the cross mark on the end of the ossuary is intentionally related to the inscription alongside which it stands, and therewith perhaps possible to understand it as the Jewish *taw* mark which has been discussed above (p. 235). But in this case a simpler explanation may be more acceptable. In 1903, at which time she was in possession of this ossuary, Miss Gladys Dickson (see the Literature under No. 263) observed that the cross mark on the end of the ossuary and the cross mark on the end of the lid of the ossuary appeared to correspond, and she suggested that together they simply showed the proper way to turn the lid when placing it in position.

Photograph: courtesy the Trustees of the British Museum.

The Ossuaries on the Mount of Offence

265. Inscription with the Name of Judah and Cross Mark on an Ossuary from the Mount of Offence

In 1873 a rock-hewn chamber was found on the Mount of Offence (cf. No. 107), to the southeast of Jerusalem, not far from the road to Bethany. This chamber gave the impression of being a storehouse for ossuaries collected from other burial places, for it contained at least thirty of these burial chests. Although the ossuaries were soon dispersed and many of them broken, Charles Clermont-Ganneau was able before this happened to make squeezes of their inscriptions and ornamentation and to compile a detailed description of the entire group. Most of the ossuaries had rosettes (cf. No. 251) on one side, and many of them had inscriptions on a long or short side or on the lid. The inscriptions were scratched on with a sharp instrument, or painted with a pen, or written on with charcoal. Both Hebrew (or Aramaic) and Greek were found. As deciphered by Clermont-Ganneau the inscriptions contained the following names in Hebrew (or Aramaic): Shalamsion, the daughter of Simeon the priest; Judah, the scribe; Judah, the son (*bar*) of Eleazar, the scribe; Simeon, the son (*bar*) of Jesus; Eleazar, the son (*bar*) of Natai; Martha, the daughter of Pascal; and Salome, the wife of Judah; and in Greek: Jesus; Nathanael; Moschas; Mariados (which could be a genitive meaning "of Marias"); Kyrthas; and Hedea. At least three of the inscriptions are accompanied by cross marks and the first of these, as copied from the squeezes of Clermont-Ganneau, is reproduced here. The Hebrew characters are undoubtedly to be read as יהודה, *yhwdh*, and so we have the familiar name, Judah. The same name occurs on another ossuary; on the lid of yet another there is a carefully cut inscription, "Judah, the scribe," and on a small end probably belonging to the same ossuary a carelessly made inscription, "Judah, son of Eleazar, the scribe." Eleazar is also a familiar name (e.g., II Macc 6:18), and is found in abbreviated form as Lazarus (e.g., Josephus, *War* v, 13, 7 §567; Jn 11:5ff.). On another ossuary and lid we have also the name of "Salome, the wife of Judah." Carefully placed beneath the name of Judah in the present inscription, and therefore probably to be taken as a symbol in some way connected with the name, is an equilateral cross.

C. Clermont-Ganneau in PEFQS 1874, pp. 7-10 and specially p. 8 No. 2; Clermont-Ganneau I, pp. 381-412; Frey II, p. 288 No. 1306. Photograph: Clermont-Ganneau I, p. 403 No. 11, courtesy Palestine Exploration Fund.

In this case the well-known OT name, Joshua (יהושע), occurs in the later form of Jeshua to which, in Greek, the name Jesus corresponds. The text reads, then, Simeon *bar* Jeshua, or, Simeon, the son of Jesus. In the inscription illustrated here, however, the name Jesus is written twice on the same line which is, at least, unusual (cf. Nos. 269, 270 below). At the left is also a cross-shaped mark of which the transverse bar runs somewhat obliquely and is relatively dim.

Frey II, p. 295 No. 1327. Photograph: Clermont-Ganneau I, p. 409 No. 22, courtesy Palestine Exploration Fund.

267. Inscription and Cross Mark on an Ossuary from the Mount of Offence

This text consists of only two Greek capital letters, Eta and Delta, cut deeply into the front of an ossuary. On another ossuary in the same group are the letters HΔHA, which could be a variant spelling of a woman's proper name, Ἡδέα, Hedea. Since the first two letters

266. Inscription with the Name of Jesus and Cross Mark on an Ossuary from the Mount of Offence

Here we have the name IECOYC which is presumably a variant spelling of Ἰησοῦς, Jesus. The same name occurs in Hebrew (or Aramaic) in one other of these inscriptions, where we read:

שמעון   בר   ישוע

of this name are the same as the two letters in the text here illustrated, the latter could be an abbreviation of the same name. Or the two letters could have some totally different significance, but what that might be it is difficult to say. At any rate above the two letters, and also deeply cut in the stone, is a cross of which the vertical member is longer than the horizontal, i.e., a *crux immissa* or Latin cross (cf. p. 231). To Clermont-Ganneau (I, p. 404) this cross seemed to be unmistakably the Christian symbol and confirmed the probable Christian significance of many other of the marks on the Mount of Offence ossuaries. It also seemed to him (in PEFQS 1874, p. 10) not less than a "singular coincidence" that this whole group of inscriptions, found near the Bethany road and near the site of that village, contain nearly all the names of the persons in the Gospels who belonged to that place, namely, Eleazar (Lazarus), and Simon, and Martha. He therefore described these (in PEFQS 1874, p. 9) as "monuments belonging to the beginnings of Christianity, before it had any official position, coming from the very soil where it had its birth," and he wrote: "The cave on the Mount of Offence belonged apparently to one of the earliest families which joined the new religion. In this group of sarcophagi, some of which have the Christian symbol and some have not, we are, so to speak, assisting at an actual unfolding of Christianity." Needless to say, this interpretation has been contradicted by others, yet remains deserving of very careful consideration. It is also true that Clermont-Ganneau (I, p. 404) thought it necessary to put the latest of these monuments later than the reign of Constantine, but that can hardly be allowed in view of the opinion that the use of ossuaries at Jerusalem only continued up to A.D. 70 or 135 (cf. above p. 218). Whatever their significance, the inscriptions and the marks accompanying them are according to that dating not later than about the first century of the Christian era, and it is this early date which is im-

portant and remarkable if their Christian character can be substantiated. Comparison with the Talpioth (Nos. 268ff.) and Dominus flevit (Nos. 272ff.) ossuaries appears to go far toward such substantiation.

Clermont-Ganneau in PEFQS 1874, pp. 9-10; Clermont-Ganneau I, pp. 403f., 411f.; Goodenough I, p. 131; André Parrot, *Golgotha and the Church of the Holy Sepulcher.* New York: Philosophical Library, 1957, pp. 110f., 116, 118 note 2. Photograph: Clermont-Ganneau I, p. 411 No. 29, courtesy Palestine Exploration Fund.

The Talpioth Ossuaries

268. Plan of the Tomb at Talpioth

The tomb represented by this plan was found in 1945 near the Talpioth suburb south of Jerusalem and beside the old road to Bethlehem. The tomb is entered from a courtyard. In the main burial chamber (labeled I in the plan) a rectangular depression allows for headroom and provides a bench on three sides. In the walls are five loculi of the kokim type, two in the eastern wall, two in the southern, and one in the western. In the tomb were fourteen ossuaries. Three were taken out by the workmen who found the tomb. The other eleven were recovered by E. L. Sukenik and N. Avigad in an excavation conducted very soon after the original discovery. The places where the eleven ossuaries were found are indicated by the numbers 1-11 on the plan. There was evidence that the tomb had been entered once by robbers, who had broken into several loculi and had taken out several ossuaries. Evidently disappointed at finding nothing but bones, however, they left the other ossuaries as they were and thus the archeologists found them. In the tomb was a coin of Herod Agrippa I dating from A.D. 42/43. The pottery was Late Hellenistic and Early Roman. Thus the tomb appears to have been in use from sometime in the first century B.C. until no later than the middle of the first century of the Christian era. On three ossuaries are roughly incised inscriptions in Hebrew characters which may be read and translated as follows: on ossuary No. 1, שמעון ברסבא, Simeon Barsaba; on ossuary No. 4, מרים ברת שמעון, Mariam, daughter of Simeon; and on ossuary No. 10, מתי, Matai, which can be an abbreviated form of Matthias. On two ossuaries, namely, Nos. 7 and 8, are Greek inscriptions, and on one of these, namely, No. 8, are large cross marks. As may be seen in this plan, these two ossuaries were found in what was evidently their original position at the back end of a loculus on the eastern side of the tomb. Both will be described more fully (Nos. 269, 270).

E. L. Sukenik, "The Earliest Records of Christianity," in AJA 51 (1947), pp. 351-365. Photograph: courtesy Department of Archaeology, The Hebrew University of Jerusalem.

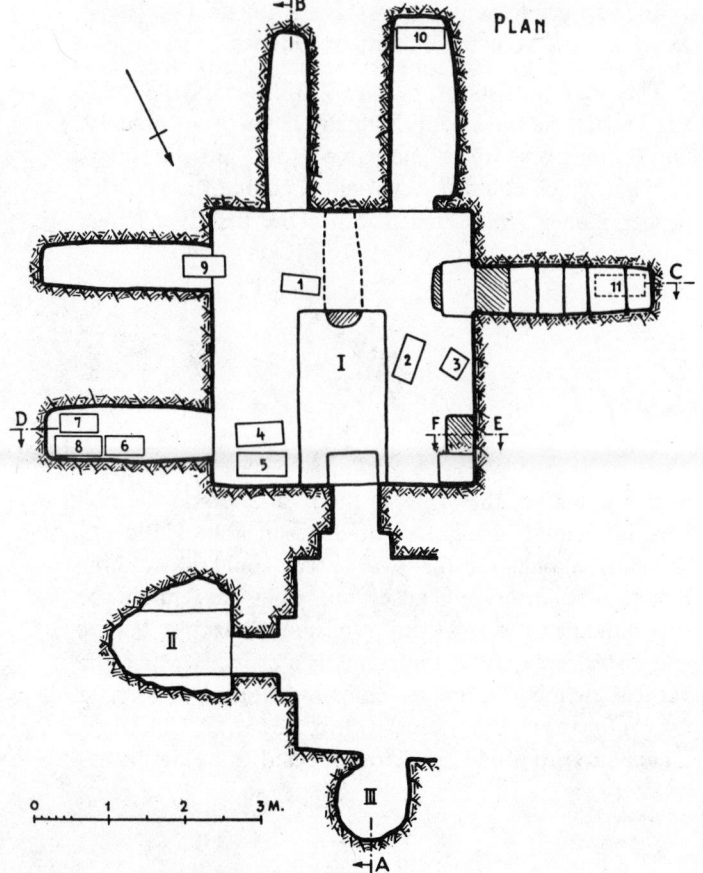

PLAN

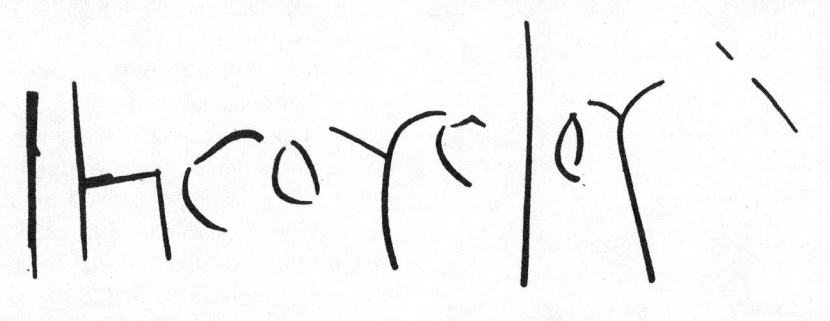

269. Photograph and Drawing of Inscription on Ossuary No. 7 from Talpioth

This ossuary is decorated on the front side with carved panels and two rosettes, a type of decoration familiar on other ossuaries of the time (cf. No. 251). On the back is the inscription shown here, drawn in charcoal and written in Greek in a single line. As far as can be seen it reads:

IHCOYC IOY

Ἰησοῦς ἰού

Jesus iou

Sukenik says flatly that there are absolutely no letters after "iou" (AJA 51, p. 363), but in his facsimile drawing of the inscription (*ibid*., p. 358) he shows a diagonal stroke to the right of the Upsilon. Hempel (ZAW 62, p. 274) thinks a character stood here, and Bagatti (p. 170 No. 17) restores two characters to read the whole as IOYΔA. If this restoration is correct then we would presumably have here the name of a certain Jesus, the son of Judah, although the reading would be more unambiguous if we had Ἰησοῦς τοῦ Ἰούδα (cf. Lk 3:33) or Ἰησοῦς υἱὸς Ἰούδα (cf. Frey I, pp. 24-25 No. 31). If, however, the name of Jesus is only followed by three letters, namely, Iota, Omicron, and Upsilon, then the

question arises as to what word these could comprise. For one thing, "Iou" represents a possible spelling of the OT name, Jehu, which is found in Greek OT manuscripts in several forms, Εἰού, Ἰηού, and Ἰού (see, e.g., IV K 9:2 LXX). In that case the inscription could be translated, "Jesus, the son of Jehu." But the spelling of the OT name in Josephus (*Ant.* VIII, 13, 7, §352; IX, 6, 1f., §§105, 110, etc.) is Ἰηοῦς and, as far as is known, Jehu was not a name in current usage at the time of this inscription. Another possibility arises in connection with the fact that "iou" is also a common ejaculation in Greek. It is a cry of woe and an expression of sorrow and grief. As such it is often twice repeated, but is also used as a single interjection (Aristophanes, *The Thesmophoriazusae*, 245 LCL III, p. 152). It is also a cry of joyful surprise (Aristophanes, *The Knights*, 1096 LCL I, p. 230), and a Scholiast says that it is written ἰοὺ ἰού when it is of woe but ἰοῦ ἰού when it is of joy (Aristophanes, *The Peace*, 317, 345 LCL II, pp. 30, 32). In the present funerary context "iou" may well be an expression of grief. To assess the significance of the entire inscription it is necessary to consider also the inscription and marks on Ossuary No. 8.

Photograph: courtesy Department of Archaeology, The Hebrew University of Jerusalem.

241

270. Inscription on Ossuary No. 8 from Talpioth

The inscription is cut with a sharp instrument into the lid of this ossuary. It reads:

IHCOYCAΛΩΘ

'Ιησοῦς ἀλώθ

Jesus aloth

The word ἀλώθ transliterates the Hebrew noun אהלות, meaning "aloes," in ss 4:14, but where the same fragrant plant is mentioned in Ps 45:8 the LXX translation (44:8) is στακτή, a word which suggests how the plant's aromatic sap oozes out in drops, and in Jn 19:39 the word for aloes is ἀλόη. Even if the word on the ossuary could be connected with "aloes," it is difficult to see what relation this word could have with the personal name which precedes it, although some think it might have been some kind of a nickname. Another suggestion sees the Greek word as the rendering of the Hebrew verb עלה in the infinitive form עלות. This verb is familiar in the OT where, in various contexts, it carries the idea of upward movement. In particular it is the verb found in Ezk 37:12-13 in the phrase, "raise you from your graves."

If the inscription on Ossuary No. 7 is to be read as "Jesus, the son of Jehu," or "Jesus, the son of Judah," and if this inscription on Ossuary No. 8 is to be read as "Jesus Aloth," with the supposition that "Aloth" is in some manner a designation of this particular person, then we presumably have in the two ossuaries the last resting places of the bones of two separate persons, each bearing the name of Jesus, a name familiar enough at that time. If, however, the words "iou" and "aloth" have some other meaning, then it may appear remarkable, as Sukenik (AJA 51, p. 363) pointed out, that the name Jesus occurs here on two ossuaries found, evidently in their original positions, side by side in the same loculus. In family graves, such as the tombs with ossuaries seem usually to be, it could of course be possible that a grandfather and a grandson might bear the same name (rarely a father and a son), but the bones of separate generations would hardly be collected at the same time and deposited thus in the same place. It was likewise observed with respect to the ossuary from the Mount of Olives (No. 266), that the occurrence on the same ossuary of the name Jesus repeated twice was very unusual. The possibility arises, therefore, that the name Jesus stands on the present two ossuaries (even as on the ossuary in No. 266 above) not as the name of the person whose bones were collected there, but in some quite different connection. In other words it is possible that there is a reference here to the Founder of Christianity, and it is possible that in each case (on the two ossuaries here and on the one in No. 266) there is intended some kind of an appeal to Jesus on behalf of the deceased one whose bones are contained in the chest. In this light it is possible to interpret the first Talpioth inscription (No. 269) as calling upon Jesus with a word of lament for the deceased one, and to interpret the second (No. 270) as appealing to Jesus with a request that the deceased one may arise: "Jesus, help!" and "Jesus, let (him who rests here) arise!" (Gustafsson). If these inscriptions are to be read as Christian, it may also be significant that Ossuary No. 1, found in the main burial chamber of the same tomb, bears the name Barsaba (cf. above No. 268), a family name otherwise known only from the NT (Ac 1:23; 15:22, Barsabas or Barsabbas).

E. L. Sukenik in AJA 51 (1947), pp. 363-365; Berndt Gustafsson in NTS 3 (1956-57), pp. 65-69. Photograph: courtesy Department of Archaeology, The Hebrew University of Jerusalem.

271. Cross Mark on Ossuary No. 8 from Talpioth

In the center of each side of Ossuary No. 8 is a large cross mark, drawn with charcoal. The one shown here, on one long side of the ossuary, has bars of quite equal length. The other three have bars of somewhat irregular length. The large size and prominent placement of the cross marks makes it evident that they have a definite purpose. Probably they were drawn by the same person who wrote the inscription (No. 270) on the lid of the ossuary. That the marks were simply intended to show that the ossuary was in use (Willoughby) is, therefore, unlikely. That they represent the Jewish *taw* (Dinkler) is possible if the tomb is only the burial place of a Jewish family. But that the marks are Christian cross marks is also possible and would be in harmony with the pos-

sible Christian interpretation of the accompanying inscriptions; in that case, this could be considered as the tomb of a Jewish family, at least some members of which were of the Christian faith.

Carl H. Kraeling, "Christian Burial Urns?" in BA 9 (1946), pp. 16-20; Harold R. Willoughby in JBL 68 (1949), pp. 61-65; J. Simons in *Jaarbericht No. 11 van het vooraziatisch-egyptisch Genootschap Ex Oriente Lux* (1949-50), pp. 74-78; J. Hempel in ZAW 62 (1960), pp. 273-274; Ethelbert Stauffer in ZNW 43 (1950-51), p. 62; B. S. J. Isserlin in PEQ 1953, p. 79; Erich Dinkler, "Zur Geschichte des Kreuzsymbols," in ZTK 48 (1951), pp. 148-172; and in JAC 5 (1962), pp. 109-110; Goodenough I, pp. 130-132; Duncan Fishwick, "The Talpioth Ossuaries Again," in NTS 10 (1963-64), pp. 49-61. Photograph: courtesy Department of Archaeology, The Hebrew University of Jerusalem.

The Dominus Flevit Ossuaries

272. Plan and Sections of a Portion of the Cemetery at Dominus flevit

When a new wall was built at the Franciscan sanctuary of Dominus flevit (see above No. 123) on the Mount of Olives, a previously unknown ancient cemetery was discovered and, beginning in 1953, excavated by Father Bagatti of the Studium Biblicum Franciscanum in Jerusalem. The cemetery is very extensive and comprises more than five hundred known burial places. The evidence shows (Bagatti pp. 43-44, 163-164) that it was in use in two different periods. In the first period the graves were of the kokim type, the coins are from the time of the Hasmoneans to the second year of the Procurator Valerius Gratus, i.e., from 135 B.C. to A.D. 15/16, and the graves were used probably up to A.D. 70 (possibly A.D. 135) at the latest (cf. p. 218). In the second period the graves are characterized by arcosolia, the coins are from Gallus (A.D. 251-253) to the

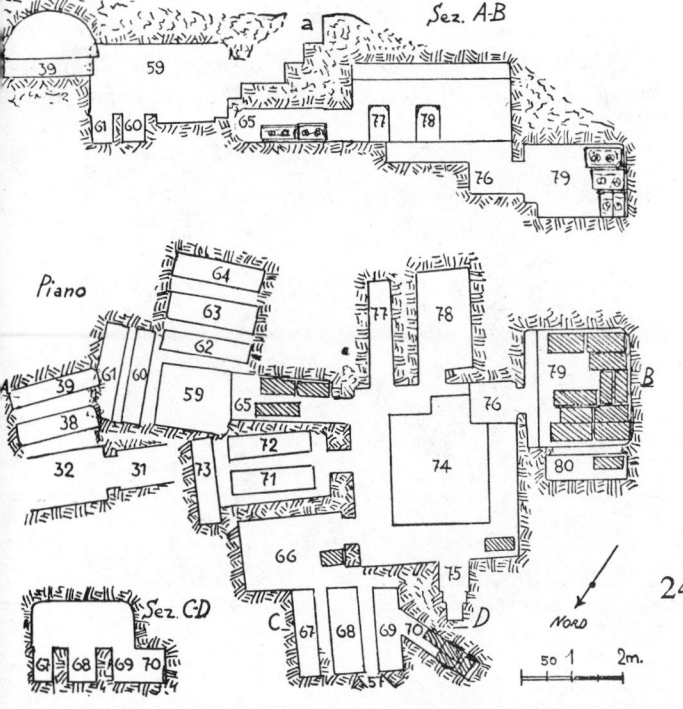

sixteenth year of Heraclius (A.D. 626), and the use of the cemetery was at its height in the third and fourth centuries, especially the fourth. Besides the coins there were pottery lamps and jars and other objects of glass and stone. In the graves were seven sarcophagi and 122 ossuaries or fragments thereof, all from the first period of use of the cemetery. Inscriptions and signs on the ossuaries will be considered in what follows. The illustration represents only a small portion of the entire cemetery, lying near the southeast corner of the region excavated. In this area, shown here in both plan and sections, are the burial places numbered 65 to 80 by the excavators, which will be mentioned frequently below. The area comprises a central chamber (No. 74) from which there is access to burial places on all sides and notably, through a descent to the south, to a grotto (No. 79), measuring 2.20 by 2.10 meters, in which were stored no less than fourteen ossuaries (Nos. 12-25 Bagatti pp. 52-53).

RB 61 (1954), pp. 568-570; A. Ferrua in RAC 30 (1954), p. 268; P. B. Bagatti, "Scoperta di un cimitero giudeo-cristiano al 'Dominus flevit,'" in *Studii Biblici Franciscani Liber Annuus* III (1952-53), pp. 149-184; B. Bagatti and J. T. Milik, *Gli scavi del "Dominus flevit" (Monte Oliveto–Gerusalemme)*, Part I, *La necropoli del periodo romano*. PSBF 13. Jerusalem: Tipografia dei PP. Francescani, 1958 (= Bagatti); J. van der Ploeg in JSS 5 (1960), pp. 81-82; M. Avi-Yonah in IEJ 11 (1961), pp. 91-94; Bagatti p. 7 Fig. 3. Photograph: courtesy Terra Santa.

273. Inscription with the Name Menahem from Dominus flevit

More than forty inscriptions have been found on the "Dominus flevit" ossuaries (Milik in Bagatti pp. 70-

109). They are either roughly incised or drawn in charcoal, and written in Hebrew, Aramaic, or Greek. There are fewer inscriptions in Hebrew, but about the same number in Aramaic and in Greek. As is customary in ossuary inscriptions (cf. No. 257), these ordinarily give the name of the deceased, and sometimes indicate a family relationship. Sometimes they also specify his work in daily life, as is the case in this inscription, No. 22. It was found on ossuary No. 83 in burial place No. 299, which is a considerable distance to the northwest of the group of burial places already mentioned, Nos. 65-80 (above No. 273). The Hebrew text, incised in the stone, may be transcribed as follows:

$$\text{מנחם מן}$$
$$\text{בנא יכים}$$
$$\text{כהן}$$

The first word in the first line is the name Menahem, a name found also in Inscription No. 26. This name is known in the OT (II K 15:14ff.) where, in LXX manuscripts (IV K 15:16), it is rendered Μαναήμ or Μαναήν. In the last form it is found in Ac 13:1. This Menahem in the present inscription is then identified as being from among the Bene Yakim, "the sons of Yakim," probably the family of Jachin (יכין LXX Ἰαχίν, Ἀχίμ) mentioned in I Ch 24:17. Finally in the last line he is described as a *cohen* or priest. While most of the ossuary inscriptions at Dominus flevit probably belong to the first part of the first century of the Christian era, this one is thought to come from before the turn of the century and to be one of the oldest of the entire group.

Bagatti p. 73 Fig. 18, 1, pp. 89f. No. 22, Tav. 29 Fot. 85. Photograph: courtesy Terra Santa.

274. Inscription with the Names Martha and Mary from Dominus flevit

This is inscription No. 7 b on ossuary No. 27 in burial place No. 70 (see above No. 272). It is cut in

large but shallow grooves on a long side of the ossuary. It is read by Milik as follows:

מרתה
מרים
Martha
Miriam

The first name is also found in Aramaic as מרתא and in Greek as Μάρθα. The second name is found as given here in both Hebrew and Aramaic. In Greek it is found in the same form Μαριάμ (indeclinable); with the *m* omitted to make Μαρία, Μαρίας; with a vowel added and the *m* sometimes doubled too, Μαριά[μ]μη, Μαριά[μ]μης; or with an *s* added to make Μαριᾶς, Μαριάδος. The same two Hebrew names are also found on the cover of the ossuary and on the other long side. In the last case we have the spelling מריה for the second name, corresponding to Μαρία, Maria.

Bagatti p. 75 Fig. 19, 3, pp. 77-79 No. 7, Tav. 28 Fot. 77. Photograph: courtesy Terra Santa.

275. Inscription with the Name Simeon Bar . . .
    from Dominus flevit

This is inscription No. 11 found written in charcoal on ossuary No. 19 in burial place No. 79 (see above No. 272). Milik reads the first five characters as Shin, Mem, 'Ayin, Waw, Nun, and the next two as Beth and Resh written together. Thus far, then, we have:

שמעון בר
Simeon Bar

The last four characters are difficult to be sure of but could be Yodh, Waw, Nun, and He, to give:

יונה
Jonah

Simeon and Jonah are Hebrew names of the OT, and Bar is the Aramaic "son." In the Greco-Roman period Simeon was a specially popular name, probably in part because of its equivalence to the Greek name Σίμων, Simon. In the Greek of Mt 16:17 we have Σίμων Βαριωνᾶ (or Βὰρ Ἰωνᾶ), which would be the exact equivalent of the above. It must be emphasized, however, that the reading of the last word in the ossuary inscription remains uncertain. The name Simeon occurs also in inscription No. 5 on ossuary No. 8 in burial place No.

65, and in inscription 34 a and b on ossuary No. 107 in burial place No. 437.

In addition to the names just mentioned there are many other names in the Dominus flevit inscriptions which are familiar in the NT as well. A tabulation follows:

Name	Original Form	Inscription No.	Ossuary No.	Burial Place No.
Eleazar (Lazarus)	אלעזר	25	52	376
Jairus	Ιαειρος	1	31	42
John	[Ιω]ανης	18	68	280
Jonathan (Ac 4:6 D)	יהונתן	16	36	80
Joseph	יוסף	20	75	297
Judah (see below No. 278)	Ιουδα	13 a	21	79
Judas	Ιουδας	18	68	220
Martha (see above No. 274)	מרתה	7	27	70
Miriam (Mary) (see above No. 274)	מרים	7	27	70
Mattia (Matthias)	מתיה	3	33	55
Menahem (see above No. 273)	מנחם	22	83	299
Salome	שלום	8	29	70
Sapphira (see below No. 278)	שפירא	13 b	21	79
Simeon (see above No. 275)	שמעון	11	19	79
Yeshua (Jesus)	ישוע	29	93	425
Zechariah	Ζαχαριου	30	95	431

In comparison with this list there may also be recalled the NT names found on the ossuaries from the Mount of Offence (see above No. 265) and from Talpioth (above Nos. 268-270):

Mount of Offence	Talpioth
Eleazar (Lazarus)	Barsaba
Jesus	Jesus
Judah	Judah (?)
Martha	Mariam (Mary)
Marias (Mary)	Matai (Matthias)
Nathanael	Simeon
Salome	
Simeon	

As for the frequency of occurrence of the several names on the ossuaries and in the NT, it is about the same.

Bagatti p. 83 No. 11, p. 86 Fig. 22, 1, Tav. 29 Fot. 81; Milik in Bagatti p. 108. Photograph: courtesy Terra Santa.

276. Inscription with the Name Shalamsion and a Cross Mark from Dominus flevit

There are also a number of signs on the ossuaries which, like the inscriptions, are either incised or drawn in charcoal (Bagatti pp. 63-69). Some of these appear to have served only a practical purpose. In several cases, for example, there is a mark, perhaps a triangle or a curved mark, on the end of the chest and a corresponding mark on the end of the cover just above, these evidently being intended to show how the lid is to be placed on the chest (cf. No. 264) (see ossuary No. 64 from burial place No. 459, Bagatti p. 54 No. 64, p. 65 Fig. 17, 17 and 18, Tav. 27 Fot. 74, and p. 100 inscription No. 43, Tav. 37 Fot. 117; ossuary No. 89 from burial place No. 301, Bagatti p. 55 No. 89, Tav. 27 Fot. 72; and ossuary No. 115 from burial place No. 437, Bagatti p. 54 Fig. 16, 115, p. 57 No. 115, and pp. 97-98 inscription No. 37, p. 91 Fig. 23, 6, Tav. 34 Fot. 105). But other signs, in the absence of any apparent utilitarian significance, appear to be intended as symbols. On ossuary No. 12 from burial place No. 79 there is a large, erect, approximately equilateral (the vertical and horizontal members measure 13 and 10 centimeters respectively) cross mark incised on the end of the chest, and a somewhat smaller cross mark incised in the sideways position on the end of the rounded cover (Bagatti p. 52 No. 12, p. 54 Fig. 16, 12,

246

pp. 64-66 Fig. 17, 2, 8). This ossuary is otherwise undecorated and without any inscription, but in other cases a crossmark accompanies an inscription. The illustration shows inscription No. 17 on ossuary No. 1 from burial place No. 84 at Dominus flevit. The Hebrew name which is cut with deep, broad strokes into the upper right-hand portion of one long side of the chest, and repeated in somewhat smaller carving on the corner of the lid above, is read as follows: שלמצין.

This name plainly incorporates the word *shalom*, meaning "peace," and the name of the holy hill at Jerusalem, Zion (spelled ציון in the OT, cf. No. 137). That it is indeed a personal name is shown by its occurrence in the same Hebrew form on an ossuary from the Mount of Offence (cf. above No. 265), where the name is followed by the designation, "daughter of Shimeon the Priest" (Clermont-Ganneau I, pp. 386-392). The same name in Greek is to be read, with restorations, on another ossuary from Dominus flevit (inscription No. 2 on ossuary No. 32 from burial place No. 42; Bagatti pp. 71-74, Tav. 35 Fot. 109): [Σαλα]μσι[ων]. In Josephus (*Ant.* XVIII 5, 4 §130) the same name occurs as that of the daughter of Herod the Great and Mariamme, Σαλαμψιώ. We may render the name, therefore, as Shalam-Zion or Shalamsion, and understand it as meaning etymologically, "Peace of Zion." Looking again at the name on the side of the chest in the photograph (No. 276), we see that immediately under the Lamedh and the Mem is an approximately equilateral cross mark carved in the sideways position.

Bagatti pp. 67, 75 Fig. 19, 6, pp. 87-88 No. 17, Tav. 29 Fot. 84. Photograph: courtesy Terra Santa.

277. Inscription with the Name Diogenes and a Cross Mark from Dominus flevit

This is inscription No. 21 a on ossuary No. 81 from burial place No. 299 at Dominus flevit. The text is cut deeply into the cover of the ossuary, and reads:

ΔΙΟΓΕΝΗΣΠΡΟΣΗΛΥΤΟΣ
ΖΗΝΑ
Διογένης προσήλυτος
Ζηνᾶ

On the edge of the chest is the similar incised inscription:

Διογένης Ζηνᾶ π[ρ]οσήλυτος

This was, therefore, the ossuary of a man with the widely used Greek name, Diogenes, and he was probably the son of a certain Zena. He was also a proselyte, i.e., a convert to the Jewish faith (cf. Mt 23:15). In two other Dominus flevit inscriptions there is also mention of a proselyte, namely, in inscription No. 13 which will be cited below (No. 278), and in inscription No. 31 on ossuary No. 97 in burial place No. 432 (Bagatti p. 82 Fig. 21, 6, p. 95 No. 31, Tav. 32 Fot. 97), which reads:

שלם הגירה
Salome the proselyte

Returning to inscription No. 21 a with the name of Diogenes the proselyte, it may be noted in the present photograph that there is a cross mark, incised in the sideways position, considerably below and to the left of the inscription. Likewise the similar inscription on the edge of the ossuary is followed by a similar cross mark.

Bagatti p. 89 No. 21, Tav. 36 Fot. 113. Photograph: courtesy Terra Santa.

278. Photograph and Drawing of Marks on Ossuary
No. 21 from Dominus flevit

Ossuary No. 21 (Bagatti p. 52) is one of the fourteen ossuaries found in burial place No. 79 at Dominus flevit (cf. above No. 272). It is painted in red with rosette decorations. On the center of the cover an inscription (Bagatti pp. 84-85 No. 13 b, p. 86 Fig. 22, 3, Tav. 29 Fot. 82) is traced in charcoal with a single name:

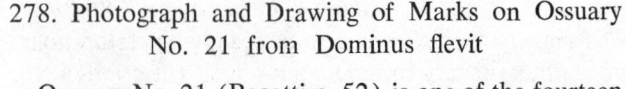

שפירא
Sapphira

Inside the ossuary, below the edge of one long side, is a longer inscription in Greek (Bagatti pp. 84-85 No. 13 a, p. 91 Fig. 23, 4, Tav. 35 Fot. 112):

ΙΟΥΔΑΝΠΡΟCΗΛΥΤΟ
ΤΥΡΑ

The name Ἰούδα with which the inscription begins can be the genitive of Ἰούδας, which can be rendered either Judah (cf. Mt 1:2, etc.) or Judas (cf. Mt 13:55, etc.). The abbreviation ν stands for νεώτερος, "younger." The next word is plainly προσήλυτος, "proselyte" (Mt 23:15), in the genitive, lacking only the final Upsilon. The word in the second line presents difficulties. If it could be read as Τύρου it could be the genitive of Τύρος, the city of Tyre, and could refer to the man's place of origin. The word is more probably τυρα, however, and one interpretation sees this as the genitive of τυρᾶς and the latter as a popular form of τυροποιός, which means a cheese maker. In this case the text reads:

Ἰουδᾶ ν(εωτέρου) προσηλύτο[υ] τυρᾶ
(Bones) of Judah the Younger, a proselyte,
a cheese maker

This ossuary is of special interest for the signs, traced in charcoal, on one short end; the fragments bearing the signs are shown in this photograph and drawing. The sign at the right is composed almost unmistakably of the Greek letters Chi and Rho written together as a monogram. Attestation of the use of this monogram long before the time of Constantine has been presented above, and several possibilities of its interpretation have been given (see pp. 233f.). Among the several possibilities of interpretation there is some reason for taking the sign here as an abbreviation of "Christian," i.e., Χρ(ιστιανός). This designation for followers of Jesus was used at Antioch about A.D. 44 (Ac 11:26) and at Rome about A.D. 64 (Tacitus, Annals xv 44, *Christianos*), hence was probably well known in many places by the middle of the first century. At both Antioch and Rome it was applied primarily to persons who had come from paganism (cf. Adolf Harnack, *The Mission and Expansion of Christianity in the First Three Centuries*, 2d. ed. 1908, II p. 126) and, according to the inscription inside this ossuary, this Judah was a proselyte, i.e., he had been a pagan before coming into Judaism and (if the monogram indeed indicates this) into Christianity. Yet a reading of the monogram as an abbreviation of "Christ," i.e., Χρ(ιστός), is also possible, and the occurrence of the monogram with this meaning seems otherwise to be attested earlier and more frequently than for any other meaning. Moreover, understandings based upon taking the Rho as standing for one hundred and therewith for the promise to Abraham, or for the word "help," remain possible.

The sign to the left of the Chi and Rho is scarcely to be made out in the photograph, but close inspection reveals it as reproduced in the drawing. It appears that it could be an eight-pointed star or a monogram of some sort. If it is of Christian significance it could be the familiar combination of Iota and Chi to stand for Jesus Christ (cf. above p. 232) plus a horizontal stroke for the addition of a cross mark or, more simply stated, a combination of two cross marks, Χ and +.

Burzachechi in *Atti della Pontificia Accademia Romana di archeologia, Rendiconti* XXVIII (1954-55), pp. 200-201 No. 6; Bagatti pp. 64-65 Fig. 17, 1, pp. 178-179, Tav. 27 Fot. 75, and Frontispiece; Testa pp. 137-139 No. 25, pp. 401-402 No. 16; Dinkler in JAC 5 (1962), pp. 96, 111. Photograph: courtesy Terra Santa.

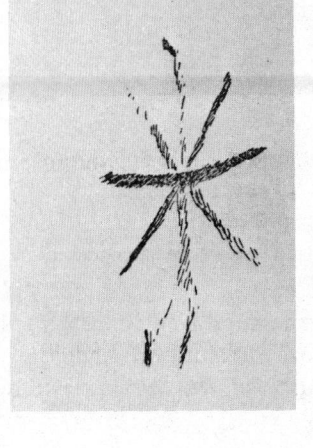

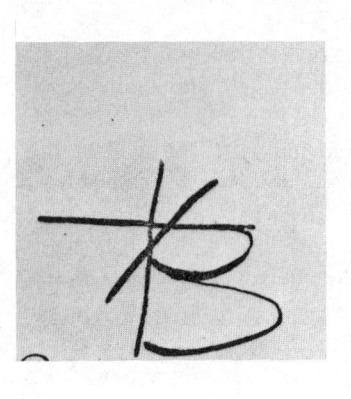

279. Photograph and Drawing of Marks on Ossuary No. 18 from Dominus flevit

Ossuary No. 18 (Bagatti p. 52) was also found in burial place No. 79 at Dominus flevit. Cut into the cover of the ossuary, near one corner, is the combination of marks shown in this photograph and drawing. Disregarding the crack toward the right, we see a roughly vertical and equilateral cross mark. From the right arm of this a stroke descends in two curves to complete what appears to be the capital letter Beta. Then a diagonal stroke is cut deeply across the whole. All this together can be seen as a monogram comprising the letters Iota, Chi, and Beta. In the light of parallels noted above (pp. 232, 234), it can be understood as standing for Ἰησοῦς Χριστὸς Βοήθια, with some such meaning as "Jesus Christ (is our) help." For the concept of "help" (βοήθεια) reference may be made to Heb 4:16, and to the saying of Justin Martyr (*Dialogue* 30, 3): "For we call him Helper and Redeemer (βοηθὸν γὰρ ἐκεῖνον καὶ λυτρωτὴν καλοῦμεν), the power of whose name even the demons fear."

With respect to the items which have now been shown from Dominus flevit (Nos. 273-279) it is of interest to note that many of the signs which are capable of a Christian interpretation and many of the names which are also known in the NT come from the group of burial places Nos. 65-80 and in particular from the one burial place No. 79 (cf. No. 272). In burial place No. 79 were ossuaries No. 12 marked with + and X, No. 18 with Iota, Chi, and Beta in a monogram, No. 19 with the name Simeon Bar . . . , and No. 21 with Chi and Rho in a monogram and the names Judah and Sapphira; while also in burial places 65-80 outside of 79 were ossuaries No. 1 with a cross mark accompanying the name Shalamsion, No. 27 with the names Martha and Mary, No. 29 with the name Salome, and No. 36 with the name Jonathan. Where there are, thus, signs that can be Christian, and names that are frequent or prominent in the NT and therefore might have been preferred by Christians, it surely comes within the realm of possibility that at least this area in particular is a burial place of Jewish families some of whose members had become Christians.

Bagatti pp. 64-65 Fig. 17, 3, Tav. 27 Fot. 71; Testa pp. 396-398 Figs. 145, 10, Tav. 41 Fot. 4. Photograph: courtesy Terra Santa.

Herculaneum

280. Wall Mark at Herculaneum

For comparison and elucidation with respect to the marks which have been noted in Palestine, brief mention may also be made of some similar marks from outside of Palestine. In Italy the town of Herculaneum lies at the foot of the volcano Vesuvius and, like the city of Pompeii ten miles to the east, was destroyed by the eruption of that volcano in A.D. 79. The cross-shaped mark shown in the photograph was found in 1938 in an upper room of the so-called Bicentenary House. It is a depression in a stucco panel and could be where an object of the same shape had been affixed to the wall

and then removed. There are nail holes in the depression and also elsewhere in the panel. The shape seems unmistakably to be that of a Latin cross (cf. p. 231). If a wooden cross had been nailed to the wall at this point, then removed and a wooden covering nailed over the area, it would account for what can still be seen. The upper room with the cross could then have been some sort of a private Christian chapel. The removal of the cross and the covering over of the area could have been done either by the Christians themselves or by others, and a likely time for this might have been during persecution such as that by Nero in A.D. 64. At any rate the mark certainly antedates the year 79.

Amadeo Maiuri in *Rendiconti della Pontificia Accademia Romana di Archeologia* 15 (1939), pp. 193-218; L. de Bruyne in RAC 21 (1945), pp. 281-309; Erich Dinkler in ZTK 48 (1951), pp. 158-159; William L. Holladay in JBR 19 (1951), pp. 16-19; André Parrot, *Golgotha and the Church of the Holy Sepulcher*, p. 117. Photograph: courtesy William L. Holladay.

281. Stand at Herculaneum

The piece of wooden furniture shown in this photograph stood against the wall beneath the panel with the cross mark in the upper room in the Bicentenary House at Herculaneum. When found it was entirely covered with the deposit of the volcanic eruption of A.D.

79. From its position at the foot of the cross it could have been a sort of altar. These two items taken together, the cross mark left in the wall above and this stand and possible altar beneath, strengthen the likelihood that the upper room was indeed a small chapel used by some early Christian or Christians.

Photograph: courtesy William L. Holladay.

Cross Marks in the Catacombs

282. A Painted Inscription in the Jewish Catacomb in the Villa Torlonia

In the Jewish catacombs at Rome (cf. Nos. 242-249) very few marks in the form of a cross are to be found, but this photograph shows one example. In the cata-

comb in the Villa Torlonia this inscription, painted in red, was found on a broken piece of stucco grave closure in a loculus at the point numbered 24 on the right side of the corridor letter C-G on the Plan (above No. 247). So far as it is preserved the text reads:

ΠΑΓΧΑΡΙΟC Παγχάριος
ΚΑΛΩC ΕΝΘΑΔΕ καλῶς ἐνθάδε

How much more of the original inscription is lacking at the left or right or both is uncertain. By comparison with many other examples (above No. 243, etc.), it may be supposed that the word κεῖται was used, or may be understood, so that the translation can be: "Pancharios lies here honorably." In other examples, however, the word βιώσας is connected with the word καλῶς. Thus an inscription on a marble plaque in the Jewish catacomb in the Vigna Randanini on the Via Appia (Frey I, pp. 81-82 No. 118; cf. also Nos. 9, 23, 82, 117, 119, 336, 353, 411, 509, 537) begins:

ΖΩΤΙΚΟΣ ΑΡΧΩΝ ΕΝΘΑΔΕ
ΚΕΙΜΕ ΚΑΛΩΣ ΒΕΙΩCAC

Ζωτικὸς ἄρχων ἐνθάδε κεῖμ(αι) καλῶς β(ε)ιώσας

(I,) Zotikos, an archon, lie here, having lived well (*or*, honorably)

By this analogy we could supply both words in the inscription shown above, to read: βιώσας] καλῶς ἐνθάδε [κεῖται, and then the translation would be: "Pancharios, having lived honorably, lies here." Beneath the text are three drawings also in red paint. The one at the left represents something which it is difficult to identify, but which may be a fruit, and, if so, perhaps an *ethrog* (cf. No. 243). The one in the middle appears plainly to be an ivy leaf, as is found elsewhere very frequently (cf. No. 243). The one at the right is a swastika or *crux gammata* with the outer arms turned to the right (cf. p. 231). These outer arms appear, however, to be painted in more lightly than the main branches of the cross, and the one at the bottom cannot even be made out with certainty. It could be surmised, therefore, that the outer arms were a later addition, and that there was originally here an equilateral cross. In that case the question could be raised as to whether this is an example of the Hebrew *taw* used with connotations of deliverance as an appropriate symbol to accompany a grave inscription (cf. p. 235). Also it could be asked if the alteration to a swastika was made after the original cross mark had been too widely recognized as a Christian symbol to be any longer appropriate in a Jewish catacomb.

Beyer and Lietzmann, *Die jüdische Katakombe der Villa Torlonia in Rom*, pp. 5-6, p. 32 No. 24, Pl. 16 No. 24; Frey I, pp. 32-33 No. 48; Goodenough II, p. 43. Photograph: Beyer and Lietzmann, *op.cit.*, Pl. 16 No. 24, courtesy Walter de Gruyter & Co., Berlin.

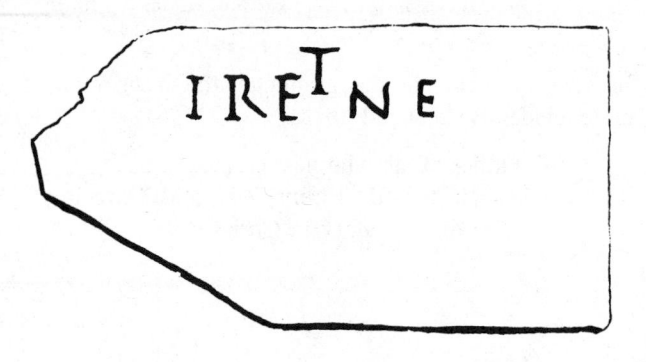

283. Rufina Inscription in the Catacomb of Lucina

Of the Christian catacombs at Rome the four oldest are those which have the names of Lucina, Callistus, Domitilla, and Priscilla, all of which probably originated at least by the middle of the second century (FLAP pp. 456ff.). In the Lucina catacomb the inscription shown in this photograph was found still in its original place on the closure of a loculus. It is a simple epitaph containing the name of the deceased ΡΟΥΦΙΝΑ, Rufina, a feminine name (Preisigke, *Namenbuch*, col. 355), and the single word ΕΙΡΗΝΗ, peace. Beneath is an equilateral or Greek cross (cf. p. 231). The date is about the middle of the second century (Wilpert) or at the turn from the second to the third century (Styger).

De Rossi I Pl. XVIII No. 1; Wilpert, "La croce," p. 5; DACL 3:2 col. 3056; Styger p. 28. Photograph: Styger Pl. 5 fac, p. 32 (Berlin: Verlag für Kunstwissenschaft, 1933).

284. Irene Inscription in the Catacomb of Callistus

This inscription was found in the oldest part of the Catacomb of Callistus and may date from the middle of the second century (Wilpert). The epitaph consists only of the name of the deceased, IRENE, but between the third and fourth letters and raised above the line is inserted a Latin letter T, corresponding to the Greek Tau, and constituting a form of the cross. In this connection it will be remembered (above p. 230) that Tertullian (*Against Marcion* III 22) spoke of "the mark Tau" on the foreheads of the men of Jerusalem (Ezk 9:4), and added: "Now the Greek letter Tau and our own letter T is the very form of the cross."

De Rossi I Pl. XLIII No. 14; Wilpert, "La croce," p. 13. Photograph: De Rossi, *ibid.* (1864).

285. A Cross in Anchor Form in the Catacomb of Domitilla

This broken marble plaque is also found in the Catacomb of Domitilla. Here the cross is in the form of an anchor, with a fish on either side. In this case perhaps the fishes are Christians caught by the cross. The circle on the upper part of the cross can be a sun disk. At the right can be also an Alpha and Omega combined with a cross.

Emil Bock and Robert Goebel, *Die Katakomben, Bilder aus der Welt des frühen Christentums.* Stuttgart: Urachhaus, 1930, p. 27 and No. 27. Photograph: JF.

286. Painted Sign in the Catacomb of Priscilla

This sign is painted in red on a tile found still attached to a loculus in the Catacomb of Priscilla. The date is probably the middle of the second century (Wilpert). What the marks at the right should signify is not evident. The marks at the left consist essentially of the letters Iota and Eta, the two first letters of the name of Jesus in Greek. These are combined in a way somewhat like that in the monogram already mentioned (above p. 232), but in this case the letters may be considered to be set one after the other, with a horizontal stroke extended through and beyond both, resulting in the ap-

pearance of three Greek crosses set side by side and connected.

G. B. de Rossi, "L'epigrafia primitiva priscilliana," in BAC 1886, pp. 34-171, especially p. 78 No. 101, p. 171 Pl. XI No. 3; Wilpert, "La croce," pp. 5-6; DACL 3:2, col. 3056. Photograph: Wilpert, *op.cit.*, p. 6 Fig. 1 (1902).

287. Trisomus Inscription in the Catacomb of Priscilla

The oldest area in the Catacomb of Priscilla is the so-called Hypogeum of the Acilians. A grave for three bodies (*trisomus*) was dug in the floor of one passageway and must, therefore, represent a second period in the utilization of this area. The inscribed marble plaque shown in the illustration was found still in its original position over this grave. The date is probably still in the second century or in the third (de Rossi), but not as late as the fourth. In the following transcription of the Greek text spaces are left between words in correspondence with the original, in which a small conventional sign marks the spaces in each case except the first (after the first two words). In the two cases where the connective καί occurs it is abbreviated with a stroke over the Kappa. Ligature of Nu and Pi and Nu and Tau will be noted in the first line, and of Eta and Nu in the second line (three times). The inscription terminates with two signs of which at least the first, the Chi Rho monogram, is to be read as a part of the text.

ΟΠΑΤΗΡ ΤΩΝΠΑΝΤΩΝ ΟΥΣ ΕΠΟΙΗΣΕΣ $\overline{\text{Κ}}$
ΠΑΡΕΛΑΒΗΣ ΕΙΡΗΝΗΝ ΖΟΗΝ $\overline{\text{Κ}}$ ΜΑΡΚΕΛΛΟΝ
ΣΟΙΔΟΘΑ ΕΝ ☧

ὁ πατὴρ τῶν πάντων οὓς ἐποίησες καὶ
παρελάβης Εἰρήνην, Ζόην, καὶ Μάρκελλον
σοὶ δόξα ἐν Χριστῷ

In spite of errors in the grammar, the inscription is quite evidently intended to say:

> O Father of all, who hast created and
> taken (to thyself) Eirene, Zoe, and Marcellus,
> to thee be glory in Christ.

The sign which follows the Chi Rho monogram is an anchor. According to Heb 6:19 hope is the anchor of the soul, and the anchor therefore became a symbol of confidence that the deceased was safe in the harbor of eternal peace. Like other appropriately formed objects connected with a ship (see above p. 231), the anchor was also recognized as a form of the cross. In this light the anchor says that the cross is the foundation of Christian hope. If, in the present inscription the anchor is to be read as a part of the text, the last line could be taken to say: "To thee be glory. In Christ (is) our hope." But if the last line is read as in our translation above, then the anchor can be taken as a separate sign, a mark accompanying many other epitaphs in the catacombs, expressive of the Christian hope, founded in the cross, that the deceased will arrive safely in the port of eternal peace.

De Rossi in BAC 1888-89, pp. 31-33; DACL 1:2, col. 2027; Styger pp. 104-105. On the fact that the cross mark is found in the catacomb inscriptions but scarcely at all in the earlier catacomb paintings, see Joseph Wilpert, *Die Malereien der Katakomben Roms.* Freiburg im Breisgau: Herder, 1903. Textband, p. 496. Photograph: Styger Pl. 18 fac. p. 112 (Berlin: Verlag für Kunstwissenschaft, 1933).

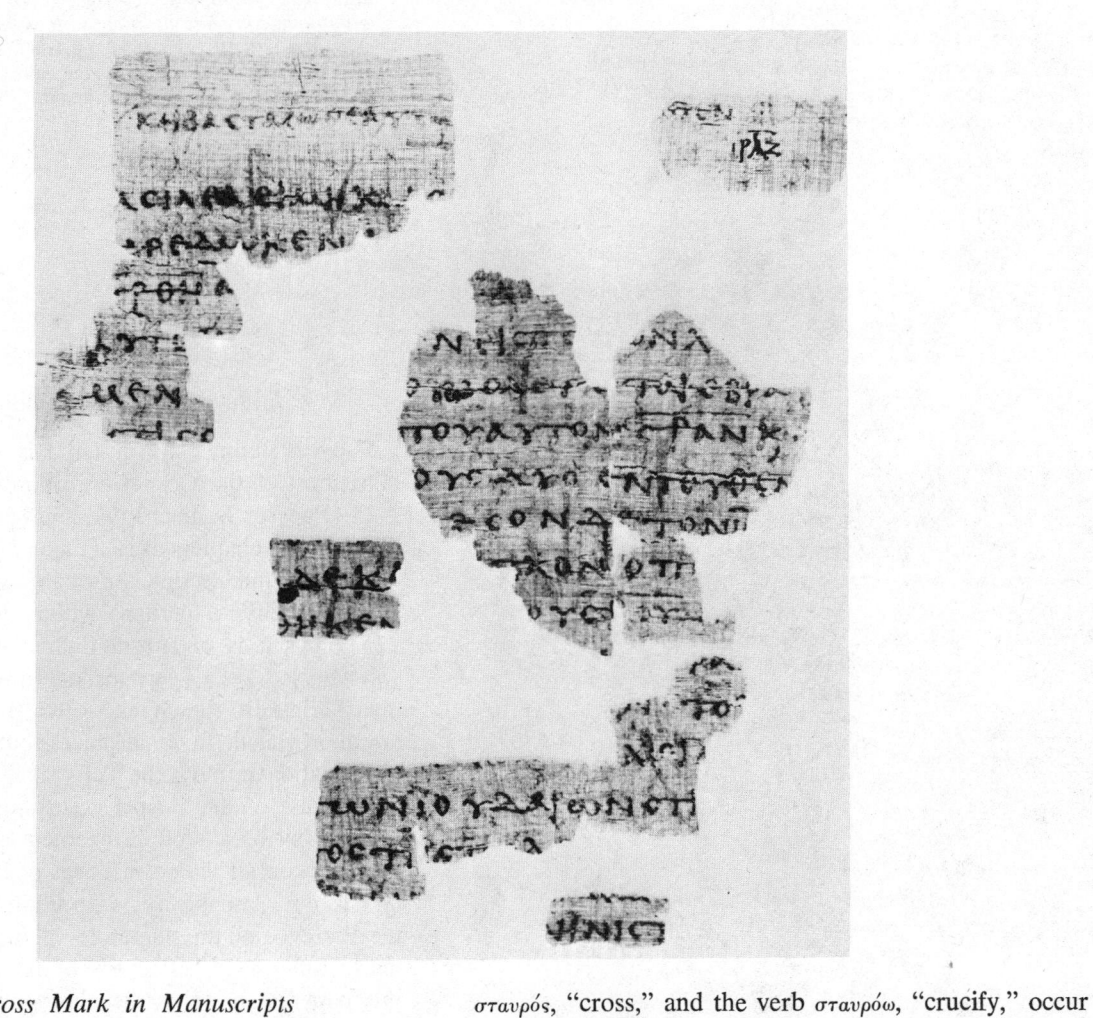

The Cross Mark in Manuscripts

288. A Page in Papyrus Bodmer II (P⁶⁶)

Papyrus Bodmer II (P⁶⁶) is a manuscript in codex form with numbered pages which contains most of the Gospel according to John, Chapters 1-14, and fragments of the rest of the Gospel through Chapter 21. It was probably written about A.D. 200 if not even earlier. In the manuscript at most of the places where the noun σταυρός, "cross," and the verb σταυρόω, "crucify," occur an abbreviation of the word is employed in which the Tau and the Rho are written together to make the sign ⳨ (cf. above p. 234). The present photograph shows the extant fragments of page 137 (ΡΛΖ) in the codex. The beginning of Line 3 contains that section of Jn 19:16 where it is stated that Pilate delivered Jesus "to be crucified." Here the verb σταυρωθῇ is abbreviated σ ⳨ θη. The initial Sigma is badly preserved but the

253

remaining letters are plainly legible together with the line over them which marks the abbreviation. Line 6 contains the mention of Golgotha in Jn 19:17, and continues with the opening words of Jn 19:18, "where they crucified him. . . ." Here the verb ἐσταύρωσαν is abbreviated $\overline{\varepsilon\sigma\,ρ\,αν}$, the initial Epsilon being lifted above the level of the other letters as shown. Line 10 contains a portion of Jn 19:19 where Pilate wrote a title "and put it on the cross." Here, although it is more difficult to make out because of the break in the papyrus, the noun σταυροῦ is abbreviated $\overline{\sigma\,ρ\,ου}$.

Victor Martin, *Papyrus Bodmer II.* Cologny-Genève: Bibliothèque Bodmer. *Evangile de Jean, chap. 1-14,* 1956; *chap. 14-21,* 1958; Victor Martin and J. W. B. Barns, *Nouvelle édition augmentée et corrigée avec reproduction photographique complète du manuscrit (chap. 1-21),* 1962; Kurt Aland in NTS 10 (1963-64), pp. 62-79, especially p. 75, and note the rejection of Sulzberger's position on p. 79. Photograph: Martin and Barns, *op.cit.,* Pl. 133, courtesy Bibliotheca Bodmeriana.

289. A Page in Papyrus Bodmer XIV (P⁷⁵)

Papyrus Bodmer XIV-XV (P⁷⁵) is a codex which contains most of the Gospel according to Luke, chapters 3-24 (Papyrus Bodmer XIV), and of the Gospel according to John, chapters 1-15 (Papyrus Bodmer XV). The date of the manuscript is probably at the beginning of the third century, perhaps within the range A.D. 175-225. Thus it is of substantially the same age as P⁶⁶ (above No. 288), perhaps not quite as old. In this manuscript also the Greek words "cross" and "crucify" are abbreviated. In some places, but not in others, the abbreviation employs the ⳨ sign, the same as in P⁶⁶. In the case of the Gospel according to John, Papyrus Bodmer XV breaks off in chapter 15, and chapter 19, in which are all the occurrences of "cross" and "crucify," is not available for inspection. The examples of the abbreviation are, therefore, all in the Gospel according to Luke, i.e., in Papyrus Bodmer XIV. The page of this papyrus shown in the photograph contains Lk 9: 23-33. In Line 8 is a portion of Lk 9:23 where Jesus says that if any man would come after him, "let him . . . take up his cross daily." Here the noun σταυρόν is abbreviated $\overline{\sigma\,⳨\,ον}$.

Victor Martin and Rodolphe Kasser, *Papyrus Bodmer XIV, Evangile de Luc. chap. 3-24.* Cologny-Genève: Bibliothèque Bodmer, 1961; Kurt Aland in NTS 11 (1964-65), pp. 1-21, especially pp. 1-3. Photograph: Martin and Kasser, *op.cit.,* Pl. 19, courtesy Bibliotheca Bodmeriana.

Luc IX :

290. A Page in the Gospel of Truth (Codex Jung)

The Gospel of Truth (cf. FHRJ §§336ff.) is one of the works contained in the Coptic Gnostic manuscripts from Nag Hammadi. It is the second work in Codex I, and was probably copied in the middle of the fourth century. Although the work has no title it begins with the words, "The Gospel of Truth is joy . . . ," and is therefore probably to be recognized as the book of that title which Irenaeus (*Against Heresies* III 11, 9), writing about A.D. 180, says had been composed recently among the Valentinian Gnostics. The pages of this codex are carefully numbered at the top, and this page, which is the *verso* of folio x, has the letter Kappa which numbers it as Page 20. In Line 27 the text is making a statement, evidently based on Col 2:14, to the effect that when Jesus was crucified he also fastened the deed of disposition (διάταγμα) which came from the Father "to the cross." Here, as may be seen in this line in the photograph, the word "cross" is abbreviated C✝OC.

Michel Malinine, Henri-Charles Puech, and Gilles Quispel, *Evangelium Veritatis*. Zürich: Rascher Verlag, 1956. Photograph: *ibid.*, f. xᵛ p. 20, courtesy Rascher Verlag.

The Ankh-Cross

The ligature of Tau and Rho in the foregoing abbreviations (Nos. 288-290) forms a sign which, at least when it stands alone, we have called a cross-monogram (see above p. 234). As a sign by itself this is decidedly reminiscent of the Egyptian ankh sign which became a form of the cross and is known as the *crux ansata* or handled cross (see above p. 232). Because of this similarity, and because the Tau-Rho monogram occurs in the papyrus manuscripts just mentioned which must have been copied in Egypt, the possibility is suggested that this form of monogram may have originated in Egypt and under the influence of the ankh sign. Since the cross-monogram is found in the copy of the Valentinian Gnostic *Gospel of Truth* contained in the Jung Codex, the question could further be raised whether the development of this sign is to be attributed specifically to the Valentinian Gnostics. Since the sign is also used in the Bodmer papyri of the Gospels according to John (P⁶⁶) and according to Luke (P⁷⁵), however, it is probably not possible to narrow down the origin of the cross-monogram to so specific a point. At any rate we will turn now to Egypt and see there examples of the ankh (Nos. 291-292), of the cross-monogram (No. 293) and of the *crux ansata* which in Egypt, the land of its origin, we will call the ankh-cross (Nos. 294-296).

Jean de Savignac, "Chronique," in *Scriptorium* 17 (1963), pp. 50-52 (note that Savignac also criticizes the position of Sulzberger); Kurt Aland in NTS 11 (1964-65), pp. 2-3.

291. Slate Dish Embodying the Sign of the Ankh

The ankh is the name of a sign very widely found in Egyptian art and writing. From its form it appears to have been first of all a knot and then perhaps a knotted amulet. Used in hieroglyphic writing it is the sign ☥, and means "life." The slate dish in the photograph is from the Early Dynastic period; it embodies two hieroglyphic signs, and combines them to make a monogram. The raised back edge of the dish is continued around the two sides in the form of arms which terminate in hands. This is the hieroglyph for *ku* or *ka*, which probably designates the configuration of characteristics of a person and is sometimes translated "spirit." It does not concern us further here. The other hieroglyph is the ankh. It is contrived to provide the

handle and remaining side of the dish, and the circular portion of its interior. It looks like a knotted tape and appears to confirm the theory that the sign originated as a knot, perhaps the knot in a sandal strap or in a headband.

William C. Hayes, *The Scepter of Egypt.* New York: The Metropolitan Museum of Art, I, 1953, pp. 42-43, 79; Maria Cramer, *Das altägyptische Lebenszeichen.* Wiesbaden: Otto Harrassowitz, 1955. Photograph: courtesy The Metropolitan Museum of Art, Rogers Fund, 1919.

292. The Ankh Sign in Ancient Egypt

As the sign of "life" the ankh appears on the monuments of ancient Egypt in all periods. Here it is carved with other characters on a column of the famous terraced temple of Queen Hatshepsut (fifteenth century B.C.) at Deir el-Bahri in Upper Egypt. Elsewhere it is often held in the hand of a god or a king. In this its conventional form the ankh can be described most simply as like a Tau cross with a loop at the top. As such it lent itself to adoption by Christians as a form of the Christian cross. In its meaning of "life" it was also appropriate for such adoption. The connection between the cross and life is implicit in much of the NT and is brought out by Ignatius (*To the Ephesians* XVIII 1) in a passage in which there are manifold echoes of NT language and thought: "My spirit is devoted (περίψημα, cf. I Cor 4:13) to the cross (τοῦ σταυροῦ, cf. I Cor 1:18), which is a stumbling-block (σκάνδαλον, cf. I Cor 1:23; Gal 5:11) to those who do not believe (τοῖς ἀπιστοῦσιν, cf. I Pet 2:7), but to us salvation and life eternal (ζωὴ αἰώνιος, cf. Jn 6:54, etc.)." It is undoubtedly to this sign that Socrates (*Ch. Hist.* IV 17) and Sozomen (*Ch. Hist.* VII 15) refer when they tell how, at the destruction of the Serapeum in Alexandria by the patriarch Theophilus (A.D. 391), hieroglyphic characters were found which had the form of crosses, and pagan converts to Christianity explained that they signified "life to come" (ζωὴν ἐπερχομένην) (FHRJ §85). It is also hardly to be doubted that the potential of the ankh-sign for adaptation to Christian meaning had been observed and acted upon long before this. As noted just above (p. 255), the Tau-Rho abbreviation and cross-monogram may well reflect the ankh and are attested in Egypt at least by the third century in the manuscripts cited above (Nos. 288-290) as well as in the next inscription to be shown (No. 293). The ankh-cross itself appears on monuments for which dates are commonly held which push back at least into the fourth century (No. 295) and which, one suspects, could in some cases be even earlier.

DACL 3:2, cols. 3120-3123. Photograph: JF.

293. Inscription from Gabbari

Gabbari is a suburb of Alexandria lying on the narrow strip of land between Lake Mareotis and the Western Harbor. On the seaside to the northwest of Gabbari a hypogeum was found in 1876 which appeared to go back to the fourth century and contained a Christian inscription. In the vicinity and even with the ground was an inscribed marble tablet, 19 by 21 centimeters in size, which is now in the Greco-Roman Museum in Alexandria (Inventory No. 11706) and is shown in the photograph. The character of the letters is judged similar to that in inscriptions of the time of the Emperor Gordian III (A.D. 238-244). The Greek text is as follows:

KYPIOCMNHCΘI
THCKOIMHCEOC
ΘEOΔOTHC
KAIANAΠAYCEWC
NIΛAMMWNOC

In the last line (Line 5) the first two or three letters can only be made out with some difficulty, and some have wished to read MΛ or MA instead of NIΛ. The present reading appears to be correct, however, and gives a name (Νιλάμμων) that is otherwise known (Preisigke, *Namenbuch*, col. 235), which is not the case with the other combinations. Furthermore a single word consisting of a single name at this point balances perfectly with the same in Line 3. The Greek text may therefore be repeated and translated as follows:

Κύριος μνησθὶ
τῆς κοιμήσεος
Θεοδότης
καὶ ἀναπαύσεως
Νιλάμμωνος

Lord, remember
the repose
of Theodota
and the rest
of Nilammon

Beneath this text and comprising the sixth line of the inscription is the cross-monogram with Alpha and Omega on either side (cf. above, p. 233).

Lefebvre p. 5 No. 21; DACL 1:1, col. 1151. Photograph: courtesy Greco-Roman Museum.

294. Inscription from Tehneh

Tehneh is an ancient site on the east side of the Nile some ninety-five miles below Asyut and across from Minieh. At the foot of a mountain called Jebel el-Teir is a Roman necropolis and, to the north of this, a Christian necropolis, in which were found many funeral stelae with short inscriptions in Greek. One of these (Lefebvre No. 146 cf. p. xxv) is dated in the year 239 of the Era of the Martyrs (cf. FHBC §217), which is equivalent to A.D. 522/523. This suggests a probable date for the cemetery in the fifth and sixth centuries. In a number of the inscriptions small, plain incised ankh-signs accompany the text. They are probably from the fifth century (Cramer, p. 48). The inscription (Lefebvre No. 138) shown in the illustration is from this cemetery and is now in the Greco-Roman Museum in Alexandria (Inventory No. 27867). The piece of limestone, 27 by 18.50 centimeters in size, is only a fragment. It bears traces of red color.

ACETE
HKAI♀
AMWNIA
HC L'IA
EN KW
N♀IY

257

In Line 3 and ending in Line 4 we probably have the name Amonilla in the form Ἀμωνίλ[λη]ς (cf. Preisigke, *Namenbuch*, col. 29). This is followed by the angular sign for "year," or "years," and this by the number eleven (ı=10 + ᴀ=1). Then in Line 5 we have, abbreviated, ἐν κυ[ρίῳ] "in the Lord"; and in Line 6, also abbreviated, Ἰ[ησο]ῦ, "of Jesus." In addition, there is at the end of Line 2 and prior to the abbreviated name of Jesus in Line 6 the ankh sign which, in this context, may be recognized as the ankh-cross. Since the inscription is not more fully preserved it is not possible to tell whether this sign is simply inserted at places where the wording allows gaps in the lines or whether it can be read as a part of the text itself.

Gustave Lefebvre, "Inscriptions grecques de Tehnéh (Égypte)," in ʙᴄʜ 27 (1908), pp. 341-390 and specially p. 375 No. 118; Lefebvre p. 29 No. 138; Cramer p. 8 and Abb. 2. Photograph: courtesy Greco-Roman Museum.

295. Inscription from the Vicinity of Armant

Armant, the ancient Hermonthis or On of the South (in contrast with On of the North, i.e., Heliopolis), is on the west bank of the Nile some fifteen miles above Luxor. On the edge of the desert to the west of Armant are many cemeteries which date from Predynastic times onward, and among the finds are many Coptic tombstones. The stone (55 by 20 centimeters in size) with the Greek inscription shown in this photograph was said to have been found at Armant, was obtained in the neighborhood of that place, and was reported on to the Royal Irish Academy in Dublin in 1892. The text is cut into the stone inside an incised border, and is accompanied by several signs. The date of the inscription is judged to be between the fourth and sixth centuries. The text, which is rather poetical in character, may be transcribed and translated as follows:

πρίν σε λέγειν ὦ τύμβε τίς ἢ τίνος ἐνθάδε κεῖται
ἡ στήλη βοαᾷ πᾶσι παρερχομένοις
σῶμα μὲν ἐνθάδε κεῖται ἀειμνήστου Μακαρίης
ὡς ἔθος εὐσεβέων γευσάμενον θανάτου
αὐτὴ δ' οὐρανίην ἁγίων πόλιν ἀμφιπολεύει
μισθὸν ἔχουσα πόνων οὐρανίους στεφάνους

Before you say, O tomb, who or whose lies here,
  the stela proclaims to all who pass,
the body lies here of the ever-remembered Makaria;
  as is the custom of the pious, having tasted death,
she is herself busy in the heavenly city of the saints,
  having heavenly crowns as a reward of her sufferings.

The four signs which accompany the inscription are arranged inside the incised border, one at the left end of the last line of text and the other three underneath that line. From left to right they are a Christ-monogram (Chi-Rho), a cross-monogram (Tau-Rho), an ankh-cross, and another Christ-monogram (Chi-Rho).

Charles H. Keene in *Proceedings of the Royal Irish Academy*, Third Series, Vol. ıı (1891-1893), pp. 295-298 (Feb. 8, 1892), and Pl. xı: Carl Schmidt in ᴢᴀ̈ꜱ 32 (1894), p. 59; Lefebvre No. 423; Cramer pp. 8f. Photograph: *Proceedings of the Royal Irish Academy*, 1892, Pl. xı.

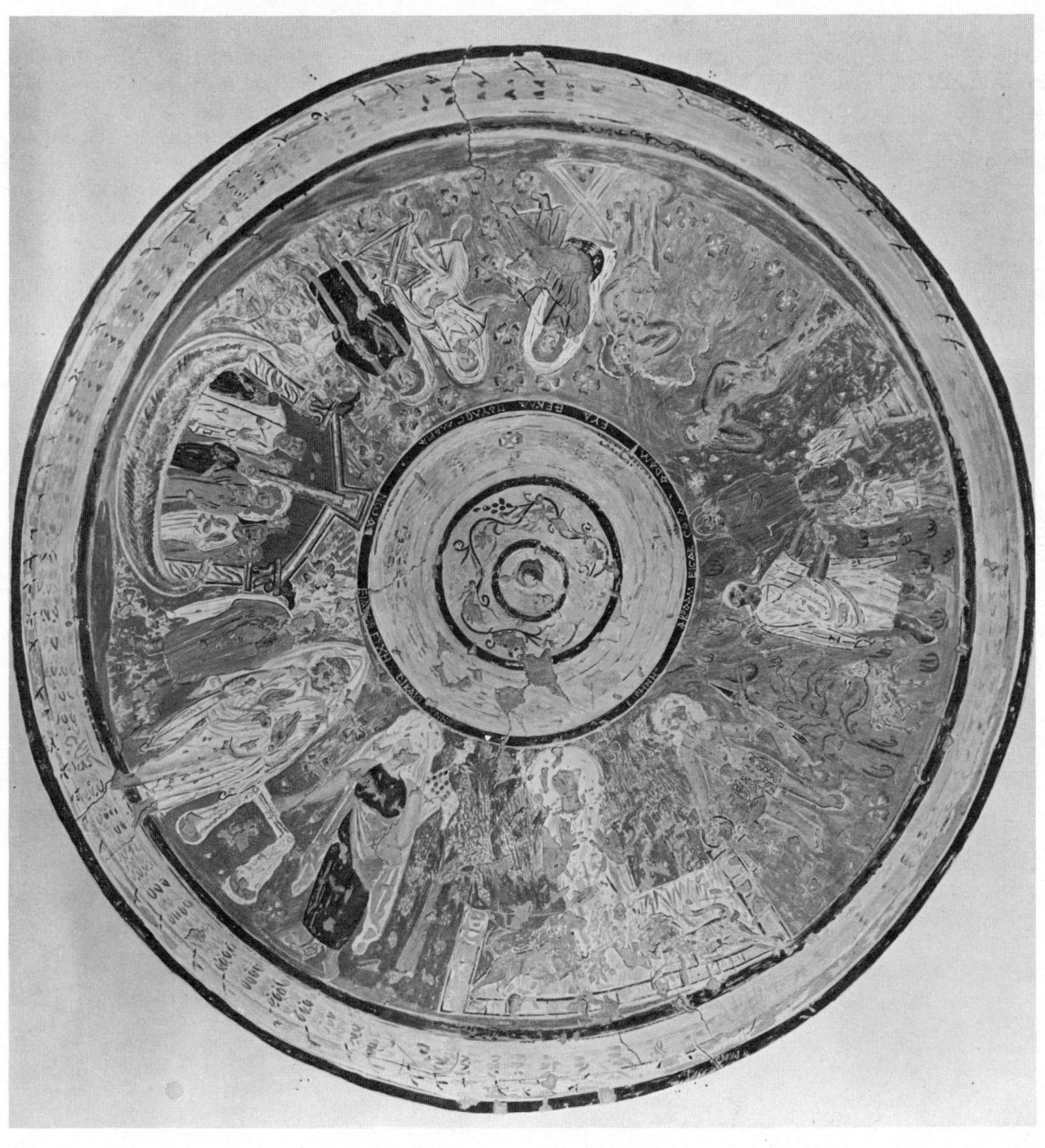

296. Painting in a Tomb Chapel at the Oasis of Khargeh

Finally we show a painting found at Khargeh, an oasis 150 miles south-southwest of Asyut. There is a large Egyptian temple here dating from the Persian period, a smaller one from the Roman period and, in some distance to the north, a large Christian necropolis. The necropolis, known locally as el-Bakawat, comprises many hundreds of brick tombs. These structures are in fact tomb-chapels, each a chamber surmounted by a dome, with an apse that is apparent on the exterior, paintings in the interior, and sometimes with an antechamber too. The date of the paintings is probably not later than the late fourth and early fifth centuries. The finest preserved paintings are in a tomb-chapel on a bluff at the south end of the necropolis. The dome painting in this tomb-chapel is shown in the photograph. It is divided into four concentric bands, separated from each other by rings of red; three bands are purely decorative, but the widest band shows biblical incidents and other figures. The names of the figures are written in Greek on the accompanying red ring. The subject first seen upon entering the room, at the bottom in our illustration, is Daniel in the lion's den.

259

To the right is a tree and then a feminine figure identified as ΕΙΡΗΝΗ, Peace. In her left hand she holds a scepter or torch. In her right hand, precisely as if she were a figure on an ancient Egyptian monument, she holds a large, plainly drawn ankh which in this case must be an ankh-cross. Continuing around the circle of the paintings we find in succession: the Sacrifice of Isaac; Adam and Eve; Thecla and Paul, two early Egyptian saints; the Annunciation to Mary; Noah in the Ark; Jacob with arms lifted in prayer; then a symbolical figure representing Prayer, and finally another symbolical figure representing Justice holding a balance in one hand and a cornucopia in the other.

The fact that in Christian understanding the ankh-cross signifies "life to come" (cf. No. 293), means that, even though its external form is so different, this form of the cross-sign too is not unrelated to the primitive *taw*-mark of salvation. That mark, derived from Jewish background and perhaps already used by Jewish Christians on ossuaries in Palestine in the first century, stood for the divine name and for the eschatological deliverance; recognized also as a representation of the instrument of the death of Jesus it showed that death as an expression of the divine power, effective for redemption. With this meaning, the *taw* sign, vestiges of which may remain as the earliest surviving memorials of the earliest church, became, above all others, the symbol of the Christian faith.

C. K. Wilkinson, "Early Christian Paintings in the Oasis of Khargeh," in *The Bulletin of the Metropolitan Museum of Art, New York.* 23 (1928), pp. 29-36; Daniélou, *Primitive Christian Symbols*, pp. 141f., 145. Photograph: courtesy The Metropolitan Museum of Art.

INDEX OF SCRIPTURAL REFERENCES

Index

All references are to pages

264